Anti-Judaism

ALSO BY DAVID NIRENBERG

Communities of Violence:
Persecution of Minorities in the Middle Ages

Judaism and Christian Art:
Aesthetic Anxieties from the Catacombs to Colonialism
(*with Herbert L. Kessler*)

Anti-Judaism

THE WESTERN TRADITION

David Nirenberg

W. W. NORTON & COMPANY

New York • London

For information about permission to reproduce selections from this book, write to
Permissions, W. W. Norton & Company, Inc., 500 Fifth Avenue, New York, NY 10110

For information about special discounts for bulk purchases, please contact
W. W. Norton Special Sales at specialsales@wwnorton.com or 800-233-4830

Manufacturing by RR Donnelley, Harrisonburg
Book design by Dana Sloan
Production manager: Devon Zahn

Library of Congress Cataloging-in-Publication Data

Nirenberg, David, 1964–
    Anti-Judaism : the Western tradition / David Nirenberg. — 1st ed.
        p. cm.
    Includes biographical references and index.
    ISBN 978-0-393-05824-6 (hardcover)
    1. Antisemitism—Europe—History. 2. Civilization, Western—Jewish influences.
    3. Europe, Western—Ethnic relations. I. Title.
    DS146.E85N57 2013
    305.892'405609041—dc23

                                                    2012031082

W. W. Norton & Company, Inc., 500 Fifth Avenue, New York, N.Y. 10110
www.wwnorton.com

W. W. Norton & Company Ltd., Castle House, 75/76 Wells Street, London W1T 3QT

1 2 3 4 5 6 7 8 9 0

For Isabel, for Ricardo, and for Alex

CONTENTS

He that doth love, and love amisse,
This worlds delights before true Christian joy,
Hath made a Jewish choice . . .

And is a Judas-Jew

—GEORGE HERBERT, "SELF-CONDEMNATION" [1633]

Introduction

THINKING ABOUT JUDAISM, OR
THE JUDAISM OF THOUGHT

FOR SEVERAL THOUSAND years people have been thinking about Judaism. Ancient Egyptians spent a good deal of papyrus on the Hebrews; early (and not so early) Christians filled pages attempting to distinguish between Judaism and Christianity, the New Israel and the Old; Muhammad's followers pondered their Prophet's relation to Jews and "Sons of Israel"; medieval Europeans invoked Jews to explain topics as diverse as famine, plague, and the tax policies of their princes. And in the vast archives of material that survive from Early Modern and Modern Europe and its cultural colonies, it is easy enough to demonstrate that words like *Jew*, *Hebrew*, *Semite*, *Israelite*, and *Israel* appear with a frequency stunningly disproportionate to any populations of living Jews in those societies.

We all know that there are differences as well as similarities between these words. *Jew* is not the same as Hebrew, *Israelites* are not Israelis, *Israeli* need not mean Zionist or Jew (or vice versa), and many who have been called "Jew" or "Judaizer" in no way identify with Judaism at all.

Yet all of these and numerous other words exist in close proximity to each other, and have so often bled together across the long history of thought that, for the sake of simplicity, we can call our topic the history of thinking about "Judaism."

Why did so many diverse cultures—even many cultures with no Jews living among them—think so much about Judaism? What work did thinking about Judaism do for them in their efforts to make sense of their world? Did that work in turn affect the ways in which future societies could or would think with Judaism? And how did this history of thinking about Judaism affect the future possibilities of existence for living Jews?

These are the questions I take up in this book. They are dauntingly, even laughably, large: roughly equivalent to asking how what people have thought in the past—the history of ideas—affects what and how people think in the future. That question once animated the discipline of history. It is seldom asked explicitly today, both because it is so large and because many historians, philosophers, and other students of human cognition have become (rightly) suspicious of any easy answers to it. And yet, even if such questions have no easy answers, without asking them we cannot become self-conscious about how we think, either about past worlds or about our own.

It is with that dilemma in mind that I offer you this account of the labor done by Judaism in the workshops of Western thought. (I will argue that, at least for our topic, Islam should be included within the rubric.) The book is intended above all to suggest some of the important ways in which "Jewish questions" have shaped the history of thought. But it is also, and more generally, an argument for the vital role that the history of ideas can play in making us aware of how past uses of the concepts we think with can constrain our own thought.

I am certainly not the first person to suggest that questions about Judaism are inculcated into the habits of thought with which people make sense of the world, or to ask how we can become critical of those habits. The term *Jewish question* (*Judenfrage* in German) itself was first brought into general circulation in the middle of the nineteenth century by a group of young German philosophers who imagined themselves to be the pioneers of what they called "critical critique." The most famous participant in their discussions was Karl Marx, whose 1844 writings "On the Jewish Question" and (together with Friedrich Engels) *The Holy Family, or Critique of Critical Criticism* intervened in a heated debate about whether German Jews needed to convert to Christianity in order to be emancipated from their legal disabilities and become citizens.

Marx insisted that this was the wrong question to debate. According to him, conversion could neither emancipate the Jews of Germany nor free Germany of Judaism, because Judaism is not only a religion but also an attitude, an attitude of spiritual slavery and alienation from the world. This alienation is not exclusive to the Jews. Money is the god of Judaism, but it is also the god of every man, no matter what his confessed religion, who alienates the products of his life and his labor for it. So long as money is god, which is to say so long as there is private property, neither the emancipation of the Jews nor the emancipation of society from Judaism can ever be achieved, for Christian society will continue to "produce Judaism out of its own entrails."[1]

Marx's fundamental insight here was that the "Jewish question" is as much about the basic tools and concepts through which individuals in a society relate to the world and to each other, as it is about the presence of "real" Judaism and living Jews in that society. He understood that some of these basic tools—such as money and property— were thought of in Christian culture as "Jewish," and that these tools therefore could potentially produce the "Jewishness" of those who used them, whether those users were Jewish or not. "Judaism," then, is not only the religion of specific people with specific beliefs, but also a category, a set of ideas and attributes with which non-Jews can make sense of and criticize their world. Nor is "anti-Judaism" simply an attitude toward Jews and their religion, but a way of critically engaging the world. It is in this broad sense that I will use the words *Judaism* and *anti-Judaism*. And it is also for this reason that I do not use *anti-Semitism*, a word that captures only a small portion, historically and conceptually, of what this book is about.[2]

Marx's insight, that our concepts can themselves create the "Judaism" of the world to which they are applied, seems to me critical. It is a necessary prerequisite for any awareness of how habits of thought project figures of Judaism into the world. From this insight Marx could have proceeded to a criticism of these same habits of thought. He might, for example, have asked why it was that Christian European culture thought of capitalism as "Jewish," and written a critical history intended to make his contemporaries more reflective about the association. Famously, he chose instead to exploit these habits, putting old ideas and fears about Jewishness to a new kind of work: that of planning a world without private property or wage labor.

We will spend more time on Marx in chapter 13. Here, I just want to suggest that both aspects of Marx's work on the Jewish question are instructive. On the one hand, his insight that our tools of cognition, communication, and interaction project figures of Judaism into the world has provided some stimulus for reflection on the functions of Judaism in modern thought. That stimulus is obvious, for example, in the title of the Jean-Paul Sartre essay written at the very end of World War II: "Reflections on the Jewish Question" (1945). It is also obvious in the essay's famous argument that the thinking of the anti-Semite produced the Jew, to such an extent that "if the Jew did not exist, the anti-Semite would invent him."

On the other hand, Marx's messianic desire (itself quite "Christian") to present his own revolutionary economic and political project as a liberation of the world from Judaism set sharp limits to the depth of his Jewish questions. His writing certainly raised critical consciousness about important subjects like class and labor, but it only tended to reinforce basic conceptions about the role of Judaism in the world—for example, its alignment with money and alienation—and to confirm the sense that in a better world that role would disappear. We can see some of the more awful potential consequences of these tendencies in the actions of some later regimes that claimed to speak in Marx's name, and more subtle consequences in the difficulties Marxist critics have continued to have with Jewish questions.[3]

Marx's example demonstrates that these questions about the roles played by figures of Judaism in our thinking about the world have the power to stimulate the type of reflection we need in order to become conscious of some of our own habits of thought. But it also points to a real danger in asking such questions: the danger that, like Marx, we stop asking them too early, as soon as we reach an answer that harmonizes comfortably or usefully with our own view of the world. Such questioning gives us the illusion of engagement in critical thought, while in fact only confirming our prejudices, this time even more strenuously defended by the conviction of being "critical."

I have set out to write a history of how critical thought has been produced by thinking about Judaism, and has therefore also generated the "Jewishness" it criticizes in the world. But unlike Marx, I have tried not to stop this history too early, pressing instead further and further into the past until "Jewish questions" are nowhere to be found. My goal in each place and period, from ancient Egypt to the twentieth century, is to demonstrate how different people put old ideas about Judaism to new kinds of work in thinking about their world; to show how this work engaged the past and transformed it; and to ask how that work reshaped the possibilities for thought in the future.

We will begin among the pharaohs circa 700 BCE, where some Egyptians transformed traditions about Moses and the Hebrews into ways of making sense of their own history of subjection to foreign powers from Alexander the Great to the Roman Empire: a transformation with important consequences, not only for the possibilities of life for Jews in Egypt, but also for the history of thought about Jews and Judaism. Then we will cross the Sinai, to Palestine and later to Arabia, and watch first Christians and then Muslims reinterpret the history of Israel—both the kingdom and the "chosen peoples"—in order to make new sense of the cosmos and its powers, human, demonic, and divine: again, with momentous consequences, not only for the work that could be done by thinking about "Jews," but also for real Jews living in the Christian and Muslim worlds shaped by that thought.

In later chapters we will see very different societies—medieval

Europe, inquisitorial Spain, Luther's Germany, Shakespeare's England, the France of Voltaire's Enlightenment and Robespierre's Terror—put these ideas to new kinds of work, using them to think about topics as diverse as politics and painting, poetry and property rights. We will see how many medieval and early modern people, on occasion, imagined their critical task as Christian or Muslim worshippers, as artists, writers, philosophers, as citizens and politicians, to be the identification and overcoming of the threat of Judaism within their ranks. We will trace the translation of this imagination into modern scientific disciplines and systems of thought—into theologies, philosophies, and political sciences, into theories about language, economics, mathematics, biology— in order to explain why so many moderns, as the philosopher Arthur Schopenhauer complained circa 1818, "equate Judaism and Reason."

We will watch these systems of thought generate so much Judaism out of their own entrails that by the twentieth century any domain of human activity could be thought of and criticized in terms of Judaism. "Culture," as an Austrian politician quipped in 1907, "is what one Jew plagiarizes from another." We will ask how the work done by all these figures of Judaism in the history of ideas contributed to what remains one of the darkest questions of modernity: how, in the middle of the twentieth century, an astounding number of the world's most educated citizens were willing and able to believe that Jews and Judaism posed so grave a threat to civilization that they needed to be exterminated. And throughout all these chapters we will insist that anti-Judaism should not be understood as some archaic or irrational closet in the vast edifices of Western thought. It was rather one of the basic tools with which that edifice was constructed.[4]

I am by profession a historian, and this is a history book. This means, among other things, that I have based my arguments only on primary sources that I could consult in the original languages.[5] Perhaps even more important, it means that in each chapter, and for each time and place, I have attempted to understand those sources as they might have been understood within the contexts in which they were produced or circulated. This historicism, as it is sometimes called, is itself a potentially powerful test of our habits of thought. It can remind us, for example, that the way believers today read Jesus's or Saint Paul's words was not necessarily the way that their followers in first-century Palestine, or in other times and places, might have read them.

But I do have three methodological deviations from contemporary professional history to acknowledge, and I confess them proudly because they are programmatic. The first, which will trouble historians of the Jews, is that my history of thinking about Judaism speaks scarcely at all about the thoughts and actions of people who would have identified themselves as Jews. My focus here is on how people—only a tiny minority of whom were Jews or descendants of Jews—thought with and about Judaism, and how that thinking affected (and was affected by) the possibilities of existence for Judaism in the world. Sometimes that thinking took place in interaction with living Jews, but often it did not.

The second, which will bother many social, political, and economic historians, is that mine is a history of thought, one that, while not treating ideas as protagonists of history, does grant them sufficient power to shape our perceptions of and actions in the world. And the third, which will scandalize all alike, is the three-thousand-year sweep of this history, which may wrongly suggest to some readers either that I take ideas to be eternal and unchanging or that I am engaged in a genealogy, an evolutionary history, a quest for the origin of the species.

These three deviations sin against some dearly held convictions of contemporary historians. In the mid-nineteenth century Jules Michelet, one of the founders of "professional history," articulated the historian's task in terms of a violent conflict: "With the world began a war which will end only with the world: the war of man against nature, of spirit against matter, of liberty against fatality. History is nothing other than the record of this interminable struggle." There is a great deal to worry us in Michelet's Manichaean dualism, which is itself a product of the history of thought we need to describe. (In fact, Michelet claimed that throughout this war Judaism always stood on the side of tyranny.) But his formulation had the virtue of viewing the battle as interminable, with history the chronicle of both sides. Historians of my generation, on the other hand, see history as the record of liberty (or "agency" and "contingency," as it is called by historians nowadays). To grant any power to the past over the future (Michelet's "fatality") smacks today of treasonous allegiance to a toppled tyranny.[6]

The enthusiasm for liberty has yielded a rich harvest. For example, the view that power should not be thought of as monolithic or monopolized by elites, but rather as dispersed and "contested" across societies, led American historians of slavery to begin asking questions about slave strategies of resistance, and to stress processes of reciprocal influence and interpenetration as the basis for the formation of cultures both black and white. Historians of European colonialism reversed their emphasis on imperial projections of power to study how the colonized transformed the colonizers, and to demonstrate that "subalterns" could speak as well as conquerors. Scholars of Jewish history began to assign a new and positive importance to the score of centuries that Jews spent living as minorities in lands ruled by others, and demonstrated that many central aspects of Judaism emerged from relationships of imitation and rejection, acculturation and differentiation, with surrounding non-Jewish cultures. Others—myself included—dismantled historical teleologies that pointed all of the Jewish past toward the Holocaust.

But our enthusiasm for liberty has also had three significant costs. First, it has blinded us to asymmetries of power. Our eagerness to discover agency for all makes it difficult to account ethically for differences in power between master and slave, or to consider the possibility that Christian ideas about Judaism might have a greater impact on the conditions of life for real Jews than anything those Jews might actually do. Second, it has blinded us to the power of ideas. If ideas are thought of as determining or constraining freedom of action and experience, then a history that stresses liberty must minimize the place of ideas. Interests, agency, strategic action: the contemporary historian's trinity looks almost the inverse of the one articulated by the founding father of sociology, Max Weber, in his "Introduction" to *The Economic Ethics of the World Religions*:

> *Ideas, not interests (whether material or ideal) intuitively control the actions of men. But: the "worldviews" which are fashioned through ideas, these have often served as switchmen for the tracks on which the dynamics of interests have moved action.*[7]

Finally, too much "liberty" has blinded us to the power of the past, to continuity, to the possibility that we are somehow constrained by what has been done or thought before us. My three-thousand-year history will perhaps offend most against the current conviction that, as Michel Foucault famously put it in the late 1960s, "history is for cutting." That conviction is strong among historians of ideas, some of whom go so far as to suggest that to guard against false continuities, we should treat texts and ideas—especially the most classical and seemingly enduring—as "speech-acts," their meaning to be interpreted only within the immediate historical context of their utterance.

Certainly the task of cutting is critical: the mid-twentieth century, for example, experienced the depth of horror that can be produced when nations fantasize their ancestry in the past. But no amount of cutting can eliminate the historian's need to generalize, that is, to create connections and continuities between nonidentical things. And cutting also has its risks. In the sixteenth century Montaigne mocked a similar tendency in his age, citing words of the ancient Roman philosopher Seneca: "Cut anything into tiny pieces and it all becomes a mass of confusion." Nor are the risks only epistemological, for fantasies of freedom from the past can be as dangerous as fantasies of continuity with it.[8]

Friedrich Nietzsche, the nineteenth-century philosopher from whom Foucault derived his dictum, did not forget this danger. He ridiculed the tendency to fantasize certain types of identity between present and past, but he also insisted on elements of formal continuity. "All great things must first wear terrifying and monstrous masks in order to inscribe themselves on the hearts of humanity." The forms in which ideas presented themselves were not incidental to their future. On the contrary, great ideas impress themselves upon generations of human memory in part by concealing their transformations behind the abiding terror of their masks.[9]

My pages will treat anti-Judaism as mask, that is, as a pedagogical fear that gives enduring form to some of the key concepts and questions in the history of thought. But at the same time they will point to the constant change taking place behind the mask—that is, to the unceasing transformation of these concepts and questions, and of the figures of Judaism through which they were so often articulated. The method, like the metaphor, is intended to help us recognize the potential meaningfulness of similarities we think we see across wide swaths of time, while simultaneously protecting us against the all-too-human tendency to build bridges of causality far too heavy for the inevitably frail foundations of our knowledge.

A provocative example might help make the point. Some of the gospels characterize Jewish sects like the Pharisees as desiring empty wisdom and striving for reputation and titles, and indeed condemn the Jewish "scribbling classes" more generally: "I bless you father . . . for hiding these things from the learned and the clever and revealing them to little children." Some eighteen hundred years later, on May 10, 1933, Joseph Goebbels celebrated his National Socialist Party's rise to power with a proclamation at the Nazis' "Burning of Un-German books": "The age of rampant Jewish intellectualism is now at an end."[10] There may well be *some* historical relation between the gospels' ways of representing the "Jewishness" of certain ideas (see chapter 2) and those of Germans (and many others) in the twentieth century (chapter 13), just as there may well be a relationship between the Qur'an's worries about the Sons of Israel (discussed in chapter 4) and those of some contemporary Islamists. That relationship is not straightforward. The teachings of a Goebbels are not necessarily implied in the gospels (nor those of a Bin Laden in the Qur'an). Nor is the relation causal, clear, evolutionary, or unidirectional. "The past," as T. S. Eliot put it, may be "altered by the present as much as the present is directed by the past." But if there is *any* relation, we need to be able to recognize it in order to understand ourselves as well as the past.

My long view into the past is intended to make these relations visible. Each chapter therefore attempts to treat its material both in the context of its own time and with an awareness of potential futures—that is, of how that material will be put to the work of generating different worldviews in later periods and other places. I recognize, and you should too, that there is a danger here. In the words of Walter Benjamin (himself a victim of Goebbels's and his colleagues' efforts to end the age of "Jewish intellectualism"),

> *Just as a man lying sick with fever transforms all the words that he hears into the extravagant images of delirium, so it is that the spirit of the present age seizes on the manifestations of past or distant spiritual worlds, in order to take possession of them and unfeelingly incorporate them into its own self-absorbed fantasizing.*

But as Benjamin himself also stressed, our study of history must be fed with the blood of the living, our questions driven by our sense of the future's needs: "[C]riticism and prophecy must be the two categories that meet in the salvation of the past."[11]

It is my sense—and I do not insist that you agree—that at this particular moment, and on these particular questions, the peril of fantasizing our freedom from the past is great. The "critical thinkers" of our present age increasingly reject the possibility that history can tell us anything vital about many of the questions that seem most pressing to us. Particularly on the questions with which this book is concerned, many see the mere invocation of the past as a symptom of special pleading (as, for example, when histories of anti-Semitism or the Holocaust are invoked to silence criticism of the State of Israel). Far too often they are right: history can easily become unreflective, pathological, impeding criticism rather than furthering it. And yet the study of the history of our ideas is also a powerful stimulus to consciousness about the ways in which we see the world. We cannot afford to live without it.

My history, perhaps like all histories, is indeed a form of special pleading. But it is not pleading on behalf of Jews, Judaism, or Israel, or for that matter against them. It is pleading for the possibility of thinking critically about our own habits of thought and the history of our ideas, for the possibility of reflection, even on "Jewish questions" that have a long history of resistance to it.

Chapter 1

THE ANCIENT WORLD:
EGYPT, EXODUS, EMPIRE

"The Egyptians began the slanders against us."

—*Against Apion*, 1.223

F LAVIUS JOSEPHUS WAS near the end of his life when he wrote these words, and that life had been eventful. A descendant of high priests and Judean kings, Josephus served as a rebel general during the great Jewish revolt that erupted against Rome in the 60s and 70s of the Christian era. He survived battles, murder plots, and suicide pacts until, encouraged by both prophetic dreams and personal defeat, he switched to the Roman side. It was from that side that he witnessed the siege, conquest, and destruction of Jerusalem by the Roman armies in 70 CE. Clearly his collaboration impressed the conquerors, for the emperor Titus took him to Rome in his victorious entourage and provided him with pension. It was in this Roman retirement that Josephus undertook what he felt to be the urgent task of defending his people by explaining Jewish history to the victors. In two massive works, *The Jewish War* and

The Antiquities of the Jews, he set down much of what we today can know about ancient Judaism, and about the world in which Christianity was born. But even after that herculean effort of historical defense, the elderly chronicler still felt, as he looked about his contemporary world, that he and the Jewish people were threatened by "malicious calumnies."[1] It was to answer those calumnies that he set about his last significant historical project, *Against Apion*, in which he undertook to reveal the Egyptian roots of the hostile discourses about Judaism circulating in his Greco-Roman world, and found their origins among the Egyptians.

Ours is not a quest for origins. Nevertheless we will follow Josephus into Egypt, and let that land provide us with our first example (the first in this book, not necessarily the first in human history) of how ideas about Jews and Judaism become tools with which a culture—in this case Egyptian—makes sense of the world, and how those ideas form and transform as they are put to work across time and space.

But first a disclaimer. The ancient world has bequeathed us countless artifacts of antipathy toward Jews: negative stereotypes, conflict and conquest, even expulsion and extermination. Yet these can rarely be reassembled into anything resembling the foundation of an ideology. Most ancient cultures attributed relatively little importance to the difference between Jew and non-Jew. For hundreds of years, for example, the Israelite kingdoms were at war with Assyrians and Babylonians. After the Babylonian conquest of Jerusalem in the sixth century BCE, thousands, perhaps even hundreds of thousands, of Jews lived in slavery, exile, or willingly in Diaspora in Babylon, with many assimilating into Babylonian society. The encounter was so central to the Israelite experience that Babylon assumed cosmological significance in biblical prophecy: think of Jeremiah, Isaiah, Daniel, Ezra, and Nehemiah.[2] But the reverse is untrue. The Babylonian kings certainly celebrated their victories over the many peoples they defeated, Israelites included. But so far as we know, the Israelites played no special role in shaping how Babylonians thought of themselves, their polity, or their cosmos.

Given our subject, our own voyage to the ancient world will avoid these vast seas of indifference toward Judaism in favor of the few places where our subject became prominent. We begin in Egypt because it is one such place. But we should not forget that by comparison with the cognitive spaces that anti-Judaism would later colonize, those that it occupied in pre-Christian antiquity were tiny islands. It is only thanks to the effects of historical projection that they loom so large.[3] In the maps historians draw of the past, the landscape is always deformed by its future.

A Garrison on the Frontier

Let us nevertheless begin our travels on one such island: in this case the literal island of Elephantine at the southern limits of ancient Egypt, where we find an Israelite garrison and an Egyptian one defending the frontier side by side against Nubian incursion. Scholars more or less agree that their collaboration probably began some 650 years before the birth of Christ, as part of a strategic alliance between the rulers Manasseh of Judah (699–643 BCE) and Psammetichus I of Egypt (664–609 BCE).[4] We know that the Jews and Egyptians of Elephantine not only waged war together but also worshipped in close proximity. A "Temple of the Jewish God YHW" (as the Jews of Elephantine spelled God's Hebrew name, in their characteristically unorthodox way) was located near the temple of the local Egyptian deity, the ram-god Khnum. There the Jews of Elephantine made offerings to their God and carried out sacrifices to him.[5] This was a highly unusual arrangement. Because the Temple in Jerusalem increasingly monopolized the privilege of sacrificing animals to God, such sacrifices were rarely carried out in the "Diaspora," that is, in a largely non-Jewish environment. Elephantine was exceptional. But the exception persisted for some two centuries, so far as we know, without incident.

Incidents were, however, brewing. In 525 BCE the Persian king Cambyses invaded and conquered Egypt.[6] For over a century (until 404 BCE) Egypt remained under Persian rule. For a considerable part of this period, from roughly 495 until 400 BCE, we are fortunate to possess an extraordinary "archive" of papyrus documents written in Aramaic by or for the Jews of Elephantine. The archive consists of three different collections: from the temple official Ananiah, a woman called Mibtahiah, and Jedaniah, a communal leader. It is thanks to these that we know something about the coexistence of Egyptians and Jews in Elephantine, about the Jewish temple there, and about the events that led to the destruction of both.[7]

Those events may have been precipitated by the Persian invasions. One of the papyri claims that during Cambyses's conquest he destroyed the temples of the Egyptian gods (including Khnum's at Elephantine), but spared that of the Jews.[8] Assuming that the story is true (and that is a large assumption), the Persian king's discriminations in favor of YHW may have been motivated by a sense of monotheistic solidarity with Judaism (the king was a Zoroastrian monotheist), or by a desire to encourage Jewish loyalty to the new regime. If the latter, his expectations were not disappointed. The Jews of Elephantine did not take part in Egyptian revolts against Persian domination, such as the one that took place in 425 BCE, during the chaotic transition from the rule of King Artaxerxes I to that of Darius II. "[When] the Egyptians rebelled we did not leave our posts," one papyrus from the Jews reminds the Persian rulers. One wonders how the Egyptians felt about this loyalty.[9]

Passover Problems

Nevertheless, the first hint of trouble comes not during the civil wars that marked Darius's accession, but from a document dated to the fifth year of his rule: 419 BCE by our reckoning. In that year a man called Hananiah wrote a letter to the Jewish garrison of Elephantine that has come to be known as the "Passover letter," because it contains a decree of King Darius stipulating the proper observance of the Jewish festival of Passover.[10] Like so many ancient documents, this one raises as many questions as it answers, not least because the papyrus itself is full of holes. Anything that can be said about it is controversial, since so much depends on how those lacunae are filled. We will avoid as much of the controversy as possible by focusing only on the opening lines, following the standard modern reconstruction: "And now, this year, year 5 of the king Darius, it has been sent from the king to Arsames the prince, saying: keep away from the Jewish garrison."[11] Hananiah is quoting here from a letter that the king sent to Arsames (also known as Arsham), his satrap, or governor, in Egypt. In that letter, it seems that the king is ordering the Egyptians of Elephantine to stay away from their Jewish neighbors during Passover.

This might not be so remarkable if we did not know that nine years later, when Arsames was absent from Egypt, the Egyptians destroyed the Jewish temple of Elephantine. Two papyri tell us of the destruction:

> *In the month of Tammuz, year 14 of Darius the king, when Arsames had departed and gone to the king, the priests of Khnub the god . . . , in agreement with Vidranga, who was chief here, (said), saying: 'The Temple of YHW the God which is in Elephantine the fortress let them remove from there.' . . . [They] broke into that Temple, demolished it to the ground, . . . But the basins of gold and silver and the (other) things which were in that Temple—all (of these) they took and made their own.*[12]

Other documents tell of the execution of Vidranga and his accomplices after order was restored, and of the diplomatic missions sent by the Jews of Elephantine to the high priest in Jerusalem, and to the governors of Judah and Samaria, in order to gain permission to rebuild the temple. Permission was eventually granted in 407 BCE, this time notably *without* the privilege of carrying out animal sacrifices that the Elephantines had previously enjoyed and specifically requested.[13] Here the documentary trail ends. Our last document is dated 399 BCE. Thereafter the Jewish garrison at Elephantine vanishes from the historical record.

Why did the Egyptians destroy the temple of the god YHW in 410 BCE? One answer, often given and perhaps true, is that Egyptians resented the Jews as allies of the Persians, whom they viewed as their oppressors. The violence at Elephantine is thus only the first instance of a pattern we will see often repeated, in which Jews are attacked because they are perceived as agents of a hated imperial power. This type of explanation treats attacks on Jews as strategic rather than structural, as motivated by politics rather than by any foundational ideology or deep antagonism.

Yet there are hints that more than politics polarized Egyptian views of Jews. The most important of these clues comes from that "Passover letter" King Darius sent nine years before the destruction, in which he commanded the Egyptians to stay away from the Jews on Passover. Why Passover? Some have suggested that the festival provided a special point of friction because the traditional Jewish sacrifice of a paschal lamb at the temple of YHW offended the Egyptian priests in the temple next door. These were, after all, acolytes of the ram-god Khnum, to whom sheep were holy. Hence the priests of Khnum and their Egyptian followers attempted to interfere with the celebration, finally succeeding when the satrap Arsames was away visiting the king. Later, aware of this irritant, the authorities of Judah refused to grant the right of animal sacrifice when they authorized the rebuilding of the temple. This explanation, elegant and economical, has the added virtue of confirming biblical prophecy. Already in Exodus 8:22, Moses had objected to the pharaoh's request that the Hebrews remain in Egypt rather than go out into the desert to make their sacrifice: "Lo, if we shall sacrifice the abomination [sacred animal] of the Egyptians, will they not stone us?"

I would propose a less vivid but more general explanation. The Egyptians were offended not only by the sacrifice but also by the very nature of the Passover festival as a reenactment of the Exodus from Egypt. What was for the Jews a commemoration of liberation and of the victory of monotheism over idolatry, was for the Egyptians an offensive celebration of the destruction of Egypt and the defeat of its gods. As Josephus put it in the first century,

The Egyptians had many causes for hatred and envy. The first was our ancestors' domination over their country, and then their prosperity upon returning to their own land. Then too, the opposition between

them created bitter enmity among them, because our religion is as different from that which is law among them as the nature of God differs from that of irrational beasts. For them it is the custom of the fatherland to think of animals as gods.[14]

It would not be surprising if the priests of Khnum sought to disrupt such a holiday with violence. Nor would it be surprising if they began to develop their own pro-Egyptian versions of "Passover," their own traditions and commemorations interpreting "the Exodus," in dialogue with the Hebrews' version but from an anti-Hebrew point of view. From this perspective, the Passover attacks at Elephantine were not merely strategic acts, but expressions of a developing sense of history in which the Jews were beginning to be understood as enemies of Egyptian piety, sovereignty, and prosperity.

The Emergence of an Anti-Jewish Tradition

My proposal must remain conjecture: the priests of Khnum have left us no papyri, no version of the events in their own words, and no evidence for the existence of an Egyptian "negative Exodus" tradition at Elephantine. It is only in the following century, the fourth before the Christian era, that we start to find evidence of such traditions. But in the intervening century Persia has been defeated. Alexander the Great and his armies conquer Egypt in 332 BCE. For the next three centuries, until Cleopatra's famous suicide in 30 BCE, Alexander's Hellenistic (Greek) heirs will occupy the pharaoh's throne.

The change is not only political, for there was a good deal of culture stuffed in the backpacks of Alexander's soldiers. The Greeks brought with them new ways of thinking about governance in what we might today call a "multicultural" empire, new forms of colonization—such as the establishment of the new Greek city of Alexandria—and new strategies of taxation and domination. But they also brought with them new questions about the world, new tools (such as philosophy and history) with which to work on those questions, and even a new language

(Greek) in which to ask them. These new questions and tools would prove highly significant for the kinds of thinking that could be done with Judaism.

We will return to politics and philosophy, but consider first the question of our own genre. Historians staffed the rearguard of Alexander's armies, their presence motivated not only by curiosity or commemoration but also by the strategic need to provide a suitably multicultural history for Alexander's vast new empire. In this history the many peoples under Greek rule needed to be intertwined, not just by conquest but also by a shared sense of origins and destiny: an "imagined community," as historians too often say nowadays, capable of giving suck and succor to newly cosmopolitan visions of the polity.

It was precisely this process of reimagining the past that produced the earliest surviving nonbiblical version of the Exodus story. It comes to us not from a native Egyptian, but from Hecataeus of Abdera, a member of the first generation of Greek historians to travel in Egypt after Alexander's conquest. Hecataeus did not speak Egyptian. As a foreigner he had little access to the traditions preserved by the Egyptian priests in their temples and in their memories. Nevertheless the history of Egypt that he wrote circa 320 BCE, the *Aegyptiaca*, represents the first close encounter of Greek historical writing with Egyptian wisdom.[15]

The work has not survived in its entirety, but only as excerpts quoted in the works of later historians. In one of these excerpts, Hecataeus describes a distant time when Egypt was afflicted by a terrible plague:

> *The common people ascribed their troubles to the workings of a divine agency; for indeed, with many strangers of all sorts dwelling in their midst and practicing different rites . . . their own traditional observances in honor of the gods had fallen into disuse. . . . At once, therefore, the aliens were driven from the country. The most outstanding and active among them banded together and, as some say, were cast ashore in Greece and certain other regions. . . . But the greater number were driven into what is now called Judaea, which is not far dis-*

tant from Egypt and was at that time utterly uninhabited. The colony was headed by a man called Moses, outstanding both for his wisdom and for his courage.

Moses, Hecataeus tells us, also founded a new religion, banning the worship of images "being of the opinion that God is not in human form; rather the heaven that surrounds the earth is alone divine, and rules the universe." In addition to their iconoclasm, Hecataeus found Moses's people noteworthy for their nastiness, "for as a result of their own expulsion from Egypt he [Moses] introduced an unsocial and intolerant mode of life."[16]

This brief account, the earliest evidence we have for the existence of an Egyptian version of the Exodus story, is dwarfed by the vast amount of commentary it has inspired. Scholars argue, for example, over its sources. Does it faithfully reflect Egyptian traditions about the Jews that Hecataeus might have gathered? Or do parts of it reflect Greek prejudices? The argument is heated by the moral implications with which it is often invested: Does ancient Egypt bear the full responsibility for the invention of what would become a fundamental concept of anti-Judaism—Jewish misanthropy—or is Greece complicit?[17] The argument is further complicated by the nature of Hecataeus's project, which was not the accurate transmission of Egyptian stories about the past, but the provision of a braided history appropriate to a vast multiethnic empire. Hence he enthusiastically adopted and elaborated stories about expulsion and migration that might help him tie together the many peoples under Alexander's rule. The literal truth of Hecataeus's history matters less for us than two interrelated facts. The first is that in order to compose it, he seems to have drawn on (among other things) an Egyptian version of the Exodus story, one in which the Hebrews are not liberated but expelled from Egypt, whence they emerge as enemies of the gods and of all other peoples. And the second is that the genre into which he translated those traditions, that of Greek history writing, gave them new reach, new (and newly authoritative) meaning, new form.

Manetho's History of Mosaic Misanthropy

The innovation inspired. We have no native Egyptian version of such a story predating Hecataeus, but we do have one from roughly a generation after him, that is, from the early third century BCE. Its author was Manetho, a native Egyptian priest of Heliopolis during the reign of the Greek pharaoh Ptolemy II Philadelphus (282–246 BCE). As with so many ancient texts, its transmission poses problems: the only portions that survive are those quoted by much later authors such as the Jewish historian Josephus, and these may have been altered in the intervening time, or even by Josephus himself.[18] But let us not become paralyzed by philological anxiety. We shall plunge into the story, and see what it can tell us about the role of the Jews in Egyptian perceptions of their own history.

Josephus attributes to Manetho, "who had undertaken to translate the history of Egypt from the sacred books," two very different versions of the Exodus, one of which Josephus thinks of as historical, the other as defamatory and polemical, and both as deliberately conflated by Manetho. The first is the story of a people called the Shepherds who invaded Egypt "with many tens of thousands and gained the mastery over its inhabitants." Later, after they had been defeated and "driven out of the country, [they] occupied what is now Judaea, founded Jerusalem, and built the Temple." Josephus understands this first account as more or less historical: "Up to this point he followed the chronicles." This "Exodus" account does not attribute any particular evil to the invaders, apart from that of being foreigners to Egypt.[19]

But then comes the second version, in which, "having assumed the power to write down the legends and sayings about the Jews, [Manetho] took the liberty of inserting incredible stories."[20] According to this second story, the Egyptian pharaoh Amenophis was advised that "he would be able to see the gods if he purified the entire land of lepers and other unclean people," and so he "gathered all the maimed bodies of Egypt: in total, a multitude of 80,000 persons." As in Hecataeus's account, religious concerns (this time a desire to see the gods rather

than to appease divine anger) incite the Egyptians to segregate a suspect people (this time the sick rather than the stranger). In Manetho's
version, however, that segregation goes badly wrong. King Amenophis
sends the lepers to labor in the stone quarries, before finally assigning
to them as habitation the "deserted city of the Shepherds." There the
oppressed lepers form a society of their own under the leadership of one
Osarseph, a renegade Egyptian priest from Heliopolis. Osarseph's first
law was that "they should not worship the gods nor abstain from any
of the animals sanctified by law in Egypt . . . , that they should not have
any contact except with those of their own sworn confederacy . . . [and]
many other laws like these, entirely the opposite of Egyptian custom."
He then went to Jerusalem to form an alliance with the Shepherds who
had settled there and who seem to share his iconoclastic views. Together
the lepers and Shepherds conquered Egypt

> *and treated the population so impiously that the earlier dominion [of
> the Shepherds] seemed like a golden age to those who were witnessing
> such sacrilege. For not only did they set fire to cities and villages, unre-
> strainedly attacking the temples and mutilating divine images, but
> they also used the sanctuaries as roasters in which to cook the sacred
> animals which were revered by the people; and they forced the priests
> and prophets to sacrifice and slaughter the beasts, afterwards casting
> the holy men out naked.*[21]

Finally, Manetho returns again to the subject of the renegade priest
Osarseph: "[W]hen he changed to this people, he changed his name
and called himself Moses."

These "incredible stories," as Josephus called them, came to be
widely accepted as fact in the ancient world. Many pagan writers of
the period (Posidonius of Apamea, Lysimachus, Chaeremon, Apion,
Tacitus) quoted or adapted some version of the story as a historically
accurate description of the origins of the Jewish people.[22] Few scholars
would do so today: Josephus turns out to have been right about the
compound nature of the tale. Nevertheless the story remains especially

important for anyone interested in our topic, as *an early example of how a people's sense of their past and present place in the world could be articulated through the construction of a fundamental opposition to Jews and Judaism*. In order to demonstrate this, however, we will need to spend just a little more time studying how these Egyptian stories about the Jews were put together, and why they proved so useful to Egyptians living under Greek and (later) Roman rule.

The Crafting of an Anti-Jewish Cosmology

Manetho was well positioned to write a history of Egypt (called, like nearly all Egyptian histories of the period, the *Aegyptiaca*). As an ethnic Egyptian and a priest, he had much greater access to informants and information than did a Greek like Hecataeus, and he had the linguistic skills to profit from that access. Manetho took up his brush (Egyptians wrote with brushes, Greeks with a calamus, or reed pen) surrounded by the physical and textual remnants of some two thousand years of history.[23] He used a number of these remnants in the construction of his narrative, ranging from the king-lists and religious manuals in his temple's library, to the statues, inscriptions, and narrative carvings on the buildings and monuments he visited. It is quite possible, even probable, that the story he told about the origins of the Jews was not his but rather borrowed from some older source since lost. But it is clear that whoever first composed the story did so by drawing on a number of traditional themes that were much older still, themes that had long shaped the ways in which Egyptians thought about the ups and downs of their history.

One of these themes is that of foreign invasion. The prototypical example of such invaders were the Shepherds, known to Egyptologists today as the Hyksos, who swept into Egypt from Palestine and ruled Egypt for more than a hundred years circa the seventeenth century BCE.[24] Stories about the Hyksos invasions and about the subsequent restoration of Egypt after their defeat and expulsion became an important motif in Egyptian political and historical thought. In the New Kingdom, after the expulsion (ca. 1555 BCE),[25] the Hyksos story served as an expression of triumphant self-confidence. But from the sixth century BCE forward, during periods of extensive northern (first Assyrian, then Persian) immigration and domination, the story became an increasingly xenophobic vehicle for the expression of Egyptian resentment of foreign power. The theme of impurity and disease, associated early on with the Hyksos, was amplified and became, along with "foreignness," an important way of characterizing those perceived as a threat to Egyptian rule.[26] The story of the Hyksos was used to emphasize the dangers "aliens" posed to Egypt, to rally resistance to them, and to cast contemporary Asian invaders as descendants of degenerates expelled by Egypt long ago. The story even inspired works of prophetic literature like the *Oracle of the Lamb* that "foretold" invasion and promised liberation.[27] In short, a tradition of stories about the Shepherd invaders from the distant past was constantly reworked to make sense of the political vicissitudes of the present.[28]

Another important strand of thought reflected in Manetho's account (as in Hecataeus's) was religious. Like many other peoples, Egyptians often understood catastrophe, whether military, meteorological, or medical, as a product of divine wrath. Angered by neglect or impiety, the gods withdraw from their temples and abandon the land, allowing anarchy or alien peoples to reign. This motif is very ancient: we have examples of laments that follow this form from the First Intermediate Period (ca. 2220–2040 BCE) and perhaps earlier.[29] A little later, during the Middle Kingdom, the pharaohs sponsored a useful variation of this logic: the bad times are now viewed in retrospect, with an emphasis on the steps taken by the king to restore order, health, and bounty to the land. Not the earliest but certainly the most famous example of this type of "historical propaganda" comes from inscription known as the Tutankhamun Restoration Stela:

> *Now His Majesty appeared as king at a time when the temples of the gods and goddesses from Elephantine as far as the Delta Marshes . . . had fallen into ruin, and their shrines became dilapidated. They had turned into mounds overgrown with weeds, and it seemed that their*

sanctuaries had never existed. . . . This land had been struck with catastrophe: the gods had turned their backs upon it. If [ever] the army was dispatched . . . they would have no success; if [ever] one prayed to a god to ask something of him, he never would come at all. . . . Their hearts had grown weak in their bodies, because they had destroyed what had been created.[30]

The point of such historical propaganda was to demonstrate how, through careful attention to the proper maintenance of temples and their cult, the good king regains divine favor. His armies become once more victorious, the land returns to health, and catastrophe becomes prosperity.

A number of Egyptologists have argued that the theme of restoration from a period of "anti-religion" and anarchy is patterned after a historical event, just as the theme of the expulsion of aliens is patterned on the Hyksos episode. They point to the reign of the pharaoh Amenophis IV, also known as Akhenaten ("Beneficial for the Aten"), who ruled Egypt for a period of some seventeen years in the mid-fourteenth century BCE. The monotheistic religious revolution that this pharaoh carried out was a violent one. He forbade the feasts and sacrifices of the traditional gods, destroyed their images, shuttered their temples. He replaced their worship with that of the sun Aten, maker of all, and built a new capital and liturgical center at Amarna: hence the religion he advocated is often called the Amarna cult. That cult was short-lived, for the religious counterrevolution after Amenophis's death was as violent as his own had been. His monuments were destroyed, his name excised from the king-lists, and the worship of the old gods was restored. He and his religion sank into oblivion, lingering only as a memory of a time of blasphemy and impiety, when men had attacked the gods. In fact it seems that within two generations of Amenophis's death the memory of his aggressive monotheism had already been displaced backward in time, and attributed to . . . the alien Hyksos! They had been long since expelled, but Amenophis's "impieties" became yet another crime in the ever-longer list of abominations with which they were charged.[31]

Manetho's Moses: Creative History versus Historical Memory

Manetho's creative genius (or that of his source) lies in the way he deployed these traditional motifs, born from conflicts long forgotten, in the service of new struggles. That creativity is too often treated as historical fact or confused with memory. Many scholars have spent the century since the rediscovery of the Amarna documents trying to prove that Manetho's account is historical, and that Judaism is really descended from the Amarna cult. Some look for parallels between the Amarna hymns and the Hebrew Bible: Did the pharaoh's Great Hymn to Aten inspire Psalm 104?[32] Others, most famously Sigmund Freud, argue not just for influence, but for identity. In *Moses and Monotheism*, a "historical fiction" that Freud wrote in exile after Hitler had annexed his native Vienna, he suggested that the Moses who organized the Hebrews and took them into exile from Egypt was an official or high priest of the monotheist pharaoh Amenophis.[33] According to Freud, the Hebrews eventually rebelled murderously against Moses and later repressed the memory both of their crime and of Moses's Egyptian roots.

The specifics of Freud's reconstruction have not found much favor with Egyptologists, but his arguments about memory and history have been very influential. Freud suggested that, much like individuals who have suffered trauma, societies repress the memory of horrific events in their past because these are too painful to confront or document directly. According to Freud, these repressed memories often resurface in distorted ways that, if analyzed carefully, can help to uncover the original trauma and bring it back into conscious memory. For Egyptologists sympathetic to it, Manetho's story represents a resurfacing (ca. 300 BCE) of a long-repressed memory from the distant past (ca. 1400 BCE). His account therefore gains value as a description of the original events. Moses really *is* Amenophis. Or at the very least (for few scholars would go so far), Manetho's "Egyptian memory" is a more accurate version of the historical origins of monotheism than the confused recollections that reached the Jews in the shape of the Exodus story.[34]

Of course Freud's is only one way of thinking about Egyptian memories of the Exodus. Another possibility was suggested by the rabbis who commented on the biblical book of Lamentations in the second or third century of our Common Era.[35] They asked themselves why no Egyptian army had appeared to help the Israelites defend Jerusalem against Nebuchadnezzar in 597 BCE, as their alliance required. Their answer:

> [Pharaoh] did send soldiers. But as they sailed the Holy One signaled the sea, and it brought up before their eyes distended leather skins, which looked like human corpses, their entrails floating in the water. The soldiers asked one another, "What are these corpses?" They were answered: "These are the remains of your ancestors who enslaved the ancestors of the Jews to whose aid you sail. As soon as the forebears of the Jews were redeemed from your forebears, they rose up and drowned them in the sea." At that, the Egyptian soldiers said, "Jews acted in this way to our ancestors, and we are going to help them?" They returned at once.[36]

It would be difficult to convince a modern reader that Manetho's version of the past was prompted by such miraculous mnemonics. It seems to me equally difficult to prove that it represents the surfacing of ancient memories of trauma after a millennium of repression. I suggest instead that we should treat Manetho's text as the work of an ancient historian. It is not the "collective memory" of a society, but the creative redeployment of stories about the past in order to make sense of the present. His account of Jewish origins, most likely borrowed from an older source, was assembled from a kit of traditional Egyptian themes. It draws on post-Amarna motifs of impiety and rebellion against the gods in order to present the Jews and their monotheism as "completely opposed to Egyptian custom," the negative image of Egyptian religiosity. And it draws on post-Hyksos motifs about diseased and cruel Asiatic invaders in order to associate the Jews with Egypt's ur-enemy, and to present them as a mortal threat to the Egyptian community. In short, Manetho (or his earlier source) took up the traditional tools with which Egyptians fashioned images of their political and religious enemies, and applied them in new ways to the Jews of his day.

There is nothing unique about this historical "working over" of the Jews. As we have seen, other aliens and invaders had been blackened by charges of association with the Hyksos, of impurity, and of impiety. Nor was Manetho's portrait of Moses and the Jews the only one circulating in Egypt. Josephus obviously had different stories in mind when he wrote that the "Egyptians . . . regard that man as remarkable, even divine."[37] Egyptian stories about Moses's divinity have not reached us, but we do hear their faint echoes in the works of obscure figures like Artapanus, who lived in the Ptolemaic era at some point between 250 and 100 BCE. According to him, Moses was the founder of Egyptian as well as Jewish culture. It was he who established the annual flooding of the Nile when he struck it with his rod, summoning the first plague; he who assigned to each *nome*, or district of the Egyptians, the gods and animals that were to be worshipped there; he who taught the Egyptians how to use hieroglyphs. Playing on the similarity of names, Artapanus identifies Moses with the god Thoth-Mosis, scribe of the Egyptian pantheon. Moses is also the Greek Musaeus, teacher of Orpheus and therefore founder of Greek culture. Artapanus's Moses is born from the creative reworking of ancient Egyptian, biblical, and Greek traditions, just as Manetho's was. He is, however, the mirror image of Manetho's: a teacher to the Egyptians, a benefactor of all mankind.[38]

I mention Artapanus only to remind us that there were multiple "Egyptian" versions of the Moses story in circulation, not all of them invoking the politics of enmity. Moreover, by Manetho's day Egyptian versions of Moses's story had to compete directly with Jewish ones. For the first time in their history, Egyptian scholars could read the Exodus narrative for themselves in the Greek translation of the Hebrew Bible known as the Septuagint. According to ancient Egyptian Jewish tradition this translation was undertaken in Alexandria at the behest of

Ptolemy II Philadelphus—that is, at the very time that Manetho was composing his own history.[39] Some have suggested that the systematic access to Jewish scriptures that the Greek Septuagint provided to non-Jews may well have inspired and shaped the production of anti-Jewish narratives among Egyptians offended by its representations of their country and their ancestors. But my point here is a simpler one: there was more than one Moses walking about in ancient Egypt. We do not know much about how contemporaries identified him or reconciled his different faces, but we should not assume that the dominance of any one image was easy or assured.[40]

The Victory of Manetho's Vision

It is therefore all the more significant that over the course of some three centuries of Hellenistic and then Roman rule in Egypt, the "Manethine" negative image of Moses and the Jews became so dominant that it exiled its more attractive brethren, and came to constitute what we can properly call an Egyptian school of anti-Jewish ideology. Of course the school's authors vary in the details. Lysimachus, for example, who probably composed his *Aegyptiaca* sometime in the second century BCE, maintained that it was Pharaoh Bocchoris who undertook the segregation and expulsion of the Jews, not from any desire to see the gods, but because of the Jews' illness and impiety. The expulsion was an easy one: there was no alliance with the Shepherds, no period of Jewish rule over Egypt. But on the essentials of the Jews' character and mission, Lysimachus agreed entirely with Manetho: "to have good intentions toward no man, to give not the best but the worst advice, and to tear down the temples and altars of the gods which they might find."[41]

This Egyptian tradition's characterization of the Jews is easily outlined, and proved remarkably stable across time:

1. The Jews are a people once driven out of Egypt.
2. Their practices are diametrically opposed to those of all other peoples, especially Egyptians and Greeks.

3. They are enemies of all the gods.
4. Whenever and wherever they rule, they rule brutally and tyrannically.
5. They are misanthropes, enemies not just of Egypt, but of all mankind.

The first of these basic points was of interest primarily to Egyptians; the others proved so useful that they continue to provide cornerstones for ideologies up to the present day. All five were disseminated with such rapidity that we can only assume they were already widespread when Hecataeus and Manetho encountered them.

The best evidence for this early and rapid spread comes not from the writings of Egyptians, but from Jewish sources like the Septuagint. Consider the decisions of its translators to render the commandment of Exodus 22:28, "you shall not revile God," in the plural, "you shall not revile the gods [of others]." The multiplication took advantage of the well-known but rarely translated fact that Elohim, the Hebrew name for God used in this passage and many others, is grammatically plural. Here the effect was to transform what had always been understood as a prohibition of blasphemy into a commandment for cultural tolerance, and to provide an argument that the Jews were not enemies of the gods, as their detractors claimed.[42]

Even more telling is the way that the Greek translators of the Hebrew book of Esther, writing some time between the fourth and second centuries BCE, seem to have imagined Esther's Persian difficulties in particularly Egyptian terms. In the Hebrew version of the story, so familiar to modern Jews from the celebration of Purim, the wicked Haman tells King Ahasuerus,

Dispersed in scattered groups among the peoples throughout the provinces of your realm, there is a certain people whose laws are different from those of every other people. They do not observe the king's laws, and it does not befit your majesty to tolerate them. If it pleases your majesty, let an order be drawn up for their destruction.[43]

The Greek version is chillingly different. Here, Haman accuses the Jews of being a "hostile" people, whose laws are "opposed" "to any other people." They are ready to attack "always and against everyone," committing evil deeds against the kingdom's affairs. "They all—wives and children included—should be utterly destroyed . . . so that those who have been hostile and remain so in a single day go down in violence to Hades, and leave our government completely secure and untroubled hereafter." The Jews who rendered Esther into Greek seem already to have been acutely aware of the Egyptian charges against them—that they were enemies of all mankind whose extermination would bring perpetual peace and security—and they retold Esther as a story of victory over those calumnies.[44]

But the translators' victory was only rhetorical. The Egyptian idea that enmity could best be imagined in Jewish terms gained strength over the centuries that followed, and we start to find not only Esther's story but also many others from Jewish history being retold across the ancient world with a distinctively Egyptian nastiness. For example, Diodorus Siculus reports that when the Hellenistic Persian king Antiochus conquered Jerusalem in 134 BCE (a conquest best known to modern Jews through the story of Hanukkah),

> the majority of his friends advised the king to take the city by storm and to wipe out completely the race of Jews, since they alone of all nations avoided dealings with any other people and looked upon all men as their enemies. They pointed out, too, that the ancestors of the Jews had been driven out of all Egypt as men who were impious and detested by the gods. For by way of purging the country all persons who had white or leprous marks on their bodies had been assembled and driven across the border, as being under a curse; the refugees . . . having organized the nation of the Jews made their hatred of mankind into a tradition, and on this account had introduced utterly outlandish laws: not to break bread with any other race, nor to show them any good will at all.
>
> . . . Rehearsing all these events, his friends strongly urged Antiochus to make an end to the race completely, or, failing that, to abolish their laws and force them to change their ways.[45]

In stories such as these we see how the expanding Egyptian conviction that Jews brought misery into the world was written into the past. In these texts and others, it was also foretold for the future. A prophetic papyrus from the Roman period warns Egyptians of impending disaster, when "impious people will destroy your temples," "your largest temple will become sand for the horses," and Jews will inhabit the sacred city of Heliopolis. The solution? "Attack the Jews," "lawbreakers" who have already been "once expelled from Egypt by the wrath of Isis."[46] By the first century of the Common Era, Egyptians no longer made sense of their vicissitudes by telling stories about the Hyksos or about general neglect of the gods. Instead they used Jews to do much of the ideological work of these earlier motifs. In this sense we can say that they defined their own sense of status against the Jews, and that it is onto the Jews that they projected responsibility for the straitened circumstances of Egyptian power. But what remains to be explained is, why this shift?

The Politics of Difference in a Multiethnic Empire

Of the motives for native Egyptian anti-Judaism during the period of Persian domination we can say nothing more convincing than the musings with which we surrounded Elephantine: perhaps the Jews' loyalty to the rulers who "imported" and supported them earned them Egyptian resentment; perhaps the particular shape of their sacred history and their cult stimulated an Egyptian counternarrative. As the anonymous author of the book known as 3 Maccabees put it in explaining a later persecution of the Egyptian Jews by the pharaoh Ptolemy IV Philopator (221–205 BCE), "But the Jews were maintaining good will toward the kings and unswerving loyalty, while at the same time, worshiping God and conducting their lives according to God's law, they maintained a separation in the matter of foods, for which reason to some people they appeared hostile."[47]

The same theories might help to explain why native Egyptians like Manetho continued to attack the Jews during the Ptolemaic period of Greek domination. After all, Egypt's Greek rulers, like the Persians before them, were always on the lookout for foreigners they could use as a counterweight to the conquered native population. For this purpose Jews and other peoples from the area of Syria-Palestine were close to hand. Thus, according to one ancient source, Ptolemy I Soter (305–282 BCE), Alexander the Great's successor in Egypt, returned from his wars against Alexander's heirs in Persia with a hundred thousand slaves he had captured in Judea. The same source claims that another thirty thousand Jews were employed in the Ptolemaic armies.[48] Other Jews came to Egypt seeking refuge from political turbulence in Judea. In around 162–160 BCE, for example, a failed candidate for Jerusalem high priest named Onias fled to Egypt with many of his followers. He was warmly welcomed by Ptolemy VI Philometor and sent as garrison to Leontopolis, a strategic site near Manetho's ancient home of Heliopolis. (The temple that Onias built at Leontopolis outlasted the one in Jerusalem: it was destroyed in 73 CE.)[49] Many other Jews were probably attracted by the glories of the Ptolemaic kingdom and of its new city of Alexandria, already recognized as "the first city of the civilized world, . . . far ahead of all the rest in elegance, size, riches and luxury."[50] So many Jews moved to Egypt that by Roman times Philo of Alexandria could claim that there were a million Jews living in the kingdom.[51]

Of course not all of these Jews were alike. Moreover, they were often not sharply differentiated from their non-Jewish Egyptian and Greek neighbors. Some poor artisans, like the Jewish family that shared a pottery factory with an Egyptian neighbor in a small Fayûm village, spoke no Greek and adopted Egyptian names like Horos and Paous. At the other end of the social scale, some Jews were so fully assimilated into Greek society that they could scarcely be recognized as such. Figures like Aristobulus and Dositheus son of Drimylus not only bore Greek names but also served as eponymous priests of the royal cult of Alexander and the Ptolemies. Even in death it is not always easy to tell where the boundaries lay: a Jewish mummy label from the first or second century CE uses the same phrasing as many Egyptian mummy labels ("may her soul live eternally"), and may even suggest that, like their neighbors, some Jews of Egypt practiced mummification.[52]

In other words, Jews fell on either side of the sharp divide between conquered Egyptian and conquering Greek in the Ptolemaic kingdom. Nevertheless it is not too difficult to imagine native Egyptian resentment of these newcomers, and of the political privileges that they and their communities sometimes possessed. We do not need merely to imagine it, for it surfaces occasionally in the surviving papyri, which preserve complaints about the privileges acquired by "undesirable and ineligible aliens." The papyri also contain some evidence of generalized resentment, most famously in a private letter from the first century BCE, in which a man called Heracles (plausibly Jewish himself) writes to "the manager Ptolemaios" asking him to look after a Jewish priest traveling in the Egyptian heartland of Memphis: "[for] you know how they loathe the Jews [there]." Such resentments may have honed the cutting edge of Manethine anti-Judaism.[53]

What is much more difficult to understand is the enthusiasm with which these ideas were adopted by the citizens of the Greek cities (and especially by those of "Alexandria by Egypt," as she came to be known). It was not the Egyptians of the heartland, but the privileged Greek citizens of Alexandria who distilled native anti-Jewish motifs into their most potent form and preserved them for posterity.[54] Why should this be so? The answer most often given is political. If we imagine the political hierarchy of Hellenistic Egypt as a pyramid, then the Ptolemaic pharaoh is at the top, followed by Greek citizens, then Jews, with the mass of native Egyptians at the bottom. This pyramid, however, was unstable. The citizens of Alexandria, for example, often attempted to increase their privileges and freedoms from royal power, while the pharaohs, to the contrary, struggled to reduce them. Of course the Jews, too, were interested in augmenting their privileges, but this desire rarely brought them into conflict with the monarchy. On the contrary, the Jews were by and large not citizens, and the privileges enjoyed by their communities were not constitutional (in the loose sense of the word). Jewish communities depended much more directly on royal favor than Greek cities did, and therefore sometimes sided with the pharaohs and against the citizens in civil conflicts.[55]

The adventures of Onias's Jewish garrison at Leontopolis provide one example of this triangular relationship. When Ptolemy VI Philometor welcomed Onias to Egypt, he was a pharaoh very much in need of friends. Raised to the throne as a child, he was constantly engaged in civil war against his younger brother Euergetes (also known as Physkon, "Potbelly"), and twice defeated by the Syrian king Antiochus IV. He would not find much sympathy among the Greeks of Alexandria, who saw in his travails an opportunity to strengthen their own power by supporting Euergetes. Nor could he embrace the native Egyptian population, who detested the foreign monarchy. Abroad, Rome intervened to save him from Antiochus. At home, he depended on his newly settled Jews for support. They were so dependable that after Philometor's death in 145 BCE, when Potbelly and Alexandria rebelled against his widow Cleopatra II, the Jewish army of Onias besieged the city. Enraged, Potbelly is said to have ordered the Jews of Alexandria trampled to death by drunken elephants.

The story, which goes on to report that the elephants attacked Potbelly's men instead, reflects how serious the consequences of participating in internal politics could be for the Jews. But once Euergetes won the war, married Cleopatra, and became pharaoh, he too found it convenient to build up the Jews as allies. His conflicts with the Greek citizens of Alexandria were strenuous ("frequently he surrounded the gymnasium of the [Greek] youths with flame and weapons, killing some of those within with steel, others with fire"), and he needed support wherever he could find it. When Euergetes himself died and his widow Cleopatra III in turn confronted rebellion (in the form of her own son, the future Ptolemy IX Lathyros), the pattern repeated itself: the garrison of Leontopolis again remained loyal, this time under the command of Onias's sons. And again, the Jews of Alexandria paid the price in violence when Ptolemy Lathyros ascended the throne, in 88 BCE.[56]

This exceptional relation between (some of) Egypt's Jews and (some of) Egypt's monarchs itself became a meaningful and useful target for citizens of Greek cities in their constant efforts to expand the power and privilege of those cities within (and often at the expense of) the monarchy. Native Egyptian motifs proved useful for this purpose in that they could be deployed to criticize the pharaoh who employed these "enemies of all mankind." The power of that critique could also be amplified by international affairs. In 175–167 BCE, the successful revolt of the Maccabees against Seleucid Persian domination and the formation of a Hasmonean kingdom in Judea allowed Alexandrian Greeks to argue that Egypt's Jews were a potential "fifth-column" that might ally with the Hasmoneans or the Seleucids against the Ptolemaic pharaoh.[57] But the most dramatic example of this amplification, and the one with the greatest impact on the development of Egyptian anti-Judaism, was the rise of Rome to empire.

Rome's power in the region was already obvious in the second century BCE: in 168 BCE, for example, she supported Pharaoh Ptolemy VI Philometor against Antiochus IV. By the mid-first century BCE, she effectively controlled the entire region. But Roman intervention only heightened the tensions I have been describing. In 55 BCE, for example, the Alexandrians attacked Pharaoh Ptolemy XII Auletes (80–51 BCE) as a Roman puppet and expelled him from the city. Roman and Jewish troops quickly returned him to power.[58] We can only imagine how events such as these might have emboldened claims that Jewish malignity, Ptolemaic monarchy, and Roman power were conspiring against Alexandrian liberty.[59]

The Emperor Is a "Jew": Anti-Judaism as Anti-Tyranny

We can only "imagine" because we do not have (so far as I know) any surviving evidence from the Ptolemaic period that explicitly documents these associations. But our imagination is not fantastic. It is guided by rich evidence from a slightly later period, that of Egypt's subjection to Rome's imperial rule after the defeat of the famously beautiful Cleopatra VII and her Roman lover Mark Antony. Consider the behavior of Isidorus, a leading Greek citizen of Alexandria, before the emperor Claudius (who ruled from 41 to 54 CE). Isidorus, it seems, brought an accusation against the Jewish king Agrippa, an accusation that, if proved true, could be punished by death.[60] Three papyri inform us of what followed, and each tells a slightly different story, but all agree on a few things. Isidorus beseeched Claudius to listen to his account of "my native city's sufferings." Claudius agreed but ordered him to "say nothing . . . against my friend" Agrippa. In every version, Isidorus responds to the emperor's order with insolence: "What do you care for a three-penny Jew like Agrippa?" "I am . . . the gymnasiarch of the glorious city of Alexandria. But you [Claudius] are the cast off son of the Jewess Salome!" The emperor was not amused: Isidorus and his co-plaintiff Lampon (nicknamed "pen-slayer" for his habit of doctoring evidence in capital cases) were executed.[61]

The records that preserve these accounts are not court records but martyrologies. They are known to historians as "The Acts of the Alexandrine Martyrs," and the stories they tell are of heroic citizens risking death to defend their city's freedoms (often freedom from financial exaction and taxes) by telling truth to tyrannical power. Often in these stories that power is presented as Jewish, or as corrupted by Judaism. Claudius is a Jew-lover, or born of a Jewess. Hermaiscus, the Alexandrine delegate in a later embassy (sometime between 105 and 112 CE), attacked the emperor Trajan in similar terms:

> Hermaiscus: "Why, it grieves us to see your Privy Council filled with impious Jews." Caesar said: ". . . I am telling you Hermaiscus: you are answering me insolently, taking advantage of your birth." Hermaiscus said: "What do you mean, I answer you insolently, greatest Emperor? Explain this to me." Caesar said: "Pretending that my Privy Council is filled with Jews." Hermaiscus said: "So then, the word 'Jew' is offensive to you? In that case you ought rather to help your own people and not play the advocate for the impious Jews."

A miracle may have saved Hermaiscus's head: the statue he carried of the goddess Serapis, patroness of Alexandria, impressed the emperor by bursting into a sweat.[62] Others were not so lucky. When the emperor Commodus (180–192 CE) sternly asked the Alexandrian Appian if he knew to whom he was speaking, Appian replied, "Yes, I do: Appian speaks to a tyrant." Appian was executed a century after Isidorus, and by now it seems that there is an established tradition of "Alexandrian martyrs," for Appian (or at least, the author of Appian's martyrology) speaks of "those who died before me, Theon, and Isidorus and Lampon."[63]

More earnest historians have wondered which Salome could have been Claudius's mother (Salome I would be too old, while Salome II, the daughter of Herodias famous from the story of John the Baptist, was born a generation after Claudius), or whether the Roman Senate of Trajan's day might indeed have been full of Jews. (It was not.)[64] But the search for a Roman reality behind the charges very much misses the point of these texts: they are the product of an ideology that represented the struggle against tyranny in terms of a struggle against the Jews. That representation drew its explanatory power from the confluence of three interrelated traditions. There were the prophetic traditions we explored earlier, about how the presence of Jews imperiled Egypt's sovereignty and its gods. "Attack the Jews," as a papyrus from the Roman era puts it, already "once expelled from Egypt by the wrath of Isis." There was also the long association of certain groups of Jews with monarchical power, and their perception as instruments of that power. And finally, there was a Hellenistic political philosophy, most famously systematized by Alexander the Great's great contemporary Aristotle, and widely disseminated throughout the world ruled by Alexander's heirs, that understood tyranny as a form of misanthropy. The tyrant is self-interested, one whose catering to his own needs and appetites at the expense of his people makes him the enemy of his subjects. The good sovereign cares not for himself but for the common wealth and well-being of his people.[65]

The confluence of these traditions provided Alexandria's Greek citizens with a new and slightly overdetermined way of explaining Egypt's political fate, and of representing Roman injustice and their own resistance to it. Overdetermined in the sense that on the one hand it is the malevolent influence of the Jews that inclines Rome against Egypt and makes its government tyrannical. But at the same time, to the extent that the emperor is tyrannical, he is acting like a Jew and can be criticized as such. Within the logic of these texts, complaints about the Jews before the emperor, or complaints about the emperor's Jew-loving or Jewishness, become an exemplary exercise of what Greek Alexandrines called "*parrēsia*," the courage to speak truth to power: what we today might call "free speech." But in fact a particularly important virtue of this ideology of freedom was that it so rarely demanded the martyrdom of its heroes, or required of them much courage. On the contrary, more often it allowed the Alexandrians to focus their attacks on a suspect and subject people, rather than on a powerful emperor or empire, while at the same time still believing that in so doing they were defending their most vital principles and privileges. The political magic of Egyptian anti-Judaism lay precisely in its ability to produce this contradiction.

Apion's Embassy against the Jews

For a brilliant (and brilliantly documented) performance of that magic we need only join the martyr Isidorus on an earlier embassy than the one that cost him his life. Two rival delegations set sail from Alexandria in the winter of 38 or 39 CE, bound for Rome. Philo of Alexandria headed one. A prolific author of biblical commentaries much influenced by Greek philosophy, Philo belonged to one of the wealthiest and most influential Jewish families of the city, one of those few Jewish families, it seems, that also enjoyed citizenship. The other delegation (the one that included Isidorus) was led by Apion, an immigrant to Alexandria famous in his day as a scholar of Homer, a historian of Egypt, and a composer of treatises against the Jews. The wind that filled their sails was a violent one. The previous summer the Jewish king Agrippa, just raised to the throne of Judea, had passed through Alexandria en route to his new kingdom. While the Jews of Alexandria celebrated, the kingless and resentful Greeks dressed up a local lunatic named Carabas (whose name means either "cabbage" or "boatman") in a purple blanket, gave him a papyrus crown and a papyrus branch as scepter, then paraded him about town while saluting him mockingly as "Lord."

In the ensuing riot hundreds of Jewish homes and shops were looted, their occupants killed or forced to move into a quarter of the city identified as a Jewish "ghetto." Jews caught in the streets outside that quarter were set on fire or dragged into a bloody pulp along the pavement. Crowds of Alexandrians burst into the synagogues and decorated them with statues of the Roman emperor Gaius, also known as Caligula. The Jews dared not remove these (fans of *I, Claudius* will understand their fear), but neither could they worship with them there. Flaccus, the then governor of Egypt, gave them little aid. He stripped the Jews of their political rights and declared them "foreigners and aliens."[66] He seems also to have accused the Jews of inciting the riot themselves. In any case he had thirty-eight of their elders whipped in the theater, and honored the emperor's birthday (August 31) by having a number of others executed in the most exotic ways he could think of.[67]

This violence provided the immediate context for the arguments of the two delegations. But their complaints and countercomplaints went far beyond assigning responsibility for the riot. The more basic issue dividing them concerned the political rights and privileges of citizenship. Egypt's Roman rulers sought to separate their non-Roman subjects into two classes: citizens of Greek cities and foreigners. In a sense the division continued—but sharpened—the distinction of privilege that had existed under the Ptolemies between Egypt's Greek rulers and the non-Greek peoples—that is, native Egyptians, as well as others—they had conquered. Greek citizens had political rights. They could inscribe their children in the *ephebia* (the gymnasium, or educational institution that prepared them for leadership and political participation), and they were exempt from certain taxes (such as the *laographia*, or poll tax). "Foreigners" (that is, foreign to Greece and Rome) lacked these rights and paid the tax. Into the first category fell all the citizens of Alexandria who were accounted Greek; into the second, all native Egyptians.

But the Jews were an anomaly, an exception. For centuries they seem to have occupied an intermediate category, with only a few Jews (such as Philo) possessing citizenship in the Greek *polis* (city), but with the Jewish community as a whole forming its own distinct polity (*politeuma*).[68]

This polity was in some ways independent of the Greek polis, with its own rights and privileges guaranteed first by Ptolemaic and then by Roman authority. The Greek Alexandrines sought to prevent any Jews from holding citizenship and to strip the Jewish community of self-rule: a goal the governor Flaccus had temporarily fulfilled for them. Now the question was put before the emperor. Could Jews be citizens? Could their community have rights?

Apion's own account of his embassy on behalf of the Greek Alexandrines does not survive. But we can reconstruct a hypothetical version of his arguments from the treatise that Josephus wrote to rebut Apion's views on the Jews, called *Against Apion*. According to Apion, the Jews had come to the city from Syria and therefore could never be called Alexandrians, no matter how long they had lived there. Indeed they could more properly be characterized as enemies of the city than as citizens, for had not the Jew Onias marched against Alexandria during the war between Cleopatra II and Physkon? Had not Cleopatra VII "in time of famine refused to give the Jews any rations of corn"? And "why . . . if they are citizens, do they not worship the same gods as the Alexandrians?" Moreover, the Jews are a seditious people who obey no laws but their own, laws that are not only ridiculous (insisting on circumcision! refusing to eat pork!), but also opposed to those of all other peoples. They are not "masters of an empire, but rather the slaves, first of one nation, then of another." How is it that a slave people clamor for the privileges of citizenship? Moreover this same people refuse to erect statues to emperors who have conquered them, claiming that it would violate their law against images, although in their own temple they worship a golden statue of an ass's head! The real reason that they honor no one is that they are misanthropes, hating all but themselves.[69]

In his writings Apion provided many "historical" examples of former kings who hated Jews, examples that he might have held before Caligula to buttress his points. It is Apion who tells the infamous story about King Antiochus's conquest of Jerusalem in 134 BCE. The king, according to Apion, found a miserable man inside the Jews' Temple, sitting before a magnificent feast. The man revealed a horrible secret.

Each year the Jews kidnap a Greek, fatten him up, then kill and eat him as part of a ritual in which they swear an oath of hostility to all aliens, especially Greeks. "The man . . . begged the king, out of respect for the Greek gods, to defeat this Jewish plot . . . and deliver him from his pitiable predicament." Roman rulers, too, had recognized the Jews' rebellious misanthropy and treated them with appropriate contempt, according to Apion. Caligula's own father, Germanicus, for example, had refused to include them in the distributions of food he made to all other Alexandrines. How could one doubt that the notoriously seditious Jews had started the riot? How could one consider admitting such people to citizenship or allowing them political rights? It was a wonder that they were tolerated in the city at all. The Alexandrians were right in detesting the Jews, and the emperor should follow their example.[70]

We know a great deal about how a Jew like Philo would have answered these accusations, not only because Philo himself left us two accounts of his embassy but also because many of the prolific writings of Philo, Josephus, and other Jews were dedicated to countering what they called "the lies of the Egyptians." But the Jews' version of history is not our subject here, and in any event Philo's delegation was allowed few arguments. When, after five months' wait, they were finally granted an audience with Caligula, it was during his inspection of some new villas, and the emperor gave them no time to state their case. His greeting was disconcerting: "Are you the god-haters who do not believe me to be a god, a god acknowledged among all the other nations but not to be named by you?" His questions ("Why do you not eat pork?") seemed designed to provoke his courtiers' laughter. And he interrupted all the delegation's answers with instructions to his decorators about how to glaze the windows and where to hang the pictures.[71] For five long months Philo had worried that the influential Alexandrines in Caligula's court were filling the emperor's ears with such stories about the Jews, and here his worst fears seemed confirmed. Fortunately (from Philo's point of view) Caligula was assassinated before he could decide the case. The emperor Claudius listened a little more patiently than his predecessor to a fresh round of delegations, and issued a ruling in 41 CE. Jews were forbidden admission to the citizenship in Alexandria, but the traditional political rights of the Jewish community were upheld.[72]

From Exception to Exclusion and Extermination

Those of us brought up in mass democracies, with their ideals of widespread and homogeneous political rights, will need to work to understand the exclusionary logic of Apion and his delegation. For the proud citizens of Alexandria, the exclusion of Jews and native Egyptians from the privileges of citizenship (such as participation in the civic athletic contests, education in the gymnasium, possession of honorable titles such as *gymnasiarch*, or membership in one of the many "Greek clubs" of the city) was vital to maintaining their sense of themselves as a sovereign people with an imperial history. That sovereignty and that history were under attack. Of course the real threat came not from native Egyptians (who remained safely subordinated and relatively powerless) nor from Jews, but from Rome. Yet it was by attacking the Jews that Greek Alexandrians like Apion and Isidorus managed to criticize Rome and secure their own greatness.

The point is not new: Apion's near-contemporary Josephus made a similar claim in his *Against Apion*. According to Josephus, Apion was a native Egyptian whose own citizenship was deceitfully obtained, and so he attacked the Jews to draw attention away from his own base origins. Josephus was probably wrong about Apion's "native" origins (since both Greek and Jewish Alexandrians agreed on the low status of native Egyptians, they often tried to assimilate their rivals to that group).[73] But he was right on two important counts. Apion's attack did draw heavily on "native" Egyptian negative traditions about the Jews (although these traditions had by now been so often repeated by Greek historians that perhaps only the Jews were still aware of their Egyptian origins). And he was very much motivated by status anxiety. His anxiety was not, however, that of a parvenu about his roots. It was rather the anxiety of a conquered elite watching its privileges erode from above.[74]

Such attacks did not end with Claudius's compromise. In 66 CE the citizen body of Alexandria met to elect delegates for a mission to Rome. The crowd spotted three Jews, assailed them with cries of "spies" and "enemies," and burned them to death. During the ensuing riot Roman legions and Alexandrines entered the Jewish quarter, met stiff resistance, and slaughtered some fifty thousand Jews.[75] A few years later, after the Jewish revolt against Rome in Judea had been defeated and Jerusalem conquered, the citizens of Alexandria sent a mission to the victorious emperor Titus asking him to deprive the city's Jews of their remaining rights. In 115 CE the citizens of Alexandria again attacked the Jews and called in the Roman legions, claiming that "impious Jews" were planning to invade the city.[76] In the urban warfare that followed, a number of the city's most magnificent monuments were destroyed (the Greeks' Serapeum, the Jews' great synagogue), and the Jewish population of Alexandria more or less eliminated.[77] An armed uprising of Jews in the rest of Egypt, as well as in Cyrene and Cyprus, created a state of civil war that lasted until 117 CE. Roman Egyptian sources tell how the Jews slaughtered their Egyptian neighbors, tore down Egyptian temples, and destroyed statues of the gods: a list of horrors suspiciously akin to those attributed to Moses and his followers by Manetho and the Egyptian Exodus tradition.[78] We cannot know whether these accounts were inspired by events or by traditional Egyptian stories about the Jews, but we can trace the fear they aroused. Mothers prayed to the gods, begging them to protect their children from being defeated by the Jews.[79] Native Egyptian priests mobilized peasant armies, Greek citizens formed militias, and an expeditionary army under Marcius Turbo reinforced the regular Roman legions. The Jews of Egypt, city and countryside, were destroyed. Only a small fraction of Philo's "million" survived, but the memory of their defeat remained to be savored. Some eighty years later in the town of Oxyrhynchus (and presumably in others like it?) an annual festival still celebrated the "day of victory" in the war against the Jews: the only victory we know of to be honored by such a holiday in the entire history of ancient Egypt.[80]

• • •

The stories that native Egyptians like Manetho or Greek Egyptians like Apion told about the Jews were popular in the ancient world, and they were read and repeated far beyond the boundaries of Egypt. They became standard fare in the histories and ethnographies produced by Greek and Roman scholars of the ancient world, who did not hesitate to apply them to the peoples and events of their own day. A Roman historian like Tacitus, for example, might articulate them with particular violence in order to explain the obstreperous rebelliousness of Judea against Roman power.[81] Yet despite the frequent deployment of these stories and stereotypes, the Jews would remain for several centuries more or less irrelevant to how Romans thought of themselves. Egyptians, on the other hand, assigned to the Jews a larger, and largely negative, role in how they imagined the fate of their kingdom and its gods in the past, present, and future. The causes of this centrality (the negative image of Egypt in Hebrew scripture? the large population of Jews in Egypt? the power of ancient Egyptian patterns of thought about invasion and impiety? the anxieties of elites under colonial rule?) are not simple, nor are they recoverable from our scarce and fragmentary sources. But though the causes of Egyptian anti-Judaism must remain conjecture, the shape and legacy of that anti-Judaism are relatively clear. The characteristics of misanthropy, impiety, lawlessness, and universal enmity that ancient Egypt had occasionally assigned to Moses and his people would remain available to later millennia: a tradition made venerable by antiquity, to be forgotten, rediscovered, and put to new uses by later generations of apologists and historians. In this sense we can agree with Josephus's claim that "the Egyptians began the slanders against us." As for the political logic of Egyptian anti-Judaism, it also had a future. The Greeks of Alexandria had focused their ambitions for sovereignty and freedom not on their conquerors (Romans) nor on their conquered (natives), but on the Jews: neither disenfranchised nor citizen, neither conquered nor conquering, neither powerless nor free. In the end, the Jews proved so useful to the Egyptians precisely because they were an anomaly and an exception. The extent to which Egypt put this exception to work was unique in the ancient world. This, however, was about to change. While Philo and Apion argued in Rome, a new movement was forming in Judea, and that movement would transform the meaning of Jews and Judaism forever.

Chapter 2

EARLY CHRISTIANITY:
THE ROAD TO EMMAUS, THE ROAD
TO DAMASCUS

The Road to Emmaus

Two men—or is it a man and a woman?—are talking on the road to Emmaus. It is seven miles to their destination, but they are oppressed by disappointment, not by distance. A third figure, a stranger, appears on the road. "What are all these things that you are discussing as you walk along?" "They stopped, downcast. Then one of them answered him: 'you must be the only person staying in Jerusalem who does not know the things that have been happening there these last few days. . . . All about Jesus of Nazareth, who showed himself a prophet powerful in action and in speech . . . and our leaders handed him over to be sentenced to death, and had him crucified. Our own hope had been that he would be the one to set Israel free.'"

Contrary to their first impression, their new companion proves to be quite well informed. "'You foolish men! So slow to believe all that the prophets have said! Was it not necessary that the Christ should suffer before entering into his glory?' Then, starting with Moses and going through all the prophets, he explained to them the passages throughout the scriptures that were about himself." "About himself," the gospel says, because the stranger was the risen Jesus, although his two disciples did not recognize him till dinnertime and journey's end (Luke 24:13–35).[1]

Jesus's presence on the road to Emmaus was a miracle, testimony to his conquest of death. But as miraculous as his feet on the road was the conversation that murmured across the miles. That conversation taught the world a new way to read the scriptures of the Jews—which is also to say, the scripture of Jesus and his followers. The miracle was repeated a short time later, when Jesus appeared to the disciples gathered in Jerusalem in order to ease their doubting hearts. "Touch me and see for yourselves," he tells the agitated disciples. Other gospels might focus more on this sense of touch (think of John's emphasis on Thomas's doubting fingers, in 20:24–29). Luke, however, dwells on the exegesis, the biblical interpretation:

"This is what I meant when I said . . . that everything written about me in the Law of Moses, in the Prophets and in the Psalms, was destined to be fulfilled." He then opened their minds to understand the scriptures, and he said to them, "So it is written that the Christ would suffer and on the third day rise from the dead, and that, in his name, repentance for the forgiveness of sins would be preached to all nations, beginning from Jerusalem." (Luke 24:44–47)

First on the road and now here in the city Jesus is performing a miracle of pedagogy, teaching his disciples how to read the old scriptures in new ways, ways that in turn transform the meaning of Israel's past and the possibilities for its future.

That pedagogy and those transformations, as they emerge after the death of Jesus in the documents that we today call the New Testament, are the subject of this chapter. But already we have stumbled on a difficulty: the story with which we have begun, the story of Jesus initiating his postmortem pedagogy on the road to Emmaus, is not in fact the beginning of our story. The Gospel of Luke was written circa 90 CE, more than half a century after Jesus's death. And although it deploys older material, it orients that material toward the burning questions of its own place and age. What were some of those questions? Jesus's followers believed him to be the Jews' Messiah, come to free Israel from Roman domination and be its king: "Our own hope had been that he would be the one who would set Israel free" (Luke 24:21). Yet by the time the Gospel of Luke was written it was clear that most of Israel did not share that belief. Moreover, Jesus had been crucified (a punishment the Romans reserved for rebels and political agitators). How could such defeat be reconciled with the prior messianic hope? If Jesus was not recognized as king by the people of Jerusalem, then who were his people, and what relationship did they have to the Jews? The Emmaus story is not a report of contemporary events, but a retrospective account that is already engaged in shaping a past capable of addressing the problems of its own present: in this case, the scandal (Greek *skandalon*) of the crucified Messiah and the apparent parting of the ways between the "New" and "True" Israel, and the "Old."[2]

The general problem is well known: Jesus left no written records that have reached us, and neither did any of the disciples who heard him speak. The anonymous authors of all our canonical gospels (their ascription to "Matthew," "Mark," "Luke," and "John" appears first in Irenaeus circa 180 CE, generations after the gospels were composed) wrote long after Jesus's death, from lands and in a language (Greek) that the founder of their religion may himself never have known.[3] Of course they did not write in a vacuum: they drew on multiple gospels and traditions—many now lost—about what Jesus had said and how he had lived. As Luke puts it in his first line, "[M]any others have undertaken to draw up accounts of the events that have reached their fulfillment among us, as these were handed down to us." The gospel authors chose among these traditions, editing, emending, arranging, and retelling them in a way that fit both their understanding of what Jesus's world must have been like and the needs of the world they lived in.

This means that when it comes to our specific questions—how the rise of Jesus's movement and the dissemination of his teachings throughout the ancient world transformed the ways in which that world could think with and about Judaism—we cannot start with the gospels' stories. But between the teachings of the historical Jesus prior to 33 CE—to which we have no direct access—and those of the gospel authors after 70 CE, another teacher took up these questions, and his teachings proved so influential that they greatly affected how gospel authors like "Luke" could imagine the past they were writing about. So let us change the scene for a moment, to another meeting on another road, this one leading to Damascus, somewhere between 33 and 39 CE.

The Road to Damascus

Whether the Jew is on foot or—as Michelangelo, Caravaggio, and many other painters imagined him—on horseback, we do not know, and it does not much matter. He is animated by righteous indignation, and the miles from Jerusalem to Damascus pass by unnoticed. Perhaps he is so absorbed in plots of punishment that he does not even notice his destination growing in the narrowing distance. The encounter, in any event, is unexpected: a flash of light knocks Saul to the sand-strewn stones of the highway. It is not the sand that blinds him, nor the sun, nor shock of the fall, and yet he cannot see. But he can hear: "'Saul, Saul, why do you persecute me?' 'Who are you, Lord?' Saul asked. 'I am Jesus, whom you are persecuting,' he replied. 'Now get up and go into the city, and you will be told what you must do'" (Acts 9:4–6).[4]

Again we have a problem: the story of this encounter, like the description of the meeting on the way to Emmaus, comes long after the fact. It is drawn from chapter 9 of the Acts of the Apostles, a text often associated with the Gospel of Luke, and generally dated to the first quarter of the second century. In his own letters, Paul (he never calls himself Saul in his own writings) does not place himself on any particular road, nor even outside Damascus, and of his vision tells us only that he saw the risen Christ (1 Cor. 9:1, 15:3–8; Gal. 1:11–16). But whatever the occasion for it, we should not doubt that Paul's encounter with Jesus circa 36 CE, and his calling "last of all" as an apostle, produced the earliest documents that survive from the Jesus movement. These documents helped to transform the meaning of Jews and Judaism forever, for Paul began to preach, perhaps first to the Jews (if we believe Acts' anachronistic picture) but certainly to the gentiles (if we follow Paul himself at Gal. 1:15–16). And among the topics that he taught about early and often is the one that interests us: how followers of Jesus should think about their relationship to the traditions that the God of Israel had enjoined on his covenant people.

We will never know as much as we would like about the nature of Paul's teaching, partly because only a fraction of it survives. What we have are seven extraordinary epistles, written between 50 and 60 CE. Their goal is not, like the gospels, to tell us about Jesus's words (Paul writes little about his savior's birth, teaching career, or death),[5] nor to provide a comprehensive outline of his own gospel, but to address questions about his teaching that have arisen in communities he has visited or is planning to visit. Each letter is pitched to a very particular context, and that context is largely lost to us, except as represented in the letters themselves. Nor, given the eventual form of the published corpus, is it even easy to know whether it is really Paul that we are reading. Such was the prestige of Paul's name that within a generation or two of his death many editors and writers (scholars call these pseudepigraphers) were sheltering beneath it, the former inserting (or deleting) words and lines into authentic writings, the latter producing epistles out of whole cloth, while still others raised the hue and cry for forgeries and alterations.[6]

But perhaps the greatest challenge to our understanding of Paul's writings is the fact that they have been read by so many millions of people before us, and continue to be read by so many millions today. Some of those readings—such as that of the author of Acts—became influential, so influential that they in turn shaped the meaning later readers could find in Paul's texts.[7] Subsequent chapters will touch on some later readings—those of Saint Augustine, for example, Martin Luther, and Karl Marx—and see how they have activated certain potential interpretations of Paul's words and repressed others. But in this chapter, at the very beginnings of what will come to be called Christianity, we will see how Paul's earliest readers (and even Paul himself) debated his meaning. We will find traces of those arguments in Paul's own writings and in those of his successors, including in some of the canonical gospels themselves. And we will see how some of these arguments helped to transform thinking about Judaism into a way of thinking about the world.

"A Scandal to the Jews, to the Gentiles Foolishness"

Paul's writings are, among many other things, manifestos of a cognitive revolution. In the ringing words of the first chapter of the first epistle to the Corinthians,

> *"I am going to destroy the wisdom of the wise and bring to nothing the understanding of any who understand." Where are the philosophers? Where are the experts? . . . Do you not see how God has shown up human wisdom as folly? Since in the wisdom of God the world was unable to recognize God through wisdom, it was God's own pleasure to save believers through the folly of the gospel. While the Jews require signs (sēmeia) and the Greeks look for wisdom (sophia), we are preaching a crucified Christ: a scandal to the Jews, to the gentiles foolishness. But to those who have been called, whether they are Jews or Greeks, a Christ who is both the power of God and the wisdom of God (1 Cor. 1:19–24; quoting Isa. 29:14).*[8]

The death and resurrection of Jesus Christ mark a total transformation of what it is that humans can know and how it is that they can know it. Throughout the letter Paul amplifies his teaching of the new knowledge, "the mysterious wisdom of God . . . that was hidden . . . before the ages began." This knowledge comes "not in terms learnt from human philosophy, but in terms learnt from the spirit," not from the wisdom of the world but from the "foolishness" of Christ crucified. Those who would have this knowledge must unlearn everything they had learned before:

"[T]he wisdom of the world is folly to God. Any one of you who thinks he is wise by worldly standards must learn to be a fool in order to be really wise" (1 Cor. 1:27, 2:1, 2:4, 2:7, 2:13, and 3:18).[9]

Already we can see that Paul is asking fundamental questions about human knowledge, and that he is answering these questions partly in terms of Jews and Judaism. But in this passage of Corinthians at least, these epistemological questions are not necessarily or even primarily "Jewish." "Jew" and "Greek" stand together in companionable error, with "Jewish signs" and "Greek learning" just two versions of the world's wisdom, two forms of knowledge that need to be superseded by the would-be follower of Jesus. The philosopher and the Jew emerge as equally foolish and equally arrogant in their misunderstanding of the cosmos.[10]

If 1 Corinthians had been Paul's only letter, the place of Judaism in the history of thought might look very different. But Paul asked other questions about the nature of human knowledge, and in answering these he characterized Judaism in specific ways and assigned it specific roles in God's plan for the history of salvation. One of these questions was similar to that staged on the road to Emmaus. What guidance could the follower of Jesus, in learning to think about and act in the world, find in the ancient promise given to Abraham, in the Hebrew Bible—Paul calls it simply "the scriptures"—as written expression of that promise, and in the many different "commandments" and "works of the law" derived from that scripture?

These questions were not Paul's alone. (See, for example, Gal. 2:11–13 on Peter.) But it was Paul, in his role as apostle to the gentiles, who confronted these questions most urgently, and it was he, in his epistles to the Galatians and the Romans, who provided the first explicit and extended meditations on them. His answers were sometimes obscure, at least in the sense that from the moment of his offering them, followers of Jesus have differed on what he might have meant. As the author of 2 Peter would later put it, "His letters contain some things that are hard to understand (*dysnoēta tina*), which ignorant and unstable people distort, as they do the other Scriptures, to their own destruction" (2 Pet.

3:15–16). But difficulty did not make Paul's writing less influential: on the contrary, it was through debates over his meaning that generations of his readers carved out the exceptional space that Jews and Judaism came to occupy in Christian thought.[11]

The urgency Paul felt about these questions is already evident in his earliest letter on the subject, to the young community in Galatia. Paul is "astonished" (1:6), disappointed in his flock ("you stupid people in Galatia!" [3:1]), indeed furious with his opponents ("I wish that they would mutilate themselves" [5:12]), who are apparently preaching that the non-Jewish believers in Galatia should, like their Jewish savior, be circumcised.[12] Paul's rebuttal is fierce, and famously articulated in an attack against the significance—for the believer—of the particular identities that his society held most sacred: "There is neither Jew nor Greek (Hellene), there is neither slave nor free, there is neither male nor female; for you are all one in Christ Jesus" (Gal. 3:28).[13] Jesus's "gospel" has overcome all these particularities, made all such distinctions meaningless. As Paul puts it in his postscript, "It is not being circumcised or uncircumcised that matters; but what matters is a new creation" (Gal. 6:15).[14]

According to Paul, the categories of classification that comprise the old world no longer matter in this new creation—that is, in Christ. This is yet another revolutionary claim about the nature of knowledge, but this time not as revolutionary as we might think. "Jews" might have recognized in it many of their own beliefs about the messianic ingathering of gentiles. And "Greeks" were quite familiar with widespread philosophical dualisms (many of them associated with Platonism, or in this period, "middle-Platonism") that stressed the existence of an idealized brotherhood in the spirit, and emphasized the superiority of that spiritual state over the many differences of body and of circumstance that marked the flesh of living beings. But the real limits to revolution here have less to do with originality than with cosmology. The new creation may be the only one that truly matters, but the old creation is still here: Paul and his followers are still living in it, and Paul cannot leave it entirely behind. Hence, although he insists that many classifications and oppositions—Jew/Greek, barbarian/Scythian, slave/free, male/female, circumcised/uncircumcised—have been overcome in Christ, these continue to matter a great deal in this world-not-yet-fully-left-behind. The ongoing relevance of one of these classifications became an especially important target of Paul's eloquence, an eloquence that inspired many early Christians to begin imagining the difficulty of overcoming the particularities of the flesh and of this world in terms of one particular status: not "Greekness" nor gender nor condition of liberty, but "Judaism."

This is clear even in the structure of Galatian's celebrated chapter 3, verse 28 (cited earlier), which concludes an argument (begun at 3:6) in pointed fashion: "And if you are Christ's then you are Abraham's offspring, heirs according to promise." Paul's "universalism" is here being constructed in terms of a struggle for control of the scriptural inheritance, an inheritance he claims for himself and his converts. In that construction the category of Jew, of descendant of Abraham, is not overcome or rendered immaterial, but rather appropriated and redefined, in order to make room for "all who believe" (3:7). To the extent that Jews refused to surrender their ancestors, their lineage, and their scripture, they could become emblematic of the particular, of stubborn adherence to the conditions of the flesh, enemies of the spirit, and of God. I say "could become" because it is not clear that Paul intended to cast them as such, although many of his later readers would make precisely that move in his name.

"Cast Out the Slave and Her Son"

The complexity of Paul's position was motivated in part by a tension that emerged between two desires: the desire to understand Jesus's gospel as the fulfillment of God's promise to Abraham (and the ongoing relevance of "the scriptures" that later Christians would call the Old Testament), and the desire to extend that promise beyond Abraham's descendants in the flesh. Had Paul dreamed of abandoning Hebrew scripture or condemning it as false (as the Marcionites and some other followers of Jesus would soon do), "Judaism" might indeed have become no more important to ancient Christians than any other of the myriad ethnic identities they were capable of ignoring as spiritually insignificant, such as the Scythians (see Col. 3:11). But he did not. Instead, as the gospels would later do through stories like that of the road to Emmaus, he taught his followers a new way to unlock the meaning of scripture and its promises. Paul was a pedagogue, his letters primers for the practice of reading he was advocating. In them we can see the principles of a new science of scriptural interpretation—exegesis, hermeneutics—being built on a foundation of questions about the believer's relationship to "Judaism."[15]

Galatians provides a good vantage point from which to watch the construction work, as here, in Paul's reinterpretation of Abraham's biography: Abraham's families—one slave, one free—form part of a chain of oppositions (reaching back to 2:6 forward), a table of antinomies each with allegorical significations. Hagar and Ishmael represent flesh and slavery, Sarah and Isaac promise and freedom. Thus far the reading would not have surprised its audience. They were presumably familiar with philosophical arguments made up of contraries (Greek *ta enantia*) arranged into tables of opposites (*systoichiai*), and with exegetical ones about the implications of Hagar's slavery and Sarah's freedom. But next comes an earthquake. Hagar and Ishmael, flesh and slavery, are associated with the law given on Mount Sinai and "the present Jerusalem." Sarah and Isaac, spirit and freedom, are a new covenant and a heavenly city. One bold allegorical stroke reverses the traditional readings of this story. The Mosaic law and the Jewish people and polity that possess it ("the present Jerusalem") are not the heirs of God's promise to Abraham, but are condemned as "of the flesh," sentenced to slavery and exile. This terrestrial Jerusalem is to be cast out, replaced by the spiritual Jerusalem, set free by faith in Jesus.[16]

The theory of interpretation and practice of reading that Paul deployed to achieve this revaluation of promise in the flesh and promise in the spirit was not a novel one. He arrayed word and meaning against each other in a set of aligned and hierarchically ordered polarities—at times expressed as a "table of oppositions"—explicitly mapped onto the distinction between flesh and spirit. The task of a reader was to penetrate beyond the letter, the sign, the outer body of a text or symbol, and into its inner or spiritual meaning. Thus in Galatians, Paul distinguishes between "flesh" and "spirit" (sarx/pneuma [see 4:23, 29]), and even makes a pun between circumcision and "flesh" to underscore its dangers for gentile believers. Similarly later in Paul's writing, Abraham's circumcision will be transformed by the pressure of Paul's stylus into a fleshy symbol of a spiritual state, a "sign or seal of the righteousness which he had by faith while he was still uncircumcised" (Rom. 4:11). Such flesh/spirit or body/spirit interpretive practices were standard among both Jews and gentiles familiar with Hellenistic philosophy, perhaps even for anyone with a secondary or tertiary education in the ancient world. Philo of Alexandria, whom we met defending the Jews before Caligula in chapter 1, was himself one of its primary practitioners, exhorting his coreligionists to read the Torah for "the hidden meaning that appeals to the few who study soul characteristics, rather than bodily forms."[17] Indeed Philo, writing a little earlier than Paul, had already discussed the signification of circumcision in terms similar to those the apostle would later use.

The difference was this: for Philo, circumcision's spiritual meaning increased, rather than lessened, the necessity of the outer practice. As he put it in *On the Migration of Abraham*,

> [W]e should look on all these [outward observances] as resembling the body, and [these inner meanings as resembling] the soul. It follows that, exactly as we have to take thought for the body, because it is the abode of the soul, so we must pay heed to the written laws. If we keep and observe these, we shall gain a clearer conception of those things of which these are the symbols.[18]

The literal and the spiritual, body and soul, were intimately bound together and mutually reinforcing. Paul's method in Galatians was similar, but his conclusions were very different. Once the inner meaning of circumcision was understood, the literal meaning became immaterial for Galatian believers living "in the new creation": "It is not being circumcised or uncircumcised that matters" (Gal. 6:15). In fact Paul went even further: some literal meanings were not merely irrelevant to those who had accepted the gospel, but positively dangerous. For gentile converts, circumcision was one of these: "Now I, Paul, say to you, that if you receive circumcision, Christ will be of no advantage to you" (5:2). When gentile followers of Jesus treated circumcision as necessary for their justification, they placed mistaken emphasis on the material sign, and thereby revealed themselves as "severed from Christ" and Spirit by the "desires of the flesh" (5:4, 16–18).

Note my emphasis on gentile converts. A modern school of scholarship known as the "New Perspective" has argued that Paul was unconcerned about and may even have approved of the ongoing observance of Jewish law by Jews and Jewish followers of Jesus. Thus, when he talked of the slavery of the earthly Jerusalem, and of the need to "cast out the slave and her son," he did not mean the Jews, whether believing or unbelieving in Jesus, but only the teachers among the Galatians who maintained that gentile converts should be circumcised. Nor is he criticizing the observance of Jewish law in general, but only its application to non-Jewish believers. In other words, Paul did not intend his letter as an attack on Judaism, though that is precisely how many later Christians would read it. He sought only to explain to the gentile Galatians, in scriptural terms, why their justification did not require them to observe these aspects of the Law.[19]

Paul may well have intended his polarized alignment of the terrestrial Jerusalem, circumcision, letter, flesh, slavery, and death to be read rhetorically and locally. But even if he did, it is easy enough to see how such opposites produced the potential for more polarized readings and more general critiques of Judaism. Equally productive of such potential readings was the word Paul coined to describe slippage from the saving to the killing side of his table of antinomies. In Galatians 2:14, he admonished Peter for refusing to eat with gentile converts who did not observe Jewish dietary laws: "Since you, though you are a Jew, live like the gentiles and not like the Jews, how can you compel the gentiles to live like the Jews [literally "to Judaize"]?" Later readers would debate extensively what it meant for one apostle to criticize another in such terms (in 2:13, Paul even called Peter's behavior "hypocrisy"). But what those later readers would not often doubt was that the verb *to Judaize* provided an accurate and useful characterization of the erroneous passage from soul to flesh, from spirit to letter, from eternal truth to the mere appearance of truth. Not merely erroneous, but deadly, for as Paul would pithily put it in his second epistle to the Corinthians, "the letter kills, the spirit vivifies" (2 Cor. 3:6).[20]

The importance of this adaptation for the history of our subject cannot be overemphasized. Paul took all the errors of relating incorrectly to the fleshy things (texts, bodies, objects) of this world and provided for them—whether intentionally or unintentionally—a "Jewish" name. It is true that for Paul, "Judaizing" was a gentile error, not a Jewish one. Neither a Jew nor a Jewish follower of Jesus "Judaized" by being circumcised, and there is little evidence in Paul's own letters that he disapproved of the observance of Jewish law by members of either of these two groups. Nevertheless, his logic identified with Jews and Judaism a cardinal category of error for the believer in Jesus—that of giving excessive attention to the "flesh" of the text and of the person. Over time, the effect of this identification would be the opposite of the one that Paul perhaps intended, for far from making "Jewishness" an irrelevant particularity ("there is neither Jew nor Greek") in the new creation, Paul's letter to the Galatians would help to turn it into a key term of epistemological and ontological critique.[21]

"They Are Enemies, but for Your Sake"

Even in his own day Paul felt compelled to correct what he saw as misinterpretations of his argument. In his letter to the Romans, he condemned those who believed that in Galatians he had encouraged baptized gentiles to demonstrate their freedom from Jewish law by doing evil (Rom. 3:8). In the generations after Paul's death, as we will see in the next chapter, plenty of readers would nevertheless stress Paul's rejection of letter, flesh, and Jewish law, embracing him as an apostle of radical dualism. Given these futures, I had best be clear: the historical Paul valued the spiritual world more highly than the phenomenal and material one through which it was perceived, but he did not represent the world and its necessities as evil. In his letters to the Corinthians, for example, the body appears, not as the "tomb" favored by so many ancient authors (including Philo), but as a sheltering tent (2 Cor. 5:1–4). And if on the one hand, Christians "look not at the things which are seen, but at the things which are not seen" (4:18), yet conversely the spiritual requires the physical. "If there is a physical body, there is also a spiritual body. . . . But it is not the spiritual which is first, but the physical, and then the spiritual" (1 Cor. 15:42–50).[22]

Paul believed that the end of the world was near—"the time has become limited. . . . This world as we know it is passing away" (7:29)— and that the new creation was at hand. But he also believed that in the meantime, while Jesus's followers continued to dwell in the body and in the company of other human beings, they should not only observe the laws of the world, but sometimes might even prefer its signs, symbols, and conventions. Thus Paul congratulated believers who spoke in tongues, doing without the mediations and limitations of human language. But he stressed that human language was to be preferred. Speaking in tongues cannot build up community because the other cannot understand it: "I am a barbarian to the person who is speaking, and the speaker is a barbarian to me" (14:11).

In short, and unlike some of his successors, Paul did not imagine that the followers of Jesus should or could completely sever their relationship to the world and its laws. In this sense we can, if we like, call him a "moderate dualist." But he did think that misplaced attention to the world of law, letter, and flesh was exceedingly, even lethally, dangerous. "The letter kills." Or as he put it in his epistle to the community in Rome, "To set the mind on the flesh is death, but to set the mind on the Spirit is life and peace. For the mind that is set on the flesh is hostile to God . . . and those who are in the flesh cannot please God" (Rom. 8:6–8). The historical question of what Paul himself thought he meant by "being in the flesh" remains a thorny one. But what is absolutely clear is that he thought the condition perilous, developed a fearsome pedagogy against it, and assigned to Judaism a special place in that pedagogy.[23]

Galatians represents an early lesson in that curriculum, the much longer letter to the Romans a later one. The context is now quite different—the Romans are a mixed community of gentile believers and Jewish ones, and moreover, unlike the Galatians, they have not previously been taught by Paul—but the questions and the answers are similar, suggesting that Paul's thinking on these issues was as systematic as it was circumstantial. And again, neither the questions nor the answers are simple, perhaps in part because Paul had in the meantime learned (3:8) that he needed to guard against the willingness of some readers to push his writings on these questions toward extremes.

Like 1 Corinthians, Romans begins with a thumbnail sketch of humanity's cognitive errors: those of the pagans, whose misinterpretation of God's creation leads them to sodomy, polytheism, and perdition; and those of the Jews, whose misinterpretation of God's scripture leads them to prefer death under the Law to life in Jesus. Like Galatians, Romans treats Judaism as an especially meaningful cognitive category, because it is especially instructive about how the follower of Jesus should and should not interpret the world. In Romans, as in Galatians, Paul maps the dangers of seeing, reading, and believing "after the flesh" onto Israel, but this time placing more stress on the honor due Israel in the history of salvation. He emphasizes, for example, that "the glory was theirs and the covenants; to them were given the Law and the worship of God and the promises. To them belong the fathers and out of them, so far as physical descent is concerned, came Christ who is above all" (Rom. 9:4–5). Some later Christians (such as the author of the Gospel of John, in 12:43) would read these words as a condemnation of the Pharisees' pride in their descent from Abraham, but Paul most likely intended them as praise. Similarly, he insisted that God has not rejected his people. "Out of the question!" They still have an ongoing role in salvation history. "Since their rejection meant the reconciliation of the world, do you know what their reacceptance will mean? Nothing less than life from the dead!" (Rom. 11:1, 11:15).

These chapters of Romans can be read—and perhaps should be read, by those interested in the historical Paul—as affirmative and conciliatory toward Judaism. They can also be read—and were, by many of the readers we will encounter in this and later chapters—as critical and condemnatory. Even the promise of reacceptance could be, would be, turned into the claim that genuine conversion from Judaism to Christianity will *only* be possible at the end of time. How could Paul's words generate so many different, even opposed, meanings? One answer, very general but nevertheless true, is that like all texts, their meaning shifted with their contexts: different communities of readers, living under different historical conditions, generate differing understandings. In this sense the potential meanings of Paul's words are as inexhaustible as an ocean of ink.

Another only slightly less general explanation is that Paul's surviving texts provided later readers with too little information to reach definitive conclusions about his intended meaning. Who does Paul mean when he speaks of "their rejection," or of "branches cut from the vine"? All the Jews, or just specific figures among them? And if the latter (as seems most probable historically), then who? Those who resisted Jesus's message? Or those who accepted it but opposed Paul's mission to the gentiles? And who does he have in mind when he speaks of "their reacceptance"? All of Israel, or just a portion? And if the latter, how small a remnant? And when? It is easy enough to see how later readers could reach very divergent answers to these important questions, which are unanswerable from within the framework of the letters themselves.

But it is also true that for all its insistence on the ongoing merits of Israel, the structure of Paul's argument in Romans also depends on the tables of "contraries" and "opposites" he had established in Galatians. And despite his criticism, in Romans, of those who had interpreted Galatians as advocating the deliberate disobedience of the law, the later letter still seems to demand that the stigmatized side of the *systoichiai*, the opposites, somehow be left behind: "For when we were still in the flesh, our sinful passions, stirred up by the law, were at work in our members to bear fruit for death. But now we are fully freed from the law, dead to that in which we lay captive. We can thus serve in the new being of the Spirit and not the old one of the letter" (Rom. 7:5–6). Or rather, we *must* thus serve, for any persistence of these categories in the new creation is not simply a matter of indifference, but of death. It is not just "the law" that threatens the spiritual believer and reader, but also the companions that Paul everywhere associates with it: the letter, and even the flesh itself. Perhaps it is therefore not so surprising that whatever Paul's intention, many readers would learn from him to associate all these dangers with Judaism and Judaizing.

Moreover, in his attempts to explain why so many of his own people had rejected and continued to reject Jesus as their promised Messiah, Paul produced some very ambivalent locutions. Already in what is probably his earliest letter, Paul had described the Jews (or perhaps only the Judeans) as the special enemies of God and humanity. They "put the Lord Jesus to death, and the prophets too, and persecuted us also. Their conduct does not please God, and makes them the enemies of the whole human race, because they are hindering us from preaching to gentiles to save them. Thus all the time they are *reaching the full extent of their iniquity*, but retribution has finally overtaken them" (1 Thess. 2:14).[24] Now, in one of his most mature writings, he theorizes this enmity and gives it cosmological implications. He sees in the enmity of "my blood-relations" toward Jesus a repetition and fulfillment of ancient prophecy. His Jews, like those of Elijah's day, have "put your prophets to the sword, torn down your altars" (Rom. 11:3; citing 1 Kings 19:10). This fulfillment is a necessary stage in salvation history. Their blindness and hardness of heart are like the pharaoh's, produced by God for the salvation of the world (Rom. 9:17, 11:15). At present, during this birthing of the new creation, they are being punished for their persecution of the prophets and are cut as a dead branch from the vine (11:17–24). But this inanimate enmity will be temporary, for the Jews still have one more cosmological role to play. When the new creation is fulfilled and the old world comes to an end, then a remnant of the Jews will receive mercy, be grafted back again, and their reacceptance will mean "nothing less than life from the dead" (9:28, 11:15). Hence Paul's extraordinary formulation: "As regards the gospel, they are enemies, but for your sake; but as regards those who are God's choice, they are still well loved for the sake of their ancestors" (12:28).

Both sides of this doubly ambivalent formulation would receive much attention across the ages, and both remain mysterious. If the rest of this book focuses less on "love's" future than on the ways in which the "enmity" will be put to work, it is not because "love" had no future, but because I believe we do not yet appreciate the critical work done by that "enmity" in the history of human thought. We must move onward in the history if I am to convince you of that. But before we leave Paul on his way to Rome, we can ask him for an example of how he himself put that enmity to work, and on no less a question than that of reconciling God's justice with human freedom, agency, and will.

The question: Why did so many of the Israelites, children of God's promise to Abraham, fail to accept the Messiah they were seeking? Paul's answer: Because God did not choose or call them. Instead, he hardened their hearts, as he had the pharaoh's. But "then you will ask me, how then can God ever blame anyone, since no one can oppose his will?" (9:19). Is God unjust in cutting these branches from the vine? "Out of the question!" says Paul, responding as the book of Job dictates he should: "[C]an the pot ask the potter why did you make me this way?" (Rom. 9:20; Job 9:12). The ways of the creator are beyond the ken of the created. But then Paul points to an exception, a special kind of pot created by the potter precisely in order to make his cosmic intentions clear. "But suppose that God, . . . has with great patience," put up with certain "vessels of wrath designed for destruction," "so that he may make known the glorious riches ready for the people who are the vessels of his faithful love and were long ago prepared for that glory?" (Rom. 9:22–23). The outcasts of Israel are these instructive vessels of wrath, whose wretched status makes God's plan for salvation knowable on earth.[25] Their "destruction" is exemplary and their "enmity" to the gospel pedagogical. These ideas themselves were not "new," in that they drew extensively on concepts drawn from scriptural traditions ("Old Testament") of prophetic criticism. Even the images of accursed wretchedness that Paul favored for fallen Israel—such as "May their eyes grow so dim they cannot see, and their backs be bent forever" (Rom. 11:10)— were often citations from that scripture (in this case, Ps. 68:24). But in the context of the tensions between gentile and Jew in the "New" Israel, these ideas would do new kinds of labor, work whose enormous productive potential we can already see in the gospels.[26]

"As for My Enemies . . ."

These ideas were already at work in Luke's meditations on the nature of Christian freedom and its enemies with which this chapter began. Luke's gospel opens with the hope of freedom: "Blessed be the Lord, the God of Israel, for he has visited his people, he has set them free" (1:68). It was this hope that the disciples on the road in the closing chapters (24:21) had given up for lost. Of course if they had read more closely the gospel in which they themselves appeared, the disciples would have understood that enemies of freedom were foreordained. What else had Simeon meant when he prophesied with the infant Jesus in his arms during the presentation at the Temple? "Look, he is destined for the fall and for the rise of many in Israel, destined to be a sign that is opposed" (2:34).

But who were these enemies that opposed the sign? Here Luke reports a range of answers. For the Jewish disciples on the road to Emmaus, it was only "our leaders" who had opposed Jesus. Jesus sometimes agrees: "The Son of man is destined to . . . be rejected by the elders and chief priests and scribes and to be put to death" (9:22).[27] But he also assigns blame more broadly and diversely. Occasionally homeland defines enmity: "No prophet is ever accepted in his own country," he tells his native synagogue of Nazara. Appropriately, his audience responds by attempting to kill him (4:24).[28] At other times enmity is generational ("faithless and perverse generation!" [Luke 9:41, 7:31, 11:29, 50])[29] or inherited ("This was the way their ancestors treated the prophets" [6:22–23, 26]). Profession, too, is a variable. Not only are Pharisees, scribes, and lawyers singled out as Jesus's most adamant opponents (for example, see 11:37–12:3), but also we can detect a strong anti-intellectual prejudice, with the scribbling classes in general stigmatized as unable to see the true wisdom: "I bless you father . . . for hiding these things from the learned and the clever and revealing them to little children" (10:21).[30] Finally, resistance to prophecy can be geographic. Jerusalem, in particular, occupies a special place in the divine plan: "I must go on, since it would not be right for a prophet to die outside Jerusalem" (Luke 13:33).

Every one of these enmities deserves a history of its own. The centrality of Jerusalem, for example, is not arbitrary. Already in the Hebrew Bible, she is the appointed enemy of prophets, as Luke's Jesus knew well: "Jerusalem, Jerusalem, you that kill the prophets and stone those who are sent to you!" (13:34). The gospel authors wrote after the great war of 66–70 in which Roman armies led by the emperors Titus and Vespasian destroyed Jerusalem and razed the Temple of the Jews. For them, these events transformed the many prophetic chidings of Jerusalem into proof of the truth of Jesus's mission. Hundreds of years before Jesus, for example, Jeremiah had warned Jerusalem of her sin, and predicted destruction at the hands of Babylon if she did not mend her ways: "In vain I have struck your children, they have not accepted correction; your own sword has devoured your prophets like a marauding lion" (2:30). He too had promised her redemption in exchange for true repentance, redemption, and the conversion of all the nations to her God: "When that time comes, Jerusalem will be called: the Throne of Yahweh, and all the nations will converge on her, on Yahweh's name, on Jerusalem, and will no longer follow their own stubborn and wicked inclinations" (3:17). The gospel authors drew on these scriptural templates. Unlike Paul (who wrote before the Roman war) they presented Jesus as a prophet who warned of Jerusalem's destruction. Luke has Jesus weep for Jerusalem as he approaches her gates, and prophesy what in their own times is already past:

If you too had only recognized on this day the way to peace! But in fact it is hidden from your eyes! Yes, a time is coming when your enemies will raise fortifications all round you, when they will encircle

you and hem you in on every side; they will dash you and the children
inside your walls to the ground; they will leave not one stone standing
on another within you, because you did not recognize the moment of
your visitation. (Luke 19:41–44)[31]

Every enmity deserves its own history, but our space is limited and
our question more general. The gospels provide literary caricatures
(remember, they are not historical reports contemporary with the events
they purport to describe) of characters interacting with Jesus. Most of
these characters are Jews of one sort or another. Many of these Jews
oppose him, and even among the supporters, many are criticized for
not understanding him. We want to discover what these characters and
literary caricatures can tell us about the critical work ideas about Judaism did in the worldview of the communities that produced the gospels.
But we also want to recognize some of the potential meanings these caricatures might generate for later communities of readers—that is, how
these texts (like Paul's) could authorize different readings in different
times and places.[32]

The task is as impossible as trying to map all the uses of a given
word in history. The concept of "enmity" alone is enough to suggest the
scope of the problem. Plenty of Second Temple Jewish sects espoused
a sharply oppositional vocabulary of enmity toward Jews who did not
share their views: a cosmological zero-sum perhaps reflected in Jesus's
"anyone who is not with me is against me" (11:23).[33] But Jesus was also
a teacher of love and forgiveness, and it is this position that certain
communities choose to emphasize. Luke tells us that Jesus prayed on
the cross that his crucifiers be forgiven (23:34). Does this mean that
we should forget—or attempt to circumscribe through exegesis—the
conclusion of his last lecture before ascending to Jerusalem? "As for
my enemies who did not want me for their king, bring them here and
execute them in my presence" (19:27). Since these words appear in a
parable, many modern readers prefer to separate them from Jesus, but
we know that some ancient ones understood them as instructions, and
applied them to the Jews (we will see Saint John Chrysostom do so in

chapter 4). Our goal is not to determine who is right, but to understand how all these views could come to seem authoritatively grounded in gospel. For that, we need to ask the gospels, in more or less chronological order, how they represent Jewish resistance to Jesus, and how they deploy that resistance to help their Christian readers make sense of their victories and disappointments in the world.[34]

"Beware the Yeast of the Pharisees and Sadducees"

The authors of the synoptic gospels (in chronological order, Mark, Matthew, Luke) seldom refer to "Jews" in general: the word appears almost exclusively in the mocking inscription hung on the cross: "King of the Jews." They speak instead of different groups (scribes, Sanhedrin, priests, chief priests, leaders, elders, Sadducees, Pharisees) and different collectives (the crowd, the people, Jerusalem). The choice of term is not consistent across the synoptics: in narrating the same event, one gospel has "crowds" where the other has "Pharisees and Sadducees"; where one has "elders," another has "scribes."[35] Such differences are meaningful: tracing them, we might learn something about the specific settings in which each gospel was composed, and the particular conflicts they reflect and represent. But our approach will be blunter: we will focus on the treatment of one prominent group, the Pharisees. Matthew refers to them twenty-nine times; Luke, twenty-seven; the much briefer Mark, a proportionally more meager eleven (and the non-synoptic John, for sake of reference, twenty times). And though their image and roles do vary from gospel to gospel, we will focus our attention on Matthew— probably the most widely read gospel in the second century, as well as the one most intensely interested in the Pharisees—while making regular comparisons with Luke and occasional nods toward Mark.[36]

Let us begin in the beginning, in the days before Jesus's ministry, when John the Baptist appeared in the desert of Judea. "Repent," he proclaimed, "for the kingdom of Heaven is close at hand." These words were the first rumor to reach Judea of the coming revolution, a fulfillment (according to the gospels) of Isaiah's prophecy: "A voice of one that cries in the desert, 'prepare a way for the Lord'" (Matt. 3:1–3, Luke 3:1–4, Mark 1:1–3, Isa. 40:3). But these were not the only words of prophecy John uttered. According to Matthew,

> *When he saw a number of Pharisees and Sadducees coming for baptism he said to them, "Brood of vipers, who warned you to flee from the coming retribution? Produce fruit in keeping with repentance, and do not presume to tell yourselves, 'We have Abraham as our father,' because, I tell you, God can raise children for Abraham from these stones. Even now the axe is being laid to the root of the trees, so that any tree failing to produce good fruit will be cut down and thrown on the fire." (Matt. 3:7–10)*[37]

The Baptist's aggression here is curious, since he himself had warned his audience to "flee." Why berate those who heed his call? But as a prophet John foresees that those running to him now will stumble before they reach the savior, and prove their repentance false. The rock that will trip them, he predicts, is pride in their descent from Abraham—that is, pride in their Jewishness. Such pride, John warns, is misplaced. The time is coming when God will choose his children from any peoples (even from stones!) that produce good fruit. He will extend no special mercy to Abraham's seed after the flesh.

In other words, John the Baptist is prophesying the Pharisees' and Sadducees' rejection of Jesus. From the historical (rather than the prophetic) point of view, these words look forward into the future of a faith not yet established. As we have already seen, it was not Jesus's immediate followers, but only later generations of believers who felt so acutely the need to explain why Jerusalem and its Temple had been destroyed, and why the majority of Jews still failed to worship the Christ while so many gentiles were heeding the call. It is they, and not the historical Jesus, who put that question at the center of Christian scriptures.[38]

Such distinctions matter a great deal to anyone interested in the important task of discovering differences between the gospels' portrayal of the Jews and the likely views of a historical Jesus, himself also a Jew.[39]

In this book, however, we are less interested in recovering the relationships Jesus might historically have had with his coreligionists, than in the gospels' portrayal of those relationship forty to one hundred years after his death and resurrection. Our goal is to understand how those portraits generated the potential for the powerful interpretations they would produce over the next two thousand years. For our purposes, then, what is interesting about John the Baptist's prophecy according to Matthew is not that it is ahistorical, but that it shows us how, before Jesus has preached a single word, the Gospel of Matthew has already focused the hot glare of its spotlights on the Pharisees and Sadducees, who are identified as advocates of an exclusive Jewishness and as poisonous opponents of the coming Messiah.[40]

Like the statements of most prophets, John the Baptist's was blindingly clear but also cryptic and compressed, a flash of dry lightning in the desert. The meaning and truth of its words only gradually unfold as the gospel narrative progresses. Jesus's first sustained address, the Sermon on the Mount, represents an important step in that unfolding. The last of its opening beatitudes is a statement much like John's, albeit more veiled: "Blessed are you when people abuse you and persecute you and speak all kinds of calumny against you falsely on my account. Rejoice and be glad . . . ; this is how they persecuted the prophets before you" (Matt. 5:11–12). Persecution is prophesied, but who is the "they" that will prosecute? There follow some disturbing words. "You are salt of the earth, but if salt loses its taste . . . it is good for nothing, and can only be thrown out to be trampled under people's feet" (5:13). "You are a light for the world," but that light becomes useless when it is hidden under a tub (5:14). These are not blessings but warnings, warnings that all is not well with Israel. The theme here is akin to John's: do not presume on inheritance, for "any tree failing to produce good fruit will be cut down."

Jesus then utters words that have convinced many scholars to call Matthew a "Jewish gospel": "Do not imagine that I have come to abolish the Law or the Prophets. I have come not to abolish them but to complete them" (5:17–19). But it is clear from the context that Jesus's idea of law and prophecy will not be the same as those of his audience, for he claims to be restoring flavor to their tasteless salt, so to speak. A distinction follows quickly: "For I tell you, if your uprightness does not surpass that of the scribes and Pharisees, you will never get into the kingdom of Heaven" (5:20). Jesus then presents a reformulation of the laws of vengeance, divorce, adultery, and oath-taking, one that to his mind clearly surpasses that of the scribes and Pharisees, and that can be reduced to the golden rule: "Always treat others as you would like them to treat you; that is the Law and the Prophets" (7:12). (Tradition attributes a similar statement to the leading "Pharisee" of Jesus's day, Rabbi Hillel [ca. 50 BCE–ca. 10 CE]: "Do not do to your neighbor what is hateful to yourself. That is the entire Torah.")[41]

Finally, the sermon introduces the theme of hypocrisy as an explanation for the tension Jesus sees between what the synagogue is and what it should be, between the piety he advocates and that of his rivals. The "hypocrites in the synagogues and the streets" (6:2, 5) give alms, fast, and pray in public. They care for "human admiration," and that is all that they will receive (6:2). But real devotion is motivated by desire for heavenly reward and is done privately, away from human eyes: "your Father who sees all that is done in secret will reward you" (6:4, 6, 18). Hypocrisy becomes the defining difference between those who "store up treasures . . . on earth" and those who "store up treasures . . . in heaven" (6:19–21), between devotion to the world and devotion to God, between salt with flavor and salt without, between, in short, the true Israel and the false.

These are distinctions that become clearer as the gospel progresses. Over and over again Jesus predicts that the citizens of the coming kingdom will prove quite different from those of the present Israel. The faith of a Roman centurion, for example, provides him with an opportunity to prophesy the Roman destruction of Jerusalem and the expulsion of the Jews from the kingdom of heaven: "In truth I tell you, in no one in Israel have I found faith as great as this. And I tell you that many will come from east and west and sit down with Abraham and Isaac and Jacob at the feast in the kingdom of heaven; but the children of the kingdom will be thrown out into the darkness outside, where there will be weeping and grinding of teeth" (8:10–12). Once Jesus reaches Jerusalem he sharpens the point through parables: the two sons; the wicked tenants ("the kingdom of God will be taken from you and given to a people who will produce its fruit" [21:43]); the guests who refuse to come to the wedding feast ("The king was furious. He dispatched his troops, destroyed those murderers and burnt their town. Then he said to his servants: The wedding is ready, but as those who were invited proved to be unworthy, go to the main crossroads and invite everyone you can find" [22:7–9]). All of these parables prophesy the Jews' rejection of Jesus and their subsequent punishment by Titus and Vespasian.

Just as Israel's future becomes clearer, so do its failings. In the case of the Pharisees, these are not immediately evident, for their piety was so conspicuous that it sometimes made that of Jesus's disciples seem wanting. Matthew records, for example, that a follower of John the Baptist asked Jesus, "[W]hy is it that we and the Pharisees fast, but your disciples do not?" (Matt. 9:14; Mark 2:18). Jesus does not attack either John or the Pharisees in his reply, but merely predicts that his disciples will fast after he is gone. This restraint is soon replaced by a more marked antagonism. Matthew has the Pharisees criticize Jesus's disciples for violating the laws of Sabbath, and ascribe his exorcisms to demonic intervention (9:34, 12:2, 12:24). Jesus responds by suggesting that if the Pharisees speak thus of Jesus, then it is they who exorcise with the help of the devil (12:27). The world becomes increasingly polarized within the narrative of Matthew's gospel, until eventually there can be no middle state: "Anyone who is not with me is against me, and anyone who does not gather in with me throws away" (12:30). It is here that Jesus first declares openly the important theme already foreshadowed by John the Baptist: the gap between what the Pharisees *claim* or *seem* to be and what they *are*: "You brood of vipers, how can your speech be good when you are evil? For words flow out of what fills the heart" (12:34).

The author of Matthew, like the authors of the fourth gospel and of the "War Scroll" of the Dead Sea Scrolls, as well as many other "apocalyptic" writers of his day and age, takes it for granted that the world is divided in cosmic struggle between the subjects of the Kingdom of God and the subjects of the evil one, between the wheat seed and the darnel seed, as Jesus put it in parable (13:24–30, 36–43). He is likewise confident of the Pharisees' place in this polarity. His originality lies less in the clarity of the oppositions he draws, and more in the way he makes sense of the fact that what is clear to him and his fellow sectarians is not clear to so many others: he uses the Pharisees to exemplify the dangerous disjuncture that exists in the world between appearance and truth. To explain why light and darkness are not always recognized for what they are (and hence, why darkness sometimes seems to triumph over light), Matthew develops a distinction—found already in Hebrew scripture as well as Hellenistic philosophy—between exterior and interior moral states. Exterior beauty can conceal interior horror, just as much that what seems fair in the world is foul when seen from a cosmic perspective. In other words, not all that glitters is gold. Matthew illuminates the problem through a theory of hypocrisy. "Hypocrites!" Jesus condemns the "Pharisees and scribes from Jerusalem" who criticize his disciples for not washing their hands before meals. "How rightly Isaiah prophesied about you when he said: 'This people honors me only with lip-service, while their hearts are far from me'" (15:7–8; Isa. 29:13). The exterior, Jesus goes on to explain, is unimportant. It is what is inside that counts: "What goes into the mouth does not make anyone unclean. It is what comes out of the mouth that makes someone unclean. . . . Whatever comes out of the mouth comes from the heart, and it is this that makes someone unclean" (Matt. 15:10–18).[42]

Over and over again Jesus teaches the distinction between outer "seeming" and inner "being" through the example of the Pharisees. "The scribes and the Pharisees occupy the chair of Moses," he tells the crowds and his disciples, but "they do not practice what they preach" (Matt. 23:2–3). With this observation he launches into "the seven woes of the Pharisees," seven indictments, six of which begin with "Alas for you, scribes and Pharisees, you hypocrites." (The opening of the one exception is "Alas for you, blind guides.") These describe in deafening crescendo the different ways in which the Pharisees confuse appearance with reality, pretense with piety. The last phrases are too memorable to summarize:

> *Alas for you, scribes, and Pharisees, you hypocrites! You clean the out-side of the cup and leave the inside full of extortion and intemperance. Blind Pharisee! Clean the inside of the cup and dish first so that it and the outside are both clean.*
>
> *Alas for you, scribes, and Pharisees, you hypocrites! You are like whitewashed tombs that look handsome on the outside, but inside are full of the bones of the dead and every kind of corruption. In just the same way, from the outside you look upright, but inside you are full of hypocrisy and lawlessness.*
>
> *Alas for you, scribes, and Pharisees, you hypocrites! You build the sepulchers of the prophets and decorate the tombs of the upright, say-ing, "We would never have joined in shedding the blood of the proph-ets, had we lived in our ancestors' day." So! Your own evidence tells against you! You are the children of those who murdered the prophets! Very well then, finish off the work that your ancestors began. (23:25–32)*

We should not overlook the artistry of these passages. The Pharisees pride themselves as heirs of the prophets and guardians of their tombs, when in fact they are tombs themselves. They are about to prove their own hypocrisy by sending yet another prophet to another tomb. How fitting, from a narrative point of view, that the Pharisees now disappear from Matthew's gospel until that tomb is occupied. They are absent from the Passion story, where the guilt is placed squarely on the shoul-ders of the people as a whole: "And the people, every one of them, shouted back, 'Let his blood be on us and on our children!'" (27:25). The Pharisees appear just once more, after Jesus is dead and buried. There, in a swan song before Pontius Pilate, they give advice which underscores once more how deeply they confuse appearance and reality: "Therefore give the order to have the sepulcher kept secure until the third day, for fear his disciples come and steal him away and tell the people, 'He has risen from the dead.' This last piece of fraud would be worse than what went before" (27:62–64).[43]

The use of Pharisees (but not only Pharisees) to represent this cognitive confusion is, for our subject, one of the most important characteristics of the synoptic gospels, because it creates figures of Judaism capable of being deployed in the service of a Christian epistemology and ontology: a theory of knowledge and of being. In a moment we will see how the Gospel of John explains Jesus's death via a highly polarized polemic between darkness and light, Jew and Jesus, this world and the world of spirit. The synoptic gospels are less dualistic, in part because of the explanatory power provided by their emphasis on what we might call a Pharisaic zone of confusion. The existence of hypocrisy, of darkness that looks like light, helps to explain blindness by deriving it in part from cognitive error. It is the complexity of the world itself, and not only some a priori commitment to Satan, that blinded Israel to God. At the same time, hypocrisy also makes judgment more difficult, darkness much more dangerous. Insofar as the foul can appear fair, even the best-intentioned follower of Jesus can be misled.[44]

The concept of hypocrisy allows Mark, Matthew, and Luke to develop what we might call an infectious theory of knowledge, an anxiety about the ease with which "Jewish" cognitive attributes can overwhelm the Christian. They summarized this theory in a biological metaphor. In Mark's words, "Then he gave them this warning, 'Keep your eyes open; look out for the yeast of the Pharisees and the yeast of Herod" (8:15). Luke's version is more explicit, and more apocalyptic: "Be on your guard against the yeast of the Pharisees—their hypocrisy. Everything now covered will be uncovered, and everything now hidden will be made clear" (12:1–2). But it is Matthew who gives us the fullest and most terrifying example:

The disciples, having crossed to the other side, had forgotten to take any food. Jesus said to them, "Keep your eyes open, and be on your

*guard against the yeast of the Pharisees and the Sadducees." And they
said among themselves, "It is because we have not brought any bread."
Jesus knew it, and he said, "You have so little faith, why are you talking among yourselves about having no bread? Do you still not understand? . . . How could you fail to understand that I was not talking
about bread? What I said was: Beware the yeast of the Pharisees and
Sadducees." Then they understood that he was telling them to be on
their guard, not against yeast for making bread, but against the teachings of the Pharisees and Sadducees. (16:5–12)*

Here, at the very moment that Jesus warns his closest associates of the
danger posed by the "Pharisaic" world, they fall into the trap. Rather
than understanding his statement metaphorically and spiritually, as he
intends it, they understand it literally and materially, in the context of
their own bodily hunger.

The danger lies at the very heart of the Christian community: even
the disciples, under Jesus's careful tutelage, can become Pharisees,
Sadducees, or Herodians, and this at the very moment that they are
being warned of the risks of infection! Worse, the danger seems to be
contained in the nature of language itself. When speaking of "yeast,"
of "bread," or of "Pharisees" and "Sadducees," did the gospels' Jesus
speak literally or metaphorically? Could the two forms of meaning be
separated from one another, and if so, how? The relationship between
the "thing" a word referred to ("yeast," for example) and the "higher
meanings" (metaphorical, allegorical, spiritual) that it was capable of
generating was imagined as similar to the relationship between perishable fleshy things of this world and eternal spirit. These linguistic
questions were therefore capable of encapsulating for Matthew, Mark,
and Luke (as they had, in different ways, for Paul and Philo) the difficulty of determining the proper relationship between the world of
human communication and community, and the word of scripture.
And at the crossroads of these questions, representing the possibility of confusion in its purest form, stood figures of Judaism like the
Pharisees.

"You Are from Your Father, the Devil"

The most sharply drawn sketch of the Jew as enemy comes from the fourth gospel, the one "according to John." This is the gospel most explicitly focused on the Jews (the word itself appears some sixty-seven times in the text, far more than in all the synoptics combined). It is also, of all early Christian texts that have become canonical, the one most thoroughly saturated by the theme of enmity. Already in the prologue a sting of conflict rides on the tail of every verse. "In the beginning was the Word . . . life that was the light of men . . . and darkness could not overpower it" (1:1–5). The bitter flavor of a cosmic dualism is beginning to emerge: light and darkness, life and death. The next verses add more elements:

> *The Word was the real light . . . he was coming into the world . . . that had come into being through him, and the world did not recognize him. He came to his own, and his own people did not accept him. But to those who did accept him, he gave power to become children of God . . . who were born not from human stock . . . but from God himself. (1:9–13)*

The world joins darkness in opposition to the word, and within the world "his own people" are the most ferocious opponents of the life-giving light. "His own people" refers to the Jews, who are of his lineage according to the flesh, though here we can see that the claim is canceled as soon as it is uttered: the "children of God" are no longer of "human stock."[45]

In these first lines we can already see a cosmic battle taking shape, one in which word, light, and life confront world, darkness, death, and the Jews in a struggle to the finish. The Gospel of John is not only an assessment of the forces arrayed on both sides of this struggle. It is also an assertion of their irreconcilable enmity, and a description of the most strategic engagement in their war: the confrontation with Jesus.

The world hates Jesus and his followers because they are alien to it: "Because you do not belong to the world . . . that is why the world hates you" (15:18). "The world can never accept" the spirit of truth, since "it neither sees nor knows him" (14:17). This hatred will result in the bitter persecution of Jesus and his followers, but the good news is that the world's victories and the word's sufferings are only apparent. Insofar as God and God's children are not of this world, their death on it is only an illusion, and their life in the higher world of truth is eternal. Jesus puts the point rather cryptically to his followers: "I shall not talk to you much longer, because the prince of this world is on his way. He has no power over me" (14:30).

If the prince of this world has no power, then how can he interrupt our conversation and deprive us of our beloved leader? The disciples do not explicitly ask this question, but it is implicit throughout the gospel's attempt to make sense of the death of God's son. Jesus's answer is implicit as well: because the prince of this world can persecute the flesh, it may seem that he has power over the godly. But because the godly are actually from the world of spirit, in truth he cannot touch them. Granted, from the vantage point of this life the immunity of God's children is not always clear. Hence Jesus reassures his disciples. He is going away, but his departure constitutes a victory, not a defeat: "The prince of this world is already condemned" (16:11). Not only is Jesus's death really a victory, but the same logic of split reality will apply to the sufferings of the disciples: "In the world you will have hardship, but be courageous: I have conquered the world" (16:33). It is perhaps an acknowledgment of how difficult it is to achieve conviction about this disjuncture between defeat in the world and victory in the spirit that Jesus compromises a bit in a prayer he addresses to his Father on behalf of his followers: "I am not asking you to remove them from the world but to protect them from the Evil One. They do not belong to the world anymore than I belong to the world" (17:15).

If Jesus and his followers do not belong to the world, precisely the opposite is true of the Jews. John treats the Jews in general (we will

return to the seeming exception of Nicodemus) as servants of the world
and its prince, intent from the beginning on confuting and killing the
Son of God. From the first narrative sentence, in which "the Jews" send
priests and Levites from Jerusalem to interrogate Jesus (1:19) to the cli-
mactic scene in which the crowd of "Jews" rejects Pilate's exhortation
and demands that Jesus be crucified (19:14–16), the "Jews" work for
Jesus's death and destruction (see, for example, 5:18, 7:1). Certain groups
do come in for special criticism. Like Luke or Matthew, John specifically singles out the Pharisees, although he does so in terms of a cosmic
dualism quite characteristic of him: "You are from below; I am from
above. You are of this world; I am not of this world. I have told you
already, you will die in your sins" (8:22–24). It is clear, however, that this
criticism applies to Jews in general, and not just Pharisees. As he puts it
later, when prophesying the persecution of his followers and their expulsion from the synagogue, "[T]hey have never known either the Father
or me" (16:2–3).

Strong as these words are, John has even stronger ones, and he aims
them at a surprising and significant subset of the population: those
Jews who *claim to believe* in Jesus. Chapter 8 contains an extraordinary
exchange that begins at verse 31: "To the Jews that believed in him Jesus
said: If you make my word your home . . . the truth will set you free."
Jesus's conditional "if" marks some skepticism about the possibility
of any Jew finding a home in his word, rather than in the world. That
skepticism is more fully expressed in the following verses. When these
"believing" Jews wonder how they could need emancipation, since they
are a free people descended from Abraham, Jesus answers with impa-
tience: "I know that you are descended from Abraham; but you want to
kill me because my word finds no place in you. What I speak of is what
I have seen at my Father's side, and you too put into action the lessons
you have learnt from your father" (8:37–38).[46]

The problem is in some sense "genealogical": the Jews, even those
who are said to believe in Jesus, do not seem to have the same father
as the "children of God." To this harsh insinuation the Jews respond,
but "our father is Abraham!" Not so, Jesus replies, for you do not "do

as Abraham did. As it is, you want to kill me. . . . You are doing your father's work."

> *You are from your father, the devil, and you prefer to do what your father wants. He was a murderer from the start; he was never grounded in the truth; there is no truth in him at all. When he lies he is speaking true to his nature, because he is a liar and the father of lies. . . . Whoever comes from God listens to the words of God; the reason why you do not listen is that you are not from God. (8:39–47)*

For John, the Jews, even these "believing" ones, are not children of Abraham but of the devil.

The author of the fourth gospel, like Paul and all the other gospel authors we have encountered thus far, is writing within a particular context and in response to a particular conflict—in this case, the ejection of Christ-believing Jews from the synagogues (9:22, 12:42). "John's" response seems to be an adaptation of Paul's argument that one can be Abraham's heir in the spirit as well as in the flesh. But Paul had made the distinction in order to make room for the gentiles within Christianity while at the same time maintaining the traditional paternity of the Jews. John does quite the opposite. Just as he denies the flesh any significance in the history of salvation ("It is the spirit that gives life. The flesh has nothing to offer" [6:63].), he strips the Jews of their lineage, assigns to them a demonic spiritual paternity, and insists on their eternal role as enemies of God. From within such a polarity, the "believing Jew" becomes something of a genetic impossibility.[47]

Of course the author knows that Jesus was born a Jew, of the lineage of David, "for Salvation comes from the Jews" (4:22), even if it does not come to them. And of course he knows that the disciples were themselves Jews. We could exploit this seeming contradiction to argue that John does not condemn the Jews, but rather allows them an ongoing role in redemption. But by "Salvation comes from the Jews" John meant Jewish prophecy, and his audience would have seen no contradiction in the stark separation John drew between Jewish prophets and their words on the one hand, and the Jews that reject Jesus and later his believers on the other. Early in his mission Jesus tells the Jews "intent on killing him" that his mission is entirely in accordance with their law and prophecy: "You pore over the scriptures, believing that in them you can find eternal life. It is these scriptures that testify to me, and yet you refuse to come to me to receive life!" This testimony, however, only makes the Jews' crime greater, for now they have become traitors to their own law: "You have placed your hopes on Moses, and Moses will be the one who accuses you. If you really believed him you would believe me too" (5:39–45).

Like the authors of the other gospels, like Jesus on the road to Emmaus, John rereads the Jewish scriptures to show how all the details of Christ's passion, from his mounting a donkey at the entrance to Jerusalem to his death-draught of vinegar and gall, were in accordance with ancient prophecy. But John places much greater stress on enmity: "[A]ll this was only to fulfill the words written in their Law: *They hated me without reason*" (15:25; citing Ps. 69:4). And he insists as well on much greater distance between Jesus and Jewish law. "Your law" (John 8:17), "their law" (15:25), John's Jesus calls the Mosaic strictures, and he makes clear that neither he nor his Father observe them (5:16–18). In John, it sometimes seems that what is most relevant about Jewish prophecy is its prediction of Jewish enmity toward God and his Son.

John explains the death of Jesus and the persecution of his early followers by viewing history through the polarizing lens of a dualist cosmology. He divides the cosmos into world and word, into a realm of flesh, falseness, and death, and one of spirit, truth, and immortality. The suffering of Jesus and his disciples is the consequence of a war between these two realms, but that suffering is also in some sense only apparent, not real. The children of God have conquered the world: the world has no power over them. What is not only apparent but also very real is the enmity the world feels toward the word, the revulsion of darkness for light. John expresses that revulsion most explicitly through the "Jews" he constructs. Their actions and their enmity fully explain the tribulations of God and God's children in the world. John's Jews are as close as canonical scripture ever comes to the embodiment—Satan aside—of a purely negative principle.

When the authors of Matthew, Luke, Mark, and John asked themselves—like the disciples on the road to Emmaus—why Jesus had lived and suffered as he did, they all agreed that he lived and suffered as he did because scripture and prophecy required that he should. They agreed as well that his opponents had failed to read scripture correctly, and had not recognized that his life and death fulfilled prophecy. Enmity was a form of illiteracy. To put it more positively, the recognition of Jesus depended on the correct interpretation of both scripture and the world. The gospels presented themselves as the classrooms in which Jesus taught this special literacy. In them, his worst students were the "professors" of the old school, the Jews, Sadducees, and Pharisees, their arrogant but false erudition a source of doubt and dangerous attraction to those struggling to learn the grammar of the new faith.

The educational metaphor is meant to remind us of Paul's pedagogy, from which some of the gospel authors learned a good deal. But they also took those teachings in directions that Paul himself might not have recognized. The Paul who appears in the Acts of the Apostles, written circa 115–120 CE, is very different from the Paul of his own letters some sixty or more years earlier. In Acts, he adopts a tone more familiar to us from the gospels than from Paul's letters (except perhaps 1 Thess. 2:14): "And Paul and Barnabas spoke out boldly, saying, 'It was necessary that the word of God should be spoken first to you. Since you thrust it from you and judge yourselves unworthy of eternal life, behold, we turn to the Gentiles'" (Isa. 49:6; Acts 13:46).[48] Here, unlike in Romans, Paul is preaching supersession: the Jews' unbelief is the prerequisite and the rational for the gentile mission. Acts is as much a rewriting of the historical Paul's message as Luke is of the historical Jesus's. Its author presents the Jews as enemies not only of God but also of all other prophets, including Paul: "You stubborn people . . . you are always resisting the Holy Spirit. . . . Can you name a single prophet your ancestors never persecuted? They killed those who foretold the coming of the Upright One, and now you have become his betrayers, his murderers" (Acts 7:51–53).[49] The Jewish people are here separated from the Jewish prophets, the truth of the latter confirmed always by the former's falsity. In this way Jewish hatred becomes proof of Paul's message, as it had been of Jesus's and of the prophets' before him. It is by Jewish persecution, according to Acts, that the gentile Christian community is defined as one of spirit.[50]

I do not mean to suggest that the authors of the gospels (and all later readers under their influence) misread Paul. I mean only that when they read him (how much they did is debated), they read him in a time and for purposes very different from his own, developing his thought in directions he had not taken, amplifying some potential implications, suppressing others. Paul the Pharisee, writing before the destruction of Jerusalem and before the predominance of gentiles in the church, had never aligned the Jews with Satan, nor opposed their world of Temple and covenant to God's. He never declared the mission to them closed nor lost sight of their reacceptance, though he conditioned that acceptance on their conversion to Christ. Finally, he never rejected the practice of Jewish law and ritual by Jewish believers in Christ. To the contrary, it was to the Jewish Christians of Jerusalem that he sends his charity and that of the gentiles among whom he preached, a charity that manifested itself in both material and spiritual terms. The gospels approached all these positions. But above all, they amplified an association Paul *had* made in order to explain to the gentile Christians why they should not observe Jewish law: the association between Judaism and the flesh, with all that the flesh stands for (the material world, the Old Testament, the literal meaning of texts). It was through Judaism that they chose to make the flesh and its tools appear in their most dangerous, most infectious ("Beware the yeast of the Pharisees!"), and most explicitly stigmatized guise. As the danger of Judaism was amplified, the possibilities for the Jews' redemption and conversion decreased. Christians came to fear rather than admire Jewish followers of Christ who practiced their old law. This fear so changed the world that within a little more than a century after Paul's death, his own spiritual itinerary had become suspect. If Paul had converted in Christianity's second century rather than its first, he would have been declared a heretic.[51]

By moving more or less chronologically through the New Testament canon, from Paul to the Gospel of John, from a conditional and godly Jewish enmity to an essential and demonic one, I have tried to emphasize the contingency of the ideas whose history we are studying, by which I mean the combination of chance and hard work that transforms the possible into the real. Increasingly historians, archaeologists, and theologians are making that hard work clear. Thanks to their efforts, and to the discovery and deciphering of ancient collections of texts like the Dead Sea Scrolls, we now know more about late Second Temple Judaism and early Christianity than any previous generation. We have learned to try to read Paul's struggles with "works of law" through eyes innocent of later writers. And we are provided with a glittering generation of scholarship that helps us to realize how the gospels' treatment of the Pharisees (to pick but one example) reflects the polemics of late-first-century Christians, writing in an increasingly gentile church after the destruction of Jerusalem, and not those of the historical Jesus. We have been offered, in short, the greatest relief that history can offer: the knowledge that, for good or ill, things did not need to turn out as they did.

This is important research. Its goal is historical truth, by which I mean a history that is not anachronistic, a history that is true to the evidence and conditions of Jesus's day, of Paul's, of the gospel authors', each in their own terms and not in terms of their futures. But it also seems ethically important to remember that the power of these historical truths pales next to the power of the figures of Judaism we have seen emerging in this chapter. The logic that animated those figures was an anachronistic one, developed by gospel authors adapting old materials to make sense of their own present, with all of its questions and quarrels. Yet it was also a conquering one, whose power would come over time to structure our cognition and our vocabulary. The *Oxford English Dictionary* entry for *Pharisee*, gives "hypocrite."

The evangelists' views of Jews and Judaism were no more immune to the mutations of interpretation than were the views of the historical Jesus or of the historical Paul. The Christian history of thinking about Judaism does not end with the first century. It only begins there, and a great shift still lies ahead. For Jesus's disciples, as for Paul and probably for a number of the gospel authors, the struggle with "Judaism" and the Law was both real and specific. Real in that it was part of their lived experience (some of Paul's communities, or *ekklesiai*, aside) in predominantly Jewish contexts. Specific in that it provided answers to particular questions raised by that lived experience: Given that Jesus was crucified and not enthroned in Jerusalem, how can he be the Jewish Messiah?[52] Should gentiles who worship Jesus also practice Jewish law as all Jesus's disciples (as Jews) had? Why do some synagogues exclude followers of Jesus from their fellowship, and even persecute them? These questions ceased to be as pressing in the second, third, and fourth centuries, when the Jesus movement had become a vastly gentile church independent of Jews and their synagogues. The Jews were by then a twice-defeated people without political power: persecution of Christians came not from Jerusalem but from Rome. Yet the logic of Jewish enmity and the killing carnality of the Jews only grew stronger, driven now not so much by conflict with real Jews, but because it proved ever more generally useful for thinking about God, the world, and the nature of the texts and powers that mediate between them.

Chapter 3

THE EARLY CHURCH: MAKING SENSE OF THE WORLD IN JEWISH TERMS

THE PREVIOUS CHAPTER focused only on the scripture Christians today know confidently as the "New Testament": four gospels plus Acts, fourteen "Pauline" epistles, seven additional letters, and one Revelation, all carefully edited, translated, printed, bound. There was no such confidence among the early Christians, no agreement about what constituted Christian scripture or how it should be read. From its very first moments, the Jesus movement was marked by a struggle between "true teaching" and "false." As Paul put it in one of our earliest texts, "If anyone preaches to you a gospel contrary to that which you have received [from me], let him be anathema" (Gal. 1:9). Today's New Testament contains those teachings certified by centuries of conflict. Its pages preserve only a few of the many voices raised in a long and clamorous debate. Early Christians had to choose among the many, and the penalty for a wrong choice was high: nothing less than eternal damnation.

Early Christian Polyphony

What did this deadly cacophony sound like? Of course the now "canon-ical" (from the Greek word for the chalked string carpenters use to mark a straight line) texts circulated, once they were written, in many versions (abridged, expanded, synthesized) and with countless variants. But there were also many other gospels, epistles, and acts in circulation. These often came attributed to a founding figure of the movement: a beloved disciple or apostle. Such attribution, however, was no guaran-tee of truth, for even the disciples were prone to error. The Gospel of Matthew tells us that when Jesus called the eleven to "make disciples of all nations . . . and teach them to observe all the commands I gave you," "they fell down, though some hesitated" (28:17–20). Who were these hesitant apostles? Matthew did not name names, but authors of other gospels often told the story of Jesus and his disciples in such a way as to put the putative authors of rival writings in the worst possible light.[1]

The Gospel of John, for example, repeatedly portrays the disciple Thomas as a stubborn doubter who refuses to believe in the corporeality of the risen Christ. John's attack seemed unmotivated until 1945, when an Egyptian peasant digging for fertilizer in the valley of Jabl al-Tarif discovered a jar under a boulder. The jar contained some forty-five lost gospels, apocalypses, and epistles buried in the late fourth century, dur-ing a period when such writings, which we now call "extra-canonical," were being condemned as heretical. Among them was the Gospel of Thomas, a collection of Jesus's sayings that presented Thomas as a dis-ciple favored with a special teaching. Thomas's teaching urged each Christian to discover the Christ hidden within himself. Read deeply, drunk like living water, Jesus's words would orient that search within, leading the believer to salvation.[2]

This promise disturbed the author of John, for whom God was not to be found in "Everyman." For him, Jesus was not just a teacher of sal-vation, leading the believer to the divine within himself. He was divin-ity itself, man's only gateway to eternal life, the Word and Son of God. John's articulation of Jesus's identity with God was unique even among the four now canonical gospels, but it seems to have especially targeted teachings like those of Thomas. Hence in the stories John's author told about Jesus's life and death, he took particular care to cast Thomas as a doubter of Jesus's divinity and resurrection in the flesh. An approximation is implicit. Thomas, like anyone else who hesitates at Jesus's identity with God, comes perilously close to the Jews, whose rejection of God is paradigmatic.[3]

The nature of Jesus's divinity was only one of the subjects on which early Christian texts disagreed. The Gospel of Mary Magdalene, and the Acts of Paul and Thecla, for example, granted women a public spiritual authority denied by texts like 1 Timothy (attributed by Christian tradition to Paul but by New Testament scholarship to a later writer). The Didache, or "Teaching of the Twelve Apostles," a text that may predate some of the now canonical gospels, preached an attitude toward observance of ritual law quite unlike that of Acts: "For if you can bear the whole yoke of the Lord, you will be perfect, but if you cannot, do what you can" (6:2). In short, the first followers of Jesus had many more, and more varied, "early-Christian" teachings available to them than we do now.[4]

Moreover, texts were not the only, perhaps not even the primary, harbingers of the gospel to these communities. The good news came as well on foot and in the flesh, in the form of apostles and prophets. The number of these was not limited, as it sometimes is in our modern understanding of the terms, to Paul and Jesus's companions. On the contrary, myriad now nameless teachers traveled the sea roads and byways of the Mediterranean, shaking off the dust of many a village along their route. Their teachings were often incompatible, their preachings often aimed against each other. To the villagers fell the task of distinguishing between true prophet and false, between apostle of Christ or one of deception.

Confronted with an abundance of contradictory testimony, early Christians developed tests to probe their prophets. The Didache, for example, provided a brief manual of instruction on how to distinguish apostle from fraud:

Let every apostle who comes to you be welcomed as the Lord. But he should not remain more than a day. If he must, he may stay one more. But if he stays three days, he is a false prophet. When an apostle leaves he should take nothing except bread, until he arrives at his night's lodging. If he asks for money, he is a false prophet. Do not test or condemn a prophet speaking in the Spirit. For every sin will be forgiven, but not this sin. Not everyone who speaks in the Spirit is a prophet, but only one who conducts himself like the Lord. Thus the false prophet and the prophet will both be known by their conduct. No prophet who orders a meal in the Spirit eats of it; if he does, he is a false prophet. Every prophet who teaches the truth but does not do what he himself teaches is a false prophet. . . . Do not listen to anyone who says in the Spirit, "Give me money" (or something else). But if he tells you to give to others who are in need, let no one judge him. Everyone who comes in the name of the Lord should be welcomed. Then, when you exercise your critical judgment, you will know him; for you understand what is true and what is false.[5]

Like the Gospel of Matthew, the Didache urged its readers to detect falsity through the gap between word and deed, between prophecy and behavior. It offered numerous specific tests to determine who was truly moved by the spirit, and who was a materialistic "Christmonger." The Didache inveighed constantly against the latter group, whom it called the "hypocrites," and warned against keeping company with them. But no matter how good the advice and how vigilant the faithful, the task of distinguishing the true teacher from the false would only get harder:

For in the final days the false prophets and corruptors of the faith will be multiplied. The sheep will be turned into wolves, and love into hatred. For when lawlessness increases they will hate, persecute, and betray one another. Then the world-deceiver will be manifest as a son of God. He will perform signs and wonders, and the earth will be delivered into his hands. He will perform lawless deeds, unlike anything done from eternity.[6]

Like the authors of our canonical gospels, and like the many other early Christians who railed against "anti-Christs," "first-born of Satan," "beasts in form of men," and "ravening wolves," "The Twelve Apostles" understood their world to be besieged by hypocrites and false teachers. Like many others, they dreamed of the day when outer appearance and inner reality would become one, when all dissimulation and false teaching would cease. In at least one important sense, however, the Didache was quite different from our canonical texts: it did not characterize the terrible gap between outer appearance and inner reality as "Pharisaic" or "Jewish," as did (for example) the nearly contemporary Gospel of Matthew. The followers of Jesus who produced and read the "Teachings of the Twelve Apostles" did not require a negative Jewish foil in order to articulate their messianic faith. They seem not to have understood the dangers of their world in terms of Judaism or Judaizing. To the contrary, they advocated the fulfillment of as much of the law as possible: the more of the Lord's yoke you can bear, the more perfect you will be.[7]

The point is worth emphasizing in the wake of the previous chapter. Not all of the many doors that led into early Christianity opened onto the Jews in the same way that the canonical gospels eventually did. Many of these doors are now lost. Others are buried in fragments of papyrus known only to scholars. We may well wonder to what Christian worlds these other doors might have led, had they remained open. On the subject of Judaism (as on every other) early Christianity had many possible futures, and there is real relief in knowing that there was nothing inevitable about the paths it eventually trod. But this book does not seek such relief. It is written, as it were, with an eye on the rearview mirror: a history of roads heavily traveled, not of might-have-beens. Over the next three centuries Christianity rose to become the religion of emperors, and the Didache fell along with many other "teachings" to the cutting-room floor. Christians resorted ever more systematically to a logic that treated the relative "Jewishness" of a teaching as the best test of its truth or falsity. "Jews" multiplied as negative types in Christian writing, and the living Jew (as opposed to the prophets of the past) became in the Christian theological imagination the enemy of the Christian.

The Church of Martyrs and the Threat of Judaism

In what sense were the Jews the enemies of the early Christians? The question will strike readers brought up in certain Christian traditions as absurd. Was not the early church a persecuted church, and weren't the Jews first and foremost among the persecutors? The gospels, after all, are full of stories in which Jews seek the lives of Christians, beginning with Jesus himself and continuing with Stephen, Paul, and others preachers of the good news. If early Christian authors wrote frequently of persecution at the hands of Jews, it must be because martyrdom at the hands of Jews was a paradigmatic experience for early Christians.

Difficult as it may be to believe given the development of later tradition, aside from the gospels only a few early Christian texts speak of physical persecution at the hands of Jews. Moreover, the handful of martyrdom accounts that assign a role to Jews in their narrative generally treat them only as "spectators": joyful witnesses of persecution, but not active participants in the killing.[8] Even in this limited role, we may wonder how "real" the Jews' participation was. As Christians understood it, both scriptural promise—"which of the prophets have you not persecuted?"—and Jesus's example demanded persecution at the hands of Jews as a sign of righteousness and a seal of good prophecy. Perhaps this prophetic need itself generated the presence of Jewish enemies in Christian narratives of persecution.[9]

Justin Martyr, whose *Dialogue with Trypho, a Jew* (written circa 150 CE) we will explore further in these pages, provides an excellent example of this general tendency to produce persecutory figures of Judaism. He accuses the Jews of being the worst enemies of the Christians: "[O]ther nations have not inflicted on us and on Christ this wrong to such an extent as you have, who in very deed are authors of the wicked prejudice against the Just One." But Justin is speaking here of an already distant past, of the Crucifixion and of the attacks against the first generation of Jesus's followers narrated in the Acts of the Apostles. Justin happily recognizes that in his own day "you [the Jews] have not the power to lay hands upon us, on account of those who now have the mastery."

He knows that Jews were not martyring Christians after the Roman conquest of Jerusalem. Nevertheless Justin understands the "genus" of the Jews as the "seedbed of all the calumnies against us." The same is true of later Christians, so much so that one Christian group can even attack another as false by claiming that it has been insufficiently opposed by the Jews: "Is there anyone among the Montanists who has been persecuted by the Jews or killed by the lawless?" asks Eusebius in the fourth century.[10]

Eusebius's example reminds us that anti-Jewish logics were not necessarily nor even primarily the product of confrontations between real Jews and followers of Jesus. Rather, they were often developed among Christians in their struggles with each other over which teachings to follow and (once teachings were cast into texts) how these should be read. In other words, whatever its origins might have been in the early Jesus movements, the logic of Jewish enmity in the second, third, and fourth centuries—that is, the period of the "church fathers"—drew much of its nourishment not from Christian conflict with Jews, but from Christian conflict with other Christians.

A similar difficulty confronts us with the "Judaizers" so frequently mentioned in our early texts. The threat posed by "Judaizers," like the threat posed by Jews, was often produced by pressures of scriptural interpretation in intramural Christian conflicts. What do early Christians mean when they speak, as they do constantly, of the Judaizers who threaten the faithful? In the rest of this chapter we will see just how complicated the answer to this question is. But of one thing we can be certain: their complaints do not necessarily mean that the early Christian world was threatened by real "Jewish Christians"—that is, people of Jewish origin who accepted Jesus as Messiah but also advocated the observance of laws and rituals from the Torah.

There were certainly many such people in the first generations of Christianity, though the number probably dropped sharply with the destruction of Jerusalem in 70 CE (Josephus describes the Romans' slaughter of crowds of messianic Jews, sometimes interpreted by scholars as Jewish followers of Jesus.) The demographics are unknowable.

But regardless, we should never assume that the "Judaizers" and "Jewish Christians" who appear in our texts came from this group of people. For example, when—some forty years after Paul—Ignatius of Antioch attacked "Judaizing" preachers in his letter to the Philadelphians, the error did not coincide with Jewish ethnicity, rather the opposite: "[I]f anyone should interpret Judaism to you, do not hear him. For it is better to hear Christianity from a man who is circumcised than *Judaism from one who is uncircumcised.*"[11]

Beginning in the mid-second century, writers like Justin Martyr and the chronicler Hegesippus began to describe what they called "Jewish Christian" sects like the Ebionites and the Nazarenes, but their purpose was not ethnographic. Rather, they sought to develop a "history of error" through which they might tarnish their Christian rivals as "Jews." Hegesippus (ca. 120–ca. 180), for example, went so far as to derive every Christian "heresy" from the seven "Jewish Christian" sects that he claimed arose after the passing of the apostolic generation. It is not clear that these writers of the second and later centuries often encountered living, breathing, examples of the dangerous "Jewish Christians" they wrote about. Like Amazons, these monsters may have been good to fear and think about, but never quite in sight.[12]

"Judaizing" became a basic negative charge because it proved tremendously useful for Christians debating profound questions about the nature of God and God's action in the world. Given how often it is denied, the point is worth repeating. In the centuries after the destruction of Jerusalem, Christian portrayals of Judaism were largely driven not by confrontation with Jews and Judaism, but by Christian engagement with non-Jews. We have already seen how, as gentiles began to join the Jesus movement, they debated the extent to which doing so required adopting some of the practices (especially circumcision and dietary laws) that marked Jewish identity in the ancient world. After the destruction of Jerusalem, as the demographic balance in the movement shifted sharply toward gentility, such questions multiplied, for educated gentiles both Christian and non-Christian were greatly troubled by much that Jesus's Jewish disciples had taken for granted.

Greek philosophical ideas about the nature of divinity were one important source of worry. As any student of mythology knows, the Greeks had no difficulty imagining active gods: gods who were men writ large, moving among us, helping those whom they favor, harming those who displease them, even—like Zeus—raping those whom they fancy. Beginning around the fifth century BCE, however, some Greek philosophers began to think of divinity as perfection.[13] The cosmos may well be full of all sorts of gods—demons, demiurges, assorted deities—some of whom may act in the world, and even be acted upon. But the highest among these gods must be perfect, unmoved and unmoving, eternally rather than contingently true, suffering none of the constant change to which the physical world and the passions of men are subject. It was for this insight—sometimes called the invention of pagan monotheism—that later Christians like Saint Augustine would praise the Greeks: "These pagan philosophers, so deservedly considered superior to all the others . . . , well understood that no material thing could be God . . . and that no mutable reality could be the most high."[14]

Despite Augustine's retrospective enthusiasm, these philosophical ideas are not obviously compatible with Judaism or Christianity. For a follower of Plato the highest god should be completely immaterial, unchanging and unchangeable. Such a god would not, could not, create matter. For that work lesser divinities were necessary, subcontractors if you will: emanations, archons, demiurges.[15] Yet Genesis and its accompanying books present themselves as the account of a creator god, and worse, one seemingly subject to the vagaries of human passion and changes of mind (witness, for example, his extermination of most of creation in the flood, and his desire to wipe out the Israelites after the incident of the golden calf). Can these then be scriptures of the highest god? The nature of Jesus Christ raised similar questions. If god is unchanging and unchangeable, if divine reason is incorruptible and immaterial, if even the intellectual part of the human soul, is in Aristotle's words perfectly determined and abiding, unmixable and immortal, then how should one approach the life and death of Jesus? Can one who suffers be divine? If Jesus Christ suffered as a man, could he also be a god?[16]

These were some of the enormous challenges that Hellenistic cosmology and philosophy posed to those of Jesus's followers who were
versed in Greek learning. But the Greek tradition also offered some
solutions to these challenges. After all, the Greeks too had learned about
their gods through ancient stories about their actions in the world. Philosophy had not required that these stories—and these gods—be discarded: divine perfection and divine action could also be reconciled.
One way to address the problem was to develop new techniques with
which to read old texts. Allegory—from the Greek *allos*, "other," and
agorein, "to speak," or "otherspeak"—was one of the most important
of those techniques, a way of moving from what a text "literally" said
to what it "truly" meant. In "otherspeak," Zeus's rape of Ganymede
signifies the rapture that seizes the soul when it contemplates the divine
being, the one. Such methods of reading rescue the text by dividing it
into two parts, literal and allegorical, outer and inner, or—in the terms
that Greek philosophy applied to the human being—body and soul,
flesh and spirit.[17]

We have already seen Philo of Alexandria use allegory to reconcile
the Hebrew scriptures with Greek philosophy. And in chapter 2, we saw
how Paul put "otherspeak" to work in order to expand Jesus's promise
from the descendants of Abraham in the flesh and emancipate gentile
converts from circumcision and other aspects of Jewish observance. As
the Jesus movement became more and more Greek in later generations,
questions about Jewish observance became less pressing, but "Christological" questions about the meaning of Jesus's suffering and the nature
of his divinity became more urgent. Paul's "otherspeak" proved invalu-
able in addressing these questions, but in the process it also made these
questions "Jewish," because it made it possible to map any difference of
interpretation generated by the tension between literal and allegorical
onto the difference between Jew and Christian.

Among the early Christians there were three broad solutions to the
"scandal" (the word is Paul's) of Jesus's crucifixion. There were those
who avoided the scandal by making Jesus a man and not a god; those
who solved it by making him a god and not a man; and those who

heightened it by making Jesus both a god and a man. The first of these schools probably included many of the first Jewish followers of the historical Jesus, who did not require that their messiah be divine. But this position was overrun early, overwhelmed by the Roman legions who destroyed the earthly Jerusalem and the gentile converts who swelled the heavenly one. Henceforth it was abandoned to heresies: to "Jewish" messianic sects such as the Ebionites, to Islam's prophet Jesus, and to the ethical Jesus of Enlightenment and modernity. The conflict between the second and third schools (both of which claimed Paul as their headmaster!) proved more stubborn, and generated most of the vast variety of texts and teachings that characterize early Christianity.

The second school included diverse groups who believed Christ to be entirely a god, incapable of suffering or death, only appearing human for the sake of his audience. Some of these groups were dualists, for whom the world of flesh and the world of spirit were so distinct that they could not have been created by the same god; some were not dualists but Docetists (from the Greek *dokein*, to show, seem, appear, think), who accepted God's participation in creation but not his assumption of mortal humanity. We see traces of the struggle against this view in New Testament texts, such as 2 John 7–8: "For many deceivers have gone out into the world, men who will not acknowledge the coming of Christ in the flesh. Such a one is the deceiver and the antichrist."[18]

The author of 2 John, like the authors of many of the other texts eventually classified as "orthodox" (from the Greek for "straight thinking"), subscribed to the third broad school, a position that seemed to many at the time paradoxical and incoherent but that became dogma: Jesus was both fully man and fully God.[19]

Anti-Jewish Solutions to Christological Questions

To demonstrate how a logic of anti-Judaism could be deployed as a tool in these debates over the nature of Christ—debates that had nothing to do with real Jews or Jewish Christians—let us focus on a second-century Christian called Marcion (fl. 139–156). Marcion quickly became known as a most formidable opponent of the man/God paradox. Irenaeus, whose encyclopedic treatise *Against Heresies* (ca. 180) helped establish the contours of what would become orthodoxy, tells a story about his own teacher of blessed memory, the martyr and prominent advocate of paradoxical Christology, Polycarp. One day Polycarp was relaxing at the baths when Marcion entered the same chamber (*frigidarium*? *calidarium*? we are not told). "Do you know who I am?" Marcion asked Polycarp. "Yes," replied Polycarp, "you are the Antichrist."[20] Antichrist because for Marcion the tension between flesh and spirit was so severe that it called for complete separation. The highest God could neither produce nor assume a corruptible body. A lesser, evil "creator" god was the author of the flesh and everything material. The savior god was a "stranger" to the world, concerned only with soul and spirit. And just as there were two creations there must also be two scriptures. The materialist god's scripture was the Hebrew Bible. The stranger's scripture was a gospel (exactly which is unknown; Irenaeus says Luke) and ten Pauline epistles, all purged of "Jewish" traits (such as quotations from the Hebrew Bible) that might lessen the starkness of the oppositions Marcion understood them to contain.[21]

Marcion read Paul as a dualist. What we today may characterize as Paul's ambivalence toward flesh, he and many others saw as utter condemnation.[22] Marcion systematically expressed his rejection of material creation in terms of a rejection of letter, law (meaning Jewish scripture), and above all, Judaism. In this again he believed he was following Paul, whose clear opinions had been obscured by the textual tampering of Judaizing Christians intent on concealing the message of the savior god. No ancient source suggests that Marcion's predilection for distilling the evils of flesh into Judaism had anything to do with his experiences of, or competition with, real Jews. (This silence has not stopped modern scholars from hypothesizing that if Marcion attacks the Jews so violently, it must be because he himself was Jewish or descended from Jews!)[23] Rather it was driven by his readings of the Pauline passages, especially in Galatians and Romans, that described the existence of a "law of the flesh" and expressed the dangers of that law in terms of

Judaizing. According to Marcion and the many dualists who would follow him, Christians who believed that god had come in the flesh were
not Christians but "Jews," still clinging to carnality and Hebrew scripture, still in need of de-Judaization. This reading, like so many others
produced in the second century of Christianity, turned Jews and Judaism into a popular arena for contests over the relationship between matter and spirit, man and God, and over the texts and sacraments that
mediate between them.

One of the most important of these contests was over the "canon"—
that is, over the content and the meaning of scripture. Marcion entirely
rejected the books of the Jews, attributed their authorship to the evil
creator of the material world, and purged his own collection of any references that obscured the sharp distinctions he saw between the scriptures of spirit and the scriptures of flesh. In the words of one prominent
scholar of early Christianity, "A Christ without human flesh heralded a
Christianity without Judaism." Marcion's expulsion of the Jewish scriptures was, in fact, the first systematic attempt to delineate the form and
boundaries of a Christian canon, and it precipitated an explosion of
debate and activity, ranging from forgery to philology, out of which the
canonical New Testament was born.[24]

The largest questions Marcion raised about the shape of the Christian canon was over the status of the Hebrew Bible. As the first of the
great Christian Latin writers, Tertullian (ca. 160–ca. 225 CE), put it in his
Against Marcion (written in 207 CE),

> *The separation of Law and Gospel is the primary and principal exploit
> of Marcion. . . . For such are Marcion's* Antitheses, *or* Contrary Oppo-
> sitions, *which are designed to show the conflict and disagreement
> of the Gospel and the Law, so that from the diversity of principles
> between those two documents they may argue further for a diversity
> of gods.*

It was in its response to this separation, and in defense of the unity of
law and gospel, that Christianity elaborated its most fateful attitudes

toward the Jew. Justin Martyr, a contemporary and outspoken opponent of Marcion's, is exemplary in this regard. His rebuttal of the dualists, an inspiration to like-minded polemicists for centuries to come, was
revealingly staged, not as a "dialogue with Marcion, a dualist," but in
the form of a "dialogue with Trypho, a Jew." According to Justin, dualists like Marcion reject the Hebrew Bible and its God because they do
not know how to read it. Justin Martyr agreed with Marcion that the
law, understood literally, is indeed carnal. God gave it in this literal form
because of the Jews' hardness of heart: the Jews had not been capable of
understanding a gentler teaching. But the law's true meaning was always
spiritual. Reading it allegorically, rather than literally, could access this
meaning. The circumcision of the heart, the Sabbath in Christ, these
were the true messages revealed through the ancient prophets. According to Justin Martyr the Jews themselves had never grasped this. Because
they read literally and believed carnally, they failed to see that the pre-
incarnate Christ had authored their scriptures in order to proclaim his
truth, and failed as well to recognize their God when he walked among
them in the flesh. The Marcionites, Docetists, and dualists, in their literal reading of the law, simply repeat this error and become "Jewish."
Tertullian's reformulation of this position some fifty years later was characteristically pithy: "Let the heretic now give up borrowing poison from
the Jew."[25]

Again, the anti-Jewish focus of polemics such as *Dialogue with Trypho, a Jew* was not the product of conflict with real Jews or Judaizing
Christians. It was rather a strategy to defend certain (eventually "orthodox") Christian readings of the Jewish scriptures from the Christian
dualists' charge of Judaizing and demonic carnality, and to return that
same charge to the dualists themselves. The Law understood literally
was indeed a curse. Read spiritually, however, it was a blessing. Because
the Jews had never understood this, they had never been the true Israel.
But the Law's spirituality was concealed only by the blindness of its
readers. Here is the sharp point of the argument: if dualists like Marcion
reject the Jewish scriptures as materialist, this is because they themselves
are like the Jews, creatures of pure carnality.[26]

This same argument proved useful against another great danger confronting early Christians: pagans and pagan philosophers. In the second century, as Christianity became widespread, they began to mount systematic attacks against the movement, which many viewed as a naive but dangerous novelty. Justin's "dialogue" with the "Jew" Trypho was meant as a bulwark against these philosophical attacks as much as it was a defense against heresy. This is why the dialogue begins with a debate about philosophy, rather than with a critique of heretics or Jews. Trypho "the Hebrew's" first words ("Hail, O philosopher!") are not spoken as a Jew, but as an advocate of philosophy's importance in understanding the deity, whereas Justin dedicates his opening speeches to making the opposite point. Indeed, Justin's first narrative is of his own conversion from philosophy to prophecy. The ancient prophets, not the philosophers, saw God and are capable of teaching about him. Trypho should cease studying philosophy and become a Christian.[27]

At this point the dialogue does begin to look like a conflict between Jew and Christian: Trypho and his companions start to laugh. As a philosopher, Trypho asserts, Justin might achieve knowledge of God and salvation. But as a Christian follower of the prophets, he cannot hope to do so since he does not "observe what ordinances have been enacted with respect to the Sabbath, and the feasts, and the new moons of God; and in a word, do all things which have been written in the law." Justin casts Trypho as an enlightened man who does not credit the stories circulating about Christians: that they eat men and engage in promiscuous orgies. Trypho's problem with the Christians is simply this: "[Y]ou expect to obtain some good things from God, while you do not obey His commandments. Have you not read, that that soul shall be cut off from his people who shall not have been circumcised on the eighth day?"[28]

Though the conflict is now explicitly staged as a confrontation between Judaism and Christianity, the polemic with the Jew is in fact also a proxy for engagement with pagans and their critiques of Christianity. To understand how this is so, we need to listen for a moment to the pagans. One particularly biting line of pagan criticism went something like this: Jews were bad enough, a miserable and rebellious people. But if, as some Christians claimed, Christians were the "New Israel," then they were even worse. Since these Christians did not observe any of the commandments that God had ordained for the Jews, they could be considered only bad Jews, with an illegitimate claim on God's covenant. After all, God does not change his mind. On the other hand, if, as other Christians (like Marcion) claimed, Christianity had no relationship to Judaism, then it was merely a new superstition, one that should be suppressed as impiety.[29]

In other words, the relationship of Christianity to Judaism was as central to pagan attacks on the young church as it was to dualist ones. For this reason Justin could meet the pagan offensive with the same strategy he used against the Marcionites: by attacking the Jews. In texts like his *Apology* addressed to the Roman authorities, Justin did exactly that. If pagans believed that Jews had a better claim than Christians to the covenant of Abraham, it was because they (like the Jews) misunderstood the past. Christianity was in fact older than Judaism. Ignatius of Antioch had made a similar claim in his letter to the Christian community of Magnesia (ca. CE 108): "[T]he divine prophets lived according to Jesus Christ." "Christianity did not base its faith on Judaism, but Judaism on Christianity."[30] From this claim Justin built a theory of history. Jesus Christ was not merely a historical figure, crucified under Pontius Pilate. He was also the Son and the Word of God, and as such had been available to all men in all times. Even before the birth of Jesus, any man who lived according to the Word of God was a Christian. Socrates and Heraclitus were examples of such Christians, as were the prophets beginning with Abraham.[31]

The Jews, on the other hand, had never understood their prophets (or "rather not yours, but ours") nor lived according to the true meaning of their words. The law was given to them not as a privilege, but on account of the hardness of their hearts and as a mark of their future punishment. Indeed their circumcision was ordained only so that they could be easily identified when the time came for the Romans to bar them from Jerusalem.[32] Their killing of Jesus, the Word of God made flesh, was the climax of their murderous misunderstanding and the turning point of history. A turning point because Jesus rose from the dead, appeared to his apostles, "taught them to read the prophecies in which all these things were foretold as coming to pass," and sent them out into the world in triumph. "[T]o every race of men they taught these things, and were called apostles." At the same time, the falsity of the Jews was made manifest. Jerusalem was laid waste by the Romans, just as the prophets had foretold, and its people were exiled. Justin quoted Isaiah 1:7: "Their land is desolate, their enemies consume it before them, and none of them shall dwell therein." He appealed to the Roman (not Jewish!) target audience to see confirmation of this claim in the political realities of their own day: "[Y]*ou* know very well that [Jerusalem] is guarded by *you* lest any one of them dwell in it, and that death is decreed against a Jew apprehended entering it."[33]

Justin's argument reconciled two seemingly incompatible positions: Christians could claim the Jews' ancient prophecies without assuming observance of their laws. And it found proof for that reconciliation in a verifiable political history: the Roman conquest of Jerusalem, the homelessness of the Jews. Justin even introduces Trypho as a refugee from the disastrous Bar Kochba revolt, which ended with the death of perhaps as many as half a million Jews, the permanent exile of the remainder from Judea, and the building of a temple to Jupiter on the Jews' sacred Temple Mount. Justin's condemnation of Trypho as a deicide is therefore all the more cutting: "[T]hese things have happened to you in fairness and justice, for you have slain the just one, and his prophets before him, and now you reject those who hope in him."[34]

Justin, like a number of his predecessors and contemporaries, met the very different challenges posed by Christian dualists and pagan philosophers in the same way: by heightening the blindness of the Jews in the prophetic past, and the misery of the Jews in the political present. These two strategies proved popular with later writers locked in struggle, again not only with Jews but also with Christian and pagan rivals. Writing roughly a half century after Justin, for example, Tertullian penned a polemic entitled *Against the Jews*. We can debate whether this work was the result of conflict with real Jews (its modern editor suggests that the book's intended readers were gentiles considering conversion to Christianity). But what is undebatable is that Tertullian developed and deployed his anti-Judaic arguments much more broadly in the many other treatises he wrote, works whose titles make quite clear that their concerns were not with real Jews: *To the Nations*, *Against Marcion*, *Apologetic against the Pagans*. For Tertullian as for Justin and many other "church fathers," anti-Judaism was a tool that could be usefully applied to almost any problem, a weapon that could be deployed on almost any front.[35]

The significance of these strategies cannot be exaggerated. The first turned Jews and Judaizing into the standard diagnostic test for the reading of scripture, a balance in which spiritual and literal meaning could be weighed against each other. Every interpretation of scripture could be (and was) evaluated against a negative index of Jewish carnality and spiritual blindness. And insofar as every Christian was also a reader of scripture, the individual believer could be diagnosed in the same way, and placed somewhere on a continuum between Jewish "flesh" and Christian "spirit." In fact all of human history could be made legible in terms of the Jews' history: their prophecy in ancient times making known God's plan for the world, and their suffering in the present serving as the most visible proof that God had transferred his favor from the Old Israel to the New.

No one understood the productive potential of these techniques better than the first great systematizer of early Christian philosophy, Origen of Alexandria (ca. 185–252/3). Origen devised an anthropology that spanned the continuum between pure flesh and pure spirit, dividing mankind into three classes: the hylic (from Greek *hylē*, matter), or materialist, who were pagans and Jews; the psychics (from *psyché*, soul), who corresponded to the average Christian; and the pneumatics (from *pneuma*, spirit), which included only the most spiritual and ascetic of Christians.[36] This taxonomy of humanity corresponded to a taxonomy of scriptural literacy, with each type of person reading according to their class: the Jews literally, and the Christians at the level of spiritual meaning appropriate to their own spiritual state and abilities. And these levels of scriptural literacy reflected the nature of the Bible itself, whose words are, like living humans, divisible into matter and spirit. Their secrets are not revealed on the "surface of the letter." They are rather "a treasure in earthen vessels," their "spiritual meanings" woven in a "garment of letters." This is what Matthew's Jesus meant when he said that "the kingdom of heaven is like treasure hidden in a field": "the soil and surface of Scripture" is "the meaning according to the letter . . . while the deeper and more profound spiritual meaning is 'the treasures of wisdom and knowledge'" (13:44) promised by Paul in Colossians 2:3. In short, the word of scripture, like the human being, should be divided into three levels. For the lowest there is "the body of scripture, what we call the ordinary and narrative meaning." As readers progress they can be "edified by the soul of scripture." As for the "perfect," they shall be edified by the spiritual law, Paul's wisdom "that is not a wisdom of this world, or of the rulers of this world . . . but a secret and hidden wisdom of God, which God decreed before the ages for our glorification."[37]

Origen engaged in this elaborate mapping of the word onto the human in order to propose a theory of knowledge that could defend the humanity and divinity of Jesus Christ on three fronts. Against the Jews he maintained that Jesus was divine. Seeing only letter and flesh, the Jews had overlooked this divinity and crucified their god. Against the dualists he maintained that Christ was man. Seeing only letter and flesh, the dualists had discarded the Hebrew Bible and with it God's promise of humanity. And against the philosophers he maintained that, read in the best Hellenistic fashion, scripture demonstrated that Christianity was not a new religion but rather the true and ancient Israel whose prophecies were more ancient than Homer's and whose teachings, understood allegorically, were not only consonant with but superior to those that philosophy could offer. Moses's laws were better than Plato's, his cosmogony more reliable. In fact, says Origen, Plato borrowed much that was good in Greek philosophy directly from the Israelites—which is to say, in Origen's schema, from Christianity, the true Israel—whose teachings he encountered during a tour that (according to an ancient tradition) he had made of Egypt.[38]

The system of Christian interpretation that Origen constructed on the Jews and their literalism was clearly productive, but it was problematic as well, for if matter, letter, and history all march under the banner of Judaism, then why isn't it the task of the Christian to leave these behind as much as possible, and of the perfect Christian to abandon them altogether? And if that is the case, what separates the perfect Christian from the dualists, with their total rejection of flesh, Judaism, and Hebrew scripture? Origen clearly associated the letter with Judaism: he even used "Jewish" as a synonym for *literal*. So why, in the interests of de-Judaization, shouldn't both the Jews and the literal meanings associated with them be abandoned altogether? Origen fought against this dualist strategy. But he also maintained that there were certain passages of scripture in which "the body, that is a logically coherent narrative meaning, is not always to be found," and "only soul and spirit may be understood."[39] Again that same slippery slope: if some passages can be stripped of the Judaizing letter, why not strip them all, thereby protecting Christianity from the threat of Judaism? Origen includes flesh and letter in his incarnational Christianity, but he also stigmatizes them as "Jewish," and imagines the perfection of the Christian in terms of liberation from this Jewishness: a strategy that has the potential to revive the dualism and antinomianism that it is meant to contain.

The "Jewishness" of Earthly Politics

One way to make the danger clearer is to think of it in political terms. What should the Christian's attitude be toward the powers and principalities of this world of flesh? There were, of course, passages in Christian scripture that legitimated governments regardless of creed (for example, Paul: "Let every soul be subject to the governing authorities" [Rom. 13:1ff).[40] But others hinted at important distinctions (like Matthew's "render unto Caesar the things that are Caesar's but unto God the things which are God's" [22:21]), and still others tended to associate the powers of this world with those of the devil and his servants. The Gospel of John, for example, imagined a conflict between the power of the word and the "prince of this world" that would end only with the complete defeat and disappearance of the latter. Similarly, the Revelation of John understood the relationship between church and empire as analogous to that between Christ and Satan. Some early Christian writers found the polarity attractive. For Tertullian, church and empire were opposed as castle of light to castle of darkness, banner of Christ and banner of demons. "The kingdom of this world" according to Hippolytus of Rome "rules through the power of Satan."[41]

Not all early Christian thinkers were so dualistic in their thinking about pagan Rome and its emperors. All, however, tended to think of the princes and principalities of this world in carnal, and therefore potentially "Jewish," terms.[42] The logic of this politics derived from the same Greek philosophical ideas about the hierarchical relationship between body and spirit that we first encountered in the reading methods of Philo of Alexandria and Saint Paul in the previous chapter. Again, Origen was its master expositor.

Wary of dualism, he understood the relationship between Christian church and Roman state in incarnational terms, with the empire as fleshy body and the church as inner spirit. "Render unto Caesar," says the Gospel of Matthew, and Origen agreed entirely. But according to Origen, Caesar's claims were only on the body. Those who are of the body need render unto him: Jews, pagans, and average Christians. But what about the "perfect," the "pneumatics" who dwell truly in the spirit? The apostles Peter and John had rendered nothing ("Gold and silver have I none" [Acts 3:6]) because their business was not of this world. Origen thought that it should be every Christian's goal to become similarly tax-exempt.[43]

You see the danger: allowing the "pneumatic" to dwell purely in the spirit implies as an ideal the same dualist antinomianism, the same overthrow of all the constraints of earthly law, that Paul had at first seemed to suggest in Galatians and then condemned in Romans. Origen saw the danger too, at least at the level of politics. Hence he sometimes stressed that all living men, no matter how spiritual, must pay "tribute to Caesar," because all bodily things "bear the bodily image of the Prince of

Bodies." Jesus's flesh was the sole exception: it had not been stamped by the prince of this world. But even Jesus had nevertheless *chosen* to pay Caesar, drawing from the mouth of a fish a coin, which he gave to the tax collector (Matt. 17:24ff). Origen's point was a cautionary one, meant to avoid both dualism and anarchy. To make the caution stronger, Origen sometimes gave Christian political error a Jewish face. Those Christians who resisted the state he called "Zealots," and those who (like dualists) denied too strongly their debt to the flesh, "Pharisees."[44]

"In Origen's politics the state is related to the Church, very much as in his exegesis the letter is related to the spirit." The same general claim could be made of many other theologians that came after him. So it is worth stressing that the same difficulties afflict Origen's political theology as afflicted his system of scriptural interpretation. To the extent that our theology marks as "Jewish" the flags of flesh flown by the princes of this world, our politics can always be criticized as "Judaizing," even when that politics consists of a total "dualist" rejection of politics itself. This political problem did not bother Origen very much. Commenting on the teachings of the Greek philosopher Pythagoras—whom he probably believed had been influenced by Moses—Origen invoked the ancient sage's famous but obscure ban on the eating of beans. The prohibition should be interpreted allegorically, he explained, as an admonition to Christians that they should not participate in politics. For Origen and for the church of the martyrs, the pressing question was not how to engage worldly power, but how to avoid it.[45]

Christian Empire: The Danger of Judaism in the New Jerusalem

Origen of Alexandria died a martyr like his father, in the Palestinian city of Caesarea where he had long taught, of wounds sustained during the persecutions of Decius in the 250s. Between the time of his father's death and his own he is said to have written some six thousand scrolls, including his massive multilingual edition of scripture known as the Hexapla, "six-fold," for the six languages included. Though most of these scrolls are lost, the surviving fragments suffice to crown him as an exemplary teacher to the church of martyrs. But that church was about to disappear. To get a sense of how quickly it vanished, consider the career of the most famous graduate from Origen's school, the scholar and bishop known to history as Eusebius "of Caesarea."[46]

Born in Caesarea just a few years after Origen's death, the young Eusebius studied under Origen's successor, Pamphilus. He absorbed the teachings of the Alexandrians, often reading them in the same books Origen had used, for that Alexandrian exile had left his library as a legacy to the Christian community of his adoptive city. Like Justin, Clement of Alexandria (Origen's teacher), and Origen, Eusebius set out to make the history of the world legible in Christian terms. In massive works such as his *Gospel Preparation*, his *Gospel Demonstration*, and his *Ecclesiastical History*, he reread the history of prophecy and of philosophy, indeed the history of the world, presenting it in its entirety as an arrow pointing to Christ. But in one important sense he was different from all of his predecessors: he wrote his history in a Christian empire, or better put, in an empire with a Christian emperor. For Bishop Eusebius of Caesarea, the task was not simply to point the past toward the kingdom of Christ, but to help Christian history incorporate the kingdom of Caesar as well.

In Eusebius's case, that Caesar was Constantine, whose conversion to Christianity in the second decade of the fourth century transformed a minority religion, still subject to periodic state persecution as seditious, into a public cult called to intimate association with imperial power. Eusebius was a leading impresario of that transformation. He was an active participant in its politics and in its new institutions—such as the "ecumenical council" of Nicaea, that massive assembly of bishops summoned by the emperor in 325 to decide the debates over the nature of the man/God Jesus Christ. But above all, he developed the new ways of understanding the relationship between the promises of scripture and the events of this world, and the new exegetical techniques that were necessary to reconcile the history of politics with the history of salvation.

The novelty of Eusebius's methods is most obvious in the writings he dedicates to the emperor himself. As with saints' lives, martyrdom accounts, or indeed the gospel accounts of Jesus's career, works like Eusebius's *Life of Constantine* cast the emperor's curriculum vitae as a chronicle, prophetically foretold, of the victory of God's servant over the persecuting princes of this world, but with this difference: Constantine's triumph, unlike Christ's, redeemed the power of those princes and made it sacred.

Every sentence of Eusebius's *Life* of the emperor, as well as his *Oration in Praise of Constantine*, attests to this marriage of politics and theology. Let's look at one of those many sentences, Eusebius's report of the words, drawn from the end of Constantine's life, with which the dying emperor called for baptism: "It is our time too to enjoy the seal that brings immortality, time to enjoy the sealing that gives salvation, which I once intended to receive at the streams of the river Jordan, where our Saviour also is reported to have received the bath as an example to us." Note how the emperor here presents Jesus as the "type"—prefiguring example or model—of which Constantine is the fulfillment, just as the prophets were the "type" for Jesus. All of our "Jewish questions" about the relationship between scripture and the world of flesh emerge in this word, but with a novel twist: the "type" of Christ is imagined as fulfilled by an emperor who emerges, dripping, from the same river in which John baptized Jesus. The sovereignty of Christ is visibly realized in the kingdom of man.[47]

For Constantine and for Eusebius, this meant that the landscape of the historical kingdom of Jesus—Jerusalem, Judea, the "Holy Land"— had to be appropriated and made legible as Christian, just as the prophetic landscape of the Hebrew scriptures had been. One way to do this was through projects of scholarship such as Eusebius's Onomastikon, a "gazetteer" that identified all the places in Palestine with prophetic implications, locating and explaining them for the Christian tourist to experience in the flesh. Another was to rediscover the topography of the Passion and mark it with triumphal monuments, as Constantine did by building a massive church over the new-found site of Jesus's tomb.

Eusebius, at least, was in no doubt about whose defeat was being celebrated: "New Jerusalem was built at the very Testimony of the Saviour, facing the famous Jerusalem of old, which after the bloody murder of the Lord had been overthrown in utter devastation, and paid the penalty of its wicked inhabitants. Opposite this [the Temple Mount] then the Emperor erected the victory of the Saviour over death with rich and abundant munificence, this being perhaps that fresh new Jerusalem proclaimed in prophetic oracles!"[48]

"Perhaps" indeed. It is always difficult to determine definitively whether a new heaven and a new earth are being realized in the polities of our own time and place. The church of martyrs had been pessimistic on this score. Its one point of historical certainty—as we saw in the case of the gospel authors, Justin, and Origen—had been the significance of the defeat and exile of the Jews. The young church of empire was much more optimistic. It too saw the state of the Jews as a point of certainty ("the facts about the Jews are obvious to practically everyone") and a barometer in which the proximity of end-time could be clearly read ("if the Anti-Christ comes as Christ . . . he will be very zealous to rebuild the Temple"). But unlike the church of martyrs, the church of empire had gained the power to transform this state of the Jews, in order to make Christian victory more evident.[49]

Eusebius used the imperial construction projects of Jerusalem to make scripture and history became mutually legible and intelligible. It is true that the specifics of his approach were soon outmoded. His reputation withered as shifting Christological winds left him in the vicinity of heresy, and as the changing fortunes of Rome led some to question his messianic imperialism. But as we will see, the historical utility of the Jews did not disappear: to the contrary, it would only gain power in the theological debates that continued to swirl after Nicaea. Soon other projects would be added: legislative projects (such as imperial restrictions on Jews visiting Jerusalem, circumcising slaves, marrying or exercising authority over Christians), even programs of exile and outright violence. All of these aimed at the same goal: to make sense of the flesh in terms of the spirit, of the earthly city in terms of the heavenly one, of the political order in terms of the prophetic oracles, through the perpetual defeat of the Jews.

Saint John Golden Mouth: "Bring Them Here and Slay Them"

The church could now bring real power to bear on the Jews' defeat. This does not mean, however, that the Jews to be defeated grew more "real." Quite the contrary: the logic of "Judaizing" grew stronger and the slippage between Christian "Judaizer" and "real" Jew increased simultaneously. John of Antioch, better known as Saint John Chrysostom (the name means "Golden Mouth"), was a master of this logic. In the summer of 386, newly ordained as presbyter and with his bishop out of town, John stepped up to the pulpit to answer challenges from a rival Christian group called the "Anomoeans." John and the Anomoeans disagreed on the nature of the relationship between God the Son and God the Father. John adhered to the position of the Nicene Creed, proclaimed at the Council of Nicaea held under the emperor Constantine in 325 CE, that Son and Father were "of one substance." The Anomoeans were one of many Christian groups, of which the Arians were the most influential, that condemned the Nicene position itself as a heretical innovation, a nonscriptural solution to problems of Trinity that compromised the unity of God by making the Son equal to the Father. Christ, according to most Arians, was the divine Son of God, but he was not identical in substance and power to the Father. Their view was not marginal: Eusebius, for example, had been an Arian, and although he had failed to convince his emperor on this score—Constantine presided over the council at Nicaea that ruled against the Arians—later emperors like Valens (364–378) were more sympathetic. The present emperor Theodosius, was a staunch Nicene, but the Arians remained strong in the Syrian city of Antioch, long one of the most important Christian centers of the Eastern Empire. Of these Arians, the Anomoeans (from Greek *an-homoios*, "unlike/dissimilar") represented the hard core, clinging to what they considered to be Arius's original position and rejecting his later "compromise" of similarity, which they saw as an accommodation made under pressure of persecution. In 386, according to John, the Anomoeans of Antioch dared him to preach against them, hoping to make of him a "victim of countless jeers and complaints."[50]

John took up the challenge, promising a series of sermons against the Arians and their errors. His first sermon was blistering, and the audience must have returned full of anticipation for the second.[51] Perhaps they speculated as they jostled through the church doors: What aspect of Trinitarian theology would he take on this time? What rhetorical devices, gestures, inflections of voice, would this master of oratory use to seduce his audience and topple the teachings of his adversaries? All must have been surprised at the words with which John greeted them. He had intended to continue attacking the Arians, he explained, "but what can I do? Another very serious illness calls for any cure my words can bring." What was this disease? "The festivals of the pitiful and miserable Jews" are coming up. Some Christians go to watch the Jews celebrate, others even observe their fasts. These people are "sick with the Judaizing disease." Hence John will not preach against the Arians, but against the Jews.[52]

The sermons that follow bear the traditional title *Discourses against the Jews*, and have been called "the most horrible and violent denunciations of Judaism to be found in the writings of a Christian theologian."[53] Certainly they are not friendly. The first section of the first sermon alone rehearses many of the standard themes of Christian invective against Jews (obstinate, stiff-necked, murderous, always rebellious against God, etc.) and amplifies them. The Jews are brute animals, concerned only with food and lust, unbreakable to God's yoke. "Israel is as obstinate as a stubborn heifer," an "untamed calf."[54] John's use of these prooftexts from the Hebrew Bible is common to Christian polemic, but his conclusions from them are uncommonly harsh: "Although such beasts are not fit for work, they are fit for killing. . . . This is why Christ said: 'But as for my enemies, who did not want me to be king over them, bring them here and slay them.'"[55]

John presented the Jews as the antitype, not just of Christians but of humans. "Their condition is no better than that of pigs or goats."[56] In fact it is considerably worse, because unlike animals, the souls and synagogues of Jews are the dwelling place of demons. John's eight sermons *Against the Jews* are full of arguments like these, which are perhaps more hyperbolic than those of most of his contemporaries. You can read them for yourselves in John's Greek, in Erasmus's Latin translation, or in the sympathetic English version published by the Catholic University of America Press. But we are less interested in the relative scale of John's assault than in the reasons for it. Why did John attack the Jews?

For many scholars the answer is obvious: "Judaizing must have caused a perilous situation for the Antiochene Christians." "Everywhere they encountered the distractions and temptations of the pagan and Jewish world; they were surrounded on all sides by perils calculated to endanger their souls . . . ," but "the pagans do not seem to have proselytized; the Jews did." Most scholarship on the sermons strives toward more modestly phrased but similar conclusions: 1) the Jews must have been strong in Antioch, 2) they must have attracted many Christians to their practices, and 3) this attraction posed a threat to a young and vulnerable church. In short, John attacked the Jews because Judaism posed a real and present danger to Christianity that had to be defeated.[57]

This was, of course, John's own position. Over and over again he insisted on the terrible threat Christianity faced in the poisonous enmity of the Jews, a threat to which his sermons were intended as the antidote. In this he was not at all original: a great many attacks on Jews or Judaism, from ancient times to the present, have understood or justified themselves as self-defense against a pressing danger. In terms of physical or political peril, the claim that the Jews posed a grave danger was already dubious in Justin Martyr's day, all the more so in John's two centuries later. John's entire life was spent in a Christian empire (with the brief exception of Julian "the Apostate's" nineteen-month reign [361–363] when John was twelve or thirteen). He knew well the imperial legislation favoring Christians and disabling Jews. He had seen synagogues seized and turned into churches, had preached victorious sermons over relics (like those of the Maccabees) confiscated from Jews and turned into objects of Christian cult. John had plenty of evidence of Christianity's triumph over Judaism. If he feared the Jews, it was because his theology had taught him to view other dangers in Jewish terms.

John makes these other dangers clear in his very first sermon. He was interrupting his preaching against the Anomoeans in order to attack Jews because, as he put it,

> *the danger from this sickness is very closely related to the danger from*
> *the other; since the Anomoeans' impiety is akin to that of the Jews,*
> *my present conflict is akin to my former one. And there is a kinship*
> *because the Jews and the Anomoeans make the same accusation. . . .*
> *That He called God His own Father and so made Himself equal to*
> *God.*[58]

John has not shifted his aim by turning from Arians to Jews; he has merely changed ammunition. The target remains those who, in his judgment, have an improper view of Christ's divinity. Sometimes these are pagans, sometimes Arians, sometimes heretics of another stripe. All are called to see their true reflection and their fate (should they not repent) in the demonic figure of the wretched Jews, who doubted Jesus's divinity and thereby lost their sovereignty and their souls. The Jews here represent a general problem of knowledge in its most virulent form. In this world, truth is mixed with falsehood "in the same way that those who mix lethal drugs smear the lip of the cup with honey to make the harmful potion easy to drink." "This is why I hate the Jews."[59]

"Poison smeared with honey": the simile was old long before John used it. To Christians it meant a deadly "heretical" teaching covered in the pious pretence of "orthodoxy." The use of such similes brought Pharisees and "heretics" into useful proximity. We can accurately paraphrase John's "this is why I hate the Jews" as meaning "this is why you should hate those that I call Judaizers: Arians, pagans, and any others who disagree with me about the nature of Jesus' divinity and thereby become God's enemies." Of course John's rivals, Christian or pagan, were not really Jews, any more than the Jews were John's real rivals.

Rather John, like many a Christian exegete before and after him, called his opponents Jews and then worked them over until they resembled the image.[60]

By John Chrysostom's time this working over was no longer confined to the basement boxing rings of small sectarian subcultures. It reached rather into the highest courts of the land, touching even the emperor himself. In his confrontation with the Arians John did not lay a glove on his own emperor, Theodosius, who was a strong Nicene. He did, however, attack Theodosius's predecessor, Julian "the Apostate." Julian had been educated as a Christian under Constantine's influence, but he attempted a pagan restoration after becoming emperor. According to John, Julian decided to let the Jews rebuild their Temple in Jerusalem. It is not entirely clear how seriously Julian and the Jews really undertook such a task, or whether the accusation was an invention or exaggeration of Christian polemicists.[61] Regardless, what is revealing is that the restoration of Jewish worship in Jerusalem seemed to a Christian (Saint John) the most obvious way for a pagan (Julian) to strike directly at Jesus's divinity. If the Jews were no longer Temple-less exiles from Jerusalem, then Christ's version of prophetic history as told on the road to Emmaus was proved false. In the event, God struck back. According to John the construction site was destroyed by earthquake, the laborers devoured by fire. Once again, the defeat of the Jews provided the best evidence, "clear and obvious even to the very young,"[62] that Christ, not Caesar Julian and his Jews, was king.

Chrysostom's "Judaizing" of Julian may not seem like news. After all, the church had long been accustomed to condemning its princely pagan oppressors with brands of flesh. But the world had changed. Chrysostom and many of his fellow churchmen now expected that it should fulfill the promise of spirit. What happened when it didn't? If the Christian empire's triumph was proclaimed through the defeat of the Jews, then might not the reverse also be true? Might not the victories of "Jews" in this world constitute evidence of Christianity's defeat? I put "Jews" in quotes because, once again, we are not talking of hordes of rabbis confronting the legions of Rome. Power is firmly within Christian hands. But within a system of thought in which law, language, and flesh are typed as Jewish, every Christian politician, even—as we will see—the most orthodox of emperors, can become a Jew.

Saint Ambrose: "That King Has Become a Jew"

In 388 CE, a year or two after John Chrysostom preached his sermons in Antioch, an armed mob of monks burned down a Jewish synagogue and a Valentinian Christian church (the Valentinians were one of many gnostic Christian sects) in the Mesopotamian city of Callinicum. The arson was illegal, and the military official in charge of the region (the Count of the East) ordered the monks' punishment, instructing the local bishop, who had apparently incited the attacks, to pay for the reconstruction of the synagogue. The incident might have remained a local and minor one were it not for the intervention of Saint Ambrose, bishop of Milan, and leading churchman of the Western Empire. In letter and sermon addressed to Emperor Theodosius, Ambrose opposed the military count's orders, and on the broadest possible grounds.[63]

Ambrose's letter (number 40) begins with a disquisition on freedom. A good priest is defined by his insistence on expressing the truth freely, a good emperor by his willingness to allow "liberty of speech." "For this is the difference between good and bad princes, that the good love liberty, and the bad slavery. And there is nothing in a priest so full of peril as regards God . . . as not freely to declare what he thinks."[64] The first five paragraphs sketch the outlines of a split model of sovereignty that Christian political history would become familiar with. The monarch has the power to compel obedience "in state causes"; the priest has the obligation to state the will of the king of kings, "one whom it is even more perilous to displease."[65]

Only once he has established this framework of dual offices, imperial and priestly, with their incipient dual sovereignties and freedoms, does Ambrose take up the case at hand. It is not some overzealous bishop in an obscure province who ordered the synagogue burning. The synagogue "began to be burnt by the judgment of God."[66] Behind this judgment stood the entire church. The bishop and his monks were but the instruments of God's justice, their violence a proclamation of his sovereignty, for insofar as the synagogue represented an exceptional space outside the law of Christ, its existence diminished that sovereignty.

The emperor and his count clearly believed the synagogue affair to be a matter of public order, and acted to defend that order and their own sovereignty from the monks' claims to place both themselves and their victims outside the law. Ambrose's response is breathtaking. He claims that this very insistence on upholding the letter of the law is Judaizing, and pointedly reminds the emperor of a predecessor's unhappy fate. The emperor "Maximus . . . hearing that a synagogue had been burnt in Rome, had sent an edict to Rome, as if he were the upholder of public order. Wherefore the Christian people said, No good is in store for him. That king has become a Jew."[67] The threat rests in implication: a monarch who reads literally, upholding the letter of the law over the demands of spirit, deserves deposition as a Jew.

Ambrose's rhetoric entirely transforms the stakes from a conflict over the relative power of governor and bishop, emperor and church, into a contest over sovereignty between Jew and Christian. "The people of the Jews will set this solemnity amongst their feast days, and they will doubtless number it amongst those on which they triumphed either over the Amorites, or the Canaanites, or were delivered from the hand of Pharaoh, King of Egypt, or Nebuchodonosor, King of Babylon. They will add this solemnity, in memory of their having triumphed over the people of Christ."[68] Ambrose might have added to his list the story of Queen Esther that doubtless inspired him. In any case his message is clear. Any defense of the Jews, no matter how small, represents a Jewish victory that, once granted, will be memorialized as long as the Jews should last.

These are three distinct claims. 1) The existence of places like synagogues where Christ's power is denied diminishes his sovereignty. 2) To defend the Jews is to become one of them. 3) The conflict should not be understood as a struggle among Christians between the claims of the emperor and those of the church to be the ultimate arbiter of law. It is rather part and parcel of Christendom's mortal struggle with its eternal enemy the Jew. All three of these claims placed the Jew completely outside the law. The Jews, Ambrose argues, "deny that they themselves are bound by the Roman laws,"[69] and by rejecting God's Son they have set themselves outside his law as well: "Will God the Father avenge those who do not receive the Father, since they have not received the Son?"[70] His sermon described the exclusion in terms of love rather than vengeance: "[T]he Church alone has kisses as a bride, for a kiss is as it were a pledge of espousals and the prerogative of wedlock. Whence should the Jew have kisses, who believes not in the Bridegroom?"[71] Regardless of the metaphor, the claim is central. Christian sovereignty demands the complete exclusion of the Jew.

By asserting the church's power to exclude the Jews from the protection of law, Ambrose sought to articulate a hierarchy of sovereignty in Christian politics. He eased the sting by presenting the conflict at Callinicum as one resolvable entirely within the confines of the prince's will. "How can your piety avenge them, seeing it has commanded them to be excluded . . . ?"[72] Since the emperor's law itself commanded the exclusion of the Jews, the emperor's decision not to defend their rights at law did not represent a retreat from that law. This argument may seem a bit tortured, but his larger point was clear. Imperial will is sovereign only insofar as it accords with the will of God, "[w]ho is rightly set before even emperors,"[73] and with the church that communicates that will. The Jews, with their peculiar status as enemies of God and as vessels of letter, law, and flesh, seemed to him a decisive point of engagement in the struggle for sovereignty between divine and secular power. It was by excluding or expelling the Jews that the supremacy of heavenly over earthly law could most clearly assert itself in the politics of Christian empire.[74]

Over the course of this chapter we have seen how, from the first to the late fourth century of Christianity, hypocrisy, carnality, literalism, and enmity were strategically distilled into the figure of the Jew. Like all distillation, this one was a risky business. If Judaism was, in Christian parlance, an attitude of excessive engagement with world and word, then no one was above reproach. In their attempts to purge the world of error Christians constantly applied the negative label "Jew" to others, even as they competed to adopt its positive sense (as the true and the New Israel) for themselves. One danger of this approach is that it could fill the world with "Jews."[75] This danger should very much worry modern historians who might want to distinguish between real Jews and Jews as figures of thought. But it is not the one that occupied the best minds of late antiquity. They worried about a different danger, and that worry in turn transformed once more the place of Jews and Judaism in Christian thought.

To understand this danger, we need only recall the method of the church fathers we have discussed thus far. All more or less agreed that the prophets themselves, properly (that is, spiritually, allegorically, typologically) understood, had never really been Jewish. "Jews" were those—whether Jewish or Christian—who misunderstood prophecy (that is, read it literally) and were condemned for it.[76] By insisting on a thoroughly "spiritual" reading of the Hebrew Bible, these theologians deprived the Jews of their scriptures, and the scriptures of their Jews. Such thoroughgoing "de-Judaization" helped Christians widen the gap between literal meaning and spiritual truth, thereby neutralizing the "Judaizing" potential of Hebrew scriptures and allowing Christians to claim them as their own. It had the added value of "Judaizing" anyone who rejected that claim. We who read scripture spiritually are Christian. You who read it literally, whether to reject parts of it (like dualists) or to take up some of its commandments, are "Jews." The argument proved persuasive, but it was also dangerous, for if Christians did not sufficiently devalue the literal and the carnal, they themselves risked becoming "Jewish." And if they devalued it too much, like the dualists, they ran the same risk.[77] Was it possible to get the balance right? The careers of Saint Jerome and Saint Augustine, two of the pillars on which the western church was built, provide a good example of the difficulties.

Saint Jerome: "A Notable Hatred for the Circumcised"

Saint Jerome (ca. 340/2–420) is a foundational figure in the Christianity of the Latin-reading West, in great part because of his role in mediating between scriptural languages and cultures. In this he was, in many ways, Origen's heir. His willingness to learn Hebrew in order to ground Christian scripture in the historical authority of the Hebrew text was, he sometimes confessed, inspired by Origen and his Hexapla.[78] Jerome's own version of that project resulted in the translation of the Bible—known as the Vulgate—that became the standard text of the Catholic Church for more than a millennium. His exegesis of scripture was similarly inspired: indeed many of Jerome's early commentaries, such as his commentary on Ephesians, reproduced Origen's allegorical interpretations without attribution, presenting them as his own. And again like Origen (and many other Christian writers), Jerome did not hesitate to deploy Judaism as a way of characterizing Christians whose sense of the balance between flesh and spirit, letter and figure, man and God, was different from his own. For example, a letter he wrote to a certain Bishop Nepotian in 394 was scathing on the vexed question of whether or not Christians should decorate churches with sacred images or artifacts. He knew that many Christians justified such things on the grounds that the Temple of the Jews had contained them. Those things of the Temple, Jerome explains, were "but a figure 'written for our admonition upon whom the ends of the world are to come.'" "But today" the Christian who *lives in that future* "must count riches to be but dirt." Today "the Law is spiritual." If Christians "follow the letter" in this, they must follow it in everything, embracing the Jews and adopting their rituals.[79]

Here the "Jews" are those who cling to representations of the divine deemed to be excessively material: too much letter, too little spirit. But who establishes the correct balance? Who decides who is a "Jew"? A few years later it was Jerome's turn to be accused of "Judaizing," this time by his former friend, Rufinus of Aquileia.[80] Rufinus was, like Jerome, an important translator and mediator between eastern and western Christianity, translating works by Origen, Eusebius, and many others from Greek into Latin. But a bitter controversy had come between the two colleagues. According to Rufinus, Jerome had surrendered to the wisdom of the Jews and the philosophers. Rufinus, a good Christian, "preferred to appear ignorant and unlearned rather than to be called

a disciple of Barabbas." The jibe is a cruel one. Rufinus knows that
Jerome's Hebrew teacher was a Jew called Baraninas, and he has twisted
the name into Barabbas, the criminal chosen by the Jews to be released
instead of Jesus in the Passion narrative.[81] According to Rufinus, Jewish
learning has transformed Jerome into an enemy of true teaching. "Who
else would dare to tamper with the tools of the church . . . but that Jewish spirit? It is they, brother most dear to me before you were captured
by the Jews, they who are rushing you into these evil matters."[82]

What evil matters? The same ones we have seen concerning Christians since the beginning of these chapters: conflicts over the nature of
God, and the implications of that nature for how man should interpret the letters of scripture and the things of this world. In this case
the conflict—known today as the Origenist controversy—was over the
teachings of Origen. In the third century those teachings had offered
advocates for Incarnation a powerful tool with which to answer Jews,
philosophers, and dualist Christians. But in the imperial church of the
fourth century, consumed as it was by debates over the doctrine of
the Trinity and the exact relationship between Father, Son, and Holy
Spirit—debates in which imperial coercion and episcopal violence were
deployed with increasing frequency—powerful factions began to be suspicious of Origen's allegories. To some, his emphasis on soul and spirit
smacked of Gnostics and dualists. His emphasis on the incorporeality of
God looked vaguely Arian to others, seeming to interpose a hierarchical
separation between Father and Son.[83]

Both Rufinus and Jerome were heavily influenced by Origen, but
with this difference: as the controversy grew sharper and more dangerous, Rufinus defended the teachings of the master, while Jerome repudi-
ated and attacked them. Matters came to a head in 399, in a dispute over
images—material and mental representations—of God. In his paschal
letter of that year, Bishop Theophilus of Alexandria emphasized the
incorporeality of God—a position that many associated with Origen—
and condemned the devotional use of images because they implied
otherwise.[84] When copies of the letter reached the monks of the Egyptian desert, it split their community. A minority of "Origenists" among

them celebrated. But a majority—like the elderly monk Serapion, who cried "[T]hey have taken my God away from me, and now I don't have anything to lay hold of"—felt bereft and outraged.[85] Like the monks whom Ambrose defended for burning down synagogues and "heretical" churches, these were men of action. They had recently marched into Syria and torn down the great pagan Temple of Serapis stone by stone. Now they marched out of the desert, laid siege to Theophilus in his palace, and threatened to kill him. Confronted by their piety—"[s]eeing you I behold the image of God," the bishop is reputed to have said— and also encouraged by Jerome and his allies, Theophilus reversed the edict and condemned the Origenists, who were expelled from the community by the triumphant monks on their return to the desert.[86]

It was in this context that Rufinus accused Jerome of having been "captured by the Jews," a charge meant to indict the plaintiff not merely of having had Jewish teachers, but of adopting an excessively carnal attitude toward God and his teachings. Jerome responded in a way that should already be familiar to us. On the one hand, he insisted that he did right in "having had a Jew as a teacher," for the appropriation of the Jews' texts and knowledge is necessary to provide Christians with uncorrupted scriptures, and "to disclose with pure and faithful speech the mysteries of the Church." On the other hand, he reiterated with apotropaic intensity his hatred of Judaism: "If it is expedient to hate any people and to detest any nation, I have a notable hatred for the circumcised; even now they persecute our Lord Jesus Christ in the synagogues of Satan." It is as if proclaiming one's hatred for the Jews could provide protection from whatever risks of "Jewishness" came with appropriating their texts.[87]

Saint Augustine: "Paul Was Indeed a Jew"

Rufinus pointed to Jerome's "Judaism" to defend Origen against him. Others did so because they found him too sympathetic to Origen and his methods. Among these was the fervent debater of heretics and future saint, Augustine of Hippo (354–430 CE). Augustine had been born into an orthodox Christian family in North Africa, a region where the Manichaean dualists were particularly strong. In his youth he had been attracted to their teachings—partly out of disgust with the apparent stupidities of the Old Testament, as he later explained—and studied with their masters. It was only in his thirties, while in Milan pursuing imperial patronage for a career as a rhetorician, that he encountered Saint Ambrose and heard some of his sermons. Those sermons, studded with glittering allegories, helped him to realize the value of the Hebrews' books, and moved him away from the Manichaeans: "I was delighted to hear Ambrose in his sermons to the people saying, as if he were enunciating a principle of exegesis: 'the letter kills, but the spirit gives life.' Those texts which, taken literally, seemed to contain perverse teachings, he would expound spiritually, drawing aside the mystical veil."[88] "The absurdity which used to offend me in those books . . . I now understood to signify the profundity of their mysteries."[89]

Ambrose's allegories gave Augustine the courage to defect to Catholicism, a defection his dualist former friends and colleagues represented as a far worse conversion: "You have gone over to the barbarous tribe of the Jews!"[90] But as a recovering dualist, Augustine was all too aware of the addictive nature of "otherspeak." He worried that the brilliant readings of Origen, Ambrose, and Jerome transformed absurdity into profundity, but at the cost of pushing letter and spirit further apart. The danger was one we've already encountered: the more these defenders of the Incarnation stigmatized the literal and elevated the allegorical, the more they approached dualism themselves.

Of course Augustine agreed that making the distinction between the literal and the figurative meanings of God's words was crucial:

> *The ambiguities of metaphorical words . . . demand extraordinary care and diligence. What the Apostle says pertains to this problem. "For the letter killeth, but the spirit quickeneth." That is, when that which is said figuratively is taken as though it were literal, it is understood carnally. Nor can anything more appropriately be called the death of the soul than that condition in which the thing that distinguishes man*

*from beasts, which is the understanding, is subjected to the flesh in
pursuit of the letter.*[91]

Like his predecessors, Augustine agreed that salvation depended on distinguishing between letter and spirit, and like them, he too understood
figurative interpretation as spiritual, and the "letter" in terms of the flesh,
a realm of animals and Jews.[92] To read "carnally" was to become a beast
like the Jews, circumcised in the flesh but not in the heart. It is to ward
off such danger that Augustine begins his interpretation of Genesis in his
Confessions with a prayer for God's help: "From all temerity and all lying
circumcise my lips, both my interior and my exterior lips."[93]

But as Augustine's choice of metaphors here suggests, he was not in
agreement with the many orthodox theologians who tried to solve the
problem by eliminating either lips of flesh or the literal meanings such
lips represent. Precisely because he knew how slippery the slope toward
dualism was, Augustine always battled the tendency to draw too easy
or too sharp a distinction between "Jewish" law and letter, and "Christian" faith and spirit: "One might hastily conclude that the law of works
belongs to Judaism and the law of faith to Christianity, on the ground
that the Jewish law prescribes circumcision and suchlike works, which
Christian practice has abandoned. The error in this distinction is what
we have all along been endeavouring to prove."[94]

In the 390s, while Jerome was busy marshalling forces against Origen
and his defenders, Augustine was engaged in a series of public debates
with his former Manichaean teachers. It is from the perspective of those
debates against the dualists that he took notice of Jerome's work, and
found aspects of it troubling. Augustine had never met his irascible
senior colleague, but he did not hesitate to send him a series of critical letters (dating from 395 to 404). One criticism, related to Rufinus's,
was that Jerome utilized the original Hebrew of the "Old" Testament
for his translation, rather than relying on the Greek Septuagint translation. Perhaps because he shepherded a community more troubled than
most by Manichaean charges about the "Jewishness" of the Old Testament, Augustine worried that Jerome's choice would create scandal by

empowering the Jews as arbiters in debates among Christians over the true meaning of scripture. To add teeth to those worries, he reported rumors he had heard of just such a scandal in the church of Oea: when Jerome's translation was read, a Jew suggested that a certain word in it was incorrect, and many Christians were thrown into confusion. But Augustine's principle complaint was a more basic one about the interpretation of biblical words: he objected to Jerome's claim, following Origen, that certain passages of scripture were not literally true but had only allegorical meaning.[95]

Flushed from his debate with the dualists, Augustine insisted that no passage of scripture can be accounted literally untrue, lest "nowhere in the sacred books shall the authority of pure truth stand sure."[96] "If he wrote what was false here, when did he say what was true?" (Ep. 40, 3.3).[97] Denial of the literal truth of any word of scripture, whether Old Testament or New, opens the door to "perverse men" like the Manichaeans, who deny the Hebrew Bible and dismiss the literal meaning of Pauline passages awkward to their cause as falsehoods uttered for some strategic purpose. "I would devote all the strength which the Lord grants me, to show that every one of those texts which are wont to be quoted in defense of the expediency of falsehood ought to be otherwise understood, in order that everywhere the sure truth of these passages themselves may be consistently maintained."[98]

The Lord granted Augustine a great deal of strength. From *On Genesis, against the Manichees*, written shortly after his conversion in 387, to the *City of God* and the *Sermons against the Jews* completed shortly before his death in 430, the saint and his scribes produced countless works—some five hundred pages per year on average—touching on the relationship between letter and spirit, law and gospel, Old Testament and New. Hundreds of these works survive, and more are still being discovered. But in his correspondence with Jerome, Augustine concentrated his efforts on a single line, one we have already encountered, that was often cited by the allegorists precisely because it synthesized the problem of Judaizing and the problem of reading into one potent and apostolic conflict. The text was Paul's exhortation to Peter in Galatians 2:14: "If you, though a Jew, live like a Gentile and not like a Jew, how can you compel the Gentiles to Judaize?" Following Origen, Jerome denied that Peter could ever have required gentile Christians to live according to Jewish law.[99] It was absurd to believe that either Paul or Peter would have recognized the ongoing validity of the law and its practice, either for Jewish Christians or for gentile ones. Paul had not meant his reproach of Peter, but had merely said these things in order to "soothe troublesome opponents," just as he sometimes pretended to observe Jewish law, not out of principle but to escape persecution.[100]

Augustine's position was a radically different one. "Paul was indeed a Jew; and when he had become a Christian he had not abandoned those Jewish sacraments which that people had received in the right way, and for a certain appointed time."[101] Paul, like Peter, observed Jewish laws, "but with this view, that he might show that they were in no wise hurtful to those who, even after they had believed in Christ, desired to retain the ceremonies which by the law they had learned from their fathers."[102] Peter's error consisted only in this: out of fear he had agreed to compel gentile converts to observe Jewish ceremonies, and in so doing gave the false impression that these were "still necessary for salvation."[103]

Perhaps the best evidence for the sting of Augustine's argument was the grace with which it was met. For years Jerome did not answer Augustine's letters, judging them "tainted with heresy."[104] When in 404 he finally did reply, it was ungenerously. Augustine was insisting, Jerome claimed, that Jewish law remained binding on all Jews, even after they converted to Christ. In this he was "reintroducing within the Church the pestilential heresy" of the Ebionites and other Judaizing sects. If such opinions were countenanced, Jerome warned, Judaism would destroy the church. "If . . . it shall be declared lawful for them to continue in the Churches of Christ what they have been accustomed to practice in the Synagogues of Satan, I will tell you my opinion in the matter: they will not become Christian, but will make us Jews."[105]

Perhaps Jerome, already sensitive to accusations about his Hebrew learning, felt that Augustine's criticisms were simply a more polite version of the same. In any event, his counterattack was ferocious, nothing less than an accusation of Judaizing. The ferocity is itself a symptom of the importance of the logic we are exploring, although it may seem in retrospect unwarranted. Augustine was not claiming that observance of the law was binding on converts from Judaism. What he did say, most clearly in the treatise *Against Faustus the Manichee* (*Contra Faustum*) of 398 as well as in his correspondence with Jerome, was that such observance was not prohibited to the apostolic generation; that it was understandable as the product of habit and custom; and that the apostles had favored it as a theologically advisable approach toward the Torah, "lest" (as he put it in his debate with Faustus the Manichaean) "by compulsory abandonment it should seem to be condemned rather than closed."[106] The ritual practice of the apostolic generation served as widow's weeds, a reminder of the Law's former place in sacred history and a reproach to those—that is, the dualists—who would deny that it had ever been beloved. But such behavior was acceptable only for this first generation of mourners. After the burial of the Synagogue, Torah observance became a type of necrophilia, the fruitless loving of an empty letter.

Augustine's defense of Jewish law here has nothing to do with the Judaism of his day. His position is not the result of contact with Jews (so far as we know the only living Jew he ever met was one who appeared in his court as plaintiff, to complain that another bishop had illegally seized his lands).[107] It is entirely the product of the theological exigencies of his debate with the Manichaeans. We have already seen Augustine's Manichaean friends characterizing his return to Catholicism as a conversion to Judaism. Similar themes emerge again and again in the debate with Faustus in 399, with the Manichaean champion stressing the "Jewishness" of the orthodox position: "Your Christianity, just like mine, is based on the belief that Christ came to destroy the Law and the prophets."[108] And again: "You cannot blame me for rejecting the Old Testament, because you reject it as much as I do. . . . You deceitfully praise with your lips what you hate in your heart. I'm just not deceitful, that's all."[109]

We know how Augustine's predecessors (for example, Justin Martyr, Tertullian, and Origen) met those charges: by invoking allegory and accusing the dualists of Judaism for reading literally. Without the pressure of debate, Augustine might have responded in much the same way, attacking the Jews as proxies for the dualists. (This had in fact been his strategy just two years before, in the first drafts of *On Christian Doctrine*, where he insisted that Jesus had deliberately shown flagrant disrespect for Jewish law.)[110] But under heavy "Jewish" fire from Faustus in 399, Augustine seems to have realized the risks inherent in the flight into allegory, and developed the new defense we have seen him suggesting to Jerome. Every word of the old Law was good. Every word of it was literally true, even if allegory was necessary for the Christian to find salvation in it. The coming of Jesus and his gospel closed the Law as a path to salvation, but it did not condemn it. No word of it was to be dismissed as false or—as Origen and many others had suggested, and as the Qur'an would later insist—as falsified by the Jews. On the contrary, says Augustine, the Jews are the best guarantors of the Law's truth. Long ago defeated, they survive for two reasons only. First, their existence testifies against all who might ever maintain—as Faustus does—that the ancient scriptures were false or falsified. Second, the misery of that existence testifies against all who might ever maintain—as the Jews and the pagans do—that Jesus was not the Messiah. Like fossils for the naturalist, the Jews continued presence on the earth is proof of an earlier stage, now superseded, in salvation's evolution.

"Outcast on the Earth"

Of course Augustine did not speak of fossils or evolution. Instead he developed a new set of metaphors, comparing the status of Judaism after the Crucifixion to that of Cain after the killing of Abel.[111] Like Cain, the Jews of Christendom were carnal tillers of the earth who killed the very flesh they had been meant to cultivate. In punishment for this killing, the Jews became, like Cain, both hyper-carnal and alienated from the world: "[Y]ou are cursed from the earth . . . , for you shall till the earth, and it shall no longer yield onto you its strength. A mourner and an abject shall you be upon the earth." Not even their law would give them fruit any longer: "[T]hey continue to till the ground of an earthly circumcision, . . . while the hidden strength or virtue of making known Christ, which this tilling contains, is not yielded to the Jews. . . . The veil which is on their minds in reading the Old Testament is not taken away." Carnal as they are, the Jews are in the end alienated even from their own mortal flesh, as Cain had been:

> So Cain . . . said: . . . "I shall be a mourner and an outcast on the earth, and it shall be that everyone who finds me shall slay me." . . . "Not so," [God] says; "but whosoever shall kill Cain, vengeance shall be taken on him sevenfold." That is . . . not by bodily death shall the ungodly race of carnal Jews perish . . . So to the end of the seven days of time the continued preservation of the Jews will be a proof to believing Christians of the subjection merited by those who . . . put the Lord to death.[112]

Augustine's position was significantly different from that of his predecessors, and it proved tremendously influential in shaping how Christendom would think with Jews. The Marcionites, Manichaeans, and other dualists had excised the Torah in the interest of a "Docetism" that emphasized Christ's divine spirit while stripping him of his flesh. Their eventually "orthodox" opponents had responded with a reading of scripture that retained the Old Testament but tended to strip it of its literal meaning and of its Jews, and thereby incurred the same charge of "Jewish Docetism" with which it attacked its rivals. Against both of these, Augustine posed a historical realism, one that restored a literal and spiritual value to the Hebrew Bible and its people.[113] His approach to reading scripture domesticated (though it could not entirely tame) the tendency of letter and meaning, flesh and spirit, Old Testament Jew and New Testament Christian, to fly toward opposite poles. He did so by alienating from their own texts and history the Jews who walk the earth after Jesus, converting them into corporeal shells of flesh without spirit. A series of linguistic metaphors drives home the point. "Like milestones along the route the Jews inform the traveler, while they themselves remain senseless and immobile." The Jews are "desks" of the Christians, adhering fruitlessly to "Jewish form" but knowing as little of its content as a blind man knows of his face in the mirror.[114]

In all of this, Augustine's concern was not with the fate of the Jews, but with the creation of a more durable paradox, one that could resist the attacks of the dualists without threatening to become dualist itself. More than any other church father, Augustine was master of the union of material and divine. It is true that he achieved his alchemy in the same alembic as his predecessors, distilling the danger of flesh and letter into an exceptional condensate of the Jew. There was, however, a vital difference: unlike John Chrysostom and Ambrose of Milan, Augustine did not imagine a Christian world rid of this Jewish residue. On the contrary, for him it was the continued existence of that residue that guaranteed the intelligibility of scripture and the world.

"Cain," "milestones," "exiles," "desks": Augustine found many ways to characterize the exemplary exceptionality he assigned to the Jews after the coming of Jesus. He found yet another late in his career. Commenting on a line from Psalm 59—"Slay them not, but scatter them in your might, lest your people forget your Law"—Augustine reminded his readers that, according to Paul in Romans 9:22, God had poured his message into two vessels, one of mercy, the other of wrath, the former perceptible through the latter. "For so God, willing to show wrath, and to manifest His power, has brought in with much patience the vessels of wrath, which have been perfected unto perdition." These vessels of wrath were God's enemies the Jews, destroyed spiritually but preserved in the flesh ("dead men") that his sovereignty might be known. Exiled yet ubiquitous, conquered but still a distinct nation, enemies of God that adhere to his laws, the Jews serve as the best evidence for the nature of Christ's sovereignty over the world, and as a lesson for heretics everywhere. Hence the Psalmist sang, "Slay them not." And hence (as he had put it earlier in *Against Faustus*), "[N]o emperor or monarch who finds under his government the people with this mark [of Cain] kills them, that is to say, makes them cease to be Jews, separate in their observance and unlike the rest of the world."[115]

It is important to remind ourselves, once again, that Augustine was not moved to invent this exemplary exile by any encounter with real Jews, nor was he setting out to articulate a "Jewish policy" for the empire. "Slay them not" emerged from the exegetical requirements of his debate over free will and predestination with the "Origenist" Pelagius, much as Cain the Jewish exile had emerged from his debate with the dualist Faustus. It was not as a living people that Augustine thought of the Jews, but as fleshy relics of a scriptural revolution. His "vessels of wrath" preserved the Jews, so to speak, in formaldehyde: inert witnesses, like Einstein's brain in a jar, of a transformation in man's understanding of the cosmos.[116]

And yet it is also important to realize that the "hermeneutic Jews" invented by Augustine and other church fathers had a real impact on future possibilities of existence for their brethren of flesh and blood. In the Middle Ages, Augustine's heuristic exile *did* become a cornerstone of "Jewish policy." In 1146, for example, some seven hundred years after Augustine's death, soldiers marching to the Holy Land on the Second Crusade paused in the German Rhineland to massacre the Jews, just as their predecessors on the First Crusade had done. This time, according to Rabbi Ephraim of Bonn, the Jews were saved by the preaching of Bernard of Clairvaux, who warned the crusaders that "[w]hosoever touches a Jew to take his life is like one who harms Jesus himself . . . , for in the book of Psalms it is written of them, 'Slay them not, lest my people forget.'"[117]

Some have seen in this anecdote proof that Augustine's teaching "saved Jewish lives," facilitating the survival of the Jews in Christendom. It is never easy to assign a clear valence—good or bad—to the fate of an idea, and a different choice of anecdote might lead to a less positive conclusion. In the same year (1146) that Bernard was restraining the crusaders, another great churchman of his age, Peter the Venerable, abbot of Cluny, was admonishing King Louis VII of France. Peter asked the king why the Jews were allowed so much freedom in the kingdom. Had the king forgotten the message of Psalm 139:21: "[S]hall I not hate those who hate you and be consumed with enmity for your enemies?"

Quickly Peter invoked Augustine's tag from Psalm 59. "Slay them not," he said, then continued: "For God does not wish them to be entirely killed and altogether wiped out, but to be preserved for greater torment and reproach, like the fratricide Cain, in a life worse than death."[118]

We will leave questions about the future of Augustine's ideas to chapters about that future (such as chapter 5 on the Middle Ages, and chapter 7 on Luther and the Reformation). But even without peeking too far ahead, we can already see that while Augustine's deployment of Jews and Judaism eased some of the "Jewish questions" with which the corpus of scripture and the body of God confronted early Christianity, it exacerbated others, not least those associated with the body politic.[119] Insofar as, in Augustine's system, the power of law was manifested through the Jews' peculiar status, that peculiar status could also put the Jews at the center of debates over power.

Some of these debates might involve "real" Jews. Whereas, for example, Ambrose's *exclusion* of the Jews from protection by imperial law resulted in a clear assertion of Christ's sovereignty, Augustine's *inclusion* of the Jews as imperially protected exiles created new problems. The paradoxes of exile as a status constituted by the law as outside the law had long been fertile ground for ancient legal theorists. Similar paradoxes inhered in the Augustinian position. Did, for example, the "mark of Cain" relieve the Jews from the obligations of the Christian law that protected them? If so, then the Christian "protected exile" of the Jews would have the unacceptable result of giving God's defeated enemies more freedom than his victorious faithful: precisely the sort of problem that we have already seen Ambrose and Peter the Venerable so exercised about.[120]

But once again the problem went far beyond Jews of flesh and blood. The transformation of the Jews into living relics of God's law, combined with their placement under the sign and power of earthly legislators, created political difficulties analogous to and even sharper than the exegetic ones created by holding together the Old Testament and the New. Analogous in that in order to articulate God's sovereignty, the laws of "emperor or monarch" had to contain Judaism within themselves, much as Christian scripture needed to contain the Hebrew Bible. Sharper in that unlike biblical exegesis terrestrial politics always took place in the "Jewish" world of flesh, and beneath the curse of Cain, its first practitioner.

Like Cain, the founder of every polity is of necessity "a fratricide." (Augustine gives the example of Romulus, the founder of Rome!) Like Cain, who sinned by subjecting his reasoning soul to the desires of his flesh, every earthly city "has its good in this world, and rejoices in [the material world] with such joy as such things can afford," so that it will at the end of time be "committed to the extreme penalty." Secular power could never quite escape Cain's conjoined significations, as both "founder of the earthly city" and "a figure of the Jews."[121] Sovereigns therefore trod a path haunted by monsters of Judaism even more ferocious than those that beset readers of biblical texts. Augustine did not seek to slay these monsters. Instead he tried to immure them, like the furies under Aeschylus's Athens, at the foundations of the Christian city. Of course other Christians with different interests would work just as hard to set them free. This struggle to control the power of "Judaism" will turn out to be one of the most persistent and explosive themes of Christian political theology, from the Middle Ages to Modernity. But before we leap into those futures, let us move to a remote corner of the late antique world, where a new religion and a new political theology is being born, one that will eventually conquer all of Augustine's beloved North Africa and much of the world beside.

Chapter 4

"TO EVERY PROPHET AN ADVERSARY": JEWISH ENMITY IN ISLAM

*Likewise did we make for every prophet an adver-
sary—evil ones among humans and Jinns, inspiring
each other with flowery discourses by way of deceit.*

—QUR'AN 6:112[1]

CARAVANS ARE ALWAYS passing the cell of Bahira, the Christian
monk of Syrian Busra. Lost in his book, he never pays attention.
His absorption is understandable: the book is ancient, handed down
from monk to monk, full of the learning of the Christians. But on this
late-sixth-century day, discerning approaching dust on the distant hori-
zon, Bahira is restless. Either his sleep or his waking (we are not told
which) has been troubled by visions of an apostle coming shaded by
cloud from the desert sun. Cloud and caravan are somehow conjoined
in his consciousness. He busies himself, prepares a feast, and steps out
to greet the riders as they pass by. "I have prepared food for you, O men
of the Quraysh, and I should like you all to come, both great and small,

bond and free." The riders, surprised by this unaccustomed solicitude, gladly dismount for the banquet, leaving the youngest boy to watch the baggage. Bahira hurries to and fro, serving his guests, but also scrutinizing, searching for and not finding the cloud or other marks of prophecy his books prescribe. Could his visions be wrong? "Do not let one of you remain behind and not come to my feast," he urges. The riders remember the boy and call for him; Bahira stares, questions, tests. Then he summons Abu Talib, the boy's uncle and guardian. He has only one bit of advice for him, but that bit is pressing: "Take your nephew back to his country and guard him carefully against the Jews, for by Allah! if they see him and know about him what I know, they will do him evil."[2]

This story comes from one of the first biographies (Arabic *Sīra*) of the apostle Muhammad, written sometime before 768 CE—that is to say, roughly 150 years after the event from which Islam traditionally dates its birth: Muhammad's flight or emigration (*hidjra*) from the Arabian town of Mecca to the more hospitable oasis of Yathrib, an event so momentous it earned Yathrib a new name (Arabic *Medina*, "the city") and the year a place at the beginning of the Muslim calendar: year 1 of the Hidjra [AH], 622 CE by the Christian reckoning.[3]

The story comes, in other words, not from the Qur'an, but from the vast mass of material scholars of early Islam call "the Islamic tradition." Later we will explore how this tradition is related to the Qur'an: a topic of central importance to the question of how Islam learned to think with and about Judaism. But first let's just admire the narrative simplicity with which this anecdote reminds us of what believing Muslims and critical scholars alike too often forget. Like the adherents of early Christianity, Rabbinic Judaism, and many other "sectarian communities," those of the early Islamic community lived surrounded by, and in dialogue with, many groups making competing claims to a partially shared realm of revelation. Like the monk Bahira, they made their claims–and rejected or appropriated those of others—by poring over old prophecies and relating them to new, constantly making sense of the revelations granted Muhammad with reference to those given earlier to Christian and Jew. To this task they brought not only some distinctive tools and cognitive habits, but also many that they shared with or learned from the other religious communities around them, including ideas about the roles available for Jews and Judaism in the cosmos. In short, from its earliest beginnings Muhammad's community of Believers had already plunged into the mosh pit of Jewish questions that interests us.

I say "Believers" (*mu'minun*) rather than "Muslims" (*muslimun*, "those who submit") because that is the term preferred by the Qur'an itself, occurring more than a thousand times (as opposed to fewer than seventy-five instances of the word for Muslim). Fred Donner has recently built on the term to argue that for the community in which the Qur'an was revealed, the boundaries of belonging had not yet hardened into those that later Muslims took for granted. By the early ninth century the great systematizers of Islamic law would condemn the suggestion that there had ever been a Jewish or Christian member of Muhammad's original community (*umma*). But Muhammad's world—the world of the western Arabian Peninsula circa 620–700 CE—might have been in this sense more like Saint Paul's: capable of imagining that individuals could remain committed to many of the practices of the particular sectarian community into which they had been born, while still believing in the new revelation or, at least, joining the new community. In this world—if we accept the thesis—"Jewish Believer" would be no more a contradiction than "Jewish Christian" had been in early Christian Jerusalem, Galatia, or Corinth.[4]

However that may be, this was also a world in which the claims of new revelation had to be justified and differentiated from those of the old. Like the early Christian communities, the early Qur'anic ones appropriated and adapted the texts and reading practices of their "predecessors," but also stigmatized some of those reading habits and their practitioners as damning or death-dealing, and this especially in the case of the Jews, considered as guardians of the founding scriptures. My goal in this chapter is to describe this process of appropriation and stigmatization, both in the Qur'an and in the early Islamic tradition. But it is also, and much more controversially, to suggest that the roles assigned to figures of Judaism in this process were every bit as important in shaping Islamic ideas about how both scripture and cosmos should be interpreted, as they had been for the early Christians, from whom in this respect early Islam borrowed a great deal.

Scriptural Community, Scriptural Conflict

To understand this process, we need first to understand the scriptural sensibilities of the community among whom the Qur'an was first revealed or produced. This is not an easy task, both because virtually no documents (aside from the Qur'an itself) shed direct light on the first fifty years or so of that community, and because the Qur'an tells us so little about the temporality of its own revelation or redaction. Unlike the gospels, for example, it is not a narrative, unfolding within the temporal frame of the life of Jesus. Nor, like the epistles, does it attribute itself to an author situated in historical time. In fact the Qur'an is almost totally unconcerned with the context within which, or even the person to whom, it is revealed. Only rarely does the Qur'an explicitly situate its message within the context of the life of the prophet who receives it, and even then it does not name him. The name *Muhammad* occurs only four times in its text.[5]

The voice of the Qur'an is not that of a man in historical time, but that of God or a mediating angel handing down instructions to a nearly anonymous prophet. "Say . . ." begin many of its commandments. We as readers (and editors/translators) tend to add "O Muhammad," but in fact the Qur'an claims the voice of all prophets, and articulates its message through their stories. Noah, Abraham, Moses, Lot, Jonah, Joseph, Jesus, and various prophets of the Arabs (Hud, Salih, Shu'ayb): their names (and especially that of Moses) occur much more frequently in its pages than that of Muhammad. It is through the repetition of their messages, as well as through stories about the rejection they encountered ("Prophets have been persecuted before thee"), that the Qur'an issues its timeless warning calling men to God.[6]

The plethora of prophets in the Qur'an does not by itself tell us much about the religious diversity of the community that first received it, just as the presence of Israelites, Egyptians, and Babylonians in the Book of Mormon need not necessarily correspond to the diversity of early-nineteenth-century Palmyra, New York. But if we listen carefully to the subtexts and intertexts of the Qur'an, we can find many traces of diversity, of dialogue, and of struggle. Consider just this one verse, focused on the initial moment of scriptural revelation:

> *And remember We took your Covenant and We raised above you (the towering height) of Mount (Sinai); (saying): "Hold firmly to what we have given you, and hearken (to the Law)." They said: "we hear, and we disobey:" And they had to drink into their hearts of the taint of the Calf because of their faithlessness. (Q 2:93)*

This verse (like many others, as we will see) is clearly reproaching the Jews, or as it often calls them, "the Children of Israel."[7] Were these "real" Jews, living neighbors or members of the community, or were they "figures of Judaism" produced from the entrails of scripture itself? The verse suggests that the answer is simultaneously both. Look, for example, at the way in which it names the mountain of Moses's revelation: Tur [Sinin], Mount Sinai. The Arabic for mountain is *jabal. Tur* is either Aramaic, the language of the rabbis of Muhammad's day and age, or Syriac, the language of the Christians. Strikingly, the Qur'an consistently refers (with one exception) to the site of revelation with this non-Arabic word, as in the opening of sura ("chapter") 52: "By the mount (*Tur*)! By a Decree inscribed in a Scroll unfolded!" It is as if memory of the origins of revelation remains lexically tied to the rabbis' (or the Christians') tongue.[8]

And what of this strange (but thrice repeated: cf. Q 2:60 and 4:153) image, "We raised above you Mount Sinai?" The line turns out not to be an error or corruption, but rather to reveal a deep knowledge of Judaism, although it is not found in the five books of Moses or the Hebrew Bible. It comes rather from an interplay with texts from other religious traditions (what I am calling "intertexts"), in this case, from Rabbinic Jewish stories about the handing down of the Torah, as in this commentary from the Babylonia Talmud, commenting on verse 19:17 of Exodus:

"And they stood beneath the mount": Rabbi Abdimi b. Hama b. Hasa said: This teaches that the Holy One, blessed be he, overturned the mountain upon them like an inverted cask, and said to them "If you take upon yourselves the Law, good. If not, here you will find your grave." Rabbi Aha b. Jacob observed: "This furnishes a strong protest against the Law."[9]

Even the devastating line "we hear and we disobey" suggests a dialogue of sorts between "Jew" and "Believer" in the Qur'anic community. Recall the Israelites' response to Moses in Exodus (24:7) and Deuteronomy (5:24): "we hear, and we obey" (in the Hebrew of Exodus, *n'aseh v-nishma'*; in that of Deuteronomy, *v-shama'nu v-'asinu*). The Qur'an transforms the phrase through a multilingual pun, playing on the homophony between Hebrew *shama'nu v-'asinu* (we hear and obey) and Arabic *sami'ina- wa-'asayna* (we hear and disobey). The Qur'an's play on words reveals the shared linguistic, cultural, and scriptural space of the diverse community that receives it.[10]

But we must not fail to notice how the Qur'an shatters this shared space at the same time that it reveals it. The verse declares the new revelation's continuity with Moses's message, but it simultaneously accuses the Jewish communities that preserved that earlier message of disobedience, misreading, and even falsification. As sura 4:46 has it, "Of the Jews there are those who displace words from their right places, and say: 'We hear and we disobey.'" Here our multilingual pun explicitly underwrites the Islamic doctrine of *tahrif*—the charge of Jewish (and Christian) alteration and falsification of previous scriptures. It is this doctrine that eventually allowed the Islamic community to develop its particular position regarding the scriptures of its predecessors. On the one hand they could honor the Torah (unlike, for example, the Marcionites and Gnostics in early Christianity, who had denied that the Hebrew Bible was a revelation of God). On the other, they could set it aside as unreliable because it was corrupted by its Jewish guardians, and therefore nonauthoritative (in contrast, for example, with orthodox Christianity's canonization of the Old Testament).[11]

Thousands of the Qur'an's verses had similarly rich intertextual early lives. As modern scholarship begins to recover the memories of those lives, we are increasingly discovering within the Qur'an an intimate familiarity with many different Jewish and Christian texts and traditions. Indeed as we learn more about ancient Judaism and Christianity, Qur'anic passages that had previously seemed eccentric—such as the repeated account of the infant Jesus making birds out of clay, which then fly away—we can now recognize as coming from the early community's vast store of sacred lore from those traditions. The birds, for example, come from the Infancy Gospel of Thomas, later marginalized within Christianity as uncanonical.[12]

The Qur'an had room for the prophetic traditions of Rabbinic Jews, Samaritans, Christians of many different stripes (including perhaps "Ebionites" and other "Judaizing" Christians), as well as earlier Arab prophets.[13] "Of the People of the Book," the Qur'an tells us, using its distinctive title for the followers of the earlier scriptural traditions it presents itself as fulfilling, "are a portion that stand (for the right); they rehearse the signs of God all night long. . . . They believe in God and the Last Day. . . . They are in the ranks of the righteous" (Q 3:113–116). Of course as we have seen it do with the Jews, the Qur'an also marks its differences with those traditions at the same time that it honors them. The Qur'anic Jesus, for example, can work miracles, be born of a virgin, and even emerge unscathed from the Jews' plot to murder him. But since God is one, he cannot be God or the Son of God. It is on this point, the Qur'an insists, that Christians have misread and mishandled their scriptures: "They do blaspheme who say: 'God is one of three in a Trinity': for there is no God except One God" (Q 5:73).

"Be Not First to Disbelieve"

The Qur'an's appropriation (and criticism) of the traditions of each of these communities deserves its own history, but we must focus on that of the Jews, not only because that is our subject, but also because its place in the Qur'an is unique, both in terms of scale and in terms of the work to which it is put. That work, as we have already seen in sura 2:93, is double. Israel serves both as the foundation of God's communication with humanity and as the fundamental example of humanity's resistance to that communication. As we expand our reading within sura 2, the scope of that work expands as well. For within this sura—the Qur'an's longest, called "The Cow"—as within many others, the frustrating cosmological question of why the world so often seems not to conform to the divine will is explained through figures of Judaism.

"The Cow" begins by announcing itself as a revelation addressed to the god-fearing: "This is the Scripture wherein there is no doubt, a guidance unto those who ward off (evil)" (Q 2:2). Initially it has, however, less to say about God's friends than about his enemies, whom it divides into two classes of people. One is more or less straightforward: "As for the disbelievers, whether you warn them or not, it is all one for them; they do not believe. God has sealed their hearing and their hearts, and on their eyes there is a veil. Theirs will be an awful doom" (Q 2:6–7). The other is more complex: "And of mankind are some who say, 'We believe in God and the Last Day,' when they do not believe. They think to trick God and those who believe, and they trick none save themselves; but they see not. In their hearts is a disease, and God increases their disease. A painful doom is theirs because they lie" (Q 2:8–10).

God has, in other words, two types of opponents, those who are open and obvious (the disbelievers) and those who are disguised or hidden (the "liars"). Like the early Christians, the Qur'an will call these "liars," who seem godly but are not, the "hypocrites." Their importance in Islamic thought will be considerable, for it is through the concept of "hypocrisy" that Islam, like Christianity, developed a critical language capable of accounting for conflict and adversity *within* Islam, and of helping to distinguish truth from falsehood in this dangerous world of "illusion" (Q 3:185). We are not far from the gospel world of "rabbis" and "Pharisees." But before we jump ahead, we should read further, to see how "The Cow" gives form and flesh to these categories of God's enemies.

Believer, disbeliever, liar: after this tripartite anthropology the sura provides a brief but exemplary history of the world. First comes the creation of man and its consequences: the fall of Iblis/Satan (the proud angel who refused to bow before Adam "and so became a disbeliever") (Q 2:34); Satan's vengeance on mankind; Adam's expulsion from the Garden, armed with a revelation from God. God promises Adam that those who believe in this revelation shall neither fear nor grieve. "But those who disbelieve, and deny our revelations, such are rightful owners of the fire" (Q 2:39). The next line identifies Satan's followers in disbelief with the vocative: "O Children of Israel! Remember my favor . . . and fulfill your part of the covenant . . . ! Believe that which I reveal, confirming that which you already possess (of the Scripture), and do not be the first to disbelieve, and do not part with my revelations for a pittance, and keep your promise to me. Do not confound truth with falsehood, nor knowingly conceal the truth" (Q 2:40–42).

Peeking out from beneath these negative commandments are four fundamental assertions, the last two prophetic: 1) The present revelation is a confirmation of God's covenants with (among others) Adam and Moses. 2) Those prior covenants contain prophecies about the truth of the present revelation. 3) To hide that fact, the Jews will sell their scriptures, altering them to conceal their confirmation of the latest revelation. 4) They will do so knowingly, and be the first to disbelieve, the first to confound truth with falsehood. Much of sura 2 elaborates this theme and puts it to work. It revisits all the episodes we have encountered in Christian exegesis: the Israelites' complaints about eating nothing but manna in the desert ("Would you exchange that which is higher for that which is lower?") (Q 2:61); the episode of the Golden Calf ("they said: we hear and we rebel.") (Q 2:93, 2:51–54); the Jews' attack on prophets ("Is it ever so, that when there comes to you a messenger [from God] with that which you do not desire, you grow arrogant, and some you disbelieve, and some you slay?") (Q 2:87).

The general point should already be familiar: the role of the Jews in sacred history is to reveal truth by attacking its prophets. Over and over again the Qur'an echoes the Acts of the Apostles: "You stubborn people . . . you are always resisting the Holy Spirit. . . . Can you name a single prophet your ancestors never persecuted? They killed those who foretold the coming of the Upright One, and now you have become his betrayers, his murderers" (Acts 7:51–53).[14] Jewish persecution marks all prophets. "Who is an enemy to God, and His angels and His messengers, and Gabriel and Michael? Then, behold! God is an enemy to the disbelievers" (Q 2:98). Further, each new revelation makes its divinity and truthfulness historically and sociologically legible, in good Augustinian fashion, by defeating and humiliating this Jewish enemy. "And humiliation and wretchedness were stamped upon them and they were visited with God's wrath. This was because they disbelieved in God's revelations and wrongly killed the prophets. It was for their disobedience and their transgressions" (Q 2:61).[15]

Insofar as the Jews suffer the visible consequences of their disbelief, they are not so different from the other communities of unbelievers. "Systems have passed away before you. Travel the earth and see the consequences for those who rejected the messengers" (Q 3:137). The claim that the fate of peoples who reject God is clearly legible in the form of their ruined towns and cities (recall Christian exegesis of the conquest of Jerusalem) is a frequent, even formulaic, assertion in the Qur'an, used not only of Jews, but also of pre-Islamic Arabian cities that rejected prophets. It is a comforting position, insofar as it implies the promise that evil is punished and good rewarded in this world, and in historical time. The problem with the Jews was that they could not be so easily classified.

To begin with, not every Jew is an enemy of God: the Jewish prophets, particularly Abraham and Moses, are the very paradigms of godliness and prophecy. "And who is there that is better in religion than he who . . . follows the way of Abraham, a man of true faith?" (Q 4:125).[16] The Qur'an presents its own prophet as in every sense the colleague and successor of the Hebrew prophets, indeed as a second Moses. Moses and his revelations are everywhere in the Qur'an, rearticulated through the voice of this new prophet sent first to the Arabs and then to the world. In this sense the Jews and their holy books lie at the very origins of truth and cannot be wholly excluded from it. The task for the new scripture is to contain the implications of this centrality.

"The Cow" does so by separating the Jewish prophets from the Jews of their own day (who rejected them) and from those who came after. Like Paul and the evangelists, the Qur'an insists that lineage gives Jews no special claim to the covenant God made with Abraham: "[Abraham] said: of my offspring, will there be leaders? [God] said: my covenant does not reach to wrong-doers" (Q 2:124). Conversely, while the Jews were wrong-doers more or less from their first reception of revelation, the Qur'an claims—like Clement, Justin Martyr, Eusebius, and other church fathers—that their prophets were in some sense "Muslims" from the beginning, even before the coming of Muhammad: "Abraham was not a Jew, nor yet a Christian, rather he was a Muslim *hanif* (*hanifan musliman*), and not one of those who associate other beings with God (*mushrikun*)" (Q 3:67).[17] Nor do Jews have any privileged knowledge of scripture. In sura 62:5 their relationship to scripture is put in terms strikingly reminiscent of Saint Augustine: "The likeness of those who were charged with the Law of Moses, but who failed it, is as the likeness of an ass carrying great books. Evil is the likeness of people who deny the revelations of God."[18] There the Jews are blind but accurate transmitters of scripture. Other suras, including sura 2, stress instead their untrustworthiness. Because the Jews rejected, concealed, sold, and falsified Moses's message, they have no claim to scriptural authority.

A second complication stems from the fact that some Jews do heed the prophet's call: "They are not all alike. Of the People of the Book there is an upright portion who recite the revelations of God . . . falling prostrate before him" (Q 3:113, 199). Who belonged to this "upright portion"? According to the traditionist Muqatil ibn Sulayman (d. AH 150), whose Qur'anic commentary is among the earliest to reach us, a small group of Jews was disgusted by the prophet-killing of their brethren among the Children of Israel. In answer to their prayer that they be separated from the rebellious, God opened a tunnel through the earth from the Temple in Jerusalem to China, and closed it behind them after their exodus. The righteous Jews have lived in China ever since, from whence they will return only to fight against the Antichrist. Others put the righteous community of Moses at the opposite end of the world, beyond al-Andalus (the Iberian Peninsula), the western limit of Islam and of the then known world.[19]

Modern scholars have debated whether these passages refer to real communities of Jewish "sectarians" who had a profound influence on the material contained in the Qur'an. Some associate this righteous remnant with "Judeo-Christians," a hypothetical community of Jews who (like the Ebionites that Jerome feared) accepted Jesus as Messiah and now accepted Muhammad as well. Others have suggested that they are Samaritans, an ancient group claiming descent from the Northern Kingdom of Israel, which fell to the Assyrians in 721 BCE. The Samaritans oriented their prayer toward their former temple on Mount Gerizim in Nablus, not Jerusalem, and believed that their version of scripture, handed down from Aaron's grandson, was more accurate than that possessed by the Jews of Judah, handed down through Ezra.[20] The Qur'an does indeed contain prophetic material that probably originated in such communities. But it is not much concerned with identifying who the "righteous" among the Children of Israel might be. Given that "most of them are perverted transgressors" concealing hatred in their breasts (Q 3:110), the Believer had better avoid them altogether: "O believers! Take not for intimates people other than your own. . . . When they meet you they say: We believe, but when they are alone they bite their finger tips at you in rage" (Q 3:118–119). For all practical purposes, the "righteous" among Moses's people might as well live in China.

Zones of Confusion: Jew and Hypocrite

We can generalize and say that the posture of the Qur'an toward the Jews is a double one, simultaneously of inclusion and exclusion. Precisely because the Qur'an adopts as its prophetic heart what it understands as "true Judaism," it exiles as false and corrupt the "real" Jews it encounters. Exiles, but does not kill: Jewish enmity exists in the Qur'an to be combated and defeated, but not necessarily exterminated. The humiliation of the Jews, their preservation in a state of abjection, provides proof of the sovereignty and truth of Islam. As sura 9:29 has it, "Fight against those who do not . . . practice the true religion from among the People of the Book, until they pay the *jizya* [poll tax] from their hand, with due submission." This passage provides the Qur'anic basis for the continued existence of Jews (and Christians) in Muslim society, in a protected but humiliated status known as *dhimma*. From our perspective, this status seems designed to resolve many of the same paradoxes of "included exclusion" that Saint Augustine had approached through the figure of the Jew as "Cain." And indeed, the Qur'an seems familiar with Augustine's association. In sura 5, for example, it explicitly derives the Jew's status as slayers of prophets from that of Abel's murderous brother.[21]

But Islam, like Christianity, also faced a more serious "Jewish" problem, one that could be neither contained nor exiled, and this was the problem of the outer versus the inner, the appearance of belief versus its reality. We have seen how early Christianity deployed the figure of the Pharisee to think through this problem. Early Islam developed that of the "hypocrite." Sura 2 became a prooftext for this category in Islam, although the Qur'anic words for hypocrisy and hypocrites (*nifaq*, *munafiqun*) do not appear in it. Instead, "The Cow" speaks of deceitful "People of the Scripture" who long ago hardened their hearts to Moses's message, and today pretend to believe: "And when they meet the believers, they say: We believe, But when they go apart in private . . . Do they not know that God knows that which they conceal and that which they proclaim?" (Q 2:75–79).[22]

Here the disease of the hypocrite is put in purely Jewish terms. It is, however, highly contagious, so much so that anyone who challenges the prophet risks catching it: "Or would you question your messenger as Moses was questioned of old?" (Q 2:108).[23] "People of the Book" spread the sickness because they "wish they could turn you back to infidelity after you have believed, from selfish envy, for the truth has become manifest to them" (Q 2:109). Note how the two categories are already overlapping: the People of the Book are also hypocrites, knowing but concealing. The disease is so dangerous that it requires powerful diagnostics. God even changes the direction of prayer in order to make physically visible the recalcitrance of the unfaithful: "And we appointed the *qiblah* [direction of prayer] which you formerly observed only so that We might test those who follow the messenger, from those who turn on their heels. In truth it was difficult, except for those whom God guided" (Q 2:143).[24]

The concept of the hypocrite flows through many suras of the Qur'an. For example, when sura 3 sets out to explore the relationship between Torah, gospel, and Qur'anic revelation, it introduces both the word "hypocrisy" and new tests for it. One of the most significant of these tests is war: "That which you suffered on the day when the two armies met, was by permission of God, so that he might test the true believers. And that he might know the hypocrites" (Q 3:166–167). Battle comes "in order that God might test what is in your breasts and prove what is in your hearts" (Q 3:154). By revealing the different behavior of those who strive in the way of God, and those who, like the Jews, fear the fight because they are "greediest of mankind for life" (Q 2:96), war makes visible the hidden inner doubt harbored by the hypocrite.

In the development of a vocabulary of hypocrisy in sura 3, we might see a distinction or evolution from the lying Jew of sura 2. Distinction, however, is not emancipation. Within the Qur'an the concept of hypocrisy is closely tied to Judaism. The hypocrite is *like* the Jew, sometimes *seduced* by the Jew ("O you who believe! If you obey a party of the People of the Book, they will make you disbelievers after your belief") (Q 3:100) or *related* to the Jew ("Have you not seen the hypocrites say to their misbelieving brethren among the People of the Book, 'If you are expelled, we too will go out with you.'") (Q 59:11). But, and the distinction is crucial, the hypocrite is not necessarily a *real* Jew.

On the contrary, the concept of hypocrisy developed in the Qur'an is useful precisely because—much like Saint Paul's "Judaizing" of Galatians 2:14—it explains how "Jewish" attributes (lying, envy, enmity, greed, cowardice, materialism, preference for this world over the next) can infect the "non-Jewish" followers of God. It provides a theory of seduction capable of accounting for the fact that despite the warnings of the prophets and the revelation of this "scripture wherein there is no doubt," the world remains a place in which truth and falsehood are easily confused. We are familiar with the principle from the gospel treatment of the Pharisees: the hypocrite looks fair but is foul. In the words of sura 63, "The Hypocrites,"

> *When the hypocrites come to you they say: "We bear witness that you are indeed God's messenger. . . . They make their oath a screen so that they may turn [men] from the way of God. Truly their deeds are evil. That is because they believed, then disbelieved, therefore a seal was set on their hearts so that they do not understand. And when you see them their exteriors please you; and if they speak you listen to their words. [They are] like blocks of wood in striped cloaks. They think that every shout is against them. They are enemies, so beware of them. The curse of God upon them! How they are perverted! (Q 63:1–4)*[25]

It is not difficult to see the resemblance between the similes of sura 63 and those of, for example, Matthew 23. The work done by these similes is also similar: the Qur'anic concept of the hypocrite made it possible (though not necessary) to understand the dangerousness of the world in terms of the danger of Judaism. Later traditionists (as we will see in the next section) would put that possibility to work in order to construct a history for the Qur'an and a biography for its prophet. As a result, and from its opening pages to its last sura (112, *al-Ikhlas,* "The Sincerity," traditionally understood as revealed against the rabbis), Jewish duplicity and enmity would become a basic axiom of Qur'anic ontology.

The Role of Jewish Enmity in the Construction of Muhammad's Biography

In its use of the Jews as figures for the confusion of godliness and falsity, and as an explanation for the vicissitudes of prophetic truth in this world, the Qur'an is quite similar, and much indebted, to the canonical gospels. But there is also an important difference. The gospels use Jewish enmity to narrate the life and the death of Jesus. In the Qur'an, the enmity of the Jews is not tied *explicitly* to events in the life of the prophet Muhammad or of his community. It is not historical but constant, the screen against which man's progress toward prophetic truth is projected.

This "timelessness" of the Jews and their enmity is in some ways a general characteristic of the Qur'an itself: a book that does not unfold as a narrative in historical time, and provides no explicit account of its own revelation. Remember that although we read the Qur'an as a book, organized by chapter (*sura*) and verse (*aya*, "sign"), Muhammad did not receive it as a continuous text, according to Islamic tradition, but in poetic fragments of vision. The first of these fragments, "The Blood Clot," was (quite typically) only a few lines long: "Proclaim! in the name of your Lord and cherisher, who created, created man out of a leech-like clot of congealed blood: Proclaim! And your Lord is the most bountiful, He who taught by the pen, taught man that which he did not know" (Q 96:1–5).[26]

From the reference to the Lord "who taught by the pen" in this first vision, we can see that the importance of previous scriptures appears already here at the beginning of Muslim prophecy. We can also see, from the fact that "The Blood Clot" comes in sura 96 and not in sura 1, that the Qur'an as scripture is not organized in the order in which it was received as revelation. It is not a requirement of revelation that it must organize itself chronologically or place itself historically. But how then did it come to be organized, and by what principle? According to Islamic tradition, the ordering, editing, and standardization of the Qur'an were carried out less than a generation after the Prophet's death, at the command of the caliph 'Uthman (AH 23–35/644–655 CE), who was troubled by the proliferation of variant versions. The caliph gathered together those who faithfully remembered both the content and the context of Muhammad's recitations. With their advice he created the standard text, after which he had all the other versions destroyed.

Of course, scholars should not accept the claims of the Islamic tradition about the authorship and transmission of the Qur'an any less critically than they accept traditional Christian claims that the gospels as we have them were written by Jesus's disciples; or traditional Jewish claims that the Torah was written by God before the creation of the world and handed to Moses at Mount Sinai. But even if we accept the traditional Islamic account about when and to whom the Qur'an's fragments of revelation were revealed (that is, to Muhammad between 610 and 632 CE), and about when and by whom they were joined together and redacted into their canonical written form (by the caliph 'Uthman between 644 and 655 CE), we still need to wonder about the principles that guided that redaction. How was this ordering achieved?[27]

The question is not a matter of idle historical curiosity, but a prerequisite for proper belief. After all, the Qur'an understands the entire prophetic tradition—including itself!—as containing revelations that are obsolete, that have been superseded or replaced: "Those of Our revelations that we abrogate or cause to be forgotten, We replace with one better or similar" (Q 2:106). The Qur'an itself suggests that chronology is crucial to faith: to know how to act we need to determine which revelation is the most recent, and therefore the one still in effect. But it gives Believers almost no guidance in making this determination.

We have already encountered one of the most famous cases of "abrogation," the establishment of a new direction of prayer (*qiblah*) for Believers in sura 2:142–145. Centuries of Islamic tradition have understood this as representing a shift from Jerusalem to Mecca, a shift undertaken to confound the Jews and the hypocrites. But the Qur'an itself never mentions Jerusalem, and says only that a controversial change has occurred, that "the fools among the people" will complain about a change from a customary (but unspecified) direction of prayer; that "to God belongs both East and West"; that you should "turn your face in the direction of the sacred mosque" (what mosque that might be is not further specified); that this change was made to separate those who follow the Messenger from those who turn on their heels; that although God has taught them the truth, the People of the Book will refuse to agree to this or any other *qiblah*; and that the Believers should on no account follow the various *qiblah*s of the People of the Book.[28]

It is not obvious what these verses should mean, or which one should supersede or abrogate the other. What was the old *qiblah* that must now be avoided? Or does the verse that to God belongs all East and West suggest that whereas once a direction was privileged, God is now indifferent to direction? Or is the verse about the sacred mosque the most recent one? And in that case, does that mean that one should pray in the direction of the closest mosque, or is there one mosque, known specifically as the sacred one, to which all must turn their faces? And what does any of this have to do with the "People of the Book" who know the truth but refuse to admit it, and why should Believers never follow their example? The Qur'an provides no guidance on these vital questions.[29] It is Islamic tradition that will come to the rescue here, explaining that the "fools" are Jews and hypocrites, that the old *qiblah* was Jerusalem, that the last and definitive revelation is the one enjoining prayer toward the sacred mosque, and that this means the pre-Islamic sanctuary known as the Ka'ba, in Mecca. In this case, as in countless others, it is the task of the tradition to give the Qur'an's revelations a temporal dimension and place them within a historical context. And given that the Qur'an is itself extensively structured as a polemic against the Jews, it should not surprise us that, as in this case, the tradition frequently takes up the cutting edge of Jewish enmity as it strives to carve eternal prophecy into an historically recognizable shape.[30]

The monk Bahira's warning about the threat posed by the Jews to the child Muhammad is just one example of how Jewish enmity could be used to fill in the Qur'an's silence about its messenger, providing it with a narrative time-line in which to situate the revelation of its verses, and providing Muhammad with a biography appropriate to a prophet. Bahira appears in the most famous such biography, attributed to the "traditionist" Muhammad Ibn Ishaq. "Traditionist" refers to those early Muslims who dedicated themselves to collecting, classifying, preserving, and transmitting traditions about what the Prophet Muhammad had said or done during his life. Those traditions became tremendously important, not only because they served to establish the context for the revelation of the various verses of the Qur'an (a genre known as *asbab al-nuzul*, "occasions of revelation"), but also because the Prophet's life, teachings, and example became the normative source for knowledge about how every Muslim should behave.

Early Islam did not function according to modern Protestant rules of *sola scriptura*: on the contrary, Muhammad's teachings and example, which came collectively to be known by the later tradition as *sunnah*, were as (or more) important for the establishment of Islamic law and practice as the Qur'an itself. But how were those traditions to be established? The task was not trivial, not least because it seems to have begun late. Ibn Ishaq, for example, died 151 years after the Hidjra (768 CE).[31] By the time he began his work, a vast chronological gulf separated him from his subject. In between Muhammad's death and Ibn Ishaq's, the Prophet's legacy had transformed the world. Conquest had swept the centers of Islamic power far beyond lands the Messenger himself had trod, embracing territories stretching from the Indian Ocean to the Atlantic. Ibn Ishaq's own curriculum vitae attests to the wideness of that world: he was of Persian ancestry (his grandfather had been captured during the Muslim conquest of Persia in the mid-seventh century CE and sent to Arabia as a slave), grew up and spent much of his life in the Arabian Peninsula, studied in Egypt, and died in Iraq.

Not only geography, but politics had also been transformed in the momentous years since Muhammad's death. Heirs to his authority had risen and fallen: caliphs had been murdered, even the Prophet's close relatives had been killed, as the leading descendants of clans that traced their lineage back to Muhammad's Arabia struggled among themselves for power. In the course of that struggle one family, known as the Umayyads, had established itself in Damascus less than a generation after the Prophet's death (AH 41/661 CE), and proceeded to consolidate its authority over rival centers of power in the rapidly expanding Muslim world. As part of this consolidation the Umayyads even besieged Mecca and sacked Medina in AH 63, killing many who had been Companions of the Prophet and might have remembered his teachings. In the middle of Ibn Ishaq's career (AH 132/750 CE) the Umayyads were themselves overthrown by the 'Abbasids, descendants of a rival Meccan clan now based in Baghdad, a revolution that itself required, like most revolutions, a rewriting of history.

In short, even before our biographer drew his first breath, the Islamic past had already been deeply marked by the conflicts that would give shape to much of its future: conflicts between eminent clans and families, some claiming descent from the Prophet; between the aspirations of rival cities and centers of power (Medina, Mecca, Damascus, Kufa, Baghdad); between the claims of those lands and peoples who came early to Islam and those who came late. In the prosecution of all of these disputes, stories about the life and example of the Prophet were a powerful witness, interrogated by all sides for testimony helpful to their cause. Rivals remembered, reinterpreted, and even invented such stories to make good certain claims and tarnish others. It is not surprising, given these many diverse interests, that by Ibn Ishaq's day there were many conflicting stories about how the prophet had lived, what he had said and done.

Ibn Ishaq was an early member of a group of collectors and transmitters of tradition—the "traditionists"—who hoped and claimed to impose order on this confusion. He is said to have studied the traditions collectors before him had transmitted, and to have spent much time in Medina (the city famous for being the first to acknowledge Muhammad as prophet), gathering stories from people who had known people who might have known the Prophet, or who had heard stories about him. The stories he gathered were expressed (or at least recorded) as memories of conversations (I once heard so-and-so say that he heard from so-and-so that she heard 'A'isha, the wife of the Prophet, say that the Prophet, peace be upon him, once said . . .). Ibn Ishaq evaluated the traditions according to his criteria of credibility, and arranged those he considered sound into the narrative form of a biography of the Prophet, a history of the founding of Islam.

In that history the Jews loom large as opponents of the Prophet. Their enmity begins, as we heard from Bahira, before the start of Muhammad's mission. But once Muhammad began to receive revelations, the Jews quickly emerged as his principal "testers." Of course in Mecca it was Muhammad's own tribe, the Quraysh, who were troubled by and often opposed his prophecy. But it was to the Jews, according to the tradition, that the Quraysh turned for ammunition:

> *They sent . . . to the Jewish rabbis in Medina and said to them . . . "You are the people of the Torah, and we have come to you so that you can tell us how to deal with this tribesman of ours." The rabbis said, "Ask him about three things of which we will instruct you." . . . They came to the apostle and called upon him to answer these questions. He said to them, "I will give you your answer tomorrow," but he did not say "if God will." So . . . the apostle, so they say, waited for fifteen days without a revelation from God on the matter, nor did Gabriel come to him, so that the people of Mecca began to spread evil reports. . . . This delay caused the apostle great sorrow, until Gabriel brought him the Chapter of the Cave [sura 18], in which he reproaches him for his sadness, and told him the answers of their questions.*[32]

Ibn Ishaq then proceeds to explain the sura almost line by line, making sense of it through constant reference to this non-Qur'anic story. Obscurities in the prophetic material (in this case, allusions to some youths who slept for more than a century in a cave) are explained by tying them to a specific context of Jewish interrogation. The (again non-Qur'anic) story of Gabriel's tardiness makes clear the mechanics: Muhammad brings Gabriel the Jews' queries, and Gabriel brings Muhammad back answers that become the material of the Qur'an. Even during these difficult early days in Mecca, it is clear (to the later tradition, at least) that Jewish harassment is a good stimulus for prophecy. But that harassment reaches its peak with Muhammad's reception as prophet and ruler in Medina after—according to the tradition— members of rival polytheist clans in the city of Medina met Muhammad just outside Mecca, at a place called 'Aqaba, and promised to follow him faithfully as one, if he would come govern them. Muhammad came, the clans (known collectively as the Ansar) brought their murderous rivalry to an end, and Medina became the first Muslim polity.

There were, however, also several Jewish clans in Medina and its environs, tied by bonds of oath, trade, feud, and marriage to the various polytheist ones. The Jews, we are told, were not pleased by the arrival of Muhammad, for they had always reveled in their prophetic superiority to the Arabs. Moreover, Muhammad's revelations threatened to unmask their own corruption, for there was much in their own scripture that they neglected to practice, and much else that they had altered for their own ends. Therefore though they knew full well his godliness, they set themselves in deadly opposition to him. The traditions reported by Ibn Ishaq stage the point frequently and explicitly. He even reports a story in which one Jew asks another, who has just visited Muhammad, "Is he *he* [that is, the Prophet announced in the Torah]? Do you recognize him, and can you be sure?" "Yes!" "And what do you feel about him?" "By God, I shall be his enemy as long as I live!"[33]

The Jews did not proclaim this enmity openly. Instead, they pretended to follow their allies in supporting Muhammad, agreed to provide him financial support, and swore to treat his enemies as theirs. Behind his back, however, they constantly belittled him and schemed against him. When, for example, Muhammad's trusted companion Abu Bakr went to gather money from them, Rabbi Finhas scoffed that since Muhammad was begging from the Jews, his god must be poorer than they were. Abu Bakr punched Finhas in the face, and the rabbi complained to Muhammad, denying what he had said. The resulting condemnations echo those of the Pharisees in chapter 2:

> God sent down refuting him and confirming what Abu Bakr had said: "God has heard the speech of those who say: 'God is poor and we are rich.' We shall write what they say and their killing the prophets wrongfully and we shall say, Taste the punishment of burning." (Sura 3.181) Then He [God] said . . . : "And when God laid a charge upon those who received the book: You are to make it clear to men and not to conceal it, they cast it behind their backs and sold it for a small

price. Wretched is the exchange! Think not that those who rejoice in what they have done and want to be praised for what they have not done—think not that they will escape the punishment: theirs will be a painful punishment." (Sura 3.187) He means [Ibn Ishaq explains] . . . the rabbis . . . who rejoice in what they enjoy of worldly things by making error attractive to men and wish to be praised for what they have not done so that men will say they are learned when they are nothing of the kind, not bringing them to truth and guidance and wanting men to say that they have done so.[34]

Islamic tradition created a biography of the Prophet through stories like these, which gave Jewish names and faces to Muhammad's enemies. On their heads, as on rocks spaced in a shallow river, Muhammad steps along the course of his prophetic career. The reconstruction of that career, achieved in large part through the naming of these enemies, helped the traditionists of early Islam to provide a context for the revelation of each Qur'anic passage: helped them to provide, in other words, a sense of time and place to the Qur'an. As Ibn Ishaq puts it, "It was the Jewish rabbis who used to annoy the apostle with questions and introduce confusion, so as to confound the truth with falsity. The Qur'an used to come down in reference to these questions of theirs, though some of the questions about what was allowed and forbidden came from the Muslims themselves." The task of traditionists like Ibn Ishaq was (in part) to build a "reception history" for the Qur'an through the construction of a prophetic biography propelled by Jewish enmity.[35]

The crimes of the Jews were manifold. Though they knew from their own scripture that Muhammad was a true prophet, greed, jealousy, and hatred made them deny the fact to everybody else. They fortified the Meccans in their persecution of the Prophet by claiming that he contradicted Hebrew scripture. And they sowed dissension among the Ansar in Medina by mocking and criticizing Muhammad's revelations, and by harping on the danger of fighting against Mecca. Better to stay home and live, they murmured, than to die needlessly supporting the false claims of a prophet whose own people had rejected him. Many among the Medinans were influenced by the malicious lies of their Jewish allies, and came to harbor doubts about Muhammad and his mission: these were the "hypocrites," "whose inclination was towards the Jews," as Ibn Ishaq put it, "and [who] strove against Islam." The Jews even cast spells on Muhammad, making him impotent for a year.[36] Finally, not satisfied with egging on Muhammad's enemies and sowing doubt among his friends, they resolved to kill him themselves, though they never quite had the opportunity to do so. (Or did they? We will return to this point.)

How, in the traditionists' accounts, did Muhammad react to this constant persecution by the Jews? Of course he exhorted them to be true to the promise of their own scripture, and recognize him as prophet. Like Jesus, he debated with their "rabbis," pointing out the contradictions and omissions in their interpretation of Hebrew scripture, and receiving Qur'anic revelations to confound them. But he also took strategic action. The first Jewish tribe he turned against was the Banu Qaynuqa'. When they refused his exhortation to convert to Islam, he besieged them until they surrendered unconditionally. Muhammad intended to execute them, but a leader of a Muslim tribe with whom these Jews were allied interceded on their behalf, grabbing the Prophet by the cloak: "I will not let you go until you deal kindly with my clients. Four hundred men without mail and three hundred mailed protected me from all mine enemies. Would you cut them down in one morning?" The apostle spared the Banu Qaynuqa', but the Muslim leader's intercession was not approved of. He was associated with the Jews and hypocrites, and it is in response to this event (according to the tradition) that sura 5:56 was revealed: "O you who believe, do not take Jews and Christians as friends. . . . Who takes them as friends is one of them."[37]

The Jews suffered different fates. One prominent warrior, for example, was assassinated at Muhammad's command so that "there was no Jew in Medina who did not fear for his life."[38] According to the tradition, Muhammad explicitly authorized lying and deceit to entrap the Jewish leader, and even told the Believers to "kill any Jew that falls into your power." The willingness of his followers to do so was considered so striking by some pagan Arabs that it prompted them to convert to

Islam: "By God! A religion which can bring you to this is marvelous!" one is said to have exclaimed, after watching his brother kill a Jewish friend and partner.[39]

By and large, however, the Jewish problem was solved tribe by tribe. For example, Muhammad received news "from heaven" that the Jewish tribe of the Banu Nadir planned to kill him, so he sent out his army against them. Abandoned by their "hypocrite" allies among the Muslims, the Jews begged Muhammad to send them into exile, and their property became the Prophet's, "to dispose of as he wished." It is said that sura 59, "Exile," was revealed about them: "He it was who hath caused those of the People of the Scripture who disbelieved to go forth from their homes unto the first exile." Thus "the Rabbis were disgraced through their treachery."[40]

All of this only hardened the Jews in their deceit. Determined to put an end to Muhammad, leaders of a Jewish tribe known as the Banu Qurayza went to the pagan tribes that most bitterly opposed him (including his own tribe of the Quraysh in Mecca), and formed an alliance to attack Medina. Their siege was broken by many miracles (a handful of dates that fed an army, a dust storm that blinded the enemy), the sowing of dissension in enemy ranks ("War is deceit," as Muhammad put it), and the defensive ditch Muhammad ordered dug around the city (hence the name "Battle of the Ditch"). The pagan tribes returned home in disgust. But for the righteous there was no rest. Immediately the angel Gabriel appeared to Muhammad. The angels, he told the Prophet, "had not yet laid aside their weapons." They rode in pursuit of the Jewish instigators. "God commands you, Muhammad, to go to the Banu Qurayza."

Their fort surrounded by armies of Muslims and angels, the Jews were in a difficult position. Should they acknowledge what (according to Ibn Ishaq) they knew to be true, that Muhammad was the prophet promised in the Torah, and convert to Islam? Or should they, echoing the zealots in Masada, sacrifice their own women and children and then perish in a last suicidal sally? In the end, they decided to surrender unconditionally. Their fate was decided by an arbiter among their former allies, and confirmed by heaven and Muhammad, though it was unheard of in the long history of feud and warfare in the region: "[T]he men should be killed, the property divided, and the women and children taken captive." "The apostle went out to the market of Medina (which is still its market today) and dug trenches in it. Then he sent for [the Jews] and struck off their heads in those trenches as they were brought to him in batches.... There were 600 or 700 in all, though some put the figure as high as 800 or 900." According to other traditions it was ʿAli who struck off their heads, and their blood flowed like a river to the olive groves.[41]

The Politics of Anti-Judaism

By calling these stories "traditions," I do not mean to imply that they are less authoritative or more fictional than the Qurʾan. On the contrary, it is out of such accounts about what the Prophet had said or done that much of Islamic law and practice was derived, and within their context that the Qurʾan itself was interpreted. Moreover, the question of which came first, traditions or codified prophecy, is itself a vexed one in the academic study of Islam. But there are important differences between the traditional and the prophetic material. Two are particularly relevant for our topic. First, more than the prophetic texts of the Qurʾan, the traditional material is explicitly interested in using the Jews and the hypocrites to make claims about the sovereignty of Islam, and to explore what the politics of that sovereignty should look like. Second, again more than the prophetic texts, the traditional material struggles to maintain the tension between conquering the Jews and exterminating them.

First, politics: there are few pillars of the Islamic political order that were not explicated by the traditionists through stories of Jewish opposition. We have already seen, for example, how the story of Rabbi Finhas "Judaized" fiscal intransigence and tax resistance. Similar stories "Judaized" resistance to Muhammad's other claims to rulership. For example, the Prophet's judicial supremacy had been a main point of the "Constitution of Medina": justice and sovereignty go hand in hand. But according to one important tradition, the hypocrites preferred to take their disputes to Jewish "Cohens" and pagan sorcerers, rather than to the Prophet. It was in response to this resistance that, according to the traditions, Qur'an 4:63 was revealed: "Have you not seen those who pretend that they believe in that which is revealed to you . . . [?]" Such incidents of jurisdictional "Judaizing," as we remember from John Chrysostom, arouse the ire not only of God but also of the godly. Sure enough, in some traditions 'Umar (the future caliph) beheads the leader of the hypocrites. In return he receives from Gabriel the highest praise an angel can give: he is called a man who knows how to distinguish between truth and falsehood.[42]

In each conflict with the Jews, a different aspect of the early Islamic "state" articulates and solidifies itself. The exile of the Banu Nadir, for example, provided the Prophet with the first "public treasury," the first property he controlled as sovereign. Similarly the massacre of the Banu Qurayza provided the occasion to articulate the proper balance between the claims to property of the sovereign and those of the soldier in the wars of Islam: "Then the apostle divided the property, wives, and children of B. Qurayza among the Muslims, and he made known on that day the shares of horse and men, and took out the fifth. . . . It was the first booty on which lots were cast and the [prophet's/sovereign's] fifth was taken. According to its precedent and what the apostle did the divisions were made, and it remained the custom for raids." The principle (eventually known in Christian Europe as "the king's fifth") will remain an important one for many economies based on the profits of battle and the conquest of land and labor.[43]

We can easily understand the elaboration of these traditions as the political expression of a prophetic concept: truth and right order express themselves in opposition to the Jews. Like Christianity before it, early Islam understood its conquest of the Jews as proof, both prophetic and political, of Muhammad's claim to succeed Moses. Just as the Qur'an did the work of "incorporating" the Hebrew patriarchs into an Islamic prophecy, so the tradition sought to do the work of incorporating the Jews into an Islamic polity. But precisely because the prophetic takeover had been so hostile (depending as it did on the idea that the Jews have always been the bitterest enemies of their own prophets), the political one would not be easy. As we have already seen, the political solutions to the "Jewish problem" represented in the traditions are much tenser and more violent than the prophetic ones in the Qur'an. Perhaps Qur'anic prophecy, being timeless, could simply appropriate the patriarchs and declare victory. For politics, on the other hand, the corrupting power of Judaism was a more abiding worry.[44]

The ambivalence is most beautifully staged in traditions about the Prophet's conquest of the Jewish fortifications of Khaybar (in AH 7/629 CE). In one sense, the conquest of the most powerful Jewish community in the region provided Muhammad's followers with the strongest evidence they had had thus far of their prophet's sovereignty. Muhammad performed the subjugation of the community in the time-honored way: by having sex with the daughter of its slain leader. In the political language of the day, his marriage to the Jewess Safiya, orphaned and widowed in the Muslim attack, was the most telling sign of his power. Hence it was vaunted in the announcement of his victory to his enemies in Mecca: "Muhammad has conquered Khaybar, and has left married to the daughter of their king."

But the traditionists also transmitted plenty of suspicions that the marriage would not be an easy one:

> When the apostle married Safiya ... [he] passed the night with her in a tent of his. Abu Ayyub ... passed the night girt with his sword, guarding the apostle and going round the tent until in the morning the apostle saw him there and asked what he meant by his actions. He replied, "I was afraid for you with this woman for you have killed her father, her husband, and her people, and till recently she was in unbelief. ..."[45]

Safiya did not slay Muhammad. But according to the traditions Zaynab, another captured Jewess of Khaybar, poisoned a roast lamb she prepared for Muhammad. One of his companions ate greedily, and died of the meal. Muhammad himself "took hold of the shoulder and chewed a morsel of it, but he did not swallow it." His prophetic prudence saved his life, though the poison began the illness that would eventually kill him. It is because of the Jewish poison he ate on the victory field of Khaybar that "the Muslims consider that the apostle died as a martyr, in addition to the prophetic office with which God honored him."[46]

Traditional accounts of the conquest of Khaybar express ambivalence about the inclusion of Jews in Islamic polity and prophecy in yet another significant way. When the people of Khaybar surrendered themselves and their property to Muhammad, they begged to become sharecroppers, working the land in exchange for half the produce. The apostle agreed, on the condition that "[i]f we wish to expel you we will expel you." He reserved for himself, in other words, the power of exile over the Jews. According to one tradition, he exercised that power on his deathbed, when he decreed that "two religions should not be allowed to remain in the peninsula of the Arabs." According to another, his words were, "May God fight the Jews and the Christians! They transformed the tombs of their prophets into mosques. Two religions will not remain in the land of the Arabs."[47]

The traditions give no reason for Muhammad's dying wish, but (given the stories about what caused his death) we can imagine that it represents Muhammad's awareness of the danger posed by the ongoing presence of Judaism in Islam. Islam, like Christianity, staked its claims in the name of Jewish truth, but guaranteed those claims with Jewish falsity. Godliness, in other words, contained within itself the source of its own corruption. It is to cure this paradox that Islamic tradition focuses not so much on the conversion of the Jews, as on their exile or execution. Muhammad's dying words, as represented by the traditionists, reached for the political prophylactic of exile, hoping to preserve the purity of prophecy by expelling the Jews from the homeland of Islam (which had not yet spread beyond Arabia).

It was, however, far too late. According to tradition, all the remaining Jews in Arabia were indeed expelled after the Prophet's death, by

the caliph 'Umar I (634–644 CE). But precisely because of the importance of Jewish prophecy and enmity in Islam, no massacre or expulsions could ever succeed in ridding Islam of "Judaism." The Qur'an
itself recognized the impossibility of solving the problem within the limits of this world: "The Jews say: God's hand is bound. Let their hands
be tied and they be accursed for saying so. . . . We have placed among
them enmity and hatred till the day of final judgment. As often as they
light the fire for war, God extinguishes it. Their effort is for mischief in
the land, and God does not love mischief makers" (Q 5:64). Islamic tradition, too, acknowledged that the problem would not be solved until
the end of the world. When the Antichrist comes, says one eschatological tradition, Jesus will return to slay all the Jews, and even the rocks
will call out to betray where they are hiding. Until then, Muhammad's
dying injunction remains nothing but a dream, a dream of the emancipation of Islam from Judaism.[48]

Over the course of the previous pages we have watched the prophetic material contained in the Qur'an and the life story of Muhammad become mutually intelligible through the creation of a narrative
of confrontation between prophecy and its enemies. "[W]e make for
every prophet an adversary," in the words of our Qur'anic epigraph,
"evil ones among humans and Jinns, inspiring each other with flowery discourses by way of deceit" (Q 6:112). In the case of Muhammad,
as in that of Jesus and some of the Hebrew prophets, that enemy was
given a "Jewish" face, a face whose epistemological and ontological
features were to some degree already familiar from the Christian and
the Hebrew prophetic tradition. We have seen these Jewish figures put
to particular kinds of work by the early community of Believers as it
sought to appropriate the prophetic traditions of Judaism while at the
same time distancing itself from them. We have touched on some of the
problems—some of them very similar to those faced by early Christian
communities—that this work produced: how to appropriate the prophetic claims of Jewish communities without "Judaizing" Islam? How

to contain or exclude them without severing Islam from its Abrahamic foundations?

Judaizing and De-Judaizing Islam

Neither the utility of Jewish enmity, nor the problems it posed, ceased with the passing of the Prophet. On the contrary, the Jewish ambivalences produced in the prophetic generation came to serve as paradigm or pattern of thought for the Islamic community as it expanded with almost unimaginable rapidity into an empire whose borders surpassed even those of Alexander's Hellenistic empire or Augustus's Roman one. The simultaneous inclusion and exclusion of Judaism became for Islam—as it had been for Christianity—a structuring principle of the world, one through which Islamic truth was explored, discovered, and articulated.

The incorporation of Jerusalem into the sacred topography of Islam provides a good example of this structuring principle. As we saw already in the case of the direction of prayer (*qiblah*), the Qur'an never mentions the city of David, Solomon, Jesus, and many other prophets. The opening verses of sura 17 (called alternately "Children of Israel" or "The Night Journey") perhaps hint that Muhammad miraculously journeyed from Mecca to Jerusalem and back in one night: that, at least, is how the tradition came to interpret the cryptic verses "Glory to God, who took his Servant for a journey by night from the sacred mosque to the farthest mosque" (Q 17:1).[49] But it was not until the reign of his second successor, the caliph 'Umar (the same who was said to have expelled the Jews from Arabia) that Jerusalem was conquered from the Christians.

What to do with this prophetically overdetermined city? The question posed problems for Islam similar to those posed to Christianity, first by the conquest of Jerusalem by the Romans and later by Constantine's imperial appropriation of the city's Christological symbolism. In the event, 'Umar and his followers seem to have set out to discover the site of the Jewish Temple so long ago destroyed by the Romans. For this, according to tradition, they called on the services of a Muslim convert from Judaism called Ka'b "of the Rabbis." The place he identified was being used by the Christians as a garbage dump. The caliph ordered it cleaned and had a small place of prayer built on it, precursor to the al-Aqsa mosque. The subsequent Umayyad caliphs went even further, building on the site (by 691) the monument we know today as the Dome of the Rock, and decorating it with Qur'anic inscriptions asserting Islam's continuity with and fulfillment of Jewish and Christian revelation.[50]

We know from contemporary Christian chronicles that Christians of the day, stunned by the Muslim conquest of Jerusalem and so many other places, sought to "Judaize" the Muslims by claiming that they were simply rebuilding the Temple of the Jews, much as Julian the Apostate had been accused of doing some three hundred years before. The Muslims undoubtedly understood things very differently. They were appropriating the power of Jewish prophecy, not of Jews. Their building on the Temple Mount was every bit as much a monument to the supersession of Judaism as the Christians' garbage dump had been.[51]

If we focus for just a moment on early Islamic traditions about the event, we can see just how delicate and difficult this work of appropriation and supersession was. Many of those traditions involve the figure Ka'b of the Rabbis, or, Ka'b al-Ahbar. Ka'b was an early Jewish convert to Muhammad's teachings who plays an important role in the early traditions as an "indigenous informant" about the deep Abrahamic past of Islam. It was he, according to these traditions, who identified the Christian garbage dump as the site of the ancient Temple Mount. But given everything we have seen, we should not expect the tradition to rest easy with this identification, and the following early tradition does not disappoint:

When [the caliph] 'Umar . . . approached the gate of the Temple complex he said, "Keep an eye on Ka'b for me." And when he passed the gate, he said, "I am at your service, O God. I am at your service in whatever is you most desire." Then he made a beeline for the . . . Mihrab of David (peace and blessings upon him). That night he prayed in it, and

soon he climbed up the outcropping and . . . led the people in prayer,
and he recited with them [sura 38, about David and Solomon], and
he sat with them. He then rose and recited with them on the second
prostration the Sura "Children of Israel" (sura 17). Then he whistled
and said, "Ka'b with me!" and Ka'b was brought to him. And he said,
"Where do you think we should make our place of prayer?" And Ka'b
said to him, "Toward the Rock." And ['Umar] said, "By God, Ka'b, you
imitate Judaism! . . . Nay, rather, we shall make its qiblah *facing in the*
way the Messenger of God made the qiblah *of our mosque."*[52]

This story about the precursor to the Al-Aqsa mosque is striking for
the way in which it appropriates Jewish learning, while at the same time
stigmatizing the expert in that learning. Here, at the very moment that
Ka'b is asked to establish the *qiblah*, he fails the test we saw set up in
sura 2: he "turns on his heels" in the wrong direction, and thereby aligns
himself with the Jews and the hypocrites. Through this alignment the
tradition proclaims its supersession of what has come before. It is not
the informant's Jewish learning but 'Umar's inspired guidance that orients the Jerusalem mosque's prayers in a direction that is neither "Jewish" nor "Christian," but Muslim and true.

We could say that Ka'b personifies the plight of "Judaism" in early
Islam: both necessary and noxious, prophetic and pernicious. He is
often called on by the tradition to authorize a given practice and eluci-
date its prophetic origins, but he is equally often suspect, even cursed:
"God damn this rabbi (*habr*) and rebuke his rabbinic learning (*hab-
riyya*)!" In this he can be made to stand for the problem that "Jewish
lore" (called *isra'iliyyat* in Arabic) posed as a whole to early Islam. This
lore cannot be purged from the traditions of Islam any more than stories
about Jewish prophets can be purged from the Qur'an. Yet it threatens
to convert Islam into "Judaism," and hence must be differentiated, stigmatized, and contained.[53]

This double gesture toward Judaism permeates early Islam. As a last
example, let's touch briefly on a later development: the role of Judaism in the formation of Islamic law. We saw in chapters 2 and 3 just

how important Judaism was in Christian thinking about the law. Early Islam also put Judaism to legal work, but unlike early Christianity, Islam seems not to have had "antinomian moments" in which it imagined the possibilities of a world free of law. It strove instead to differentiate Islamic law from what had come before. Muslim exegetes did not hesitate to formulate this as a claim of supersession: "The faith of the Jews prescribed cleaving to the Torah and to the *sunna* of Moses until Jesus came. Once Jesus came . . . whoever did not reject these and follow Jesus was condemned to perdition. The faith of the Christians consists of adhering to the Evangel and to the laws of Jesus (*shara'i' 'Isa*) until Muhammad should come. Once Muhammad came, whoever of them did not follow Muhammad . . . was lost." In theory, this claim of supersession applied to Christian as well as to Jewish law. But early Islam focused on the latter, and once again with its characteristic double gesture: on the one hand condemning Judaism as a negative foil for Muslim law, on the other incorporating that Judaism within itself.[54]

Already the Qur'an begins this process, presenting its Messenger as one who mercifully ameliorates the strict laws that came before. Some of these specific ameliorations, like the abolition of many dietary restrictions associated with Judaism—"O People! Eat the lawful and good things from what is in the earth, and follow not in the footsteps of Satan" (Q 2:168)—are familiar to us from texts like the Acts of the Apostles in the Christian tradition. But the Qur'an also approaches the general principle that Jewish law was a punishment imposed on the Jews for their hardness of heart. The Messenger, says the Qur'an, "makes lawful to [the People of the Book] the good things and prohibits to them the bad, and removes from them their heavy covenant and the shackles that were upon them" (Q 7:157).[55]

The Islamic tradition presents many particular laws or rulings of the Prophet as ameliorations or abrogations of Jewish norms. This one is fairly typical in form if not in content:

A group of the Prophet's companions were sitting around one day, and a Jew was nearby, and one of the Companions said to the others: "I have sex with my wife lying down." Another said: "I have sex with her standing." A third said: "As for me, I take my wife while she's on her side or on all fours." The Jew came over and exclaimed: "You people are no better than animals! We Jews have intercourse in only one position." In response to this God revealed: "Your wives are a tilth for you; come to your tilth in any manner that you please." (Q 2:223)

The example is typical, too, in the deep dialogue with Judaism it encodes. For in fact the Muslim traditionists are here adopting and adapting the various arguments that emerge in the rabbis' debates on the topic. They take the liberal majority position that the Talmud had in fact settled on—"whatever a man wishes to do with his wife, he may"—and attribute it to Muhammad's "amelioration." And they take a view reported by the Talmud as that of an overruled minority of one—that sex in any position other than the "missionary" results in deformed off-spring—and project it onto Judaism as its normative law.

The textual details of this engagement reveal just how well informed by Judaism the Islamic legal traditions on this subject were. (The debate on whether husbands are permitted anal intercourse with their wives—a question on which the Talmud is unequivocally more liberal than the Islamic tradition—is particularly revealing of the interpretive principles at stake.) But my point is not whether Rabbinic Judaism is really more liberal sexually than Islam or vice versa. I want only to note once again how early Islam makes its claim to truth through a logic of supersession that appropriates "Judaism" and includes it within itself, while at the same time defining itself against that Judaism as a perversion of prophecy—stigmatized, enslaving, hostile—to be left behind by the Believer.[56]

It is this double gesture of inclusion and exclusion that made it possible—though not inevitable—for Islam to produce "Judaism" out of its own entrails, much as Christianity had done before. Again and again the Islamic tradition invoked the threat of Judaism to make critical sense of its cosmos. We have already seen how the prophetic material contained in the Qur'an and the history of early Islam (understood as the life story of Muhammad) became mutually intelligible through a narrative structure of confrontation between prophecy and its "Jewish" enemies. This utility did not cease with the passing of the Prophet. Of course the young and rapidly expanding religion had many enemies, including the empires of Rome and Persia. All of these enmities, however, tend to resolve themselves within the early tradition. Even the emperor Heraclius, who led the first fruitless decade of Roman military resistance against the forces of the new religion, turned out to be a closet Muslim according to traditionists like Ibn Ishaq.[57] The position assigned to the Jews, however, was more productive, for their prophetic legacy and their irreducible enmity could be combined to explain not only truth and falsity, but all the complex and confused space in between, the space in which all human life takes place.

The fate of the Umayyads, the first dynasty of sovereigns over Islam, provides a good example. Like Muhammad and his immediate successors, the Umayyads appropriated aspects of Judaism to claim authority over prophecy. We have already mentioned one such appropriation: the caliph 'Uthman's production of a canonical text of the Qur'an. In retrospect that redaction may seem uncontroversial, but it was resisted in its own day, perhaps because it was thought to represent an extension of the caliph's power over prophecy. According to the critics, rather than reconciling conflicting texts, the caliph had "mutilated and destroyed the divine word."[58]

From what we have seen of how early Muslims thought about prophecy, we can already guess the form that this accusation of mutilation of scripture took. 'Uthman's edition of the Qur'an was attacked as Jewish. According to one strand of the tradition, the Prophet Muhammad's own scribe condemned Zayd b. Thabit, the editor picked by the caliph: "I read the Qur'an while this Zayd was still a boy with two sidelocks playing among the Jewish children in their grammar school." It may seem shocking that the tradition preserves the claim that the standard edition of the Qur'an is corrupted by Judaism, but in fact the charge should not be so surprising, for two reasons: because of the process of simultaneous inclusion and exclusion that we have already discussed, and because both the falsification of scripture and the "false" claim to control its text were so thoroughly typed as Jewish in the Qur'an itself.[59]

But the tradition did not stop there. Most of the traditionists whose work has reached us lived after the overthrow of the Umayyads by the rival Meccan clan of the Abbasids. They therefore worked hard to justify that overthrow, putting the Umayyads in the worst possible light. Thus we find Ibn Ishaq—who lived through the Abbasid revolution—stressing in his life of Muhammad the Prophet's constant persecution by the Umayyad clan in Mecca. It is because of this persecution, he explains, that Muhammad ordered the execution of 'Uqba, a leading member of the clan captured in the Muslim victory at the Battle of Badr (624 CE). "But who will look after my children," pleaded the prisoner. "Hell," answered Muhammad.[60] After their overthrow, the traditionists develop such stories into a narrative of feud between the Umayyad clan and the Prophet. Ibn Ishaq memorably depicts the mother of the first Umayyad caliph seeking vengeance at the battle of Uhud. She is shown leaping into the thick of the fray to exhort the pagan troops to fight harder against Muhammad's forces, and then, after the pagan victory, chewing exultantly on the bloody liver of the Prophet's beloved uncle Hamza, slain in the battle.[61]

Ibn Ishaq's alignment of the Umayyad ancestors with the most persistent enemies of the Prophet already puts them in proximity to the Jews. Other traditionists went so far as to unite them. According to one important tradition 'Uqba, whom we just saw unsuccessfully pleading for his life with the Prophet, did so not on account of his children, but by reason of their shared tribal membership. "'Shall I be killed, although I am of the Quraysh?' The prophet replied, 'But are you not merely a Jew, from the Jews of Sepphoris?'" The question was a genealogical one, and the story goes on to explain that it was settled in the manner that the Quraysh settled such questions: with divining arrows. The arrows were cast, and the way in which they pointed determined whether one was of the tribe. In this case the arrows pointed thumbs down: 'Uqba was determined a Jew, not Quraysh, and was killed.[62]

This "Judaizing" of Islam's first sovereign dynasty is only one example of the way in which the traditionists put the threat of Judaism to work in making prophetic sense of their world and its politics. In fact association with Judaism became for the traditionists a crucial critical principle in their own work, as they struggled to distinguish sound (*sahih*) Islamic traditions from unsound ones, good from bad transmitters of Muslim memory. The two tasks were interrelated. The reliability of a tradition about what the Prophet Muhammad had said or done was only as strong as the reputation of the Muslims who claimed to remember and transmit it. Each tradition was therefore accompanied by an *isnad*, or list of names of those Muslims who had passed it from one to another across the space of time. These lists were carefully scanned for (among many other things) evidence of Judaism, with traditions handed down in the name of transmitters thought to be descended from Jews (or to have been friendly with them, as the hypocrites had been) potentially suspect.

In other words, the soundness of a tradition or text was determined by studying the genealogy of the people who transmitted it. The early traditionists generated countless (often conflicting) genealogies in their attempts to establish the truth or falsity of the traditions they codified. Jews are everywhere in these genealogies: even the Prophet's own tribe of Quraysh intermarried with them (as did Muhammad himself). It is thanks to this genealogical methodology that historians know much of what they think they know about the figures that people the history of early Islam. But it is also thanks to this methodology that many of these figures became "Jewish."

Were these figures really descended from Jews, or were they "Judaized" by the power of a critical language that understood both prophecy and falsity as "Jewish"? Stories about divining arrows do not suggest incorruptible genealogical memories. Nor does the frequent accusation among traditionists of manufacturing genealogies in order to flatter friends or attack enemies. For example, one eminent transmitter is said to have had the best information about who fought for and against the Prophet at the Battle of Badr. Allegiance at Badr had become an index of nobility in early Islam so that the testimony of this venerable trans-

mitter—he died in AH 123 at over a hundred years old, having known
'Ali and many other Companions of the Prophet—was very valuable.
But everything he said was considered suspect by later traditionists
because he was poor, and it was feared that he switched people's sides
depending on the size of the presents they gave him. Of course the poor
were not the only ones with vulnerable memories: it is well known that
genealogies were widely manipulated in the course of the sectarian and
political conflicts that roiled early Islam.[63]

Even in cases where the transmitter's own genealogy was not suspected of Judaism, the accusation of Judaism remained a powerful
tool in the critical work of distinguishing truth from falsehood within
Islamic tradition. Ibn Ishaq himself became a victim of this logic
when a rival who also worked in Medina, the great traditionist Malik
b. Anas, pronounced him an "antichrist" (*dajjal min al-dajajila*) and
drove him out of the city. Malik denounced Ibn Ishaq, not because
he was descended from Jews, but because he "reports traditions on
the authority of Jews" (that is, he collected traditions transmitted by
descendants of converts). The verdict stung as much in death as in life.
While Ibn Ishaq was cited constantly by later authors of Qur'anic commentary (*tafsir*) and prophetic tradition (*hadith* and *sira*), his reputation
remained suspect. Of course, his defenders claimed that the charge was
false, triggered by fear of Ibn Ishaq's phenomenal genealogical memory. According to them, Malik believed that Ibn Ishaq had spread the
rumor that he was the descendant of a slave and not an Arab, thereby
besmirching his lineage. Given the highly charged genealogical atmo-
sphere of early Islam, the charge is certainly plausible. Nevertheless, to
this day Ibn Ishaq remains associated with the introduction of dangerous "Jewish knowledge" into Islam.[64]

Muslim traditionists strained to purge Islam of "Judaism" by using
genealogy to identify and quarantine "Jews" and transmitters of "Judaism." Their efforts had the reverse result—much as similar efforts would
have in late medieval Spain or modern Europe—of spreading "Judaism" rather than purging it. But even if they had heeded the warnings
of the Qur'an and paid less attention to lineage, they would not have

avoided this dangerous diffusion of Judaism, for in Islam, just as in the Hebrew Bible and early Christianity, the errors that revelation locates in the specific flesh and lineage of the Jews are cognitive failings that affect everyone in the corporeal world.[65]

Like Jewish and Christian scripture, the Qur'an contains the awareness that the problem is one of language: "He . . . revealed unto you the Scripture in which there are verses of clear meaning [*muhkamat*] . . . , and others which are ambiguous [*mutashabihat*]. But those in whose hearts is perversity pursue the ambiguous, looking for discord [*fitna*] and seeking to interpret it" (Q 3:7).[66] Interpretation, the human desire to make sense of communication, is the wellspring of discord. Like so many Qur'anic passages about the sowing of scriptural confusion, this one referred to the Jews' inability to read correctly.[67] The Jews' "reading disability" was paradigmatic, so strong that at times God gave up on their literacy altogether and turned them into apes. But the same risks applied to non-Jewish readers: "Lo, the worst of beasts with God are the deaf and the dumb who do not understand" (Q 8:22). Tradition relates that Muhammad meant here "the hypocrites, whom I have forbidden you to imitate." But if hypocrisy means falling like an animal into the trap of language—recall Jesus's warning to his disciples about the "yeast of the Pharisees!"—then no human except perhaps the Prophet himself is exempt.[68]

According to a famous tradition, Muhammad recognized the danger: "There will come out of my community people in whose souls these deviations will spread like rabies." The "heretical" movement of the Khawarij that arose after his death was often interpreted as the first such deviation. The Khawarij emphasized the reading and interpretation of the Qur'an over the following of traditions about the Prophet. Their enemies said of them, alluding to sura 3:7, that "[t]hey believe in the *muhkam* [of the Qur'an], but perish in its *mutashabih*." They are "people who speak eloquently, but act badly; they recite the Qur'an, but it does not extend past their throats . . . they invoke the book of God, but are not related to it in any way. Whoever fights them will be closer to God than they are." Even if we did not know that by alluding to this verse their critics were assimilating them to Jews, the images of hypocrisy should alert us to the possibility. In fact, not only sura 3:7 but many other Qur'anic texts about Jews and Judaism were explicitly applied to the Khawarij, to convince them (as 'Ali is said to have told them) that "they [the Jews] are you."[69]

In turn, the followers of 'Ali themselves suffered this same fate of "becoming Jewish." According to (Sunni) critics, the elevation of 'Ali by the early Shi'i movements was an imitation of the Israelites' worship of the golden calf. These critics even went so far as to give Shi'i Islam a specifically Jewish paternity, claiming that it was the Jew 'Abd Allah ibn Saba' who convinced the Muslim community to elevate 'Ali. The Shi'i, of course, attacked the Sunni with the same ammunition. So powerful is the logic that, in the words of a recent historian, "it would be difficult to find a Muslim heresy that was not at one time or another traced back to a Jewish originator" by its opponents.[70] (You will recall from chapter 3 that the same could be said of the church fathers.) Muhammad himself, according to tradition, is said to have foreseen the endpoint of this process: "Those who were before you of the People of the Book became divided into 72 sects [*milla*], and this community will be divided into 73, 72 in Hell, and one in Paradise." If indeed Muhammad uttered these words, they express the prophetic awareness that the critical language of "Judaism" could turn every Muslim into a potential Jew, and "Judaize" much of Islam.[71] If, on the other hand, the words are those of later traditionists describing their own sectarian landscape, the awareness, equally melancholy, is that it already had.

Potential Futures

In the preceding pages we have explored some of the ways in which the Qur'an and the early Islamic tradition developed a tension between the truth of Jewish scripture and the falsity of Jews in order to create a complex language capable of criticizing and comprehending the confusions of their world. In this, they were no different from their Christian predecessors, nor indeed from their Jewish ones. The reason for this similarity is obvious, but it bears repeating: the many different groups of early Muslims, Christians, and Jews that peopled the histories we have been visiting all drew on the same tools. These tools were, above all, the self-critical prophetic tradition through which the many "Israels" of Hebrew scripture explained their tribulations to themselves. We feel the deep tones of that tradition already in the voice of the psalmist:

> *Hear my teaching, my people. Turn your ears to the words of my mouth. I will open my mouth in a parable. I will utter dark sayings of old, which we have and known, and our fathers have told us. We will not hide them from their children, . . . that the generation to come might know, . . . that they might . . . not be as their fathers, a stubborn and rebellious generation, a generation that didn't make their hearts loyal, whose spirit was not steadfast with God. (Ps. 78:1–8)*

This is the voice of a vision of Israel claiming harmony with God, even as it finds discord in the voices of others: "And they flattered him with their mouth, / with their tongues they lied to him, while their heart was not straight with him, / And they kept no faith with his covenant" (Ps. 78:36–37). It was because of this hypocrisy that God "rejected the tent of Joseph, and didn't choose the tribe of Ephraim, but chose the tribe of Judah, Mount Zion which he loved" (Ps. 78:67–68).

The voice of each vision speaks in a distinctive accent, and that accent does matter. Orthodox Christianity, for example, eventually settled on the Jews as faithful transmitters of scripture, whereas early Islam did not: "Some of those who are Jews change words from their contexts and say: 'We hear and disobey . . . ' distorting with their tongues and slandering religion" (Q 4:46, 2:87). The Muslim charge of Jewish alteration and falsification of scripture would come to fundamentally distinguish Islamic attitudes toward the Hebrew Bible from Christian ones. Such differences are fateful, but it is the similarities I would emphasize here. In Islam as in early Christianity, the Children of Israel are the offspring of prophecy, sometimes legitimate, often not. The many similarities between what the church fathers and early Islamic traditionists had to say about the Jews does not derive from a similarity between their respective encounters and struggles with "real" Jews. It stems rather from the fact that both were doing similar political and theological work within the same overarching prophetic tradition.

Did Islam inherit from Christianity this way of thinking with Jews and Judaism? Certainly there are many echoes of Christianity among the early Muslim traditionists. Ibn Ishaq, for example, borrowed from the Gospel of John to explain why the Prophet Muhammad had to be opposed by the Jews: "Among the many things which have reached me about what Jesus the son of Mary stated . . . to describe the apostle of God, is the following . . . : 'He that hateth me hath hated the Lord. . . . But the word that is in the law must be fulfilled, 'They hated me without a cause.'"[72] Sometimes we may even see an implicit acknowledgment of such debts in the Qur'an: "You will find the most vehement of mankind in hostility to those who believe to be the Jews, and the idolaters. And you will find the nearest of them in affection to those who believe to be those who say: We are Christians. That is because there are among them priests and monks, and they are not proud" (Q 5:82).

Nevertheless it would be misleading to understand Islam's critical use of Jews and Judaism as a "borrowing" from Christianity, or from the many forms of Judaism (Rabbinic, Samaritan, Judeo-Christian, etc.) that we find traces of in early Islamic prophecy and tradition. More than a "borrowing," it was the product of arguments about how to read prophetic texts, arguments common to all who wanted to understand themselves as the "True Israel" in a world full of competing claims to truth. To point out the importance of this reading practice in early Islam is not to say that Islam is "essentially anti-Semitic" any more than it is to say that Christianity (or Rabbinic Judaism!) is. It is only to say that Islam, like Christianity and many another "True Israel," contains within itself the potential to understand the adversity it encounters in terms of "Judaism."

That potential is not always activated in the same way: the history of Islam's engagement with its Jewish "friends" and "enemies" is very different from that of, for example, Catholic Christianity's. That difference lies, not so much in the kinds of "pre-judgments" and stereotypes about Jews that were available to Muslim thinkers, but in the kinds of cognitive work to which these concepts were put. It is easy enough to find, throughout the vast sweep and range of Islamic history, quotes saturated with certainty about the Jews' ontological status as figures of hypocrisy, such as this one from the thirteenth century:

> Know that these people are the most cunning creatures, the vilest, most unbelieving, and hypocritical. While ostensibly the most humble and miserable, they are in fact the most vicious of men. This is the very essence of rascality and accursedness. If they remain alone with a man, they destroy him . . . They are the most unbelieving and most perfidious of men. So beware of their company. They have no belief or religion.[73]

What seems to me less common (and here the accounting can be only subjective) is the application of such ideas to the "Judaizing" critique of spheres of culture.

In the following chapter, for example, we will see how many medieval Christians came to think of certain kinds of government as "Jewish," and to criticize their princes as "Jews." I do not think such a widespread "Judaization" of politics took place in the Islamic world until modernity. There were, however, exceptions, and those exceptions enable us to appreciate the *potential* power that figures of Judaism had within Islamic thought, even if that potential was not *actualized* as frequently (again, the accounting is at best impressionistic) in the medieval Islamic world as it was in the medieval Christian.

Perhaps the most remarkable of these exceptions took place in Islamic Spain. We can trace its contours clearly enough through the career of one individual, the Muslim scholar, poet, and politician ʿAli Ibn Hazm (AH 384–456/994–1064 CE). Ibn Hazm was born in the Caliphate of Cordoba, the vast (and vastly rich) Islamic state that then occupied much of what we now call Spain. He lived in an extraordinary era, often called "the Golden Age" of medieval Judaism, but a distinctly stormy period for the political elites of the peninsula. He came of age as civil war tore the caliphate into dozens of factions and competing principates, called the "party kingdoms" by historians (not for their festive but for their fractious mood). Within this fragmented politics, Ibn Hazm himself rose very high, occupying for a time the office of *wazir* or "chief minister," of the last caliph, 'Abd al-Rahman V. But he also fell very low, suffering imprisonment at the hands of his rivals, and spending a good deal of his life in exile in different "party kingdoms," such as Seville (where his books were condemned and burned) and Mallorca.

Jews were not the cause of the strife that so adversely affected Ibn Hazm's political career, but the chaos of civil war did create opportunities for some Jews. One of these was Samuel ibn Naghrila, who became *wazir* of the "party kingdom" of Granada because, as a Muslim chronicler put it, of the king's "utter lack of confidence in anyone else, and the hostility of his kinsmen."[74] Ibn Hazm's reaction to the appointment is preserved in a treatise he penned, entitled "The Refutation":

> *Oh God, we complain to Thee, for the rulers of our faith absorbed in worldly affairs neglect the observance of their religion. . . . Absorbed in piling up riches—sometimes with results fatal to their own lives and helpful to their enemies—they are deflected from their faith and people. . . . Non-Muslims become arrogant, and infidels wag their tongues.*

The complaint is addressed to God, but it was aimed at one particular ruler, the *amir* of Granada, and one particular "non-Muslim," Samuel ibn Naghrila. Samuel was, according to Ibn Hazm, "a man who is filled with hatred toward the Apostle [Muhammad], a man who is, in secret, a materialist, a free thinker, a Jew, of that most contemptible of religions, the most vile of faiths." Ibn Hazm's warning to the king on the subject of his servant lies somewhere between prayer and curse:

> *It is my firm hope that God will treat those who befriend the Jews and take them into their confidence as He treated the Jews them-*

selves. For whosoever amongst Muslim princes has listened to all this and still continues to befriend Jews . . . well deserves to be overtaken by the same humiliation and to suffer in this world the same griefs which God has meted out to the Jews, apart from their chastisement in the next world. Whosoever acts in this manner will be recompensed by suffering along with the Jews themselves. . . . Let any prince upon whom God has bestowed some of his bounty take heed . . . let him get away from this filthy, stinking, dirty crew beset with God's anger and malediction, with humiliation and wretchedness, misfortune, filth and dirt, as no other people has ever been. Let him know that the garments in which God has enwrapped them are more obnoxious than war, and more contagious than elephantiasis. May God keep us from rebelling against Him and His decision, from honoring those whom he has humiliated, by raising up those whom He has cast down.[75]

The political theory encoded in this invective does not sound so distant from that of Ambrose's warning to the emperor Theodosius ("that king has become a Jew"), or the medieval Christian critics of monarchs whom we will encounter in the next chapter. The desire for material wealth lures rulers into raising Jews from the miserable position assigned to them by God. In doing so, the ruler becomes (like the Jews) a rebel against God, and will be punished as such. Like the punishment of the Jews for their ancient enmity, which is everywhere obvious in their wretchedness, God's punishment of the ruler will also be visible in this world, in the form of abasement and defeat.

In "The Refutation" Ibn Hazm presents Jewish power as cause, as well as symptom, of a world turned upside down, a world in which Jews were becoming more powerful than Muslims, and the Muslim monarchs—or worse, all their Muslim subjects!—were becoming "Jews." In the words of one poet, the Granadans are "a people who are considered to be nothing but Jews, though they are called Berbers." The Granadans themselves apparently agreed that this "Judaism" had to be eliminated. Though Ibn Hazm did not quite live to see it, in 1066 the

Muslims of Granada revolted against their *amir*'s employment of Samuel's son Joseph, killing him and three or four thousand other Jews.[76]

We should not treat these attacks as merely strategic, although they were also that. Behind them there stood a vast intellectual edifice, an ontology. One of the most monumental wings of that edifice was erected by Ibn Hazm himself. In his encyclopedic *History of Religions*, a work that is sometimes called the first comparative history of religious ideas, the scholar devoted long pages to the Jews. On the one hand, their accursedness was obvious, apparent even in their persons: they were the filthiest and smelliest of peoples. Their intellects stank too: the equivalent, among odors, of garlic. Equally clear was the corruption of their texts. Jewish tampering with the Torah had made it an incoherent stupidity to which no Muslim should lend credence or authority, and the Talmud had obviously been written by atheists "without a law."

Nevertheless, and despite this obvious falsity, Ibn Hazm did assign to the Jews an important role in the history of religion. This role was not that of the vessel through which the written word of God was first poured into the world. Rather the opposite: Ibn Hazm's Jews moved history along through their lies. By bribing Saint Paul to spread false teachings, the Jews tricked the early Christians into believing that Jesus was divine rather than simply a prophet (as Muslims believe). Then the Jews spread schism within Islam, instigating all the principle heresies that afflicted the faith from its earliest days. Always it was the Jews' "materialism" that drove them to such deceptions: "[T]he religion of the Jews tends strongly towards that, for there is not in their Torah any mention of the next world, or of reward after death."[77]

It is not his basic conception of the Jews as figures of hypocrisy that makes Ibn Hazm's example exceptional. As we have seen, that idea was widespread already at the foundations of Islam. Nor is the problem of Jews in the service of Muslim rulers particular to Islamic Spain. Rulers throughout the Muslim world often employed non-Muslims in their service, and were commonly criticized for this practice.[78] What is unusual about Ibn Hazm and his context is that it produced not only a massacre, but also a systemized model of thought capable of explaining all of world history in terms of the ontological trickery wrought by figures of Judaism. (I say "figures of Judaism" rather than Jews because many of the "villains" in Ibn Hazm's history were Christians or Muslims, not Jews: it was the system of thought that rendered them "Jewish," not their own beliefs.)

There were not many Ibn Hazms in the medieval Islamic world, nor were there many massacres or mass expulsions of Jews. This is not to say that the status of Jews was "better" under Islam than under Christianity. It is only to say that in Islam the Jews' peculiar positions in scriptural ontology and their peculiar position in Muslim societies did not often combine in such a way as to generate politically useful general theories capable of explaining the world's struggles in "Jewish" terms—not often, that is, until modernity. But the prooftexts for such thought were widespread in the Islamic tradition. And as Ibn Hazm's example reminds us, the potential power of that thought to make sense of Muslims' place in the world was great. Neither the potential for nor the power of this struggle with Judaism can be dismissed as something extraneous to Islam.[79]

Chapter 5

"THE REVENGE OF THE SAVIOR":
JEWS AND POWER IN MEDIEVAL EUROPE

What do you think the devil can accomplish through
the Jews, who are so numerous, almost all educated
and most adept at trickery, so well endowed with the
good life and the usuries allowed them by Christians,
so loved by our princes on account of the services they
provide and the flatteries they spew forth, so scattered
and dispersed throughout the world, so secretive
in their deceptions that they display a remarkable
appearance of being truthful?

—RAMON MARTÍ,
THE DAGGER OF THE FAITH, CA. 1275[1]

BY NOW WE are used to seeing the Jews cast as confounders of truth, master hypocrites, and even agents of the devil. But none of the previous chapters has quite prepared us for the political worry expressed here by the famed thirteenth-century Dominican friar, theologian, canon

183

lawyer, and advisor to Iberian kings, Ramon Martí (whose tomb and chapel you can visit today at the Barcelona Cathedral), as an anxiety about the Jewish seduction of princes and the princely love of Jews. That love affair—I mean this as a metaphor, but as we will see, medieval people understood the love literally as well—is the subject of this chapter, which focuses on western, "Catholic," Europe in the Middle Ages.[2]

The Prince as Jew-Lover

Consider this tale told about Alfonso VIII, king of Castile (1158–1214), a generation or two before Ramon Martí's birth:

> *After the king Alfonso was married . . . he departed to Toledo with his wife. And while there he saw a very beautiful Jewess, and he became so attached to her that he left the queen his wife and secluded himself with the Jewess. . . . [H]e remained secluded with her for seven months, so that he paid no attention to himself or his kingdom or anything else, and they say that this great love that he bore the Jewess was caused by love magic and spells that she knew how to make. But the counts and knights and rich men, seeing how the kingdom was in such danger . . . agreed together how they would resolve such a bad and unconscionable situation. And the agreement was that they would kill her. And with this intention they entered to where the king was, pretending that they wished to speak to him. And after all had gone in before the king, while some spoke to him the others entered to where the Jewess was and . . . they cut her throat and did the same to the others who were with her. . . . And when the king learned this he was so unhappy that he did not know what to do, for he loved her so much that he wanted to die with her. And then some of his vassals took him and transported him to a place called Illescas. . . . And as he lay one night preoccupied by the affair of this damned Jewess there appeared to him an angel who said to him: how now, Alfonso, are you dwelling on the evil you have done, from which God received great disservice? You do ill, for know*

that He will charge you dearly for it, you and your kingdom, [because it consented to your sin].[3]

God charged dearly indeed. Versions of the story vary (some, for example, say the affair lasted seven years, not seven months), but according to most it was because of this transgression that Alfonso's army was destroyed by the Muslims at the Battle of Alarcos (1195), that all his male children died before him, and that therefore his kingdom was inherited by the son of another man.

The tale is puzzling. After all, Alfonso was a successful warrior-king. His victory over Islam in 1212 at Las Navas de Tolosa humbled forever Muslim power in the Iberian Peninsula, and ranks with the Battle of Lepanto (1571) among Christendom's most celebrated triumphs. It is true that his sons died young, but he himself lived long, and through his daughters his blood beat in the greatest crowns, not only in Castile, but also in France (Saint Louis IX, for example, was a grandson). Moreover, the sources from Alfonso's own day tell nothing of this story. About the king's love for a Jewess, about her murder by barons in the king's court, about a reproachful angel, they are completely silent. This story of royal love only begins to be told some 180 years after Alfonso's death, during the reign of King Sancho IV (1284–1295). We may well doubt that the Jewess ever existed.[4]

What we should not doubt, however, is that she was meaningful. The first person whose telling of the story has reached us, King Sancho himself, included her in a work called *The Punishments* (*Castigos*), a moral handbook for princes that Sancho (or his ghostwriters) composed for the edification of his own son and heir. The basic lesson of the handbook was clear. Kings have an obligation to rule according to God's will. If, seduced by worldly desire, they rebel against that will, they will in turn be punished by the world's rebellion. Adam, the first man, was himself the first to suffer this fate. Wanting to please Eve he gave her power over him, power that she used against him, seducing him to rebel against God. As a result, not only did the natural world become rebellious and alienated from man, but Eve and her sex did as well. "As punishment for this Our Lord God decreed that whenever man gives woman lordship over him, she will always be contrary toward him."[5]

Adam's error was not love, which Sancho (like so many other Christian thinkers) recognized as a basic principle of life both physical and spiritual. His error was excessive love, misdirected love, love turned away from God and toward the world. According to Sancho this excessive love of the carnal world was the greatest danger confronting the Christian king, and three enemies worked constantly to lead him into error: the devil, the world, and the flesh. Already in the politics of Eden these enemies of godly sovereignty had worn a female face. Now, in the politics of Christendom, a figure not just feminine but Jewish provided the purest example of deviance because the Jew stood furthest from the love of Christ. As Sancho explained, "You must never in intimacy bring your lips close to the face of a Jewess, who is of that race that spat in the face of your Lord Jesus Christ." The kingdoms of kings that "kiss Jews" will suffer grievous bodily harm in the form of divine punishments like defeat, disease, and disaster.[6]

The story of Alfonso's Jewess is unusual, both because of its long life in Castilian letters and because it was explicitly used to explain and even justify rebellion. It was not, however, unique. In the lands becoming France, Guibert of Nogent excoriated the Count of Soissons for his affair with a Jewess (and many other crimes as well). Count Thibault of Blois is said to have had a relationship with a Jewess called Pucellina, whose nasty breakup in 1171 led to his burning a number of her coreligionists alive on charges of ritual murder. According to Polish legend, King Casimir the Great (1310–1370) so loved the Jewess "Estherke" (Esther) that in 1334 he granted the Jews a new charter of privileges in her honor, and after her death kept her eyes and heart in a box by his bed.[7] Much about these stories is almost certainly fiction, but (as Sancho's example made clear) these fictions tell some basic truths about the importance of Judaism in medieval thinking about Christian kingship and political power.[8]

The Prince as Exterminator of Jews

How did Judaism achieve such an importance? When medieval Christians meditated on this question, they sometimes told a story called "the revenge of the Savior." The story came in many forms: biblical apocrypha, plays, poems, and even chivalric adventure "novels"—all recounting the conquest of Jerusalem by the Roman emperor Vespasian (and Titus) in 70 CE. Though Vespasian was not a Christian, Christians in much later centuries came to understand the emperor's actions as divinely inspired. God had afflicted him with a terrible illness, but then sent Saint Veronica bearing Christ's shroud to cure him in the name of Christ.

The miracle convinced the emperor to conquer Jerusalem as punishment for the Jews' crucifixion of Jesus. According to many medieval versions of the story, after Vespasian conquered Jerusalem he claimed all Jewish captives as his own. The vast majority he sold to his soldiers, who then disemboweled them, looking for the gold and jewels they were rumored to have swallowed. But the last 180 he retained for himself, banishing them to wander, exiled but under his protection, throughout Europe. The conquest of Jerusalem by the Romans thus came to be understood as a divinely ordained punishment of the Jews for deicide, as the origins of the Jewish Diaspora, and as the founding example of a Christian monarch's correct relationship to his Jewish subjects.[9]

We want to pursue this last point: Vespasian's behavior represented medieval ideals about the proper behavior of rulers toward Jews (the emperor here serves as a model for all such authorities, be they king, pope, bishop, magnate, or even town council). These ideals were impossibly disparate. On the one hand, the exemplary emperor is God's delegated exterminator of Jews, cleansing the Holy Land forever of their presence. On the other, he is also the guarantor of the Jews' safety, guarding them from violence with special protection, as God had guarded Cain in his exile. Vespasian, in his medieval Christian incarnation, encourages slaughter, but he ultimately subscribes to the canonical position of Saint Augustine regarding the protection of Jews in Christendom, and preserves for witness and exile his remnant of nine score.

This ambivalence was deeply felt, and acted out in violence as well as on page and stage. In some parts of Europe, for example, children and young clerics would gather during Holy Week for a ritual called "killing the Jews," in which they would throw rocks at the walls of the Jewish quarter and at the royal officials especially hired to protect it. The violence was usually constrained by custom, but it had a sharp point: toleration of the Jewish quarter was a political and spiritual compromise, a concession to king and flesh. In a redeemed world, neither concession would be necessary. The Castilian poet Juan Ruiz expressed much the same sentiment in his *Book of Good Love* (ca. 1330) when he staged life as a battle between Sir Carnality and Lady Lent. During Holy Week, Sir Carnality is at his weakest, forced to take refuge in the Jewish quarter. Lady Lent lays siege, but the triumph of purity is fleeting in this world of the body: at the end of the week Sir Carnality sallies forth on the rabbi's horse and puts her once more to flight.[10]

All these stories, rituals, and poems use the destruction of Jewish Jerusalem to imagine the moral and political struggles between body and spirit in this fallen world. Through frequent exposure, the image burned itself into the retina of the Christian imagination. In many parts of Spain, for example, the ritual of "killing the Jews" continued late into the twentieth century, a half millennium after the last Jews were expelled in 1492. Once, when I spoke on this subject in Houston, a Spaniard in the audience stood and announced, "I've killed the Jews," before adding "in effigy," as part of the Holy Week traditions in his native town.

These practices endured because they were such powerful dramatizations of the Augustinian paradox of simultaneous punishment and protection. As such, they were capable of generating startlingly different conclusions about the proper place of Judaism. They might, for example, be interpreted as endorsing and stabilizing the status quo of compromise in this imperfect world, that is, protection of the "Jews." But because they stage the eventual triumph of the spirit as the conquest of this remnant of Jerusalem, they could also support attempts to perfect the world through their elimination. Both possibilities were, as we will see, thoroughly explored in the Middle Ages.

The "Jewish" Foundations of Princely Power

Though medieval Christians were not thinking historically when they anchored their foundation myths about relations between sovereigns and Jews in the first century after the birth of Jesus, they were pointing toward an important truth. The *potential* to ask "Jewish questions" of sovereigns was perceived very early in Christian (and Islamic) politics, as we saw in the previous chapters. But in fact that potential was not often put to work in the Roman Empire or the Islamic caliphates. It began to become more useful in the "Barbarian kingdoms" that emerged after the fifth-century collapse of the Roman Empire in the West. In the Iberian kingdom that the Visigoths carved out of that declining empire, an "anti-Jewish politics" came close to becoming a platform of monarchy (and therefore also a pulpit from which the monarch could be criticized), but that kingdom was cut short in 711 by the Muslim conquests. Charlemagne stretched a polity painfully from Pamplona to Prague in the late eighth century. That "empire" abounded in theoreticians eager to provide political and theological guidance. But although these scholars produced sharp and sometimes original commentaries on, for example, the place of Jews and Judaizers in Saint Paul's writings, they rarely put Judaism to the task of making critical sense of worldly power.[11]

The Carolingian empire collapsed in the mid-ninth century under the weight of vast distances and varied dangers. The dust cloud that arose from that collapse obscures much of the following century, particularly in the more western stretches of Europe. When it starts to clear, around the year 1000, we can make out the dim outlines of figures scurrying to build new claims to sovereignty out of the rubble. It is in the echoing audience halls and throne rooms of these new claimants that the "Jewish question" was amplified from a minor quarrel in the marriage of church and empire, into a central political paradox capable of generating a critical science of power.

The acoustics of this process vary slightly across the many polities of medieval Europe, but we will focus on what all the versions have in common: across Europe, those who claimed power came to claim a special power over Jews. The few sources that survive for the earliest stages of this process vary greatly in genre. Near the eastern limits of Latin Europe, Cosmas of Prague's *Chronicle of the Bohemians* gives us a glimpse of a group of Jews and converts attempting to flee Prague in 1098, after the massacres and forced conversions perpetrated there by the forces of the First Crusade in 1096. They are intercepted by a troop of Duke Bracizlao's men, who assert (in verse!) the duke's special power over them, invoke the legacy of Vespasian, then beat them up and seize all their property. To the south, where entrepreneurial Normans such as Robert "the Cunning" are busy converting Muslim lands like Sicily and southern Italy into kingdoms for themselves, the sources are less poetic but equally practical. They tell us, for example, that the Norman lords of Sicily in the 1080s and 1090s could grant entire communities of Jews as special "gifts" to those (often bishops and churches) whom they wished to favor, and that they put those whom they chose to keep in charge of important royal monopolies (like the dye works at the hub of the kingdom's textile trade).[12]

To Europe's extreme west, where Iberian frontier lords were carving Christian kingdoms out of al-Andalus, and to its north, where William the Conqueror and his heirs were busy making England Anglo-Norman, we find sovereigns establishing their tutelage, defense, and "ownership" (more on this word below) of Jews. In central Europe (roughly modern Germany), where Charlemagne's legacy crumbled but did not quite shatter, his Ottonian successors still made credible claims to continuity with imperial practice. Nevertheless, the privileges given by the Holy Roman emperor Henry IV (1050–1106) to the Jewish communities of Speyer and Worms in 1090, though clothed in Carolingian garb, began to articulate the legal contours of a special royal protection of Jews. And in what had once been "West Francia," where the ruin of the Carolingian project was perhaps most complete, the claim to power over Jews proved especially important for the Capetian counts of Paris as they jousted with their peers in their quest to become "Kings of France."[13]

The King's "Private Things"

Understanding the many regional and temporal differences in the development of Jewish legal status across the European Middle Ages is an important comparative project for medievalists. For us a general point matters more: European sovereigns increasingly insisted that the Jews *belonged* to them in a *peculiar* way, different from that of their other subjects. If the exact terms of this peculiarity are not always clear, it is partly because medieval lawyers struggled to find an appropriate phrase in their venerable vocabulary for what was not an ancient status. In an English code known as the "Laws of Edward the Confessor" (but produced in the reign of Henry I, d. 1135) jurists spoke of the king as "tutor" and "defender" of the Jews, and of the Jews as his "possessions": "for those Jews, and all that they possess, belong to the king, . . . as if they were his private property." In 1176 those working for King Alfonso II of Aragon spoke in slightly different terms: "for the Jews are the *servi* of the king, and are always subject to the royal fisc."

This concept of the Jews as the king's *servi* (a Latin word that could mean "slave," "serf," or "servant") became very widespread in European law. The emperor Frederick II of Hohenstaufen adopted and disseminated it throughout his German and Italian lands in the 1230s and 1240s. Shortly thereafter lawyers for the Capetian kings of France began to speak of the Jews as "tanquam servi," meaning "like slaves"? "Like serfs"? "Like servants"? Much stress has been laid on qualifying words such as *tanquam* and *sicut* ("like," "as if"), and on the difficulty of translating *servi*, for the stakes are high. Should we think (at one extreme) of the Jews as abject slaves of monarchy or (at the other) as "protected dependents," favored members of the royal "household."[14]

We do not need to decide between these possibilities, each of which contains some truth. It is more important to realize that one depends on the other. Whatever exceptional protection Jews received from medieval monarchs was a product of their exceptional relation to those monarchs. Royal protection was not itself exceptional, for it could be extended to anyone, as King John of England implied in his famous edict forbidding attacks on Jews: "If I give my peace even to a dog, it must be kept inviolate." It was the peculiar justification for their particular protection that came to distinguish the Jew from every other kind of subject.[15]

We have already seen Henry I's lawyers speaking of the Jews as the king's "proprium," which we loosely translated as "property." King John's words in 1201 were only slightly different: the Jews and their property are "sicut res nostre proprie," "sicut nostrum proprium catallum": "like our own private thing," "like our chattel property." By calling Jews "res proprie," English kings were assigning to Jews a place quite different from that of their other subjects. In his *Commentaries on the Laws and Customs of England*, the learned thirteenth-century jurist Henry of Bracton explained this difference to his medieval colleagues: "The Jew can truly not have any property of his own, for whatever he acquires is not acquired by him but by the king, for the Jew *does not live for himself but for another*, and thus the other acquires, and not the Jew himself." The Jew is a "private thing" of the king. All other subjects of the sovereign partake to some degree of the "res publica," the "common/public thing," the *republic*. The Jew is of the "res proprie" alone. Hence the king can say of the Jew what he cannot say of his other subjects: "No Jew shall remain in our kingdom except those that can serve the king. . . . Other Jews, indeed, who have nothing with which they can serve the king, shall leave the kingdom."[16]

The English were precocious in their legal diction, but the idea that Jews were especially reducible to the sovereign's "things" was not confined to their sceptered isle. Cosmas's *Bohemians* again provides an early eastern example. In 1091, when King Wratislaw took up arms to assert his power over the vassals of his magnate Konrad of Brünn, his aggression was criticized on the field of battle. I paraphrase the chronicler's version of that reproach: "Why don't you attack the suburbs of Prague? There you will find Jews and merchants with gold and silver aplenty, rich plunder for your knights. If you want to repeat the sack of Troy, why don't you go there? You will say: 'I don't attack them because they are mine!' But are we, your subjects, not also yours? When you attack us, you attack your brothers, and become a fratricide. You want to treat us, not as your brother, but as your slave (quasi tuus servus)." The faint precursor of a political argument is emerging here, though without the clarity of law: the king's subjects stand in a different relation to him than the Jews do, a relationship of brotherhood, not of servitude. Their bond to him is not a private but a common one. The king errs (it is implied) by trying to equate the two, by trying to reduce his subjects into his "Jews" and slaves. In the process he becomes (like Cain?) a fratricide.[17]

It is worth pausing for a moment, though neither Bracton nor Cosmas did so, to notice that this infant politics is related to the ideas we encountered in chapter 3. The political status of the Jew as a "slave" (Latin *servus*) or chattel who does not exist for his own political good but only for that of another is very close to the theological status of Jew as the illiterate "living letter" that exists only to be read by the Christian. Because Augustine himself had used the word *servus* to describe the Jews' exegetical relationship to the Christian, medieval popes (like Innocent III in his Etsi Iudaeos of 1205) also used it in their theological justifications for the continued protection of Jews in Christendom.[18]

Historians argue about how that ecclesiastical use might specifically have influenced the contemporaneous claims of princes that the Jews were their *servi*. They should, however, accept the more general point, that the Middle Ages created for the Jews a political and legal status analogous to their hermeneutic one. The Jews already represented for Christian exegesis an exceptional form of relation to text, an extreme literalism that turned them into living flesh unconnected to spirit. Over the course of the Middle Ages they came to represent an exceptional form of relation to power, one of extreme subjection to the sovereign. This subjection turned them into the political equivalent of Augustine's "living letters": into "living private things" of the sovereign, rather than political members of the "republic."

Judaism, Fiscality, Monarchy

This special relationship between Jews and rulers proved tremendously useful to European monarchs and magnates trying to establish and expand their power in the eleventh, twelfth, and thirteenth centuries. The most notorious way in which control of the Jews served to extend sovereign power was through money lending. Any number of European princes channeled Jewish economic activity toward lending at interest to Christians, so that they could then expropriate a considerable share of the proceeds from the Jews in the form of loans, taxes, and extraordinary seizures called *captiones*, "takings." We can think of this as a novel form of indirect taxation. At a time when the power of princes to impose taxes was sharply constrained by custom and competing jurisdictions, exactions on interest collected by Jews from Christians gave lords new access to the wealth of their Christian subjects.[19]

Medieval people were well aware that it was the prince who ultimately profited from Jewish money lending. Usurers, as the learned French theologian Peter the Chanter put it in the twelfth century, "are both the coffers and leeches of princes, because all things they shall have sucked up, they vomit into the fisc."[20] It is perhaps in mid-thirteenth-century England that the system reached its starkest form. There, the pressures of royal taxation forced the Jews to sell their loans at deep discounts to members of the royal court, who would then collect the debt. Such transactions were ruinous, not only for the Jews but also for their Christian debtors. Jews rarely seized the estates of bankrupt borrowers, for they were barred by law from owning land. King and courtier knew no such limits and amassed vast landholdings from lords otherwise unable to pay their debts. The workings of the system were clear to everyone. One bureaucrat even drew it as a cartoon—in the first known medieval caricature of Jews—at the top of an English tax receipt roll of 1233. The drawing, presumably by a clerk of the exchequer of the Jews whose taxes are registered in the roll, represents a city overrun by a demonic army. In the center we have two Jews in profile, each labeled with their name, and united by a demon tweaking each of them by the nose. And towering over the city is a crowned three-faced figure—a traditional representation of the Anti-Christ—wearing the distinctive trefoil crown of the then reigning King Henry III, but bearing the name of Isaac of Norwich, one of the most powerful Jewish money-lenders of the day.[21]

Even the lighter obligations with which Jews were burdened made clear their close connection with the monarchy and its finances. The Jews of Valencia and Barcelona, for example, were responsible for the feeding and care of the royal lions.[22] In Aragon as in Norman Italy and some other areas of Europe, Jews were required to provide bedding, linens, and housing for their peripatetic lord or his officers in their travels throughout the kingdom. And on those occasions when Jews rose to high office and joined the court itself, they most often did so in capacities closely tied to the treasury: mint master, tax collector, bailiff, even treasurer. Given this close association between Jews and royal financial affairs, it is not surprising that Jewish communities were commonly referred to as the royal "treasure," "chest," or "money-bag."[23]

These were, however, moneybags with legs, and their mobility was important. Insofar as the Jews represented sovereign power in its most concentrated form, their diffusion could help to expand it. Consider the legal texts with which we began, with their assertion of royal protection of the king's Jews no matter where they were found. This was no trivial claim in the fragmented legal landscape of the twelfth and thirteenth centuries, in which the great lords sought constantly to extend their jurisdiction at the expense of the lesser, and all fought vigorously to defend their own. What happened when one lord allowed the Jews of another to lend to his vassals and dependents? In case of any dispute, the Jew's master claimed jurisdiction, but for the debtor's lord to grant the claim meant to lose power over the property of one's own subjects.

In places like England, where Jews belonged more or less exclusively to the king, these jurisdictional claims strengthened only the monarchy. The king alone claimed to decide the Jews' fate, and any attempt by other Christians to circumscribe that power through violence became a violation of the king's rights. In other lands, where counts, bishops, and other great lay and ecclesiastical lords also possessed Jews, these claims helped to extend the power of magnates as well as of the king. But even in such lands, kings found that the incipient association of Jews with sovereignty helped them to make new and powerful jurisdictional claims against their rivals. In the twelfth and early thirteenth centuries, for example, a number of the great magnates of France who gave only token recognition to the political authority of Capetian kings harbored Jews on their lands. The movement of these Jews across jurisdictional boundaries often gave rise to conflict between lords, especially when Jews attempted to escape the extraordinary "takings" of one magnate by fleeing with their goods to the territory of another.

In 1230 King Louis IX issued the Ordinance of Melun to address such conflicts. The ordinance stated that lords could seize their own Jews wherever they were found, even if they were living in another lord's territory. Even more significant: it was the king as sovereign who claimed the right to adjudicate between lords in any dispute about Jewish movement, even when neither domain belonged to the Crown. Moreover, the ordinance asserted that any magnate who resisted these claims could be punished as a rebel: "If any barons do not wish to observe them, we shall compel them. . . . We and our other barons have sworn to compel the rebels to observe the aforesaid statutes." One eminent historian has called this "the first piece of treason legislation in French history," as well as the first example of French legislation since the Carolingians. Such arguments not only extended royal authority over Jews who belonged to other lords, but also provided an entry point for new forms of monarchical power (such as the charge of treason and *lèse majesté*) that would later find much broader application.[24]

Resisting "Jewish" Government: "We Would Rather Die"

Over the course of roughly two centuries, the Jews had become a special class of "hyper-subject," put to special use in the extension of sovereign power. The needs of sovereigns, along with the rise in these centuries of guild organizations and other Christian communal structures that barred Jews from many economic activities, tended to channel Jews into specific financial functions such as money lending and tax collecting. These functions came to be associated with Jews, and even thought of as "Jewish," although Jews rarely predominated in them, and then only for short periods of time. Both these tendencies, to associate Jews with sovereign power and to associate sovereign (especially fiscal) power with Judaism, meant that Jews came to occupy a special position in the arguments of those who would resist that power as well as those who would extend it.

This resistance took many forms. Sometimes it meant attacking Jews conducting the business of monarchy, or attacking any Jew at all, as symbol of a resented ruler. It might mean casting the ruler himself as a "Jew." Conversely, it might represent his subjects as "Judaized." After all, if Jews represented complete subjection to the sovereign, then attempts by lords to achieve greater power over their Christian subjects (by, for example, imposing new taxes) could be understood as making those subjects more "Jewish." King Wratislaw's subjects already hinted at this logic on the battlefield in 1091. The city council of Valencia was more explicit when it told King Peter that his request for a new tax in 1378 was "nothing other than to make a Jewry out of each of his municipalities . . . , and we will not give way to such a demand, for we would rather die than be made similar to Jews."[25]

The point is unsurprising: "Jewish politics" served both to make claims to power and to resist them (unsurprising because "resistance" too is a claim to power). Lords who defended and profited from their Jews opened themselves to a powerful form of criticism portraying them as "Jew-lovers" and oppressors of their Christian subjects. Thus (to draw on only a few English examples) William of Newburgh tells us that Henry II favored the "unbelieving race and the enemies of Christ, that is to say, the usurious Jews," because he delighted in the money derived from their usury. The barons assembled at Runnymede in 1215 might have said the same about King John, for they were united in their disapproval of him by (among other things) his exploitation of Jewish debts. Magna Carta, the famous document limiting the powers of monarchy that they forced John to sign, included two clauses intended explicitly to frustrate that exploitation.[26]

Half a century later, the great magnate Simon de Montfort seems to have believed that because the Jews were under the sole jurisdiction of the king, their presence on his lands provided an entry point for royal power and diminished his own dominion. He therefore expelled all Jews from the city of Leicester and other of his domains. There was also a theology behind his politics of expulsion, articulated in this case by one of the greatest churchmen of his age, Robert Grosseteste. When Simon de Montfort's aunt, the Countess of Winchester, welcomed the refugee Jews of Leicester into her domains, Grosseteste wrote her a letter of unusual acrimony. The Jews, he said, were like Cain, enslaved to all nations for the murder of Christ. They were not to be killed, as Augustine had rightly said, but neither could they enjoy the protection of princes or be allowed to live a life of anything but barest subsistence. They should be forced to "work the earth laboriously, for the utility of the prince, and for some little sustenance for their miserable lives." Lords who allowed them more, or who benefited from their activities, became as guilty as the Jews themselves (a point not so different from Ibn Hazm's in the previous chapter). Grosseteste quoted words of Saint Paul: "[N]ot only those who do these things, but those who consent to them are worthy of death" (Rom. 1:32). Such lords, like the Jews, drink the blood of their subjects.[27]

This was the politics and the theology with which Montfort was girded in the rebellion he later led against the government of King Henry III, a rebellion in which attacks on Jews became a major theme. Henry himself was not spared indignities. We have already seen his crown being worn by the "Anti-Christ Jew" Isaac of Norwich. The English chronicler Matthew Paris (ca. 1200–1259) took a wittier route and circumcised the king. Here is his account of Henry's reaction (in 1255) to the news that his Jews are so poor they can no longer pay him taxes:

When the king heard their answer he exclaimed woefully: ". . . [I]t is horrible to imagine the debt to which I'm obligated. . . . I'm divided all around! I am a mutilated king and a shortened one, even cut in

half! . . . I need money . . . no matter how I get it!" Having become,
then, another Titus or Vespasian, he sold the Jews for some years to
Earl Richard his brother, that the earl might disembowel those whom
the king had skinned. The earl, however, spared them out of consider-
ation for their . . . poverty.

Matthew's mention of Vespasian is a mocking one, meant to evoke a
vivid contrast between that emperor and the king he presents as greedy,
castrated, and even cut like a Jew. (Elsewhere Matthew uses the word
circumcised to describe Henry's debased coinage.) Painting a few years
later, when the expulsion of the Jews from England had become a popular demand, the less humorous illuminator of an apocalypse manuscript invoked Vespasian's example to promote a grimmer policy. In his
illumination to Revelation 6:12 a king sits enthroned in the center. To
his left stands a group of Jewish courtiers bearing moneybags, to his
right, a knight disemboweling Jews to find the gold and jewels they had
swallowed.[28]

In all of these examples we see the exceptional status of Jews as
"royal treasure" being transformed into shorthand for royal exactions
perceived as exploitative. The negative valence that had built up around
sovereign power over Jews became a charge that could be directed at
any number of claims to administrative and fiscal authority. Arguments
about Jews arose wherever the limits of royal power were debated:
representative assemblies, civil wars, and other forms of resistance to
or negotiation with monarchy. In the thirteenth century, for example,
almost no English parliament voted its king a tax without first demanding that some steps be taken against the Jews. In the fourteenth, virtually the same could be said of the Castilian Cortes (parliament). French
kings too were used to receiving petitions like the one addressed by the
citizens of Toulouse to Philip V in 1320–1321, listing the crimes of Jews
and of royal officers and demanding the expulsion of the former. It was
through such action that Christian subjects asserted the limits of their
subjection, and therefore action against Jews became an important quid
pro quo for their grants of aid to monarchy. In certain times and places,

we could even say that anti-Judaism was one of the basic concepts (like "defense of the realm") out of which representative taxation emerged.[29]

The same power of anti-Judaism that warmed the cradles of Europe's parliaments burned in its rebellions, as we saw in the case of England. Even in places like France, where monarchs learned early to persecute their own Jews, there are examples of violent criticism aimed at the monarchy through the Jews. It is, however, in the west and east of Europe that the dependence of sovereigns on Jews lingered longest, and it is also there that the rebellious potential of anti-Judaism was longest invoked.

To the west, on the Iberian Peninsula, the "unions" of nobles and townsmen that waged war against the kings of Aragon in the late thirteenth century placed restrictions on the royal exploitation of Jews at the center of their demands. At much the same time in Castile, Prince Sancho (IV, the future author of our "Castigos" with their story of Jewish love) rebelled against his father, Alfonso X "the Wise," claiming among other things that Alfonso was a puppet of the Jews.[30] Once king, he set about reforms that were opposed by many magnates as empowering Jews: the nobleman he put in charge of royal finances was even murdered by his rivals in the king's own court. (This context may help explain why Sancho found the story about the Jewish love of Alfonso VIII so edifying.) The aristocratic factions that deposed and killed King Peter "the Cruel" of Castile in the mid-fourteenth century justified their actions by portraying him as a favorer of Jews, and even claimed that he was a cuckoo, the son of a Jewess adopted by the queen mother to conceal her inability to provide an heir. The revolt led by Prince Henry (IV) against his father, Juan II, generated the most explicit vindications of violent resistance to "Jew-loving" tyrants produced in the Middle Ages (for more on this revolt see chapter 6). Henry IV, in turn, was accused of favoring Jews and living like a Muslim. Even the "Catholic monarchs" Ferdinand and Isabel, founders of the Inquisition, conquerors of the last Muslim outpost in Spain, and expellers of the Jews (in 1492), were said by some of their subjects to be descended from Jews and to favor them in their policies.[31]

To the east, in the German lands of the Holy Roman Empire, the politics were different but equally consequential. The emperor Frederick II's designation in 1236 of all the Jews of the empire as "slaves" of his chamber coincided with increasing attacks on them. In 1235, for example, a miller and his wife went to church, leaving their five children home alone. When they returned, they found the mill burned down, the children dead. The Jews of Fulda were accused of having drained the children's blood for use in their rituals, then setting fire to the mill as cover for their crime. The commission established by the emperor to investigate the accusation found it groundless, and Frederick used the occasion to powerfully reassert his rights of protection and ownership over all the empire's Jews. He and his lawyers claimed that this power over Jews had been committed to him by "the people," but "the people" were clearly not ready to surrender it entirely. In the decades of political crisis and imperial collapse that followed Frederick's reign, Jews became a strategic target in the power struggles between emperors, electors, aristocrats, bishops, burghers and town councils, lesser knights, and laboring classes.[32]

The resulting violence rolled over the "Teutonic Kingdom" with tidal regularity. The Mainz persecutions for ritual murder in 1283, the "Good Werner" massacres of 1287 (named after a Christian boy allegedly killed by Jews), the "Rintfleisch" attacks on over 130 Jewish settlements in 1298, the "Crusade" of 1309, and the movement led by "King Armleder" in 1336–1338: each of these attacks had a different name, but all of them can be understood and analyzed as (among other things) a politics expressed in terms of the destruction of the Jews. By 1348, just a century after Emperor Frederick's claims to power over all the Jews, imperial strategy had come full circle. The Black Death was newly come, claiming perhaps a third of Europe's souls, and throughout the land Jews stood accused of having sowed it. The future Charles IV was locked in a contest with Günther of Schwarzburg for the (much-weakened) title of emperor. Günther resigned in 1349: Charles IV had won his crown, in part by using his "ownership" of the Jews in an unusual, but legally quite coherent way. He granted it back to the cities whose support he required (for example, Frankfurt, Nuremberg, and Worms) so that they could kill their Jews with full sovereign immunity, which they immediately did.[33]

Ritual Murders, Murderous Rituals

It is an understatement to say that both sides of this politics exacerbated the tensions inherent in the Augustinian paradox of "Jew as protected exile." There is perhaps no better example of this tension than the very different work two of the greatest theologians of the twelfth century did with the same quote from Saint Augustine. The Jewish writer Ephraim of Bonn tells us that in 1146, when crusaders marching to the Holy Land paused in the Rhineland to massacre the Jews who lived there, Saint Bernard of Clairvaux exhorted them: "Whosoever touches a Jew to take his like is like one who harms Jesus himself . . . , for in the book of Psalms it is written of them, 'Slay them not, lest my people forget.'" Peter the Venerable, on the other hand, writing to King Louis VII of France that very same year, used the same words to criticize the sovereign for protecting the Jews too much: "Has that which a certain holy king of the Jews once said escaped the notice of the king of the Christians? 'O Lord,' he said, 'shall I not hate those who hate you and be consumed with enmity for your enemies?' [Ps. 139:21]." Peter did not contradict Augustine, but he pushed him to an extreme. "Slay them not," he conceded, "for God does not wish them to be *entirely* killed and *altogether* wiped out, but to be preserved for greater torment and reproach, like the fratricide Cain, in a *life worse than death*."[34]

Peter's reproach drew a sharp contrast between Jewish enmity toward Christ and his people, and royal favor toward Jews. This juxtaposition remained powerful throughout the Middle Ages (we saw a thirteenth-century example in Ramon Martí's words at the beginning of this chapter). Propagandists for the princely possessors and exploiters of Jews claimed that these sovereigns were fulfilling God's will, protecting the Jews, while enforcing their abjection (through, among other things, financial exactions). Their critics claimed they had the balance wrong. Protection actually privileged the Jews, they argued, giving them power over Christians. "Why are the Jews so pitilessly persecuted by you Christians?" Johannes Pfefferkorn asked Germany's Christian princes circa 1500, on the eve of the Reformation. "As everybody knows, they have to pay high taxes for public protection and the rule of law. . . . The argument whereby you seek to justify your greed, namely, that this is a way of forcing their conversion, is not very convincing."[35] In pointing out the hypocrisy of princes, Pfefferkorn was not arguing for less persecution of the Jews. On the contrary, he was advocating greater conversionary pressure and more thorough suppression of their religion and its texts, which he argued were saturated with hatred for Christ and for Christians.

The efforts of medieval Christians to heighten the tension between royal favor toward Jews and Jewish enmity toward Christians produced new and durable ways of imagining both elements. In Alfonso's Jewess we saw an example of some of the new ways in which royal favor toward Jews was given flesh and face. Beginning in the twelfth century, the dangers that Jewish enmity posed to Christian society also found new embodiments. Jewish usurers sucked the blood and gnawed the bones of Christian peasants. Jewish blasphemers desecrated consecrated hosts and ritually murdered Christian children. Jewish men raped Christian women; Jewish doctors killed Christian patients. Jews caused plague and disease, either actively through poison or passively because Christian toleration of their malign presence angered God and roused him to punishment. By stressing that the toleration of Jews put Christian communities in terrible danger, these new representations of Jewish evil sought to recast the sovereign's dilemma in starker relief. "Protection of Jews" became a corrupt materialism that endangered the land; "persecution," a spiritual purity that protected it.

It is easy to dismiss each of these gross claims about Jewish evil as fantasy. They were that, but they were also ways of representing the theological and political conceptualizations of the struggle between world and spirit that I have been describing. It is through such representations that these complex ideas were made visible and intelligible, tangibly carnal, a part of lived experience. Stories about the ritual murder of Christian children and (later) about Jewish host desecration provide a good example of this process of representation, both because these stories have a rich theological background and because they became a common tool with which critics of monarchy represented the dangers they believed protection of Jews posed to Christian society.

Since Jesus's infancy and Jewish enmity toward him were such central themes of early Christian and medieval narrative, we might expect a linkage between them to emerge early, with Jews becoming persecutors of Christian children. There are some early tales about Jews attempting to kill children, but in the best-known and most widely circulated of these, the children are Jewish. In the late sixth century, for example, the Latin writer and bishop Gregory of Tours (in what is today France) adapted a story from the Greek east for inclusion in his "On the Glory of the Martyrs." The story was about a Jewish boy who went to school with Christians. One day he followed his schoolmates into the Christian basilica and shared with them some of "the Lord's body and blood." When he went home and told his parents what he had done, his father was furious and threw him in the oven. The mother's wails drew a Christian crowd whose mere arrival quelled the flames and revealed the boy, unharmed in the oven. He had seen, he reported, the same woman whose image stood in the basilica, a woman with an infant on a throne, and she had preserved him from the fire by covering him with her cloak. The boy, his mother, and many other Jews converted, the father was burned in the oven, and many later generations were provided with an exemplary story about the Jewish confirmation of Christian truth.[36]

This story, like most of those in this book, changed form and meaning across time and place, as different readers brought different contexts to it and put it to different kinds of work. It began to circulate widely, for example, in the collections of the Virgin Mary's miracles produced by advocates of her devotion in the late eleventh century. By the mid-twelfth century, the emphasis was becoming more Eucharistic. William of Malmesbury, writing in England before 1141, has the Jewish boy recognize that the child on the Virgin's lap is the same child he saw on the altar of the basilica, whose body was then distributed by the priest in the shape of the Eucharist: "That beautiful woman, . . . whose son was divided among the people, was with me in the burning oven." The Jewish child's story now confirmed not only Mary's miraculous powers but also that which many Christians were struggling to imagine: the real presence of the Christ-child's body in the sacrifice of the mass.

It is also in the twelfth century that a related genre of stories began to circulate. In these, Christian children rather than Jewish ones were the target of Jewish hatred. Sometime after young William of Norwich was found dead in the forest in 1144, the Jews of the town were accused of committing the murder as a necessary part of an annual Jewish sacrifice. Similar charges were made elsewhere in England before spreading to the continent, where they throve above all in the Holy Roman Empire (see, for example, the list of massacres given earlier). By the late thirteenth century, the genre had evolved yet again. Communion was now required annually of all Christians and becoming ever more the center of their piety. The Eucharist was increasingly present both spiritually and physically: hurried through the streets to the dying, paraded ceremonially in new holidays like Corpus Christi (Latin for "the body of Christ"). Now Jews were accused of attacking not just any Christian child, but the Christ-child himself, in the form of consecrated hosts purchased or stolen. The Jews might stab, burn, bury, or boil their tortured host, which might in turn transform into a child, bleed copiously, wail pitifully, and somehow attract the attention of a vengeful Christian crowd.

The rise of these stories about murderous Jewish enmity toward Christian children and the child Christ has often been studied in terms of the increasing importance of Marian devotion, of Eucharistic piety, or of the need to generate local martyrs, saints, and pilgrimage sites. For our purposes, it is equally important to stress the interdependence between the theological and the political meaning of these stories. The birth of ritual murder in England, during a period of intensive royal exploitation of Jews by the Angevin dynasty, is significant. Already on the occasion of its first telling, with the death of young William of Norwich in 1144, royal complicity had crystallized into narrative. The king's sheriff, John de Chesney, was accused of blocking the investigation, and King Stephen portrayed as doubting the accusation's truth. Three hundred years later, starting to tell a similar story long after the Jews had been expelled from England, Chaucer's Prioress still remembered royal perfidy as an indispensable detail: "Ther was in Alsye, in a greet citee / Amonges Cristene folk a Jewerye / Sustened by a lord of the contree / For foule usure and lucre of vileynye / Hateful to Cristland to his compaignye."[37]

This association between royal "greed"—we could also call it fiscality, or administrative monarchy—and murderous "Jewish" power was not incidental. On the contrary, over the course of the Middle Ages it had become a commonplace concept with which to make sense of the gap between worldly politics and some posited (albeit strategically) Christian ideal. An anonymous cartoonist expressed the association brilliantly circa 1450, when he decorated a copy of the papal bull of protection granted to the Jews of Frankfurt in 1349 (the same year in which they were massacred) with a figure seated in majesty, one Jew riding on his head, his throne balanced atop another. Accusations of ritual murder and host desecration drew on the same association. They articulated a specific vision of the terrible danger into which the materialism of rulers (represented as a spiritless "Jewish" carnality) could lead the spiritual bodies of Christ, of the Christian, and of the Christian polity. Their logic of conspiracy between Jews and the princes of this world—already a potential, as we have seen, in early Christian thinking about earthly politics—sought to unbind the furies that Augustine and others had sought to immure in the paradoxical political and theological status of the Jews, in order to direct their pent-up rage against the claims of rival powers.

We cannot analyze the context and consequences of each and every accusation of ritual murder or host desecration in order to make this claim convincing, but consider only one, from a town we visited earlier in this chapter. Throughout the 1380s, the city council (*universitas*) of Prague fought with King Wenzel of Bohemia over his protection of Jewish money lending. According to some sources the king's opponents did not mince words. They presented him as abandoned by all his Christian subjects because of the favor he showed the Jews and the pleasure he took in their usury. "Oh kings, kings! Be shamed for such a crime . . . in which you yourselves are proven to be accursed usurers."

During Holy Week 1389 the conflict took on its most revealing form.

The Jews of Prague were said to have thrown a stone at a monstrance carried in procession and to have ridiculed the host. The event was represented as a second killing of Jesus in Jerusalem, with the Jews said to be chanting, "[S]tone him, for he pretends to be God's son." Since the king wrongly tolerated such "nefarious acts against Christ's faithful," the people took it upon themselves to exact vengeance, eviscerating and dismembering the Jews, unearthing the treasures hidden in their homes, burning their bodies and their pillaged habitations. With Prague translated into Jerusalem, the rebels were cast in the role of Vespasian, and King Wenzel in that of a damned usurer and lover of Jews. By representing their actions in these terms, the people of Prague asserted that theirs was not a rebellion against divinely appointed monarchy, but rather (as Saint Ambrose had implied a thousand years before in his complaint against Emperor Theodosius) legitimate resistance to Jewish tyranny.[38]

The Sovereign's Dilemma: Protect or Persecute?

Over time, and at different paces in the varying regions of Europe, medieval princes responded to the pressure produced by these increasingly critical representations of their "special relationship" with Jews. They did so by moving toward the "persecutory" side of that relationship, invoking their privilege to punish rather than to protect the Jews, either by burdening them with ever-heavier discriminatory measures or by expelling them. Such movement should not necessarily be interpreted as a defeat for monarchy or a weakening of its powers. On the contrary, the persecution of Jews could play as important a part in the extension of royal power as did their protection.

Actions against Jews could strengthen the claims of princes in a number of ways. First, they could provide the cornerstone for the construction of a reputation as an "ideal" king. At this the French monarchy excelled. Beginning with King Philip Augustus, the Capetian monarchs attempted to make good the title of "most Christian majesty" by attacking the Jews. The most exemplary monarch in this regard was Saint Louis IX, who "so abominated the Jews, hateful to God and to man," that "he was unable to look at them." Saint Louis was quite explicit in invoking his special rights of persecution to rid his land of Jewish evil, if we are to believe William of Chartres's quotes in his "Life and Miracles of Saint Louis":

> *The matter of Christian usurers . . . seems to pertain to the . . . Church. The matter of the Jews, who are subjected to me by the yoke of servitude, pertains to me, lest they oppress Christians by their usury . . . under the shelter of my protection . . . and infect my land with poison. . . . I wish to do what pertains to me concerning the Jews. Let them abandon usury, or let them leave my lands completely, lest it be further defiled by their filth.*[39]

Throughout the Middle Ages, princes' oppression of their Jews led directly to their celebration. In 1182, when King Philip Augustus pronounced the first expulsion of the Jews from France, the monk Rigord called for panegyric: "Who alone accomplishes great miracles should be praised by the clergy and by the entire Christian populace." In 1491 Antoine Vérard turned to poetry to laud the last, Charles VIII's expulsion of the Jews of Provence: "That good king, second Vespasian, / so hated the Jews . . . , / that he is called the most Christian king, / Who expelled the Jews from his land."[40] It was to lay claim to this reservoir of royal virtue that persecutions might be undertaken in the wake of a reversal in the exercise of some other royal right. For example, it was after aristocratic reaction forced Philip the Fair to back down from his attempts to manipulate the coinage that he undertook the expulsion, not only of his Jews, but of those belonging to all other lords as well. In this case the expulsion of the Jews "allowed the king to reassert, in the immediate aftermath of his loss of dignity over the coinage reforms, the radical paramountcy of the crown."[41]

Expulsions could also be profitable. The property of expelled Jews belonged to the king, and its seizure might constitute a remarkable, albeit unrepeatable, windfall. The fifteen thousand marks Philip Augustus received from his "ransom" of his Jews in 1180, for example, "was equal to one and one-half times what Philip's government might expect in normal predictable revenue in an entire year."[42] Moreover expulsions could "launder" a negative financial right over Jews into a positive one over Christians. Charles of Anjou's expulsion of the Jews from Anjou and Maine in 1289 provides a good example. The Jews, according to Charles's edict, were enemies of all Christianity and committed any number of "crimes odious to God." He was expelling them to protect his Christian subjects, for he preferred "to provide for the peace of our subjects rather than to fill our coffers with the mammon of iniquity." He filled them instead with a perpetual capitation tax of six *deniers* and a hearth tax of three *sous*, granted by his subjects in exchange for the expulsion.[43] And when King Edward expelled the Jews from England, he received from his parliament in return the largest tax ever granted to a medieval English monarch.[44]

Given how useful expulsions of Jews proved to be, it is no surprise that so many princes eventually adopted them. Of course royal persecution was more difficult in those areas of Europe where non-Christians were more numerous, and where kings were more dependent on Jews for financial and administrative support. If King James the Conqueror of Aragon had heeded Pope Clement IV's exhortations to expel all Muslims from his realm, and to bar the Jews from office, punish them for blasphemy, and confiscate their Talmud, he would have crippled his monarchy.[45] (The fact that this same King James was the great patron of Ramon Martí, whose words about the princely love of Jews opened this chapter, reminds us that there was something of a pro forma flavor to these exhortations. Neither the preacher nor the prince was expected to take them too seriously.) Nor could Béla IV or László of Hungary have foregone the collaboration of Jews, Muslims, and Cumans, and still resisted the Mongol invasions (or at least so these monarchs argued to the pope).[46] In these religiously diverse kingdoms at the frontiers of Christendom, the protection of non-Christians seemed for a while a more solid foundation for monarchy than their persecution.

The decision on whether to protect or to persecute was to some extent a calculated one. In the midst of host desecration accusations against the Jews of Catalonia-Aragon in 1377, for example, King Peter the Ceremonious ordered the crown prince to restrain his zeal for prosecution. Such accusations were often false, he explained, and propagated by people who were not concerned with the health of the royal patrimony. The monarch's interests, he insisted, lay in protecting the Jewish community, not in persecuting it.[47] At much the same time in Castile, Henry of Trastámara, who had emerged victorious in his civil war partly by painting his foe as a lover of Jews, now found that as king he could not do without them, and refused the parliament's (Cortes) request to bar them from his service.[48]

But in the end, as we know, nearly all the western European monarchs followed the examples of their French and English colleagues.[49] In 1391 (as we will see in detail in the next chapter) a wave of massacres and mass conversions of Jews swept the lands we now call Spain. In their aftermath a few large cities (Barcelona, Valencia) obtained special royal permission to forbid Jewish habitation within their jurisdictions. Less than a century later the kings of Spain expelled all the Jews, first from the province of Andalucía, then in 1492 from their united realms of Castile and Aragon. (Portugal and Navarre shortly followed suit.) Within the fragmented politics of German-speaking lands expulsion took place at the level of more local jurisdictions. By one admittedly incomplete count, between 1388 (Strasbourg) and 1520 (Weissenbourg), roughly ninety major jurisdictions had expelled their Jews. By the end of the Middle Ages even privileges of settlement in the cities that still allowed Jews had in some sense become simultaneous orders of expulsion, stipulating their own expiration after a specified number of years.[50]

By 1500 the Jews had vanished from much of western Europe (the next chapter discusses a second wave of expulsions after 1530 in central Europe and Italy). This virtually complete victory of persecution over protection did not put an end to "Jewish politics," however, because that politics had never been entirely dependent on the presence of "real Jews." As we saw in the previous chapters, the potential to think of earthly powers as "Jewish" was encoded within foundational Christian texts, even if rarely expressed. This potential did not make inevitable the mutual embrace of Jews and princes in the young polities of

Europe. Rather, like some fairy godmother, it smiled on the romance and endowed it generously with meaning. But once married there was no divorce. In most of medieval Europe the close relationship between Jews and monarchs did not last more than a century and a half, but over the course of that time, negative manifestations of "earthly sovereignty" took on a fleshy Jewish figure that they would never later lose.

"Thy State of Law Is Bondslave to the Law"

Despite the vanishing importance of real Jews in royal government of the later Middle Ages, attacks on Jews and Judaism remained a powerful way of articulating complaints about the proper exercise of royal power. In 1321, for example, a number of French municipalities accused the Jews of plotting to poison the wells with leprosy in order to hand the kingdom over to the "Sultan of Babylon." The burghers who forged the evidence and orchestrated the violence were not worried about the financial power of what was by then a small, impoverished Jewish community, already twice expelled from France and on the brink of their final medieval exile. King Philip's proposed tax reforms were the political target of the rebellion, but because Christians had learned to think about the materiality of monarchy in Jewish terms, it was the Jews who burned.

In Spain, the "Jew" as a figure of political thought survived the mass conversions, expulsions, and exterminations of the later Middle Ages in a more complex way, by colonizing the flesh of Christians. In 1449, for example, the Jewish population of Spain was perhaps a quarter of what it had been the century before, and it was barred from any direct role in royal government. Nevertheless, when the city of Toledo rebelled that year against the administration of King Juan II and his "prime minister" Álvaro de Luna, it did so in familiar terms: killing Christian citizens descended from the many Jews who had converted over the past sixty years (for more on these conversions, see the next chapter), and passing a municipal ordinance barring any such people from ever holding public office. Some of these Christians worked for the Crown, and some may have favored the faith of their forefathers, but neither their monarchism nor their spiritual inheritance suffices to explain why and how they were worked over into the figure of the Jew.

The next chapter will focus on the why and how of this chemistry that turned Christians into Jews. Let us conclude this one with a quick preview, and look briefly at a treatise written by the ideologue among the rebels of Toledo, an obscure university graduate known as the "bachelor Marcos," to justify the killings, discriminations, and rebellion. The bachelor was writing under pressure: outside the gates were ranged the forces that would tomorrow capture the city. The entire resulting treatise is fascinating, but we do not need to read further than its first lines, with their tortured choice of address, in order to master the formula:

> *[I address this letter] to the very Holy Father . . . , and to the very high and powerful king or prince or administrator to whom, according to God, law, reason and right there belongs the administration and governance of the realms . . . , and to all other . . . administrators in the spiritual and temporal [affairs] of the universal orb, in the Church militant, which is the congregation and university of faithful Christians, [that is, those] truly believing in the birth, passion and resurrection [etc.] . . . , [but I do not address it to] the unbelieving and the doubtful in the faith, who are outside of us and in confederation with the synagogue, which is to say a congregation of beasts, for since such bind themselves like livestock to the letter, they have always given and still give false meaning to divine and human scripture. [In short, I address this letter to those] attesting to the truth and saying: "the letter kills, the spirit vivifies [2 Cor. 3:6]."*[51]

In the bachelor's desperate salvo we can easily recognize any number of distinctions borrowed from the political pyrotechnics of his age: distinctions between beast and human, material life and spiritual life, tyrant and legitimate magistrate, killing letter and vivifying spirit, all linked by the charge of "Judaism." The bachelor translates that accusation into a literacy test for sovereignty and citizenship. Those who read like Jews, literally after the flesh, deprive themselves of legitimate authority and exclude themselves from the human community, becoming beasts of the synagogue. Creatures of carnality, they have lost the human right to participate in the republic. Whatever power they wield is by definition tyrannical, not sovereign. The bachelor therefore refuses to address them.

Let me insist: the bachelor's beastly governors, the targets of his accusations of Judaism, were not "real" Jews. They were the "prime minister" Álvaro de Luna, King Juan II who supported him, and (as Marcos makes clear) even the pope, if his holiness should reject the bachelor's appeal and rule in favor of the king. "Jew" here encoded a particular position toward word and world, not a professed adherent to Judaism. It could not be otherwise, if the "Jewishness" of rulers was to be useful as a legitimation of rebellion in an ostensibly Christian world. And such legitimation was very much on the bachelor's mind. In fact his treatise concludes: if no Christian prince can be found who reads like a Christian, then the city should place itself directly under the government of the Holy Spirit.

There is very little that is new in the bachelor's basic contention that Christian sovereignty and freedom require the subjection of flesh and letter by spirit, and that the reverse produced, not sovereignty, but tyrannical materialism. The key distinction had been drawn long ago by Aristotle, whose ideas were being consumed with heightened relish by late medieval intellectuals with new access to the Greek texts. "Men form states to secure a bare subsistence; but the ultimate object of the state is the good life." For Aristotle, the chief function of the sovereign was to guide politics away from the demands of the body toward those of the immortal soul. As he put it in the *Nicomachean Ethics*, "[W]e must not follow those who advise us, being men, to think of human things, and being mortal, of mortal things, but must, so far as we can, make ourselves immortal" (1177b). The philosopher had even framed the relationship of sovereign to subject in terms of the analogy between soul and body. "[A]lthough in bad or corrupted natures the body will often appear to rule over the soul, because they are in an evil and unnatural condition. . . . It is clear that the rule of the soul over the body . . . is natural and expedient" (*Politics* 1254b). He realized that many rulers did indeed reverse these priorities, placing worldly gain ahead of a common and immaterial good, and he represented this reversal not as sovereignty but as its most basic perversion, tyranny.[52]

Of course Aristotle had never associated this perversion with Judaism. That was the work, as shown in chapters 2 and 3, of long Christian centuries of interplay between theology, politics, and Jews, both real and imagined. Already for the church fathers, that interplay had made Judaism a critical term in their negotiations between the vital poles of politics: between political existence for the sake of material life or for the sake of a higher good; between tyrant and sovereign; between political subjection and political subject; between legalism and the rule of law. Here, too, there was little original about the bachelor's understanding of political materialism as "Jewish," and of the spirit's struggle for sovereignty as a struggle against the "Jews." What was new about the bachelor's arguments, what was new more generally about the Judaizing creativity of mid-fifteenth-century Spanish politics, was its context. As we will see, mass conversion had shrunk the distance between Judaism and Christianity, and the mass assimilation of those converts had created, probably for the first (but not for the last) time in the history of Catholic Europe, the possibility for extensive doubts about who really was or was not a Jew.

The royalists soon retook Toledo, and the bachelor was hanged in the public square. His treatise became a founding document of the Castilian ideology of "purity of blood," hence of importance to anyone interested in the history of racial ideologies. But it is as an example of a particular political logic that he claims our time here. Christian sovereignty and freedom, as the bachelor expounded them, required the "spirit" to achieve the political subjection of flesh and the hermeneutic subjection of letter. The reverse produced, not sovereignty, but tyrannical materialism. Within the bachelor's political theology this materialism was best understood as "Jewish," and the struggle for Christian sovereignty could best be represented as a struggle against the "Jews."

It is worth insisting that this critical language did not require any living Jews, or even Christian descendants of converts from Judaism, to do its work. Nor was it peculiarly "Spanish," though its Spanish version was, as we will see, peculiar. Tyranny, private interest, love of the material, in short, a misplaced interest in the "flesh" rather than the "spirit," these had all become "Jewish" traits in Christian political thought, traits that themselves produced the "Judaism" of those represented as having them, regardless of the faith of the accused. A medieval Englishman like John of Gaunt would have understood this, although unlike the bachelor Marcos, he lived in a land without any real Jews. So would Shakespeare, who also lived in a land without Jews and who penned for John, some two centuries after his death, his immortal dying words in *Richard II.* Those words, spoken in defiance of a deviant sovereign, are perhaps the most famous justification of rebellion in English letters:

> *Methinks I am a prophet new inspired*
> *And thus expiring do foretell of him:*
> *His rash fierce blaze of riot cannot last,*
> *For violent fires soon burn out themselves;*
> *Small showers last long, but sudden storms are short;*
> *He tires betimes that spurs too fast betimes;*
> *With eager feeding food doth choke the feeder:*
> *Light vanity, insatiate cormorant,*
> *Consuming means, soon preys upon itself.*
> *This royal throne of kings, this scepter'd isle,*
> *This earth of majesty, this seat of Mars,*
> *This other Eden, demi-paradise,*
> *This fortress built by Nature for herself*
> *Against infection and the hand of war,*
> *This happy breed of men, this little world,*
> *This precious stone set in the silver sea,*
> *Which serves it in the office of a wall,*
> *Or as a moat defensive to a house,*
> *Against the envy of less happier lands,*
> *This blessed plot, this earth, this realm, this England,*
> *This nurse, this teeming womb of royal kings,*
> *Fear'd by their breed and famous by their birth,*
> *Renowned for their deeds as far from home,*

For Christian service and true chivalry,
As is the sepulchre in stubborn Jewry,
Of the world's ransom, blessed Mary's Son,
This land of such dear souls, this dear dear land,
Dear for her reputation through the world,
Is now leased out, I die pronouncing it,
Like to a tenement or pelting farm:
England, bound in with the triumphant sea
Whose rocky shore beats back the envious siege
Of watery Neptune, is now bound in with shame,
With inky blots and rotten parchment bonds:
That England, that was wont to conquer others,
Hath made a shameful conquest of itself.

For T. S. Eliot, these words were a paean to patriotism. For us they are something else: a powerfully Judaizing political critique. John's "prophecy" hurtles from demi-paradise, through stubborn Jewry, to a servile land bound in with parchment bonds.[53] Conquered by inkblots on paper, Shakespeare's Englishmen have become slaves to letter, shameful Jews. But the prophet does not stop here. Enter King Richard II, and John speaks, like Ambrose a millennium before but pregnant with different meaning, a certain kind of truth to majesty:

Why, cousin, wert thou regent of the world,
It were a shame to let this land by lease;
But for thy world enjoying but this land,
Is it not more than shame to shame it so?
Landlord of England art thou now, not king:
Thy state of law is bondslave to the law; And thou—

A lesser dramatist might have furnished the speech with a blunt conclusion: "art from a sovereign turned to tyrant Jew." Shakespeare leaves us hanging. But he has more to say on the subject, and so will we, in chapter 8.

Chapter 6

THE EXTINCTION OF SPAIN'S
JEWS AND THE BIRTH
OF ITS INQUISITION

*The Christian who is neighbor with a Jew will
never be a good Christian.*

—SAINT VINCENT FERRER, CA. 1400

No one quite knows when Europe ceased being medieval, but everyone is sure that it did. In late-fourteenth- and fifteenth-century Italy, we are taught in school, "humanist" scholars began to develop new practices of reading and writing oriented toward the recuperation of the wisdom of Greek and Latin antiquity. In the sixteenth century, the application of their methods to the textual foundations of Catholicism by Protestant theologians like Martin Luther and John Calvin challenged the monopoly of the Roman Catholic Church. That challenge began the debates about God's governance of the world that we call the "Reformation" and the "Counter-Reformation," debates whose

217

sharper edge was felt in the "wars of religion" that consumed Europe for the next two centuries. Simultaneously, the rise of a new empire in the east (the Ottomans), the conquest of a new world in the west (Atlantic Africa and the Americas), and the development of new attitudes toward trade within the reaches of this vast compass all contributed to the creation of novel economic, commercial, and hence political orders for which we have no single name ("capitalism," for example, being too large, and "mercantilism" too small).

All of these transformations and many more we subsume under the term *Renaissance*. This term, which few historians today would use without some sense of irony, implies the rebirth of classical civilization out of the ashes of the Middle Ages. This is not the place to argue about the accuracy of the claim. It is true, as medievalists often complain, that the Renaissance inherited from the Middle Ages a great deal of both what it claimed to have discovered and what it claimed to have left behind. But from the point of view of our project, the period from 1400 to 1600 in European history was significantly different from what came before. It was in its Renaissance that western Europe achieved what the Middle Ages had at most dreamed of: a world free of Jews. It is in the same period that this dream of freedom turned into a nightmare, and Christian Europe awoke haunted by the conviction that it was becoming Jewish. The seeming contradiction within this coincidence is striking and worth investigating. Why is it that the fear of Judaizing reached a new peak in western Europe at precisely the moment when Jews had virtually disappeared from it? We will ask this question over and over again in the chapters that follow, on Luther's Reformation and Shakespeare's stage. But there is no more dramatic place to start than with the revolution that, in the previous chapter, we saw taking place in the medieval lands we nowadays call Spain.[1]

"So That No Jew Remain in the World Henceforth"

No one, in the days before Holy Week of 1391, would have thought of the Iberian Peninsula as a land without Jews. Heirs to centuries of Islamic rule, the kingdoms of Castile and Aragon (not to mention Navarre and Portugal) housed much larger populations of non-Christians than any other region in western Europe. Even the most optimistic members of the small band that set out on the fifteenth of March to attack the Jewish quarter of Seville cannot have expected to change that, or been too surprised when their attempt was frustrated by the royal officials who customarily guarded the Jews at this volatile time of year, when ritualized attacks on Jewish neighborhoods were common (see previous chapter).[2] Nevertheless the preaching of Archdeacon Ferrant Martínez urged persistence, and on June 6 they tried again. This time the Jewish quarter was overrun, and many of its inhabitants killed or forcibly converted. Quick as rumor, the violence spread: by the end of August it had reached more than seventy other towns and cities of the peninsula.

One survivor, Reuven, son of Rabbi Nissim of Gerona, described the events of that summer in words he penned in the margins of his father's Torah scroll, which he rescued from the wreckage:

> *Wail, holy and glorious Torah, and put on black raiment, for the expounders of your lucid words perished in the flames. For three months the conflagration spread through the holy congregations of the exile of Israel in Sepharad. The fate [of Sodom and Gomorrah] overtook the holy communities of Castile, Toledo, Seville, Mallorca, Cordoba, Valencia, Barcelona, Tàrrega, and Girona, and sixty neighboring cities and villages. . . . The sword, slaughter, destruction, forced conversions, captivity, and spoliation were the order of the day. Many were sold as slaves to the Ishmaelites [Muslims]; 140,000 were unable to resist those who so barbarously forced them and gave themselves up to impurity [i.e., converted].*

Reuven's figure for converts is staggering, amounting to nearly half of the entire Jewish population we might reasonably estimate at this time for the Crowns of Castile and Aragon combined. Like him, other contemporary observers stressed the high number of converts and the disappearance of Jews from many towns and cities. The prominent Jewish courtier Hasdai Crescas wrote that no Jews remained in the Kingdom of Valencia except in the town of Murviedro. Describing the large Jewish population of Gerona, the royal chancery simply stated that the majority converted while others were put to the sword. The nobleman and chronicler Pedro López de Ayala used very similar words to describe the fate of Seville's community.[3]

Neither Reuven, nor Hasdai, nor any other contemporary gives estimates for the number of slain. Seldom do we find documents describing the massacres themselves, and even then the information is often incidental. We know how officials in Barcelona dealt with the dead only because years later the new owner of a house in the former Jewish quarter asked for permission to remove the many corpses filling the neighborhood water well.[4] Not until centuries after the events did Hebrew chroniclers begin assigning numbers to the fallen (in the case of Joseph Ha-Cohen, 150,000). Modern historians, always suspicious of premodern statistics, are right to point out that these numbers of killed and converted are implausible, and to replace them with more modest but equally conjectural estimates. However much we might reduce their toll, we should not doubt that these killings and conversions not only meant to transform the religious demography of the Iberian Peninsula, but actually succeeded.[5]

There is plenty of evidence that many of the actors in 1391 were pursuing a vision of a Christian society freed from its Jews: the cries of "let the Jews convert or die" with which the mobs assaulted Jewish quarters, and the prolonged sieges (sometimes months long) of fortifications in which Jews had successfully found refuge suggest that the passion of the attackers was oriented by visions of a world rid of Jews. Moreover, in the weeks following the massacres the municipal leaders of cities like Valencia and Barcelona undertook ongoing campaigns of conversion and expulsion. In Barcelona, for example, the governing council decreed shortly after the riots that any Christians who were hiding or sheltering Jewish survivors had to surrender them. As the council decreed a few days later, these survivors were to be housed with clerics so that they might better be instructed in the Catholic faith. Any surviving Jew who refused to convert after instruction was to be expelled from the city. In other words, whatever their causes (which were undoubtedly many and varied) the massacres and mass conversions of 1391 expressed the view of both citizens and civic leaders that separation from Judaism, and even its elimination, were structurally necessary for the improvement of the Christian community.[6]

These efforts at perfection did not end with that year. In the years immediately following 1391 the king pursued a policy of resettling Jews in cities from which they had disappeared. The governments of these cities just as actively pursued a policy of resistance to any restoration of Jewish settlement and utilized a variety of financial inducements, as well as arguments ranging from theology to public safety, to obtain from their rulers the perpetual ban on Jewish residence within their limits. Valencia, for example, received a privilege from King Martin in 1397. Barcelona struggled longer to achieve its goal. Martin granted the city a ban on Jews in 1401, but limited its duration to eight years. That year the outgoing city councilors reminded their successors to maintain pressure to make the ban permanent, since Jewish presence leads to scandal and riot, but it was not until 1430 or so that the city obtained the permanent privilege of keeping all Jews from settling within its jurisdiction.[7]

Preachers, too, moved to extend the implications of this apocalyptic moment. Shortly after the riots, Antoni Rieri of Lerida was accused, among other things, of preaching that the prophesied time had arrived "in which all Jews must die, so that no Jew remain in the world henceforth." Antoni was charged with heresy, but his eschatology was unexceptionable. Apocalyptic readings of the epistle to the Romans had long suggested that at the end of time a righteous remnant of the Jews would convert to Christianity. The remainder would be killed while fighting as soldiers for the Antichrist. Antoni's error consisted only in believing that the first half of this prophecy had been fulfilled by the events of 1391. But some of his coreligionists continued to organize attacks on the Jews of Lerida as late as 1400: "It has reached our ears," writes the king, "that some sons of iniquity, desiring the destruction of the Jewish quarter of that city, which we have newly made and commanded to be established, have several times attempted, so it is said, the aforesaid destruction." Perhaps Antoni's "heretical" views were widely shared?[8]

Without multiplying examples: the massacres and mass conversions of 1391 raised in the Iberian Christian imagination, perhaps for the first time since the Visigoths in the seventh century, the possibility of a world without Jews. With many of the largest cities of Castile, Catalonia, Valencia, and Mallorca now free, that world seemed on the cusp of becoming reality. These were exhilarating times for a Christian society trained to hear the hoof beats of apocalypse in the retreating footsteps of the Jews. But they were also highly unsettling to a society used to thinking about Christianity in terms of its difference from Judaism. How would Christianity define itself if the living exemplars of that difference vanished?[9]

The Vanishing Difference between Christian and Jew

One symptom of the anxiety provoked by this question is the letter that King Joan I of Aragon wrote to the officials of his most important cities in 1393. He informed them that it had become impossible for "natural Christians"—that is, not the converts—to tell who was a convert to Christianity and who was still a Jew. To help reestablish the difference, converts were henceforth forbidden to live, dine, or "have conversation with" Jews. The Jews were to be made to wear more conspicuous badges and Jewish hats, so "that they appear to be Jews." Failure to make the difference clearer would put the most basic boundaries of Christianity at risk. The letter concluded with worry about one of the most important of these boundaries: "[W]e order and desire that if any of these said Jews are found with a Christian woman in a suspicious place, in order to have carnal copulation with her, let them both be burned without mercy."[10]

In other words, as soon as the Jews began to disappear, contemporaries began to worry that it was becoming impossible to separate them from Christians. To cope with these worries King Joan advocated a strategy that we today would call segregation: mark the remaining

Jews more visibly and increase the social distance between them and the Christians. Perhaps because this strategy was not applied very systematically, it seems to have provided some twenty years of stability, without major outbreaks of Christian concern about the identifiability of either Jews or converts. That stability ended in 1411, when Saint Vincent Ferrer, a man widely considered the holiest of his age, pushed the logic of segregation to its limits.

Saint Vincent's worries were expressed in familiar terms. He believed that "[T]he Christian who is neighbor with a Jew will never be a good Christian," and he was convinced that the two religious groups had become too neighborly. According to him, Jews (and Muslims) were living among Christians, dressing like Christians, adopting Christian names, so that "by their appearance they are taken and reputed by many to be Christians." He even preached that as a result of this confusion, "many Christian men believe their wife's children to be their own, when they are actually by Muslim and Jewish [fathers]."[11]

Saint Vincent, like King Joan, sought to reinstate the necessary distance between Christian and Jew, but he had an additional goal as well: eliminating the Jewish antithesis to Christianity altogether. He did not advocate the killing of the Jews, as the "heretic" Antoni had done. Rather, from 1411 to 1416, the saint mounted a messianic program to achieve either their conversion or their complete isolation. On the one hand, he preached the prohibition of any intercourse across religious boundaries:

> *Jews and Muslims should be separate, not among Christians. Do not tolerate infidel doctors, do not buy victuals from them, let them be walled up and enclosed, for we have no greater enemies. Christian women may not be their wet nurses, nor should [you] eat with them. If they send you bread, throw it to the dogs. . . . for Holy Scripture says of these sins: "Do you not know that a little leaven corrupts the entire dough?" (1 Cor. 5)*[12]

To implement that separation from the Jews (Muslims were sometimes included in the rhetoric of the sermons and edicts, but almost never in their implementation) Vincent encouraged and coordinated the efforts of the pope, the kings of Castile and of Aragon, and innumerable local officials in one of the most thorough attempts at segregation before the modern era. Jews were to be moved to totally separate neighborhoods. Even commercial contact between Jew and Christian was severely restricted since the ideal was to prohibit all exchange. In some towns Christians refused to sell Jews food. Entire communities found themselves evicted, "with boys and girls dying from exposure to the cold and the snow." Writing some years after these events, one Jewish chronicler called them "the greatest persecution that had ever occurred."[13]

Simultaneous with this segregation, Vincent and his patrons mounted a massive program of evangelization. Rabbis from all the communities of the Crown of Aragon were summoned before the pope and his cardinals in the city of Tortosa, where they were required to remain for a lengthy disputation, the largest ever staged in the Middle Ages, intended to convince them once and for all of the falsity of their faith. Their communities were meanwhile compelled to attend sermons aimed at their conversions. We know from the rich archives of the Crown of Aragon that in those lands, at least, the king made extraordinary efforts to pressure the members of leading Jewish families to convert, efforts that ranged from promises of monetary reward to the imprisonment of recalcitrant relatives. The fully intended consequence of all these segregatory and evangelizing efforts was the mass conversion of tens of thousands of Jews to Christianity. As in 1391, entire populations converted in many towns, some of which (like Alcañiz) promptly obtained from the king perpetual bans on Jewish residence in order to make permanent their spiritual gains.[14]

Given the Christian triumph at the disputation of Tortosa, the increasingly effective segregation of the Jews, and the streams of neophytes in angelic garb emerging from baptismal fonts, contemporaries may be forgiven for thinking once again that they were witnessing the end of a living Jewish presence within the Christian community. But Saint Vincent's project was abandoned before it was completed. King Ferran I, Vincent's patron in Catalonia-Aragon, died in 1416. Castile and Aragon withdrew their obedience from his papal sponsor, Benedict XIII, who was deposed and declared "anti-pope" by the Council of Constance in 1417. The Jews remained, albeit much diminished, in the peninsula, and Vincent left to die out of favor in Brittany.

Saint Vincent's actions, combined with those of the earlier rioters, reduced the population of Jews living in the lands we now call Spain to a fraction (somewhere between one-fourth and one-half) of what they had been before 1391. But in many ways his activities heightened the anxieties of neighborliness that had motivated them in the first place. As in 1391, the appearance of tens of thousands of new converts seemed suddenly to diminish the distance between Christian and Jew, not increase it. On the one hand, the converts enjoyed all the privileges of a Christian. As the convert Francesch de San Jordi (known as Astruch Rimoch before his conversion) put it a bit hyperbolically in a letter to the unconverted Jew Shaltiel Bonafos,

> *Those who have emerged from the waters of baptism, from the foun-*
> *tains of salvation, are firmly established upon golden pedestals. They*
> *are all personages. In their courts and in their palaces there are ivories*
> *and monkeys and peacocks and dwarves; they divested themselves of*
> *their soiled attire . . . and donned the garments of salvation.*[15]

Of course we know that the vast majority of those who converted remained poor, without peacock or dwarf, but even the lowliest convert could now perform his Christianity by throwing rocks at Jews during Holy Week, having sex with Christian women, or working in a trade forbidden to Jews, and we know that many of them did.

Yet at the same time that converts enjoyed the privileges of the Christians, many remained close to their former coreligionists. They were, in fact, often "neighbors," since converts in many cities continued to occupy, as they had before their conversion, houses in or near the Jewish quarter. In the immediate aftermath of the 1391 riots in Mallorca, city officials asked converts whether they wished to remain in their old homes or move out into traditionally Christian neighborhoods. Most preferred to stay put, although the city soon received a letter from the king insisting that any proximity or "conversation" between converts and Jews "could not be without great peril." Even in Barcelona, where very few Jews remained unconverted in 1391, municipal officials worried about establishing sufficient distance and ordered converts to brick up any windows or doors that opened onto the houses of Jews.[16]

Proximities of residence were not the only ones to endure. Family ties, too, extended over the previously un-spanned abyss of kinship between religious communities. Perhaps the most unusual of these ties was that of marriage. During the 1391 massacres in Girona, a husband who had just converted sent messengers to the tower where his Jewish wife was still being besieged by the mob, asking her to return to him under the condition that she not interfere with his observing the Christian faith. She refused. Conversely, when Samuel Baruch's wife Aldonça converted to Christianity in 1391, her father, also a convert, publicly presented his son-in-law with two possibilities: convert to Christianity and continue the marriage, or remain a Jew but still keep her as his wife without prejudicing her Christian faith.[17] These ad hoc arrangements became formal choices during the second wave of conversions, when in 1415 Pope Benedict ruled that mixed couples could continue living together for a year from the date of conversion, so that the Christian spouse might convince the unconverted partner. But in 1417 the city of Gerona complained that within its jurisdiction, at least, the period of grace was being exceeded, and asked that "the Jewish wives of the new Christians be separated from their husbands, since they don't want to be converted and have had a long time for deliberation." The city also insisted that the new Christians should be forced to baptize any minor children in their power who remained Jews.[18]

Such "mixed marriages" were temporary and probably rare, but as the city of Gerona's complaint suggests, the problem of mixed families extended far beyond spouses. In 1393 King Juan had expressed shocked surprise that many converts in the Kingdom of Valencia "have in their homes and habitations wives, children, nephews, cousins, brothers, parents and others who are still Jews, and even infants, that is, children under seven years of age." It was this last group that particularly offended the king, who decreed that the children be baptized or removed from the Christian homes. A little later, he also decreed that converted children should be taken from the homes of their Jewish parents.[19]

In these cases the king tried to weaken family ties across confessional boundaries. Often, however, royal action reinforced them. Before 1391, for example, kings insisted that converts could not inherit from Jews. This baptismal disinheritance was meant primarily to protect the king's claims over the property of his Jews, but it also had the effect of severing many legal connections between converts and their Jewish relatives. After the mass conversions, on the other hand, kings forcefully maintained the rights of converts to inherit from Jewish kin, making the separation much less radical. Conversely, they also recognized the ongoing claims of Jewish kin on their converted brethren. Sometimes these claims could even be religious, as when King Joan compelled the new Christian Manuel Salvador (formerly the Jew Mahir Suxen) to perform the Jewish *halitza* ceremony for his widowed sister-in-law Haluha, who was unconverted and wished to marry again. Much more often they were financial. The debts, taxes, and business affairs of Jews and converts remained entangled for a generation after 1391, and those entanglements were re-created for yet another generation by the mass conversions of 1411–1416.[20]

The point, in short, is that the flood of baptism that swept over Spain in the decades around 1400 filled much of the available space between Judaism and Christianity with converts. The retreat of those apocalyptic waters uncovered a much-altered social and religious landscape. Saint Vincent's own efforts had themselves been inspired by the first wave of these alterations and the disorientations they produced. But insofar as his great victories ushered a new mass of converts into the no-man's land between Judaism and Christianity, they only increased the anxieties that they were meant to contain. In the sense that neither hyper-segregating the Jews nor converting them had solved the problem of proximity, Vincent's messianic mission was a failure. After that failure, the post-conversion generations took a very different tack. Instead of attempting yet again to contain the danger of Judaism among the Jews, they put that danger to work among themselves, threatening each other, both old Christian and new, with the fear of becoming "Jew."[21]

"Many Frequently Judaize"

Since the relapse of converts to their former religion was punishable as a crime, new Christians were obviously vulnerable to charges of Judaizing. Toward the end of the fifteenth century this vulnerability would find a famous institutional home in the Spanish Inquisition. The situation at the century's beginning, however, was very different. With tens of thousands of uninstructed converts stumbling toward Christian worship, there must have been opportunity for a litany of accusations about their Jewish errors and habits. In 1400, for example, King Martin complained that converts "frequently judaize" by celebrating Jewish holidays, and called on inquisitors to help him in "extirpating these errors." Accusations of wrongdoing were useful weapons in the countless conflicts of daily life, and we know that people often reached for them. But what is most striking about these concerns is how rarely they were voiced officially, and how moderately they were acted on. In the case of convert Judaizing, the chorus remained largely silent for some fifty years.[22]

Before the middle of the fifteenth century, the voices we hear invoking convert Jewishness are scattered, improvisational, and of little resonance. The 1407 trial of Peter Ganyiver, a tailor from Lerida, provides a good example. In November of that year he was summoned, bearing lance, sword, and shield, to serve in the local militia. Before his conversion from Judaism, Peter would not have been called to militia service. Once a Christian he was entitled, indeed obligated, to the honor, but his Jewish past marched with him. After his unit had left its bivouac in the village of Miralcamp, rumor began to spread that he had broken into the village church, smashed the chest containing the Eucharistic wafers, ripped down the crucifix, and thrown it in a bonfire.

We know from the transcript of the trial, held at Lerida after the militia's return, that Peter's accusers drew on negative feelings about converts as a class. "Oh, these converts do so much harm," the rumor's chief monger is reported to have said. We suspect as well that they were motivated by more personal vendettas, since Peter's family had persistent enemies. (His sister Franchesca had been acquitted of poisoning charges exactly a year before.) But the weapons available to those enemies, the tools with which they could exploit Peter's "Jewishness" and put it to work, were not yet standardized. Hence they pursued Peter, not with charges of Judaizing, but with denunciations of host desecration and blasphemy drawn (like the charge of poisoning against his sister) from old stock long deployed against the Jews. Peter's accusers were inventive, but unsuccessful. The native of Miralcamp that they had named as eyewitness to the desecration denied any knowledge of the affair, and Peter was acquitted.[23]

The half century after 1391 was marked by this type of creativity, as contemporaries experienced the frictions caused by the new proximity of Jewishness and Christianity, and experimented with ways of harnessing the energies those frictions released. Some of these experiments took aim at converts like Peter or their descendants. Others threatened "old Christians," "natural Christians," with new force. This should not be surprising: in the tradition of Saint Paul, Judaizing had always been a Christian vice, not a Jewish one. It had also always been understood as a linguistic error, a basic miscomprehension of how words work to relate humans to each other, their God, and their world. We should therefore expect the Judaizing experiments of Spain's fifteenth century to address the most basic questions about language and communication in Christian communities.

Putting Judaizing to Work: Poets "Stuffed Full of Jewish Sperm"

Not everyone is equally interested in thinking about how language works. Poets are among those with the most obvious stake, and their Judaizing experiments were among the most precocious. (In chapter 8

we will turn to the similar experiments of a later, and English, poet.)
A precious example is the first known "critical anthology" of Castilian poetry, the songbook, or *Cancionero*, compiled by Juan Alfonso de
Baena. The anthology contains some six hundred poems composed in
the courts of four Castilian kings, ranging from shortly before 1391 to
shortly after 1430, when Baena presented the work to King Juan II. The
anthology is critical in the sense that each poem is preceded by a short
editorial introduction noting merits and demerits, and the whole is pref-
aced with a meditation on the function of poetry and the nature of the
poet's art.[24]

The *Cancionero*'s poets, nearly all Christian, are constantly defaming
one another, and the accusation of Jewishness is prominent among the
charges they hurl. They accuse each other of Jewish ancestry, of having
too small a foreskin or too big a nose, of heterosexual and homosexual
intercourse with Jews. Indeed the collection includes many poems that
insult the editor himself. Some poets refer to his "bath in the water of
holy baptism," or to his sexual encounters with Jews, both male and
female (the Mariscal Íñigo de Astuñiga, for example, claims that the
editor is stuffed full of Jewish sperm). Poems impugn his birthplace of
Baena as a land where "much good eggplant" is grown, mock him for
having "eyes of eggplant," and even threaten to put him to flight with a
"barrage of eggplants."[25]

Each of these defamations deserves a history of its own. The attention to eggplant, for example, derives from the popular association of
this vegetable with Muslims (who introduced it into Spain) and Jews
(who were reputed to be especially fond of it). Some seventeenth-
century satirical texts suggest that individuals convicted of heresy or
witchcraft by the Inquisition might be pelted with eggplant as they did
their public penance. Sancho Panza, on the other hand, changes the last
name of the Muslim Cidi Hamete Benegali to Berengena, "Eggplant,"
because "the Moors," so he says, "are very fond of aubergine." But
none of these defamations was tied strictly to a "real" religion or a lineage. On the contrary, their "Islamizing," "Sodomizing," or "Judaizing"
charge could be widely deployed. The royal chronicler Alonso de Palen-

cia, for example, tells of a dispute between Burgos and Toledo in 1480, over which city should have the right to call itself "first city" of Spain. The procurators for Burgos won the field, in part by calling the citizens of Toledo "Berenjeneros" (eggplant eaters)—a successful strategy that gained its power, not from the religion of its targets, but from the power of the insult to summon specters of Judaism.[26]

And yet, historians and critics have often deduced from such accusations that if a poet is attacked as Judaizing, he must be a *converso*. And if the attacker himself betrays knowledge of Judaism (for example, by drawing on Hebrew vocabulary, such as *meshumad* for apostate) then he too may be presumed to have a Jewish past. The result of such logic is the conviction that, as one critic put it already in 1871, the *Cancionero* is full of "half-converted Jews." Yet in many cases where we have been able to find further, nonpoetic evidence about the poets of this *Cancionero*, they turn out not to be descended from Jews at all. How then can we make sense of the fact that in poetry they are so often insulted as converts?[27]

Like so much "Judaism" in this book, the Judaism of our Christian poets has much to do with the history of Christian thought. In this particular case, their insults are part of a strategic deployment of Judaism developed to defend Christian poetry from its critics. Following Plato, theologians from Augustine to Thomas Aquinas had attacked poetry as the use of language that came closest to reproducing through imitation the materiality of nature (mimesis). Poetry was, according to these theologians, the genre most tightly bound to literalism and to flesh, the most dangerously seductive. Poetic fictions, as Saint Thomas Aquinas put it, contain no divine truth. They "have no purpose except to signify; and such signification does not go beyond the literal sense." Saints issued similar warnings in the Spain of Juan Alfonso de Baena and his colleagues: both Vincent Ferrer and Alonso de Cartagena (the convert from Judaism who was bishop of Burgos) preached about the dangers of poetry.[28]

Of course poetic fictions also had their defenders of the day, most famously Dante, Petrarch, and Boccaccio. Like these Italian notables,

Baena and his colleagues were seeking to justify and enlarge the place of poetry within Christianity. They did so through a theory of "poetic grace" much like that of Dante, a theory that is articulated in Baena's prologue to the *Cancionero* as well as in its poetry. Two lines of Latin verse scrawled at the top of the first manuscript folio capture the general theme: "To each one grace is given / according to Saint Paul" (a paraphrase of Eph. 4:7). The proper use of poetic language was, our poets claimed, the product of divine grace and inspiration, and through this inspiration the lay poet, if he was a *good* poet, gained access to spiritual truth.[29]

In this debate over the status of poetry, the negative foil of "Judaism" was deployed by all sides. It could, for example, buttress claims that the "infused grace of God" offered poetry access to divine truths that escaped the sophisticated training of the theologian. The poet Ferrán Manuel de Lando tried this approach when he reminded Friar Lope del Monte that "God chose to reveal his secrets / to simple folk, humble, heavy, and rude, / while he left the learned nude, and hid from them his glory, / as Our Savior makes clear / in the subtle texts of His Gospel story." These verses contain an implicit accusation of "Judaism," insofar as they align the theologian with the seemingly learned but actually blind Pharisees in the gospels. Friar Lope's position in this debate, on the other hand, reiterates the traditional condemnation of poetry as "literal fictions" without hints of the divine. The poet, he says, belongs with those who have "never achieved knowledge of divine deeds: . . . the gentile, the Jew, and the tax collector." In his final riposte, Friar Lope turns Lando's implicit "pharisaization" of theologians (that is, his accusation that those who seem clothed in learning are in reality naked and blind) on its head. "God makes bears with furry skins, and makes the ignorant wise. / But few are the wise and truly learned, who have hairy chests and thighs." Whatever the limits to our knowledge in this world, Lope implies, one thing is clear: in theological matters his rival Lando, a mere lay poet, ranks with Jews and beasts.[30]

Perhaps the most important help that Judaism gave these poets, however, was in the development of their own practice of poetic criticism: that is, in deciding who really was a *good* poet and therefore not a "Jewish" one. Then, as now, poets liked to complain that bad poetry was often mistaken for good, and good poetry maligned as bad. In his own version of this plaint, Alfonso Álvarez de Villasandino, the most influential of the *Cancionero* poets, characterized what he called "meter scribblers" ("metrificadores") as tax collectors ("arrendadores"), and mockingly described the king rewarding them with "robes with badges" ("ropas con señales") like those the Jews wear. But of course Villasandino, Baena, and their colleagues were not willing to surrender poetry to these false "Jewish" poets. Instead they developed a critical framework within which to distinguish between good poems and bad.[31]

That framework is articulated in the prologue to Baena's *Cancionero*, which can fairly be called the earliest surviving poetic manifesto in the Castilian language. I already mentioned the first prerequisite for good verse articulated in that prologue: Paul's "infused grace of God." There were a number of others: 2) knowledge of rules of meter and form, 3) subtle inventiveness, 4) exquisite discretion and judgment, 5) broad reading, 6) knowledge of all languages, 7) familiarity with court life, 8) nobility and courtesy, and 9) always seeming to be a good lover, loving whom one should, as one should, where one should. The degree to which poets possessed these qualities could be diagnosed directly from their poetry. Insofar as Baena's colleagues understood the poet's state of grace as legible in the poetry itself, the poem became a literary marker of its author's place (at the moment of composition) on the continuum between letter and spirit, with the bad poet, the mis-user of language, understood as (among other things) a graceless "Jew."

Baena presents the pages of his *Cancionero* as the lists in which the mettle of each poet and each poem are put to the test of this complex standard. The martial metaphor is especially appropriate, because although the poems reach us preserved on paper, the poetic honor of Baena's authors was gained in competitive performance before a live audience. Baena himself put this wittily in his poetic challenge to the poet Ferrán Manuel de Lando: "Ferrand Manuel, for the public display / of your marvelous skill / in this great court of the King of Castile /

Someone must give you a sting." It is out of provocation, according to Baena, that good poetry is born. But the substance of the provocation itself should not be taken to heart: "Ferrand Manuel, since to each / is given [poetic] grace doubled or simple, / don't let your face turn yellow / because my tongue splashes or stains you." Insult is only a picador's prod, meant to stimulate the revelation of a poet's virtues. Its "truth claims" are not to be taken seriously but are merely a stimulus to poetry. Hence, Baena tells Ferrán Manuel in another poem, he is sending him "a dozen mule turds" in verse.[32]

The competition between the editor Baena and the most famous poet in his anthology, Alfonso Álvarez de Villasandino, is a good example of this type of poetic jousting. Baena begins by challenging this "rotten old man, whose ribs are made of phlegm" to a contest of poetry. Villasandino responds in kind:

> Sir, this vile ass with a branded face
> Twisted and stuffed with wine and garlic
> I consider on account of his foolish frenzy
> And crazed works a fine troubadour. This swells the head
>   of the dirty Jew-pig,

and he presumes to pick a fight with his betters. Whoever heeds the words of this grackle

> Must himself be blacker than a sea-faring crow.
> He who is unworthy and incapable
> Of this knowledge and art that we pursue,
> His arguments are not worth a straw
> Nor a lousy cucumber, not even a gherkin.

Baena is a "suzio cohino," a dirty Jew pig (the word plays with the proximity in Castilian between Cohen and *cochino*), with the voice of a cormorant, not a poet. He knows nothing of "this science [of poetry]," and his words are worthless.[33]

Cohino here is redolent with implications of poetic Pharisaism and pretense, but it is no more genealogical than any of the other assertions made in the course of this contest. Baena will respond by calling Villasandino (among other things) "swine sputum," a drunk, an apostate gambler; Villasandino by calling Baena a bastard and a pig (*tuerto chazino*, *gruniente cochino*). These claims drew their meaning and usefulness, not from the biography of their target, but from the rules of the poetic contest in which they were deployed, in which provocation stimulated poetry, and that poetry revealed the respective states of poetic grace of the competing poets.

For our poets, poetic incompetence, ignorance, rudeness, sexual deviance, animality, and especially Judaism are all ways of representing the lack in their rivals of any one of their multiple prerequisites for poetry. They are the negative poles of poetic virtues: divine grace, good meter and form, learning, courtesy, love, and so on. Poems often combined several of these idioms of virtue and vice. Baena and Villasandino's exchange, for example, focused on animality as well as Judaism. The Franciscan monk and theologian Diego de Valencia drew on a different combination in a glorious effort accusing the poet Juan de Espanha of being a Jew with no testicles. Although written in Spanish, the poem's rhyme scheme was made up of words borrowed from Hebrew: a brilliant etymological barb aimed at the "Jewishness" of its target.[34]

Those critics who have argued from the poem's Hebrew vocabulary that Friar Diego must have been a convert have missed the point. In these poems the discourse of Judaism, like that of sexuality or animality, was part of the language of literary criticism, not of biography. It was a key metaphor, a governing insult that carried with it a host of implications about its target's poetic skills, but it was entirely separable from the genealogy and religious orthodoxy of its object. It was even possible for a real Jew to possess the qualities of a poet, as when the same Friar Diego praised the Jew Symuel Dios-Auda for his charity, his courtesy, and his nobility ("fydalguia"): "For your word never changes or wavers / . . . / these are the markers of a noble man / to say things and do them without any doubt."[35]

Some poets of the *Cancionero* were converts, or descended from converts. But even in these cases, "Jewishness" in poetry was not the same as "Jewishness" in life. The poets of the generation following the mass conversions did not hurl accusations of Judaism in order to uncover each other's Jewish lineage or religious deviance. They were exploring and expanding the place of poetry in Christian society. Like their more famous colleagues of the early Italian "Renaissance," they were championing poetry against a well-established tradition that devalued it as literal, mimetic, and dangerously misleading. The difference is that, much more explicitly than the Italians, they relied on the charge of Judaism to do so.

As we saw in earlier chapters, the potential to evaluate language in terms of Judaism had existed since early Christianity. But the existence of a potential within a complex system of thought does not necessarily mean its actualization. "Judaism" had played a relatively insignificant role for previous generations of poets. Earlier Castilian poets, for example, did sometimes invoke "Jewish" literalism as a negative foil. But they did so from a privileged distance, confident in the ability of Christian practice to avoid the danger.[36] Baena's friends, on the other hand, worked in a very different world, one in which that privileged distance had been dramatically reduced. Within this sociologically transformed world they discovered the poetic potential of "Judaizing" and exploited it for a new kind of work, delighting in the leap from the potential "Jewishness" of their rivals' language, to the potential "Jewishness" of their bodies, and back again.

To shift the metaphor slightly: the mass conversions produced in Spain a heightened sense of just how slippery the slope was between Christianity and Judaism. Saint Vincent and his many supporters had reacted to this vertigo by attempting to eliminate the danger, working for the conversion or complete isolation of all Jews. Baena's poets, on the other hand, put the vertigo to work, exploiting the danger in the thrill ride of a poetics that threatened every Christian poet with "Jewishness." The approach was dangerous inasmuch as it made everyone vulnerable to "Judaism," but the risk was fleeting, lasting only to the end of the poem.

The obvious concern of our poets with language, and their unwillingness to tie the implications of that language too tightly to each other's life and lineage, makes them a particularly attractive example of the creativity unleashed by the mass conversions. Though their Judaizing art drew its power from the presence of tens of thousands of converts in Christian society, it was not aimed specifically at those converts and did not seek to make them over into Jews, real or imagined. But poets were not the only creative people at work with Judaism in the courts and corridors of fifteenth-century Spain. While Baena was collating his verses, prominent factions in both Castile and Aragon began adopting charges of Judaism as weapons in their increasingly high-pitched struggle for political power.

Putting Judaizing to Work: Politicians of the Synagogue

In 1434, according to one chronicler, King Juan II of Castile suppressed a plot to rob and murder the "new" Christians of Seville. In Aragon the tactics were less violent and the evidence for them more abundant, but the picture is the same. In 1433 Queen Mary decreed on behalf of the converts of Barcelona that no legal distinction should be made between "natural" Christians on the one hand and neophytes and their descendants on the other. The following year King Alfonso had to bar efforts in Calatayud to impose disabilities on neophytes; in 1436, the councilors of Barcelona moved to bar converts and those whose parents were not both "Christians by nature" from holding the office of notary; in 1437 the town council of Lerida attempted to strip of their office and license all commercial brokers who could not demonstrate at least four generations of "natural Christian" lineage.[37]

These attempts to keep converts and their descendants from positions of power were resisted not only by kings but also by the highest ranks of the church. In 1434 the prelates of Catholic Europe gathered at the Council of Basel reiterated that the regeneration of the spirit through baptism was more powerful than lineage or flesh, and should therefore bring with it all the privileges of Christianity:

Since [the converts] became by the grace of baptism fellow citizens of the saints and members of the house of God, and since regeneration of the spirit is much more important than birth in the flesh . . . they enjoy the privileges, liberties, and immunities of those cities and towns where they were regenerated through sacred baptism to the same extent as the natives and other Christians do.

Again in 1437, responding to an appeal from the converts of Catalonia and Valencia, Pope Eugene IV condemned those "sons of iniquity, . . . Christians only in name," who suggested that recent converts be barred from public office and who "refuse to enter into matrimony with them." But the contrary argument, that descendants of converts remained in some essential way Jewish and should therefore not enjoy all the privileges of Christians, was a powerful one. That power became brutally clear in 1449, when the "old" Christian citizens of Toledo rose up in rebellion against the government of King Juan II of Castile and his chief minister, Álvaro de Luna.[38]

In the previous chapter we touched on the role of Judaism in the political theology of these rebels—"Judaism," that is, as a form of interpretation, an attitude toward word and world. We saw how the bachelor Marcos aimed that charge of "Judaism" not only at converts from Judaism and their descendants, but also at the entire Christian political hierarchy of his age, including even the pope. This usage was similar to that of the poets in that it treated Judaism as a quality that threatened any and every Christian, and "Judaizing" as a critical language that could be applied to any sovereign, regardless of confessed faith. And it was the result of a very similar process, in which an ancient discourse of "Judaizing" gained new meaning and new power from the new sociological context in which it was deployed: a context in which confidence in the obviousness of the differences between Christian and Jew had been eroded by mass conversion.

But in addressing and exploiting this crisis of confidence, the rebels also made a very different argument, one we would today call genealogical, or even racial. (The Spanish word *raza*, from whence our English *race*, was in fact first widely deployed in these mid-fifteenth-century arguments.) According to them, Jewish hatred of Christianity and of Christians ran indelibly in the veins of those Christians descended from converts. Through their actions it was Judaizing government and destroying the kingdom. To counter that danger, the rebels besieged "new" Christian neighborhoods in Toledo and later in Ciudad Real, and killed dozens of their inhabitants. On June 5, 1449, the rebel government of Toledo also issued a "Sentencia-Estatuto," a statute that is sometimes called the earliest act of racist legislation in Europe. The statute decreed that descendants of converts be barred from holding office or exercising power over Christians, so that Christian society could be freed from Jewish tyranny and corruption.[39]

Unlike the creativity of the poets, that of the politicians promised to contain by force of lineage the threat of Judaism among the descendants of Jews. This promise proved false from its first utterance. Partly this was a result of the fact that over the generations the genealogies themselves had become hard to distinguish. The royal official Fernán Díaz described the problem with all the exaggeration appropriate to polemic in a memorandum he wrote against the rebels' purity of blood statutes: scarcely a noble family could be found without a convert somewhere in its tree. If Jewishness were linked to blood, he warned, the aristocracy of Spain would be destroyed.[40] The politicians' experiments did in fact fail to contain Judaism (though in the end it was not primarily the aristocracy that was affected). The causes of that failure were many, but perhaps the most fundamental was that in order to produce enough power to be politically useful, the threat of "Jewish" lineage needed to be mixed with the much more volatile and generalizable dangers of "Jewish" language that had so interested the poets and theologians. The result of this mixture was an explosion of Judaism.

Putting Judaizing to Work: The Spanish Inquisition

In their inquiry into how modernity could produce mass murder, two German-Jewish philosophers we will meet in the epilogue, Horkheimer and Adorno, proposed a metaphor for how accusations of Judaism work: "[To] call someone a Jew amounts to an instigation to work him over until he resembles the image."[41] In Spain, at least, the extent of this "working over" had been tightly circumscribed before the mid-fifteenth century. Theologians and poets might call each other "Jews," but the label was not meant to extend much beyond a specific interpretation or practice of reading. These limits collapsed under the tactics advocated by the rebels of Toledo, and in the context of a society in which mass conversion and widespread intermarriage had blurred many of the differences, including those of lineage, between gentile and Jew. Accusations of Judaism now became instigations to prove through genealogy and interrogation that their objects really were Jews in flesh and faith.

Let's take a quick look at how this process could remodel yet another sphere of culture: that of image-making itself. We have come to think of religious images—paintings and statues of Jesus or of the saints—as absolutely central to Catholic devotion. But in fact there has been criticism of the use of material representations in spiritual devotion throughout the history of Christianity. Thinkers as diverse and as foundational as Saint Paul, Saint Jerome, and Saint Bernard of Clairvaux (to mention only a few of the canonized) had criticized the use of images, and associated it with "Judaism," as a form of misplaced attention on the material rather than the spiritual, on outer appearance rather than inner truth. This critique became more muted after the twelfth century, and by the later Middle Ages religious art was ubiquitous, and largely uncontroversial, in churches. It seems not, however, to have been widespread in private households before the mid-fifteenth century, at least not in Iberia.

It was in the middle of that century that an anonymous pamphlet condemning the use of images in devotion began to circulate in Seville. The author apparently urged his fellow Christians not to contaminate themselves with idols—that is, not to pray to images—nor to fall into homosexual fornication. There was nothing necessarily "Jewish" about such a critique: in fact the author based himself on venerable Christian precedent (such as chapter 1 of Saint Paul's epistle to the Romans, with its linkage between idol worship and sodomy). But in his response to the pamphlct, Quccn Isabel's confessor Hernando de Talavera tied such criticism of Christian art to the "new" Christians, and condemned it as "Judaism." In 1478 Talavera, together with Seville's archbishop, Pedro González de Mendoza, went so far as to issue an edict without analogue in medieval or modern Europe, requiring *all* Christians to keep images at home:

> *And because it is reasonable that the houses of faithful Christians should [honor] the memory of the passion of Our Lord Jesus Christ and of his blessed Mother, we desire and declare that every Christian should have at home the painted image of the cross where Christ was sacrificed and some painted images of the Virgin and other saints that would provoke the inhabitants, arousing them to devotion.*

Shortly thereafter we begin to find descendants of converts brought before the tribunal of the Inquisition, either because, like the accusation against Donosa Ruiz in 1484, they "never had nor has at home an oratory of the Virgin Mary or Jesus Christ or of the saints, such as Christians usually have to pray in front of"; or because they misused the paintings they had, turning their backs to them, or even whipping or torturing them. [42]

Here we see how art, impressed into the service of differentiating Christianity from "Judaism," transformed what it meant to be a "good" Christian and in the process uncovered new "Jews." But now art too had to be patrolled and protected against infiltration. In 1480, Seville's city council approved ordinances regulating the production, style, and content of religious paintings, instituting a system of licenses for painters, and even appointing "painting inspectors" (*veedores*). Yet no amount of inspection could protect art from the "Judaism" it generated from its own entrails. A long history of thought (both Platonic and Christian) about the dangers of art's appeal to the senses had made "Judaism" a powerful language for criticizing the materiality and illusionism of art. The "Judaism of Christian Art" is a subject for a different book. Suffice it to say here that, over time, some of the most distinctive styles of religious art that Spain produced to defend itself from Judaism would themselves be condemned as "Jewish," their extreme emphasis on the suffering flesh of Jesus likened by pope and papal Inquisition alike with the Sadducees' rejection of the Resurrection.[43]

Painting, poetry, politics: these were just a few of the registers of Spanish culture transformed by the vast new power that critical discourse of Judaizing acquired with the disappearance of the Jews. Over time Spain developed institutions to manage the vast new power of this critical discourse of Judaism. The Inquisition was one custodian of that power, which it channeled toward the extirpation of any remnants of Judaism in Castile and Aragon. Modern historians are largely convinced that the inquisitors succeeded in this task. By 1500 they had helped to expel all unconverted Jews from Spain, and convicted nearly all of the converts and their descendants that they seriously suspected of harboring Judaism in their hearts. These turned out to be an astonishingly small percentage of converts: less than 10 percent. Apparently the Inquisition, at least, considered the vast majority of converts to be Christians of sound faith. Spain had been rid of Judaism. But none of these successes insulated Spanish Christians from the charge of Jewishness. On the contrary, they only heightened the "Jewishness" of Spain.

This "Jewishness" was in part produced by the inquisitorial methodologies themselves. Ever on the lookout for Judaizers, the inquisitors encouraged denunciation of "Jewish" practices. They filled catalogues with the resulting accusations, accusations such as (and I pluck this short list from just a few Inquisition trials) wearing clean clothes or refusing to buy an apple on a Saturday (the Jewish Sabbath); nodding one's head during prayer; eschewing religious images; or studying the Old and New Testaments in Hebrew and Greek. As we have already seen, there was nothing exclusively, or even obviously, "Jewish" about many of these practices. Saint Jerome, for example, had famously studied Hebrew in the early days of the church. Now, in the late fifteenth and sixteenth centuries, the new humanist movements were increasingly directing attention toward philology and ancient languages as tools with which to better interpret the Bible. How was the Inquisition to decide whether an interest in Hebrew was evidence of Judaism, or of a desire to study the Bible with the cutting-edge techniques of Europe's intellectual elite? Similarly, the refusal to buy an apple on a Saturday might be produced by clandestine observance of the Jewish Sabbath. But it might also simply reflect a lack of appetite.

Confronted with such questions, the inquisitors turned to genealogy. Nearly every trial transcript begins with a search for Jews or converts in the ancestry of the accused. If there were Jews in the genealogy, then there was likely Judaism in the practice, and if not, then perhaps not. The method produced a flood of practices newly considered Judaizing, from head nodding to Hebrew study. And it also produced a vast hoard of "family trees," stored in the archives of the Inquisition, detailing the bloodlines through which such practices might be transmitted.

One might think that by tying "Jewish" practices to "Jewish" bloodlines, the inquisitors were limiting the dangers of Judaism, much as the rebels of Toledo had promised in 1449. Instead the risks widened, and this for a number of reasons. To begin with, once a practice was associated with Judaizing, anyone who practiced it, even an "old" Christian, became vulnerable to accusation and stigma. No one was entirely above suspicion. After all, it did not take much Jewish blood to convey a predilection for these practices. A distant and forgotten ancestor would suffice, or perhaps just a wet nurse descended from converts, since breast milk was derived from blood according to the doctors of the day.

By the mid-sixteenth century, all candidates to positions of power in government, church, guild, military, aristocracy, university, the colonies, and so on, had to prove that their families were not infected by Judaism. Spain's archives overflow with these apotropaic "proofs of purity of blood." But these proofs, too, were quite plastic. There were plenty of people willing and able to manufacture genealogies, whether to obtain proofs of purity where there was none, or conversely, to extort money from honorable candidates. The Inquisition itself often complained of gangs of *linajudos*, "ingenius genealogists" with access to the archives who kept an eye out for people who had to prove their purity in order to blackmail them, threatening to forge proofs of taint wherever necessary.[44]   Such prophylactic genealogies had become necessary in a land where Christians had lost any immunity to Judaism, but they were also ineffective. It may be an exaggeration, but not an enormous one, to say that there is no leading sixteenth- or seventeenth-century Spanish writer or politician who entirely avoided being accused or accusing another of genealogical or cultural "Jewishness."

The "Most Catholic" monarchy of Spain had succeeded in converting and expelling all its Jews. But the result was the thorough "Judaization" of Spain. Foreigners tended to put the point most bluntly. "Spain is not pleasing," wrote Europe's leading intellectual, Desiderius Erasmus in 1517, because it is full of Jews. Such opinion became definition in *A Worlde of Wordes*, the Italian-English dictionary that John Florio published in 1598, which advised its readers that the word *Marrano* (a word for pig with which "old" Christian Spaniards insulted converts from Judaism) meant "a Jew, an infidel, a renegado, a nickname for a Spaniard." Among the French, Spain's greatest competitor in the late sixteenth-century contest for European hegemony, the Jewishness of their rival was axiomatic enough to appear as graffiti: "Pereat Societas Judaica, cum gente Ibera," Pierre de L'Estoile reported seeing on the walls of Paris in 1590: "May the Jewish Society perish, along with the people of Spain." As far as her enemies were concerned, Spain's unprecedented evangelical success had created a "Jewish" empire threatening the world with its tyranny.[45]

But let us conclude with a more discerning voice, one that came from within Spain itself. Writing in 1533, Rodrigo Manrique, himself the son of an inquisitor general, seems to have understood that the logic his father (and so many others) had championed, rather than freeing Spain from Judaism, had instead convicted vast areas of its thought and culture as Jewish. As he put it in a letter to his exiled friend, the humanist Luis Vives, in 1533, Spain has become "a land of envy, pride, and . . . barbarism. For now it is clear that no one can possess a smattering of letters without being suspect of heresy, error, and Judaism."[46]

Chapter 7

REFORMATION AND
ITS CONSEQUENCES

*He who would be a good Christian might almost
have to become a Jew.*

—MARTIN LUTHER,
"THAT JESUS CHRIST WAS BORN A JEW," 1523

*They are given to all people . . . to tread down, just
like scum in an alley, thrown out because it is of
absolutely no use to anyone, except to soil one's feet.*

—MARTIN LUTHER,
OPERATIONES ON THE PSALMS, 1519

MARTIN LUTHER, BORN a year or two after the Inquisition but at
the other end of Europe (in Eisleben, in 1483), was the rock that
shattered an age. Of course historians nowadays must add that he was
neither the first nor the last stone thrown, and that he gained momentum from the gravity of much larger forces. Nevertheless, there was

246

something revolutionary in Luther's message and in the way he delivered it. "I declare that neither pope nor bishop nor any other person has the right to impose a syllable of law upon a Christian man without his own consent." Not that Luther approved of political revolution. On the contrary, he opposed rebellion against secular authorities, condemning even the rebellions of peasants and knights that his preaching helped to inspire. Nevertheless his proclamations, written in the language of the masses and published by the thousand in cheap editions, were meant to transform the aspirations of his audiences for freedom.

In this they succeeded. Luther's writing and his preaching served as the foundation for Christian communities (Protestant and Evangelical, as they came to be called) that believed themselves radically different from the existing church. It took only a few years for those differences to seem irreconcilable, a few decades more for them to break into the sectarian wars that would shape the historical landscape of Europe and its colonies for centuries to come. Luther and his contemporaries may not have known the future, but they were perfectly aware of their claims to break with the past. Hence Luther styled himself "the Liberator" (Eleutherius), while his followers praised him as the "the Angel of the Apocalypse."[1]

Luther's innovations were many. He was, for example, the first great propagandist in the age of print. In addition to tomes of weighty erudition, he wrote hundreds of pamphlets whose brief text and bold language, illustrated with cartoons and caricatures, took his arguments to an audience that had never before been so effectively reached by text. He produced so many works (by one count, 183 editions of works attributed to Luther appeared in 1523 alone), and those works elicited so many responses, that in the first five years of his publishing career he single-handedly increased the total output of the young German printing presses almost tenfold.[2] Many of his tracts were written in German rather than in the Latin of the learned. These, combined with his efforts to translate the Bible into a language intelligible across the wide variety of dialects that stretched from the Netherlands to Poland, accelerated the birth of a modern German capable of serving as a language of culture.[3] Moreover his complaints against the Roman Catholic Church gave voice to his countrymen's long resentment of French and Italian domination, and helped to articulate their own imperial aspirations. Hence some have called Martin Luther the prophet of the German nation, much as Muhammad was "the prophet of the Arabs" nearly a millennium before.[4]

Of course what we most remember about Luther is his theology. His revaluation of the literal meaning of scripture; his rejection of tradition (including the authority of the Roman pope and church) wherever it seemed to clash with that scripture; his demotion of devotional practices considered external or ceremonial in favor of an intense stress on a personal faith in Christ gained through the reading of scripture; his belief that justification before God is gained solely through that faith and not through any works of man: these were the key notes of Luther's call for spiritual transformation. Rung in one change or another, they would for centuries summon believers to evangelical struggle. They continue to do so today.

The re-vindication of scripture's literal meaning was one of Luther's earliest and most characteristic teachings. It animated many of his major projects and ideas, including his sharpening of the distinction between law and gospel, his criticism of religious or interpretive practices and institutions that claim to mediate between the word of God and the individual believer, and his famous translation of the Bible out of learned languages and into the common German of his day. If this were a book about Luther, we would pause to examine that animation frame by frame, but my goal here is a much more restricted one. I want only to convince you that Luther's reconceptualization of the ways in which the language of scripture relates humans to their world and their God rewrote the roles played by Jews as figures of Christian thought. Like Paul and the evangelists in chapter 2, like Justin Martyr, Marcion, and Augustine in chapter 3, like Muhammad in chapter 4, Luther forged his history of reading and of the world's salvation in "Jewish" crucibles. In the process, he transformed once more the possible meanings of "Judaism" for the world, and the possibilities of life in the world for Jews.

The Distinction between the Law and the Gospel

Writing the "Introduction" to his collected Latin works in 1545, the year before his death, Martin Luther looked back over his entire career and compressed all of its discoveries into one moment. That moment was not his famous protest of 1517, in which (as later tradition has it) he nailed with "hammer strokes heard around the world" his "95 Theses" against papal remission of sins to the door of the castle church in Wittenberg. It was not his Augsburg debate with Cardinal Cajetan (1518), or his defiance of the holy Roman emperor at Worms (1521). The crucial moment came in 1519, when Luther was still a monk in the Augustinian order, and it was a solitary, not a public one. It involved no tools beyond interpretation, no materials beyond a single word of scripture, but the meeting of the two produced, at least as he remembered it, a blinding flash of revelation:

> *I was seized by an ardor to understand what Paul meant in his Letter to the Romans, but there stood in my way . . . that one word in chapter one: "The* justice *of God is revealed in it." I hated that word, "justice of God," which I was taught to understand philosophically according to the use and custom of all the learned, as referring to what they call formal or active justice, namely, that justice by which God is just and by which he punishes sinners and the unjust. But I, who lived as an irreproachable monk, felt myself to be before God a sinner with a very unquiet conscience, nor could I be confident that God was appeased by my penance. I did not love, indeed I hated the just God who punishes sinners. . . . I said, "Is it truly not enough that miserable sinners, who perish for all eternity because of original sin, are oppressed by every type of calamity by the laws of the Decalogue? Without God adding sorrow to sorrow by the Gospel, and even through the Gospel threatening us with his justice and his wrath?" . . . Meditating night and day, at last through the mercy of God, I paid attention to the context of these words: "The justice of God is revealed in it, as it is written: 'The just person lives by faith.'" By "justice of God" I began to under-*

stand that the just person lives by a gift of God, that is by faith, and
that by this verse the Gospel reveals that the justice of God is a passive
justice, namely, that by which the merciful God justifies us by faith, as
it is written: "The just person lives by faith." I suddenly felt myself to
be born again, and with the gates open, I entered into paradise itself.
Immediately all the facets of Scripture appeared to me in a different
light. . . . As much as I had previously hated these words "the justice
of God," now with love I exalted this sweetest phrase of mine. This
phrase of Paul's was for me the true door to paradise. Later I read
Augustine's "On the Spirit and the Letter," where I . . . discovered that
he interpreted "the justice of God" similarly.[5]

Luther's difficulty with the word *justice* is one that we have already
encountered in the struggles of earlier followers of Jesus to establish
their relationship to Judaism and its practices (see chapter 2). As he
states the problem, no human being, not even a "blameless monk" of
virtuous works like himself, could hope for acquittal in a formal court of
divine law. Along with the vast majority of Christians, Luther associated
the hateful age of legality with the Jews. But Paul's use of the word *justice* seems to threaten the believer with chains of Jewish law even in the
Christian era. How could the Christian be freed from these shackles?

Certainly not, according to Luther, by following the interpretive
strategies of the Roman church, or performing the devotional practices
built on them. That church, seduced by Greek philosophy, had dealt
with the difficulty by devaluing the literal meaning of the text in pursuit
of ever-higher allegorical levels considered more spiritual, a move that
only alienated Christians from their own scripture and thereby increased
the tyranny of law. Saint Augustine's attempt to limit flights of allegorical fancy and restore value to the literal sense had temporarily reversed
this process. But under the increasingly infectious influence of Aristotle,
medieval theologians (often called "Scholastics") cast aside Augustine's
restraints. They completely forgot Paul's message that salvation comes
only through faith and God's grace, and pursued it instead through the
learned "work" of philosophical interpretation, even believing that "the

just exercise of reason merits the remission of sins." Meanwhile the pope and his bishops exploited the fear produced by a legalistic understanding of God's justice in order to build up pontifical power and worldly wealth through practices such as the sale of papal justice, ecclesiastical office, and indulgences. The result was nothing but confusion about the difference between the law and the gospel, between works and faith. In this sense the Roman church had become more "Jewish" than the Jews, so that, as Luther would put it in 1523, "he who would be a good Christian might almost have to become a Jew."[6]

What was needed was a new way of reading (or rather, a return to the original apostolic way), one capable of containing God's justice within the embrace of God's grace and man's faith. The story Luther told about his troubled meditations on one word in Paul is an account of how, helped by the oil of God's mercy, he pried open gates of meaning rusted shut by bad reading, and discovered that these led directly to Paradise. Luther's student Philipp Melancthon summarized the point more dryly in the eulogy he pronounced for his teacher in 1546: "He here showed the distinction between the law and the gospel; he refuted the error then reigning in the schools and councils, which taught that men deserve the remission of their sins on account of their own works, and the dogma of the Pharisees, that men are in themselves just before God."[7]

Melancthon's "Life" of Luther is remarkable for the way in which it treats early Christianity as a template for Luther's own time. He provides a short history of how hermeneutic error entered the church, a history in which Origen is the chief villain, and Augustine's confrontation with the Origenists serves as the forerunner of Luther's struggle with the doctors of the Catholic Church. Melancthon describes that struggle and its resulting discoveries as a triumph over "law," "works," and "Pharisees," which is to say over "Judaism." But we know that, with perhaps one exception, Luther's opponents were never real Jews. Luther did, in a sermon of 1526, claim to have once debated with "learned" Jews. (His point in the sermon was that even though the Jews know the letters of the alphabet [*Buchstaben*] of the Old Testament by heart, they

cannot acknowledge its obvious literal meaning. They prefer to interpret according to the lies of the Talmud, because they are of the devil's
stock.)[8] Indeed it could scarcely have been otherwise. There were few
living Jews on the streets of Wittenberg: they had been expelled from
most of the cities and territories of the Holy Roman Empire, as well as
from England, France, Spain, and much of Italy. Luther's rivals were
almost always other Christians, whether Papists or (later) Protestants
more radical than himself. So why were Luther's conquests understood
as victories over Judaism? The reasons are very similar to those that
drove Augustine's debates with Jerome toward arguments about Judaism, but with significantly different results.

Like Saint Augustine, whose example he self-consciously invoked,
Luther realized very early that if the literal meaning of scripture was to
be amplified, its "Judaizing" potential needed to be contained. Augustine had used the passage of time to achieve this containment. By treating the literal sense of the Hebrew Bible as a description of God's "age
appropriate" relationship to the world and its various peoples (particularly the Jews) in the long eras before (but not after) the Incarnation,
Augustine had drained the literal Judaism of scripture into its historical sense. Luther wanted more. His claim would be that the story of
Christ, not the history of ancient Judaism, was the literal meaning of
even the most Hebrew of scriptures. To make that claim, he demolished
the massive Augustinian culverts that had long serviced the structures of
Christian exegesis, and tried to redirect the flow of Judaism and Jewish
history away from scripture altogether.

Draining the Jews from the Letter of Scripture

The scope and the strategy of this vast construction project are already
evident in the very first lectures that the young Luther, still a monk in
the order of Saint Augustine, gave as a newly minted doctor of theology. The lectures, held at the seminary of Wittenberg in 1513–1515, were
on the biblical book of Psalms. The project, entitled *Dictata super Psalterium*, was ambitious, modeled as it was on Augustine's own monu-

mental commentary, the *Enarrationes in Psalmos*. Its results were a vast treasure house of readings (more than a thousand pages in the modern printed edition), some entirely traditional, some startlingly original, many a studied mixture of both.

As is so often the case with Luther's work, the riches are too great for appraisal to encompass every jewel. But the general point is this: for Luther, the literal sense of the Psalms was not, as it had been for Augustine, the voice of a historical King David praising God and crying out against his persecutors, but that of the living Jesus himself. As he put it in the Preface, interpreting John 5:39, all prophecies and all prophets, including the Psalms, are about Christ. They are not to be understood in terms of the history of ancient Judaism "as Hebrew rabbis, forgers and false writers, and searchers after Jewish vanities do." The Psalms were literally about Jesus's suffering, and their historical context was not that of an ancient Israelite kingdom, but of Judea under Herod and Pontius Pilate.

If the literal sense of the Hebrew Bible was the historical life of Jesus rather than that of Israel, what place was left for the Jews in their own scriptures? Luther did give the Jews a role in his Christ-centered reading of the Psalms, but it was a purely persecutory one: wherever the voice of the psalmist cries out, it is the voice of Jesus crying out against his tormentors, the Jews. Or as he put it in a note to another theologian, "Since it [the Psalm] speaks about the Lord, therefore it speaks also about the Godless of His time." The Jews had always played such a role in the *allegorical* readings of many earlier theologians. But by moving it to the literal level, Luther made the engagement both sharper and more exclusive.[9]

As an example, we can take the first lines of the first Psalm, which Luther expounded in his first lecture as a professor of scripture: "Happy the man who follows not the advice of the wicked, nor loiters on the way that sinners take, nor takes his seat in the chair of pestilence."[10] How does the young Luther's interpretation differ from that of his exemplar, Saint Augustine?[11] Allegorically, the bishop of Hippo had identified the blessed one of the Psalm as Jesus Christ, while the three classes of error (the wicked, the impious, and the sitters in pestilence) represented col-lectively and without discrimination all those whose pride leads them astray. For Luther, the "councils of the godless" meant literally the Jews' rejection of God and their efforts to crucify Jesus. By "path of the impi-ous" the psalmist meant not only the Jews' error in this rejection, but also their refusal to acknowledge that error and their persistence in jus-tifying it through false teachings. Finally, "seat of pestilence" described the ways in which these "death-dealing" teachings of the Jews spread a spiritual plague that "corrupted, infected, and killed" countless souls.[12]

The example of these first few lines is representative of the whole work, which is comprised of *glossa*, brief explanations written between the lines or in the margins of the biblical text, and *scholia*, longer exe-getical commentaries printed on a separate page. Not all of the Psalms received their own *scholia*. But Luther's rewriting of the script is so thoroughgoing that of the roughly one hundred Psalms to which he dedicated full commentaries, only two—Psalms 97 and 112—are free of polemics against the Jews and their synagogue. It is not so much the expansion of polemic that is so important here. After all, Jews and their synagogue had long been the whipping boys of preachers and exegetes: "If hatred of Jews makes the Christian, then we are all plenty Chris-tian," as both Erasmus and Luther put it at much the same time.[13] More significant than the expansion of the polemic is the contraction of the role assigned to the Jews. If the literal meaning of the Hebrew scriptures is the life of Jesus, then Jews lose their traditional Augustinian role as guardians and guarantors of the letter, and are cast exclusively as per-secutors of Christ and (typologically) of Christians.[14] But if the Jews do not instruct through their history or their presence, and if that presence is so dangerous to Christ and to Christians, why do the Jews survive in Christendom at all?

Within Augustine's historical approach, those who lived as Jews in a Christian age played an important role as "witness." Like fossils for the naturalist, their survival provided the best evidence for the transforma-tion of God's promise in the distant past. The Jews' pedagogical useful-ness was clear in some of the similes with which he described them:

they were milestones, mirrors, vessels, desks for the Christians. That usefulness largely disappeared in Luther's interpretation. The more literally the life of Christ was legible in the scriptures of ancient Israel, the less necessary the presence of Jews to guarantee the reading. In this first commentary on the Psalms, Luther does not abandon the traditional (Augustinian) explanation for the continued presence of Jews in the world so long after their fundamental error: "[N]ow they remain as testimony to Christ's Cross." But it is clear from his metaphors that the nature of that testimony has changed. The Jews have become a useless, indeed a polluting, waste product. They are sewage, "scum in the streets." A few years later, again lecturing on the Psalms, he expanded the theme and enriched the image: "They are given to all people in the whole world to tread down, just like scum in an alley, which is thrown out because it is of absolutely no use to anyone, except to soil one's feet . . . just like anything of worth is excluded from dust and scum, so also from the castaways, so that there is nothing left among them that can still be of use to anyone." And not just useless, but dangerous: "One must beware of the shit of Rabbis, who have in a sense made the Holy Scripture into a latrine of sorts, into which they may introduce their shameful pursuits and utterly stupid opinions."[15]

Thus far I have focused only on Luther's theories of biblical interpretation. But how did these affect Luther's views on how "real" Jews, living in his world, should be treated? Luther wrote a number of treatises specifically addressed to this question, most notably "That Jesus Christ was born a Jew" in 1523, "Against the Sabbatarians" in 1538, and three treatises written in 1543, among them "On the Jews and their lies."[16] Most studies of Luther's impact on Judaism focus on these works and trace through them a shift from a relative generosity built on the younger Luther's optimism about the possibility of Jewish conversion to his gospel, to the activist anti-Judaism of Luther's disillusioned later years. I should therefore state more openly the claim implicit in my unorthodox opening emphasis on Luther's early exegetical writings: the energy necessary for Luther's transformation of the figure of Judaism was generated by the friction between "letter" and "law" in his thought, not by his collision with living Jews in the "real" world. His "Jewish problem" was the product of his theory of how biblical language works and how it should be interpreted—in other words, of hermeneutics, not of sociology.

Of course if Luther had not succeeded in moving from the one to the other, he would have remained (like his predecessor Jacob Perez of Valencia, whose Christ-centered readings of the Psalms made little impression on the future) an obscure exegete of interest only to the most specialized of historians.[17] But Luther launched an armada of arguments whose force led to the acceptance of his way of reading by many and its violent rejection by many more. It was the active prosecution of this conflict of ideas that reshaped the ways in which European Christians experienced their world, and heightened the dangerous significance of Jews and Judaism in that world.

From Hermeneutic Jews to Living Ones

It is not too surprising that an attempt to expand the domain of the letter should raise the specter of Judaism in Christian thought: remember Saint Jerome, who feared that Saint Augustine's literalism would "make us Jews." Those fears turned out to be unfounded in Augustine's case, but well placed in the very different context of Luther's world. This is not, I hasten to add, because his letter or his law were really Jewish, but because of the specific ways in which the conflict developed, the particular strategies through which it was pursued, and the long history within which it was situated.

Consider, as an example of how Luther pursued the conflict between letter and law and altered its history, his preaching on that cryptic but lapidary formulation of Saint Paul's that we have already encountered, "for the letter kills, but the spirit vivifies" (2 Cor. 3:6).[18] In his sermon on this text, Luther quickly characterizes what he sees as the chief error of his Christian rivals: "By 'literal sense' they signify the meaning of a Scripture narrative according to the ordinary interpretation of the words. By 'spiritual sense' they signify the secondary, hidden sense found in the words." Always the teacher, he then provides his audience with a pithy example, drawn from the very beginnings of scripture and of human history, of how this reading style works, taken from Genesis 3, which records how the serpent persuaded Eve to eat the forbidden fruit and to give it to Adam, who also ate. In its simplest meaning, he explains, this narrative represents what the traditional interpreters understand by "letter." By "spirit," however, they understand interpretations such as the serpent signifies evil temptation; the woman represents the human senses subject to temptation; Adam stands for reason; and the "spiritual lesson" of the passage is that when reason does not yield to the temptations of the senses, all is well, but when it wavers or consents, then man has fallen.

Luther's example is short but double-edged. Its downstroke condemns the traditional Christian system of interpretation known as the "fourfold senses of scripture." The first of those senses was what exegetes considered to be the literal meaning of what scripture states or reports, also called the *sensus historicus*. The remaining three senses were allegorical, although only one bore the name: 1) the *sensus allegoricus*, which explained the text in relation to Christology, doctrine, and dogma; 2) the *sensus tropologicus* or *moralis*, which provided the moral lesson for the individual believer; and 3) the *sensus anagogicus*, which focuses on the metaphysical and eschatological implications of the text, searching, for example, for hidden information about the Antichrist or the future of the world. The more basic division, as Luther and many others understood it, is a binary or twofold one, between the *sensus literalis* and the *sensus spiritualis* or *mysticus* in which the literal or historical meaning of a passage is identified with the killing "letter," while the layers of allegorical meaning are associated with the saving "spirit" and exuberantly explored. And the upstroke of Luther's example presents the result of such readings as a glorification of man's own powers, expressed as the delusion that through reason man is sufficient to save himself. (Recall Paul's condemnation of such confidence from chapter 2.)

This was a point Luther restated often (we met it already in Melancthon's eulogy): the reading practices of the Papists led to a fundamentally "Pharisaic" belief in the ability of man to achieve salvation through his own merits. In this sermon, he goes on to explain who invented the error, and to what end:

> *So it was Origen who first toyed this way with Scripture, and he pulled many others after him, so that it is now considered to be the highest artfulness, if one can generate so many meanings, so that the Church is filled with them. They aimed at imitating Paul, who in his Galatians v [actually Gal. 4:22–24] interprets the story that Abraham had two sons, the one by the free woman, that is, the mistress of the house, and the other by the hand-maid: that is (says Paul), that the two women represent the two Testaments: one makes only bondservants (which is precisely what he in our text calls the ministry of the letter); the other leads to freedom, or as he calls it here, the ministry of the spirit, which gives life. And the two sons are the two different peoples or nations, of which one remains only with the Law, while the other believes in and accepts the Gospel.*[19]

You recall from Galatians Paul's brilliant reading of the Abraham story, in which he set up those couples (Old Covenant and New, law and gospel, synagogue and church, letter and spirit) whose quarrels we have been following throughout this book. Luther's reading of Paul is equally audacious. It reorients once more the relationship between the couples, by putting not only Origen but also the entire Catholic interpretive tradition on the wrong side of the argument, just as Paul had done to the disbelieving Jews. The move is one of definition. According to Luther, Paul "does not say that the literal text is necessarily the letter that kills, and the allegory, or hidden meaning, the spirit." Paul's "killing letter" is not the literal sense of scripture, but rather the law itself.

> *For the word "Letter" means everything that is taught, ordered, and written there, whether it remains word, or writing, or even thoughts, that one can paint, write, or say, but not write in the heart or live in*

the heart . . . Saint Paul calls all this "the letter," or, as we put it previ-
ously, "the written sense." [20]

But, says Luther, the "false teachers" do not understand this. Instead
they claim that the text, or the record itself, of all scripture is *a dead*
"letter," its interpretation being "the spirit." In so doing, according to
Luther, they have not pushed interpretation farther than the teaching
of the law: precisely the law which Paul means when he speaks of "the
letter."

The argument is complicated, but the claim is clear. Paul did not
condemn the literal meaning of the letters, words, and texts of scripture.
What Paul meant by "killing letter" was the law, which included not
only the law of Moses but also any way of reading scripture, whether
"Old" Testament or "New," that emphasizes man's justification through
obedience of God and fulfillment of commandments. Luther's distinction here is designed to free the letter for the Christian. But it is
worth noting that he achieves this liberation by condemning his Christian opponents as "false teachers," readers after the law rather than the
spirit, followers of the "killing letter"—which is to say, as "Jews."

The strategy of Judaizing Christian "error" is as old as Christianity itself, and Luther's use of it is in some ways conventional. At the
level of the individual, for example, medieval sermons often preached
that every sinner or blasphemer is, like the Jews, a tormentor of Christ.
"The hands of the Jews, who bored through Christ, are the hands of all
the godless." So standard was the strategy that Chaucer had his Pardoner deploy it in his parodic condemnation of Christian oath-takers
as torturers of Christ: "Oure blissed Lordes body they totere— / Hem
thoughte that Jewes rente hym noght ynogh."[21] Luther could certainly
make a point like the Pardoner's (albeit without the parody), as when
he preached that "Christ is even today spit upon, murdered, whipped,
and crucified within ourselves. Nevertheless the flesh with its senses
ever plots against him without respite, as does the world with its plea-
sures, and the Devil with his suggestions and temptations, just as the

Jews plotted against Christ in the flesh." Luther's association between the Jews and the temptations of the flesh that assail the Christian is in this sense traditional. The difference is in part one of the target's scale. Where conventional preachers might indict an individual sinner, a group of people (moneylenders, for example, or blasphemers), or even a "heretical" movement as Jewish, Luther's project ends up condemning the entire existing structure of Catholic orthodoxy.

We have already seen a few examples of Luther's aligning his Papist opponents with "legalism," "Pharisaism," and "Judaism," and there are countless others. Whether early in his career or late, he was always willing to compare the teachings of his rivals with the crimes of the Jews. If the Jews deserve death for stabbing the host with little knives in their attempts at desecration, he writes in his lectures on the epistle to the Hebrews (1517/18: his allusion is presumably to the host desecration trial held in Brandenburg in 1510), how much worse do the Roman priests deserve for murdering the faithful, that is, the living children of God? And if the Jews' mistaken faith is based on their perversion of circumcision, he writes in "On the Jews and their Lies" (1543), is the Papists' perversion of the sacraments not exactly the same error? The Roman church, he wrote the same year in his treatise against the papacy, is "the Devil's Synagogue." He was equally willing to recruit the graphic imagery of anti-Judaism to the purposes of his antipapal polemic. In a print he commissioned from Lucas Cranach in 1545, for example, a bearded and hook-nosed Pope Paul III rides a sow while holding a handful of steaming feces ("Drecetta" as the accompanying Latin poem puts it, punning on "Decreta," Decretals). This "Papensau" was doubtless inspired by and meant to evoke the Jews on their "Judensau."[22]

Luther's "Judaizing" of the Roman church was in part a consequence of his particular way of reading the Bible, in part a strategic appropriation of the most powerful language of opprobrium available to any critic of the powers and institutions of this world. It was also, in part, a reaction to his rivals' attempts to Judaize *him*. Like so many other "heresies" in Christianity and Islam, Luther's was painted with the brush of Judaism. The charge that the Protestants had learnt their doctrines from the Jews was a powerful one, whether insinuated in pamphlet wars or proclaimed formally at gatherings of prelates. At the Diet of Augsburg, convened in 1530 to confront the controversial question of Luther's reform movement, rumor circulated that the Jews had encouraged Luther to rebel against the papacy. "That Jesus Christ was born a Jew," Luther's first (1523) treatise with much to say about how contemporary Jews should be treated by Christians, was clearly written in response to similar insinuations. Hence Luther begins by refuting the Catholic claims that, like the Jews, he denies the virginity of Mary. He then goes on to return fire: if the Jews stubbornly refuse Christianity, it is not only because the Christianity on offer beats and insults them, but also because it is a version of Judaism worse than their own. Given a religion of love, rather than the law, violence, and hypocrisy provided by the papacy, they might well convert. Or as he writes that same year in a letter to a recent convert from Judaism, if more Jews do not convert, it is because of the teachings of "our Sophists and Pharisees"—that is, the Pope, priests, monks, and theology students.[23]

"That Jesus Christ was born a Jew" is often described as marking an early, sympathetic stage in Luther's attitude toward Jews. Papist polemicists presumably pounced on Luther's mildness to repay him in his own coin, adducing the treatise as yet more evidence of Luther's Jew-love. Certainly the Papists wasted no opportunity to align the reformers with Christ's worst enemies. The ritual murder accusation against the Jews of Tittingen in 1540 provided just such an occasion. A treatise defending the Jews against the charge was published anonymously, without mention of either author or publisher. The author, as it happened, was almost certainly the Lutheran Andreas Osiander, and reaction to the treatise confirmed his prudence in choosing anonymity when defending Jews. A refutation commissioned from Johann Eck, a leading propagandist of the papal party, was entitled "Refutation of a Jew-Book in which a Christian, to the Dishonor of all Christendom, Claims that injustice is done the Jews in the Accusation that they murder Christian Children." It accused the anonymous skeptic of being both a "father of Jews" and a Lutheran.[24]

The pressure of such polemic may have affected Luther's attitudes. Indeed one Jewish contemporary, who had read and admired "That Jesus Christ was born a Jew," explained the increasing hostility of the reformer's later works as a reaction to his opponents' "defaming him and saying that his mind inclines to the faith of the Israelites." Luther's opinions certainly evolved markedly. By 1543, in "On the Jews and their Lies," he was advocating either a "sharp mercy" or an "utter merciless-ness" toward them. The phrase "sharp mercy" was adopted by some Lutheran theologians to characterize the reformer's late attitude toward Jews, perhaps because it sounds more loving than the "utter merciless-ness" Luther recommends later in the same treatise: "Burn their syn-agogues, forbid everything that I recommended above, force them to work, and deal with them with utter mercilessness, as Moses did in the wilderness when he struck three thousand dead." But whether mercy or not, the sharpness included the burning of the Jews' synagogues, the destruction of their houses, their concentration into one place ("under one rooftop or stall") "like the Gypsies," the confiscation of their wealth and their religious books, the prohibition of their teaching and their money lending, forced manual labor for the young, and, if all this still failed to contain their blasphemy, then "away with them."[25]

Our anonymous Jewish commentator, like other Jews of Luther's day and after, may well have experienced the impact of this sharp mercy in his daily life. Luther's words directly provoked the expulsion of the Jews from electoral Saxony in 1537 and from the towns of Thuringia in the 1540, and sparked riots against the Jews in Brunswick in 1543. Post-humously they inspired expulsions from Brunswick and a number of other duchies in 1553, the destruction of the synagogue of Berlin in 1572, and expulsion from Brandenburg in 1573 and from the (Calvinist) Palati-nate in 1575. By that point, "the Jews had been cleared from every major German secular territory except Hesse, and from every Imperial free city of any importance except Frankfurt." The handful that remained in German lands were confined to the Catholic ecclesiastical states, gov-erned by bishops under the protection of the Holy Roman emperor. When a Jewish refugee from Brunswick living in the Holy Land wrote that the author of his exile was "this foul priest Martin Luther and the other scoundrels who derive from the stock of this arch-heretic," he was not entirely off the mark.[26]

The point made earlier by our anonymous chronicler is, however, more subtle than his coreligionist's condemnation. What is remarkable about his perception of the shift in Luther's thought and his explanation for it is an awareness (lacking in many later scholars) that whether mild or harsh, Luther's words about Jews were weapons forged for service in conflicts with other Christians. In the case of "That Jesus Christ was born a Jew," early and relatively mild, those Christians were his Catholic opponents, whom he sought to portray as more "Jewish" than the Jews. In the case of his later treatises, "cruel as if written in blood," those opponents were just as often the followers of other Protestant reformers with a literalism more radical than (or simply different from) his own.[27]

"Jewish" Weapons in Christian Wars

Of such reformers there were many, for the "gates to paradise" that Luther had pried open with his readings of Paul turned out to have been holding back a flood. What authority could control the flow of interpretations once the letter was freed from Catholic constraints of custom and consensus? Luther nominated himself the lock-keeper, but on every issue of importance (Is Christ really present in the Eucharist? What is the nature of the Trinity? When should Christians be baptized? What is the proper relationship between God and Caesar? Do the Bible's commandments on how to observe the Sabbath need to be followed literally?), a boiling tide of rival readings threatened to sweep him from his high ground in Wittenberg.

Some of these readings, like John Calvin's, achieved an influence so great as to become the foundations for new communities of faith.[28] Others, like those of the obscure biblicizing Baptist Oswald Glaid, flared briefly before being extinguished by polemic. Even without a catalogue, we can imagine that the sectarianism of this moment approached an intensity unknown to western Europe since late antiquity. This sectarianism was debated in terms of Judaism, just as it had been in those earlier centuries of Christianity. Glaid's teachings, for example, were attacked in a treatise revealingly entitled "Against the Error of the Ebionites Old and New." According to the familiar logic of the treatise, the more rigorous Sabbath observance preached by Glaid would necessarily require circumcision and the full adoption of Jewish ritual. Any convert to his teachings must become a Jew. Such language was a staple of the new sectarian diet, and through it the conflict between rival visions of Christianity assumed the shape of a struggle against "Judaism."[29]

"We Should Neither Tolerate, nor Endure Them"

For Luther, however, the sectarian struggle was not only against Christian "Judaizers," but against "real" Jews. He seems to have experienced the rise of biblicist groups like Glaid's as a wave of Jewish proselytism endangering entire provinces of Christendom. His own treatise aimed at such groups, "Against the Sabbatarians" of 1538, began with the claim that Jewish missionaries were converting Christians to Sabbath observance and circumcision. The treatise therefore took the form of the question "Whom should we believe more, the true, trustworthy God or the false, lying Jews?" His answer extended for thirty printed pages of polemic against the Jews, pages that flowed directly into "On the Jews and their Lies" and his other "cruel" works of 1543.[30]

Luther defended the "sharpness" of these and other treatises by insisting that the efforts of the Jews to proselytize their poison posed a present danger to Christians. A number of eminent modern scholars have accepted the claim, explaining Luther's anti-Judaism as a response to a "wave" of conversions to Judaism.[31] For this there is little evidence. The rumor of conversion relayed by King Sigismund of Poland to the Senate of Lithuania in July of 1539 was probably related to the case of Katarzyna Wejglowa, burned at the stake in Cracow on April 19 of that year for "having fallen into a perfidious and superstitious Jewish sect." Hers is the only documented case, and there is good reason to believe that she was a Christian sectarian, not a convert to Rabbinic Judaism.[32]

The fear that the world was converting to Judaism was produced, not by this obscure and extraordinary case, but by the sectarian polemics of Judaizing. There were no proselytizing Jews of flesh and blood behind Luther's claims of "Jewish" onslaught in the east, any more than there were behind the 1551 sermon of an Augsburg Catholic that "the King of England [the Protestant Edward VI], his council and kingdom had all become Jews." The "reality" of these Jewish rivals was entirely the product of a discursive struggle against "Judaizing" projected onto the flesh of Judaism's living representatives.[33]

Neither Luther's theology nor his social context quite suffice to explain why, toward the end of his career, he became this fantasy's leading impresario. There were, after all, contemporaries with different views, in both the Papist and the Protestant camps. Among the former, for example, Johann Eck deployed a vocabulary of anti-Jewish stereotypes every bit as cruel as those of his arch-foe, and advocated a very similar program of oppression ("degrading labor," etc.), but he never abandoned the Augustinian position that the Jews should not be expelled from Christian lands. Among the latter, too, there were those who took issue with Luther's campaign against Judaism. The most notable of these was Luther's own student Andreas Osiander, who wrote a letter to the Jew Elia Levita explicitly criticizing Luther's "On Schem Hamphoras," and then had to enlist Melancthon's help to make sure that a circulating copy of the letter did not fall into his elderly and irascible teacher's hands.[34]

A full answer to this difficult question is best left to a different book. What is important here, and incontestable, are the older Luther's efforts to convince his contemporaries that "so thoroughly hopeless, mean, poisonous, and bedeviled a thing are the Jews that for 1400 years they have been, and continue to be, our plague, pestilence, and all that is our misfortune." The Jews are no longer the powerless people persecuted by hypocritical Papists that they had been in "That Jesus Christ was born a Jew." They are rather "in their hearts our daily murderers and our most bloodthirsty enemies," and therefore eminently "worthy of hatred."[35]

The aging Luther worked tirelessly to achieve the elimination of these enemies, this misfortune, from German lands. He did not seek the Jews' conversion, since he now believed that Jews could become true converts only at the apocalypse. In the interim, he once suggested, the only effective way to baptize them was in rivers with millstones tied around their necks. (It is presumably coincidence that a generation later we hear of Ivan the Terrible proceeding in precisely that manner. According to a later French traveler's account, the prince had all the Jews assembled and made to deny Judaism and accept Christianity. They were then bound hand and foot and thrown from a very high bridge into Moscow's river, "so that, he said, they would be better baptized.")[36]

Instead of conversion, Luther strove for the expulsion of Jews from Christian territories. In 1546 he even undertook the hard winter journey to his birthplace of Eisleben. A number of Jewish refugees from other expulsions had recently been granted asylum there, a grant he hoped to reverse. As he rode through the town, he wrote to his wife on the first of February, it seemed to him that the presence of the Jews and their guilt raised a bitter wind against him, one that sought to freeze his brain, leaving him weakened and ill. He would do all he could, he told her, to see that they were driven out. To this end he preached some hard-edged sermons to the faithful: "If they will not convert, we should neither tolerate nor endure them among us." Luther's chill worsened, and these turned out to be the final sermons of his life. Like so many prophets before him, he died in combat with the Jews.[37]

Already in Luther's day and ever since, generations have debated the motives, severity, and consequences of this combat. The debate is particularly sharp because Luther's words had such long futures. "Whoever writes against the Jews, and for whatever reason, feels justified in referring triumphantly to Luther," as the rabbi and historian Reinhold Lewin (1888–1942/3) put it in 1911. Lewin doubtless had in mind anti-Semitic florilegia like Theodor Fritsch's 1887 Cathechism for Antisemites (republished in 1907 with the more scientific title Handbook on the Jewish Question: The Most Important Facts Necessary for Judgement of the Jewish People), with their catalogues of Luther's condemnations. His rule applied just as well to the National Socialists at whose hands, decades later, he probably perished. Under the auspices of research centers like the "Institute for the Study and Eradication of Jewish Influence on German Religious Life," Lutheran scholars in the Nazi period produced a flurry of new editions and explications of the reformer's writings, emphasizing his campaigns to eradicate the dangers of Judaism. Even today, Luther is invoked (albeit less triumphantly) as predecessor and example on the home pages of German neo-Nazi websites.[38]

These futures were not Luther's concern, nor (in this chapter) are they ours. I am not interested in contributing to arguments, so often dominated by apologetics and anachronism, about whether Martin Luther was an anti-Semite or an architect of the Holocaust.[39] My point is simply that Luther's reconceptualization of the ways in which language mediates between God and creation was achieved by thinking with, about, and against Jews and Judaism. Insofar as these reconfigurations diminished the utility and heightened the dangers Jews posed to the Christian world, they had the potential to transform figures of Judaism and their fates. How powerful this potential might be, and what work it might perform in the future, were not Luther's to control. In the event, his teachings awoke into startled ferocity the long slumbering debate about the place of letter, law, and works in the Christian world. The conflict raged far beyond the borders of the Bible, invaded many provinces of human thought and action, and ensured that specters of Judaism would stalk battlefields in which scarcely a real Jew was left alive.[40]

Economics and its neighbor, politics, were among the largest of those provinces. Their invasion by new fears of Judaism in this period should not be too surprising. We have already seen in previous chapters the long relationship between thinking about language and thinking about politics, and the history of interaction between language and money as symbolic systems of exchange is scarcely shorter: in fact the ancient Greek term *sēmē*, from whence our "semiotics," meant coin as well as word. We might therefore expect that the heightened anxieties produced by novel ways of thinking about how biblical language works would migrate into economic thought. Luther was aware more than most of the long and porous border between the two realms, and treated them as two words at war: "Money is the Devil's word, through which he creates everything in the world, just as God creates through the true word." We could fruitfully follow the figure of Judaism in the great reformer's economic thought. But we have lingered too long in little Wittenberg, so let us trace our figure's wanderings to another stage, in Shakespeare's London, a half century after Luther's death.[41]

Chapter 8

"WHICH IS THE MERCHANT HERE, AND WHICH THE JEW?": ACTING JEWISH IN SHAKESPEARE'S ENGLAND

Enter a merchant, in the company of friends. "In sooth, I know not why I am so sad" (1.1.1). Centuries of critics have pondered the motives for the merchant's melancholy. Their explanations range from the self-alienation of the capitalist to the repressed homoeroticism of a man whose best friend wants to marry.[1] Shakespeare's own audience might have suspected yet another cause. "Our English proverb 'To looke like a Jewe'," noted Thomas Coryate in 1611, means to look like "one discontented." Even their cookbooks taught Elizabethans to associate melancholy with Judaism. As Henry Buttes's diet book put it in 1599, the Jew's "complexion is passing melancholious," a situation he attributed to an excessive fondness for goose.[2] The audience's suspicions could have increased only with the dialogue. It is worry that your ships might sink, says one companion (Salerio), which makes you so sad. You think of nothing but your money. Everything else, no matter how sacred, reminds you only that your investments are at risk:

> . . . should I go to church
> and see the holy edifice of stone
> And not bethink me straight of dangerous rocks,
> Which touching but my gentle vessel's side
> Would scatter all her spices on the stream,
> Enrobe the roaring waters with my silks—
> And in a word, but even now worth this,
> And now worth nothing?
>
> (1.1.30–37)

Exit one friend and enter another, who makes a similar diagnosis in even harsher terms:

> You have too much respect upon the world.
> They lose it that do buy it with much care.
> (1.1.76–77)[3]

In this allusion to the Gospel of Matthew (16.25–26)—"Whosoever will save his life, shall lose it. . . . For what shall it profite a man, though he should winne the whole worlde, if he lose his own soule?"—we hear the hint of a critique. Is our merchant, like the Jews and Pharisees, too concerned with earthly treasure, overly preoccupied by the material world? He objects strenuously to this critique. His investments are safe, he insists, his attachment to the world not excessive: "I hold the world as but the world Gratiano, / A stage, where every man must play a part." Gratiano, not dissuaded, takes another, equally distressing, tack:

> There are a sort of men whose visages
> Do cream and mantle like a standing pond,
> And do a wilful stillness entertain,
> With purpose to be dressed in an opinion

> *Of Wisdom, gravity, profound conceit. . . .*
> *. . . I do know of these*
> *That therefore only are reputed wise—*
> *For saying nothing; when I am very sure*
> *If they should speak, would almost damn those ears*
> *Which hearing them would call their brothers fools.*
> *I'll tell the more of this another time.*
> *But fish not with this melancholy bait*
> *For this fool gudgeon, this opinion.*
>
> (*1.1.91–105*)

If the merchant's melancholy is not the product of vulgar materialism, Gratiano implies, then it is the product of a Pharisaic hypocrisy, one that conceals inner emptiness with outer profundity in order to earn a reputation among men. Either way he appears to be, in the vocabulary of Christianity, a "Jew."[4]

We are, you will immediately have recognized, in Shakespeare's theatrical world: a world every bit as concerned with "Judaizing" as Luther's Germany, or the Inquisition's Spain, and every bit as willing to put that concern to work, albeit in its own way. It is the power of this "Judaizing" critique, I hope to convince you, that put so many imagined Jews on the new commercial stages of London, a city that had sheltered fewer "real Jews" in its long history than perhaps any other major one in Europe. And it is the power of this critique that animated Shakespeare's "Jewish questions" in *The Merchant of Venice*.

Shakespeare scholars will recognize here an explicit challenge to a venerable school of criticism, founded by Sidney Lee and Lucien Wolf and reenergized by James Shapiro, that emphasizes the importance of excavating "real Jews" as the context for *The Merchant of Venice*. Such excavators are misguided, and not only because their confidence in the "Judaism" of the few-dozen descendants of Spanish and Portuguese converts they discover living in Shakespeare's London—none of whom confessed to being anything but Christian—replicates the genealogical convictions of the Inquisition. More important, their insistence that Christian anxieties about Judaism depend on the existence of "real Jews" ignores the ability of Christian thought to generate Judaism "out of its own entrails." Even if we were to find an entire clan of Hebrews cowering in some Elizabethan estaminet, we would be no closer to understanding the work done by figures of Judaism on Shakespeare's stage. For that, we need to focus on the critical work done by "Judaism" within Shakespeare's Christian culture and that of his contemporaries.[5]

But this does not mean—and here there is a less obvious challenge to another school—that Shakespeare presents us with a healing allegory, in which "Christian" criticism achieves the overcoming of "Judaism." Certainly Shakespeare insists, as did Saint Paul, on the important difference between Israel after the flesh and Israel after the spirit. But he also insists, as Paul did too, that the threat of "Judaizing" attends every Christian act of communication, interaction, and exchange. Like everyone else in this material world, Christians are bound by necessity to promise their words, their goods, and even their flesh (as, for example, in the marriage contract). In texts like *The Confessions* and *On Christian Doctrine*, we saw how Saint Augustine had explained that love could discriminate between the killing hermeneutics of the Jew and the salvific one of the Christian. As the poet George Herbert rather savagely recognized a generation or so after Shakespeare's death, the test of love only concentrates the problem:

> He that doth love, and love amisse,
> This worlds delights before true Christian joy,
>   Hath made a Jewish choice.
> . . . He hath made a sorrie wedding
> Between his soul and gold . . .
>   And is a Judas-Jew.

How to distinguish the "Christian" from the "Jewish" choice? This is Shakespeare's Jewish question at its most basic. From its first words to its last, *The Merchant of Venice* poses this question repeatedly: the famous line "Which is the Merchant here, and which the Jew?" is only its most apothegmatic expression. The play is a drama of chronic conversion whose every participant—including playwright and viewer—moves suspended like a compass needle trembling between Judaism and Christianity. Approached in this way, the play opens a new perspective on the role of Jewish questions in Shakespeare's (and not only Shakespeare's) thinking about the rapidly changing religious, legal, economic, and poetic landscape of his age.[6]

Commerce, Theater, and Other Judaizing Exchanges

There are two businessmen in *The Merchant of Venice*, the Christian Antonio, whose entrance in act 1, scene 1, we have been describing, and Shylock the Jew. The similarity between them is deliberate, so deep that Shylock notes it with surprise when he first sees Antonio: "How like a fawning publican he looks!" This line too has perplexed its commentators. "Publican" is the gospel name for Jewish tax collectors, and in the gospel texts they play an ambivalent role: either (in Matthew's exhortation to love) as the most degrading example of people who are kind only to their friends, or (in Luke's parable of the publican and the Pharisee) as the humblest example of the meek triumphing over the proud. By and large, scholars have preferred to cleave the ambivalence rather than maintain it. Many have opted for the Lukan interpretation, and seen in Antonio's fawning an allegory of Christian virtue. But how to suppress the whiff of "Jewish" misanthropy that Matthew's "publican" emits? Perhaps, some have suggested, the line as we have it is an editing error, and Shakespeare meant "publican" to apply to Shylock, not Antonio. Such arguments seek to cut, rather than untie, the elegant knots with which Shakespeare bound Judaism and Christianity. Yet it is precisely through these knots ("publican" is only one of many), and the confusions between Christian and Jew they make possible, that the *The Merchant of Venice* does its work.[7]

By ambivalence and confusion I do not mean the often-made point that Shakespeare's Jew is sometimes sympathetic ("If you prick me, do I not bleed?"), nor the less often-made one that his Christians are sometimes not. It is true that the characters in the *Merchant* make greater claims to sympathy and humanity than those in its influential predecessor, Christopher Marlowe's *Jew of Malta* (ca. 1589), in which not only the title character, but Christian and Muslim protagonists as well, are cynical distillations of villainy. But these claims are just one symptom of a much more systematically staged confusion of Christian and Jew in the play, and it is through this more general—indeed all-pervasive—confusion that Shakespeare achieves his dramatization of a crucial question: How can a society built on "Jewish" foundations of commerce, contract, property, and law consider itself Christian?

This was, as we saw in chapters 2 and 3, a question as ancient as Christianity itself, encoded to some extent in a theology that distinguished more or less radically between the pursuit of earthly treasure and that of heavenly treasure, between loyalty to secular law and loyalty to divine love, and that understood the Jews as the prototypical example of the alienation from God and spirit that results from the wrong choice. Many medieval moralizers exploited that exemplarity, preaching that attachment to material wealth in general, and its pursuit through certain forms of commerce and monetary exchange in particular, were not Christian but "Jewish" activities. Saint Vincent Ferrer put it eloquently around 1400:

> . . . *today, nearly everything is avarice, for almost everyone commits usury, which used not to be done except by Jews. But today Christians do it too, as if they were Jews.*

Sebastian Brant's *Ship of Fools* made the same point a century later (1494), half a continent away, and in a different genre: "Most tolerable was the Jews' petition / but they could remain no longer / The Christian Jews drove them away / who themselves tilt with Jewish spears."[8]

In the theater of Shakespeare's England, yet another century and genre later, there were plenty of dramatists willing to "Judaize" credit in much the same way. In *The Jew*, for example, an anonymous and now-lost play performed sometime before 1579, the title character was meant to represent "the greedinesse of worldy chusers, and bloody mindes of Usurers." But this insistence on a bright contrast between the attitudes and practices of the spiritual Christian toward commerce, and those of the fleshy Jew, was becoming more difficult to maintain in a world in which the wheels of commerce were accelerating, and from which the Jews themselves had vanished.[9]

Beginning in 1571, the lending of money at interest became legal in England. The crime of usury remained, but henceforth it would mean only the charging of excessively high rates of interest (of which crime William Shakespeare's own father John was at least twice accused). Why was the rapidly spreading Christian practice of money lending not a "cruel" one, like the much demonized lending of medieval Jews? Some writers tried to draw a sharp contrast, claiming that "our usury in money" is not "all one with that of the Jews," and even culled medieval chronicles in an attempt to prove that the latter had charged rates of up to 80 percent. Others, like the author of *The Jew*, effaced the contrast and strove to represent Christian moneylenders as "Jewish." It was even a commonplace, so Francis Bacon reported, that moneylenders should wear Jews' hats, "orange-tawny bonnets, because they do 'Judaize.'" Shakespeare, as we will see, took a more sophisticated tack.[10]

The question of money lending provides one "Jewish" context for Shakespeare's *Merchant*, but it is far from the only one. Moralists found cause for further worry in the increasingly mercantile nature of the English economy. In the twelfth century the stigmatization of merchants had been canonical: "A merchant can rarely or never please God. And therefore no Christian should be a merchant, and if he wishes to be one, he should be ejected from the Church." Over time merchants had claimed with ever-more vigor their rights as "profitable members of the common wealth, in transporting our commodities into other lands, and enriching us with the benefits and fruits of other countries." But was a man's profitability a sufficient measure of his virtue? Might not the merchant, who grows money by buying things at one price and selling them at a higher price, also be condemned as a kind of "Jewish" usurer? The words remained near synonyms even in the seventeenth century, as when the traveler Henry Blount, describing the Egyptians, ascribed to them "a touch of the Merchant, or Iew." And what was the relationship between the merchant's profit and the commonwealth or state? Should the latter organize itself in such a way as to maximize the former? Conversely, was a man's capacity to "act for the commodity of his Countrie" a good qualification for participation in the state and its governance, or were other virtues (such as aristocratic values and Christian morality) more important?[11]

These and many others were urgent questions as England joined the fray of European mercantilism. Commerce, and the dangerous sea of contract, bond, and law on which it floated, demanded exploration. For that exploration, the city-states of Italy provided the perfect "Indies." Italian treatises on political philosophy and economy were "Englished" and consumed by the dozen. And Venice, with its commercial dominance, its merchant oligarchy, and even (at times) its toleration of Jews, provided particularly frequent examples to philosophers and divines.[12]

Dramatists too turned to these examples, not only because entertainers need to comment on their times, but also because the theaters of the Elizabethan age were among the newest barks on this dangerous sea of commerce. Vendors of words and pretense, they were as dependent on capital as any financier. Like directors of merchant companies, theatrical impresarios of the day rose and fell on their ability to obtain royal licenses and monopolies, secure cheap sources of product, and reach an audience whose hunger for that product was great enough to be turned into profit. The diaries of theatrical impresarios from the day are full of the strategies by which all this might be achieved, strategies drawn from the most up-to-date arsenals of the market. (One such strategy, relevant to the theme of our play, was that of locking up actors under contracts enforced by "bonds"—that is, threats of penalty should they be broken.) As for playwrights, could they not be thought of as Herbert's "worldly chusers," or as close kin to counterfeiters and usurers? After all, they sold their gilded words for sound silver, that "pale and common drudge / 'Tween man and man" (3.2.103–104), which they then reinvested in commodity and credit markets. Shakespeare, for example,

bought shares of theater companies, invested in real estate, and speculated in malt.[13]

Counterfeiter is not too strong a term to characterize the problems
posed by theatrical words themselves. One did not have to be a dogmatic Platonist to charge them with all the dangers of mimetic deceit (or
Pharisaism, to use a more Christian term for an excessive concern with
appearances), given that commercial drama was explicitly built, perhaps
more than any other genre of its day, on the gap between appearance
and reality. Could a theatrical word ever be true? If not, it was in the
interest of a Christian state, as some moralists argued, to suffocate this
infant language in its crib—and in fact the theaters were temporarily
closed on these moral grounds in 1642. But if so, as a playwright might
want to claim, in what sense could such words be true? These questions
about how theatrical language works were hot ones in Shakespeare's
time, and a good deal of that heat came from their connection to those
"Jewish questions" about the dangers of interpreting scripture, sign,
and sacrament which we have already found at the center of the disputes between the many flavors of Catholicism and Protestantism that
so marked the history of England in this age.[14]

Scenes of Confusion

From its opening scene, *The Merchant of Venice* inserts itself into all
these contexts and more.[15] You know the story. A rich but melancholy
merchant, Antonio, has a friend, Bassanio, who has spent all his money
trying to appear wealthier than he really is. Bassanio, however, has
"plots and purposes / How to get clear of all the debts I owe" (1.1.133–
134). His cunning plan is to marry a rich heiress, the fair Portia: "nothing undervalu'd / . . . / Nor is the wide world ignorant of her worth"
(1.1.165, 167). Bassanio proposes to woo and win this "golden fleece,"
but to do so he needs to compete with other candidates, and to compete
he needs more cash: "O my Antonio, had I but the means / To hold a
rival place with one of them, / I have a mind presages me such thrift
/ That I should questionless be fortunate" (1.1.173–176). Value, thrift,

worth, means, debts, fortune, fleece: thus far the plot sounds more like a business plan than a love story—a confusion of profit and passion that is precisely the kind of reversal of values the audience would have associated with Judaism. And to business Antonio goes. He has no liquid funds, his fortune is all at sea, but he sends Bassanio to do what businessmen do in such circumstances: borrow money.

Bassanio takes Antonio to Shylock the Jew, and it is at this point that Shakespeare's audience might expect a moralizing distinction to emerge between good merchant and bad. The expectation is not entirely disappointed. At first, for example, the Jew talks differently, in a strangely literal semi-comprehension, repeating Bassanio's statements word for word. (We will revisit Shylock's linguistics later.) Then too, the credit negotiations between the three of them recapitulate the traditional Christian view of an irreconcilable enmity between Jewish and Christian economics. The character of Shylock articulates the difference as Christians imagined it: "I hate him [Antonio] for he is a Christian: But more, for that in low simplicity / he lends out money gratis. . . . / He hates our sacred nation, and he rails / (Even there where merchants most do congregate) / On me, my bargains, and my well-won thrift, / Which he calls interest: cursed be my tribe / If I forgive him!" (1.3.37–47). But then Shylock attempts to bridge the difference with exegesis. He tells the biblical story of Jacob multiplying Laban's sheep, and interprets it as legitimating profit: "Thrift is blessing if men steal it not."[16]

Now it is Antonio's turn to reject assimilation and recapitulate the traditional claim to irreconcilable economics. He rudely dismisses Shylock's reading with a charge of Pharisaism: "The devil can cite Scripture for his purpose,— / an evil soul producing holy witness / Is like a villain with a smiling cheek, / A goodly apple rotten at the heart. / O what a goodly outside falsehood hath!" (1.3.94) He calls Shylock a hostile cur, an enemy of his customers, because (so Antonio) by charging interest he breeds lifeless money from their living flesh: "If thou wilt lend this money, lend it not / As to thy friends, for when did friendship take / A breed for barren metal of his friend? / But lend it rather to thine enemy, / Who if he break, thou may'st with better face exact the penalty" (1.3.127–132).

There is some irony here, in that Bassanio is receiving metal (ducats) in exchange for the pledge of his friend's flesh. This is why the practice of standing surety was itself controversial, condemned not only by Luther but also by contemporaries like Sir Walter Raleigh: "Suffer not thyself to be wounded for other men's faults, or scourged for other men's offenses, which is the suretyship for another. . . . From suretyship, as from manslayer or enchanter, bless thyself." Critics have also pointed out that although Antonio does not ask Bassanio for monetary interest in exchange for his money, he craves emotional interest in the form of Bassanio's love, breeding friendship from metal, so to speak. But let us set aside the irony and focus for the moment on the economics model evoked by the vocabulary of the scene itself.[17]

The passage is indigestibly rich with allusion to the tropes of pre-economic thought. "A breed for barren metal" evokes the common-place hierarchy of ways to create wealth from Aristotle's *Politics*, in which interest occupies the lowest and most stigmatized place: "And this term interest, which means the birth of money from money, is applied to the breeding of money from money because the offspring resembles the parent. That is why of all modes of getting wealth this is the most unnatural." (Or as Luther put it, "Money is a barren thing.")[18]

"Enemy," too, is an overgrown concept in the history of money lending, one whose taproot lies in God's commandment that Israelites could lend at interest to strangers but not to their brothers. Though this commandment may originally have cut only between families, the requirement of brotherhood came over time to be read as a collective metaphor for community. The Israelite could charge interest only to the non-Israelite, the Jew only to the non-Jew, and the Christian, called to universal brotherhood in the gospel, could take interest from no one. As always, Saint Thomas Aquinas summarized well the Catholic exegetical consensus: "The Jews were forbidden to take usury from their brethren; i.e., from other Jews. By this we are given to understand that to take usury from any man is evil simply, because we ought to treat every man as our neighbor and brother, especially in the state of the Gospel, where to all are called."[19]

Within this tradition, the charging of interest draws a sharp line between neighbor and alien, friend and enemy, Christian and Jew. Antonio's angry invocation of that line is intended to freeze the two merchants into starkly opposing allegories of their respective covenants: loving Christian, hateful Jew. But Shylock starts to melt the opposition as soon as it is made. He responds to Christian insult not with anger, but with love ("I would be friends with you, and have your love") and the offer of an interest-free loan. In seeming jest ("in a merry sport"), he asks only for a token penalty, a useless pound of flesh, should Antonio fail to pay. A dialogue full of double meaning convinces Antonio that "flesh" here is not meant literally, and that the contract is indeed an expression of charity: "Hie thee, gentle Jew! / The Hebrew will turn Christian, he grows kind" (1.3.173–174). The vocabulary of conversion is not coincidental, and its implications are too often overlooked: if according to our logic the wrong kind of contract can make the Christian "Jewish," so conversely can the right kind make the Jew a Christian. Now it is Bassanio's turn to worry about the "Pharisaic" possibility that the contract may be something other than it seems: "I like not fair terms, and a villain's mind" (1.3.175).

Diagnostic Failures

The problem that worries Bassanio is the same one that bothered our evangelists and church fathers in earlier chapters. If in this world of flesh the nonliteral or spiritual sense of what lies before us cannot be separated from its literal or material form, then how can we avoid the danger of interpreting it incorrectly? Shakespeare knows that many have preached easy answers to this question. He puts one of these "answers" at the center of his drama: the test of the three chests by which Portia must be won. The test is simple: the suitor swears to choose between three boxes, one of lead, one of silver, one of gold, and to abide forever by the outcome of his choice. One chest contains Portia's portrait and brings her hand in marriage. The others condemn the suitor to a loveless life, "never to speak to lady afterward" (2.1.41).

The Prince of Morocco is the first to undergo the test. His blackness, like Othello's, dramatizes the Christian ontology in question, with its tensions between exterior appearance and inner virtue. He picks the chest of gold, on the (slightly different) theory that inner and outer beauty should ideally conform. Nothing else is fair enough to contain fair Portia: "an angel in a golden bed / Lies all within." Both these positions are defensibly "Christian," yet the casket contains a damning scroll: "All that glitters is not gold, / Often have you heard that told,— / Many a man his life hath sold. / But my outside to behold.— Gilded timber do worms enfold" (2.7.66–70). We are not surprised by Morocco's failure, and neither was Shakespeare's audience. They had probably already heard the famous story of the three chests from the *Gesta Romanorum* (a late medieval collection of anecdotes for use in sermons widespread in Shakespeare's day). Even if they had not, they knew from Jesus's condemnation of the "whitewashed tombs" of the Pharisees that the "vessell of golde full of dead mennes bones" was the "Jewish" choice, not the "Christian" one. What is surprising about this scene is not Morocco's failure, but that of the test itself.[20]

We can best recognize the chests' inability to establish a distinction between "Christian" and "Jew" if we shift our focus from Morocco's choices and ontological assumptions to Portia's. Portia—like every character in this play—is at high risk of "Judaism." When we first meet her, she is melancholy, like Antonio, and again for "Jewish" reasons: unfree to "choose" love, bound by "cold decree," "curbed by the will of a dead father," she is explicitly placed under the tutelage of the law, from which only the test of the chests can free her. But Portia, too, fails the test, and more blatantly than Morocco. Portia, this "angel," "this shrine, this mortal breathing saint," this woman "of wondrous virtues," commits the "Judaizing" error of placing more value on outer appearance than on inner worth. She has already stumbled in act 1: "If he have the condition of a saint, / and the complexion of a devil, I had rather he should / shrive me than wive me." Now, with the poor prince so cruelly condemned to a loveless life, Portia pitilessly sharpens the point: "Let all of his complexion choose me so." Shakespeare sharpens his point as well: the test of the three chests, with its confident opposition of outer and inner, of material value and spiritual worth, of Jew and Christian, will not suffice. No one in this play, no matter how virtuous, is capable of fully separating the material world from the moral or spiritual one. Like the apostles who "Judaized" even as Jesus warned them against the "leaven of the Pharisees" (Luke 12:1–2, Matt. 16:5–12), the virtuous Portia opts for the "whitewashed tomb" of appearances the moment after the Moor has revealed the skeletons within it.

Shakespeare's characters repeatedly perform this problem, constantly mixing the vocabulary of outer form and material value with that of inner meaning and spiritual virtue. Equally constant is their attempt to remap the resulting confusion onto the polarity of "Christian" and "Jew." Consider, for example, the relationship between Shylock's daughter, the Jewess Jessica, and the Christian Lorenzo. From its beginning their affair is described in a double-dealing language of love and lucre. A letter Jessica writes to Lorenzo sounds—as do most declarations of passion in this play—more like a business proposition than a pledge of love: "She hath directed / How I shall take her from her father's house, / What gold and jewels she is furnish'd with" (2.4.29–31). These words move Lorenzo to rapture, and to religious confusion:

> *If e'er the Jew her father come to heaven,*
> *It will be for his gentle daughter's sake,*
> *And never dare misfortune cross her foot,*
> *Unless she do it under this excuse,*
> *That she is issue to a faithless Jew. (2.4.33–37)*

Is Jessica a "gentle" (gentile, that is, a Christian) or a Jew? The question is important, and we will return to it. At the moment, however, Lorenzo's own identity appears precarious as well. He is late to the elopement, prompting his friends to describe his ardor in terms of broken faith:

"O ten times faster Venus' pigeons fly / To seal love's bonds new-made, than they are wont / To keep obliged faith unforfeited!" (2.6.5–7). When he finally does reach Shylock's house he himself acknowledges his confused religious state: "Here dwells my father Jew." The confusion only increases: Jessica comes to the window disguised as a boy, throws down a casket of her father's jewels, and promises gold: "I will . . . gild myself with some more ducats, and be with you straight" (2.6.51–52). Now it is Lorenzo's friend Gratiano who responds to this conflation of bride and bullion in religious terms: "Now by my hood, a gentle, and no Jew" (2.6.53). Shakespeare's audience, better versed than we are in the moral hierarchies I have been describing, would have found the joke amusing. Gratiano stakes his "hood"—which is to say, the foreskin emblematic of his Christianity—that Jessica is a Christian. But he does so at precisely the moment when she is most explicitly represented in terms of metallic value, a confusion associated with Judaism throughout the play. In other words, Gratiano "Judaizes," and his faulty hermeneutics effect his own "circumcision," thereby revealing (to paraphrase Paul's Romans and Augustine's *Confessions*) that his penis may be uncircumcised, but his heart and lips remain suspect.[21]

This confusion between living being and object of value pervades the play, although Shylock the Jew is made to represent it in its purest form. Recall Solanio's report of the Jew's discovery of his daughter's deception:

> *I never heard a passion so confus'd,*
> *So strange, outrageous, and so variable*
> *As the dog Jew did utter in the streets,—*
> *"My daughter! O my ducats! O my daughter!*
> *Fled with a Christian!*
> *O my Christian ducats!*
> *Justice, the law, my ducats, and my daughter!*
> *A sealed bag, two sealed bags of ducats,*
> *Of double ducats, stol'n from me by my daughter!*
> *And jewels, two stones, two rich and precious stones,*

>Stol'n by my daughter! Justice!—find the girl,
>She hath the stones upon her, and the ducats!" (2.8.12–22)

Girl, gold, justice, gentiles, genitals: all are jumbled together in the howling sorrow of the "dog Jew," who can no longer distinguish between his financial assets and his flesh and blood. His misery unmans him in a double sense. He is castrated through the loss of his "two sealed bags," his "two stones," and he is classified (by the Christian) as un-human, a creature whose words are incapable of distinguishing between living people and material things.[22]

This confusion and the inhumanity it produces are presented in this moment as peculiarly Jewish traits. But they are also, as Shakespeare shows over and over again, to some extent characteristic of every act of communication and human interaction in the world of Venice. If Shylock brings Christian audiences some relief from this "Jewishness," it is through the extremity of the representation. The same is true of the specific form of communication and exchange through which Shakespeare chooses to explore the implications of this confusion: not tissues of lies or lace handkerchiefs as in *Othello,* but contract, oath, pledge, and promise, the legal words that relate people and property to one another. Such contracting words take many forms in *The Merchant of Venice.* Relationships of obligation between father and daughter, bride and groom, employer and employee, citizen and state, God and man: all are translated by Shakespeare into the question of how contracts should be read, explored as a quarrel between covenants.[23]

Can Contracts Be Christian?

The form of contract at the center of the play—the debt contract, or IOU—was the subject of much debate in Shakespeare's day. Throughout much of the sixteenth century, parties to such contracts had been free to specify any mutually agreed-on penalty for nonperformance, in a type of bond known as "conditional defeasance." Such bonds enabled penalties independent of—and sometimes grossly incommensurable with—the value of the debt. But increasingly, they also raised difficult questions, questions absolutely basic to economic and political life. Are there limits to the freedoms, the autonomies of soul and body, that can be alienated through contract? What legal practices, what ways of writing and reading contract and law, can help us determine these limits? By the later sixteenth century the courts were tending to decide that there were limits: Chancery (the high court of equity) began to reduce penalties to the amount of the debt on appeal, a practice (called "chancering") that became routine by 1614. Shakespeare pushed these questions to their limits, not only by staging them as "Jewish questions" but also by posing the legal alienation of self in the extreme form of a carnivorous contract, one that explicitly equates three thousand ducats of Shylock's gold with (on default) one pound of his Christian debtor's flesh.[24]

Such contracts already occupied a distinguished place in European genealogies of morals by the time Shakespeare drew his up. The most famous one stalked the primeval forests of Roman law, at the mythic origins of the European legal order. The Romans were fond of telling stories about the earliest codification of that law, which they called the Law of the Twelve Tables (because it was said to have been inscribed on twelve tables of bronze erected in the Roman Forum in 451–449 BCE). According to Cicero (106–43 BCE), "[N]o bond [*vinculum*], by the wish of our ancestors, was to be tighter in binding good faith than a sworn oath."[25] In the case of debts, the tightness of that bond deeply impressed later commentators. In his *Attic Nights*, a popular collection of ancient lore, the Roman jurist Aulus Gellius (ca. 125–ca. 170 CE) included a description of the capital punishment inflicted of old on debtors who broke their bonds:

> But it was in order to make good faith sacred . . . that they made that capital punishment dreadful by a display of cruelty and fearful by unheard of terrors. For in cases where there were several creditors to whom the debtor had been adjudged, the Board allowed them the privilege of cutting up in pieces and sharing out the body—the body of a man—of him who had been made over to them; and listen, I

will quote the actual words of the Law, lest you believe that maybe
I shrink from their odium—"On the third market day creditors shall
cut pieces. Should they have cut more or less than their due, it shall be
with impunity."[26]

Gellius treated this repayment in flesh as an extreme representation
of the sacrality of contract in ancient Rome. The Christian Tertullian,
writing a generation later, took a very different tack. His *Apologeticus*,
or "Apology," addressed in 197 CE to the judges who were condemning
Christians for violations of Rome's laws, begins with a consideration on
the nature of justice. Laws should not be enforced unless they can be
shown to be just. Enforcing the law merely because it is the law, rather
than inquiring into its higher truth, is not justice but tyranny. Of course
Tertullian was aiming at the laws by which Christians were condemned,
but the best example he could find of legal tyranny is the one that concerns us:

There were laws, too, in old times, that parties against whom a deci-
sion had been given might be cut in pieces by their creditors; however,
by common consent that cruelty was afterwards erased from the stat-
utes, and the capital penalty turned into a brand of shame. . . . How
many laws lie hidden out of sight which still require to be reformed!
For it is neither the number of their years nor the dignity of their
maker that commends them, but simply that they are just. . . . [I]t is a
positively wicked law, if, unproved, it tyrannizes over men.[27]

Today's scholars are fond of suggesting that the Twelve Tables
themselves never existed but were rather a mythical foundation for the
Roman legal order, built out of the retrospective imagination of later
lawyers. If this is so, then already within the Roman legal imagination
the butchering of the bankrupt represented a "limit case," a way of
exploring the extreme implications of basing a society on exchange,
and of society's dependence on the forms of communication (promise,
oath, contract) that guarantee that exchange. It is precisely this type

of foundational exploration that Shakespeare was engaged in through the "limit case"—equally mythic in his England—of the cruel Jew and his carnivorous contract. The answers he produced are tremendously revealing of the political and economic imagination of his age, and of the places assigned in that imagination to figures of Judaism.[28]

Christian Judgment, or Out-Jewing the Jew

The political stakes become clear in act 4's courtroom drama, which is staged as a constitutional affair, presided over by the duke. From its beginning the duke makes his opinion clear: the state cannot deny the Jew law, but nevertheless expects him to show mercy: "Shylock the world thinks, and I think so too, / That thou but leadest this fashion of thy malice / To the last hour of act, and then 'tis thought / Thou'lt show thy mercy and remorse more strange / Than is thy strange apparent cruelty" (4.1.16–121). The language ("last hour") alludes to the Christian belief that the hard hearts of the Jews will be softened at the apocalypse, bringing about their conversion and the redemption of the world. With this hope the duke ends his speech: "We all expect a gentle answer Jew!" (4.1.16–34).

The Jew does not "turn gentle" (that is, convert). He demands instead the "due and forfeit" of his bond. The duke takes yet another theological tack: "How shalt thou hope for mercy rend'ring none?" (4.1.88). Shylock responds as Christian theology dictates Jews should, by claiming to be justified by the law. "What judgment shall I dread doing no wrong?" But in a celebrated speech, he points out as well that the opposition encoded within that theology is not as stark as it seems.

> *You have among you many a purchas'd slave,*
> *Which (like your asses, and your dogs and mules)*
> *You use in abject and in slavish parts,*
> *Because you bought them,—shall I say to you,*
> *Let them be free, marry them to your heirs?*
> *. . . you will answer*

"The slaves are ours,"—so do I answer you: The pound of flesh
   which I demand of him
Is dearly bought, 'tis mine and I will have it:
If you deny me, fie upon your law! There is no force in the
   decrees of Venice: I stand for judgement,—answer, shall I
   have it? (4.1.89–102)

The Christians rail: the Jew is not a human, he is as senseless as the tide, as the mountain forests, his is the soul of a man-eating wolf, reincarnate in man's body. The Jew's position: "I stand here for law" (4.1.42).

The line recalls Portia's portentous words to Bassanio, just before his happy choice of chests: "I stand for sacrifice" (3.2.57). But with law and sacrifice now posed in intractable antithesis, the choice before the duke's court, a choice between mercy's antinomian anarchy or the tyranny of contract, seems irreconcilable. It is at this point of impasse that Portia enters the scene, disguised as a doctor of laws. It is she who will decide the case, and her decision will again make clear that (*pace* so many preachers) against the claims of law there are no easy answers, no easy distinctions between Christian and Jew. Indeed her first question will famously be, "Which is the merchant here, and which the Jew?"[29]

Portia's initial strategy, like Ambrose's so long ago, is to point earthly law toward the divine. Mercy, she tells Shylock, is the miracle that transcends the difference between giver and receiver. It is mercy that mediates between laws earthly and divine, raising "temporal power," the "dread and fear of kings," to godliness: "And earthly power doth then show likest God's / When mercy seasons justice: therefore Jew, / Though justice be thy plea, consider this. / That in the course of justice, none of us / should see salvation: we do pray for mercy" (4.1.200–204). Alongside equity Portia appeals to transcendence, to deferential emulation of a heavenly and spiritual court. But the Jew rejects the otherworldly gambit: "My deeds upon my head! I crave the law" (4.1.210). The point is clear: the legal claims of this world cannot be overcome simply by pointing to the existence of another. Bassanio pleads that Portia "[w]rest once the law to your authority, / —to do a great right, do a little wrong" (4.1.219–220). But Portia understands the antinomian danger:

> *It must not be, there is no power in Venice*
> *Can alter a decree established:*
> *'Twill be recorded for a precedent,*
> *And many an error by the same example*
> *Will rush into the state,—it cannot be. (4.1.222–226)*

In order to solve the problem, the "doctor of laws" cannot simply transcend "Judaism," "legalism," and contract. On the contrary, she must embrace them.

Embrace them she does, engaging Shylock in a battle of literalism and emerging the winner. The contract stipulates a "pound of flesh," but it does not mention blood. Therefore should Shylock shed a drop of Christian blood in cutting out his pound, or should he take a hair's weight flesh too much, "Though diest, and all thy goods are confiscate." Moreover, as an "alien" who has sought the life of a citizen, under "the laws of Venice" all his goods are forfeited, and his "life lies in the mercy / Of the Duke only, 'gainst all other voice" (4.1.330, 353–354). Order has been restored. Antonio is saved from Shylock, and the rule of law is simultaneously maintained, by the paradoxical expedient of making the Jew both supremely subject to the law and simultaneously placing him outside it, as an alien whose life is entirely in the sovereign's hands. That sovereign is merciful, "that thou shalt see the difference of our spirit" (4.1.366): the Jew's life is pardoned, but all his property is lost. Antonio adds yet another mercy: half the property will go to Lorenzo and Jessica, but the Jew must convert to Christianity.[30]

For readers who think that the courtroom scene has separated the Christian from the Jew, the fifth act that follows must seem a puzzling anticlimax. But if my interpretation is correct, the courtroom scene, like the test of the three chests, represents another failure, and the separation remains unclear. One symptom of this failure, at least for modern readers, is that the "Christian mercies"—confiscation, choice between death or conversion—seem "Jewishly" cruel.[31] But a more telling symptom for Shakespeare's audience would have been the competing poetics of conversion within the scene. The doctor's feats of literalism convert Shylock to Christianity, but they simultaneously convert Gratiano—with his eponymous claim to Christian "grace"—to "Judaism." The conversion is evident in Gratiano's diction as well as in the content of his speech. Throughout the courtroom scene he increasingly imitates Shylock's rhythms, repeats his phrases and his biblical allusions, and adopts his merciless insistence on the application of law (punning on his own name as he does so: "a halter gratis—nothing else, for God's sake!" [4.1.390]), until at last he appears as cruel as the Jew. His fall reminds us of the fundamental unclarity between "Jewish" and "Christian" approaches to the myriad forms of promise and contract inescapable in this world. The doctor has defeated the limit case, but only by resorting to a "Judaizing" hyperliterality, that is, by "out-Jewing" the Jew. The Christian difficulty with law and language remains.[32]

The Christian Problem: "For I Am a Jew If I / Serve the Jew Any Longer"

If the court fails to establish "the difference of our spirit," it is because Shakespeare, unlike some of his sources, is uninterested in minimizing the dangers of "Judaism" that haunt contract. On the contrary, he wants to extend those dangers into the contractual realm at the heart of his own practice: the promise of meaning inherent in the exchange of words themselves. Communication and interpretation have long been associated with lending and obligation, as the etymology of those words themselves makes clear.[33] In Shakespeare's age, a number of prominent theorists understood every communicative act, regardless of whether it involved words, objects, or money, as a promise of meaning to others. Words are, to quote Francis Bacon, "the tokens current and accepted for conceits," just as money is the accepted currency of value. What Bacon meant is that in order for communication to be possible, every sign exchanged (be it word or coin or ring) must bind all parties to a common understanding of its meaning. In other words, when we communicate with someone else, we enter into a type of contract with that person, promising that our words mean more or less what others expect them to mean. We pour into our sounds and symbols a significant portion of our interpretive freedom, and we subject ourselves to language's laws.[34]

Since ancient times this contractual understanding of language was thought by many to be a prerequisite for human society. An example well known to Shakespeare and his contemporaries was that of Cicero, for whom the common bond (*societas*) of political life was unthinkable without a strong common bond of language. Men were joined, according to Cicero, by the "most cheerful chains of speech." In the century after Luther, as Catholic consensus collapsed into religious and civil wars (see chapter 9 of this book), the contractual model of language offered some refuge. Hugo Grotius, for example, looking for the sources of an international law that could hold all religions and peoples (even atheists) under its jurisdiction, found that law in the contract of language. The "common usage" (*populari ex usu*) of words, according to Grotius in his *On the Law of War and Peace*, is the basis of all association:

> *There would be no obligation at all by Promises, if every man were left to his Liberty, to put what Construction he pleased upon them, therefore some certain Rule must be agreed on, whereby we may know, what our Promise oblige us to; and here natural Reason will tell us, that the Person to whom the Promise is given, has a Power to force him who gave it, to do what the right Interpretation of the Words of his Promise does require. For otherwise no Business could come to a Conclusion, which in moral Things is reckoned impossible.[35]*

This contractual linguistics produces a difficult question, one distantly related to the debates over the relative merits of literal and nonliteral readings of the Bible that divided the theologians. In exchange for a stable society, just how much of our freedom do we need to surrender to the symbols with which we communicate? For Hobbes, writing half a century after Shakespeare and anxious to augment the stabilizing powers of contract after a bloody civil war, the surrender was almost total: "Metaphors, and sensless and ambiguous words, are like *ignes fatui* [will-'o-the-wisps]; and reasoning upon them, is wandering amongst innumerable absurdities; and their end, contention, and sedition, or contempt." Shylock's warning to the Duke of Venice invokes the political danger. Deny the binding force of contract and you "let the danger light / Upon your charter and your city's freedom" (4.1.39–40). Shylock's speech itself expresses his awareness of the linguistic origins of that peril when we first encounter him, literally repeating his interlocutor's words. Hence his constant effort to stipulate his metaphors: "There be land rats and water / rats . . . —I mean pirates" (1.3.20–21); "but stop my house's ears—I mean my casements" (2.5.34). If Shylock can be said to have a theory of how language should function, it is one very close to Hobbes's: "Fast bind fast find, / A proverb never stale in thrifty mind" (2.5.54–55).[36]

But Shakespeare's linguistics is not Shylock's. A playwright cannot deny the literal and common claims of the "tokens current and accepted" (that is, words) that he depends on, but neither can he afford to invest them with too tyrannical a power over the pun and play of his poetics. How much liberty can the language of theater be allowed? This is yet another of Shakespeare's "Jewish questions," posed perhaps most explicitly in the person of Launcelot, first Shylock's servant and then Bassanio's. Launcelot is, of all the characters in the play, the most self-conscious of the danger of becoming Jewish: "For I am a Jew if I / serve the Jew any longer" (2.2.107). His awareness of the risk is as much the product of profession as proximity: he deals in words, and knows (like Shakespeare) that how he employs those words will determine whether or not he "Judaizes." In this sense, Launcelot performs the problem of theater as another version of the Jewish problem. On the one hand, he lives from mimetic deceit of the sort we have seen Christian hermeneutics associating with "Judaism." On the other, his wordplay, like that of many of Shakespeare's fools, strives toward truth telling. His claim, like that of Elizabethan theater, is of virtuous deceit, and the establishment of that claim requires distancing from the Judaism that threatens it.

Shakespeare explicitly stages this linguistic similarity between playwright, jester, and Jew when he has Launcelot "contrive confusions" on his blind father, in obvious imitation of the biblical Jacob's theft of Isaac's blessing, and in echo of Shylock's earlier conversation. But imitation is not repetition. Launcelot pretends to be other than he is only to obtain what is already his in any case (his father's blessing), not to take what belongs to another. His deceit may be similar to Jacob's or Shylock's, but it produces no theft, no false claims to identity. "Thrift is blessing, if men steal it not": the point of the Launcelot/Gobbo scene is to claim, in the moral terms of the day, that Launcelot's profit from his words is Christian and not Jewish. Shakespeare is as fond as Launcelot of this ontological trick, restaging it at the end of the play in Portia's "adulterous" oath to lie with the lad who has her ring (an oath that similarly resolves into identity, rather than the adultery it pretends to threaten, since Portia is herself that boy).

Both Launcelot and Shakespeare realize that such narrow scenes of virtuous deceit cannot serve as a general justification for theater. What underlying identity can be established between players and audience that would suffice to make theatrical deceit virtuous? Launcelot proposes one possibility. Speaking to his new employer, he divides words in two, assigning the "thingness" of words to the Jew and their spirit to the Christian: "The old proverb is very well parted between my / master Shylock and you sir, you have 'the grace of / God' sir, and he hath 'enough'" (2.2.132–134). For Launcelot, as for much of the Renaissance poetic tradition, it is "the grace of God" that separates Christian wordplay from its materialist "Jewish" neighbor, raising poetry from mere letter to spirit and thereby legitimating it as a Christian art.[37]

Shakespeare does not rest with Launcelot's solution, perhaps because its dualism produces as many difficulties as it solves. Instead, in act 5 he embarks on one more exploration of the problem: the "comedy of the rings." Portia and her maid Nerissa had given their respective fiancés an engagement ring, making them promise to keep it forever.

Then, disguised as the doctor and his clerk, they extracted the rings from Antonio's grateful friends as reward for his rescue, and hurry home to prepare their reproach. The comedy is full of double entendres that exploit the difference between appearance and reality in order to threaten infidelity, but now both "outer" and "inner" will simultaneously, even miraculously, be true. The "men" to whom the men gave the rings were really women, but they were "their" women, and so fidelity is maintained.[38]

Similarly, confusions between monetary and spiritual value begin to resolve themselves. Gratiano (as we have come to expect) remains too worldly, disparaging the monetary and aesthetic value of the ring he gave away, but Nerissa brings him up short: "What talk you of the posy or the value? / You swore to me when I did give it you" (5.1.162–164). The object of exchange has, in other words, symbolic as well as metallic value: it represents an oath of love.

We are approaching a hopeful hermeneutics. But this distinction is still not enough. Shylock, after all, had made it as well, upon hearing of Jessica's trade of one of his rings for a monkey: "I had it of Leah when I was a bachelor: I would not have given it for a wilderness of monkeys" (3.1.112–113). The distinction is not enough because excessive attachment to a "thing held as ceremony," "a thing stuck on with oaths upon your finger, / And so riveted with faith unto your flesh" (5.1.168–169), still represents a "Judaizing" literalism, a confusion between symbol and meaning almost as dramatic as that expressed in the contract of the pound of flesh. Shakespeare's players must go further. They must recognize that the Christian triumph over Judaism consists in knowing not how to keep the oath and its symbolic forms but when, in the interests of love, to let them go. Like everyone else within the material world, they too are bound by necessity to promise their words, their goods, and even their flesh (as, for example, in the marriage contract) in a vast and shimmering network of communication, circulation, and exchange that entraps even the wisest person. Within this world, Shakespeare seems to suggest, it is only the exceptional knowledge of love that can distinguish the "gentle" from the "Jew."[39]

"The Difference in Our Spirits"

At last we are in a position to identify the twin constitutional pillars of Shakespeare's imagined community: the sovereignty of love, the rule of law. Relations between man and man, man and money, man and material thing can be mediated and represented only in the language of law and contract. This language cannot be denied, hence law must rule. But among fellow Christian citizens, at least, its reading should be oriented in a particular way. The point remains that of Augustine, articulated in *On Christian Doctrine*: "To follow the letter, and to take signs for the things that are signified by them, is a mark of weakness and bondage." According to Augustine, this was the weakness and bondage of the Jews, and the only way to avoid it is for the Christian to subject all readings to the test of love. "Every man . . . has hope in his own conscience, so far as he perceives that he has attained to the love and knowledge of God and his neighbor." It is this hope, offered by Augustine to readers struggling to distinguish between the literal and the figurative in biblical texts, which Shakespeare offers to readers of contracts and the world in *The Merchant of Venice*.[40]

Of course there are many differences between Shakespeare and Augustine, but there are also some similarities worth noting. Shakespeare, like Augustine, realizes that the tendency of the material sign and its immaterial meaning to fly toward opposite poles can be combated only by holding them in close proximity. Like Augustine, he realized the risks of confusion that this close proximity of matter and spirit creates, and much more than the saint, he exploited the comic (as well as the tragic) potential of those possibilities. In the end, though, he relieved these risks in much the same way that Augustine did, by pouring their extremes into the figure of the Jew. Shakespeare's Jews remain in some sense ontologically alien, irreducibly more literal and less loving than the Christian. Shylock may bleed like a Christian, hate like a Christian, even occasionally talk like a Christian, but he most emphatically does not become a Christian, not even after his conversion. It is in this enduring distinction, with all the projections it facilitates, that we begin to see an essential "difference of our spirit" emerge.

Given the importance of this distinction, it is not surprising that the question of whether or not a Jew can "turn Christian" is a crucial one in *The Merchant of Venice*, with Jessica as its focus. Comedy requires happy endings, but Shakespeare gives us plenty of reason to doubt that even Jessica's liberality, seemingly in every way the reverse of her father's misanthropy, can ever be enough to overcome the Jewishness of her flesh. Already in the third act Launcelot joked that Jessica's only hope for salvation is a "bastard" one—namely, that she might not be the Jew's daughter (3.5.1–21). The skepticism of the fifth and final act is more serious. It opens with banter on a beautiful evening in Belmont, as Jessica and Lorenzo compare this night to nights that enveloped great lovers of the past. As the stakes rise, Jessica makes a final classical allusion:

> *In such a night*
> *Medea gathered the enchanted herbs*
> *That did renew old Aeson. (5.1.15–17)*

The allusion is appropriate, in that Medea was a sorceress who abandoned her father to elope with Jason and who used her magic to help him win the Golden Fleece. It is, however, unfortunate, since the marriage ended in betrayal, infanticide, and Medea's murderous exile. It is for this reason that Lorenzo comes crashing swiftly back into the near present:

> *In such a night*
> *Did Jessica steal from the wealthy Jew*
> *And with an unthrift love did run from Venice*
> *As far as Belmont. (5.1.18–21)*[41]

Is the momentum of Jessica's "unthrift love" enough to free her soul from the gravitational grip of Judaism and launch it into Christian orbit? Early modern Europeans like Thomas Calvert were famously pessimistic about the ability of Jews to convert sincerely to Christianity: "When a mouse shall catch a cat, then a Jew converted . . . will remain a firm

Christian." Shakespeare leaves the diagnosis open, but the prognosis is not good. At the end of their evening stroll, Lorenzo puts the problem in cosmic terms, explaining to Jessica that music causes the harmony within our souls to echo the harmony of the heavenly spheres.

> *The man that hath no music in himself,*
> *Nor is not mov'd with concord of sweet sounds,*
> *Is fit for treasons, strategems, and spoils;*
> *The motions of his spirit are dull as night,*
> *And his affections dark as Erebus:*
> *Let no such man be trusted. Mark the Music.* (5.1.91–96)

"Mark the Music": Shylock has already failed this test in the second act, when he condemned "the vile squealing of the wry-necked fife" and commanded Jessica to close the windows lest the "sound of shallow foppery / enter my sober house" (2.5.30–35). Has Jessica just failed the test as well? "I am never merry when I hear sweet music" (5.1.77). These flat words of blank verse, Jessica's last in the play, were the ones that prompted Lorenzo's leap into harmonic theory. Lorenzo tells us that even wild horses are made gentle by music. By that diagnostic, and depending on how we interpret her lack of musical merriment, is Jessica condemned to remain, like her father, worse than an animal?[42]

A great deal rides on our answer to this question. Generations of critics have debated whether *The Merchant of Venice* is anti-Semitic. Their argument is not so much about the play's reception and historical effects: few would deny, for example, that however complex a character Shylock might be, his name quickly became a popular synonym for usurious cruelty. The disagreement is rather about the range of interpretations the play can reasonably sustain and which of these interpretations Shakespeare himself might have intended. A subtle defense can even set the one against the other, suggesting, for example, that Shakespeare gave his vulgar audience the Jewish stereotype they demanded, but hollowed it out with an irony that he intended the wise to detect.[43]

It is certainly true that Shakespeare undermines the easy answers to the difficult questions he poses. Indeed, the play reminds us with its very last words that even in Belmont, the Christian can still "Judaize." Those last words are, not surprisingly, Gratiano's: "Well, while I live I'll fear no other thing / So sore as keeping safe Nerissa's ring" (5.1.306–307). A few moments before, confronted with Nerissa's playful "threat" of adultery with the young clerk to whom he gave her ring, he had responded with a brutal conflation of writing and circumcision: "I'll mar the young clerk's pen" (5.1.250). Now, with Portia's pedagogy revealed and the lovers reconciled, Gratiano's interpretation of the world remains unreformed. Not only is his conflation of Nerissa's symbol ("ring") with her sex precisely the type of confusion the play has again and again associated with "Judaism," but his notion of exchange remains fearful and contractual rather than loving, "Jewish" rather than "Christian." Gratiano's use of language remains, to adapt a formula of the French philosopher Jacques Derrida's, "an experience of circumcision."[44]

Gratiano marks one limit to Shakespeare's poetics of conversion: in this world communication cannot be purged of "Jewishness"; the Christian remains at risk. But Jessica marks a starker limit, for if we take seriously the doubts that Shakespeare has planted about her conversion, then his irony is not bottomless. The choice is not between, on the one hand, a straightforward opposition between Jewish legalism and Christian love that "ends with harmony and perfect love," as one modern critic suggested, and, on the other, "an ironic comedy" without resolution, as another counterargued. There is irony, but that irony has its limits, and the Jewish shape those limits take preserves the plausibility of Christian claims to love.[45] The Christian may be confused with "Judaism" on Shakespeare's stage, and the Jew may appear Christian, but the one cannot become the other. The Jew stands—unlike the Christian—outside the reach of Shakespeare's poetics of conversion. In this scenario, it is that poetics itself which, like Lorenzo's music, rediscovers "the difference in our spirit," the vanishing difference between Christian and "Jew."

To a Christian world increasingly convinced that (as Adam Smith would put it a good while later) "every man thus lives by exchanging, or becomes in some measure a merchant," the rediscovery of that difference brings immeasurable relief, even when it takes place in a world without "real" Jews. It is this lingering fantasy of relief based on an irreducible difference from "the Jew" that, if we wish, we can begin to call anti-Semitism. During World War II, in their *Dialectic of Enlightenment*, the German philosophers Adorno and Horkheimer wrote that "what is pathological about anti-Semitism is not projective behavior as such, but the absence of reflection in it." Are Shakespeare's projections of the contractual dangers of symbolic economies onto figures of Judaism pathological? Your answer to this final question may well come down to your explanation of one character's melancholy: not the melancholy of Antonio or of Portia, with which we began, but that of Lorenzo's "Jewess," who is never merry when she hears sweet music.[46]

Chapter 9

"ISRAEL" AT THE FOUNDATIONS
OF CHRISTIAN POLITICS: 1545–1677

> *But in that I am next to handle, which is the nature*
> *and rights of a* CHRISTIAN COMMONWEALTH,
> *whereof there dependeth much upon supernatural*
> *revelations of the will of God, the ground of my*
> *discourse must be . . . also the prophetical.*
>
> —Thomas Hobbes, *Leviathan*, 1651

W HEN INTELLECTUAL HISTORIANS want to tell a story about Europe's path to modernity, their account often goes something like this:

The tectonic stress between Reformation and Counter-Reformation opened a rift in revelation. Into this rift leapt countless explorers like Galileo, Descartes, Hobbes, and Spinoza, explorers whose discoveries gradually reduced confidence in the claims of Christian cosmology to effectively govern all aspects of human life. Correspondingly, the individual's rational faculties, rather than God and revelation, were increasingly put in charge of making order and sense of the cosmos. The goals of human knowledge, whether political, economic, historical, or natural, were slowly but steadily re-oriented from divine toward secular ends. By the late seventeenth century the more radical wings of the "Enlightenment" were demanding the complete emancipation of "reason" from the tutelage of religion, even calling into question the existence of divinity itself. The Revolution that began in France in 1789 sought to cast off all chains of faith and custom, marching into Paris with promises of freedom and the radical improvement of the world through reason. Yet many resisted this promise, or proclaimed it false. Unchecked by faith, they prophesied, reason would prove a more terrible tyrant than God, pitilessly reducing every soul to self-interested calculation and utility, and destroying the possibility of community based on love of God, of neighbor, or of any higher good. In its myriad and sometimes violent forms, this debate has continued to shape much of the history of the past two centuries.

Of course this caricature of a struggle between a dictatorship of divinity and the rule of reason leaves many of the subject's features blank. Some of these will be filled in over the course of the chapters that follow. But the detailed history of secularization and its enemies is not our focus here. The goal of the chapters that follow is to suggest that because basic ideas about human action in a divinely ordered world had long been conceptualized in terms of Judaism, revolutions and counterrevolutions in those ideas could be (and often were) fought through figures of "Judaism" descended from those that had sustained the earlier political and theological order. This is not to say that the centuries of conflict and change that produced European Enlightenment and counter-Enlightenment, modernity and antimodernism, should be understood principally in terms of "Judaism." It is only to say that neither Enlightenment nor modernity overthrew the Christian theologies of Judaism described in earlier chapters. Instead they translated them into new terms, embedding them in the philosophies and sciences with which they claimed to make a new and more critical sense of the cosmos. In the process, they simultaneously altered the work these figures of Judaism did in the world, and the possibilities of life in that world for real Jews.

We will begin in this chapter with political work, looking at the ways in which Judaism was deployed in the wars of religion unleashed by the efforts at Reformation and Counter-Reformation we first encountered in chapter 7. We will then focus on a case—the English Civil Wars—that is extreme both because of the intensity with which the vocabulary of Judaism was employed within it, and because the employment took place in a society that had not had "real" Jews living openly within it for more than three hundred years. It was in the context of those wars that Thomas Hobbes produced his *Leviathan*, a book that quickly became one of the foundations for what we today sometimes call political science, and that will serve us as an example of the work that "Israel" could be asked to do at the foundations of modern political thought.

What Firebrands of Sedition Hath Religion Kindled?

Within a very few years after Luther's death, the great princes of Latin Europe were willing to concede that after more than a millennium, Catholicism no longer had a monopoly on the Continent's Christianity. The speed with which rulers came to this conclusion is astounding. Already in 1555, the Catholic emperor Charles granted the Protestant princes of the Schmalkaldic League the freedom to choose between Lutheranism (but no other sect or faith) and Catholicism for themselves and their subjects, and promised not to interfere in their decision by force of arms. The logic behind this limited but momentous concession, known as the "Augsburg compromise," crystallized into an aphorism: *cuius regio, eius religio*, "who has the kingdom, has the religion." The faith of the kingdom was the king's to decide. This should not be confused with anything like "freedom of conscience." Subjects, if they disagreed with their princes, were granted only the right to sell their property and leave the state.[1]

The Augsburg compromise was meant to avoid religious violence between sovereigns in a world that had hardened with amazing rapidity into rival confessional blocks. But the term *sovereign* is anachronistic here. No sixteenth-century prince was "independent" in the modern sense. The various Lutheran rulers of the Schmalkaldic League, for example, owed fealty to the Holy Roman emperor, who was ruler of many other realms (including Spain and its increasingly large territories in Columbus's "New World") in his own right, and himself under a complex of obligations to the papacy. Whose then was the *regio*, the power of decision? Differences over "jurisdictional" ambiguities like these helped plunge Europe into a century of religious war. As the Flemish humanist Justus Lipsius (1547–1606) put it,

> *Good Lord what firebrands of sedition hath religion kindled in this fayrest part of the world? The chiefe heads of our christian commonwealths are at strife among themselves, and many millions of men have bin brought to ruine and do dayly perish, under a pretext of piety.*[2]

Lipsius's description might have been bleaker still had he lived to see the Thirty Years' War (1618–1648), in which many of the Protestant states allied with France to confront the global empire of Catholic Spain, and as much as a third of Germany perished. None of this violence, however, affected the general consensus about the political principle that the prince decided the piety of his people. In fact, after a century of massacre, the best that Europe's sovereigns could do was repeat that consensus. The Peace of Westphalia that concluded the Thirty Years' War in 1648 is often invoked by political scientists as the origin of the modern order of sovereign states. But it is largely a reassertion of the Augsburg compromise, and even retains the ambiguity in that compromise that had led to its collapse (namely, the emperor's right to overrule the choices of princes who owed him allegiance).

This consensus was priestly as well as political. Regardless of confession, the vast majority of theologians agreed that God expected governments to enforce religious conformity and to punish violations of his laws, without mercy or tolerance. As John Calvin put it in his *Defense of the orthodox faith* (1554),

> *Whoever shall maintain that wrong is done to heretics and blasphemers in punishing them, makes himself an accomplice in their crime and guilty as they are. There is no question here of man's authority: it is God who speaks and clear it is what law he will have kept in the Church even to the end of the world. Wherefore does he demand of us a so extreme severity, if not to show us that due honour is not paid to him, so long as we set not his service above every human consideration, so that we spare not kin nor blood nor life of any and forget all humanity when the matter is to combat for his glory?*

A similar position had been a part of mainstream Catholic Christianity since the fourth century (in the words of Saint Jerome, "There is no cruelty in regard for God's honor"). It was the duty of government to punish infractions of God's law. Failure to do so, it was widely believed, would dishonor God and bring down his wrath on the polity. Calvin's position was not "merely" theoretical. He used his own authority in Geneva, for example, to urge the city (successfully) to burn Michael Servetus at the stake for espousing anti-Trinitarian doctrines. The treatise *On Heretics* that Calvin's disciple Theodore Beza published in defense of his teacher's actions on that occasion became one of the most influential sixteenth-century Protestant defenses of "hereticide."

As "International Calvinism" grew into a potent political power in places like England and the Netherlands, these arguments for state repression of religious dissidence became particularly consequential. Late in the seventeenth century some Protestant advocates of toleration would attempt to characterize them as relics of Catholic cruelty or Jewish theocracy. None of the founding figures of Reform would have agreed. Every important theologian of what is sometimes called the "magisterial Reformation" shared the general thesis that it was the duty of the civil magistrate to punish religious error with the power of the state. Melancthon, for example, echoing his teacher Luther, wrote in 1531 that people who "proclaim tenets that are frankly blasphemous, even if they are not rebels, should be done to death by the civil authority."[3]

Of course there were practical limits to this "done to death," particularly in those (relatively few) polities where religious diversity was significant enough to prove a threat to the basic stability of the state. In France, for example, decades of civil war between Catholics and a Protestant Huguenot minority convinced some pragmatic souls that in cases where too large a proportion of the population was inclined toward an "evil" sect, the heretics should be allowed their practice lest corrective violence utterly destroy the commonwealth. This "politique" logic, argued in treatises like Sebastian Castellio's *Advice to France Laid Waste* (1562) and the anonymous *Exhortation to Princes* (1561), certainly contributed to experiments in toleration, such as the protection granted to French Protestants by the Edict of Nantes in 1598, which was revoked by Louis XIV in 1685. But even the practically minded *Exhortation* agreed that the ideal course was to exterminate early while extermination was still possible:

> *Just as in the human body one has to amputate a rotten member at an early stage before the disease spreads, . . . so the wise men of the world agree that as soon as new opinions begin to cling to a society, they should be cut off, by fire, sword, and death: that is to say, when their number is still small.*[4]

It was this ancient and ecumenical consensus about the duties of earthly powers to coerce their subjects into conformity with God's will that was the chief engine of war in early modern Europe.

Historians have long suggested that the devastation wrought by the wars of religion forced a basic rethinking of faith's place in European politics, and encouraged a turn toward greater freedom for individual reason and conscience. But what is striking from our point of view is the extent to which, for more than a century, that rethinking managed to skirt the basic consensus. Justus Lipsius, whose complaint about the "ruine" of the "Christiane commonwealths" we just encountered, is himself a good example of this rethinking and of its limits. Certainly he was a champion of individual reason. In treatises like his *On Constancy in Times of Public Calamity* (1583/4), he advocated a novel blend of philosophical stoicism with Christian faith. Borrowing from the Roman Seneca, he argued that through the use of reason humans could conquer their passions and false opinions, and achieve the peace of mind necessary to endure the many earthly tribulations to which they are subjected by God's will. This peace of mind Lipsius called "freedom," for "we are born into a kingdom wherein true liberty consists of obedience to God."

In his *Six books on politics or Civil Doctrine* (1589), Lipsius elevated this Christian Stoicism into a politics for troubled times, applying it to the question of how princes should live and rule, again with an emphasis on human reason (for if a prince "wishes to subject all things to himself, he first should subject himself to reason"). But as one might deduce from Lipsius's definition of *freedom*, none of this emphasis on individual reason implied an emancipation of the subject's religiosity from that of the state, or of the political from the divine. On the contrary, though Lipsius's princes had no "rights in sacred matters" (in other words, they should not interfere with the doctrines and governance of the church), they were obliged to maintain public religious conformity with fire and sword. As he put it in the now-familiar surgical metaphor, "Burn, cut [dissidents away], for the entire body is much more valuable than a few of its limbs."[5]

Lipsius is just one example of a faintly paradoxical but general truth: the theological heterogeneity of Europe in the age of Reform and Counter-Reform did not shatter religious homogeneity at the level of the state. On the contrary, the increasing potential for theological difference only increased the investment of the polity in the piety of its members. Hence European politics grew more, not less, confessional over the course of the sixteenth and early seventeenth centuries, and revelation grew more, not less, political. In Protestant countries especially, with their emphasis on mass access to the Bible in translation, the language and meaning of scripture itself became an affair of state. In the opinion of King James's advisors, for example, the English version most widely read in Shakespeare's day (known as the Geneva Bible) was "destructive of the person and power of kings," or as the king himself put it, "very partial, untrue, seditious." *Cuius regno, eius scriptura*, he could have said, as he commanded the new translation we know today as "King James."[6]

In short, this period from 1550 to 1670 was not (as the eighteenth century would be) an age of revolution against the rule of revelation. Its great rebellions (of the Dutch against their Spanish rulers, of the English against their king, to name only two) were carried out in the name of scripture, not against it. For although kings were the enforcers of God's laws, they were also subject to those laws. This double status, as we saw in previous chapters, had always made them vulnerable to resistance in the name of God. The clash of Reformation and Counter-Reformation only heightened the tension. Its transformation of confessional politics increased sovereign authority over scripture (*cuius regio . . .*), but its transformation of biblical reading practices increased subjects' access to that scripture, and thereby amplified the political power of God's words. At the same time that the princes of this period extended their power over prophecy, prophecy extended its power over them.

Mosaic Constitutions for Christian Polities

The Old Testament, in particular, gave specific instructions as to what God's kingdom should look like. Especially in Protestant lands, there were many who wondered whether a Christian nation should not be putting more of those instructions into practice. Already in Luther's day, the German peasants' revolt had appealed to the reformer's literalizing interpretations in order to justify their uprising in terms of "God's word." In a sermon revealingly entitled "How Christians should regard Moses," Luther had rejected the peasants' appeal: "[B]ut my dear fellow, the question is whether [God's word] was said to you." His patronizing rejection facilitated the peasants' bloody repression, but it did not stifle the revolutionary potential inherent in the increasingly intimate relationship he advocated between reader and letter of scripture.[7]

The history of England provides a good example of just how great that potential could be. Beginning with the reign of Henry VIII, the scripturally ordained relationship between sovereigns and subjects was intensely debated.[8] There were even those, like the Presbyterians decried by Bishop Sandys of London in 1573, who believed (according to Sandys) that "the judicial laws of Moses are binding upon Christian princes, and they ought not in the slightest degree to depart from them." Queen Elizabeth and her advisors probably had such people in mind when they included among the Thirty-nine Articles of their religious settlement the insistence that "the Law given from God by Moses, as touching Ceremonies and Rites do not bind Christian men, nor the Civil precepts thereof ought of necessity to be received in any Commonwealth."[9]

Both bishop and queen were right to worry. Biblical Israel had always provided a model for Christian polities. Medieval Catholic monarchs had frequently drawn on a model known (among medievalists) as "Davidic Kingship": indeed at times the English royal family even claimed to be descended from King David. The new republics of the later Middle Ages and the Renaissance also turned to Israel for inspiration: after all, before God grudgingly acceded to their requests for a king, the Israelite "nation of priests" had lived as a "republic," without a monarch and under God's immediate rule. (Recall the desperate suggestion of the bachelor Marcos in chapter 5, that Toledo should put itself under the direct rule of the Holy Spirit.) But Israel's example posed especially urgent problems for Protestants, both because, having dispensed with papal claims, they faced more open questions about the relationship between secular and divine power, and because when confronting those questions they were armed with new confidence in the possibilities of scripture.[10]

According to Thomas Hobbes, it was through this confidence that civil disorder crept into the commonwealth:

Every man, nay, every boy and wench, that could read English thought they spoke with God almighty, and understood what he said, when

*by a certain number of chapters a day they had read the Scriptures
once or twice over. . . . [T]his licence of interpreting the Scripture was
the cause of so many several sects, as having lain hid till the beginning of the late King's reign, did then appear to the disturbance of the
commonwealth.*[11]

The "disturbance of the commonwealth" of which he speaks is, of
course, the English Civil Wars (known also as the English Revolution,
the Great Rebellion, and by numerous other names) that began in 1642.
This was a time, as Hobbes put it, when England was "boyling hot with
questions concerning the rights of Dominion, and the obedience due
from subjects."[12] Before those questions were extinguished, the king and
as much as a tenth of his kingdom would perish, and England would
experiment with both parliamentary rule and military "Protectorship."

It is perfectly reasonable to ask, after this rather breathless tour of
early modern confessional politics, what any of this has to do with our
theme of thinking about Jews. Why focus, for example, on the English
Civil Wars if until their very end no living Jews confessed publicly in
England? Contemporaries would not have asked this question. They
well understood the importance of ideas about "Jews" and "Judaizing"
in the long history of Christian disputes over power. To them, it made
perfect sense to translate the disputes of their own day into those terms,
as when the author of *The Wonderful and Most Deplorable History of
the Jews* (1652/1684) explained that the city of London executed King
Charles because it was "led along by a true Jewish Spirit." At the end of
this chapter I will touch briefly on the subject of what European Christians were saying and doing about "real" Jews, whom the vast majority
of them would never meet. But first we need to understand how and
why, during the rough century between 1545 and 1677, so many of the
"burning" questions about the relationship between the rights of scripture, of sovereigns, and of subjects were posed and answered in terms
of "Judaism" even in the vast stretches of Europe where there were no
Jews. For this, the English Civil Wars provide a capital example.[13]

We are by now accustomed to seeing accusations of Judaizing thrown back and forth in disputes over power, and such was certainly the case in this long struggle over the rights of rulers and subjects. Just how extensive that usage was can be demonstrated through the massive databases of seventeenth-century text that are today available. Searching through the 37,515 texts available (in 2009) for the period 1640–1660, one recent scholar found that the words *Israel, Hebrew, Jew, Moses, Jerusalem*, or *Zion* appeared in some 3,222 records: roughly 8.6 percent of printed works produced, in any and all genres, that are fully searchable. (Subtracting mathematical, scientific, and other genres where these words rarely appear, the proportion would be considerably higher.) To put it in comparative terms, many more sources (2,271) contain Jewish keywords like *Josephus, Rabbi, Kabbala, Moses, Talmud*, and *Solomon*, than classical ones like *Plato, Aristotle, Socrates, Homer, Tacitus*, or *Cicero* (1,406).[14]

Readers interested in the full semantic field of these usages can turn to this important research: here we must remain at the level of anecdote. To give but one example, during the critical lawsuit that preceded the civil wars, over the king's rights to tax his subjects for the defense of the realm without approval of Parliament (Hampdem's case, 1637), Sir Robert Berkeley, judge of the Court of the King's Bench, could find no better term with which to characterize the opinions of those who opposed the king's claims:

> *I would be loth to irritate any differing from me with provoking or odious terms, but I cannot more fully express myself . . . than in saying, that it is a dangerous tenet, a kind of judaizing opinion, to hold that the weal public may be exposed to peril of utter ruin and subversion, rather than such a charge as this . . . may be imposed by the King upon the subject, without common consent in Parliament.*

Conversely, we are also used to messianic attempts to restructure society along the lines of ancient Israel, such as those of the "Fifth Monarchy Men" of Cromwell's time, who advocated converting Parliament into a "Sanhedrin, or Supreme Council," patterned on the biblical high court of the kingdom of Judea.[15]

What is more surprising is the systematically central role ancient Israel played in the elaboration of constitutional claims and political philosophies during the English Civil Wars, and this for all sides of the debate. While representing Oxford in the Long Parliament, for example, the eminent jurist and self-taught Hebraist John Selden undertook lengthy investigations into ancient Israelite and rabbinic legal history. He even corresponded with rabbis, such as Leon Modena in Italy, all to buttress the parliamentary claim that God intended the powers of law and its institutions to extend even over church and Crown.[16] Also in the parliamentary camp, and much influenced by Selden, was James Harrington, whose writings are often said to have translated the "civic Republicanism" and "civic Humanism" of the Italian renaissance into English terms, thereby laying the foundations, not only for many of the English Whigs but also for constitutional thought in the eighteenth-century American colonies.[17] It is certainly true that Harrington drew on a great many "republican" models, ranging from ancient Athens to the Venice of his own day, but the Hebrew example occupies a place of honor in works like his *Commonwealth of Oceana* (1651/6), intended as a blueprint for a British republic.

In it, Harrington tried to demonstrate that the Hebrew commonwealth established through Moses had been a theocratic republic of the sort he advocated for England, in which there was no distinction between the civil and the religious, and therefore no room for the claims of ecclesiastical independence and clerical privilege that had fomented the civil war. In later works, like the *Prerogatives of Popular Government* (1658) and *The Art of Lawgiving* (1659), he continued these arguments and extended them. He began, for example, to extract from Jewish history a paradigm for the rise and fall of political institutions. Among the Jews, he argued, the purity of the Mosaic republic ("the commonwealth of Israel") had given way to the compromises of the "Cabala" (which for Harrington meant the oral law as interpreted by the rabbis in what he called "the commonwealth of the Jews"). Similarly the excellence of many other communities, including the early Christian Church, had given way to priestly claims of privilege and hierarchy. For Harrington, the history of Judaism provided both a prescription for the creation of ideal republics and an etiology of their corruption.

Separating Prophecy from Politics: Hobbes's *Leviathan*

This dependence of Christian political theory on the history of Israel was entirely typical in an age whose most pressing questions revolved around the relevance of prophecy for politics. No one was more aware of this dependence, or more acute in his deployment of it, than Thomas Hobbes. Identified with the royalist side, Hobbes found it prudent to seek refuge in France during the war, where he served for a time as math tutor to the young Prince of Wales in exile. The task must not have been too time-consuming (his student is said to have been so uninterested that he masturbated during lessons), for it is during this exile that Hobbes produced his massive and most famous work, the *Leviathan* (1651). Hobbes's agenda was ambitious: nothing less than to provide a general theory of society that was robust enough to decide the clash between divine and human claims to political power decisively in favor of the latter. Professors of political science have lavished attention on parts 1 and 2 of that work, in which Hobbes attempts an entirely "rational" derivation of a contractual theory of relations between sovereign and subject. As Hobbes put it in the opening to part 3:

> *I have derived the rights of sovereign power, and the duty of subjects, hitherto from the principles of nature only; such as experience has found true or consent (concerning the use of words) has made so; that is to say, from the nature of men, known to us by experience, and from definitions (of such words as are essential to all political reasoning) universally agreed on.*

The many readers who wish to see in Hobbes a progenitor of contemporary "realist" and "rational actor" theories end their lectures here. But Hobbes (and *Leviathan*) continued:

But in that I am next to handle, which is the nature and rights of a CHRIS-TIAN COMMONWEALTH, whereof there dependeth much upon supernatural revelations of the will of God, the ground of my discourse must be, not only the natural word of God, but also the prophetical. (32.1)

Leviathan's parts 3 ("Of a Christian Commonwealth") and 4 ("Of the Kingdom of Darkness") seldom appear on syllabi, but they are crucial to Hobbes's argument, and it is in them that Israel plays a central role.

To understand why, we need only return to the central problem of Hobbes's age, and a major cause of the English Civil Wars: the relation between church and state. Hobbes had addressed the issue of rebellion against sovereigns by insisting that once a people had contracted to obey a sovereign, then (with certain exceptions such as defense of their own lives) they could not refuse to do so: "[S]ubjects owe to sovereigns simple obedience in all things wherein their obedience is not repugnant to the laws of God" (31.1) But what about those things where obedience *was* repugnant? What if the sovereign's laws were in opposition to the subject's sense of the laws of God? Does not scripture say, "[W]e must obey God rather than man" (Acts 5:29)?

Hobbes could have chosen (as Benedict de Spinoza would choose some twenty years later) to contradict this scriptural command, or to deny the possibility that prophecy makes visible God's will. He did not do so. "It is manifest enough," he wrote, "that when a man receiveth two contrary commands, and knows that one of them is God's, he ought to obey that, and not the other, though it be the command of his lawful sovereign" (43.1). But neither could he give the divine veto free rein, for in his sectarian century it was precisely this claim of repugnance that was "the most frequent pretext of sedition . . . in Christian commonwealths" (43.1). His solution was to argue that God had himself set sharp limits on his own political power, and announced these limits in the prophecies he had addressed to Israel. It is for this reason that in parts 3 and 4 of *Leviathan* Hobbes chose as "the ground of my discourse . . . not only the natural word of God, but also the prophetical."

According to Hobbes, "prophecy," or the revelation of God's word to mankind, came in two forms: the ancient prophecies preserved in scripture, and the countless noncanonical prophecies of those, like the many political millenarians of Hobbes's day and our own, who claimed to speak in God's name. The latter certainly worried Hobbes, for they could "bewitch" their "fellow subjects . . . into rebellion . . . , and by this means destroying all laws, both divine and human, reduce all order, government, and society to the first chaos of violence and civil war" (36.20). But since the power of contemporary prophets derived entirely from the authority of ancient ones, it was on scripture that Hobbes focused in posing the key question in the debate between church and state: "*[B]y what authority they [the words of God] are made law?*" (33.21).

To answer this question, Hobbes turned to the Hebrews as the paradigmatic case of prophecy as law, and to Moses as the central example of a prophet who was also a sovereign. Did Moses's political authority derive from his prophetic power? Hobbes's answer was an emphatic no:

> *His authority, as the authority of all other princes, must be grounded on the consent of the people and their promise to obey him. And so it was; for "the people, when they saw the thunderings, and the lightnings, and the noise of the trumpets, and the mountain smoking, removed, and stood afar off. And they said unto Moses, speak thou with us, and we will hear, but let not God speak with us, lest we die." (Exod. 20:18–19) Here was their promise of obedience; and by this it was they obliged themselves to obey whatsoever he should deliver unto them for the commandment of God. (40.6)*[18]

Prophecy became law, in other words, through a people's founding contract with their sovereign. It was as sovereign, not as prophet, that Moses imposed the Mosaic law on his people. Furthermore, according to Hobbes, the Mosaic law itself, like the New Testament it foreshadowed, was deeply pessimistic about prophetic reliability: "Of 400 prophets of whom the king of Israel asked counsel concerning the war he made against Ramoth Gilead only Micaiah was a true one" (32.7, citing 1 Kings 22; 43.1). Hence that law warned the people to beware of false prophets, and assigned to the sovereign the right to judge and punish any such (36.19–20).

In all of this, Israel was meant to be exemplary: in his own kingdom, in his "sacerdotal" and "holy nation," God himself had decreed that all prophecy was subject to the judgment of the civil sovereign contractually constituted by the people. But Israel had to be extraordinary as well, to prevent the extension of its Mosaic laws to the rest of the world. Hence Hobbes spent a good deal of time demonstrating that the Jews had been for God a "peculium de cunctis populis" (peculiar people to me), because they and no other people had contracted to make God their immediate sovereign, and had therefore by their "own consent and covenant" agreed to make his word their law (35.5ff.).

Within Hobbes's contractual model of the Mosaic covenant, the political problem of prophecy disappeared, at least until end-time and the coming of Christ's messianic kingdom. Since only Israel had stood at the foot of Mount Sinai and covenanted with Moses to make God its civic sovereign, only in that bygone nation could scripture "be made law." As for the possibility of ongoing prophecy, Hobbes did not deny it. An individual might receive direct revelation from God, and thereby be in a position, when faced with two contrary demands, to "know" that one of them came from God, "and not the other, though it be the command of his lawful sovereign" (43.1). But such a revelation could not carry political authority because it could not constitute certain knowledge for anyone except the individual who received it. For everyone else, God's command was whatever the sovereign decided it was, in accordance with the political theology that God himself had established in the case of his own and unique "sacred nation," Israel.

By making the sovereign the sole arbiter of scripture, Hobbes achieved a radical redefinition of the relation between church and state: "I define a CHURCH to be *a company of men professing Christian religion, united in the person of one sovereign.*" "And therefore, a Church, such a one as is capable to command, to judge, absolve, condemn, or do any other act, is the same thing with a civil commonwealth consisting of Christian men, and is called a civil state. . . . Temporal and spiritual government are but two words brought into the world to make men see double and mistake their lawful sovereign. . . . That governor must be one, or else there must needs follow faction and civil war in the commonwealth: between the Church and State; between spiritualists and temporalists; between the sword of justice and the shield of faith; and (which is more) in every Christian man's breast, between the Christian and the man" (39.5). In other words, through his history of prophecy in ancient Israel, Hobbes managed to collapse church and state into the one sword and person of the civil sovereign.

Hobbes realized that this conclusion could not be more different from that of a patristic author like Saint Ambrose (whose excommunication of the emperor Theodosius, "if it were true he did so," he calls "a capital crime" [42.135]). Where Ambrose had subjected emperor to episcopate, Hobbes subjected priests to princes. Hobbes's contemporaries realized the sharpness of this difference as well, and it led many of them to charge him with atheism and materialism. The name of "Hobbes" became, like that of Machiavelli before him and Spinoza after, an epithet whose mere mention was meant to evoke Godlessness and impiety, and this despite the fact that nowhere in *Leviathan* did its author explicitly deny the authority of scripture or challenge its claim to derive from divine revelation.[19]

In fact, what is more striking from the point of view of our subject is a very general similarity between Hobbes's method and that of a patristic politician like Saint Ambrose. Although they reached sharply divergent conclusions, both pursued their arguments about the right relation between God's law and man's through the Jews, and like nearly everyone else mentioned in this book, both assigned to the Jews and their history a role that was simultaneously exemplary and exceptional, paradigmatic and peculiar.

The role Hobbes scripted was, however, in some ways more complex than Ambrose's. For although it is clear that Hobbes "wants to draw a sharp distinction between God's relation to the Jews under the

Old Covenant and his relation to Christians under the New Covenant," it is not at all clear what his attitude toward that Old Covenant was. His insistence that the laws established by Moses for the kingdom of Israel cannot serve as constitution for a Christian polity was probably intended, at least in part, as a negative charge of "Judaizing" against the "Revolution of the Saints." But he also treated both Moses and Israel seriously as exemplary sources for constitutional thought.[20]

In short, Hobbes was neither a dualist nor a "Judaizer," though he would be accused of both. His goal was rather to articulate the relationship between the kingdoms of the Old Covenant, of the New, and of the world to come—much like Augustine of Hippo—in ways that distinguished between them but preserved (or at least, appeared to preserve) the ongoing relevance of all three. Hobbes's arguments about the Hebrews had—again like Saint Augustine's—the potential to generate many different interpretations, both in his own time and into the far future. In the 1930s and 1940s, for example, his thought would prove a battleground between the political theories of the Nazi Carl Schmitt and those of Jewish philosophers, such as Leo Strauss and Franz Neumann. In 1942, Schmitt even published an anti-Semitic "children's book" inspired by Hobbes's use of Leviathan and Behemoth as political symbols.[21]

Today there is still little agreement about Hobbes's critique of Israel. For one eminent historian, Hobbes is the philosopher who "most rigorously separated the Hellenic from the Hebraic components of his cultural tradition and went further than any major philosopher since Augustine in rejecting the former and relying upon the latter." For another, he is an anti-Jewish political theorist who "celebrates the Christian kingdom of God to come as a utopian solution to the political problems with which the Leviathan-state can more or less successfully deal, and with which the original kingdom of God notably failed to deal." We need not take sides in this debate in order to agree that, for good or ill, it was on Israel that Hobbes—like many others of his day and age—erected the foundations of his political thought.[22]

The New Sciences of Judaism

From the charges of atheism against Hobbes we can see that we are approaching the end of a world that could only imagine itself as under God's active governance, and the beginning of one in which the complete absence of divine plan or providence was becoming conceivable. Before we enter that new world, we should glance for a moment at the figures of Judaism laboring in the Reformation and Counter-Reformation landscape at our back. (I continue to emphasize figures of Judaism here, and not real Jews, in part because until the late seventeenth century there were very few openly practicing Jews in western Europe.)[23] In some ways the work that they are doing is slightly different from what they had done before, and the place that work is carving out for Judaism in Christian thought is potentially different as well.

Much of that difference (and also a great deal of the similarity) is caught in the expression "Christian Hebraism," by which we mean (loosely) a fascination in certain scholarly and theological circles with the study of the textual traditions of Judaism. The importance of "Jewish questions" to so many of the urgent political and theological issues of the day made the mid-sixteenth to the late seventeenth century a high point of this Christian Hebraism. It is in this period, for example, that "Jewish studies" entered the university, with the establishment of chairs like the Regius professorships in Hebrew at Oxford and Cambridge (1540), the professorship in "Jewish Controversies" (Controversiarum Judaicarum) in Leiden, and the professorship in Oriental languages at the Escorial in Spain, to name just a few. The efforts of their occupants, as well as those of many other Christian Hebraists, gave birth to the critical study of scripture and of Judaism.

There are many reasons for the growth of Christian Hebraism in this era, perhaps the most obvious being the heightened stakes that inter-Christian debate placed on the biblical text itself. Scholars of all confessions competed in their acquisition of the linguistic expertise that would allow them to claim the more accurate reading of God's words. Benito Arias Montano of Seville was chaplain to the "Most Catholic"

King Philip II of Spain, and a participant at the Council of Trent, which is to say he was a champion of the Counter-Reformation. Johannes Buxtorf of Basel, on the other hand, was a paladin of Calvin. But both spent their superhuman efforts on behalf of their respective causes in much the same way: studying rabbinic writings and writing histories of the Jews, to produce better editions of the Hebrew Bible. Such efforts extended to the New Testament as well, in works like John Lightfoot's *Hebrew and Talmudical Excitations upon the Gospel of Saint Matthew* (1658), which advocated the now-standard scholarly practice of reading the gospels and rabbinic literature in each other's light.[24]

Scholars such as these were often accused of Judaizing. In Spain, for example, the Inquisition sought to proscribe Arias Montano's work, while much later in England, the great historian Edward Gibbon claimed that from excessive reading of the rabbis, Lightfoot had become one himself. But none of these scholars were preaching Judaism. The common goal of their philology was to reinforce the scriptural foundations of whatever wing of the Christian edifice they lived in. The patient scratching of their quills in search of the proper vowel markings of the Hebrew Bible, or their mining of the Jewish past for evidence that might buttress their theology, was in no way intended to question the truth claims of Christianity, or to erode the hegemony of scripture. It is one of the habitual ironies of history that in the long run their work also had the opposite effect. In retrospect we can see how the discovery of the Samaritan biblical manuscripts in 1603, with their many ancient variations from the Hebrew text hitherto thought of as eternal, may have contributed as much to skepticism about the legitimacy of Christian political order as the horrors of the Spanish Catholic siege at Protestant Ostend the same year. But that skepticism belongs to the long run, and we will leave it until the next section.[25]

Humanist biblical philology was a more or less ecumenical stimulus to an interest in the Hebrews and their language, affecting Catholic and Protestant alike. Other stimuli, like the millennial interest that characterized a number of Protestant sects, were more specifically confessional. If, as Saint Paul had proclaimed, the conversion of the Jews would herald the Second Coming, then perhaps it behooved those who most anticipated that glorious day to hurry it along. There were many, particularly in sectarian England, who strove to acquire "great understanding of the Hebrew tongue" to help with "the Calling of the Jews." Significant scholarly projects, such as the translation of parts of the Talmud into Latin, were undertaken with this end in view. And of course there were those millennialists for whom the study of Hebrew served more self-interested ends: since it was the language that would soon be spoken in heaven, why not start learning it early?[26]

One did not need to be a biblical philologist or a millenarian divine to believe in the importance of Hebrew: the subject was also relevant to basic questions in a number of disciplines. We have already seen, for example, how the strong association between Judaism and law in Christian theology encouraged jurists like John Selden to build their constitutional arguments out of detailed studies of Israel's laws. Perhaps more surprising to a modern reader was the importance of Hebrew to philosophical questions about the very nature of language itself. In the previous chapter we encountered the demands of thinkers like Frances Bacon, Hugo Grotius, and Thomas Hobbes for a strong bond between words and the things they signified, so that interpretive ambiguity, contention, and strife could be avoided. One way of imagining such a bond, according to an ancient school of thought proposed (but also mocked) in Plato's *Cratylus*, was to have a language in which words resemble things as closely as possible. In the eighteenth century, *Gulliver's Travels* would make scathing fun of this "universal Language" theory, taught at the School of Languages in Laputa:

> *Since Words are only Names for* Things, *it would be more convenient for all Men to carry about them, such* Things *as were necessary to express the particular Business they are to discourse on. . . .* [I]f a Man's Business be very great, and of various Kinds, he must be obliged to carry a greater Bundle of Things upon his Back. . . . [W]hen they met in the Street they would lay down their Loads, open their Sacks, and hold Conversation for an Hour together; then

put up their implements, help each other to resume their Burthens, and take their Leave.

But in the seventeenth century the dream of such a language was still a serious one, capable of engaging the greatest minds. Thus in 1629 Marin Mersenne (described by Hobbes as "the pole round which revolved every star in the world of science") and René Descartes exchanged letters over the former's claim to have found the ur-tongue from which all others derived, a language where the relation between word and thing held true. Reading the correspondence roughly half a century later, Leibniz remained irrepressibly enthusiastic about the possible existence of such a language, which he thought would "exterminate controversy in all subjects having to do with reason. For then to reason and to calculate would be the same thing."[27]

Mersenne and Descartes were cryptic about the specifics of this semiotic holy grail, this ur-language from which a universal tongue might be reconstituted, but other scholars engaged in the topic named a variety of candidates. Johannes Goropius Becanus (1519–1572), for example, became immortal by improbably proposing his native Dutch. Others favored hieroglyphic languages, or character-based ones like Chinese. (Cratylus and Socrates, too, had discussed the relationship between words and pictures.) But according to contemporary observers like Samuel Purchas, the "common and more received opinion" concurred with Saint Augustine that the language with which God spoke to man, the language with which Adam named the animals of the Garden, the language spoken by the builders of Babel, was some pristine form of Hebrew. If Hebrew philology could recover that pristine form, it would heal the breech between sign and signified, and make possible a truly universal philosophy.[28]

These and many other examples of Christian Hebraism point to the shifting function and importance of ideas about "Jews" and about Jewish history in the early modern period.[29] Some have called this phenomenon "Philosemitism," although I hasten to add that the "Philo-" here has as little to do with the activities of real Jews as its evil twin

"Anti."[30] In some cases, such as in the Dutch Republic or in England, the importance of cognitive figures of Judaism did contribute to significant changes in the treatment of the category's living representatives. In the case of England, for example, Oliver Cromwell's negotiations with Menasseh ben Israel over the formal readmission of the Jews into England in 1655–1656 were brewed from a mix of ideas about the political, messianic, and mercantile meanings of Judaism.

But the headiness of this brew should not be exaggerated. Only in the Dutch Republic were Jews explicitly allowed to settle (albeit only in small numbers) and practice their religion (but not in public). In England, not even Cromwell could overcome the resistance of his council to the official admittance of Jews, though a handful were allowed to worship unofficially. That resistance flowed from two great fears, that the Jews would steal commerce from Christian merchants and souls from Christ himself. The fear of Jewish commercial competition was voiced even by such "philo-semites" as John Drury (known for, among other things, his advocating the translation of the Talmud). Drury wrote from Germany (where he was acting as Cromwell's agent) urging caution, on the grounds that Jews "have ways, beyond all other men, to undermine a state, and to insinuate into those that are in offices, and prejudicate the trade of others; and therefore, if they be not wisely restrained, they will, in short time, be oppressive; if they be such as are here in Germany." Among divines, there were many who, like William Prynne, believed that if the Jews were readmitted, the Christians "would sooner turn Jews, than the Jews Christians." Nor did an academic or political interest in the history of Judaism necessarily translate into a vote for readmission. James Harrington, for example, was certainly against the idea. According to him, the Bible made clear the agricultural and military potential of the Jews, and common experience testified to their mercantile skills, but he feared settlement in England would lead to the corruption of Christians there. His *Oceana* recommended instead the establishment of a colony of Jews in Ireland, where they could be profitable to the republic but safely separate from it.[31]

Outside of England such ideas had even less power, and almost nowhere else is it possible to speak of anything approaching "political Philosemitism" in this period. In French political discourse, for example, "Judaism" remained largely a category of opprobrium within which to imprison one's Christian enemies. French Catholics accused French Protestants of Judaizing, French Protestants accused the pope of favoring Jews over Christians, and Frenchmen of all faiths concurred in the "Jewishness" of their arch-enemy, Spain and its Hapsburg monarchs. The French context did produce a few lonely examples of the type we are familiar with in England, figures like Isaac La Peyrère, whose *Recall of the Jews* (*Rapell des Juifs*, 1643) argued that it was the messianic destiny of the kings of France to convert all the Jews, and that to that end they should be readmitted into the kingdom. But whereas in England such figures were part of a thriving political culture, in France they were exotics, ridiculed and suspected of being half-Jewish themselves.[32]

Moreover, nowhere in the Europe of this period did the willingness to study Judaism's dusty past necessarily translate into altered perceptions of Jews in the fleshy present. La Peyrère was perfectly capable of believing in the stereotypical blackness and bad smell of the Jews (*foetor Judaicus*), all of which he thought would disappear with their conversion, when "the whiteness of their complexion will shine the same way as the Psalmist says, as the wings and breast of a pigeon, an extremely white one at that. . . . Their breath will be sweet. Only musk and amber will exude from their clothes and their sweat." Slightly later, the encounters that the great French Catholic scholar of biblical Hebrew Richard Simon had with living Jews convinced him that he should defend the Jewish community of Metz against charges of ritual murder, but also confirmed in him the common view that Jews were devoid of reason, consumed by avarice, and full of pride and hatred toward all other peoples.

Like the scholars, the tourists of the day were also attracted to Judaism when visiting the few places that could afford them a glimpse (notably Avignon, Italy, and Ottoman Turkey). Again like the scholars, their sightseeing generally confirmed rather than altered their preconceptions of Jews in the flesh: "The Jewish quarter is a place filled with infection which I would gladly have left behind had it not been for the fact that curiosity drove me to see it. . . . It is not possible to see anything as disgusting as this whole place, as repulsive as their apartments, nothing as wretched and as stupid as the people: all these afflictions have justly befallen them for their crimes."[33] Of course there were exceptions, like the English traveler Thomas Coryate, whom we encountered in the previous chapter. Yet by and large, these tourists can stand for a more general conclusion. The distant horizons of ancient Judaism were a frequent destination in late sixteenth- and seventeenth-century Europe's critical debates about how Christian society should be structured. But the knowledge obtained on these voyages did not significantly alter the Christian figure of the Jew. Instead, it piled new meaning on him, making him bear the growing baggage of ever-more numerous and inimical political theologies.

Chapter 10

ENLIGHTENMENT REVOLTS
AGAINST JUDAISM: 1670–1789

Then dare, oh Europe! Break the unbearable yoke
of the prejudices by which you are afflicted.

—BARON PAUL THIRY D'HOLBACH,
THE SPIRIT OF JUDAISM, 1770

LUTHER AND CALVIN, Lipsius, Hobbes, and Harrington: all of these thinkers were struggling to achieve a precarious equilibrium between church and state, revelation and reason, piety and liberty of thought. It is a balancing act whose history stretches back in some form or other to our chapter 3 and the time of Constantine (we skipped over an intermediate moment of vertigo, during the Investiture Controversy between popes and emperors in the Middle Ages). The Reformation had made this equilibrium all the more improbable in at least two ways. On the one hand, as we saw in the previous chapter, it greatly heightened the importance of the sovereign's decision (*cuius regio*) in determining the subjects' religion (*eius religio*), and thereby had the potential to make religion seem

325

a mere extension of the ruling order.[1] On the other, the Reformation's transformation of biblical reading practices increased the power of God's kingdom as a template for earthly polities, and thereby had the potential to turn the secular state into a subsidiary of the heavenly one.

In retrospect (but only in retrospect) the efforts of these thinkers to maintain the previous equilibrium look like the desperate attempts of cartoon characters to keep running in the air long after they've gone over the edge of the cliff. But although many scholars have argued that the tensions introduced by the Reformation made inevitable the shattering of scripture's hold over the European mind, none of the authors we touched on from this first century after Luther and Calvin drew such conclusions (Hobbes comes closest). None of them openly recognized the danger of free-fall, or abandoned the explicit goal of balancing prophecy with politics. And though they each had a different sense of what the proper balance might be, they all set out across the tightrope with the help of the same scriptural pole, using arguments about Israel to justify their own positions and overthrow those of others. The basic Christian consensus about the tension between God and the world, and about the Jews' role in representing that tension, remained very similar to the view expressed by Augustine more than a millennium before. The Catholic philosopher and mathematician Blaise Pascal expressed this consensus admirably in his *Pensées*, published posthumously to great acclaim in 1670. According to him, the Jews were stranded symbols, simultaneously execrable and exemplary, of the great tipping point in the relationship between God and the world: "Carnal Jews are half-way between Christians and pagans. Pagans do not know God and only love earthly things; Christians know the true God and do not love earthly things. Jews and pagans love the same possessions, Jews and Christians know the same God."[2]

Theologico-Political Rebellion: Spinoza's *Treatise on the Superstitious Ceremonies of the Jews*

This consensus was about to experience a shock so great that it has sometimes been called the "crisis of the European mind." The dying third of the seventeenth century ushered in a new kind of thinker, one who not only refused to cross the tightrope, but deliberately opted to cut it. Among these the one with the sharpest shears was Benedict de Spinoza, whose *Theologico-Political Treatise* appeared furtively in Latin, under cover of anonymity and with false publishing information, in the same year as Pascal's *Pensées*. Spinoza's discretion was prudent, since his treatise was incendiary, advocating nothing less than a divorce between faith and reason, scripture and truth. Its preface began modestly, declaring itself a defense of the liberty of conscience already existing in the Dutch Republic:

> *Now since we have the rare good fortune to live in a commonwealth where freedom of judgment is fully granted to the individual citizen and he may worship God as he pleases, and where nothing is esteemed dearer and more precious than freedom . . .*

But Spinoza was not merely praising local freedoms. He was making the much larger claim that liberty of thought and conscience was a prerequisite for any peaceful polity:

> *I think I am undertaking no ungrateful or unprofitable task in demonstrating that not only can this freedom be granted without endangering piety and the peace of the commonwealth, but also the peace of the commonwealth and piety depend on this freedom.*

Moreover, he was predicating this happy state of secure freedom on a conceptual revolution:

> *This, then, is the main point which I have sought to establish in this treatise. For this purpose my most urgent task has been to indicate the main false assumptions that prevail regarding religion—that is, the relics of man's ancient bondage—and then again the false assumptions regarding the right of civil authorities. There are many who, with an impudence quite shameless, seek to usurp much of this right*

and, under the guise of religion, to alienate from the government the
loyalty of the masses, still prone to heathenish superstition, so that
slavery may return once more. (3/3.7)[3]

Who were these advocates of slavery and bondage? Spinoza
described them in terms we should recognize. They were the clergy
of every religion ("Christian, Turk, Jew, or Heathen") who had turned
their respective traditions into vehicles for "avarice and ambition."

The very temple became a theatre where, instead of Church teachers,
orators held forth, none of them actuated by desire to instruct the peo-
ple, but keen to attract admiration, to criticise their adversaries before
the public, and to preach only such novel and striking doctrine as might
gain the applause of the crowd. This inevitably gave rise to great quar-
rels, envy and hatred, which no passage of time could assuage. Little
wonder, then, that of the old religion nothing is left but the outward
form—wherein the common people seem to engage in base flattery of
God rather than in his worship—and that faith has become identi-
cal with credulity and biased dogma. But what dogma!—degrading
rational man to beast, completely inhibiting man's free judgment and
his capacity to distinguish true from false, and apparently devised with
the set purpose of utterly extinguishing the light of reason. (4/3.8)

The advocates of such religion cared only "for their own standing,"
reputations they secured with fancy speculations plundered from Greek
philosophers and imposed on a scripture they scarcely read: their "attitude to Scripture is one of abject servility rather than belief" (5/3.9).

Thus far we might think we were hearing a Luther or a Calvin, calling in Christ's name for a return to scripture, and preparing to hurl an
accusation of "Pharisaism" or "Judaizing" against a rival. (The Latin
makes the point more clearly than the English "every church": "ipsum
Templum in Theatrum degeneravit." Spinoza is presenting himself as
Christ, about to cleanse the Temple.) We would only be half right. Spinoza's treatise is indeed an extended accusation of "Judaizing," so much so

that some editions of the clandestine French translation published shortly after his death bore the title *Traité des cérémonies superstitieuses des juifs tant anciens que modernes* (Treatise on the superstitious ceremonies of the Jews, both ancient and modern). But it is certainly not a Protestant defense of scripture as the sole path to truth. On the contrary, Spinoza's Judaizers will turn out to be precisely the people who insist, "as a basic principle for the understanding of Scripture and for extracting its true meaning, that it is throughout truthful and divine" (5/3.9). It is this principle, shared by nearly everyone writing in Spinoza's day, that he took to be the cause of "the disputes of philosophers . . . raging with violent passion in Church and Court and . . . breeding bitter hatred and faction which readily turn men to sedition, together with other ills too numerous to recount here" (5/3.9). Against it, Spinoza proposed his own examination of "Scripture afresh, conscientiously and freely, and [admitting] nothing as its teaching which I did not most clearly derive from it" (5/3.9).[4]

Insofar as he "formulated a method of interpreting the Bible," Spinoza was indeed very much like a Luther or a Calvin. But as he described his motives in a letter of 1665, these were not at all the same:

> *I am now writing a treatise on my views regarding Scripture. The reasons that drove me to do so are these: 1) The prejudices of the Theologians. For I know that these are the main obstacles which prevent men from giving their minds to philosophy. So I apply myself to exposing such prejudices and removing them from the minds of sensible people. 2) The opinion of me held by the common people, who constantly accuse me of atheism. I am driven to avert this accusation, too, as far as I can. 3) The freedom to philosophize and say what we think. This I want to vindicate completely, for here it is in every way suppressed by the excessive authority and egotism of preachers.*

Moreover, his methods led to entirely different conclusions, and produced, not a revitalization of scripture as the privileged gateway to the divine will and a godly life, but a sharp restriction of its relevance and a complete evacuation of its special claims to truth.[5]

Spinoza's conclusions were manifold. First, he demonstrated that even within the canonical books of Hebrew scripture, there were very few places where scripture claimed that God was speaking in his own voice. The vast majority of prophecy came not directly from God but from men and women who (with the exception of Moses and Christ) had no special access to God, and who, as scripture itself warned, could often err. Second, the business of these prophets was not to teach truth, but merely to convey morality to those who lacked the ability to achieve it through reason or by other means. Prophets were not particularly learned, nor experts in any branch of knowledge (Joshua, for example, clearly knew little about the nature of the universe since he thought that the sun revolved around the earth). Hence revelation should not be treated as a source of knowledge: its moral principles were its sole truth content.

Third, even those moral principles could not be generalized beyond the context of those who had originally received them, since they were designed to instruct a particular people with particular problems. Moses's Israelites, for example, were slaves fresh out of bondage, an unhappy people incapable of anything but obedience to threats of reward and punishment. Hence Moses offered them the commandments in prescriptive form, and hence they were willing to surrender to him their sovereignty. It was through this surrender that "religion acquired the force of law" (214/3.230–231), but such force was meant to last only as long as the Hebrew commonwealth endured. Sounding a bit like Hobbes, he wrote, "[T]he Law revealed by God to Moses was simply the laws of the Hebrew state alone, and was therefore binding on none but the Hebrews, and not even on them except while their state still stood" (5–6/3.9–10).

According to Spinoza, even Jesus's teachings were limited by the requirements of context. Although he appealed less to the fears and more to the "reasoning faculties" of his audiences, out of necessity he too "adapted" his teachings "to the beliefs and principles of each individual," using words and examples appropriate to the cultural expectations and mental capacities of each. "For example, when he said to the

Pharisees (see Matt. 12:26), 'And if Satan cast out Satan, he is divided against himself; how shall then his kingdom stand?,' his only purpose was to refute the Pharisees according to their own principles, not to teach that there are devils, or any kingdom of devils" (33/3.43). Later generations of Christians tried to deduce general truths from words like these, words that Jesus had carefully addressed to the prejudices of particular audiences. In doing so, they succeeded only in adopting those archaic prejudices for their own—in this case, for example, foolishly populating the cosmos with legions of nonexistent demons and angels.[6]

Scripture itself made plain that its specific instructions were always addressed to such local needs and limitations, and that only the most general moral principles of Revelation were meant to be universal: "to obey God with all one's heart by practicing justice and charity" (6/3.10). Moreover, in passages like Romans 1:20, the Bible made clear that neither prophecy nor scripture was required to arrive at these universal principles: "[T]he Divine Law revealed to all mankind through the Prophets and the Apostles" does not differ in any way "from the teachings of the natural light of reason" (6/3.10). Hence it followed that the word of God "is not to be identified with a certain number of books," but could be found everywhere: in the words of the many prophets sent to nations other than the Hebrews, in the teachings of the wise, or for that matter (and this was especially important) in observation of nature itself (6/3.10).

Not even the "historical sense" of Hebrew scripture, which had been so important for Augustine, Luther, Hobbes, and many others, is particularly instructive for Spinoza: "[N]or can the belief in historical narratives, however certain, give us knowledge of God, nor, consequently, the love of God." It is always useful to study "the ways and manners of men" (51/3.61) in the past so as to know what to expect in the present, but by this standard, biblical history is neither more nor less valuable than that of "the Koran or a poetic drama or at any rate ordinary history" (68/3.79). In sum, the general moral principles that are Revelation's only universal truth are available in many different forms, and since "men's ways of thinking vary considerably" (6/3.11), each person must be free to find those truths in the form most adequate to each. For many this might be religious obedience, but for others it might be philosophizing or the study of nature. Scripture itself proclaims this freedom and teaches that people shall be judged not by the path to truth they chose, but by the fruits of that choice. This very freedom to choose one's own path was, as Spinoza put it in his preface, the most basic "freedom granted to every man by the revelation of the Divine Law" (7/3.11).[7]

"The Same Old Song of the Pharisees"

Contemporaries did not need go beyond these sentences of the preface in order to realize that they were holding a revolutionary treatise in their hands. Spinoza's treatments of politics and revelation were not entirely unprecedented. His emphasis on the complete subjection of prophecy to the political sovereign, all the way down to his condemnation of Ambrose, is very similar to Hobbes's.[8] Similarly, Hobbes's dark hints about Moses's authorship of the Pentateuch anticipate Spinoza's attack on the reliability of revelation. Both, however, fall short of Spinoza's critique. (Hobbes himself is reputed to have said, after reading Spinoza's treatise, that the work's anonymous author "had out-thrown him a bar's length, for he durst not write so boldly.")[9] And we have already met other Christian Hebraists who made similar arguments, such as Isaac La Peyrère (1596–1676), whose *Men Before Adam* created a scandal in 1655, with its argument that not only could Moses not have written the Pentateuch, but also, given the existence of ancient civilizations like those of the Chinese and the Mexicans, the creation account in Genesis must be wrong. La Peyrère's criticism had been directed only at the Hebrew Bible; the New Testament remained for him clear and salvific.[10] The same could not be said of the Quaker Samuel Fisher (1606–1665), whose massive critique of Protestant scripturalism was revealingly entitled *The Rustick's Alarm to the Rabbies* (1660). According to Fisher, there was a crucial distinction that needed to be made between God's word and scripture. The first was eternal and supernatural, the second a human copy, taken down by a particular people at a particular place and time, and subject to corruption. Scripture as we have it, including the New Testament, does not correspond to the exact or the entire word of God, and through it we cannot gain access to God's perfect word. Hence we should not seek to interpret the scriptures literally, but only according to the spirit of God's message.[11]

All of these thinkers and many others shared some skepticism about the reliability of revelation's textual record, and questioned scripture's utility as a pathway to particular truths about specific topics (such as the early history of the world, or the proper governance of the common-wealth). They did not, however, move from such skepticism to a general denial of Christianity's special claims to truth, nor of God's providence, prophetic revelation, or miraculous powers more generally. On the con-trary, even the most famous and controversial of these scriptural critics (men like La Peyrère, Fisher, Richard Simon, and Jean Leclerc) under-stood their work as a prelude to a more refined faith in Christ.

Spinoza went much further.[12] Not only did he stress the instability of scripture and sharply circumscribe its truth content, but also he denied that revelation was *required* for human blessedness, though he granted that for some people it provided an adequate path. He even sought to prove from scripture that no external or divine power was required to create, move, or animate matter, which was moved by forces produced entirely within itself. It was obvious to the *Treatise*'s earliest readers that Spinoza reduced divine providence to "nothing more than the order of nature," and that this idea struck at the most fundamental distinctions in all the religion and philosophy that we have encountered thus far: the distinctions between spirit and body, between God and creation.[13]

In short, Spinoza demolished the special claims of scripture in order to erect a new politics, a new ethics, and perhaps (Spinoza's conception of divinity is much debated) even a new spirituality on the rubble. All the more surprising that in the midst of all this iconoclasm, he left one idol conspicuously unbroken, in order to put it to new use: I mean, of course, the figure of the Jew. For the *Treatise*'s revolutionary claims to complete liberty of thought and faith, its reduction of religion to the simple rule of love, its radical circumscription of scripture's claims to power, and its complete subjection (like that of *Leviathan*) of the priest to the sovereign are all achieved against a threatening backdrop of Judaism, and a Christian axiom of supersession, adopted and adapted from the scriptural paradigms that these claims proposed to overturn.

The distinction Spinoza drew between Moses, who spoke to God only in human language, and Christ, who communed immediately with God, is one example of Spinoza's adaptation of Christian idioms of supersession. Others include his claim that the laws of Moses compelled obedience through prophetic proclamation and fear of punishment whereas Christ appealed to rational argument (138–144/3.151–158); his charge that Jews (even the rationalist philosopher Maimonides!) despised reason and philosophy, which was the province of the gentile Greeks; his insistence that the true covenant is "[d]ivinely inscribed in men's hearts" (145/3.158), not on tablets of law; his denigration as "worshippers of the letter" of those Christians who strove to establish the exact text or literal truth of scripture. In other words, the distinctions between Jew and Christian that Spinoza deploys to attack the tyranny of scripture are intimately related to those that the architects of that tyranny had long deployed before him.[14]

Spinoza's repeated attacks on Maimonides have particularly puzzled scholars, since that medieval philosopher's rationalism seems in many respects similar to Spinoza's. One recent historian, for example, suggests that "Spinoza's objection to Maimonides is primarily not philosophical but political. He regards him as a rabbinical elitist," whereas Spinoza "insists on a democratic vision of learning and study." This explanation seems strained, given that the *Treatise* proclaims itself an elitist work aimed only at philosophers, and that Spinoza explicitly accuses Maimonides of *not being elitist enough*. In my view, it is the supersessionist structure of Spinoza's own argument that pushes him to align himself (on occasion) with Jesus, and to characterize Maimonides, not just as an elitist, but as a Jew who subjects reason to law by insisting that a virtuous life is blessed only if lived in knowledge of and obedience to the Torah.[15]

Spinoza sharpens his distinctions to make them more cutting. Since his goal is to make scriptural politics less appealing in his own day, he works to make the ancient Israelite and Jewish examples of that politics more repulsive. In chapter 17, he even suggests that the theocratic constitution that God granted to the Israelites was not a blessing but a punishment. Angered by their idolatry and aware of their slavish and rebellious character, God gave them as "vengeance" a law that was deliberately flawed and would, through its separation of the priesthood from the people and the polity, inevitably produce civil war and the destruction of the Jewish commonwealth. Again, this type of argument had precedents: recall Justin Martyr's claim, in the second century, that the law was given to the Jews "on account of your transgressions and the hardness of your hearts." It could even be grounded in Hebrew scripture itself, as in that extraordinary passage from Ezekiel (20:25), in which God proclaims that "I gave them a law that was not good." But whereas the vast majority of exegesis prior to Spinoza had sought to contain this possibility, Spinoza insisted on amplifying it to the point of explosion.[16]

According to Spinoza, even the love that God commanded the Hebrews was an imperfect one, since it instructed them to love only themselves and hate all others. It was this Jewish hatred of others that generated the enmity with which they were universally and eternally met, and condemned them to perpetual separation from all other peoples of the earth. His choice of prooftext for this point is striking: "It was for this reason that they were told: 'Love thy neighbor and hate thine enemy'" (216/3.233, citing Matt. 5:43). Spinoza knew (just as Matthew's authors did) that although the Hebrew Bible often enjoins love of one's neighbor, it nowhere joins such love to hatred of one's enemy. Yet here, in a book explicitly founded on the proposition that scripture can be interpreted only within its specific context, he uses a gospel text to characterize what he presents as the essential particularism and misanthropy of Israelites and Jews.

This is not to say that Spinoza's view of the Jews was univocal. Occasionally we find him including himself among the Jews, as when he writes "in Hebrew we employ nouns more frequently than adjectives."

His love of Hebrew as a language is amply expressed in the *Hebrew Grammar* he produced. And there are even moments within the *Treatise* when Spinoza seems to hint—very obliquely—that although the Jews are stiff-necked and despicable, they may yet be closer to piety than many Christians: "Therefore if anyone by believing what is true becomes self-willed, he has a faith which in reality is impious; and if by believing what is false he becomes obedient to the moral law, he has a faith which is pious." Such moments suggest complexity in Spinoza's thinking about Judaism. But certainly we can say that for strategic purposes at the very least, in his published writing he chose to exploit a characterization of Israel and Judaism imported more or less wholesale from his Christian colleagues and predecessors.[17]

If Spinoza had been a Christian, his embrace of these standard characterizations of the Jews and their religion would be unremarkable. But he was born a Jew and remained one until his confrontation and disputation with the rabbis of his community led to his famous excommunication. Even after that excommunication he did not convert to a Christian faith. Quite the contrary, much of his work, and especially the *Theologico-Political Treatise*, was intended as a critique of Catholic, Lutheran, and Calvinist teaching (he was more favorably inclined toward less dogmatic groups like the Quakers). His contemporary biographers thought it most remarkable (as indeed it was) that he lived a life outside of every denomination, grinding optical lenses to earn what little income he needed, and was otherwise entirely devoted to the pursuit of a philosophy completely unfettered by doctrine and governed by no ethics but his own.[18]

Why then did such an exemplary iconoclast as Spinoza use the conventional Christian figure of the Jew to do so much of his polemical work? Some have suggested that he was angry at his excommunication from the Jewish community (an excommunication, however, that he seems to have provoked). Equally plausible is the possibility that through his immersion in the philosophical and theological discourses of the day, he had imbibed some of the basic Christian axioms with which those discourses were saturated. Alternatively, he may have concentrated his fire on the Old Testament because he actually believed that it played a more central role than the New Testament in the political arguments of his rivals. Or finally (and I think more likely), his deployment of the Jews may have been part of a rhetorical strategy to persuade his audience by drawing on its prejudices, much as Christ had done (according to Spinoza) when he spoke to the Pharisees about demons. Through Christian commonplaces about the nature of Jewish subjection to letter and law, Spinoza sought to lead his Christian readers to the conclusion that anyone who believes that the words of scripture articulate rational truths that bind human reason, or contain laws that should constrain the behavior of citizens, is singing "the same old song of the Pharisees."[19]

We don't need to decide between his motives in order to concede that Spinoza's otherwise bold arguments for freedom of conscience and human reason depended, at least in part, on a conventional critical representation of Jews and Judaism. This dependence is one of Spinoza's many contributions to enlightened thought. He helped teach philosophy that, for critical purposes at least, the nastiness of biblical Jews was far more useful than their godliness. Henceforth a significant wing of critical Bible studies would shift its focus away from *Hebraica veritas*, the quest for truths encoded in the Hebrew Bible by which a more perfect society might be organized, and toward what one might call *Hebraica falsitas*, a search for the origins of Christian society's present ills in the errors and superstitions of Israelites and Jews.[20] There would always be traditionists vindicating the Old Testament, but the cutting edge of philology now turned from the task of sculpting Hebrew heroes to dissecting them. Thus Pierre Bayle, the great impresario of the early Enlightenment, devoted an article in his monumental *Historical and Critical Dictionary* (1697) to the subject of "David, King of the Jews," in which he simultaneously demonstrated the corruption of the Israelite king's morals and of the biblical text's transmission. The strategy remained popular throughout the eighteenth century (Voltaire's *Saul* of 1763 is an illustrious example), perhaps because it criticized revelation without challenging Christian authority too explicitly.

The topic deserves its own book, but we can roughly say that after Spinoza (and partly in response to him) Old Testament studies divided into three strategic camps. "Radicals" adopted Spinoza's techniques to claim that, whatever its origins, the scriptural record had been hopelessly corrupted (members of this group preferred for safety's sake to remain anonymous, but some who leaned toward this camp, like Antonius Van Dale, who argued extensively against the existence of demons and angels, did publish in their own name). "Moderates" adapted Spinoza's critical methods but used them to strip away layers of corruption and argue for their denomination's particular versions of a residual core scriptural truth (the Catholic Richard Simon and the Protestant Jean Leclerc are famous examples). "Traditionists" like the French bishop Pierre-Daniel Huet formed the third camp, claiming that Moses had indeed composed the Pentateuch and that every word in it was true. All of those mentioned, it is worth pointing out, were at some point or other accused by opponents of "Judaizing."[21]

To put it bluntly, Spinoza translated Christian ideas about Jewish error and irrationality into secular terms, assigning to Jews and Judaism a role as enemy of reason that was very similar to the role of enemy of revelation assigned them by Christian theology, and using that role to "Judaize" revealed religion itself. I do not mean to suggest that Spinoza was solely responsible for this translation, or singular in his critique of Judaism, or that his critique represents the most notable aspect of his oeuvre. He does, however, provide an excellent and influential example of the ways in which the strategies of even the most radical and original of Enlightenment thinkers could help give new shape and power to familiar figures of the Jew.

"A Jew First, after a Cartesian, and Now an Atheist"

If Spinoza was not singular in his "anti-Judaism," he was nearly unique in his Judaism, and in this, too, he proved fruitful for the future of European thought. For Spinoza's friends, like his biographer Jean Maximilien Lucas, there could be no better proof of Spinoza's greatness than his

Judaism, or rather, than his ability to emerge from the blindness of that Judaism into the light of reason:

> *But what I esteem most in him is that, although he was born and bred in the midst of a gross people who are the source of superstition, he had imbibed no bitterness whatever, and that . . . [h]e was entirely cured of those silly and ridiculous opinions which the Jews have of God.*

Insofar as Spinoza (like Jesus, Paul, and Muhammad) presented his truths as both a fulfillment and an overcoming of Judaism, he sowed the seeds of a claim to status as a prophet of reason (though we should remember that "prophet" was not high praise for Spinoza!). The Christian flavor of the claim is well described by the historian Adam Sutcliffe:

> *Once again, a Jewish outcast upholds the deepest spiritual truths of Judaeo-Christianity, in rebellion against the dogmatic and primitive group that first, and most drastically, corrupted this message. The dawn of Enlightenment is thus given a subliminally millenarian tinge, with Spinoza performing the key Messianic role as its necessarily originally, and then no longer, Jewish harbinger.*[22]

To the vast majority of western Europe's scribbling classes, however, Spinoza was no savior. He was rather the false Messiah, a "prince of Atheism," a "new Mohammad" whose goal was to destroy all true religion. The reformed ministers of Leiden were clear in their verdict when they successfully urged the government to ban Spinoza's collected work in 1678: "Perhaps since the beginning of the world until the present day . . . , [this book] surpasses all others in godlessness and endeavours to do away with all religion and set impiety on the throne." According to one recent count, of the thirty published reactions to Spinoza's *Treatise* that appeared in Germany between 1670 and 1700, only three expressed even qualified approval for some part of its argument. The rest were unequivocal, even scatological, in their condemnation. The *Presentation of Four Recent Worldly Philosophers*, for example, speaks of "the abominable doctrines and hideous errors which this shallow Jewish philosopher has (if I may say so) shit into the world."[23]

Like the *Presentation*'s anonymous author, most denouncers found it easy enough to draw a straight line from Spinoza's Jewishness to his ideas. After all, Judaism had long been associated in Christian (and Muslim) thought with the murderous denial of divine truth. Christians knew that Jews believed in God, but insofar as they had preferred to crucify him rather than give up their stubborn worldliness, they could easily be aligned with atheism. Spinoza's detractors could draw on fifteen hundred years of research attributing Jewish origins to skepticism, materialism, and atheism. These genealogies could all be telegraphed in brief allusions. Henry More, for example, wrote to Robert Boyle in 1676 informing him that the author of the anonymous *Treatise* was "Spinoza, a Jew first, after a Cartesian, and now an atheist." The tag became formulaic. Even Pierre Bayle, himself considered a radical both by contemporaries and by posterity, began his article on Spinoza in the *Dictionary* (1696) by tracing the same itinerary: "Spinoza, Benedictus de, a Jew by birth, and afterwards a deserter from Judaism, and lastly an atheist."[24]

Some commentators spelled out the formula in more detail than others. One who opted for detail was the Lutheran pastor Johannes Müller of Hamburg. Müller was much concerned with Judaism, to which he had devoted a book early in his career (*Judaismus oder Judenthumb* [Judaism, or Jewry], 1644). Now, appalled at the *Treatise* and offended by its pretense to have been published in his own home town, he set out to defeat atheism in his *Atheismus devictus* (1672). For him the two threats of Judaism and atheism were closely related. Atheism, he claimed, had its roots in the long tradition of Jewish arguments against Jesus's divinity (he mentions specific works like Isaac of Troki's *Chizzuk Emunah* [Strengthening of the Faith] of 1593).

Müller was not alone in making a connection between the new philosophical atheism and the much older Jewish rejection of Jesus, a connection that brought renewed critical attention to Jewish defenses against Christianity. In a book called *The Fiery Darts of Satan* (*Tela Ignea Satanae*, 1681) the Altdorf professor Johann Christoph Wagenseil made a number of Hebrew texts available to Christians for the first time, translating lengthy excerpts from works like the *Toldot Yeshu* (an ancient and fiercely negative portrayal of the life of Jesus), Nachmanides's *Vikuach* (his account of his arguments against Christianity in the Barcelona disputation of 1263), and Isaac of Troki's *Chizzuk Emunah*. Similar logic may have inspired the Heidelberg professor of Oriental languages, Andreas Eisenmenger, to write his massive (more than two thousand pages) and highly influential *Judaism Revealed* (*Entdecktes Judenthum*, 1700), a vitriolic treasury of Jewish perfidy toward Jesus and his followers that was meant to arm Christians in their struggle against the Jews.[25]

This new wave of research into Judaism was motivated, at least in part, by the widespread conviction that the new atheistic philosophies were descendants of Judaism, and that the war against them needed to target the source. Perhaps the most explicit in making this point was another German Lutheran, Johann Georg Wachter (1673–1757), whose *Spinozism in Judaism* (*Der Spinozismus im Jüdenthumb*) was published in Amsterdam in 1699, the year before the appearance of Eisenmenger's *Judaism Revealed*. Wachter claimed that whatever true knowledge of the one God there was in the Old Testament had been stolen by Moses from the Egyptians. The Egyptians had themselves obtained it in the same way all other pagans gained their knowledge of divinity: "through the light of reason" available to all men. Among the Jews, even this borrowed light was snuffed out by the "ancient Cabbalah of the Hebrews." The Kabbalah, according to Wachter, was a mishmash of misunderstood materialist Greek philosophy that repressed the Jews' capacity for reason and left them with a soul-destroying religion in which only "the world is God." Since this (according to Wachter) was also Spinoza's claim, both Spinozism and Judaism amounted to the same irrational perversion.[26]

Wachter's is a complicated case: he himself eventually "converted" to "Spinozism." Even in this early work, he is clearly trying to preserve a place for "natural reason" as a path to God, and to protect that path from dangerous charges of Judaism, atheism, and "Spinozism." In other words, his is most definitely not a defense of Christian dogma, like Müller's or Wagenseil's, but rather of natural reason as a mode of revelation. It is all the more significant, therefore, that he pursues his agenda in the same way they do, by attacking Spinoza's Judaism. In this sense both he and they are entirely representative of the new roles assigned to figures of Judaism in the late seventeenth and the eighteenth century.

On the one hand, the philosophical friends of Enlightenment, from the most radical (for example, "Spinozists," deists, atheists) to the most moderate, thought of the Old Testament as the authoritative source of the darkness they sought to illuminate, and of Jews and Judaism as that darkness's most easily satirized by-product. On the other, the movement's many enemies saw in Jews and Judaism the source and most horrific example of the hyperrationality, self-interest, atheism, and stubborn materialism with which they believed the Enlightenment threatened the world. Hence although the battle was over a Christian edifice, all sides in this conflict focused their fire on the Hebrew foundations. Out of these many inquiries into Judaism there emerged a number of the disciplines and methodologies that we today associate with the scholarly and source-critical study of religion. It is nevertheless worth remembering that in the Enlightenment at least, that study was always polemical. *The History of the Jews, from Jesus Christ to the Present* by Jacques Basnage, for example, is often praised as the first scholarly history of Judaism, and it is indeed an achievement whose massive learning across time and space can only astound today's specialist. But we can tell from just a glance at the subject headings of the section on Moses that Basnage organized that learning in familiar ways and toward familiar ends: "He kills an Egyptian for making an Israelite a Cuckold. His reign in Ethiopia. How he went over the Red Sea. A ridiculous story. His tiranny. Crimes he committed. His miracles and his hardness." "He was ambitious, a Tyrant, and an Enemy of the People subjected to his laws." Basnage knew more about the history of Judaism than the vast majority of humankind before or since. Compared to his colleague Pierre Bayle, he was a "moderate" in the battles of Enlightenment. But like all sides in these battles, he loaded his batteries with the charge of "Judaism."[27] Or as Adam Sutcliffe put it, "[T]he ideologically necessary but philosophically impossible border between reason and unreason was repeatedly drawn through the middle of the intermediate intellectual terrain where Judaism was exiled." In this sense we can say, along with Leo Strauss, that "from every point of view it looks as if the Jewish people were the chosen people, at least in the sense that the Jewish problem is the most manifest symbol of the human problem insofar as it is a social or political problem."[28]

"Destroy That Which Is Infamous": Judaism and the Philosophes

It would be profitable to follow further the place of Judaism in each of these encampments. But since our interest in this chapter is primarily in the translation of theological figures of Judaism into philosophical ones, we will focus entirely on the Enlightenment camp, and on just one battalion within it, the French movement known as the "philosophes." Montesquieu (1689–1755), Voltaire (1694–1778), Rousseau (1712–1778), Diderot (1713–1784): collectively these luminaries and countless others gave their name to the French eighteenth century, the "century of lights" (*siècle des lumières*). The movement's partisans came from every social class, and its production ranged across all genres, from scandal rags to learned encyclopedias. It would be folly to attempt a general characterization of such diversity, except perhaps to say that all shared a common belief that critical reason could improve society by exposing error, ignorance, and superstition: "Écrasez l'infâme" (destroy that which is infamous), in Voltaire's famous motto.

However vast and varied the opinions of the philosophes, their engagements with Judaism are relatively easy to summarize. This is not, I hasten to add, because such engagements were rare. On the contrary, though living Jews were scarce in eighteenth-century France, literary ones were easy to find. Before the French Revolution there were at most forty thousand Jews in all the lands of France. More than three-fourths of those lived in provinces conquered from the Holy Roman Empire during the seventeenth century, at the far eastern margins of the kingdom: Alsace, Lorraine, and the *généralité* of Metz. Another twenty-five hundred lived in the old papal territories of Avignon and the surrounding Comtat Venaissin, while some two thousand descendants of Spanish converts were settled in Bordeaux, and another thousand in a town called Saint-Esprit, just outside the Basque port city of Bayonne. In Paris there were only a handful, all living on temporary residence permits: here a Hebrew bibliographer for the royal library, there a visiting delegation from Metz or Bordeaux. In aggregate the Jews might have accounted for a miniscule fraction (.0015, or less than one-fifth of 1 percent) of the total population of France, and if one left out the far eastern provinces, the number rushed rapidly toward zero.[29]

These vanishingly small numbers make the overrepresentation of Jewish figures in French literature of the eighteenth century all the more remarkable. Following the historian Ronald Schechter's example, I have searched the eighteenth-century volumes in the ARTFL database of French literature, and found 6,624 results for the words *Jew*, *Hebrew*, and *Israelite* in their various forms. To put this number in perspective, the word *Anglais* and associated forms occur less often (6,523 times), despite France's bitter struggle with its neighbor for hegemony in Europe. Among philosophes the interest in Jews is even more marked. The database of Voltaire's vast writings, for example, yields 4,394 references to Jews, nearly double the number of allusions to the English (2,303), a people whom he very much admired, visited, read often, and even copied from. By way of further comparison, the ARTFL authors were seventy times more likely to mention Jews than Basques, a much more numerous "stateless 'nation'" within France.[30]

These allusions to Jews may have been frequent, but they were not diverse. For the philosophes, the Jews did four basic kinds of work. First, they played an important role in debates over commerce, mercantilism, and the money economy, much as they had done on the Elizabethan stage. Like Shakespeare, the philosophes wrote at a time of rapid economic transformation. As if in some financial "big bang," the eighteenth century produced a vast expansion of the market for money. Europe witnessed the dramatic expansion of stock exchanges and credit economies as nations, corporations, and individuals all turned to bonds, bankers, and brokers to slake the growing thirst for money of statesmen and of speculators. Unlike the galleon gold that expanded the monetary supplies of the sixteenth and seventeenth centuries, the eighteenth-century explosion of liquidity was driven by paper: paper stocks, paper bonds, and above all, the paper currency that was rapidly replacing sovereign silver and gold as a medium of exchange.[31]

Earlier chapters have taught us to expect such shifts in systems of exchange to produce worries about "Judaism," and we are not disappointed. For although from an econometric point of view Jews accounted for only a tiny fraction of the circulation of commodities, credit, and specie in the globalizing economy of eighteenth-century Europe, they played a much larger role in the cultural imagination of economic exchange. In principle, the market in money could be ecumenical. In the words of Voltaire, "Enter the Stock Exchange of London . . . and you will there see assembled for the utility of men deputies from all nations. There, the Jew, the Muslim, and the Christian treat each other as if they were all of the same religion, and only call the bankrupt infidels." Voltaire was himself an enthusiastic and successful investor, so interested in lucre that his own lover called him "pierced by avarice." (His English banker independently reached the same verdict: "very avaricious and dishonest.") Nevertheless, for Voltaire this worship of the golden calf of "utility" was itself already in some sense "Jewish," and in *Candide*, Jews provided him with some of the cruelest caricatures of the conniving faithlessness that he believed devotion to commerce produced.[32]

For the philosophes as for the theologians they so often criticized, the sphere of economic circulation was thoroughly "Jewish," the difference being that the reasons the philosophes gave for this "Jewishness" were historical rather than theological. According to Montesquieu's *Spirit of the Laws*, for example, the intolerance of medieval Christians had forced Jews into the credit market, with the result that "[c]ommerce passed to a nation covered with infamy and soon was distinguished only by the most frightful usury, monopolies, the raising of subsidies and all dishonest means of acquiring money." Things had apparently not changed much since the Middle Ages. "You ask me if there are Jews in France?" Montesquieu has the fictional Muslim traveler write home in his best-selling *Persian Letters*. "You can be sure that wherever there is money, there are Jews." Similarly in the great collective project of Enlightenment knowledge known as the *Encyclopedia*, the article "Jew" treated Jews as the lynchpins of all economic circulation: "They are like the pegs and nails that one uses in a great building, and which are necessary to join all the parts."[33]

As the metaphor of "pegs and nails" makes clear, this imaginary role of the Jews as "representative" of commerce was not necessarily negative. Indeed for the Chevalier de Jaucourt, author of this particular metaphor, the role was so positive that in various other articles he contributed to the *Encyclopedia* about specific cities in which Jews lived— London and Frankfurt among others—he stressed the prosperity they there produced. The important point is not that there were positive as well as negative portrayals of Jewish commercial activity, but that figures of Judaism were proxies in an increasingly sharp struggle over what European economies should look like. Among eighteenth-century philosophes, that struggle took the shape of a debate between those thinkers—known as the *économistes* or "physiocrats"—who believed that trade was "sterile" and that all wealth derived from agricultural production, and others—sometimes called mercantilists—who stressed the importance of commerce and credit for the "wealth of nations."[34]

In chapters to come we will pay more attention to later manifestations of these struggles—such as the contest between "capitalism" and "Marxism" in the nineteenth and twentieth centuries. Here we can only pause to note that well before the French or the Industrial Revolution, "Judaism" was already a crucial figure in economic arguments about the nature of production and exchange. And already at this early date, there were some living Jews who understood just how dangerous this position could be. Historians are fond of citing Isaac de Pinto's (1715–1787) *Apology for the Jewish Nation* of 1762, addressed against Voltaire's more vitriolic statements about the Jews. But from the point of view of prescience, it is de Pinto's work on economic theory that is much more significant. In books like *An essay on circulation and credit*, he endeavored to convince readers that purveyors of credit and liquidity were vital to the economic growth and prosperity of nations; that buyers of government bonds were not "enemies of the plough," "drones" driven by "avarice," nor "devouring wolves"; that neither "manufacturers are pernicious" or "money is chimera"; that "dealers, jobbers, and gamesters may contribute to the success of those great operations of finance, by which the fate of nations is frequently determined"; and (finally) that Voltaire, like centuries of Christians before him, has misunderstood what Hebrew scripture has to say about lending at interest, a misunderstanding that resulted in a stigmatization of credit, as well as in "many atrocious calumnies against the Jews."[35]

The second basic kind of work the Jews did for the philosophes was to represent the origins of revelation, with all the ambivalence this implied, just as they had done in the work of earlier Enlightenment thinkers, such as Spinoza, Bayle, Van Dale, and Wachter. For those who hoped to preserve the authority of scripture while purifying spirituality of superstition, this meant that some "Jews" (Old Testament patriarchs, scriptural Karaites, but never the Talmud-toting rabbis of the here and now) could be celebrated as archaic examples of a primitive age when revealed religion was not yet so alienated from human reason. But for those who were determined to reduce ecclesiastical authority to rubble, it often made more strategic sense to aim at that authority's foundations. For Voltaire, the biblical Jews were the "most detestable people on the earth" who had usurped with "the most odious rapine and the most detestable cruelty that history has ever recorded" a land "to which they had no more right than they do to Paris or London." Such were the black origins, we can hear him implying, of theocracy and priestly power.

But the Jews were themselves frequent victims of persecution, which could also make them symbols of the intolerance that religious fanaticism and superstition produce. This was the third basic type of work that figures of Judaism did for the philosophes. Indeed, though few authors protested discriminations against the Jews in France, many devoted tenderly indignant pages to the suffering of the Jews at the hands of the Spanish Inquisition. The young Voltaire, for example, deployed the familiar figures of inquisitor and Jew in *La Henriade*, the poetic encomium to King Henry IV with which he earned his first literary laurels in 1714:

> *In Madrid, in Lisbon, he lights his fires,*
> *The solemn bonfires to which the unhappy Jews*
> *Are sent every year, in pomp, by the priest,*
> *For not having left the law of their ancestors.*

Similarly in his *Spirit of the Laws*, the mature Montesquieu adopted the authorial guise of an anonymous Jew in a "remonstrance" against the Lisbon Inquisition's burning of an eighteen-year-old girl. *Remonstrance* was itself a technical term at the sovereign court in which Montesquieu had been a magistrate. It designated protests against the despotic deployment of monarchical authority. By using it here, Montesquieu seems to be associating his law court in its struggles with Louis XV to the Jews in their persecution by the Inquisition.[36]

The history of Spain's cruelties provided a particularly good target for this kind of critique, in part because the theme had already been so well developed by Protestants in previous centuries, in part because it kept the point from landing too close to home. For critics who were themselves writing under the censorship of a Catholic regime, there was an obvious advantage in situating the worst excesses of Catholicism across the borders, in a region all Frenchmen could agree was fanatical. Less obvious is the way in which this move displaced Christian cruelty onto a *religion* about whose horrors there could also be consensus.

In the previous chapter we saw that Spain was a thoroughly Judaized land in the European imagination. In this one, we have seen how, in enlightened corners of that imagination, the coercive powers of clergy were becoming increasingly characterized as a Jewish invention. Perhaps—and this is speculative—we should see here a commutative effect. The focusing of critiques of religious persecution onto "Juda-ized" Spain and its Inquisition simultaneously implied a shift in the burden of responsibility for intolerance from Christianity to Judaism. (More on this later, when I address Voltaire.) The eventual transfor-mation of Spain from a land of fanaticism to one of tolerance could even be described in terms of a conversion from Judaism to Christianity. Thus the Marquis d'Argens, whose best-selling *Jewish Letters* famously adopted the fictional mask of Judaism in order to criticize Christian society, imagined a future in which Spaniards—now under the rule and tutelage of a French Bourbon king—would finally be cured of "their blindness," and shake their heads in wonder at how they could have "remained so long without making use of their reason."[37]

The Jew as paradigmatic progenitor of religious persecution and the Jew as that persecution's exemplary object: these twin figures played two of the key roles assigned to Judaism by many leading writers of this "century of lights," much as they had in the "dark" Christian centu-ries that had come before. The same continuity is evident in the fourth basic role assigned to Jews by the philosophes, and well described by Ronald Schechter in his *Obstinate Hebrews*: that of marking the limits of humanity. For Christian evangelists, Jews had represented the limits of the possibility of conversion. The philosophes, too, used the Jews to explore the limits of conversion, only now that conversion was to rationality. At its most basic, their question was anthropological: Can humans be ruled by reason? Can they be educated and their societies perfected (or at least improved) by the assiduous deployment of critical thought? Or are large parts of humanity so prone to violence and igno-rance that they cannot be freed by truth, but rather require myth, faith, and fear to restrain them? The question was as old as philosophy itself, but it became especially acute for a movement agitating to kick over the traces of tradition and piety.

This is the place to pause and remind ourselves that when we focus on Jewish questions as this book does, we risk losing sight of the gran-deur of the many intellectual projects we today collectively call the Enlightenment. The eighteenth century opened up vast new vistas in

Western (and not only Western) thought: new anthropologies, new sociologies, new typologies of civilizations, new ways of conjecturing the histories of nature and of humankind. It produced serious, systematic, and vitally innovative attempts to understand and categorize non-Western civilizations, from the Amerindians to the Chinese, as well as non-Christian religions. The motivations for these attempts varied, and so did the valorizations of these civilizations, cultures, and religions that they produced—from stigmatory classifications designed to legitimate colonial exploitation, to idealizations (such as Diderot's *Supplement to the Voyage of Bougainville*) intended to cast critical light on the West. It is because of the ways in which their engagements transformed the shape of European thought and expanded the objects of its attention that works like Montesquieu's *Spirit of the Laws*, Rousseau's *Second Discourse*, and Buffon's *Natural History* retain their central claim on our attention as students of the history of ideas.

My highlighting of certain continuities evident in the work that some of these eighteenth-century thinkers did with Judaism is not meant to deny the scope or the potentially radical nature of their broader project. Nor do I mean to put Jewish questions at the center of their interests or inquiry: the Enlightenment's interest in Jews and Judaism was by some measures disproportionate, but it was never a primary concern. Nevertheless, that work was important precisely because the horizons of Enlightenment thought were so vast. As eighteenth-century philosophers rapidly expanded their sense of the human, they sought as well for its limits. For that purpose they turned often to Jews and Judaism, and in the process, produced an excellent example of my claim that the work that figures of Judaism are asked to do in critical thought makes it difficult to become critical of those figures themselves.

Because the Jews were generally imagined as the most fanatically irrational segment of the species (indeed, as the very origins of fanatical irrationality), they provided the perfect proving ground for the powers of Enlightenment. Perfect because Enlightenment won either way. If even the Jews could be "regenerated," then there were no limits to the emancipatory powers of Enlightenment anthropology. But if they could not, it simply meant that reason had reached the boundaries of its authority, and that the Jews lay on the other side. For philosophes bent on exploring the boundaries of their anthropology, the Jews were a "limit case," an example whose pursuit charts the extremes of a concept. In this case, the limits were those of humanity, and the question "Can the Jews be regenerated?" was also the question "Are the Jews human?" In the words of the lawyer Pierre-Louis Lacretelle in his legal brief of 1776 on behalf of the Jews of Metz, "The real question in this case . . . is whether Jews are men." Or as the philosophes more often put it, "[I]s the Jew more a human or a Jew?"[38]

The word that many thinkers of the later French Enlightenment settled on to describe their anthropology's potential for the transformation of humanity was *régénération*: *regeneration*, the same word used to refer to baptism and resurrection (as well as the healing and regrowth of damaged tissue). In the words of one eminent scholar, "[A]fter making such a dark and seemingly irreversible diagnosis of their age, Rousseau and his disciples could imagine the emancipatory transformation only as a sort of miracle, on the religious model." But that model had a history, and in that history the Jews had long been type-cast. This fact alone suggests that when it came to the limit case of the Jews, the philosophes' answers to these questions would be as ambivalent as those of the priests.[39]

That ambivalence is everywhere apparent. Montesquieu, for example, believed that men were shaped by the culture and climate in which they lived, and could therefore be reshaped by alterations to those conditions. Even the Jews, he pointed out, had once been an agricultural and warlike people, becoming ruthless usurers only under compulsion from Christian tyrants. If the Christian regimes under which they lived would treat them more tolerantly, the Jews would presumably improve as well. Yet it is also true that for Montesquieu the Jews all look distressingly the same, no matter what sun or sovereign they are subject to. According to the Muslim traveler in his *Persian Letters*, "[N]othing more closely resembles a Persian Jew than a European Jew." Everywhere Jews pursue the same goals with the same obstinacy: "You can be sure that wherever there is money, there are Jews." In the face of such uniform obduracy, perhaps pessimism about potential for reform is justified.[40]

Enlightened Toleration, Jewish Intolerance

This ambivalence about the improvement of the Jews was no mere by-product of the Enlightenment, but one of its more important tools. Voltaire's celebrated *Treatise on Tolerance* (1763) provides a good example of this utility.[41] It is a call for liberty of conscience and an end to religious violence, written on the occasion of the death of Jean Calas, an elderly merchant in the city of Toulouse. He and his family were Protestants, with the exception of one son, Louis, who had converted to Catholicism some years before. One evening after dinner, Jean found his eldest son Marc-Antoine hanging by the neck in the cellar, an apparent suicide. To this terrible misfortune was added another: a Catholic crowd, attracted by the family's cries, began to murmur that Marc-Antoine had intended to convert to Catholicism. These rumors slithered into the shape of a grotesque accusation: it was said that the Protestants of the region, informed of Marc-Antoine's plans, had sent an executioner to Toulouse to assist the father in hanging his soon-to-be-apostate son. Catholic confraternities began to compete for the honor of Marc-Antoine's burial, despite the fact that he had died a Calvinist. His body was interred at the Catholic Church of Saint-Etienne, where it began to work miracles. As for his father, Jean Calas was convicted by the judges of Toulouse on the charge of murdering his eldest, and his body was broken on the executioner's wheel in the public square. [42]

None of this has anything to do with Jews, except in the sense that some elements of the horrifying narrative (the son who wishes to convert, the cruel father, the homicidal council, the miracles worked by the victim's body) may well have been borrowed from the repertory of ritual murder accusations long aimed against them. But Voltaire's treatise is much more than a vindication of Jean Calas and his family. It is above all a claim that religious toleration is commanded by natural, human, and divine law. According to Voltaire, Greece, Rome, China, India, Persia, Turkey, even Tartary all practiced tolerance, which was the rule everywhere except in the darkest corners of Catholic Europe: Portugal, Spain, and apparently Toulouse. Intolerance, on the other hand, is as absurd as it is barbaric: "[I]t is the law of the jungle. Nay, it is yet worse, for wild animals kill only to eat, whereas we have exterminated one another over a parcel of words" (chap. 6).[43]

Since this parcel of words came from holy writ, it is not surprising that a large part of Voltaire's treatise was dedicated to a reinterpretation of scripture. There was, he insists in chapter 8, no such thing as intolerance among the gentiles of Jesus's day. Both Romans and Greeks were humane and undogmatic peoples who never persecuted others on religious grounds. (According to Voltaire it was the Jews, not the Romans, who executed Jesus and martyred his disciples.) Early Christians were equally tolerant. Even fundamental differences of opinion were debated among them without disturbing the peace. Voltaire chose as an example of this tolerant debate an episode with which we are already familiar: Saint Peter's insistence that gentile converts should be circumcised, and Saint Paul's condemnation of such actions as "Judaizing" (citing Gal. 2:14). Today, he wittily observed, a Spanish or Portuguese bishop who adopted Saint Peter's position would be burned in an autodafé.

Convincing Christians of the gospels' gentleness was no great challenge. It was the Old Testament that posed the true test of Voltaire's claim that scripture endorsed toleration, and his treatise therefore hinged on the question that served as the title to his chapter 12: "whethere religious persecution was part of the divine law in Judaism, and whether it was always practiced." Voltaire conceded that "in Exodus, Numbers, Leviticus, and Deuteronomy there is mention of very severe religious laws and even severer penalties," such as Moses's slaughter of twenty-three thousand (Exodus has only three thousand!) of his countrymen for worshipping the golden calf. But in a twist by now familiar from Hobbes, Spinoza, and many others, Voltaire insisted that God required these law and punishments only of a "Jewish theocracy" whose customs, "we cannot state too often . . . bear little resemblance to those of our own day." Moreover (and this was more original), the laws themselves only served to illustrate the futility of using violence to coerce belief. Voltaire lovingly catalogued Israel's worship of idols and false deities to demonstrate that although the Jews blasphemed relentlessly throughout their history, God only rarely sent prophets to punish their infractions. One could therefore speak, even among God's most intolerant and intolerable people, of de facto toleration: "Throughout the history of the Jews you will find not one instance of generosity, magnanimity, or charity; and yet, in the fog of this long and frightful barbarism, one may always discern rays of universal tolerance."

Eighteenth-century artists were fond of painting bad weather. Perhaps Voltaire had learned from the stormy canvasses of Claude-Joseph Vernet and his colleagues that the darker the cloud, the more dramatic the piercing light. The rays he projected from Jewish darkness helped him represent Enlightenment tolerance as a universal, to be found even at the origins of monotheism and divine revelation. The depths of that darkness, on the other hand, helped him draw contrasts sharp enough to mark the boundaries of tolerance, and set his opponents outside them. Those opponents, you will recall, were the (Catholic) killers of Jean Calas and others like them, willing to do violence out of religious zeal. In chapter 18, entitled "The only cases in which intolerance conforms to human laws," Voltaire took aim at such zealots, whom he called religious "fanatics." Fanatics harm others in pursuit of their own beliefs and therefore should not be tolerated. Voltaire is far too politic to consign powerful countrymen like the judges of Toulouse to such a class, preferring to give more exotic examples, "one of the most astonishing" being a sect in Denmark that slit the throats of newly baptized infants so that they might enter heaven before having occasion to commit a sin.

But unsurprisingly, his paradigmatic fanatics are the Jews, whom for the purpose he paints very darkly indeed. The Jews, he writes, "appear to have more right than anyone to rob and murder us," for although it is true that the Old Testament contains "a hundred examples of toleration," it also contains "some instances" of rigor:

God occasionally ordered them to kill all idolators, sparing only mar-
riageable girls; they look upon us as idolators; and though we are toler-
ant towards them these days, they could easily, if they got the upper
hand, denude the world of all but our marriageable daughters. (chap. 18)

The Muslims are in even greater danger from the Jews, who are
under "an inalienable duty to murder the whole Turkish race" occupying the strip of territory promised to them by God. "If the Jews were to
argue along these lines today," Voltaire concludes, "it is clear that the
only valid response would be summary execution. These are about the
only cases in which intolerance may be sanctioned by reason."

From the point of view of a Palestinian living in the occupied territories today, such words might seem a realistic assessment of threats to
toleration in the world they live in. From that of an eighteenth-century
European writing about the violence of Christians against Christians,
in a region that allowed at most a few thousand Jews within its borders and accorded them few civic rights, the use of Judaism to represent
the existential danger posed by intolerance is a fantastic distortion of
reality. Fantastic, but doubly useful: Voltaire first impresses labor from
the mythic jungles of Jewish misanthropy to build his tolerant community of the future, and then defines citizenship in this new community
by expelling the monstrous migrants back into their archaic past. This
double utility of Judaism is already familiar to us from Christian theology. We might say that in the *Treatise on Tolerance* Voltaire attacked
the Christian order by adopting one of its most important axioms. He
"smashed" intolerance, but transplanted its beating heart.

"The Euthanasia of Judaism"

There were those who objected to the violence of Voltaire's cudgel and
the sharpness of his scalpel. Some Christian authors sought to shield the
Jews from his harsh words in order to defend church and Bible; others,
as anticlerical as Voltaire but more optimistic about the Jews, insisted
on the possibility of their improvement through reeducation. Yet all

the participants in this argument, whether Enlightenment radical, clerical apologist, or even Jew (and there were some Jewish participants),
shared the conviction that the critical anthropological and philosophical
issues at stake could be boiled down to "Jewish questions." Could the
Jews be "regenerated"? If so, then how, and if not, why not?[44]

Not every major intellect of the French Enlightenment was interested in these questions. There are plenty of writers like Jean-Jacques
Rousseau with little to say about the Jews, and that little was predictable
enough. (He was most impressed by their immutability.) Nevertheless,
the energy expended on Judaism by illustrious figures such as Voltaire,
Diderot, and many others remains astounding. In just three years, for
example, Baron Paul Thiry d'Holbach published enough on the topic to
make any professor envious. In 1768 he translated Peter Annet's *David,
the History of the Man after God's Own Heart*, a hatchet job on the
prophet's reputation in the best Enlightenment tradition. That same
year, under the title *Study of the Prophecies that serve as the Foundation
of the Christian Religion*, he translated Anthony Collins's *Discourse of
Free-thinking* of 1713, in which the English deist had demolished the
exemplarity of the Hebrew Bible by showing that the Jews were "barbarous and illiterate," "cross-grained brutes" with whom God had had
to deal "by craft rather than reason." To demonstrate that the Jews were
despised for their credulity and cruelty long before they killed Jesus,
in 1769 he edited and republished Jean Baptiste de Mirabaud's collection of texts by Roman and Greek authors, the *Opinions of the Ancients
Concerning the Jews*. Finally in 1770, he produced his own semi-original
work, *The Spirit of Judaism*, in which he marshaled the vast corpus of
anti-Jewish writings at his disposal, from Apion and the ancient Egyptians to the most recent writings of Voltaire and Diderot, and molded
them into an eternal history of Jewish threats to the destiny of Europe
and of human reason:

> *Europe! Happy land where for so long a time the arts, sciences, and
> philosophy have flourished; you whose wisdom and power seem des-
> tined to command the rest of the world! Do you never tire of the false*

dreams invented by impostors in order to deceive the brutish slaves of the Egyptians? Then dare, oh Europe! Break the unbearable yoke of the prejudices by which you are afflicted. Leave to the stupid Hebrews, to the frenzied imbeciles, and to the cowardly and degraded Asiatics these superstitions which are as vile as they are mad; they were not meant for the inhabitants of your clime.[45]

Europe, cast off your chains! Voltaire might not have admired the rhetoric, but he would have concurred with the logic. D'Holbach's call for a revolutionary emancipation from Judaism is utterly representative of one common strategy in the struggle for freedom of thought from the strictures of the Christian state. The philosophes adopted and transformed Christianity's founding enmity, the enmity of Judaism toward the spirit, then deployed that enmity against Christian priestly power. In other words, philosophy emancipated herself from theology by learning everything her tutor could teach about the Jews. Indeed the pupil surpassed the pedagogue, rediscovering ancient Egyptian, Greek, or Roman sources and mining them for whatever examples of Jewish irrationality and inhumanity they could provide.[46] The result was a unified field theory, one capable of explaining the history of human reason and the history of human faith in the same anti-Jewish terms. Henceforth it would not much matter whether future theorists of anti-Judaism spoke in the name of the sacred or of the secular. On this point, at least, their languages would be very much the same.

The French were by no means unique in the conceptual work they did with Jews. It is one of the greatest ironies of the Enlightenment (and so far as I know, not previously noted) that all its most famous treatises on toleration and freedom of thought depended on separating Judaism from Christianity, and isolating the former in an archaic and execrable past. An example from the early Enlightenment, English and very influential, was John Locke's *Letter Concerning Toleration* of 1685. Like Spinoza's more radical *Treatise* (by which it was influenced) and Voltaire's more demagogical essay (which it inspired), the logic of Locke's letter hinged on the argument that intolerance was the exception in sacred history. It had been commanded by God to ancient Israel, but had been forbidden to Christians by their Savior because it had nothing to do with "true religion." The absolute theocracy required by the laws of Moses was applicable only to Jews, and only during the period of their kingdom of God in the land of Canaan. Christian "Zealots" who coerce belief are therefore untrue to the gospels. Their actions do not produce true piety, but only foment the hypocritical conformity that arises from fear of the law.[47]

A late example, German and equally influential, is Immanuel Kant's *Religion within the Bounds of Reason Alone* (1792–1794), a work that earned the aged Prussian professor a sharp rebuke from his king, and the "request" that he never publish on the topic of religion again. The work represents a milestone in the history of relations between philosophy and theology (terms whose very meaning Kant's work fundamentally altered). It is easy enough to see how the treatise's careful separation of these realms, its sharp distinctions between what universal human reason can know about divinity and what historical religions tell us must be believed, and its bitter critique of coercive clergy who confuse the two and produce a "counterfeit service" of God, sent shudders through the quills of his Lutheran censors. But for our purposes it is also important to stress what those censors would have found entirely congenial: the philosopher's founding distinction between a Jewish "slavery" based on fear of the law, self-love, and formal ritual, and a Christian "freedom" based on love of God and neighbor and an inner yearning for morality. In fact, like the prophet of Wittenberg whom he often quoted, the philosopher of Königsberg was calling for a thorough de-Judaization of Christianity.

On this score, at least, the censors' only complaint could have been that Kant was too radical, even Manichaean, in his divorce of Christianity from Judaism. According to Kant, who here seems inspired by an extreme reading of Spinoza, "the *Jewish* faith stands in absolutely no essential connection, i.e., in no unity of concepts, with the ecclesiastical faith whose history we want to consider, even though it immediately preceded it and provided the physical occasion for the founding of this church (the Christian)." "Strictly speaking Judaism is not a religion at all. . . . Judaism was rather *meant* to be a purely secular state. . . . Judaism as such, taken in its purity, entails absolutely no religious faith," demanding only obedience to law and political hatred of all other peoples. The teachings of Jesus can therefore owe nothing at all to this Judaism, nothing at all to the context into which he was born, which is also to say, nothing at all to a particular history. (Without sensing any contradiction, Kant elsewhere claimed that Jesus's teachings were really Greek, Occidental wisdom clothed in Oriental garb.) From confusion on this score, Kant insists, flowed "so many evils that religion prompted."[48]

How had this misunderstanding occurred? How had the history of the two faiths become so inextricably linked? In order "to win over to the new faith, through its own prejudices, the nation which was accustomed to its old historical faith," Jesus and the early Christians had allowed the legalistic and unreligious scriptures and customs of Judaism to become "the foundation of a universal world-religion." This lamentable but understandable pedagogical concession had given rise to the evil tendency to give "precedence to the observance of statutory law, requiring a revelation as necessary to religion." This widespread tendency, which Kant saw afflicting the priesthood of all Christian sects equally, he called a "counterfeit service" to God, "mere fetishism." Only by denying the historical particulars of its Jewish origins could Christianity fulfill its destiny as the truly universal religion of humanity. This de-Judaization was a principal task of Kant's writings on rational religion, and he believed that, thanks to the Enlightenment, Christianity had never been closer to achieving it. "Should one now ask, Which period of the entire church history in our ken is up to now the best? I reply without hesitation, *The present*." Insofar as "reason has wrested itself free from the burden" of faith corrupted by Judaism, the "invisible kingdom of God on earth" is close to hand. And with that kingdom would come, in quasi-Pauline fashion, the redemption of Israel and the conversion of the Jews. In *The Philosophy Faculty vs. the Theology Faculty*, for example, Kant envisions the "[e]uthanasia of Jews and

Judaism" in messianic terms. The Jews, he says, will convert from their current status as "garments without a man in them (a church without a religion)" to a purely moral religion, which will then itself disappear in the "greatest drama of religious change on earth, the restoration of all things, when there will be only one shepherd and one flock."[49]

Kant considered himself the fomenter of a "Copernican revolution" in philosophy, the founder of a new form of "critical thought," and many of his contemporaries and successors were compelled to agree. For this reason he will return in chapter 12, on the new philosophies of the nineteenth century. But in this one he stands as a last representative of Enlightenment, and of its limitations. In his essay of 1784, "What is Enlightenment?" Kant proposed that it consisted in the "emergence of the human being" from "the guidance of another," in the emancipation of individual reason from bondage to cognitive "statutes" and "mechanical tools" of thought. Yet it should be clear by now, even from our brief foray into a very few of his late texts, that when it came to Judaism as a figure of thought, Kant himself wore "the foot shackles of a permanent immaturity." His philosophical revolution did not seek to shatter the chains binding Judaism in the Christian imagination, but rather reinforced them with secular steel. We will let his words be our last on the Enlightenment, not only because they are so revealing, but also because chronologically they coincide with another much bloodier philosophical revolt against Judaism, one whose convulsions are often said to have birthed modernity.[50]

Chapter 11

THE REVOLUTIONARY PERFECTION
OF THE WORLD: 1789–?

The age of chivalry is gone. That of sophisters,
economists, and calculators has succeeded; and the
glory of Europe is extinguished forever.

—EDMUND BURKE, *REFLECTIONS ON*
THE REVOLUTION IN FRANCE, 1790

IT SEEMS ODD to approach the revolution that began in France in 1789 as a revolt against Judaism. We have already seen how few Jews there were in that realm, and how powerless. The topic of Judaism may not have crossed the mind of a single member of the mob that stormed the Bastille, hated symbol of sovereign power, in the heat of that famous year's July. Unlike the Castilian rebels we met in 1449, or the Egyptian ones of the first century, the revolutionaries of 1789 did not flirt with the assertion that the king—in this case Louis XVI—was a Jew, nor did they expend much energy imagining the royal regime as a vast Jewish conspiracy. Judaism was not even mentioned in what is perhaps the most important of their manifestos, the Declaration of the Rights of Man and of the Citizen, issued by the newly constituted National Assembly on August 26. And although that document begins by placing its framers "in the presence and under the auspices of the Supreme Being," it is remarkably silent about religion, except to insist (in clause 10) that no one should be molested on account of their beliefs, unless those "disturb the public order." Even the sacred is scarcely mentioned, except in the last clause (17), guaranteeing the "inviolable and sacred" right to private property.[1]

And yet the revolutionaries sought to effect a transformation in what the (hostile) English observer Edmund Burke called "doctrine and theoretic dogma," extending "even to the constitution of the mind of man." Many of them believed that a true revolution required a people's fundamental reconceptualization of the world. That reconceptualization had already begun to take place in the more radical corners of Enlightenment philosophy. Already in 1704, Leibniz had prophesied that thinkers inspired by Spinoza's philosophical attack on divine providence were

> *inclining everything towards the universal revolution with which Europe is threatened, and are completing the destruction of what still remains in the world of the generous sentiments of the ancient Greeks and Romans who placed love of country and the public good, and the welfare of future generations, before fortune and before life.*[2]

We do not need to agree that the French Revolution was caused by philosophy in order to concede that the revolutionaries shared with these philosophers a number of basic questions about human relation, communication, and exchange. Because many of these questions had long been asked in terms of Judaism, it would not be surprising if the revolutionaries and counterrevolutionaries also engaged these terms, and even on occasion represented their conflict as a struggle against Judaism. Those occasional representations are worthy of our attention, not because they were the central concern of the revolution and its enemies (they were not), but because they can teach us a great deal about how figures of Judaism did new work and gained new meaning in moments

of radical transformation that, on the face of it, had little to do with
Israel or Israelites.

Moses, Law, and Revolution

We have just traced how the Enlightenment tradition, from Spinoza to
Kant, represented the transformations it hoped to achieve in Christian
terms, as the replacement of a "Mosaic" world of slavery to law and
letter by one of truth and human freedom. The revolutionaries were
the heirs of this radical critique. Like their forefathers, they saw themselves overthrowing the Old Covenant in favor of a new and better constitution, one based on nature and human reason. They too imagined
new and better forms of community and association in which language,
contract, and exchange were stripped of their deadly ambivalence
and became pure instruments of communication. And again like their
forefathers, the concepts through which they made sense of these new
covenants and constitutions were saturated with the Christian logic
of supersession. Even Jean-Jacques Rousseau, a thoughtful theorist of
"national physiognomy" and an author not often given to ruminations
about Judaism, imagined the founding of nations and the framing of
constitutions as "mosaic moments." As he put it in his *Considerations on
the Government of Poland and on its Planned Reforms* of 1772,

> *Moses formed and executed the astonishing enterprise of shaping into
> a national body a swarm of unhappy fugitives, bereft of arts, weap-
> ons, talents, virtues and courage . . . not having a single square inch
> of land for their own. . . . Moses dared to turn this wandering and
> servile band into a Political body, a free people . . . gave it this durable
> form . . . which five thousand years have not been able to destroy or
> even alter, and which even today retains all its strength, although the
> national Body itself no longer exists.*

The revolutionaries participated fully in this logic. Their task as legislators, like that of Jesus or Muhammad, was to be a new and better

Moses, leading the people toward true freedom. Hence, although the Declaration of the Rights of Man and of the Citizen nowhere mentions Jews or Judaism, it was famously presented and represented to the people—in a painting and in print—as two new tablets of law, replacing those handed Moses on Mount Sinai.[3]

Of course the legislator was only one part of such a covenant; the people had to subscribe as well and to participate in their own transformation. In the case of the French Revolution, this meant the transformation of a hierarchical society of "subjects" under the law of a sovereign into a state of free and equal "citizens" collectively sovereign over themselves. As the Declaration put it (in clause 6):

Law is the expression of the general will. Every citizen has a right to participate personally, or through his representative, in its foundation. It must be the same for all, whether it protects or punishes. All citizens, being equal in the eyes of the law, are equally eligible to all dignities and to all public positions and occupations, according to their abilities, and without distinction except that of their virtues and talents.

The status of the republican "citizen," in other words, was defined by his relationship to the law. The "subject" was (like the "Jew") a slave to the law; the "citizen" was (like the "Christian") a free participant in it.

The distinction is not an easy one to implement, nor are the difficulties so different from those that had confronted Christianity. How to proclaim freedom from the law, while still functioning as a state with its attendant political and legal order? Moreover the revolutionaries faced additional questions produced by what we described in the last chapter as Enlightenment anthropology. Were all humans capable by nature of achieving this conversion? If there were some who were unwilling or unable to change their mentality from that of a "subject" to that of a "citizen," how should they be treated by the nation? Did they retain their rights as "men" even if they proved incapable of assuming their rights as a "citizen"? If so, the result would seem to be a hierarchical division within the polity, a "state within a state" of the very sort that the revolution was meant to eliminate. If not, then there would seem to be an irreconcilable conflict between an individual's particular rights and duties as citizen of a nation, and their universal or natural rights as human beings.

These and many other questions about law, freedom, citizenship, and humanity spurred the legislative mania of the fledgling National Assembly. The Assembly confronted these fundamental questions in myriad forms. Could women become citizens? (No.)[4] Could slaves? (No.)[5] Could the poor? (Not until late in 1792.)[6] But over and over again it turned to the Jews as a "limit case" from which to approach the limits of citizenship and of humanity. Thus, although on Christmas Eve of 1789 the Assembly removed Catholicism as a requirement for citizenship and public office, it made an explicit exception of "the Jews, on whose status the National Assembly reserves the right to pronounce." And pronounce it did. Given the poverty of most Jews and the property requirements established by the deputies for citizenship, immediate emancipation would scarcely have produced a hundred new Jewish citizens for all of France. Yet during the two years of its existence, and with all the urgent business of building a nation from scratch to address, the Assembly took up some thirty-two times the question of whether Jews could be citizens.[7]

How can we explain this focus of revolutionary legislators on the citizenship status of a statistically nonexistent group? One explanation has to do with a phenomenon we have already observed in nearly all the previous chapters: in the Christian polities of Europe, the right to decide the fate of the Jews—to "decide the exception," in the much later words of Carl Schmitt—was a defining prerogative of the sovereign. In claiming to determine the status of the Jews, the Assembly was therefore asserting its sovereign power. But another explanation is more specific to the revolution, and returns us to a basic anthropological question of the philosophes. Can humanity and human society be perfected, "regenerated"? And if so, how can this "regeneration" best be achieved? Some of the best minds of the Enlightenment had approached this basic question through the Jews, and some of the best minds of the revolution followed their example.

Just a year before the revolution, the Royal Academy of Sciences and Arts of the city of Metz had published the names of the prize-winners of its essay contest on the question "Is there a way of making the Jews more useful and happier in France?" In 1789 the same question, and some of the same participants, moved to the remodeled riding ring in Paris that served as meeting place for the delegates to the National Assembly. One of these, the Abbé Grégoire, had been a co-winner of the Metz essay prize. Another, François Hell, had been a leader of a popular movement against Jewish moneylenders in prerevolutionary Alsace. Still others, with storied names like Mirabeau, Talleyrand, La Rochefoucauld, and Robespierre, brought the zeal of neophytes to the topic.

The arguments of the first great debate, on December 21–24, recapitulated those of the previous century of Enlightenment. Those arguing for the exclusion of the Jews from citizenship focused on their usury, their separatism, their depravity, their misanthropy. Those arguing for their inclusion argued for their common humanity, and therefore their potential for improvement. As the Abbé Grégoire put it, "I always believed that they were men; a trivial fact, but one that is not yet proven for those who treat them as complete brutes." "I had always thought that one could recreate those people, bring them along to virtue, and leave them in good will." As men, and therefore bearers of universal human rights, said Robespierre, they could not be excluded from political rights within a particular nation without a "violation of the eternal principles of justice and of reason that are the basis of all human society." Of course the possibility that the Jews might refuse to enter into the common rights of humanity and citizenship still remained. Count Stanislas of Clermont-Tonnerre dealt with this possibility much as Voltaire had done: "Every one of them must individually become a citizen. If they do not want this, they must inform us and we shall then be compelled to expel them. The existence of a nation within a nation is unacceptable to our country."[8]

In emphasizing the theoretical importance of these arguments to the revolutionaries, I do not mean to imply that they were not also important to real Jews. On the contrary, Jews sent delegations, wrote treatises, and agitated for the rights and duties of citizenship. Jews were doubtless among those most disappointed when, on December 24, 1789, the opponents of Jewish citizenship in the National Assembly carried the day, 408 to 403. Jews were also among the more elated when, on September 27, 1791, the Assembly finally voted in favor of emancipation. And, in cities that had significant Jewish populations like Metz and Bordeaux, they were prominent among those targeted by the Christian protest riots that greeted the news of that emancipation. In short, the revolutionary struggle over the place of Jews in the nation had a real impact on the lives of the forty thousand Jews living in France and those inhabiting the parts of Europe that Napoleon would conquer in the not-too-distant future. That impact has been well studied (and sometimes exaggerated). But for the purposes of understanding how the French Revolution reshaped the space available for figures of Judaism in an increasingly "modern" world, it is just as important to remember that these hothouse debates over the regeneration of a few-score Jews were a subset of and a surrogate for the much larger debate over how to achieve the conversion of tens of millions of French subjects, peasants and princes, peddlers and priests, into citizens.[9]

Paul, Conversion, and Revolution

The word *conversion* here is apt, in that the revolutionaries expressed their aspirations for the philosophical perfection of the world in the Christian vocabulary of "regeneration" (that is, baptism), "second birth," and "new creation." This should not be surprising, given their roots in an Enlightenment that so frequently encoded Christian logic in its philosophy. Like their predecessors, the revolutionaries understood their task to be the complete restructuring of the conditions for human knowledge in the world. In 1791, the National Assembly's president, Charles-Maurice de Talleyrand, had even urged that body to pursue Leibniz's quest for a universal language. By eliminating "the multitude of errors that we owe to the imperfection of our ordinary signs," he explained, and by achieving the same conformity between a word and its referent that there is between gold and goods, such a language would bring an end to the political strife afflicting the nation. (It is difficult to imagine such epistemological exhortations resounding in today's legislative chambers!)[10]

Again like their predecessors, they sometimes represented the necessary cognitive restructuring in the traditional terms of covenantal succession, conversion, and even messianic transformation. The historian David Bell has translated for us a brilliant example: the sermon delivered by Father Antoine-Pascal-Hyacinthe Sermet to the Municipal Council and National Guard regiment of Saint-Ginest (near Toulouse, in southern France) on July 14, 1790, the "Festival of the Federation." Father Sermet took as his opening prooftext a quote from Saint Paul that we encountered in chapter 2: *"So then, brethren, we are not children of the bondwoman, but of the free. Stand fast therefore in the liberty wherewith Christ hath made us free, and be not entangled again with the yoke of bondage"* (Gal. 4:31, 5:1). He left no doubt about who was bond and who was free:

> NEVER *forget, my children and good comrades, to whom the Apostle Saint Paul, the greatest Preacher to appear on earth since the birth of Christianity, addressed these words. It was, so that you may know, to our illustrious cousins, to the children of those Gauls who, around three thousand years ago, left this country, one hundred and fifty thousand of them, to journey beyond the seas, to the end of the world as it was then known, to the depths of Asia, to found the proud City of Ankara, and to populate the Province that took their name and was henceforth called Galatia.*
>
> *Barely had he made them abandon the Idols and embraced the Gospel, than a few Jewish theologians, who had also converted, but who clung to their old customs, worked to stuff their heads with the idea that there was nothing more holy or pleasing to God than Circumcision. The Apostle learned of this, and so as to prevent the Galatians*

from becoming the theologians' dupes, wrote to them strongly and firmly, telling them to guard preciously the liberty that Jesus Christ had procured for them, and to protect themselves with care from the painful and disgusting ceremonies of the old Law, which the new law had entirely abrogated.

This sainted Apostle loved them too much, not still to take an interest, from the heights of Heaven, in our own happiness. He will therefore not find it wrong that I have borrowed his words to congratulate you on the great change which the all-powerful hand of God has just brought about in this Kingdom, to acquaint you with the excellence of our new Constitution, to exhort you to observe it faithfully, and to behave in such a manner that those most interested in disparaging it will be obliged to respect and to love it; and finally, to urge you, if ever you are confronted by people scatterbrained and angry enough to attack it, to hold steady, to defend it like lions, and never to retreat.[11]

There is much that is fascinating about this sermon (including the fantastic history—based on an equally fantastic etymology—that has the Galatians be cousins of the Gauls), but for our purposes, two points stand out. One is the power of Paul's image of conversion from slavery to freedom in the particular political context of the French Revolution. For Sermet and his audience, the new France and its new constitution stood in relation to the old France and its laws much as the heavenly Jerusalem stood to the terrestrial, the Christian to the Jew. (Sermet went on to associate the ministers and courtiers of the pre-revolutionary royal government with Jewish Pharisees and hypocrites.) The second is the power that the danger of "Judaizing" retained in this revolutionary political theology. Precisely because the politics owes so much to the theology, the figures of the Jew and the Judaizer—in this case a few semi-converted "Jewish theologians"—were easily translated from their role as opponents of the Christian (or Muslim) dispensation, into representations of postrevolutionary enmity toward the new constitutional order.

But if we remember just how difficult a time Saint Paul and his early Christian readers—indeed the entire Christian tradition—had with establishing these distinctions, we will not be surprised to find that the revolutionaries also struggled. And if we recall the important place that figures of Judaism and of Judaizers occupied in Christian attempts to discover and defend differences between law, lawlessness, and freedom, we should expect that they will also play a role in the constitutional experiments of the revolutionaries.

Jean-Paul Rabaut de Saint-Étienne's "Project of National Education" provides a subtle example. In December of 1792 he promised the Legislative Assembly (the National Assembly's successor) that his project would achieve the "indefinite perfection" of mankind through a "revolution in heads and hearts." He did so in terms that evoked the covenant of Moses: "Oh cunning lawgivers, who speak to us in the name of heaven, should we not do in the name of truth and freedom, what you so often did in the name of error and slavery?"[12] The example is subtle, because although Rabaut is proclaiming the supersession of Moses's law of slavery, he is also simultaneously representing himself and his audience of legislators as Moses. There is an echo here of Rousseau's dictum in *The Social Contract* (book 2, chapter 7) that the beginnings of a constitution or law require a legislator who, like Moses or Muhammad, claims divine inspiration. According to Rousseau, individuals cannot agree en masse to cede control over their own lives to a collective will without the threat of divine force. Hence the legislator must found the law upon fear of the supernatural. Even Rabaut's "revolution in heads and hearts," the overturning of the old Mosaic covenant and its replacement with a new one, requires at least the figment of a Moses.

Rabaut and some of his fellow revolutionaries were willing to utilize the tools of Mosaic slavery to lead their countrymen gradually to freedom. The representation of the Declaration of the Rights of Man as Moses's tablets of the law (mentioned earlier) was itself an example of this willingness. So was the creation of countless political ceremonies and rituals, the act of passing and imposing an endless stream of new laws, and the ongoing project of drafting a new constitution. These

could all be considered intermediate actions, concessions to the imper-
fections of man, to the difficulty of changing long-established human
habit, and to the incompleteness of the revolution.

But there were other revolutionaries—more radical supersessionists,
we might call them—who attacked this incompleteness, and worked to
heighten the tension between the old legislation and the new freedom.
The convention's debates about the trial of Louis XVI that were taking
place at much the same time as Rabaut's speech produced a number of
expressions of this tension. In a speech against the king, Marie-Joseph
Chénier stressed both the revolutionary suspension of the old legal
order and the implementation of a different set of norms, drawn from
nature: "Listen to this natural morality, source of public morality, foundation of every social pact, model of the Declaration of Rights. This is
what, during revolutionary moments, fills the interregnum of laws . . .
consult this eternal law, this Constitution of all peoples." Nicolas-Marie
Quinette put it more bluntly in the same debates: "[D]uring political
revolutions, the only positive laws are those of nature."[13]

There is an entire history of ideas huddling in these words. Readers
interested in that history may turn to Dan Edelstein's fine book, *The
Terror of Natural Right*. To us these ideas are important because they
provide a glimpse of several potentially "Jewish" questions confronting
this and future revolutions. One of these has to do with the necessary
foundations for the revolutionary perfection of society, the other with
the necessary *radicality* of revolution and conversion.

The Terrors of Supersession: Enmity and Extermination

First, foundations: having set aside both scripture and custom as foundations for a free society, some revolutionaries pointed to the supremacy of reason. In 1793, for example, Nicolas de Condorcet (who would
die imprisoned by his revolutionary colleagues less than a year later)
proposed "[a] Constitution which, founded solely on the principles of
reason and justice, guarantees all citizens the full enjoyment of their
rights . . . in such a way that the necessity to obey laws, and to sub-

mit one's individual will to the general will, does not impede on the sovereignty of the people, the equality between citizens, and the exercise of natural liberty." The proposal sought to reconcile the freedom of the individual subject with society's need for positive law, but it did not generate enthusiasm. It was attacked by the Jacobin representative Louis Antoine de Saint-Just (who would die guillotined a few months after Condorcet) as too "intellectual," hyperrational. "The general will, purely speculative, would seem to be a mental production, and not to reflect the interests of society." Not reason but nature should serve as source of law, just as it had among "the ancient Franks, the ancient Germans."[14]

Saint-Just's fear that the sum of individual rationalities would not add up to the common good; his demotion of rationality, abstract, or speculative thought in favor of an organic sensibility and sympathy for one's society; and his invocation of the primitive nature of a people as the best basis for a polity are all ideas that would have important futures. Already opponents of the revolution were associating many of the qualities he criticized (hyperrationality, speculation, abstraction) with Judaism (see the section on Burke, later in this chapter). The association would only grow more useful in the century to come.

Equally portentous was this turn by revolutionaries like Saint-Just away from reason and toward nature as a foundation for a free society. In the future, that turn will underwrite some of the forms of romantic and folk nationalism that we will encounter in chapters 12 and 13. In the present, it permitted the revolutionaries to imagine their opponents as "enemies of humanity," outside the protection of natural law. *Hostis humani generis*: the concept had been applied to the devil and his agents by early Christian and medieval theologians, to bandits and pirates by Hugo Grotius and other natural-law theorists of the sixteenth and seventeenth centuries. For revolutionaries like Quinette and Chénier, it provided a way around the constitutional inviolability that protected King Louis XVI from prosecution. Tyrants were "enemies of humanity," and as such outside the protection of law. Louis could therefore be tried and executed without prejudice to the constitution.[15]

The trial of Louis XVI may have provided an initial impetus for the turn from reason to nature, but the move proved useful in addressing the second major difficulty as well: that of the required radicality of regeneration. Just how total a conversion did a revolution that claimed the death of the old law and the birth of the new need to effect? Paul had preached what sounded like a complete conversion—"But now we are fully freed from the law, dead to that in which we lay captive. We can thus serve in the new being of the Spirit and not the old one of the letter" (Rom. 7:6). But he had condemned readers eager to radicalize his teaching into an antinomian cult of lawlessness, and commanded his followers to respect the existing political structures of the world, at least for the short time that remained before Christ's Second Coming. This strand of Paul's teachings could support distinctly antirevolutionary arguments (as they had in Luther's condemnation of the Germans Peasants' War).

The revolutionaries faced the problem even more acutely, since they would not and could not point to the realization of their freedom in some other world, but had to achieve it in this one. Robespierre, whom we met in the National Assembly debates of 1789 countenancing no "Jewish" limits to the sovereignty of reason, was by 1793 using evangelizing terms to describe the necessary conversion: "Considering the depths to which the human race has been degraded by the vices of our former social system, I am convinced of the need to effect a complete regeneration, and, if I may so express it, to create a new people." But how best to effect that conversion? Rabaut and others like him counseled an intermediate stage of pedagogy guided by reason. But how long would conversion take? How long before revolutionary freedom and the promised perfection of the polity would be realized?

Robespierre and his faction shared the goal of converting the French with many of the revolutionary colleagues whom they would send to the guillotine in July 1793–July 1794: the period of their ascendance on the Committee of Public Safety known as "The Terror." Their model of conversion was, however, more total. "All must be new in France. We wish to date only from today," as Bertrand Barère put it in his (successful) arguments for the adoption of a revolutionary calendar beginning with the Year I. Or as the same author wrote in January of 1794, "We have revolutionized government, laws, usages, manners, customs, commerce, and even thoughts; let us therefore revolutionize the language which is their daily instrument."[16]

And yet, despite all these transformations, the revolution still faced resistance, even rebellion. The turn from reason toward nature provided one way of explaining and dealing with that resistance. If the opponents of the revolution were "outlaws" and "enemies of humanity," the task was not to rehabilitate or educate, but to exterminate them. And exterminate the Jacobins did. They burned and slaughtered their way through regions such as the Vendée, even accelerating the massacres after the rebellions had been defeated.[17]

But this brutal anxiety about the unconverted was not limited to royalists, rebels, and other avowed opponents of the revolution. The Terror was generated as much by fear of the incompletely converted within the revolutionary ranks, as of the unconverted outside them. As the view of revolution as conversion grew increasingly total and millennial, the accusation of false or incomplete conversion, of appearing on the outside to be a friend of the revolution while remaining an enemy within, became more powerful. "Let us not be fooled by the apparent conversion." This charge of pharisaic hypocrisy became a particularly cutting one during the Terror, deployed frequently by Robespierre's faction against the many rivals it sent to the guillotine.[18]

At its most general, the problem faced by the more radical revolutionaries was the same one confronting many of the advocates of a Christian politics of the spirit that we met in earlier chapters. Until the apocalypse, the "spirit" will always depend on the same "carnal" tools that produce the imperfection of the world: tools like law, symbol, ritual, ceremony, money, contract, and language. The more imminent a politics makes its claims to the world's perfection, and the more it stigmatizes these tools, the more dangerous the paradox of their persistent survival becomes for that politics, and the more pressing the drive to destroy them.

It was because Christian Europe had long addressed this general problem through the discourse of "Judaizing" that the medieval Christian pursuit of the millennium had so often expressed itself in the form of violence against Jews. The French revolutionaries faced a similar paradox. They fought to perfect the world through reason, and found that reason could not transcend the world of "habit" and "superstition." The more they claimed to be on the verge of such a transformation, the greater their violence toward those "vestiges" that so stubbornly resisted. During the Terror, for example, some 2,000 Catholic clerics were guillotined, and another 32,500 emigrated in fear, doubly stigmatized as irrational (because religious) and unnatural (because celibate). Unlike their medieval and early modern predecessors, the Jacobins did not focus their millennial pursuits on the Jews, despite all the prejudices they shared with the Enlightenment. Instead they aspired to the radical conversion not just of the Jews, but of all of society—an aspiration that seems in this case to have made their attempts at the perfection of the world less "anti-Jewish," but all the more bloody.[19]

It is worth repeating that Jews and Judaism were not the central concerns of the French Revolution. Nor does the work done by models of supersession and conversion in revolutionary thought fully explain the revolution's increasingly total attempts to transform the world and its itinerary toward Terror. I have stressed how the Christian supersession of Judaism was translated into Jacobin ideas about revolution, not because I take this translation to be of paramount importance to the history of the French Revolution, but because it is an excellent example of how ideas about Jews, Judaism, and Judaizing could underlay revolutionary thought.

Although the revolutionaries sometimes thought of themselves as revolting against Judaism, they rarely attacked real Jews, as participants in some later revolutions would. The architects of the Terror, for example, did not single out the Jews as conspicuously dangerous. The reasons for their restraint are not clear. Perhaps they were confident that they had effectively "regenerated" the Jews into citizens: "The republic does not know the meaning of the word Jew because this term no longer refers to a people but to a sect. The republic has no interest in sects and deports its votaries only when they disturb the social order." Or perhaps from the point of view of the revolutionaries, real Jews (as opposed to the revolutionaries' Judaized monarchist, Federalist, Girondist, and other enemies) were too few and too powerless to disturb much of anything. Strangely enough, it was outside of France that the French Revolution would provoke the most fantastic confusions between figures of Judaism and Jewish power.[20]

Counterrevolutionary Anti-Judaism

The French Revolution was by no means merely a French affair. From the moment of the Bastille's storming, all of Europe knew that it was witnessing a world-making moment of history. Tourists like the young poet William Wordsworth collected "relicks" of the ruined fortress as mementos of the passing of an age, just as members of my own generation did after the collapse of the Berlin Wall. And everywhere "pamphlets swarmed from the press," as the young journalistic culture that had contributed so much to the ferment of Enlightenment ideas (it is no accident that freedom of expression figured prominently among the "Rights of Man") now spread news of their explosion to every corner of Europe and its colonies. Each day, as the papers brought fresh tidings of battling speeches in the National Assembly or battling factions in the streets, thoughtful people throughout Europe thrilled with either horror or delight at the revolutionary promise that human reason could achieve universal rights, an end to poverty and inherited privilege, the brotherhood of all nations, and perpetual peace. And each day, as these events unfolded, writers and readers began to ask with new urgency a question that would be constantly repeated in the coming centuries. *Could the triumph of reason unleash even greater barbarism than what had come before?*

The Italian philosopher, jurist, and historian Giambattista Vico had posed an early version of the problem in his *New Science* of 1725, where he distinguished between the barbarism of sense (associated with the

beginnings of societies) and the barbarism of reflection (associated with
their ends). Vico predicted that the growing importance of the intellect
in the world would alienate man from nature and from his fellows, leading to the collapse of society. We have already seen the revolutionaries
themselves (Condorcet vs. Saint-Just) debating this problem, and the
question is so central to the history of modernity that we will return to it
in all of the following chapters. But once again, from our narrow point
of view here, what is remarkable is just how many of those thoughtful
voices asked this question with the help of the same vocabulary they had
earlier used to worry about the excessive power of faith and superstition: the vocabulary of Judaism and of Jews.[21]

One such voice, speaking in an Anglo-Irish accent, was that of
Edmund Burke (1730–1797). Burke was a member of Parliament well
known for both eloquence and zeal, and his *Reflections on the Revolution in France*, published in 1790, became an instant best-seller in
England. Over the course of a few decades, it came (perhaps unjustly)
to be seen in both England and on the Continent as a counterrevolutionary manifesto, and its author as the founder of English "conserva-
tism," a precursor to Count Joseph de Maistre and other reactionaries
of Europe's nineteenth century.[22]

Burke was indeed an increasingly strident critic of the French Revolution. Over time, as the revolution declared war first on its citizens (the
Terror), and then on England and the rest of Europe, his hysteria came
to seem prophetic. Within the English political context, however, he was
not a reactionary but a reformer, much of whose career was spent on
crusades against corrupt government in Britain and its colonies. Indeed
his *Reflections* was written at the request of French admirers who had
some reason to hope that he might lend his pen to their cause, as he
famously had to that of the American rebellion two decades earlier. He
was no friend of absolutist monarchy and might even have approved,
under the right circumstances and in the proper style, of regicide:

> *The punishment of real tyrants is a noble and awful act of justice; and
> it has with truth been said to be consolatory to the human mind. But*

if I were to punish a wicked king, I should regard the dignity in aveng-
ing the crime. Justice is grave and decorous, and in its punishments
rather seems to submit to necessity than to make a choice.

Nor was Burke an advocate, as de Maistre and so many others would be, of mixing politics and the sacred, or of restoring church or papacy to a supervisory role over secular sovereigns. On the contrary, he was so consistently opposed to theocracy that he accused the Jacobins of replacing the tyranny of one cult (Catholicism) with that of another (the cult of reason and of the nation). Burke was, in short, an experienced and well-connected writer working very hard to influence the politics of his time and place. His treatise is therefore an excellent example of the ways in which European thinkers made sense of what they all knew was the defining drama of their age.[23]

That sense is profoundly "Jewish." Perhaps the least significant aspect of this Jewishness is Burke's use throughout *Reflections* of the phrase "Old Jewry" to refer to the revolutionaries and their views. Scholars have always ignored this strange coinage (along with variants like "Old Jewry doctrine") as the inconsequential by-product of the fact that Burke's treatise was cast as a rebuttal of a pro-revolutionary sermon that had been given by the Reverend Richard Price at a Pres-byterian meetinghouse located on a street known to Londoners as "the Old Jewry."

A by-product it may be. Nevertheless, it cannot be denied that Burke makes the most of this happy topographical coincidence. Over and over and in varied ways he presents the preachers of revolution in "Jewish" terms. They are the dying Moses, gazing longingly at a prom-ised land he will never reach. They are, like the Pharisees, "hypocritical professors," destroying the world through their self-interested preach-ing of seemingly idealistic theories. They come from the class of "low lawyers," with "subtle litigious minds," of traders who have "never known anything beyond their counting house," of "dealers in stocks and funds." Herein, according to Burke, lies one of the chief differences between this rebellion and all previous ones. For whereas "other revolutions have been conducted" by men "of great civil, and great military talents," men whose nobility "sanctified their ambition," this one was led by "Jew brokers contending with each other who could best remedy with fraudulent circulation and depreciated paper the wretchedness and ruin brought on their country by their degenerate councils."

From this "Judaizing" of the revolutionaries, it is but a short step to associating them with the interests of "real Jews." When the National Assembly appropriated the lands of the Catholic Church property, it was (according to Burke) because the Jews wanted to buy them. Thankfully in England "[s]acrilege and proscription are not among the ways and means of our committee of supply. The Jews in Change Alley have not yet dared to hint their hopes of a mortgage on the revenues belonging to the see of Canterbury." Elsewhere Burke proposes to help the revolutionaries by sending English Jews to France, "to please your new Hebrew brethren." He goes so far as to predict that the one certain outcome of the revolution will be the triumph of "Judaism." "The next generation of the nobility will resemble the artificers and the clowns, and money-jobbers, usurers, and Jews, who will be always their fellows, sometimes their masters." Or as he puts it more abstractly a little later, "The age of chivalry is gone. That of sophisters, economists; and calculators has succeeded; and the glory of Europe is extinguished forever."[24]

In the words of J. G. A. Pocock, one of the *Reflections'* most eminent recent interpreters, Burke was "not far from that identification of Freemasons and Jews as the revolutionary underground which was to haunt the imagination of the Catholic Right for at least a century and a half." Pocock insists, however, that Burke never quite made that identification. "His references to Jews are usually contemptuous but not obsessive; he does not seem to mention Freemasons at all." Yet in comparison with French demographic, political, and economic reality, Burke's frequent references to Jewry and Judaism seem obsessive enough. Even one reference in a work like *Reflections* could be considered disproportionate, given the complete absence of Jews from the actual leadership, whether political, pecuniary, or philosophical, of the French Revolution.

What should we make of all these references to Jews? In his editorial note to Burke's "Jew Brokers," J. C. D. Clark writes that "[o]n the basis of such remarks, Burke is sometimes accused of antisemitism; yet his objections are evidently to financiers rather than to their race." It seems to me that such arguments are so busy exonerating Burke from the charge of "anti-Semitism" that they miss the point. It is the fact that Burke makes sense of the revolutionaries and their political, legal, and economic theories in Jewish terms that is significant here. And it is all the more significant precisely because neither the theories nor the financiers are "real" Jews, racial or otherwise. Is this a sign of "anti-Semitism"? I suppose that depends on how one wants to define this word. At the very least we can say that Burke displays a tendency (which we may or may not want to associate with anti-Semitism) to understand the dangers posed by the human dependence on symbolic economies as "Jewish." We need therefore to ask, Why did Burke understand—or at the very least, criticize—the revolution in such Jewish terms?[25]

The answer to this question has nothing to do with Judaism, and everything to do with the basic issues raised by the revolution, and the cognitive tools with which Burke and his contemporaries confronted them. We are already familiar with some of these issues from the debates over language, liturgy, law, and lucre that we followed in the previous chapters, and we have seen that they are all variants of a general theme: How should individuals relate to the world and one another in order to form the best-possible society? Burke was especially interested in the more constitutional variations on this theme: What type of covenant or contract best binds individuals together into a state? And what liberty do individuals have to renegotiate the social contracts in which they find themselves?

His answer to these questions was unequivocal. By breaking ancient oaths of loyalty to monarchy and nobility; by insisting that each individual enters into his own contract with society and sovereign unfettered by the obligations of his ancestors; by eliminating gold as a guarantor of monetary exchange and replacing it with paper currency; by confiscating for the state the vast landholdings accumulated by the church over a millennium of pious bequests: by all of these actions the revolutionaries had shown that they fundamentally misunderstood the nature of social contracts and political constitutions.

"Society is indeed a contract," wrote Burke, but it is not a contract like a "partnership agreement in a trade of pepper and coffee, calico, or tobacco . . . to be taken up for a little temporary interest, and to be dissolved by the fancy of the parties . . . because it is not a partnership in things subservient only to the gross animal existence of a temporary and perishable nature." The founding covenant of each state, each society, is "but a clause in the great primeval contract of eternal society, linking the lower with the higher natures, connecting the visible and invisible world, according to a fixed compact sanctioned by the inviolable oath which holds all physical and all moral natures, each in their appointed place."[26]

These words are full of familiar echoes. The tense distinction at their heart—between debasing forms of contract and relation and those leading to a higher good—is one we have already found among the ancients, encountered again in the church fathers, tracked to the bachelor Marcos and his Toledan rebels, and seen performed in Shakespeare's Venetian court. Of course it is important to insist that in each historical case the tension expressed different fears and produced different solutions. Burke's overriding fear that the revolutionaries, with their "stock-jobbing constitutions," their "metaphysics of an undergraduate, and . . . arithmetic of an exciseman," would "reduce men to loose counters, merely for the sake of simple telling, and not to figures whose power is to arise from their place in the table," is very much a product of his place in a particular political, cultural, social, and economic context.[27] So too are the solutions he advocated as the best safeguards for individual freedom against the danger posed by the base desires of the individual—an apolitical priesthood, a hereditary land-based aristocracy, a currency backed by precious metals, and a reverence (not necessarily extending to idolatry) for time-tested covenants and constitutions.

But it is also important to recognize the weathered and familiar features that Burke assigned to these newly pressing problems. He constantly aligned his opponents on the revolutionary side with figures long emblematic of misanthropic self-interest: merchants, lawyers, sophists, tax collectors, and above all, Jews. He did so, not because Jews were the real agents of the French Revolution, nor because he was "antisemitic," but because the revolution forced him and his contemporaries to confront basic questions about the ways in which humans relate to one another in society. These were questions that two millennia of pedagogy had taught Europe to ask in terms of "Judaism," and Burke had learnt the lesson well.

So had his opponents. In Prussia, for example, the aspiring professor Johann Gottlieb Fichte began his *Contribution to the Rectification of the Public's Judgment of the French Revolution*, published anonymously in 1793, with exactly the same question as Burke: "Does a people have any right to arbitrarily alter its constitution or basic political contract?" Fichte was pro-revolutionary, so from the same starting point he arrived at very different answers. Where Burke condemned philosophizing and appealed to historical experience and long tradition, Fichte praised philosophical inquiry as the only path toward truth and freedom, and mocked those who placed their "necks under the yoke" of history's authority. Those who preach reverence for history, he claimed (echoing Kant), only wanted to reduce their audiences to unreasoning habit and "animality" (*Tierheit*), the better to enslave or slaughter them. Moreover it was not the revolutionaries who thought like peddlers and shopkeepers, but rather those (like Burke) who treated constitutions like binding contracts, thinking of them (says Fichte) as price negotiations between merchants (*Handelsleute*). Such logic turns a constitution (*Staatsverfassung*) into a "dead book" made up of "hard inflexible letters" and standing in "the starkest contradiction to the spirit of mankind." As for the aristocracy, far from being a bastion of liberty against the tyranny of the petty self-interest of lesser men (as Burke had it), it constitutes a dangerous state-within-a-state, just like (says Fichte) the military, and even worse, just like the Jews.[28]

The pages Fichte composed to make this last point begin with words that rank today among his most infamous: "Through almost all the lands of Europe there spreads a powerful nation predisposed to hostility, which stands in a state of perpetual war with all the other nations and, in some, presses fearfully hard upon the citizenry: it is Jewry (*Judenthum*)." Even the footnote drips with venom, for in it he proposes to cure the danger by cutting off the heads of all the Jews and replacing them with non-Jewish ones, or by conquering "their promised land for them and sending them all there." The potency of the poison may owe something to the growing presence of real Jews in Fichte's native Prussia. But that real presence has nothing to do with the animating role that "Judaism" plays throughout Fichte's treatise. It is not his particular context or peculiar personality that leads Fichte to (for example) characterize his antirevolutionary opponents (such as Burke!) as hypocritical priests of Moses, but rather the common culture he shares with those opponents.[29]

Both Burke and Fichte feel that this common culture is undergoing dramatic change. Like many Europeans, they understand themselves to be in the midst of an earthquake, standing on the trembling threshold of a new century with large chunks of the old regime crashing down around their ears. They are sharply divided about how to answer the many questions this earthquake raises about the soundness of human society's foundations. But about certain key distinctions they are entirely in agreement. The distinctions between human and animal, freedom and slavery, universal and particular, subject and object, love and self-interest: none of these were destroyed by the successes and failures of the French Revolution, nor were the maxims that distilled them. "A good maxim," as Nietzsche would later put it, "is too hard for the teeth of time, and all the millennia cannot succeed in consuming it, though it always serves as nourishment."[30] "Judaism" is one such maxim. In its many variants, both old and new, it continued to provide food for postrevolutionary thought.

Whither Shall We Follow Our Wandering Jew?

The revolutionaries had believed that the rule of reason would perfect the world. "All follies fall before reason," as Robespierre put it in his memorandum on the cult of the "Supreme Being."[31] Within France, the hiss of the Parisian guillotines soon made it clear that heads could fall as well as follies. Outside it, France's increasingly bellicose turn demonstrated that perfection need not be philanthropic. The irenic proclamations of the republic's first years, in which the National Assembly renounced all military aggression and promised the world perpetual peace, gave way by 1793 to declarations of war against Austria, Prussia, England, Spain, and the Netherlands. By 1796 France had transformed itself into a massive military engine (musket production, for example, increased exponentially from 1789), and Napoleon Bonaparte had risen to the rank of general. By 1804 his colossal citizen-armies were marching the revolutionary constitution into distant corners of the European continent, and their commander onto an imperial throne. To some, most notably Napoleon himself, it might have seemed that the messianic dream of one world empire was finally at hand. That dream died on the fields of Waterloo in the summer of 1815, but not before more than a million French soldiers (to say nothing of the millions of their opponents or of noncombatants) had lost their lives in its pursuit.[32]

Clearly these two decades did not perfect the world, but just as clearly they changed it. The years of "total war" waged between France and its neighbors mobilized Europe's masses as workers, soldiers, and political actors on an unprecedented scale, transforming their expectations of the polities in which they lived, and transforming as well the economic and political structures of those polities. The nineteenth-century states that emerged from this pan-European struggle had very different expectations of their inhabitants than the eighteenth-century ones that entered it, and the same is true in reverse.[33]

Modern is the word we still use (albeit with increasing cavil and trepidation) to describe the world shaped by this flood of changes. It is a world in which new answers became conceivable for old questions—questions about the relationship of individuals to their property, to each other, to their state, their environment, and their God—and some old answers became inconceivable. It is also a better-documented world than those that came before, and therefore confronts us even more sharply than previous periods with the challenge of selection. How can we bring this ocean of lives and words within a slim chapter's compass and still claim to have explored it?[34]

One strategy might be to pick a theme that seems prominent—debates over the nature of the social contract, for example, or the continuing conflict between reason and revelation in the politics of Christian Europe—and hope that it carries us to hospitable shores. A different strategy might be to focus on a few particularly omnivorous and influential individuals whose unitary sense of the complex world gave impetus to new movements and schools of thought. Even here there are still many possibilities to choose from, some more attractive than others. Earlier we met William Wordsworth, collecting "relicks" from the Bastille. He was nineteen when the fortress was stormed, and had rushed to France from his native Britain to take part in the making of a new world order. A few short but eventful years later he abandoned the young republic—and the even younger family he had begun there—not just because he was out of money but also, as he described it years later in his poem "The Prelude," because his optimism had deflated.

Would it not be delightful to overleap the gates of time and Racedown Farm in 1797, to join William and his sister Dorothy on their summer walks with Samuel Taylor Coleridge through Dorset fields? We could share in their disappointment with the French Revolution, listen to their discoursing on man's increasing alienation from language, from nature, from the world and its "One Truth," and preview their earliest plans for a new poetry capable of overcoming that alienation: the poetic movement we today call English Romanticism. We could watch each of them at their respective desks, struggling to produce their first collaborative example, full of figures of Judaism, a ballad called "The Wandering of Cain." We could hear how, after the failure of that first project, "thou" (as Wordsworth put it years later writing of Coleridge) "[d]idst speak the vision of that / Ancient Man, / The bright-eyed mariner": yet another figure of Judaism. And given the subject of this book, we would certainly ask them why, as they set out to chart the reaches of the new poetic sensibility to nature and self that they claimed to be discovering, they so often chose as the subject on which to anchor their imagination the "ribbed sea sands" of the wandering Jew.

What answer would Coleridge and Wordsworth have given to such a question? How conscious were they of the work they were asking Judaism to do at the foundations of their poetics? I do not pretend to know how they would have responded to such an inquiry, but I suspect their reply would not have been in the language of poetry. They would themselves have turned to that of a different discipline, one that claimed to have a more specialized interest in questions about the state of the world, and more systematic answers to them. So instead of following our poets into the forests of the Quantock Hills or the fells of the Lake District, in our next chapter we will turn toward the starker landscape of philosophy, and particularly to the new philosophy emanating from Germany, which inspired not only our poets—Coleridge, for example, translated large chunks of Fichte—but so many other participants in the cultural, political, and economic history of the nineteenth and twentieth centuries.[35]

Chapter 12

PHILOSOPHICAL STRUGGLES WITH JUDAISM, FROM KANT TO HEINE

*With [Kant's Critique of Pure Reason] . . . there
began a mental and spiritual revolution in Germany,
one which bears the most peculiar analogies with
the material revolution in France, and which must
appear to deeper thinkers to be just as important. It
developed in the same stages, and between the two
the most remarkable parallelism rules.*

—HEINRICH HEINE, *ON THE HISTORY OF RELIGION
AND PHILOSOPHY IN GERMANY*, 1834

IT DID NOT take long for German philosophy to become disappointed with the French Revolution, though not with the idea of revolution itself. Fichte, for example, living in Berlin under Napoleonic occupation, lost all his sympathy for the Gauls and their Enlightenment. The events of the last decade—especially Napoleon's victories over Prussia and his coronation as emperor—confirmed Fichte's conviction that the world was standing on the threshold of a new age, but they also transformed his sense of what that new age would look like and who its heroes would be. In works like *Characteristics of the Present Age* (1804–1805), he began to reconsider the history of the human spirit's progress, from its origins to eternity. He arrived at a scheme—in some ways novel but in others quite traditional—in which an original state of human innocence was all too quickly succeeded by a long ice age of blind faith and obedience, which ran from the beginning of recorded history until the Enlightenment. The third and present age was one of "completed sinfulness," in which men's souls are entirely ruled by materialism and self-interest: a tyranny incarnate in Napoleon. But the light of liberation kindles in the deepest dark. A new people being born will make the coming age the real age of reason, in which man's rational faculties will be lovingly oriented toward true knowledge rather than selfishly toward utility and gain.

Fichte's "Science of Hating Judaism"

Of course before this struggle for the world's soul can be won and a new age can dawn, its partisans have to be rallied, its enemies identified and overcome. This role of philosopher-prophet Fichte assumed for himself. King Frederick William III ignored his request to be appointed field-preacher to Prussia's defeated armies. So instead Fichte lectured at noon on successive wintry Sundays in 1807/8, to the largely empty amphitheatre of the Berlin Academy. The resulting *Addresses to the German Nation* is a fascinating fusion of many of the ideas we have touched on in previous chapters.[1] Like so many earlier ideologies, these lectures interpret the history of the world as a long-running war between love and self-interest. Only if the first is victorious can man reach true knowledge rather than ignorance, ideal reality rather than the mere "shadow and phantom" of the material world of appearances (39). Now, with Napoleon's ascendance, the critical moment in this world war has come, and the entire future of humanity is at stake.

Fichte took great care to describe the battlefield. On one side are arrayed the slaves of a cold and calculating universal reason, concerned only with practical power over transient things in the world. These creatures can scarcely be considered human: they do not even have true language, for they speak in "dead" tongues—Fichte is here taking aim at French and other languages descended from ancient Latin—and have already forgotten the true meaning of their own words. They can exchange practical, even rhetorically elegant utterances, but they can never achieve authentic communication, never know or feel what they really mean (53–55).

Opposed to these are the members of a new society, one that speaks a pure and unalienated language (German), and that is on its way to becoming a "totality of men continuing to live in society with each other and continually creating themselves naturally and spiritually out of themselves." This totality will achieve a synthesis every bit as miraculous as that of Jesus Christ, a synthesis of the worlds of appearance and of the eternal, so that "in the phenomenal world neither can be separated again from the other." The result of this synthesis will be a "people" who love each other with a "love that is truly love." Man's "love for his people" will in turn make him eternal, not only in his invisible or heavenly life but also in his visible and terrestrial one. In his "fatherland" man experiences "eternity visible and made sensuous," a "precious possession" that he can pass "unimpaired to his posterity" in his last drop of blood.

Fichte did not claim that Germans were the only ones with a capacity for this patriotic love, but he did draw a sharp contrast between Germans, with their authentic language, simplicity, and Greek love of beauty, and other peoples—he meant above all the French—of a "deadly foreign spirit" who believe "only in an eternal recurrence of apparent life." Like the Jews, these last "are in the higher sense not a people at all. As they in fact, properly speaking, do not exist, they are just as little capable of having a national character" (115–117). We should step back a moment to admire Fichte's achievement here: remaining entirely within Saint Paul's vocabulary of a Christian synthesis of love, he has turned Galatians' formula of "neither Jew nor Greek" on its head. It is now the "particularist" love of the Germans for their soil, tribe, and nation that is associated with love for the divine and eternal, whereas the French advocates of Enlightenment "universalism" are aligned with loveless nonexistence and become, as the Prussian poet Ernst Moritz Arndt put it a few years later, "an empty, hollow, doll-like, formless, contentless Nothing," "a Jew People."[2]

There were plenty of preachers willing to translate the political, economic, and military conflicts of these decades into spiritual terms—in 1806, for example, the Holy Synod of the Russian Orthodox Church convicted Napoleon of conspiring with the Jews against the Christian faith, and condemned him as a false Messiah—and plenty of poets singing songs to new nations. Fichte's addresses are exemplary for our purposes not only because of their explicit nationalism or their implicit anti-Judaism, although each of these left weighty legacies, but because of the new philosophy through which they arrived at and justified both. The danger was well noted by Saul Ascher, a young Jewish bookseller and avid reader of philosophy living in Berlin. In 1794 he published a remarkable book entitled *Eisenmenger the Second*, in which he celebrated Kant's discovery of "critical" philosophy but condemned Kant's followers, especially Fichte, for misusing that philosophy to develop an "entirely new species" of Jew-hatred. Comparing Fichte to Eisenmenger (whose encyclopedia of anti-Jewish lore, *Judaism Revealed*, published in 1700, we encountered in chapter 11), Ascher suggested that thinkers like Fichte used the new philosophy to cloak Jew-hatred as "critical reason" rather than as religion, and thereby achieved a tremendous advance in "the science of hating Judaism and its followers."[3]

Ascher's indictment points toward an extraordinary half century of German thought, stretching from the first appearance of Kant's *Critique of Pure Reason* (1781, 1787)—with its modest claim that before its appearance there had been no reliable basis for metaphysics, to Hegel's lectures on the philosophy of history (1822), which announced with equal humility that "philosophy has now come to its end." During this intensely competitive period, new schools of philosophy rose to and fell from the "cutting edge" with a rapidity that provoked dizziness in even the most self-confident of contestants. Though each of these schools thought of itself as superseding its predecessors—that is, as being the first to offer humanity a true "system of human freedom," as Fichte put it in his modestly titled "First Introduction to the Theory of Knowledge"—they also had much in common. All shared a commitment, inherited from both Enlightenment and revolution, to the emancipation of the human mind: "Reason and freedom remain our principles," as a young Hegel wrote to an even younger Schelling in 1793. More important, they shared a very distinctive sense of what this "reason" and "freedom" should look like. It is because of this distinctive sense that we call the whole movement German Idealism, and it is on this sense that we need to focus in order to understand how Idealism contributed to Ascher's "science of hating Judaism."[4]

Kant's Revolution: Freedom, Law, and Human Thought

That distinctive sense of freedom and reason begins with Kant. Like many philosophers and scientists of his time (and ours), Kant understood the material world, the world of "things," to be governed by the laws of nature. Some of these philosophers and scientists thought of this subjection of the world to natural laws as an opportunity rather than a problem. In his *Discourse on the Method* (1637), for example, René Descartes had celebrated a practical philosophy by means of which "we could know the power and action of fire, water, air, the stars, the heavens and all the other bodies in our environment . . . and we could use this knowledge—as the artisans use theirs—for all the purposes for which it is appropriate, and thus make ourselves, as it were, the lords and masters of nature." Closer to Kant's day, a number of British philosophers like Locke and Hume, whom we call "empiricists," proposed that human reason was itself produced by our experience of this material world and its laws. Humans create thoughts and concepts out of their experience of this natural reality in order to make sense of it, but these thoughts and concepts are "the inventions and creatures of the understanding, made by it for its own use, and concern only signs."[5] In other words things, not ideas, are the primary reality.

Kant revolted against this empiricism. If human reason were produced by the world of objects, he conjectured, then it must also be subject to the laws of nature. But if human reason is subject to the laws
of nature, then it is—like an object or an animal (or a Jew)—a slave
to necessity. Man becomes a mere creature, eking out existence within
a deterministic universe. Human liberty, according to Kant, requires
freedom from necessity, and this freedom is possible only if reason
transcends the world of "things" and the laws that govern them. In his
Critique of Pure Reason, Kant proclaimed the discovery of a philosophy
of mind—a theory of how we know what we think we know and what
relationship this knowledge has to what really "is"—that freed reason
from this bondage to the material world.

Our determinate knowledge of an empirical "thing," he argued, is
not the product of the unmediated experience of that thing, but rather
is itself produced by what he considered to be pure forms of understanding—sensible intuition, space, and time—which he called "the
categories." We can only know objects of experience as subject to such
forms. In other words, according to Kant, we have no knowledge of
things in themselves, considered independent of our forms of intuition
and knowledge.[6]

From the philosophical perspective I have been describing, the
advantage of Kant's theory is that it makes man the creator, rather than
the creature, of the laws of nature. The empirical world is now the product of human reason, rather than the other way around. Released from
slavery to the laws of nature by the "critique of pure reason," humanity can now produce a true metaphysics of freedom. But this freedom
comes at a price: it radically circumscribes what we can know about
the world. At best, according to Kant, empirical knowledge can tell us
only about phenomena, about the "appearance" of things, not about
noumena, or what Kant called "things-as-they-exist-in-themselves."
The "thing-in-itself" always remains "an unknown something." Any
philosophy that fails to recognize this (and here Kant would include
all previous philosophy, since he was by his own reckoning the first to

discover this truth) is—like the Pharisees—confusing the "appearance" of a thing for its reality.[7]

Following on the success of his *Critique of Pure Reason*, Kant further developed his philosophy of mind, striving to demonstrate that even "practical reason" should not be understood as dependent on empirical conditions. He did the same in his moral philosophy—his ideas about how people ought to behave in relation to one another, and what it is that constrains them to behave in this way. Morality must be "carefully cleansed of anything empirical." If morality is to be compatible with freedom, then it must be entirely the product of reason, not of external necessity or fear of punishment. Morality must be separate from law, and ethics separate from submission. In effect, Kant is trying to translate Saint Paul's distinctions (between inner and outer circumcision, between hearers and doers of the law) into the secular language of rational philosophy. Man cannot become ethical through obedience to the law, he insists. But Kant was no anarchist or antinomian: he was equally certain that humans must act ethically toward each other, and observe the laws they have established in their societies. What compels them, however, is not some law external to them but the internal rules produced by their own human reason (recall Condorcet's very different attempt, during the French Revolution, to deal with a similar problem), which he called the "categorical imperative." Kant thought he had developed an argument to show something like the *practical necessity* of our subjection to the categorical imperative: from the first-person point of view, we must act as if subject to a universal moral law posited by reason itself. He called this argument for such a practical necessity "the fact of reason."[8]

Kant compared his exposition of these transcendental principles to Copernicus's discovery that the heavens do not revolve around the earth. He was proposing a fundamental realignment of the relationship between the human mind and the world, and hence also between one human subject and another. Before we can ask any empirical or philosophical question—any question about the world, about knowledge, about the good—Kant insisted that we must first ask how it is that the human mind "knows" anything at all. Once we ask that most basic question, we discover that the possibility of objective knowledge depends on the human subject's active establishment of its relation to the world. In that active engagement lies the possibility of human freedom. We must therefore become radically reflexive, completely critical of the conditions of cognition. *Sapere aude!* "Dare to know!" Only thus can we arrive at a rational and self-authorizing philosophy. Such a philosophy can simultaneously free us from enslavement to dogma (whether religious or philosophical) and to nature's laws, and generate the common norms necessary to keep relativism and antinomian anarchy at bay. A Copernican revolution indeed!

Idealism's "Christian Problem": The Persistence of the Law

Yet for all their novelty and their revolutionary potential, Kant's theories about how human reason related to the material world depended on the same basic hierarchical distinctions—"between spirit and matter, soul and body, faith and intellect, freedom and necessity"—that we encountered in our previous chapters on Christianity.[9] The theologians we met in those earlier chapters had discovered the difficulty, in this world, of fully overcoming law, letter, and other categories stigmatized as "Judaizing" within their Incarnational dialectic. They had tried to contain those difficulties by pouring concepts associated with law and the material world into Jewish vessels. Similarly Kant and the many Idealists who were influenced by him would quickly discover the impossibility of entirely replacing the law with love. They made sense of that failure through familiar figures of Judaism, so much so that their own debates sometimes recapitulate the Christian deployment of those figures.[10]

Kant himself did not hesitate, in *Religion within the Bounds of Reason Alone*, to portray Jesus as a Kantian, a rebel against Jewish materialism, a revolutionary who "opened the doors of freedom to all who, like him, choose to die to everything that holds them fettered to earthly life to the detriment of morality." In chapter 11 I called Kant a "Manichaean" on the narrow grounds of this treatise and its treatment of Judaism as a nonreligious system of mere earthly life. Now we can see that his dualism was in fact more systematic, indeed central to his philosophy, with its divorce of human reason from the world of "things-in-themselves," and of morality from law.[11]

Given the tendency of earlier dualisms to cast their criticism of the material world and its laws into anti-Jewish terms, we might expect Kant's "critical reason" to have the same potential, and in this we are not disappointed. Kant often used Judaism to represent a state of pure submission to the demands of the material world, and measured humanity's progress toward truth in terms of its distance from that state. The Christian world had not, in Kant's opinion, gotten very far, and his philosophy was designed to take it one giant step further away from the Judaism and materialism that still haunted it. Like Martin Luther, his great predecessor in this task, Kant was confident that once the cognitive revolution was accomplished, the Jews—or at least the more reasonable among them—would convert and disappear. If the most "enlightened" Jews of his day, like the philosopher Moses Mendelssohn, still refused the call to convert, it was only because the philosophical revolution was still not complete. "Christians," he imagines Mendelssohn saying, in words borrowed from Luther, "first take the Judaism away from your own faith, and then we will abandon ours."[12]

The analogy between Kant's dualism and that of the Manichaeans is not rigorous, but it is useful because it helps us to notice how "critical reason" recapitulated some basic Christian debates about the relationship between the human spirit and the material world, debates in which "Jews" and "Judaism" had played important roles. The point sharpens if we press the analogy. The protagonists on both sides of the early Christian struggles between dualists and anti-dualists had fought to cast their rivals out of Christianity and into "Judaism." Likewise in their struggle to perfect the new philosophy, the giants of German Idealism tried to wrestle their opponents out of the circle of critical reason and into "lower" categories of knowledge that they characterized as materialist, dogmatic, and "Jewish." Fichte's two introductions in *The Sci-*

ence of Knowledge (1794, 1797) provide a capital example, although they never mention Judaism. They divide all of philosophy into two types: those whose starting point is the "thing-in-itself," which Fichte (like Kant) called "dogmatism," and those that begin with the human subject, which he called "Idealism." Idealism leads to freedom. Everything else yields only determinism, fatalism, and slavery.

Like Marcion and other early Christian dualists, Kant and Fichte sought to overcome and "Judaize" the empiricists' emphasis on the material world by positing a sharp divide between the spirit of human reason and the world of things. But their overcoming of the law foundered precisely on the sharpness of that divide, and they in turn became vulnerable to charges of "borrowing poison from the Jew" very much like those that Tertullian and other early Christian defenders of the Old Testament and the Incarnation had used against Marcionites and other dualists. It was this sectarian dynamic within the critical discourse of German Idealism that amplified the language of anti-Judaism into what Saul Ascher called the new "science of hating Judaism."[13]

With appropriate equipment we could graph the increase in decibels across many debates of the day. An obvious and early symptom, detectable even to the naked ear, is the explosive return of Spinoza and Spinozism to the philosophical stage almost immediately after Kant's publication of the *Critique of Pure Reason*. Spinoza's "Judaism," you will recall from chapter 10, had been eagerly deployed by those who wanted to condemn radical critiques of revealed religion. Now Spinoza was resuscitated to serve once again as the bogeyman in debates over the proper limits of reason. In 1783 F. H. Jacobi (1743–1819) initiated an epistolary debate with Moses Mendelssohn, which he published under the title *On the Doctrine of Spinoza, in Letters to Herr Moses Mendelssohn* (1785, second edition 1789). The work became an immediate *cause célèbre*, propelling both Jacobi and Spinoza to the center of philosophical attention. The work's celebrity stemmed in part from the hard questions that Jacobi posed about the position of the "thing-in-itself" in Kant's system, a position that Jacobi claimed put the world of objects at an infinite regress from human cognition. But if the *Letters* on Spinozism "touched everyone in their deepest convictions," as Goethe later put it, it was because of the way in which Jacobi indicted the entire project of "critical reason" itself. Kant's systematic philosophy, he argued, was a fanatic "Jewish" formalism, a rule-bound game of logic whose end result was to reduce humans to the mechanistic products of external causes. All "consistent philosophy," in Jacobi's words, "is Spinozist, hence pantheist, fatalist and atheist."[14]

Jacobi's philosophical polemic with Mendelssohn was an early salvo in the debates sparked by Kant's "critical reason." Its precocity demonstrates just how quickly concepts associated in Christian theology with Judaism—concepts like materialism, dogmatism, Spinozism—became keywords in those debates.[15] We could trace the echoes of Jacobi's accusations among the many philosophers—like Fichte, anointed the false "Messias of speculative Reason" by Jacobi in 1799, or Schelling, labeled by him a "Spinozist"—who attempted, in the decades around 1800, to close the problematic gap in Kant's system between man and nature, "reason" and "thing-in-itself."

These echoes would make clearer how Kant became, in the words of the great philosophical poet Friedrich Hölderlin (1770–1843), the "Moses of our nation": a philosopher-prophet leading human thought to freedom, according to his advocates, or into slavery and Judaism, according to his critics (like Hölderlin). But rather than multiply examples of philosophers pointing to the "Jewish" errors of those systems they sought to discredit, I will leap to the conclusion of our analogy in the personage whose attempts to reconcile all the apparent antinomies of the cosmos made him the most influential philosopher of the age. I mean, of course, Hölderlin's friend and fellow seminarian, Georg Wilhelm Friedrich Hegel (1770–1831).[16]

Hegel's Overcoming of the "Jewish Principle"

Hegel was, like Saint Augustine, a convert from "dualism" to synthesis. In youth an ardent Kantian, by his early thirties he was convinced that Kant's "ideal does not come to terms with reality . . . the real remains absolutely opposed." This opposition, he claimed, was simply a new version of "the Jewish principle of opposing thought to reality, reason to sense; this principle involves the rending of life and a lifeless connection between God and the world." This "Jewish" opposition of thought to reality could lead neither to religion nor to philosophy, for the one task of every living religion and true philosophy was to "[strip] off the forms of dualism from its extremes, rendering the opposition in the element of Universality fluid, and bringing it to reconciliation." Christ had once shown humanity how to achieve this reconciliation through his crucifixion. Now it was Hegel's calling to do so through his philosophy.[17]

If today some scholars do not hesitate to describe Kant as a "Judeo-Prussian," or to speak of "the system of Jewish—and Kantian—ethics" in the same breath, it is largely because of the sharp pages that Hegel tilted against his elderly predecessor on that quest. Among those pages, perhaps the most striking are those of the first essay in which Hegel announced the full extent of his defiance: *The Spirit of Christianity and Its Fate*, written in 1799 but not published until the beginning of the twentieth century.[18] This inspired essay takes the form of a re-narration of the entire history of revelation, beginning with the great flood of Genesis. Already in the different responses of Noah and of Nimrod to that first catastrophic confrontation between God, man, and nature, Hegel sees clearly two opposed paths opening before humanity in its struggle with the natural world. Nimrod and the empiricists strove to master the world with the material strength of his body. Noah, like the Kantians, allied himself to some vast and abstract power—God, Thought, Reason—and opposed it to the world (184).

Of course the essay will conclude with Jesus—and Hegel—teaching the overcoming of this opposition. But first Hegel must demonstrate the errors of the religion and philosophy that came before, that is to say, the errors of those who take the path of Noah. (He leaves Nimrod's road aside because, like a good Idealist, he does not believe that it can lead to anything that could properly be called philosophy.) This is the task he undertakes in the first section of his essay, a section entitled—predictably to our now-tired eyes—"The Spirit of Judaism."

That spirit begins with the patriarch Abraham, who abandoned family and fatherland to wander alone, "a wholly self-subsistent, independent man, to be an overlord of himself." Independence of this sort is not a positive value for Hegel, because it destroys community. "The entirety of the relationships in which he had hitherto lived with men and nature, these beautiful relationships of his youth, he spurned." It is one thing to make such a rupture because of insult, want, or unrequited love, as Achilles, Meleager, or some other Homeric hero might—whenever Hegel says "beautiful" he means Greek—before returning once more into society. But Abraham made himself "a stranger on earth, a stranger to soil and men alike," in order to worship a distant divinity, a "perfect Object on High," an "Ideal."

> *The whole world Abraham regarded as simply his opposite. If he did not take it to be a nullity, he looked on it as sustained by the God who was alien to it. Nothing in nature was supposed to have any part in God; everything was simply under God's mastery. . . . Moreover it was through God alone that Abraham came into a mediate relation with the world, the only kind of link with the world possible for him. His Ideal subjugated the world to him, gave him as much as he needed, and put him in security against the rest. Love alone was beyond his power. (187)*

Abraham's rejection of the world in favor of a sublime God makes him the "progenitor of a nation," but not of a happy or beautiful one. All of that nation's future miseries are contained in its foundation: "The subsequent circumstances of the Jewish people up to the mean, abject, wretched circumstances in which they still are today, have all of them been simply consequences and elaborations of their original fate." His rupture with creation alienated the Jews forever from the beauty of nature, and made them incapable of any loving relation with the world around them. But the distant perfection of his ideal estranged them as well from the love of God, making their relationship to divinity one of slavery. "In this thoroughgoing passivity there remained to the Jews, beyond the testification of their servitude, nothing save the sheer empty need of maintaining their physical existence and securing it against want."[19]

Judging from the many erasures, insertions, and corrections in the manuscript, Hegel worked hard to expand the stock of metaphors with which to represent this peculiar state of the Jews. Some of the ones he came up with are indeed startling. In one, for example, he adapts the Hebrew Bible's description of Moses's education of Israel—"As the eagle enticing her young to fly, and hovering over them, he spread his wings, and hath taken him and carried him on his shoulders" (Deut. 32:11)–into a very different image: "In relation to their God [the Jews] rather afford the image of an eagle which by mistake warmed stones, . . . and took them on its wings into the clouds, but never raised their weight into flight or fanned their borrowed warmth into the flame of life" (199). Another simile draws less inspiration from Augustine and more from Shakespeare, made newly fashionable as an example of genius in Germany by Schiller and Goethe: "The fate of the Jewish people is the fate of Macbeth who stepped out of nature itself, clung to alien Beings, and so in their service had to trample and slay everything holy in human nature, had at last to be forsaken by his gods (since these were objects and he their slave) and be dashed to pieces on his faith itself" (205).

Defenders of Hegel—like Walter Kaufmann, whose flight from Hitler in 1939 proved so fortunate for the popularity of German philosophy in the United States—rush to dismiss "the ridiculous anti-Semitism of these pages" as an unpublished youthful indiscretion that anyhow "played no part in the vast Nazi literature about the Jews." But our goal is not the absolution (or the condemnation!) of Hegel as a precursor of the Nazis. We are interested only in understanding the work done by "Judaism" in his thought, and this requires taking seriously the hard philosophical labor he assigned to the Jews in *The Spirit of Christianity and Its Fate*.[20]

Perhaps the typological wrappings of the essay have insulated modern readers from the coldness of its philosophical steel, for they seldom note that Hegel has just made Abraham the founder of Kantian idealism, and derived the entire grim fate of the Jews from that philosophical error. What critique could be more crushing? Far more ruthlessly than Jacobi had, Hegel's section 1 pushes Kant into the alienated "Spirit of Judaism." Then in section 2—"The Sermon on the Mount Contrasted with the Mosaic Law and with Kant's Ethics"—he leaves him standing among the Pharisees, stubbornly refusing to hear the message of Jesus. Like a Jew who can think only in terms of law, Kant misunderstands Jesus's teaching to "love God above everything and your neighbor as yourself" as a "command requiring respect for a law which commands love," the equivalent of his "moral imperative" (213). The resulting morality, says Hegel, is merely a "fulfillment of duty," the same as the Pharisees' "hypocrisy" (220).[21]

Jesus's message was entirely different. He was not issuing some new set of commands, perhaps more Kantian than the old, but nevertheless continuing to set the domains of love and of law against each other and thereby perpetuating slavery. He wanted instead to "strip the laws of legality" (212), to achieve freedom through a synthesis of love and law, subject and object, universal and particular. Hegel adopts Jesus's phrase the "fulfillment" of the law to describe this synthesis. Sections 3 and 4 of his essay ("The Moral Teachings of Jesus: Love as the Transcendence of Penal Justice and the Reconciliation of Fate," and "The Religious Teachings of Jesus") are devoted to expounding Jesus's instructions— drawn largely from the Gospel of John—for how to achieve it.[22]

Finally section 5 ("The Fate of Jesus and His Church") outlines why these teachings have never before been correctly understood or completely implemented. His explanation here sounds much like that of Kant or Spinoza, in its focus on the limitations imposed by Jesus's Jewish audience. Jesus addressed a people whose "loveless nature" had entirely alienated all "love, spirit, and life" (240–241, citing John 2:25). To reach "the impure attention" of even the most receptive among them— namely, the apostles—Jesus had to adulterate his message and speak to them in terms and oppositions that they could understand (282).

The poverty of Jewish culture affects even John. Hegel cites John constantly as the most spiritual of the evangelists. Nevertheless, "[h]owever sublime the idea of God may be made here, there yet always remains the Jewish principle of opposing thought to reality, reason to sense; this principle involves the rending of life and a lifeless connection between God and the World" (259). Hence "in all forms of the Christian religion which have been developed in the advancing fate of the ages, there lies this fundamental characteristic of opposition." In other words, all the progress of Christianity—from the "servitude" of Catholicism to the various relationships between God and the world envisioned in different Protestant sects—has not yet sufficed to overcome the Judaism at work within it, so that until now (Hegel concludes the essay) "church and state, worship and life, piety and virtue, spiritual and worldly action, can never dissolve into one" (301).[23]

We cannot dismiss these pages as "ridiculous anti-Semitism" without missing both what is banal and what is remarkable in their uses of Judaism. Banal, or at least well worn, is their deployment of a derogatory vocabulary of Judaism in order to criticize a rival philosophy. Remarkable is what Hegel has discovered by taking the typology so seriously and pushing it to its limit. By harnessing the anti-Judaic potential of Christology into an extreme critique of Kant's "dualist" idealism, he has arrived at an "Incarnationist" idealism. Far from ridiculous, Hegel's insistence on the poisonous (190) harvest of Judaism helps him to find within *The Spirit of Christianity* nearly all the fruit—unripe but recognizable—of the philosophy that will make him famous.

That philosophy posits as its goal the dialectical overcoming of all oppositions, a process explicitly patterned on the overcoming of the difference between God and man, in the Incarnation and Passion of Jesus Christ. By writing the man-God union across all the fundamental oppositions of religion and philosophy—infinite and finite, love and law, spirit and letter, reason and nature—Hegel seeks to synthesize (the technical word often used in English is *sublate*) all of them in the dialectical movement of the spirit across the ages. Even Kant's limit case, the "thing," the "object," is transformed by this Christological dialectic, achieving its true being when it "itself puts forth the necessary relation of itself to its opposite."

If the phrase just quoted seems obscure, that obscurity is entirely representative. Hegel was famous for the difficulty of his expression even in his own day—Goethe and Schiller once debated with each other how he might best be taught to communicate more clearly—but the pages he devotes in his *Logic* to the proper understanding of "Relation" are among the most impenetrable of his oeuvre. Not even the heroic oversimplifications of Herbert Marcuse have succeeded in making them clear: "The object, in other words, must be comprehended as a 'subject' in its relations to its 'otherness.' As an ontological category, the 'subject' is the power of an entity to 'be itself in its otherness'." In the face of such failures, I will not attempt to unpack the Hegelian vocabulary, but I will simply note that in this case the obscurity is patterned on a genuine mystery: that of the Incarnation. Hegel's "things" must recognize their "others" in themselves, and overcome the difference by suffering their own destruction. In this sense all "things" are like Jesus, just as all of world history is for Hegel an *imitatio Christi*, an "imitation of Christ." Or as he put it in his 1827 *Lectures on the Philosophy of Religion*:

> *It is in connection with a true understanding of the death of Christ that the relation of the subject as such in this way comes into view . . . The highest knowledge of the nature of the Idea of Spirit is contained in this thought.*[24]

Once we take seriously the Christology of Hegel's dialectics, it is easier to understand the stigmatized place of Judaism in his philosophical system. Specialists will protest that this place evolved over the course of Hegel's career. It is certainly true, for example, that his rhetorical marriage of Kant and the Jews loses its passion in later work. Kant's dualism becomes less "Jewish," and Judaism becomes less abject. In the *Lectures on the Philosophy of Religion*, for example, Hegel implicitly places Kant and Fichte alongside the Persian Manichaeans in the section on "Oriental dualism," not in the section on Judaism. He now calls Judaism "the religion of sublimity" and treats its radical subjection of the material world to an ideal God as a necessary step in the dialectical evolution of the spirit across the ages, rather than an alienation from all that is human. The same move allows him to defend Spinoza against the charge of atheism and pantheism by pushing him to the other extreme: "There is [according to Spinoza] therefore no such thing as finite reality. . . . What is, is God, and only God. Therefore the truth is the opposite of what they maintain, who charge him with atheism: in Spinoza there is too much God." Since this is the philosophical position Hegel associates with Judaism, we might simply say that Hegel defends Spinoza from the charge of atheism by calling him a Jew.[25]

But these changes in tone and vocabulary do not solve Hegel's "Jewish problem." On the contrary, in some ways they only make it more "Christian." Once he assigns Judaism a necessary place in the unfolding history of salvation, he is forced to confront the question of why the Jews were not caught up in that history: why, in Christian terms, they refused to be superseded. In other words, the refusal of the Jews to convert to the spirit of a new age becomes as problematic in Hegel's philosophy as their refusal to convert to Christianity had been in Luther's theology. Hegel tries to explain this refusal in ways familiar to us from theology. For example, he now calls the Jews "the most despicable" of peoples because they had been the first to open "the door to salvation" but then refused to pass through it. Throughout his career Hegel continues to try to make sense of the Jews' refusal to exit the stage of history once their assigned moment was over. But Judaism after Christ will always remain for him a type of necrophilia: a dead man walking, an undigestible remnant expelled from the guts of history.[26]

In this he was much like Augustine and his heirs, and for much the same reason: having described the flow of history in terms of the overcoming of an opposition between law and love, he discovered the difficulty, in this imperfect world, of replacing the law with love. In what sense, for example, is the punishment of criminals not a necessary product of positive law? The problem pushed Hegel into considerable contortions. Hegel tried to argue that the criminal wills his own punishment as a free self-authorizing subject, but there is reason to believe that even he found his own argument unconvincing. There is no "dialectical synthesis" that can completely overcome the opposition between "law" and the "freedom" of the subject. But if the plenitude of freedom can never be reached, if the remainder of "Jewish" law cannot be reduced, then the unintended result of Hegel's patterning the history of philosophy on the history of salvation turns out to be that every philosophical step, no matter how "progressive," remains "Judaizable," just as every theological step had proved to be in Christian theology. Hegel's dialectic had given a new power to the dangers of Judaism.[27]

There are, however, important differences between the theologian and the philosopher. One of the most important is this: the theologian speaks in the name of God, whereas the philosopher speaks in the name of reason. Hegel's models of history, for all their theological borrowings and resonances, claim the status of critical scientific research, rather than of religion or superstition. The inability of history to overcome Judaism and digest the Jew is thereby translated from an article of faith into an axiom of science, the new "science of hating Judaism" that the prescient Saul Ascher had warned about in 1794.

Ascher was quite right to worry that "a totally new kind of adversary is developing before our eyes, one who is armed with more awful weapons than his predecessors, and whose principles are still in their germinating stage." But this potential for anti-Judaism was not—as Ascher hoped—the result of tendentious misreadings of Kant by scurrilous followers. It was rather endemic to the whole project of German Idealism. That project confronted many of the same cosmological abysses—between spirit and matter, the eternal and the perishable, what really "is" and what only appears to be—that we know from all of our previous chapters. The new philosophers attempted to bridge those impasses with new versions of tools—such as dualism and dialectic—developed during these earlier encounters. "Critical" philosophy transformed these distinctions and devices into a secular "science," and thereby gave them vast new powers: among them, the power to generate "scientific" figures of Judaism.[28]

This is not to say that philosophical ideas about Judaism *determined* the political or social stances of individuals toward real Jews in any triv-

ial or obvious way. Hegel is himself a good example. His rise to philosophical prominence occurred at the same time that the number and
the importance of Jews were beginning to rise in German lands, and
he himself lived to witness the first convulsions of what we might call
"political anti-Semitism" when, after the defeat of Napoleon, German
nationalists made repeal of the rights that he had extended to the Jews a
rallying cry in their campaign for "German-ness." Hegel saw this not as
"German-ness" but as "German-stupid-ness," and his response to it in
the *Philosophy of Right* was categorical (and familiar). "The fierce outcry
raised against the Jews . . . ignores the fact that they are, above all, men;
and manhood . . . [is] itself the basis of the feeling of selfhood." During
Hegel's brief stay at the University of Heidelberg, he even supported
the attempts of his student Friedrich Wilhelm Carové to translate these
principles into action. Carové lobbied for the admission of Jewish students into Heidelberg's "student union," which indeed became the only
German union to pass such a measure.[29]

According to one influential scholar of Hegel and the Jews, support
for Jewish political rights is "a better test of anti-Semitism than any theoretical speculation." Perhaps this is so. But we are not asking whether
Hegel or any other thinker was or was not an anti-Semite. We want only
to see if Judaism did any special work in the systems that our various
thinkers devised in order to describe and understand the world, and to
ask how that work affected the ways in which the place of Jews in the
world could be conceived and understood. From this point of view, the
ways in which Hegel articulated his resolution of the ancient tension
between the ideal and the real, and the ways in which he explained and
represented the ongoing failure of these resolutions through figures of
Jews and Judaism, were of tremendous significance, not only because of
the specific work they assigned to figures of Judaism, but also because
they had such widespread influence on the ways in which Europeans
(and later, people in other parts of the world) came to think about their
history and culture.

Hegel wrote at a time when, as he put it during Napoleon's invasion
of Germany, "the connecting bonds of the world are dissolved and have

collapsed like images in a dream." He taught a generation increasingly desperate about what they perceived to be the resulting alienation of man from the world—from things, from other people, and from the signs and symbols that mediate between them—that the collapse itself represented a great stage in the human spirit's overcoming of this alienation: that the dialectical movement of the human spirit was marching toward freedom. He helped his followers understand how the entire history of human existence in the world could be understood as the development of the human spirit's unity with the absolute, that history was working toward a future in which, as the American poet Walt Whitman would put it several decades later,

> All these separations and gaps shall be taken up and hook'd
> and link'd together,
> The whole earth, this cold, impassive, voiceless earth, shall
> be completely justified.
> . . . Nature and Man shall be disjoin'd and diffused no more,
> The true son of God shall absolutely fuse them.

The mature Hegel did all this philosophically and "scientifically," without requirement of scripture or benefit of prophecy.[30] But he did, as we have seen, need his "Jews," and in this he both reflected and shaped the ways in which Europe could envision the place of Judaism in its future as well as in its past.

"Philosophy Must Be Something Entirely Other Than Jew-Mythology"

Reflected and shaped: the ambivalence is deliberate. Philosophers like Kant, Fichte, and Hegel did not "invent" the cognitive work to which they put Jews and Judaism, nor were their ideas necessarily the principle engines propelling the future of that work. On the contrary, figures of Judaism played these roles in the thinking of philosophers precisely because they had already played such principal parts in the history of thought about the basic questions with which our philosophers were concerned: questions about how the freedom of the individual subject and the seemingly deterministic laws of nature could be reconciled; how the particular and the universal could be consonant; how the world of things and the world of spirit could be made one. Our philosophers' ideas were fashioned in part from a conceptual toolkit drawn from Christian culture, and their success owed a good deal to the ways in which they resonated with parts of that culture. But at the same time that our thinkers were embedded in a history of thought, they also discovered new uses for the conceptual tools they deployed, articulated the crucial questions in new ways, and reshaped the ways in which these questions could be conceived and expressed within a given community.

It is important to insist on this ambivalence in order to avoid the twin temptations that confront the "historian of ideas": on the one hand, that of subjecting ideas to the tyrannical sway of an overdetermining past; on the other, that of granting them too much freedom, emancipating them excessively from what has been thought before. The avoidance of that temptation is made all the more difficult in the case of the thinkers studied in this chapter, who themselves insisted on the radical novelty of their thought and succeeded in making that claim good. On the maps philosophy departments draw of human thought, the appearance of Kant's *Critique of Pure Reason* constitutes the frontier of modernity, and the forty years to Hegel's *Philosophy of History* take us deep into its heartland. This periodization, however justified it is in some respects, has made it difficult to recognize the extent to which these thinkers impressed "Jewish" labor from the "Old World" of the Christian theological imagination in order to settle the new territories of critical and philosophical thought that they discovered.

Just as Hegel (for example) did not "invent" this Jewish labor, its usefulness did not end with him. Nor was it confined to philosophers who shared his sense that the unfolding history of the spirit should be understood in terms of the imitation of Christ. Even those who disagreed sharply with his use of Christian salvation history as a model for Idealism could agree that the Jews provided the best example of the stumbling blocks on the road to philosophical truth. Arthur Schopenhauer (1788–1860), for example, was interested in the same Kantian questions that concerned Fichte, Schelling, Hegel, and other German Idealists. Are there some basic principles, or some laws of thought, that can explain how we experience the cosmos—the world of objects, of living creatures, of other people—in a way that preserves the thinking subject's freedom from the determinism of those laws? Or are we and our thoughts, as the empiricists might have it, produced and determined by the actions of the external world on our senses? Kant's answer to these questions in the *Critique of Pure Reason* had attempted to preserve the possibility of freedom by concluding—his so-called Copernican revolution—that it is we who create the laws of nature, rather than the other way around. Hegel, you will recall, had been inspired by Kant's conclusions but found them excessively "Jewish"—that is, insufficiently optimistic about the possibility of overcoming the difference between ourselves as thinking subjects and the things-in-themselves of the external world—and had suggested instead an unfolding history of the spirit in which that difference was continually and successively sublated, synthesized, overcome.

Schopenhauer agreed with Kant (and other Idealists) that the world and its laws are created out of our thought. In his most famous work, *The World as Will and Representation*, he attempted to demonstrate that creation out of the "principle of sufficient reason" (that is, the claim that everything must have a reason or a cause). But unlike many of Kant's successors, Schopenhauer totally rejected the sense that this process of willful creation unfolded in a teleological (whether positivistic, Incarnational, Trinitarian, dialectical, or otherwise) progress toward truth. On the contrary, according to him, the will produces—through individuations and objectifications—the very oppositions and differences that need to be overcome. The extension of our will through thought (especially practical and scientific thought)—that is, the very action by which we make sense of the cosmos and our place in it—itself creates the violence of our world. Our willfulness is self-wounding. We are like the Australian bulldog ant when it is cut in half: its head and tail engage in a battle to the death.

Life in the "real" world, the created world of objects and individuation, is a life of suffering. But we can ease this suffering by shifting our attention away from the individual, away from the world of particulars and spatiotemporal objects, and toward the universal and undifferentiated. We can, for example, study the teachings of what Schopenhauer called the "Vedic" religions—Christianity, Hinduism, and Buddhism— all of which taught (according to him) that the world is mere appearance, and that being (*Dasein*) in this world of appearance is the root of evil. Or we can attend to the fine arts, to works of genius (especially musical ones), which always point beyond their own particular materiality toward the universal. Asceticism and the self-denial of fleshly desires is also helpful. But no matter how hard we try, Idealism and the relief from suffering that it brings will remain a "paradox" in the West, "as a consequence of the present and unavoidable realist Jewish position." According to Schopenhauer, Europe is so thoroughly infected with Jewish realism that she is condemned to a bipolar oscillation between the errors of subjectivism and those of materialism. In India, by way of contrast, where there were no Jews but only Brahmins and Buddhists, "Idealism was even the folk religion."[31]

Schopenhauer found symptoms of infection throughout the history of thought. He wrote frequently of a *foetor Judaicus*, "a Jewish stench," emanating from this or that person, text, or idea. Even philosophers he admired were at risk. Though he sometimes thought of Spinoza's writings as in some ways a precursor to his own, the margins of those writings in his library are blazed in his own hand with notations like *ecce Judaeus*, "behold the Jew." Not surprisingly, however, his harshest diagnoses were aimed at his rival Idealists, the followers of Fichte, Schelling, and Hegel teaching in the German universities. Schopenhauer had many names for these competitors: lectern philosophers, he often called them, but also more insulting names like "plaster daubers," "pillpushers," "administrators of enemas." But above all they were "Jews," followers of "the Old Jew" or "the Jewish God"—not because of their religious beliefs or ancestry, but because of the habits of philosophical thought they had acquired. Schopenhauer mockingly marveled in one of his attacks on the Hegelians dominating the universities, at the power those habits acquire over thought. After all, he wrote, "men are born into the world uncircumcised, that is, not as Jews."[32]

Schopenhauer was fond of insults, but it would be a mistake to treat his charges of Judaism as a content-less rhetoric of denigration. On the contrary, the place of "Judaism" was just as central to his thought, and its deployment against the Hegelians just as systematic, as it had been in Hegel's engagement with Kant and the Kantians. It was in the Hebrew Bible and its opening account of the creation of the world—"And God saw that it was good"—that Schopenhauer saw the birth of the mortal enemies of human happiness: "realism" and "optimism," cognition oriented toward the things of this world. Even at the very end of his life, after hundreds of attacks on "the old Jew" and his stench, he still spoke of redoubling his engagement with the "entire Old Testament . . . in order to criticize Judaism even more insistently." Theism, theodicy, free will, and all of the many other metaphysical errors oriented toward the worship rather than the overcoming of creation: these were in their origin and in their essence "Judaism." It was Kant, according to Schopenhauer, who had first articulated the truth that "philosophy must be something entirely other than Jew-mythology." Schopenhauer was the paladin of this de-Judaification, and the Hegelians, with what he saw as their theology masquerading as philosophy, were his greatest enemies.[33]

The intertwined cognitive and rhetorical power of this "Judaism" is perhaps most spontaneously evident in Schopenhauer's letters, such as this one upbraiding a philosopher who had written that the "Thing in Itself is the eternal, ungenerated, imperishable primordial Being":

> *That is the Thing in itself?! The devil, too! I'll tell you what that is: it is the well known* Absolute, *that is, the beheaded cosmological argument upon which the* Jew-God *rides. And you go before him, like* King David *before the ark of the covenant, singing and dancing. . . .*

*We know already everything that hides behind that: it is the Lord of
the Absolute. . . .*

   It is the Lord of the Absolute!

   That means, it is the Old Jew!

   *Who in the beginning made the heavens and the earth, amen,
amen! On the basis of such definitions you go on to argue . . . "this all
follows* analytically *from the concept of the Thing in itself." Sure, out
of* your *[concept], that* you *fetched from the Synagogue. . . . Have a
nice trip to Cloud-cuckoo-heaven! Greet the* Old Jew *from me and
from Kant. He knows us.*

Such letters make clear the degree to which Schopenhauer thought of
these struggles within Idealism as part of a cosmological battle with
Judaism. This one is all the more interesting in that it is addressed,
not to some inimical Hegelian, but to the philosopher's beloved "arch-
apostle" (as he called him) and literary executor, Julius Frauenstädt,
himself a convert from Judaism.[34]

The fact that Frauenstädt was a convert, like several other of Schopenhauer's "apostles," reminds us once again that the way in which
thinkers deploy "Judaism" in their thought does not map easily onto
their thinking about or dealing with Jews and Judaism in their every-
day world. Schopenhauer could wage war against "Judaism" in European thought while at the same time counting converts among his
most beloved disciples, even if (like Jesus's) those disciples occasionally stumbled. At a time when many of his contemporaries stigmatized
converts and complained about "insincere" conversions, he welcomed
even the most opportunistic baptisms as a step in the right direction.
(He was, however, against the granting of civic rights to Jews if they did
not convert, on the grounds that they would remain "recht Juden.") He
complained often about "Jewish stench," but did not tie that malady to
lineage or confession but to ontology: to a way of living and thinking
about Being.[35]

Schopenhauer's philosophical uses of Judaism had a future, but it
would be misleading to declare them or that future as especially fateful

or exemplary. His was only one of the many such systems of thought: indeed we have already seen his rivals, the Hegelians, deploy Judaism quite differently, though just as centrally. The point here is not to anoint heroes or villains; to uncover hidden "anti-Semites" in the history of thought; or to provide a forensic accounting of the impact of a given idea on the possibilities of existence for Jews. We want only to make plausible the thesis that widespread habits of thought about Judaism shaped philosophers' potential understandings of the world. The effects of those habits were not simple, and the potential understandings of the world that they generated were many (with many more as yet still un-thought and unrealized). We cannot multiply examples without tedium, so let us conclude this chapter with a Hegelian admired by Schopen-hauer as a humorist (albeit one with a "Jewish stench"), whose exam-ple will also help to make clear how difficult it is to assign a decisive valence—"positive" or "negative"?—to any deployment of "Judaism" in dialectics.[36]

"The Assigned Task of the Whole of European Civilization": Heinrich Heine

Unlike Schopenhauer, Heinrich Heine (1797–1856) did not think of Juda-ism as Europe's stumbling block on the path toward idealism. On the contrary, for him the world-historical significance of Europe consisted precisely in its capacity to achieve the synthesis of Jew and Greek: "Per-haps such a harmonious mixture of both elements is the assigned task of the whole of European civilization?"[37] His views on these topics were not marginal: although Heine's place in the pantheon of German letters is due above all to his lyric poetry, his mordant wit and acute political sensibilities—so acute that they drove him into exile in France—made him a celebrated commentator on the politics and culture of his age. Among those comments were many about Jews and figures of Judaism, both those he knew from his own society and those he imagined from other times and places. In fact in his essays and in his poetry, Heine explored many of the places we have ourselves visited in this book—the ancient world, early Christianity, Islamic lands, medieval Spain, Luther's Germany, the markets of Shakespeare's Venice, German philosophy— and many we have not.

Heine's lifelong interest in "Jewish questions"—the phrase is for the first time in this book not anachronistic, since Marx's essay "On the Jewish Question" appeared next to an article by Heine in the *Deutsch-Französische Jahrbücher* of February 1844—doubtless owed a great deal to the fact that he was himself a convert, a German Jew turned Protestant. But it also owed a great deal to the philosophical thought of his age, and above all, to Hegel's treatment of Israel as a stage in the dialectical unfolding of the spirit. Heine was influenced by Hegel's thoughts about Judaism throughout his life (except perhaps at its very end), but a single paragraph suffices to make their importance clear:

> As the prophet of the Orient [Muhammad] called them "the people of the book," so the prophet of the Occident [Hegel!] ... called them "the people of the spirit." ... Their whole religion is nothing but a dialectic act by which matter is separated from spirit and the absolute is recognized solely as spirit.... In what a dreadful opposition they must have stood to colorful Egypt, the Temples of Joy of Astarte in Phoenicia, lovely, fragrant, Babylon, and finally to Greece, the flourishing home of art.[38]

The paragraph is quite typical of Heine, both in its wit—Muhammad and Hegel as prophets of East and West!—and in the easy strokes with which it synthesizes the gist of Hegel's teachings on Judaism, from the youthful *Spirit of Christianity* to the late *Lectures on Fine Art*. Of course influence does not mean tyranny. Heine put Hegel's system to work in original and idiosyncratic ways. Among the most important of these idiosyncrasies was that, unlike Hegel, Heine did not confine the Jews' dialectical importance to the distant past. Instead he claimed that Europe's Jewish affliction was also the seedbed of its greatness. He treated Jews and Judaism not as vestigial remnants of a bygone age, but as a vital organ of a living Europe.

Which organ? Hegel had once commented to Heine—or at least so the latter reported—that the penis provided a remarkable example of dialectics, in that it served both man's basest and his highest needs: material waste and divine reproduction. Heine expanded the analogy. Like the penis, the Jews produced both peddlers and prophets, "the shabbiest of filth" and "the highest pinnacles of humanity." And he insisted that this dialectical process had not ended with Jesus. "Golgotha is not the only mountain where a Jewish god has bled for the salvation of the world." Jews remained "the people of spirit," and an ongoing source of inspiration to Europe. In fact for Heine, as we have seen, the specific historical mission of Europe consisted in achieving precisely this dialectical synthesis of the Jews' devotion to the absolute and the Greek cultivation of beauty.[39]

It is easy to see how important Hegel's dialectical philosophy was in helping Heine (and many others) think about the place of Judaism in the cultural history of Europe. Like Hegel (and many others), Heine believed that the categories designated by terms like *Jew* and *Greek* derived from ancient historical distinctions between two cultures: according to Heine, historical Jews really had been "abstract" and "otherworldly," and ancient Greeks had really delighted in the beauty of the world. Like Hegel (and many others), he called "Jews" those he associated with "ascetic, iconoclastic, and other-worldly-addicted drives and impulses," and contrariwise called "Greeks" those who were "life-loving, proud of human achievements, and of a realistic nature." Finally, like Hegel (and many others), he constantly deployed "Jew" and "Greek" as critical categories that could be used to analyze and classify people and ideas in the past and present. Even the ur-Germanic world of folk and fairy tale could become an allegory for the dialectical struggle between these two cultures. In his essay *Elemental Spirits*, for example, he uses a folk tale about the banishing of the dwarves from the world of men, in order to point to the European history of Jewish expulsions. The whole realm of German myth and fairy tale becomes, in that essay, a stage set for the question "of whether the morbid, meager, anti-aesthetic, overly legal Judaism of the

Nazarene, or Greek joyousness, love of beauty, and blooming lust for life would rule in the world."[40]

Heine made clear—more explicitly than some of his contemporaries— that these categories no longer corresponded to separate confessional communities, as they might have done in the ancient world. "The beard does not make the Jew, nor the wig the Christian," he quipped in a critique he wrote against the revolutionary journalist Ludwig Börne in the 1830s. On the contrary, words like *Jew* and *Greek* (as well as related terms like *Nazarene, Christian, Pharisee*, and others) designated ways of thinking about and relating to the world—asceticism versus worldliness, faith versus reason, the sublime versus the beautiful, and so on—rather than adherence to a particular religion. The struggle between the outlooks they represented was ongoing in every thinker and in every artist regardless of confession or nation, their synthesis the achievement of every genius. From this point of view we can understand the ironic work behind the brutal stereotypes with which he begins his essay *Shakespeare's Maidens and Ladies*:

> *I know a good Hamburg Christian who can never reconcile himself to the fact that our Lord and Saviour was by birth a Jew. A deep dissatisfaction seizes him when he must admit . . . that the man who deserves the highest honor as a pattern of perfection, was kin to those snuffling long-nosed fellows who go running about the streets selling old clothes. . . . As Jesus Christ is to this excellent son of Hammonia, so is Shakespeare to me. It takes the heart out of me when I remember that he is an Englishman, and belongs to the most repulsive race which God in his wrath ever created.*[41]

Determining the outcome of the struggle between the "Jewishness" or "Greekness" of a given thinker or artist, explaining how a "nation of shopkeepers" gives birth to a Shakespeare, how warring strands of worldviews give rise to new manifestations of the human spirit: these were for Heine a basic task of cultural critique.

The ideal outcome of this struggle was supposed to be synthesis.

Heine's criticism of Börne, for example, was that rather than striving for such synthesis, he had opted for Judaism. Börne was "Jewish," not because he, like Heine, was a convert from Judaism, but because he thought and wrote like a "Jew," incapable of appreciating the world in its beauty. Again, this literary criticism of "Jewishness" was not aimed only at "ethnic" Jews like Börne. In the same essay, Heine specifically attacked "the Jew Pustkuchen, the Jew Wolfgang Menzel, the Jew Hengstenberg," all Christian writers who "raise their pharisaic hue and cry" against the joyful worldliness of "Athens." Shakespeare, on the other hand, though by religion a Christian, was for Heine "simultaneously Jew and Greek," because he had achieved Heine's (and Hegel's) ideal, integrating "Jewish" spirituality with "Hellenic" worldliness, and thereby elevating both to a "higher Whole."[42]

Like Hegel (and like Shakespeare, Saint Paul, and nearly everyone else we have encountered in this book), Heine built a wide-ranging system of cultural critique out of the difference between Christian and Jew. His dialectical synthesis of Hebrew and Hellene shared many assumptions with those of his teachers: assumptions about the essential nature of the differences between Jew and Greek, and about the overcoming of these differences through history's unfolding. This meant that Heine could not completely escape the difficulties implicit in Hegel's notion of the spirit's progress. Of these, perhaps the most dangerous was dialectic's destruction of the antinomies that it reconciled. Theoretically, at least, Heine's synthesis required the sacrifice of both Hebrew and Hellene.

The Hebrews here required a heavier sacrifice than the Hellenes. "When we speak of the Greeks"—to invoke the ever-quotable Nietzsche, himself a great admirer of Heine—"we unwittingly speak simultaneously of today and yesterday. Their universally known history is a blank mirror that always reflects something that is not in the mirror itself. . . . Thus do the Greeks lighten for modern man the exchange of much that is ominous and difficult to communicate." We might say the same of their dialectical opposite, the Jews, with some important differences. First, the Jewish mirror was not meant to be blank, or flattering,

or even particularly reflective. Rather, the image of everything gross in
European culture was projected on it, in the hope that it would absorb
some of that grossness back into itself. Second, the Jewish mirror was
not made of polished bronze or silvered glass, but of living flesh. There
were few Athenians in togas wandering the streets of nineteenth-century
Paris, London, or Berlin. Things were otherwise with Judaism. There
were increasing numbers of kaftaned and bearded Jews who refused
(unlike Heine or Börne) to convert or disappear. What place was there
in Heine's dialectics for the survival of these un-sublated, unrepentant,
Talmud-toting Jews?[43]

That question does not have any one answer, in part because Heine
was more uneasy than most of his contemporaries about the relationship between "Jewish" ideas and Jews of flesh and breath. Sometimes he answers it in terms that sound like those of many a Hegelian.
"Whither now the Talmud?" he asks in *On the History of Religion and
Philosophy in Germany*. "Moses Mendelssohn earned great praise, in
that he toppled this Jewish Catholicism [that is, the Talmud], at least
in Germany. For what is superseded is harmful." The Talmud's "Jewish
Catholicism"—that is, its legalism and emphasis on works and ritual
practices—had once been necessary as a defense against "Christian
Catholicism," he explains, but in a modern world in which the Vatican
entrusts its money to the Jew Rothschild, such a defense is as baneful as
it is superfluous.

But on the other hand, Heine seems resistant to the fantasy that the
world can be perfected through the elimination of Jews or "Judaism." He
places the contributions of Judaism to the formation of European culture in the ongoing present as well as in the distant and completed past.
Moreover, he is terribly aware of the danger that philosophical thinking
poses. "Do not laugh at my advice," concludes the *History of Religion
and Philosophy in Germany*, "the advice of a dreamer who warns against
Kantians, Fichteans, and [pantheist] philosophers of nature. Do not
laugh at the visionary who anticipates that the same revolution will occur
in the world of appearances, as has already taken place in the world of
mind and spirit. Thought precedes deed as lightning precedes thun-

der. . . . Such a drama will take place in Germany, that in comparison the French Revolution will look like an innocent idyll."[44]

A "Creeping Calamity"

This chapter has focused on the ways in which a few thinkers—Kant, Fichte, Jacobi, Hegel, Schopenhauer, Heine—thought with and about Judaism. Their selection is not meant to imply that they were "worse" or "better" in this regard—or more or less anti-Semitic—than the many other thinkers of their day. To quote one of their heirs, Friedrich Nietzsche, "I only avail myself of the person as of a strong magnifying glass with which one can render visible a general but creeping calamity which it is otherwise hard to get hold of."

The method may seem old-fashioned: we are nowadays more skeptical of the claim that the ideas of a philosophical "individual" tell us anything important about the "general." Few contemporary intellectual historians would agree with the young Karl Marx that, as he put it in 1842,

> [p]hilosophers do not rise by themselves out of the earth like mushrooms. They are the fruits of their time and of their people [Volk], whose subtlest, most precious and least visible sap runs in philosophical ideas.

But in defense against too relentless a skepticism, we should remember that philosophy was not always the academic discipline it is today, so strictly segregated from religious piety, bourgeois culture, or mass ideology. In the next chapter Marx himself will provide us with a powerful example of the ties that bound the pages of nineteenth-century philosophical treatises to those of political manifestos. In this one, it is enough to grant that each of the writers we have touched on had some influence on the ways in which culture could be conceived in the future.[45]

Schopenhauer's writings, for example, inspired (among many others) the German composer Richard Wagner's meditations on music as an escape from the problem of being, and moved him to his own influential meditation (*The Jews in Music*) on the need to "de-Judaize" music and the arts. The British critic Matthew Arnold (1822–1888) was only one of many who adapted (in *Culture and Anarchy*) Heine's thought, launching a wide-ranging critique of "Pharisaism" in England's increasingly industrial society.[46] In fact the idea that European culture's goal is the dialectical overcoming of the difference between Jew and Greek became so common in Victorian intellectual circles that James Joyce could mock it "with saturnine spleen" as a representative idiocy of the age: "Jewgreek is greekjew. Extremes meet. Death is the highest form of life. Bah!"[47]

This defense is important, but it is also a little beside the point. Even if this or that thinker's ideas had little or no impact on the future of thought in the world—even if they languished unpublished in the obscure pages of a private diary—they could still reveal to us the "creeping calamity" we have in mind, for that calamity does not consist in the triumph of a particular idea. Indeed it would be difficult to declare "triumphant" or hegemonic any of a particular thinker's ideas about Judaism, and not because many of the ones we have described seem in some ways contradictory: Schopenhauer's Jews are "realists" while Heine's are "antirealists"; Schopenhauer's are Europe's unavoidable stumbling block on its path toward Idealism, Heine's are the generative organ of Europe's greatest syntheses.

These apparent contradictions should not be too surprising. After all, early Christianity had also generated views of the Jews' role in history as different as those of the Manichaeans, who saw Jews as witnesses to the demonic origins of the material world, and Augustine's, who cast them as essential witnesses to God's incarnation in his own creation. Nor had centuries of theologians seen any insurmountable difficulty in simultaneously understanding Judaism as too realist ("carnal Israel") and too symbolic ("the letter kills"). As in Christianity so in Idealism: different deployments of Judaism within dialectics could produce seemingly contradictory results, but these contradictions did not undermine confidence in the coherence of the dialectic itself.

Hence nineteenth-century critics—to continue with our example of "Jew" and "Greek"—rarely complained that European culture was growing too "Greek." But they worried constantly that it was growing too Jewish, a worry that expanded throughout the century, even into areas of cultural production where it had hitherto been little known. When critics did attack the dominance of attributes generally associated with "Greekness," they often did so by recasting those attributes as "Jewish." "Reason," for example, was a quintessentially Greek attribute for the nineteenth-century philosophers and divines we have discussed. Yet at the same time, many of these thinkers worried about the increasing materialism, self-interest, and disenchantment, which they frequently associated with hyperrationalism. One way in which they criticized these tendencies was by associating them with Judaism (hence Schopenhauer's complaint that "one should not identify reason with Judaism"). Another was to subdivide reason to contain its excesses within less exalted categories of cognition, such as "instrumental reason," which could then be associated with "Judaism" and projected onto the living representatives of that class.[48]

In short, our "creeping calamity" is a thought process, not an idea. It is the translation of theologies of supersession into modern science; the smuggling of "Jewish" laborers from the overpopulated lands of the Christian imagination into the booming markets of critical and philosophical thought. Throughout this chapter we have watched the infant disciplines of critical modernity learn from their parents—Christian theology and Enlightenment philosophy—to think of certain basic problems of cognition as "Jewish," and to imagine a more perfect future in terms of the overcoming or the elimination of this Judaism.

That pedagogy was all the more dangerous for taking place at precisely the moment when Europe was flooded by two new tidal waves of Judaism: one figural and one of flesh. First the figural: across the long nineteenth century—from 1789 and the French Revolution to 1914 and the First World War—mass politics and mass markets transformed the European (and not only the European) world. Different aspects of this phenomenon have different names: industrialization, urbanization, proletarianization, nationalism, to name a few. But for many thinkers, ranging from reactionary counterrevolutionaries (such as Joseph de Maistre) to proto-anarchist ones (like Max Stirner), all these aspects threatened to dissolve the bonds of love and obligation that tied man to man and (for the more conservative) man to God. These thinkers worried that the result would be an egoistic, materialistic world of self-love and self-interest in which only the desire for property and the circulation of money linked man to man. And—like Shakespeare's contemporaries tossing on the seas of mercantilism a few centuries before—they imagined the dangers of such a world in terms of "Judaism."

The second wave came in the flesh and yammering in Yiddish, in the shape of the immigrants from the shtetels, towns, and cities of eastern Europe. Over the course of the nineteenth century, and for a variety of reasons, the Jewish population of those regions had more than doubled, and a substantial portion of that population—again for a variety of reasons—had chosen to emigrate. Between 1848 and 1914, hundreds of thousands of Jews migrated westward within Europe, multiplying many times over the ranks of living Israelites in Vienna, Berlin, Paris, and London. (Millions more braved the Atlantic for the Americas, but we cannot follow them there.) The demographic results of this human wave were evident to contemporaries, and have been well studied by historians. But we are more interested in the confluence of the two: just when it became most necessary to perceive the differences between real Jews and figures of Judaism, critical thought blurred them once again into one.[49]

The next chapter will explore some of the consequences of this confluence in modernity. But in this one, let us give the last word to Heinrich Heine, himself a great impresario of this confusion, as well as one of the most sensitive to the calamities it might incubate. Standing outside the gates of the Venice ghetto—or so he pretends in the penultimate page on "Portia" in *Shakespeare's Maidens and Ladies*—he was moved to prophesy: "[I]f Satan, or the sinful pantheism—from which may all the saints of the Old and New Testament as well as the Koran protect us!—should conquer, there will fall on the heads of the poor Jews a tempest of persecution which will far surpass all their previous sufferings."[50]

Chapter 13

MODERNITY THINKS
WITH JUDAISM

*The age of rampant Jewish intellectualism
is now at an end.*

—JOSEPH GOEBBELS, MAY 10, 1933

So BEGINS THE speech with which the propagandist-in-chief of
the Nazi Party addressed the students of his nation, some four
scant months after his party's rise to power. The speech (you can hear
as well as read it, for with this chapter we reach the age of film and
radio) announced a revolution "from below." With a PhD in German
literature, Goebbels was himself something of a recovering "intellectual." But now he exhorted his audience to don brown shirts and stand
side by side with the German worker, rebelling against domination by
machines; with the German burgher, straining against the financial burden of war reparations; with the German soldier, revolting against the
dishonorable defeat of the Great War.

The newly coined Minister of Folk-Enlightenment and Propaganda also gave the students an assignment: to clear the way for a true German spirit and a new German man, a man capable of facing death without fear. They were to perform a "strong, symbolic act," one that would show the world that the old order lay in flames, and that the new was being born in German hearts. What act would symbolize the destruction of the "Un-Spirit of the past" and the shattering of the "Un-State's" (namely, the liberal Weimar Republic) "fetters of tyranny"? What act could best symbolize the destruction of all of the "old" and all of the "Un-"? Goebbels proposed a bonfire of "Jewish intellectualism," a "Burning of Un-German books."[1]

The book burning was only a small part of the Nazis' initiative for the "de-Judaization" of German education. A few weeks before, the first of many "Un-German" professors had been purged from the universities. And the "de-Judaization" of university education was only a small part of the Nazis' plan for the de-Judaization of German society and culture as a whole. Still, small as it was, this "strong, symbolic act" can serve as something of a synecdoche not only for the Nazis' larger project but also for mine. "Rampant Jewish intellectualism" stands here explicitly as a figure of thought. The Jewishness with which it explains the world is not limited to real Jews, but threatens everyone. According to the Nazis, it had infected the entire liberal Weimar state. Goebbels expected his audience to understand what this "Jewish intellectualism" was, and to perceive how it menaced them as individuals, as classes (students, workers, burghers, soldiers), and as a German nation. He also expected them to be moved by this understanding to political action. We know that he was not disappointed. So our question must be, How could "Jewish intellectualism" provide so many people—not only Germans, as we will see, but also many of the greatest thinkers of the modern age—with such a satisfying explanation for the condition of their world?[2]

Modern Transformations

To answer that question, we need to look, however briefly, at the transformations that made that world seem, both to many of its inhabitants and later to its historians, something quite different from what had come before. We call one of those transformations "the Industrial Revolution." The phrase cloaks many subsidiary revolutions, for the age of steam, steel, and machine power touched every aspect of human life, and that impact was everywhere reflected in society and culture. Statistics tell of a rapid expansion of population in the industrializing world. City life became a defining feature of Europe (and North America) in this period. The populations of the great capitals—London, Paris, Berlin—exploded, but so did the populations of many more provincial towns, such as Birmingham, Lyons, and Bielefeld. And as we saw at the end of the previous chapter, in many of these urban agglomerations the population of Jews rose significantly as well.

Industrialization and urbanization left few corners of these city dwellers' lives untouched: where workers lived, what they ate and wore, the number of children they had and what those children were (or were not) taught, when they died and how they were buried, and of course, how, how much, and by whom they were paid, and who was enriched by their labors. We have endless witnesses to these effects, such as the study that Friedrich Engels wrote in 1844 (just before he became Karl Marx's coauthor and collaborator) on living conditions in Birmingham. But we should not forget that property and capital were transformed as much as labor. A steady stream of financial innovations, from the spread of paper money to the rise of a stock-capitalized banking system, constantly refashioned the nature of risk; the opportunities for investment, brokerage, and arbitrage; and the very notion of private property. If in the previous centuries every man had become, in Adam Smith's words, "in some measure a merchant," now every man became willy-nilly a speculator: every citizen subject to the slings and arrows of financial fortune—from market bubbles to international depressions—in a hugely complex interpenetration of private interest and nation-states whose thirst for modernization required long draughts of capital.

And with all these transformations, as in every period we have touched on in this book, came a heightened attention to communication, circulation, and exchange: to the words and objects that mediate human community. Some of these questions are already familiar to us from previous chapters because they are questions of the sort so often addressed in terms of Judaism across the history of Western thought. The limits of contract, for example, were a key concern of modernity, though they took a different form from Shakespeare's or Hobbes's. What kinds of rights did an employer gain over an employee, and what kinds of rights could employees alienate to their employers? Was wage labor a form of slavery, as many argued, or a legitimate contract between two parties? And what kinds of powers did debt contracts give creditors over the bodies of their debtors? Should, for example, bankruptcy be punished by prison? Or were there limits to the rights that workers and borrowers could alienate through contract? And what of the debts (or assets) of states? How did these oblige (or belong to) their citizens? Was there a social contract? Was there a sovereign one? And if so, how far did the powers of these "contracts" extend, what were their limits?

These questions may sound abstract to many readers today, in an age more strongly committed to the axioms of liberal capitalism than perhaps ever before, but in the nineteenth century they burned every bit as hot as the Bastille had in the French Revolution. Pope Leo XIII put it well at the end of that century, in his encyclical on the wage contract entitled "On New Things: Rights and Duties of Capital and Labor":

> That the spirit of revolutionary change, which has long been disturbing the nations of the world, should have passed beyond the sphere of politics and made its influence felt in the cognate sphere of practical economics is not surprising. The elements of the conflict now raging are unmistakable, in the vast expansion of industrial pursuits and the marvelous discoveries of science; in the changed relations between masters and workmen; in the enormous fortunes of some few individuals, and the utter poverty of the masses; the increased self-reliance and closer mutual combination of the working classes; as also, finally, in the prevailing moral degeneracy. The momentous gravity of the state of things now obtaining fills every mind with painful apprehension; wise men are discussing it; practical men are proposing schemes;

popular meetings, legislatures, and rulers of nations are all busied
with it—actually there is no question which has taken deeper hold on
the public mind.[3]

In chapter 10 we approached these questions through a work of art:
Shakespeare's *Merchant of Venice*. In this chapter, too, we could treat
works of art as "mirrors of the gigantic shadows which futurity casts
upon the present" (words Shelley wrote about poetry). We could even
focus entirely on nineteenth- and twentieth-century performances of
Merchant (such as the German performances that so impressed Heinrich Heine and Ludwig Börne in 1828), or on modern rewritings of
Shakespeare's works, such as Richard Wagner's early (and thankfully
only once performed) opera of 1834, *Das Liebesverbot* (The Prohibition
on Love), a neo-Manichaean massacre of *Measure for Measure* that ends
with the overthrow of the legalistic tyrant and a rousing chorus of "We
want nothing of your law. Our only law is love."[4]

In this chapter, however, we will focus more directly on the ways in
which these questions about contract, communication, and exchange
were addressed in political and economic thought. After all, these were
the questions that articulated the great political divides of modernity.
Putting it crudely: liberals, their political parties, and their newspapers
and ideologues emphasized the right to enter freely into contract and
tended to orient the powers of the state toward enforcing those contracts, rather than limiting them. Conservative and reactionary parties—
from the monarchist, counterrevolutionary, and Catholic parties of
the early nineteenth century to the fascist parties of the twentieth—
embraced more corporatist views that represented unrestrained rights
of contract as a threat to the right order (natural, moral, and divine)
of society. Socialists of all stripes—including Henri de Saint-Simon
(1760–1825), who invented the word; Marx and Engels; Anarchists, and
Catholic and Christian socialists—had a very different vision of right
order than the conservatives did, but like them, they thought of the liberal emphasis on contractual forms of exchange as destructive of community. And as they thought through these questions about what the

English call "political economy," all of them drew on the theological and philosophical discourses we have encountered in earlier chapters. Which is also to say that as they thought through these questions, they often found themselves thinking, like so many of their predecessors in the long history of thought, with and about "Jews."[5]

I put the word once more in quotation marks just to remind us that this thinking did not need to be about "real" Jews. Consider, from the very beginning of our period, this letter to the editor of the newspaper *Boston Patriot*, dated October 31, 1810 (p. 2):

"The Ten Lost Tribes"
Mr. Editor— . . .
There is in Boston a numerous class of very singular and mysterious people, whose origins no heraldry can trace, and who, with all their arts of concealment, betray such striking marks of resemblance to the children of Israel, that they have obtained the name of Jews with no small portion of the inquisitive populace of the place. The point of character, which betrays them, is the art of spunging, shaving, *or as it is most commonly called,* jewing, *in money matters.—In other words, the mystery of getting usury, or more than lawful interest for money. This unconscionable, antichristian practice is not the only peculiar characteristic of this mysterious people. To accomplish their sordid purposes, they resort to necromancy, and whether from an intercourse with evil spirits, or by what charm I know not, transform themselves into any shape that suits their design. Not choosing to appear among christians in the odious character of* spungers, shavers, *or* jews, *nothing is more common than for these grub-souled, proteus-jugglers to transform themselves into some new shape; and assume in all things so exactly the appearance of some of our most respectable citizens, that it is next to impossible to discover the imposition till too late. . . .*
When and how did they get among us?—Whether smuggled into our country under the alien law? Rained down from the clouds like toads?—Whether they ate their way through the earth from its centre or opposite side, like moles?—Or were sent from no one knows where,

like the locusts of Egypt, to devour the land?—are questions which I
shall leave with the curious at present. I cannot, however, avoid draw-
ing one conclusion—that this recent race of people, distinguished by
those striking peculiarities, and gaining such an unaccountable ascen-
dancy among us, must be the lost tribes of Israel.

　　What will be their effects upon our manners, morals, and religion,
it is difficult to determine, but if we may judge from their impunity
and success for a few years past, it is very evident, that in spite of the
boasted habits of our forefathers, and all the efforts of our missionary
and bible societies, they will progress much faster in converting us to
jews, than we shall in converting them to christianity.[6]

I quote the letter so extensively because it provides an excellent (and
relatively lighthearted) example of the ways in which the application of a
Christian discourse of "Judaizing" to new forms of exchange could produce new perceptions of the dangers of Judaism, and generalize those
dangers to all of society. The letter is part parody: the author's genealogical explanations for the presence of Judaism ("the lost ten tribes")
are no more earnest than his meteorological ones ("a rain of Jews"). He
does not seriously believe that the bank directors and "influential citizens" he is criticizing have been possessed or demonically impersonated
by real Jews (of which there were almost none in New England in 1810).
But he does seriously believe that certain forms of finance and contract
are "Jewish." And he insists—even quoting as his last line Saint Jerome's
response to Saint Augustine that we encountered in chapter 3—that
engaging in these types of exchange will Judaize Christian society.

　　The editorialist is here exploiting a venerable Christian confusion
between the figural Jew and the real in order to make critical sense of
the changing world of circulation and exchange. In the process he con-
tributes to the creation of new possibilities for confusion between the
figural and the real, confusions that can in turn have powerful consequences for the "real life" of both Christians and Jews. Just how powerful those consequences could be will become clear if we jump to
the work of one of the most influential thinkers on the subject of how

humans should exchange the fruits of their labors, a thinker whose logic is in some ways very similar to that of our anonymous correspondent. I mean, of course, Karl Marx.

Marx's "Emancipation of Mankind from Judaism"

Karl Marx considered himself a "critical thinker," and as such, a harsh opponent of many of the habits of thought discussed in this book. In fact his first collaboration with Friedrich Engels, *The Holy Family, or Critique of Critical Criticism* of 1844, opens with a blast aimed at one of our founding distinctions: "The letter kills, but the spirit vivifies." "Real humanism has no more dangerous enemy," they write, than this "spiritualism." And yet . . . listen in for a moment as the young Marx—he was twenty-six—takes notes that same year in his 1844 "Paris Notebooks" on James Stuart Mill's *Elements of Political Economy*, one of the founding texts of classical economic theory. Yes, agrees Marx, as he parses the arguments of the great Scottish utilitarian, "man as a social being must proceed to *exchange*." But as Marx perceives it, exchange is a means, not an end, and indeed some forms of exchange militate against, rather than aiding, human and social life. Specifically, in a society with private property "the mediating process between men engaged in exchange is not a social or a human process, not *human relationship*."

> [T]*he* mediating activity *or* movement, the human, *social act by which man's products mutually complement one another, is* estranged *from man and becomes the attribute of money, a* material thing *outside man. Since man alienates this mediating activity itself, he is active here only as a man who has lost himself and is dehumanized; the* relation *itself between things, man's operation with them, becomes the operation of an entity outside man and above man.*

Money becomes God in such a world, says Marx: a formulation he will frequently repeat.

In his notes, Marx allows himself to imagine instead a society without private property, one that "carried out production as human beings," for the sake of relation rather than exchange. In such a world of exchange, "in my production . . . I would have been for you the *mediator* between you and the species, and therefore would become recognised and felt by you yourself as a completion of your own essential nature and as a necessary part of yourself, and consequently would know myself to be confirmed both in your thought and in your love." Only such a society, Marx concludes, can realize "my true nature, my *human* nature, my *communal* nature."[7]

Mediation, recognition, love: these terms resonate strongly with the theological and philosophical discourses we have encountered in earlier chapters. At times Marx will embrace those resonances, as when, in the *Economic and Philosophical Manuscripts* he produced from these notebooks a little later in the year, he credits Shakespeare with "depicting the real nature of *money*." Often he will deny them. Indeed one of his most insistent claims in his various writings of 1844 is that his predecessors and rivals—including and especially Hegel and a group of his followers to whom Marx initially belonged called "the Young Hegelians"—are insufficiently emancipated from the long tyranny of Christian forms of thought. Their "philosophy is nothing else but religion rendered into thoughts and thinkingly expounded, and . . . it has therefore likewise to be condemned as another form . . . of the estrangement of man."[8]

After seeing in the previous chapter just how much the new philosophy had drawn from the old theology, we have sympathy for the criticism. Yet from the point of view of our subject, we should also notice that Marx's own philosophy here depends on and reproduces deep continuities with Christian figures of Judaism. To see how this is so, we need to unpack a little the resonances in Marx's language. The invocation of "recognition" in economic exchange, for example, should remind us immediately of Hegel, and in particular, of his most explicitly political work, *The Elements of the Philosophy of Right* (1821). Again, Hegel's goal was to emancipate the individual from positive law, so that the necessary ordering of society became a product of love and freedom rather than subjection to or observance of an external law. You remember from the previous chapter the example of the criminal who has to will his own punishment. Hegel faced a similar problem with property and contract, which on the face of it seem to impose external constraints on the freedom of the individual (and hence can be thought of as "Judaizing"). Hegel tried to solve the difficulty by understanding the contractual exchange of a thing between individuals as a form of "recognition" and relation—that is, as a form of love. Insofar as each individual "recognizes" the other as a proprietor of the thing exchanged, through the exchange they "really exist for each other." This form of recognition mediated through the thing exchanged is Hegel's way of attempting to resolve the constitutional tension between law and love, necessity and freedom, in the all-important sphere of property, markets, and contractual exchange.[9]

As we can see from Marx's own vocabulary, for all his criticism of the religious roots of philosophy, he has abandoned neither Hegel's dialectics, nor his "Trinitarian" ideas about the ability of the object to mediate between the individual and the world. Like Hegel, he too posits a type of exchange that produces love, and opposes it to another that produces alienation and enslavement. Where he differs is on the type of exchange he favors. For Hegel, property is a crucial attribute, not only of individuality but also of intersubjectivity: "[T]he origin of property is personality, the individual's freedom. Man in so far as he is a person, essentially has property." Marx insists instead that private property is not a prerequisite of human subjectivity, nor does it entail or generate the recognition both philosophers hold as a common good. On the contrary, property is a perversion of relation, a perversion that produces only enslavement, estrangement, alienation.

Perhaps the most striking continuity, from the point of view of our subject, is the way in which both philosophers imagined error. When Hegel, for example, wanted to provide an example of an incorrect relation to things and property, he turned to the Jews. Their "mind," he explains, "is completely held fast to one side" by legalism and contract. In "this firm bond there is no freedom," and virtually no humanity: "Man has as yet no inner space, no inner extension, no soul of such an extent as to lead it to wish for satisfaction within itself, but rather it is the temporal which gives it fullness and reality." The Jewish "people" become "identical, inseparable," from their "possessions." Following Kant, Hegel says "possessions" rather than "property" in order to mark the vast difference he sees between Christian and Jewish economics. The Jewish people serve God as an absolute master, in "a fanaticism of stubbornness," with fear "the basic element of its dependence, namely its serfdom." As slaves and serfs of God they do not properly have property but only possessions, temporary holdings. Hegel here sounds a bit like our medieval lawyers from chapter 5, except that he assigns the Jews' possessions to God rather than to the king.[10]

Marx's views on property were more or less the opposite, but his negative exemplars were the same. We have already taken a quick look, in our Introduction, at the essay on the Jewish question that Marx published in the same year (1844) as he took his notes on Mill and wrote his *Economic and Philosophical Manuscripts*. We need to return to that essay, not because of its immediate influence in its own time (the tract had almost no circulation, since the German police confiscated nearly the entire print run of the journal in which it appeared), but because it provides such a powerful example of the phenomenon this book is about.

"Bruno Bauer: The Jewish Question" (as the piece was entitled, although it is generally published with the title "On the Jewish Question") and its sequel, *The Holy Family*, were meant (among other things) to show Marx's fellow critical thinkers and rival radicals among the young Hegelians that they were not being critical enough. These writings took aim at an essay by one of the more famous of these, Bruno Bauer, on the question of whether the Jews should be emancipated and receive the rights of citizens within the state, without first having to convert to Christianity. Bauer replied in the negative—How could the Jews ask the Christian state to give up its religious convictions, while at the same time holding on to theirs?—while simultaneously arguing that this was the wrong question. The real question and the real task, according to Bauer, was the emancipation of the state from religion. Once the German state was emancipated from Christianity, it could then emancipate the Jews, but only if the Jews first emancipated themselves from Judaism—that is, ceased to be Jews.

Bauer's argument depended, like so many others in this book, on a number of un-self-consciously borrowed Christian concepts, such as the casting of the Jews as figures of anti-universalist particularism. They are egoists who demand emancipation for themselves as Jews, rather than, as Germans, political emancipation for all Germans or, as human beings, the emancipation of all mankind.[11]

Marx does not object to these borrowings. What he objects to is the level of the critique. The real question, he writes, is not that of the relationship of political emancipation to religious emancipation, but that of the relationship of political emancipation to *human* emancipation. The mental bonds of religion are only symptoms of a deeper alienation:

> *The members of the political state are religious through the dualism between the individual and the species-life, between the life of civil society and the political life; religious in that they hold the political life of the state, something outside their true individuality, to be their true life; religious insofar as religion is here the spirit of civil society, the expression of the separation and distancing of man from man . . . man as he has been corrupted by the entire organization of our society, as he is lost to himself, alienated, and handed over to the rule of inhuman circumstances and elements—in short, man who is not yet a true species-being.*[12]

There is a vision of two cities on offer here: one a truly political city, oriented toward man's social and species-being, his love of neighbor; the other a city in which civic life, built on egoistic foundations of private property and mediated by money and market, has alienated man from man. So long as civic life continues to contaminate the political, Marx claims, no true politics, no politics oriented toward the real being of man, is possible. Both the dualisms and loving mediations he imagines necessary to overcome them seem to me an example of what Marx mocked in his rivals: "religion rendered into thoughts and thinkingly expounded." But we need not agree on the theological flavor of Marx's ideas (and many Marxists would not). What is undeniable is the "un-critical" continuity inherent in the name Marx gave to the inhuman confusion he was criticizing. Read on just a bit more:

> *We are attempting to break with the question's theological formulation. The question of the Jews' capacity for emancipation transforms itself for us into the question: What specific* social *element needs to be overcome in order to dialectically overcome Judaism? For the contemporary Jews' capacity for emancipation is the relation of Judaism to the emancipation of the contemporary world. This relation necessarily results from the peculiar place of Judaism in the contemporary enslaved world.*
>
> *Let us consider the real worldly Jew—not, as Bauer does, the* Sabbath *Jew, but the* everyday Jew.
>
> *Let us look for the secret of the Jew not in his religion, but let us look for the secret of religion in real Jews.*
>
> *What is the worldly basis of Judaism?* Practical *need,* individual utility. *What is the worldly cult of the Jew?* Haggling. *Which is his worldly God?* Money.
>
> *So now! Emancipation from* haggling *and from* money, *that is to say, from practical, real Judaism, would be the self-emancipation of our time.*
>
> *An organization of society that overcomes the preconditions for haggling, that is, the possibility of haggling, would make the Jew impossible.... Contrariwise, if the Jew recognizes this* practical *nature of his as futile and works for its dialectical overcoming, he works himself out of his development up to that point, works for simple* human emancipation, *and converts himself against the* supremely practical *expression of human self-alienation.*
>
> *We therefore recognize in Judaism a generalized* contemporary anti-social *element, which through historical development—to which in this negative respect the Jews have eagerly contributed—has been driven to its current high level, to a height, from which it must of necessity disintegrate.*

The emancipation of the Jews, *in its ultimate meaning, is the emancipation of mankind from Judaism.*

The Jew has already emancipated himself in a Jewish way. . . . The Jew has emancipated himself in a Jewish way, not only insofar as he has acquired financial power, but also insofar as, through him and without him, money *has risen to world power and the practical Jewish spirit has become the practical spirit of the Christian peoples. The Jews have emancipated themselves to the extent that the Christians have become Jews.*

. . . Yes, the practical domination of Judaism over the Christian world has achieved as its unambiguous and normative expression in North America, so that the preaching of the Gospel *itself and the Christian ministry have become articles of trade, and the bankrupt merchant does with the Gospel the same as the rich preacher does with business deals.*

Between Marx's words here, and those from the anonymous letter written to an American editor some thirty years before, we can perceive a common register of thought. "Judaism" is, for both authors, a type of engagement with the world and one's neighbors, an excessive and misplaced attention on the accumulation of the signs, tokens, and objects of exchange. For both of them (as for Paul, Jerome, Luther), the danger of this "Judaism" is not limited to Jews: on the contrary, it threatens every Christian with "Judaizing." In fact in both authors we can already see, long before any substantial migration of living Jews across the Atlantic, how this logic is beginning to transform the United States into a "Jewish" land. (We will return to the future of this transfiguration.)[13]

There are, however, differences between the Boston editorial and Marx's treatise, and one of the more important has to do with the centrality of the "real." The reality of Judaism is not a serious concern in the anonymous letter: the sharpness of its Pauline point does not require the presence of real Jews, nor does it depend on a historical account of the true Jewishness of the practices it condemns. Its Judaism is more a moral and epistemological category than a people. Marx, on the other hand, requires the reality of his Jews and his Judaism. He claims to be providing both a sociology and a theology: a description of how *real* Jews live, and of the religion that makes them live this way. "What, in itself, was the basis of the Jewish religion? Practical need, egoism." "The bill of exchange is the real god of the Jew." "Money is the jealous god of Israel, in face of which no other god may exist." After establishing this "reality," he then makes it commutative, infectious: money, the true god of Israel, makes all of its users Jewish. "Money degrades all the gods of man—and turns them into commodities. . . . Money is the estranged essence of man's work and man's existence, and this alien essence dominates him, and he worships it. The god of the Jews has become secularized and has become the god of the world."

In my introduction I called "fundamental" Marx's insight that "the Jewish question" was as much about the basic tools and concepts through which individuals in a society relate to the world and to each other, as it was about the presence of real Judaism and living Jews in that society. Marx understood that some of these basic tools—such as money and property—were thought of in Christian culture as in some way essentially "Jewish," and that these tools could therefore produce the "Jewishness" of those who used them, whether those users were Jewish or not. "The Jew," he wrote, "is perpetually created by civil society from its own entrails." But Marx also seems to have understood the Judaism of these tools as *real*, with *real* Jews their priests and acolytes. "From the outset, the Christian was the theorizing Jew, the Jew is, therefore, the practical Christian, and the practical Christian has become a Jew again." In other words, Marx's "critical thought" provided a new and powerful confusion of the figural and the real, a confusion all the more credible for being articulated in terms of science rather than theology. Worse, his conflation elevated the specific and particular "Jewish question" posed by Bruno Bauer, about the social emancipation of the Jews, to a universal and revolutionary question, with its solution (in Marx's emphatic words) "the *emancipation of society from Judaism*," a solution all the more dangerous because of the reality it claimed for the Judaism it targeted.[14]

What led Marx to embrace these confusions and amplify them? Why did Judaism come to occupy such an important role in the criticism of society that he elaborated? Many scholars have asked these questions and come to varied answers. For some, Marx's radical critique of Judaism was simply an adaptation of Christian interpretations of the Old Testament such as those we encountered in chapter 3. For others, he is the continuator of an Enlightenment tradition, stimulated by works like Spinoza's *Theologico-Political Treatise* (which Marx had been reading prior to writing his essays of 1844) and systematized into moral philosophy by Kant and Hegel. Still others point to more contemporary intellectual influences, such as the writings of Ludwig Börne, the "radical critic" we met in the previous chapter. And many point to Marx's own Judaism, for Marx—like Börne, Heine, and a number of other radical critics—was himself the son of a Jew, his father a lawyer who had successfully striven (among other things, by converting to Christianity) to enter the world of bourgeois commercial society. Perhaps there is an oedipal force and flavor to the engagements of Marx and other radical critics who were Jews or descendants of Jews: "[F]ew generations of patriarchs were as good at raising patricides and grave diggers as first-generation Jewish liberals."[15]

We should not ask for a single explanation of the critical engagement with Judaism in these thinkers' thoughts, for the problem is "overdetermined," to borrow a word from Freud. How can we distinguish, for example, the young Börne's wounded sense that in his Jewish father's heart "[m]oney rules as law in the place of Love," from his critical interpretation of *The Merchant of Venice* as a play in which father Shylock learns that "gold is not the Lord of the world, as the Jew believes, but that love is mightier than gold"? And how do we distinguish either of these from his acute awareness of the economic and political transformations of his age? Freudian "family romance," inherited cultural forms, the rapid evolution of new types of economic and labor relations: we cannot ignore any of these if we want to understand why Börne, Marx, and many other refugees from Judaism found it as easy to theorize the evils of capitalism in terms of Jews and Judaism as non-Jews did. Moreover, the explanations are interrelated. Rebellions against Jewish fathers, "Jewish" property, "Jewish" money, the "Jewish" state: all were made meaningful—perhaps even necessary—by long habits of thought that understood human life and history in terms of the struggle to achieve the proper relation between law and love, thing and person, letter and spirit, and called the failure to achieve that ideal "Judaism." These dialectical concepts, to paraphrase Marx against his will, produced the Judaism of society out of their own entrails.[16]

"Judaism" in the Social Sciences of Modernity

My focus on Marx in these last few pages should not mislead: it is not meant to suggest that these theological habits of economic thought were particularly powerful among radicals or Marxists, or among Jews and descendants of Jews, or any other specific group. Marx deserves our attention not as an exemplary "anti-Semite," but because he is such a good example of how these habits of thought, put to work in changing historical circumstances, can create new and powerful ways of thinking about the modern world. The habits themselves, however, were widely diffused, and deployed in the service of the entire spectrum of arguments about economy and society, from the most reactionary to the most radical.[17]

Again, there are countless examples. In fact it is difficult to think of a financial innovation, practice, or crisis that was not discussed in terms of Judaism in the nineteenth and the early twentieth century. The wave of antiliberal and anticapitalist critique precipitated in German-speaking lands by the *grosse Krach*, the "great bankruptcy" of 1873, drew so insistently on that vocabulary—"Ninety percent of the jobbers and promoters are Jews!" "Semitism is subverting Germandom!"—that it has often been understood as the beginning of "political anti-Semitism" in Central Europe. Of course the crash also precipitated many defenses of liberal capitalism. These defenses, not surprisingly, also had to grapple with Jewish questions. Hence when the prominent German economist Wilhelm Roscher (1817–1894)—founder of what came to be known as "the historical school" of political economy—felt moved to respond to these anticapitalist attacks, he did so with an article entitled "The Jews' Function in the Evolution of Medieval Life."[18]

Few read Roscher and his rivals nowadays, so we will turn to two of his more famous intellectual heirs—Max Weber and Werner Sombart— to demonstrate the logic of these attacks and defenses, as well as the impact of that logic on the development of what we today call "the social sciences." It is as a founder of those sciences that Max Weber (1864–1920) appears on so many undergraduate syllabi today, where he occupies a proud place beside Karl Marx and other patriarchs of critical thought. Like many of those patriarchs, Weber was interested in the processes that seemed to characterize modern life: processes of secularization, rationalization, bureaucratization, alienation, industrialization, and state formation. These were, as Pope Leo has already told us, some of the key political questions of his age. Because the answers Weber provided to them have since become the familiar tools of social theory, we tend to forget that they were produced by, and themselves encode, many of the "Jewish questions" that marked the politics of their place and time.

Within that politics, Weber would be classified as a liberal: he even helped to draft the Weimar Constitution of 1919, the founding charter of Goebbels's "Un-Statt."[19] But long before Goebbels or the National Socialist (Nazi) Party were even dreamt of, Weber understood the threat that "Judaism" posed to liberal versions of modernity—that is, he knew that the opponents of the liberal capitalist and political order routinely attacked that order as Jewish. Weber wrote the first of his major works, *The Protestant Ethic and the Spirit of Capitalism*, as a defense against the dangers posed by such attacks. That work, whose first edition appeared in 1905, set out to defend capitalism much as Hegel had done: first, by differentiating Christian from Jewish attitudes toward property, and second, by casting capitalism not as the victory of "Jewish" materialism and literalism over Christian asceticism and spirituality, but as an Incarnational (the word is mine, not Weber's) synthesis of seeming opposites. According to Weber, Luther and Calvin's Protestantism had attained what no religion had heretofore achieved: a union of a spiritualized and transcendent religiosity with a disenchanted and rationalist ethics. The result, according to Weber, was a Protestant (and specifically Puritan) "worldly asceticism," a faith capable of reading the divine in the material, possessing a soteriology of prosperity, a "capitalist spirit."[20]

Through familiarity that famous phrase has lost its paradox, but this was not the case in 1905. To a society trained by conservative and Marxist alike to associate capitalism with the "Jewish" world of flesh and letter and not the Christian world of spirit, Weber's thesis (or rather, synthesis) was an invitation to polemic. The invitation was most famously accepted by Weber's fellow champion of historical social science, Werner Sombart (1863–1941). Sombart was at the time perhaps even more famous than Weber. His *Modern Capitalism*, first published in 1902, had immediately become a reference point on the subject (Weber's *Protestant Ethic* was in part a response to this work), but in 1911 he intervened directly in the debate with his *Jews and Economic Life* (*Die Juden und das Wirtschaftsleben*, translated in 1951 as *The Jews and Modern Capitalism*). His rebuttal of Weber was direct. The history of capitalism had nothing to do with Christian theology. It was driven instead by the migrations of the Jewish people. Wherever in the world's history economies flourished and profit grew, there could be found the Jew. "Israel passes over Europe like the sun: at its coming new life bursts forth; at its going all falls into decay." Capitalism did not develop through Christian synthesis, but from the progressive colonization of the world by the Jews.[21]

Sombart trotted through the history of Europe and its colonies in search of evidence for his thesis, with the United States as chief witness. Weber (a bit like Hegel, Börne, and Marx) had looked to North America and its Puritan settlers for the most extreme examples of his Protestant synthesis. For Sombart, American capitalism was instead the product of heavy initial settlement by Jews and crypto-Jews (by which he meant, for example, Marranos, Huguenots, and Puritans): "America in all its borders is a land of Jews." " [T]he United States (perhaps more than any other land) are filled to the brim with the Jewish Spirit." "In the face of this fact, is there not some justification for the opinion that the United States owe their very existence to the Jews? . . . For what we call Americanism is nothing else, if we may say so, than the Jewish spirit distilled."

All the various components of Sombart's ideas will be familiar to us, although like many writers on our subject, he was holding together seemingly incompatible positions. On the one hand, he wanted to insist on the "difference of our spirits"—that is, on the antagonism between "Jewish" materialism and "Christian" spirituality. The Jewish "attitude of Mammon was as opposed to [the Christian] as pole to pole." But simultaneously, he put so much stress on the infectiously Judaizing power of capitalism that the "Judaizing" Christian actually became the Jew: "All that Weber ascribes to Puritanism might . . . with equal justice be ascribed to Judaism, and probably in greater degree; nay, it might well be suggested that that which is called Puritanism is in reality Judaism." Or as he puts it in a lapidary sentence, "Puritanism *is* Judaism." We might think of Sombart's "reality" as the product of Marx's "Jewish Question" run amok, with the result a total confusion of the figural and the real. And unlike the lighthearted meteorological theories of our Boston correspondent in 1810, Sombart a century later meant his history of migration in earnest. We are not far from the animated maps of the Nazi movie *The Eternal Jew* (*Die Ewige Jude*), with its cartoon rats running along arrows meant to represent the routes of Jewish migration.[22]

For all its conventionality (or perhaps because of it), Sombart's charge of capitalism's and Puritanism's "Jewishness" had wide resonance.[23] Weber himself took it so seriously that he dedicated years of research into Jewish history and sociology to respond to it. In *Ancient Judaism* (1917–1919) and *The Sociology of Religion* (1922) he grappled again and again with the role of Jews and of the Old Testament in the genealogy of capitalism, incorporating his results into the much-revised final version of *The Protestant Ethic* (1920–1921). Throughout these works Weber deployed a number of solutions to his Jewish problem. One was to delimit the impact of Judaism on Christianity through historical periodization. Thus Weber emphasized that it was the *ancient* Israelite religious ethic of worldly action "free of magic and all forms of irrational quest for salvation" that mattered for the future of ascetic Protestantism. This ethic had been transmitted, not through contact with Rabbinic Jews, but via Christian textual engagement with the Old Testament:

> *The world-historical importance of Jewish religious development rests above all in the creation of the Old Testament, for one of the most significant intellectual achievements of the Pauline mission was that it preserved and transferred this sacred book of the Jews to Christianity. . . . Yet in so doing it eliminated all those aspects of the ethic enjoined by the Old Testament which ritually characterize the special position of Jewry as a pariah people.*[24]

A second strategy was to insist on the falseness of any apparent similarities between Rabbinic Judaism and Protestantism. For example, while it might seem that the two shared an understanding of "formal legality as a sign of conduct pleasing to God," Jewish observance of the law was in fact not the same as Protestant inner conviction, and Puritan morality had nothing to do with Talmudic legalism. Above all, Weber stressed that Jewish economic activity was fundamentally different from Protestant and bourgeois capitalism. According to him, Jewish economic thought assigned no ethical value to the outcome of transactions with non-Jews, was speculative rather than productive, and did not result in any innovations in the organization of labor.

Finally, not only were the economic ideologies different, but the one owed nothing to the other. It was in order to make this point, and thus quarantine the "spirit of capitalism" from those who would infect it with Jewish influence, that Weber invented the sociological concept of the "Jew as Pariah." The model was asserted in the opening paragraph of *Ancient Judaism*: "The problem of ancient Jewry . . . can best be understood in comparison with the problem of the Indian caste order. Sociologically speaking the Jews were a pariah people, which means, as we know from India, that they were a guest people who were ritually separated, formally or *de facto*, from their surroundings." This self-imposed "pariah" marginality meant that Diaspora Judaism had "a high capacity for innovation" but "a low capacity for diffusion." In other words, not only are the Jews not real capitalists, but they so isolated themselves that their activities contributed nothing to the economic and cultural transformation of Christendom.[25]

Weber's argument here is diametrically opposed to Sombart's: the "pariah status" in which he places the Jews serves as a *cordon sanitaire*, keeping Christian rationalism and materialism free from Jewish infection. The technique is reminiscent of Saint Augustine's, Luther's, and Hegel's. Weber posits a dialectical messianism, a fusion of godliness and worldliness in the form of an economic spirituality, and defends it from the charge of Judaizing by banishing the living Jew from dialectic, expelling both the Jews and the types of exchange negatively associated with them into an exceptional status of alien. Augustine had called that status Cain; Weber names it "pariah." Once again sociology recapitulates soteriology and draws its tools from the same kit.[26]

This technique was, as we have seen throughout this book, an infinitely flexible way of "Christianizing" relation, communication, and exchange, while projecting the inescapable residue of stigmatized materialism, literalism, or abstraction into figures of Judaism. Sombart himself would eventually embrace this flexibility. Whereas in his early writing he treated the "capitalist spirit" as entirely inimical to the true "German spirit," he later split capitalism into two "spirits," the entrepreneurial versus the commercial, trader, or bourgeois. The bourgeois commercial spirit he called "homo Judaeus," as if it were a species. The entrepreneur he identified with the German Spirit (*Volkgeist*) and turned into a Nietzschean superman, "equipped with extraordinary vitality . . . a passionate joy in work, an unbounded *drive for power* . . . a strongly developed emotional and spiritual life; a robust nature . . . men carved with an axe; smart men." This division destigmatized the economic rationality of Sombart's countrymen, so necessary to Germany's geopolitical might, while simultaneously casting England and the United States as Jewish lands: no small advantage at the time Sombart was writing, during the titanic economic and military struggles we today call World War I.[27]

The Power of Ideas

Once more I have availed myself of individual thinkers "as of a strong magnifying glass with which one can render visible a general but creeping calamity," in this case, the translation of figures of Judaism into tools of social science and economic thought. Most historians will not be satisfied with such "high intellectual" history. They will want to ask how the ideas of these thinkers participated in (which is to say, influenced and were influenced by) the ideologies of their age. To put the question in excessively zero-sum (but quite common) terms: Did these ideas influence the many millions whose actions in aggregate make up the flow of history? Or are they an effect rather than a cause, mere second-order reflections or reifications of processes determined by more powerful forces?

It is crucial for historians to reflect on such questions about the origins and causal power of ideas, but it is also crucial for them to remember that these questions are in some sense unanswerable even at the level of an individual, let alone a complex society of tens of millions. Joseph Goebbels himself provides us with an excellent example of the problem. Certainly he ranks among the most effective mobilizers of the masses in history, but he was also an "intellectual"—albeit perhaps an apostate one—who reflected a great deal on precisely these questions. He chose as the epigraph of his 1922 Heidelberg doctoral dissertation a particularly zero-sum formulation, a line plucked from Dostoevsky's *Demons*: "Reason and knowledge have played only a second-order, subordinate, servile place in the life of a Folk, and it will always be so!"

And yet the dissertation itself—on the playwright Wilhelm von Schütz (1776–1847)—depends entirely on the history of ideas. Beginning from the conviction that the early-nineteenth-century Romantics were a "mirror" for "the current decade," its central claim is that they were led astray by a philosophical error: Friedrich Schlegel's attempt to achieve a synthesis of art and philosophy, a marriage of Goethe's poetry with the thought of Fichte. This *mésalliance* produced the Romantics' alienation of the German creative spirit from true art: a Jewish "dancing before the Golden Calf" in which "irony" was raised to a central value and "matter" and "form" enslaved the spirit of the poet. Goebbels condemned all of this as false critical intellectualism, which he called "a new type of Philistinism." (*Philistinism* was a term closely related to *Judaism* in late-nineteenth- and early-twentieth-century cultural theory.) His own dissertation, he proclaimed, was part of a struggle for freedom from this "tyranny," its goal nothing less than the "overthrow" of the false synthesis.[28]

The thesis is saturated with the high-intellectual pieties of a certain segment of the age: pieties about the crisis of culture, about the yearning for higher meaning, about the grounding of poetry and art in phenomenology rather than intellect, criticism, and form. (And I hasten to add that those pieties were not only the province of third-rate minds: in a moment we will see them deployed by some of the finest philosophers of the century.) But however "high intellectual" they may be, these commitments also bear an obvious relation to the kinds of arguments that Goebbels and his associates would put at the center of their propaganda in the early 1930s, including the "rampant Jewish intellectualism" with which this chapter began.[29]

In fact, for all that Goebbels's epigraph belittled the motive force of ideas, not only his dissertation but also his propaganda constantly drew on that force. It is easy enough to show that the concept of "Jewish capital" played a central role in the National Socialists' platform and propaganda, both during the Weimar electoral campaigns of the 1920s and 1930s, and in its later efforts to mobilize German society for war. The Nazi Party wanted the German people to understand the dangers of the world they lived in through the lens of Jewish power, and to that end they produced a vast amount of propaganda materials that survive for our analysis, ranging from leaflets and posters (such as an election poster from 1924, showing a Jewish financier astride a German worker, with the words "Down with Finance Enslavement! Vote National

Socialist!"), to films like *Jüd Sus* and *Der Ewige Jude*. Thanks to meticulous record keeping, we know how these ideas were disseminated: the numbers of posters printed, the numbers of cinemas in which the movies played each week.

In the archives of the Reich's Ministry for Folk-Enlightenment and Propaganda we can even document how Goebbels and his staff mobilized some of the more academic ideas we have been exploring. During the "Battle for Britain," for example, the Reich Press Office together with the Office of Anti-Semitic Action in Goebbels's Propaganda Ministry attempted to coordinate the widespread diffusion of Wolf-Meyer Christian's *English-Jewish Alliance*, a book that explained "the inner-Jewification of English politics" by elaborating Sombart's theories about the intimate relationship between Judaism, Puritanism, and capitalism—theories that Sombart himself had aimed at the "Anglo-Saxons" during the previous Great War.[30]

And finally, plenty of evidence survives—from voting records to Anti-Semitic postcards—that can give us some access to the ways in which "ordinary people" took up the ideas on offer. We can also go to the Göttingen University Library and leaf through the children's books of the Seifert Collection—such as Ernst Hiemer's *Der Giftpilz*, "The Poison Mushroom," of 1938—to see how these ideas were offered to young minds as explanations of the world. Or at a moment when that world seemed on the point of collapse, we could join in his basement the elderly Bremen businessman Friedrich Köper, sitting out the British and American air raids of early 1945, typing away at his memoirs.[31]

Those memoirs are depressing reminders of the hold that habits of thought have over the human mind. Looking back over his life, Köper tried to describe the malignant adversary that had always opposed him, from his youth in Bremerhaven, through his successful career as an import-export merchant in Central America, to the carpet bombings of his retirement back in Germany. He called that enemy America, he called it Big Capital, but above all he called it "the Jew, "whose implacable advance he tracked from Galicia to Berlin and Hamburg, then New York, then Central America (El Salvador he identified as an especially

"Jewified" place), where they tricked the natives by appearing indistinguishable from more honest races. It was the Jews who had driven the Germans out of the world economy, and who (despite their almost total extermination from Europe by this time) were now incinerating German homes.

How much was Goebbels's propaganda influenced by the high-intellectual culture in which he himself was so well trained? And did that propaganda in turn create, amplify, or merely reflect the prejudices of the masses at which it was aimed? What, in other words, is the relationship between the ideas Goebbels discussed in the lecture halls of Heidelberg, and those that gave solace to an elderly Nazi enduring the destruction of his world? We have mountains of material from which to minc the habits of thought that interest us, but none of this material allows us to answer these questions definitively. We can choose, as so many social scientists do today, to minimize the power of ideas, making them subordinate to other (often material) interests. We can also choose to maximize the power of ideas, and treat people "deterministically" as prisoners of their forms of thought. And of course there are many less zero-sum choices we can make, each producing a different approach to history.

Which choice we make may depend on the type of question we are asking, the historical problem we are working on. On this score the historian should be reflective rather than dogmatic. But for the questions addressed in this chapter and throughout this book, it seems to me particularly important to stress the potential for interplay between the history of ideas and the ways in which individuals think about their world in any given time or place, precisely because those ideas were so widespread and so central to so many of the different discourses those individuals could draw on in order to descry and describe their world.

Another way to make my point is to reverse the question, for it is just as difficult to separate the critical ideas of intellectual elites from the political pieties of the day, as it is to do the reverse, and separate propaganda and ideology from ideas. How do the mass convictions of an age influence the inquiries of even its most critical intellectuals? The history of all the Western academic disciplines demonstrates how easily critical thought can collude with, rather than corrode, the cognitive claims of anti-Judaism. The history of early-twentieth-century philosophy provides a good example, for in it we can see some very familiar figures being deployed to explore a terrain of thought that was in some ways quite new. Familiar, for example, was the stigmatization of abstract, logical, or allegedly hyperrational thought as "Jewish." In the debates provoked within German philosophical circles by the outbreak of the First World War, it is hard not to hear echoes of Hegel's "Jewish principle of opposing thought to reality, reason to sense," his conviction that "this principle involves the rending of life," and his suggestion that Kantianism could be understood in terms of this "Judaism." With increasing stridency as defeat approached and nationalist anti-Semitism increased, critics like the philosopher Bruno Bauch attacked the teachings of the dominant neo-Kantian school of philosophy as "Jewish formalism," and derided the editorial board of the journal *Kantstudien* as "Jew-ridden." No less distinguished a scholar than Weber's colleague Ernst Troeltsch condemned the scholarship that appeared in its pages as "Jewish terrorism."[32]

We can clarify the philosophical meaning of these attacks—for we should not doubt that they were philosophically meaningful—by focusing on a slightly later episode that burned itself more deeply into historical memory. The event was a staged debate at the Swiss spa town of Davos in 1929, between Ernst Cassirer, white-haired dean of the neo-Kantians, and the young Martin Heidegger, freshly famous from the publication of his *Being and Time*. Many years after the confrontation Emmanuel Lévinas, who had been a young (and Jewish) philosopher in the audience, and very impressed by Heidegger, would recall that "a young student could have the impression that he was present at the creation and the end of the world."[33]

Why did the stakes seem so high to the participants? The Weimar context of political crisis surely contributed to the temperature. In the political imagination of the day, Cassirer and his school were associated with the old liberal order. Just a few months before, the Catholic philosopher Othmar Spann had denounced neo-Kantianism and its "foreign"

leader Cassirer (who was Jewish) before a meeting of the Kampfbund
für deutsche Kultur (Fighting League for German Culture). And even
without taking into account possible rumors about Heidegger's anti-
Semitism (Cassirer writes explicitly about such rumors in 1932) or back-
dating his embrace of the Nazi regime, already in 1929 his writings and
seminars made clear his views on liberal modernity's pernicious and
alienating effects on Germany's youth and culture.

Politics is relevant. But my point here is that the energies swirling at Davos were also generated by philosophy itself: that the power
inherent in the philosophical questions being debated, and the potential to turn those questions into "Jewish" ones, were in part generated
by the conceptual tools with which philosophers had learned to ask
and answer their questions. In 1929, those questions seemed to many
more pressing than ever. In the words of the philosopher Max Scheler
(the subject of the future Pope John Paul II's doctoral dissertation),
"[A]t no time in history has the human being become so *problematic* as
in our contemporary age." *Problematic*: perhaps an understated word
to describe a world whose confidence in the progressive promises of
modernity had been shattered by the Great War, and that nevertheless
found itself caught in a sharp struggle between new articulations—
such as capitalism and Marxism—of that modernity.

Philosophers, not surprisingly, tended to explain the crisis of modernity by criticizing the nature of modern thought. And among these
explanations, one particularly resonant one was the sense that "rationality" had overstepped its boundaries, that the claims of reason and
of science—which underpinned both capitalist and Marxist ideologies,
as well as many others—had grown so great as to threaten humanity.
One science above all was particularly disturbing to the participants at
Davos: not the new science of evolutionary biology, whose claims about
the human animal were causing consternation in the courtrooms of Ten-
nessee, but the old science of mathematics, whose victories in explaining the universe threatened to turn everything, even "thingness" and
matter itself, into symbol and form.

Think, for example, of how the new physics of the late nineteenth and the early twentieth century increasingly mathematicized the objects it studied, from the smallest (elementary particles) to the largest (the universe itself), until the quiddity of the cosmos, the very idea of metaphysical substance, disappeared into conceptual function. In the words of Albert Einstein—who had entertained the crowds at Davos the year before, lecturing on relativity and playing the violin in a trio—"[N]o sort of things are truly invariant but always only certain fundamental relations and functional dependencies retained in the symbolic language of our mathematics and physics." Space, time, matter: these were not metaphysically real substances or containers, but ideas of relation conceived of and expressed in the formal and rule-bound language of mathematics. By now it should not be too difficult to see how these conquests of symbolic thought could potentially resonate with habits of thought about Jewishness, and seem to threaten humanity with a new tyranny of "Jewish" letter, "Jewish" law.[34]

The threat is not hypothetical. In just a few years, for example, the German physicist and Nobel Prize laureate Philipp Lenard would be warning physics students not to take too much mathematics, because it carried Jewish intellectual influences that killed "feelings for natural scientific research."[35] Even German mathematicians were increasingly preoccupied with understanding their own discipline in these terms, seeking to distinguish between the fruits of the German spirit, concrete and creative, and those of Jewish intellectualism. Certain branches of mathematics, such as Georg Cantor's set theory and its axiomatization by Ernst Zermelo (who would be dismissed from the University of Freiburg in 1935 for refusing to use the Hitler salute), or invariant theory and the axiomatic abstract algebra that David Hilbert and Emmy Noether developed from it, were particularly suspect.

The classification of this mathematics as "Jewish" did not derive from the genealogy or religion of the mathematicians (Noether was Jewish; Cantor, Zermelo, and Hilbert were not). It stemmed rather from the habits of thought available to make sense of new styles and novel forms of proof in mathematics. In the new set theory, for example, the existence of a mathematical object with certain properties could be logically demonstrated without the mathematical object itself ever being exhibited. Thus Zermelo's "Axiom of Well-Ordering" proved that a well-ordering of all real numbers exists, a finding of importance to set theory and to mathematics more generally.[36] But although it makes logical sense within the axioms of the theory to say that a well-ordering of real numbers can be found, that sense is strangely unintuitive. Even if we were immortal and we spent our whole lives trying to describe such an ordering, we could not succeed. That was the basis of Henri Poincaré's objection to such axioms in his *Last Thoughts* (*Dernières pensées*) of 1912. What human sense can there be, asked the greatest French mathematician of the previous generation, in saying that something exists when that something cannot possibly be identified in any finite number of words, not even in any infinite but countable number of words?

Poincaré invoked no figures of Judaism. But in the 1920s and 1930s, some German thinkers assigned a specific name to the "un-human" sense of such axiomatics: "Jewish mathematics." The struggle between *Deutsche Mathematik* (German Mathematics) and "Judaism" in the 1920s, 1930s, and 1940s is a fascinating example of the new work that figures of Judaism could do in every corner of human thought. Readers can pursue it further in Sanford Segal's monumental *Mathematicians under the Nazis*. But what we need to note here is that this work was not some Nazi aberration, discontinuous with all previous philosophy, but rather it was rooted in a long history of addressing certain basic questions—such as the question of the relation between objects of thought in the human mind and objects as such in the world—in terms of Judaism. Rooted, but not determined. If we return for just a moment to Davos in 1929, we can see how what was being staged was a confrontation between two different visions of what the German philosophical tradition had to say about the victories of mathematics and the modern conquests of the human mind.

Cassirer saw the striving toward infinity as humanity's highest achievement, and the mathematicization of matter as the "logical conclusion of an intellectual tendency characteristic of all the philosophical and scientific thought of the modern age." This intellectual tendency was but one manifestation—the crowning one—of a basic attribute of the human condition that Cassirer, following Kant, called "spontaneity": the principle that only through the shaping of the world by forms projected spontaneously by the mind does the world appear as ordered or objective. Hence the key term of his masterwork, the three-volume *Philosophy of Symbolic Forms*:

> By symbolic form is meant that energy of the spirit through which a mental meaning-content is attached to a sensual sign and inwardly dedicated to this sign. . . . [O]ur consciousness is not satisfied to receive impression from outside, but rather it permeates each impression with a free activity of expression. In what we call the objective reality of things we are thus confronted with a world of self-created signs and images.

Symbolic form, according to Cassirer, was humanity's defining gift, and his trilogy was dedicated to documenting the unfolding of its energy of the spirit across all periods of history and domains of thought—myth, religion, philosophy, art, poetry, mathematics.

For Heidegger, by contrast, man was "the lieutenant of nothing." Finitude was the fundamental and proper attribute of the human: "the essential *dependency* of the human being on what is disclosed within experience." After the Davos debates, both in his seminars and in writings, such as *What Is Metaphysics?*, he insisted that the attempt to overcome this finitude through logic, mathematics, and scientific reason is in fact one of the greatest obstacles between us and the ground of our being. According to Heidegger, by peddling the fantasy that through reason humanity could achieve freedom from finitude, Cassirer and the neo-Kantians (like all previous practitioners of metaphysics) were producing instead the tyranny of thought.

Heidegger did not, on the public stage in 1929, put his critique in terms of Cassirer's Jewishness. But I suspect that his audience could hear a resonance between his claim that Cassirer's philosophy "blocks the path" to a deeper understanding of our humanness, that it "unties

ANTI-JUDAISM: THE WESTERN TRADITION

us from ourselves . . . [so that] our flight and disorientation, the illusion and lostness, become more acute," and the more explicitly anti-Jewish critiques of modernity that were everywhere swirling in the political discourse of the day. It is precisely because financial brokerage and modes of rationality deemed "hyperrational" were all tarred with the same brush of "Judaism" that contemporaries would have felt the anti-Jewish sting in Heidegger's curt dismissal of Cassirer's life-work on the importance of symbols and language as mediators of experience: "Mere brokerage will never amount to anything productive."[37]

Writing years later, in 1948, Cassirer's widow Toni describes the couple's feelings on the eve of the Davos meeting: "We knew of [Heidegger's] . . . hostility toward the neo-Kantians. . . . And his tendency toward anti-Semitism was not unknown to us." They feared, she writes, that Heidegger meant to drag the work of the philosopher Hermann Cohen, the (Jewish) founder of neo-Kantianism, "into the dust and, if possible, to obliterate Ernst." The year 1948 was a very different one from 1929: perhaps Mrs. Cassirer's choice of the word *vernichten* so many years later is "burdened with all the complications of historical hindsight." But in 1929, Cassirer did not need hindsight to sense that the philosophical forces arrayed against him were rooted in a long history of Judaizing symbolic mediation and exchange, and that those roots had found new nourishment in the political movements of the day.[38]

The "Jewishness" of Thought

What is true of philosophy and economics is true of many other fields as well. Most notorious are the roles played by fears of Judaism in the development of natural history and the "race sciences": biology, medicine, psychology, and evolutionary theory. Almost as well known is the work done by anti-Judaism in the scientific study of religion, a discipline whose fundamental insights sometimes seem driven by the efforts of scholars to Judaize or de-Judaize Christianity. Contemporary Jews themselves could feel an anti-Jewish animus to some of the most important developments in the field. The German scholar Julius Wellhausen's methodology, for example, produced the fundamental discovery of the "documentary hypothesis" about the origins of the Hebrew Bible. Wellhausen's school was known as "the higher criticism," and its discoveries remain important. But it was famously described by Solomon Schechter, himself a towering figure in Hebrew Bible scholarship at Cambridge and later the influential president of the Jewish Theological Seminary in New York, as "the higher Anti-Semitism" because of its stated goal of diminishing the importance of the Hebrew Bible, which (according to Wellhausen) "blocks up the access to heaven, . . . and spoils morality." Similar critiques could be made of other monumental contributions to the history of early Christianity, such as Adolf von Harnack's reconstruction of the history of Manichaeism, with its hints of nostalgia for a religion purged of the Old Testament god. And of course there were much more frankly anti-Semitic efforts at "scholarship," such as those of the Protestant "Institute for the Study and Eradication of Jewish Influence on German Religious Life" under National Socialism.[39]

We might be tempted to treat the centrality of Judaism in these disciplines as specific to them: it is after all not so surprising that racial anti-Semitism nurtured and was nurtured by biology, or that a perhaps lamentable but nevertheless legitimate religious Christian logic of supersession should be translated into science by modernity. But what should be surprising, and bears stressing, is the sheer number of fields of modern thought in which figures of Judaism were put to work, and this long before the Nazi assumption of power made such labor expedient in so much of Europe. In the world of art, for example, a thick line of scholarship—from Friedrich von Schlegel's *Paintings of the Old Masters* (1803), through Heinrich Wölfflin's *Sense of Form in Art* (1931)—made "Judaism" a respectable, meaningful, indeed even crucial term of criticism. There were of course interventions, such as Hans Günther's *Race and Style* and Paul Schultze-Naumburg's *Art and Race*, whose explicit racism made them less academically respectable. But even those who considered racial rhetoric vulgar could still share with the racists a common negative sense of the "Jewishness" of certain styles and movements. Visitors to Goebbels's monumentally successful "Degenerate Art" exhibit of 1937 (the Munich exhibit broke all modern records) might agree that modern art was in a crisis that could be explained (at least in part) in Jewish terms, even as they could disagree about the specific "Jewishness" of the 112 artists condemned in that exhibition.[40]

And of course by now we should not be surprised that of those artists, only six were Jews by "race." It was the logic of art criticism that produced "Judaism," not the real beliefs or genealogy of its object. Similar logics unfolded in all the humanistic disciplines—literary studies and music criticism, philology, historical linguistics, history—and the scientific ones as well (see the earlier discussion on mathematics and physics). These logics Judaized and de-Judaized every department of the modern German university: no discipline proved immune to them.[41]

What were the consequences of this resonance between the critical disciplines of modernity and the anti-Semitic ideologies of the same era? Again, no definitive answer to such a question is possible. A maximalist might claim that the victories of Nazi anti-Semitism were inconceivable without the conceptual work of thinkers working within a history of ideas. A minimalist might insist that the ideas of university professors were irrelevant to a mass politics driven by deeper structural or material conflict. But both would, I hope, agree that this resonance helps to explain why the German academy failed to fulfill one of the most important ideals by which universities justify their existence in the modern world: the ideal of providing the societies that support them with a space of reflection in which to put even their most sacred certainties to the test of criticism. At the very least then, we can say that what is perhaps the most spectacular modern failure of critical thought was constituted in large part by a failure to think critically about the history of its own ideas about "Judaism."

I should stress that mine is not a "deterministic" argument, whether at the level of the individual or at that of the nation. To stick with philosophy for a moment, I am not claiming that the work of Judaism across the history of ideas *determined* Heidegger's philosophical thought, or Cassirer's, or any other thinker's. Nor am I suggesting that a given philosophical position translates automatically into a political one, or vice versa. Kant did not inoculate against Nazism, and enthusiasm for Heidegger was not an index of anti-Semitism. But I am claiming that the history of ideas shapes the possibilities of thought. To borrow words yet again from Karl Marx, this time from his "Eighteenth Brumaire":

> [M]en make their own history, but they do not make it as they please; they do so not under circumstances chosen by themselves, but under circumstances . . . given and transmitted from the past. The tradition of all the dead generations weighs like a nightmare upon the brain of the living. And just when they seem engaged in revolutionizing themselves . . . creating something that has never yet existed . . . they anxiously conjure up spirits of the past to their service.

The many uses of "Judaism" in the history of ideas smoothed certain paths for critical insight and littered others with stumbling blocks. This approach helps explain, for example, why the translation of philosophical questions into Jewish ones could so easily take place, and how it could become so meaningful to so many of Germany's (but not only Germany's) philosophical minds.[42]

Nor is mine an argument for determinism at the level of the collective. I am not claiming that the long history of thinking with and about "Jewish questions" inevitably led to or caused the "Final Solution." Quite the contrary: although I have focused on Germany in this chapter because it was in fact the German government and its people who planned and implemented the Holocaust, the habits of thought that I have been describing were, with local variants, widespread throughout Europe and the United States. When, for example, English publicists wanted to criticize financial markets and economic structures in the period between 1873 and 1939, they used a rhetoric of Judaism very similar to that of the German commentators we have touched on. An observer of western European politics around 1900, asked to predict where mass political violence against the Jews was most likely to erupt, might well have nominated France. And American citizens, asked to name the greatest threat to the United States in a series of polls taken by the Opinion Research Corporation between 1939 and 1946, consistently chose "the Jews" over the Japanese or the Germans, with fear peaking in June of 1944, just as the Jewish population of Europe was close to fully exterminated.[43]

We know from internal correspondence of Goebbels's conviction that "German" habits of thought about Judaism were widely shared by the English and American people. Perhaps he was right. Where he proved wrong was in his optimism that anti-Semitism would serve as a basis of solidarity between the German and Anglo-Saxon peoples sufficient to keep the latter out of the war, a failure he explained with his usual logic. "Astonishing," he notes in his diary entry for March 7, 1942—after the House of Lords reacted to emerging rumors of genocide by observing a moment of silence for the victims—"how much the English people, above all the upper classes have become Judaized and scarcely have the English character anymore." They "have been so Jewishly infected . . . that they can scarcely . . . think as English people."[44]

In pointing to this common history, I do not mean to intervene in what German historians call the "Sonderweg" debate—that is, the question of whether the structural "Peculiarities of German History" condemned it to a unique attitude toward fascism and anti-Semitism.[45] My point is only that the long history of thought I have described was broadly shared. It shaped the worldview of many people, both among those who came with more or less willingness under Hitler's rule and among those who successfully opposed and defeated him. Perhaps that commonality can help to explain why the Germans found so many willing collaborators for their projects of extermination in many of the lands they occupied. Perhaps it explains as well why even some of the nations that most firmly resisted the German armies (the United Kingdom, the United States, and immediately after the war, the Soviet Union) nevertheless adopted important anti-Semitic measures of their own, such as closing their borders to Jews seeking to escape their executioners. But what it cannot explain is why Germany and not, say, France.[46]

In short, I do not believe that the history of thought I have attempted to sketch in these pages *determined* why Germany moved from anti-

Semitism to genocide, and other nations did not (setting aside the question of collaboration). The West's long history of Jewish questions did not "cause" the "Final Solution" or make it inevitable. It is easy enough to imagine that with only a slight alteration to just one of the countless variables at play in any given moment—What if, for example, the advocates for lower reparations had prevailed in the negotiations after Germany's surrender in World War I?—none of the many modern peoples who thought of their world in terms of "Judaism" would ever have moved to exterminate real Jews from that world.

But I do believe that the Holocaust *was inconceivable and is unexplainable* without that deep history of thought. There are undoubtedly many reasons why the extermination of millions of Jews became not only imaginable but also implementable in mid-twentieth-century Germany and not in some other place and time. But none of those other factors functioned independently of the history sketched in this book. The "Jewish" terrors that assailed Germany and many of its neighbors in the first half of the twentieth century were not reflections of reality, or eccentric fantasies imposed on a populace by a powerful propaganda machine, or even of a profound but temporary demonic possession of the German nation between 1933 and 1945 (as a synod of Catholic bishops declared immediately after the war). They were rather the product of a history that had encoded the threat of Judaism into some of the basic concepts of Western thought, regenerating that threat in new forms fitting for new periods, and helping far too many citizens of the twentieth century make sense of their world. We will fail to understand those terrors or their effects if we sunder them from what came before.

Epilogue

DROWNING INTELLECTUALS

"A PERSON STRUGGLING TO save himself from drowning becomes an intellectual, insofar as he is thinking about the conditions of his existence." The quip has been attributed to W. H. Auden, but I cannot imagine that particular poet so callously oblivious to the powers of terror, or so optimistic about intellectuals. The life of the mind is lived swaddled in habits, like any other. And although sometimes thinkers *in extremis* become capable of questioning the deepest foundations of their thought, often enough greater peril produces only a greater allegiance to previous commitments. In apocalyptic times, as William Butler Yeats put it, "The best lack all conviction, while the worst / Are full of passionate intensity."

The careers of four German-Jewish intellectuals who lived through the mid-twentieth century provide a vivid enough illustration of the very different effects that terror can have on the interrogation of Jewish questions. Hannah Arendt, our first example, abandoned her studies with the philosopher Martin Heidegger and fled Nazi Germany for Paris in 1933. It was there, while working for a Rothschild-funded initiative to help refugees, that she wrote (but never published) an essay on a

461

topic very much on her mind, entitled "Antisemitism." France soon fell, and Arendt fled once more, this time to the United States, where she became famous as a philosopher, journalist, and "public intellectual." After the war, in "Part One" of the now-classic *Origins of Totalitarianism*, she again took up the subject of anti-Semitism, this time with full knowledge of the horrors that it had generated.[1]

In both the earlier and the later essay, her question was more or less the same as mine has been throughout this book: How and why do ideas about Jews and Judaism become convincing explanations for the state of the world? She rightly stressed the failure of "Antisemitism" as a sufficient explanation. The term *anti-Semite* effectively labels its targets as enemies of Jews and Judaism, but it does not do much to explain the nature of or reason for that enmity. On the contrary, it strongly implies that there is *no reason* for that enmity, that the enmity is *irrational*. She used a joke from World War I to describe the limitations of such an approach: "An antisemite claimed that the Jews had caused the war; the reply was: Yes, the Jews and the bicyclists. Why the bicyclists? asks the one. Why the Jews? asks the other."[2]

According to Arendt, this joke sums up the main problem with the irrational "scapegoating" model of anti-Semitism: it cannot account for why one group is singled out to be the scapegoat and not another. The model "upholds the perfect innocence of the victim, an innocence which insinuates not only that no evil was done [by the victim] but that nothing at all was done [by the victim] which might possibly have a connection with the issue at stake." In other words, it completely severs what is being said about the Jews from anything that "real" Jews say or do. But if that is the case, then why pick the Jews as scapegoat?

Arendt was surely right that "an ideology which has to persuade and mobilize people cannot choose its victims arbitrarily." The choice must make cultural sense if it is to prove convincing and effective, capable of moving masses. But *why* do ideologies make cultural sense? In previous chapters, I suggested that the sense that "anti-Semitism" made in the nineteenth and twentieth centuries had much to do with the habits of thought it appealed to, and with the history of the ideas from which it was fashioned. Arendt, on the other hand, believed that the ideology made cultural sense because it described something that the Jews *really* were, something that they *really* did. The victims shared "responsibility" (her word) for the worldview built on their backs. Arendt found her strong link between ideology and reality in what she considered to be "specifically Jewish functions" related to commerce and economic circulation that developed in the modern nation-state. It was in their special commitment to bourgeois capitalism that the Jews were "co-responsible" for the reality to which they fell victim: "[A]ll economic statistics prove that German Jews belonged not to the German people, but at most to its bourgeoisie."[3]

It is a bit surprising that Arendt so often drew the necessary statistics from work produced by Nazi economists in support of party propaganda. It was, for example, to the "fighting scholarship" of Walter Frank and his "Reichsinstitut for the history of the New Germany" that she owed her indictment of the Rothschilds and other nineteenth-century Jewish bankers as "reactionary," "parasites upon a corrupt body."[4] But even if her statistics had been less obviously partial and partisan, their selection out of the world's infinite sea of significance would still be shaped by what her conceptual framework encouraged her to recognize as meaningful. In this case her negative view of "bourgeois capitalism" and its role in the nation-state, the ease with which she was willing to assume that Judaism was especially bound to money, her insistence on the "co-responsibility" of the Jews for the economic order within which they function: these were among the a priori ideological commitments that structured her selection and interpretation of "facts" about the Jews.

And here we come upon a problem as basic as the nature of knowledge itself: all of our prodigious cognitive and computational abilities are inadequate to a full comprehension of our complex world. As humans, we remain heavily dependent on certain tools of perception and conception that our cultural and biological heritages have taught us are useful. These tools—such as language, causal logic, religion, mathematics—are indeed powerful, but they are powerful precisely because they reduce complexity to intelligibility by projecting our mental concepts onto the world. One consequence of this is that our recognition of significance is always what some philosophers call "theory laden," meaning that it is shaped by what our theoretical framework and cognitive tools encourage us to recognize as meaningful. Anti-Judaism, as have argued throughout this book, is precisely this: a powerful theoretical framework for making sense of the world.

Dependent as we are on such concepts, we can also test them against our evolving experience, refining, transforming, even abandoning them. Such efforts are probably as old as human cognition itself, but scientific modernity has raised them to a defining value. In fact it is precisely this effort of testing that intellectuals and professors invoke when they claim to be engaged in "critical thought." It is therefore remarkable that Arendt clung to the views on Jewish reality and co-responsibility that she elaborated in the late 1930s, even after the full extent and fantastic projective power of Nazi anti-Semitism (including its vast exaggeration of the Jews' economic importance) became clear. After the war she applied some of these same views to a new "Jewish question," engaging in an ongoing critique of Zionism and the State of Israel—most famously in *Eichmann in Jerusalem*—that remains a touchstone for debate today.

Moreover she had little patience for those who questioned the relationship between anti-Semitism and the real. She scorned the French philosopher Jean-Paul Sartre's understanding of Judaism as a category of fantasy and projection in the thought of non-Jew (as she put it, "the Jew as someone who is regarded and defined as a Jew by others"). And her pithy mockery of approaches that looked to the long history of ideas about Judaism in order to understand modern ideologies—she dubbed these approaches "Eternal Anti-Semitism"—could serve as an ironic title for my own book. All of these attempts at reflexive criticisms of anti-Semitism she repeatedly rejected throughout the 1950s and 1960s on the grounds that they sought to deny "specific Jewish responsibility" for the phenomenon.[5]

There are many ways to explain this refusal of reflection on the part of so critical a thinker. Some have invoked Arendt's autobiography, pointing to her assimilationist childhood, to her long relationship with Heidegger, or even going so far as to suggest that she had read so much anti-Semitic literature that she began to believe it.[6] But a much more basic explanation, and one that helps us to understand not only Arendt's attitudes to Jewish questions but also those of a great many other highly intelligent people (including many Jews) of the modern era, has to do with the critical concepts with which they worked: concepts themselves produced by a history of criticizing Judaism, and hampered by that history when it came to producing a critique of the anti-Jewish critique.

My point here is similar to one made by Arendt's compatriots, Max Horkheimer and Theodor Adorno, who provide our second example. Before the war Horkheimer and Adorno had, like Arendt, explained the explosion of anti-Semitism they felt themselves to be witnessing in terms of the "real." They too criticized their fellow Jews' eager partici- pation in what they called "the sphere of circulation"—that is, finance and commerce—and understood this participation as the cause of the hatred against them. Like Arendt, they survived the war in the United States, moving in circles of refugee intellectuals that overlapped with hers. (Arendt would later describe Adorno as "one of the most repulsive human beings I know.") But they were apparently much more struck than she was by what the 1930s and 1940s revealed about the fantastic power that ideas about Jews had acquired in European thought.[7]

That power seemed to them far in excess of any "real." After all, no matter how overrepresented the Jews may have been among the Euro- pean "bourgeoisie," they remained a tiny minority of that class. How could that tiny minority convincingly come to represent for so many the evolving evils of the capitalist world order? More broadly, how could untold millions of Europeans (and not only Germans) come to believe—or act as if they believed—the claims of the Nazis (and not only the Nazis) that Jews and their conspiracies so threatened the secu- rity of the world that they needed to be excluded, expelled, or extermi- nated? According to Horkheimer and Adorno, the liquidation of the Jews of Europe was not grounded in "reality." It took place in the vast gap between an explanatory framework ("anti-Semitism") that made satisfying sense of the world to a significant portion of its citizens, and the complexity of the world itself.

They set out to explore that gap in a philosophical history of modern thought drafted in 1944 and later published as *Dialectics of Enlightenment*. Their final chapter, "Elements of Anti-Semitism: Limits of Enlightenment," suggested that what gave anti-Semitic ideas their power was not so much their relation to reality, but rather their exemption from reality checks—that is, from the critical testing to which so many other concepts were subjected. "What is pathological about anti-Semitism is not projective behavior as such, but the absence of reflection in it." In their terms, the problem is a heightened resistance to reflection about the gap between our ideas about Jews, Judaism, or Jewishness, and the complexity of the world. From their point of view, anti-Semitism provides its adherents with a cognitive comfort: the fantasy that the gap between our understanding of the cosmos and its fearful complexity does not exist.[8]

Clearly we do not want our decisions about the world to be made in the grips of fantasy or pathology. But how can we tell whether we are being adequately reflective in our "projective behavior," that is, in our deployment of our concepts into and onto the world, in order to make sense of it? The decision is all the more difficult the more such claims are made in terms consonant with our own understandings of reality. In such cases we need a point from which we can reflect on our own habits of thought. The difficulty lies, of course, in finding such a platform for perspective. On this issue, our fourth drowning intellectual expressed a profound lack of conviction. "The challenge," explained the literary scholar Erich Auerbach, writing from exile in Istanbul in October of 1938,

> is not to grasp and digest all the evil that is happening—that is not too difficult—but much more to find a point of departure (Ausgang-spunkt) for those historical forces that can be set against it. . . . The consequence: I am a teacher who does not concretely know what he should teach. . . . I could be immediately active again, if I concretely

knew how and what, in the light of every life circumstance in which I
happened to find myself—and this now hidden not only from me but
from everyone in similar circumstances, that is, from everyone who
cares for the dignity and freedom of man.[9]

In retrospect we can see that even as he wrote these words, Auerbach
was discovering the solid ground that would serve as his point of departure. He had just finished "Figura," an essay about the system of textual
interpretation at the foundations of Western Christianity. In that essay
he argued that "the Church Fathers" did not adopt a classical model of
allegory, in which the first occurrence (in this case the Old Testament) is
treated as a fiction designed to illustrate a given proposition of reality (in
this case, Christ and Christianity). Instead, they had devised a system of
interpretation in which "both occurrences are vertically linked to Divine
Providence." He called this system "figural" rather than allegorical: "Figural interpretation establishes a connection between two events or persons, the first of which signifies not only itself but also the second, while
the second encompasses or fulfills the first. The two poles of the figure
are separate in time, but both, being real events or figures, are within
time, within the stream of historical life." By opting for the figural over
the allegorical, the great architects of early Christian thought allowed the
historical truth of "Old" Israel to persist along with the spiritual truth of
the "New," rather than seeking to cast it off or leave it behind. Out of
this generative duality—according to Auerbach—there flowed the well-
springs of a specifically Western understanding of reality.[10]

Over the next four years, as German armies converged on his Turkish refuge from both north (the Balkans) and south (North Africa),
Auerbach strove—I cannot say with what level of desperation—to
expand his inquiry into what we might call the conditions of his existence. Those armies were eventually defeated, Auerbach moved to Yale,
and the results of his researches were published in 1946 as *Mimesis:
The Representation of Reality in Western Literature.* The book began
with Genesis and the Odyssey, ended with Proust and modernity, and
quickly became a classic of literary studies.[11]

It is easy enough to imagine Auerbach's Nazi-era projects as a response to those, such as the anti-Semitic ideologue Alfred Rosenberg and the "German Christians," who fantasized the perfection of the new through the elimination of the Old: "The Old Testament as a book of religious instruction must be abolished once and for all. With it will end the unsuccessful attempts of the last one-and-a-half millennia to make us all spiritual Jews." I say *imagine* because oddly enough nowhere in these published works did Auerbach himself explicitly relate his questions about the Western "representation of reality" to "Jewish questions," although we know from his letters that precisely such a relation weighed heavily on his mind. *Jews*, *Judaism*, *Judaizing*: these terms are curiously absent from his pages.[12]

Nevertheless it should not be difficult to see how those pages—as well as the very different ones of his three colleagues in exile—have inspired mine. Throughout this book I have tried to show how, across several thousand years, myriad lands, and many different spheres of human activity, people have used ideas about Jews and Judaism to fashion the tools with which they construct the reality of their world. The goal of my project, like Horkheimer and Adorno's, is to encourage reflection about our "projective behavior," that is, about the ways in which our deployment of concepts into and onto the world might generate "pathological" fantasies of Judaism. And my choice of method owes something to Auerbach's conviction that the study of a given moment, problem, or even a single word in the distant past can teach us something about a much longer history, extending even to our own.[13] As he put it in the concluding words of "Figura,"

> *Our purpose was to show how on the basis of its semantic development a word may grow into a historical situation and give rise to structures that will be effective for many centuries.*

In *Mimesis* Auerbach gave this starting point a new name: not the *Ausgangspunkt* of his despairing letter of 1938, but a near synonym, *Ansatzpunkt*: a semantic point of departure from which major historical movements become visible. The concept has proved fruitful, not least for the literary theorist and advocate for Palestinian rights Edward Said, who found in it a methodological foundation for his famous history—*Orientalism* (1978)—of Western ideas about Islam. From the beginning of his career to its end, Said found stimulus in Auerbach's work, which offered him a way to approach questions fundamental to historical thought. In *Beginnings: Intention and Method*, for example, he provided one version of those questions: "Is the beginning simply an artifice, a disguise that defies the perpetual trap of forced continuity? Or does it admit of a meaning and a possibility that are genuinely capable of realization?"[14]

I would adopt the formulation, though without the emphasis on origins. Like all books, mine began because books must. But it started in the present, and its first destination in the past was a matter of choice rather than necessity. We could as well have begun among the Greeks, debating distinctions between body and soul in their philosophy, or with the biblical Hebrews complaining about the many crimes and hypocrisies of Israel, as on the sand-strewn island of Elephantine on the Nile. Perhaps some histories can be tied to an origin or an *Ansatzpunkt*, but this is not one of them. The history of thinking with Judaism is too overdetermined to admit of one "point of departure." The question for us is not one of beginnings, but of what Said elegantly called meaning, possibility, and realization.

My history of thinking with and about Judaism has been animated by the conviction that there is a relationship between past and present—in this case, a relationship between the ways people have thought with and about "Judaism," "Israel," "Jews," and "Judaizing" at different times and places. By *relationship*, I mean that some aspect of the past may contribute to the possibility of (or be realized in) a given future, and that conversely, we can gain some sense of the possibilities of our present by thinking critically about our past. This is (to repeat my cautions from the introduction) certainly not to say that the relationship is one of responsibility, causality, or necessity. I am, for example, not suggesting that the gospels caused genocide, or that Saint Paul is responsible for the many futures of his warning that "the letter kills, but the spirit gives life."

What then *is* the relationship? For as long as they have been writing, historians have attempted to describe it, primarily through metaphors (the notion of "beginning" itself being such a metaphor). None has proved adequate. Least adequate of all are those—sometimes called "positivists"—who claim to deduce a future or end condition from some given moment in the past. Postmodern historians have tended to refuse this temptation, but their own proposals remain insufficient. In the conclusion of my first book I embraced one of Walter Benjamin's metaphors:

> *History rests collected in a focal point, as formerly in the utopian images of thinkers. The elements of the end condition are not present as formless tendencies of progress, but instead are embedded in every present as endangered, condemned, and ridiculed creations and ideas.*[15]

But even Benjamin's metaphor gives too strong a sense of direction to history. We know from bitter experience that communities can invent their past; that historians can find hoary hat pegs on which to hang new headgear. If we have the power to project into the past (at least some of) the elements of our present condition, then the "embedding" in every moment of some germ of futurity does not suffice as a metaphor for the relation between past and present.

There are good reasons for our inability to stipulate the relationship between past and present, reasons that have to do not only with the complexity of history but also with the nature of historical knowledge, and of the objects with which it is concerned. We can leave those reasons to different authors and different books. To justify this one, we need only agree that the difficulty of describing a relationship does not mean that a relationship doesn't exist, or that it isn't meaningful or important. We cannot document precisely how nineteenth- and early-twentieth-century debates over the "Jewishness" of rational thought contributed to the appeal of mid-twentieth-century anti-Semitic ideologies, any more than we can easily explain last night's troubling dream in terms of the day, the week, or even the lifetime that came before. But we would not therefore be entitled to assert that there is nothing to be learned from dreams, or from thinking about possible connections across historical time. Even less would we be justified in insisting that thinking about such connections would itself constitute an egregious historical mistake.

There is no metaphor, no model, no formula that can securely relate to one another all the moments in this long history that I have produced, or for that matter in any other history. Does this mean that we historians should sever all the more severely, isolating each moment from all others? As I wrote at the beginning of this book, that depends on whether you think the greater danger lies in inventing continuities or in forgetting them. For many historians who came of age in the 1960s and after, the most urgent task seemed to be the dismembering of a tradition of history writing whose continuities and genealogies they thought underpinned colonialism, imperialism, and racism, to name just a few of the -isms they sought to combat.

I don't claim to speak for a generation, only for myself. To me it seems that—at least in terms of the work that figures of Judaism do in our thinking about the world—the risks of hyper-sectioning the history of thought are once again as real as those of overdetermining it. We live in an age in which millions of people are exposed daily to some variant of the argument that the challenges of the world they live in are best explained in terms of "Israel." For this reason I have chosen to write a history that takes seriously the possibility that how we have thought about the world in the past affects how we think about the world in the present, while at the same time attempting not to forget that how we are thinking about our present affects how we think about the past. Holding both those possibilities in balance—exploring past ideas about Judaism and their many futures, while at the same time insisting that those futures themselves affect how we can think about the past—is the greatest challenge of this history, as it is of any other.

I may be wrong about the risk, wrong in my sense of where the greater danger lies, and therefore wrong in how I have chosen to approach the past. The same could and should be said of any history worthy of the name, for on these vital matters all historians' choices depend on their sense of the future. This is one meaning of the words from Walter Benjamin cited already in the Introduction: "[C]riticism and prophecy must be the two categories that meet in the salvation of the past." My sense of the future's dangers, like every other historian's, may well turn out to be untrue. But in such matters of prophecy, as God explained to Jonah, we should take joy in being proved wrong.

David Nirenberg
Abbey of Montserrat,
January 27, 2012

ACKNOWLEDGMENTS

A BOOK AS BROAD as this one must depend more than most on the kindness of colleagues. I am all the more grateful to those who read drafts of chapters and did their generously critical best to keep me from error: Antón Barba-Kay, David Bell, Paul Cheney, Jeremy Cohen, Michael Cook, Bradin Cormack, Fred Donner, Michael Geyer, Sean Hannan, Galit Hasan-Rokem, Richard Jasnow, Meirav Jones, Sara Lipton, Yitzhak Melamed, Margaret Mitchell, Angelika Neuwirth, Isabel Nirenberg, Ricardo Nirenberg, Robert Pippin, Eran Shalev, Brenda Shapiro, Andrea Sterk, Richard Strier, and Sofía Torallas Tovar. I have surely forgotten to mention others who offered council over the decade it has taken me to write this book. I hope they will forgive me.

I thank as well the institutions that supported my work over these years: the Johns Hopkins University, the Wissenschaftskolleg of Berlin, and the University of Chicago. It is humbling to think of how much each of these great communities of learning has contributed to the world's collective intellect, let alone my own. The world of publishing is also an important part of that collective intellect, and there too I have been fortunate. Georges Borchardt and my editor, Steve Forman, showed faith in the project from the start. Every reader of this book (and of many others) should be as grateful as I am to Steve's persistent advocacy for clarity. Where I have failed him, it is no fault of his own.

Perhaps parents are the beginning of every book, certainly of this one. It is to them, and to my son Alexander, whose ever-waxing soul has inspired and sustained me for years, that I dedicate this book. And to Sofía: the least of my debts to you is that without your love this book would never have been finished; the greatest, that with it a new life has begun.

NOTES

INTRODUCTION: THINKING ABOUT JUDAISM, OR THE JUDAISM OF THOUGHT

1 Karl Marx, "Zur Judenfrage," in Karl Marx and Friedrich Engels, *Werke*, 43 vols. (Berlin: Dietz, 1956–1990), 1:347–377, here 374.

2 For a recent history of anti-Semitism, readers can turn to Robert S. Wistrich, *A Lethal Obsession: Anti-Semitism from Antiquity to Global Jihad* (New York: Random House, 2010). Mine is a different project.

3 Even Jean-Paul Sartre, writing passionately about the need to welcome returning Jews to a newly liberated France, could not let go of the conviction that in a more perfect world the particularities of Judaism would vanish into one universal French identity—and this at a time when, in the not-yet-liberated East, Jews were still being liquidated in the name of a competing program for the improvement of society.

4 "Kultur ist was ein Jud' vom anderen abschreibt": Reichsrat Deputy Bielohlawek, quoted in Friedrich Heer, *Land in Strom der Zeit* (Vienna: Herold, 1958), 295.

5 This also means, however, that I have had to neglect important areas where my linguistic competence is inadequate, most notably Byzantium and eastern Europe.

6 Jules Michelet, *Introduction to Universal History*, quoted in Edmund Wilson, *To the Finland Station* (1940; New York: New York Review of Books, 2003), 10. The passage is striking, not least because of its terms of martial dualism, which, as we will see in chaps. 2 and 3, came early to be thought of as a war of Christian spirit and liberty against Jewish matter and fatality. On Michelet's association of the Jews with slavery and tyranny, see Jacob Katz, *From Prejudice to Destruction: Anti-Semitism, 1700–1933* (Cambridge, MA: Harvard University Press, 1980), 131–132. The German philosopher Georg Wilhelm Friedrich Hegel (whom we will meet again in chaps. 12 and 13) proposed an (equally Christian) "union of *freedom* and *necessity*" as one of the universal aims of "the process of World History." See Hegel, "Introduction," in his *Philosophy of History*, trans. J. Sibree (Amherst, NY: Prometheus, 1991), 25–26.

7 Max Weber, *Einleitung in Die Wirtschaftsethick der Weltreligionen*, Max Weber Gesamtausgabe [MWG], sect. 1, vol. 19 (Tübingen: Mohr Siebeck, 1989), 101. I trust it will be clear that my position is not Weber's. Neither is it that of Jacob Katz: "It is, of course, important to know the sources of anti-Semitic ideologies, how their ideas were passed down from one source to the next, who was influenced by whom, and the like. However, the more significant question is what were the social intentions and political goals that motivated the ideologues to use these ideas, and how did they adapt them to the needs of the situation at each particular time." Katz, *From Prejudice to Destruction*, 9. I am not attempting to trace the dissemination of ideas, nor do I understand them primarily as the tools of ideologues. I am interested in how the possibilities of thought about Jews and Judaism are transformed by individuals putting their fundamental concepts and habits of thought to new kinds of work.

8 Seneca, *Epistulae Morales* 89.3, cited by Michel de Montaigne in "On Experience," in *The Essays: A Selection*, trans. M. A. Screech (London: Penguin Books, 2004), 3.13, 366.

9 Following Nietzsche, Michel Foucault (somewhat confusingly) used the term *genealogy* to describe his antithetical alternative to the histories produced by this fantasy, a history that does not "go back in time to restore an unbroken continuity that operates beyond the dispersion of forgotten things . . . [that] does not resemble the evolution of a species or map the destiny of a people." See M. Foucault, "Nietzsche, Genealogy, History," in D. Bouchard, ed., *Language, Counter-Memory, Practice* (Ithaca, NY: Cornell University Press, 1977), 154, 162; and Foucault, *Il faut défendre la société*, Cours au Collège de France, 1976 (Paris: Gallimard, 1997), 10. Masks: I take the liberty of personifying concepts here, a liberty authorized by Nietzsche's aphorism in "Beyond Good and Evil," sect. 40, on the mask as a necessary form of presentation for every "great spirit." Quote "All great things" is from Nietzsche's "Preface" to the same work.

10 On Pharisees as strivers after reputation for wisdom, see Matt. 23:5–12. Quote with "little children" is from Luke 10:21; Matt. 11:25–26. Goebbels's speech is discussed in chap. 13, 423–424.

11 "Just as a man": Walter Benjamin, *The Origin of German Tragic Drama*, trans. John Osborne (London: Verso, 1977), 53–54. "[C]riticism and prophecy": R. Tiedemann and H. Schweppenhäuser, eds., *Gesammelte Schriften* (Frankfurt: Suhrkamp, 1991), vol. 1, pt. 3, 1245.

CHAPTER 1: THE ANCIENT WORLD

1 Josephus, *Against Apion* 1.1. I translate from the Greek text in Josephus, *The Life: Against Apion*, ed. H. St. J. Thackeray, Loeb Classical Library 186 (Cambridge, MA: Harvard University Press, 1926).

2 On the figure of Babylon, see Ulrike Sals, *Die Biographie der "Hure Babylon": Studien zur Intertextualität der Babylon-Texte in der Bibel* (Tübingen: Mohr Siebeck, 2004); and Alice Ogden Bellis, "The Changing Face of Babylon in Prophetic/Apocalyptic Literature: Seventh Century BCE to First Century CE and

Beyond," in Lester L. Grabbe and Robert D. Haak, eds., *Knowing the End from the Beginning: The Prophetic, the Apocalyptic, and Their Relationships* (New York: T & T Clark, 2003), 65–73.

3 Interest in this afterlife animates studies such as Peter Schäfer's *Judeophobia: Attitudes toward the Jews in the Ancient World* (Cambridge, MA: Harvard University Press, 1997).

4 See Daniel Kahn, "Judean Auxiliaries in Egypt's Wars against Kush," *Journal of the American Oriental Society* 127 (2007), 507–516; Bezalel Porten, "Settlement of the Jews at Elephantine and the Arameans at Syene," in Oded Lipschits and Joseph Blenkinsopp, eds., *Judah and the Judeans in the Neo-Babylonian Period* (Winona Lake, IN: Eisenbrauns, 2003), 451–470; and Pierre Grelot, "Elephantine: Araméens et Juifs en Egypte," *Monde de la Bible* 45 (1986), 32–35.

5 On religious practices in Elephantine, see Thomas Bolin, "The Temple of YHW at Elephantine and Persian Religious Policy," in Diana Edelman, ed., *The Triumph of Elohim: From Yahwisms to Judaisms* (Kampen: Kok Pharos, 1995), 127–142; Paul-Eugène Dion, "La religion des papyrus d'Éléphantine: un reflet du Juda d'avant l'exil," in Ulrich Hübner and Ernst Axel Knauf, eds., *Kein Land für sich allein: Studien zum Kulturkontakt in Kanaan, Israel/Palästina und Ebirnari für Manfred Weippert zum 65. Geburtstag* (Göttingen: Vandenhoeck & Ruprecht, 2002), 243–254; Ingo Kottsieper, "Die Religionspolitik der Achämeniden und die Juden von Elephantine," in Reinhard Kratz, ed., *Religion und Religionskontakte in Zeitalter der Achämeniden* (Gütersloh: Kaiser Gütersloher Verlagshaus, 2003), 150–178; and M. Alyoueny, "The Religion of the Elephantine Jews," *Beit Mikra* 26 (1981), 217–230.

6 On Cambyses's conquest, see Heike Sternberg-El Hotabi, "Die persische Herrschaft in Ägypten," in Kratz, ed., *Religion und Religionskontakte*, 111–149; and Edwin Yamauchi, "Cambyses in Egypt," in Joseph Coleson and Victor Matthews, eds., *"Go To the Land I Will Show You": Studies in Honor of Dwight W. Young* (Winona Lake, IN: Eisenbrauns, 1996), 371–392. For discussion of the chronology, see D. Devauchelle, "Un problem de chronologie sous Cambyse," *Transeuphratène* 15 (1998), 9–17.

7 Ananiah's collection was edited by Emil G. Kraeling, *The Brooklyn Museum Aramaic Papyri: New Documents of the Fifth Century B.C. from the Jewish Colony at Elephantine* (New Haven, CT: Yale University Press, 1953); the collections from Mibtahiah and Jedaniah were edited by A. Cowley, *Aramaic Papyri of the Fifth Century B.C.* (Oxford: Clarendon Press, 1923). Further documents were discovered at Hermopolis. All these collections have been republished, together with Hebrew and English translations, by Bezalel Porten and Ada Yardeni, *Textbook of Aramaic Documents from Ancient Egypt*, vol. 1: *Letters* (Winona Lake, IN: Eisenbrauns, 1986), and vol. 2: *Contracts* (Jerusalem: Hebrew University, 1989) [henceforth *TAD* and cited as A and B, respectively, followed by document number]. The entirety is translated in Bezalel Porten et al., eds., *The Elephantine Papyri in English: Three Millennia of Cross-cultural Continuity and Change* (Leiden: Brill, 1996). In subsequent notes, I cite first Cowley (C), followed by Porten et al. (B), and then Porten-Yardeni's *TAD*. On the archive generally, see

Bezalel Porten, *Archives from Elephantine: The Life of an Ancient Jewish Military Colony* (Berkeley: University of California Press, 1986).

8 C30/B19/*TAD* A4.7.13; C31/B20/*TAD* A4.8.

9 C27/B17/*TAD* A.5; C27/A4.5:1–2.

10 C21/B13/*TAD* A4.1 On the status of this text, see Erasmus Gass, "Der Passa-Papyrus—Mythus oder Realität?" *Biblische Notizen* 99 (1999), 55–68.

11 C21/B13/*TAD* A.4.1. The reconstruction of line 3 is from Porten, *Archives from Elephantine*, 129 and 311–312, following suggestions by Grelot, "Études sur le 'papyrus pascal' d'Éléphantine," *Vetus Testamentum* 4 (1954), 349–384; and K. Galling, *Studien zur Geschichte Israels im persischen Zeitalter* (Tübingen: Mohr, 1964), 152ff. See also Schäfer, *Judeophobia*, 124–126.

12 C30/B19/*TAD* A4.7, 14–43. See also C31/B20/A4.8.

13 See James Lindberger, "What Ever Happened to Vidranga? A Jewish Liturgy of Cursing from Elephantine," in P. M. M. Daviau, John Wevers, and Michael Weigl, eds., *The World of the Aramaeans* (Sheffield: Sheffield Academic Press, 2001), 3:134–157.

14 Josephus, *Against Apion* 1.224–225.

15 On multicultural history, see François Hartog, *Mémoire d'Ulisse: Récits sur la frontière en Grèce ancienne* (Paris: Gallimard, 1996), 73–75. On Hecataeus specifically, see also Donald Redford, *Pharaonic King-lists, Annals, and Daybooks: A Contribution to the Study of the Egyptian Sense of History* (Mississauga, Ontario: Benben, 1986), 281–282.

16 Hecataeus of Abdera, *Aegyptiaca*, excerpts in Diodorus, *Library of History*, 40.3, here 3, 1–3, trans. Diodorus Siculus, *The Library of History*, ed. F. R. Walton and R. M. Geer, Loeb Classical Library 423 (Cambridge, MA: Harvard University Press, 1967), 12:279–283. The Greek description of unsociability: "apanthrōpon tina kai misoxenon bion." On the complexities of this fragment, see Lester Grabbe, "Hecataeus of Abdera and the Jewish Law: The Question of Authenticity," in Ingo Kottsieper, Rüdiger Schmitt, and Jakob Wöhrle, eds., *Berührungspunkte: Studien zur Sozial- und Religionsgeschichte Israels und seiner Umwelt* (Münster: Ugarit, 2008), 613–626; Rainer Albertz, "An End to the Confusion? Why the Old Testament Cannot Be a Hellenistic Book!" in Lester Grabbe, ed., *Did Moses Speak Attic? Jewish Historiography and Scripture in the Hellenistic Period* (Sheffield: Sheffield Academic Press, 2001), 30–46; and Doron Mendels, "Hecataeus of Abdera and a Jewish 'Patrios Politeia' of the Persian Period (Diodorus Siculus XL 3)," *Zeitschrift für die alttestamentliche Wissenschaft* 95 (1983), 96–110.

17 On this debate, see John Gager, *The Origins of Anti-Semitism: Attitudes toward Judaism in Pagan and Christian Antiquity* (Oxford: Oxford University Press, 1983), esp. 39–40, 69–76; Gager argues that Hecataeus's "noncondemnatory" rhetoric was transmuted into anti-Judaism by subsequent Greek writers. Against this, see Schäfer, *Judeophobia*, 15–39, who contends that the basic elements of anti-Judaic rhetoric can already be found in Hecataeus and Manetho. See also Katell Berthelot, "Hecataeus of Abdera and Jewish 'Misanthropy'," *Bulletin du Centre de Recherche Français à Jérusalem* 19 (2008), at http://bcrfj.revues.org.

18 In subsequent notes, citations for quotes from Manetho are given by fragment (frag.) number from W. G. Waddell, *Manetho with an English Translation*, Loeb Classical Library (Cambridge, MA: Harvard University Press, 1948), followed by the passage of Josephus that cites them. On Josephus's Manetho, see Lucia Raspe, "Manetho on the Exodus: A Reappraisal," *Jewish Studies Quarterly* 5 (1998), 124–155; Miriam Pucci Ben Zeev, "The Reliability of Josephus Flavius: The Case of Hecataeus' and Manetho's Accounts of Jews and Judaism," *Journal for the Study of Judaism in the Persian, Hellenistic, and Roman Periods* 24 (1993), 215–234.

19 Manetho, frag. 42; Josephus, *Against Apion* 1.228.

20 Josephus, *Against Apion* 1.229.

21 Manetho, frag. 54; Josephus, *Against Apion*, 1.232–249.

22 For these and other examples, see Menahem Stern, ed. and trans., *Greek and Latin Authors on Jews and Judaism*, 3 vols. (Jerusalem: Israel Academy of Sciences and Humanities, 1974–1984).

23 On brush versus calamus, see J. Manning and J. D. Sosin, "Palaeography and Bilingualism: P.Duk.inv. 320 and 675," *Chronique d'Égypte* 78 (2003), 202–212; and W. J. Tait, "Rush and Reed: The Pens of Egyptian and Greek Scribes," in *Proceedings of the XVIII International Congress of Papyrology*: Athens, 25–31 May 1986 (Athens: Greek Papyrological Society, 1988), 2:477–481. Presumably Manetho used a calamus when he wrote Greek.

24 On the Hyksos, see Raymond Goharghi, "The Land of Goshen in Egypt: The Hyksos," *Bulletin on Biblical Studies* 18, no. 1 (1999), 99–131. The association of Hyksos ("rulers of foreign lands") with "shepherds" is a false etymology. See "Hyksos" in Donald Redford, chief ed., *The Oxford Encyclopedia of Ancient Egypt*, 3 vols. (New York: Oxford University Press, 2001). The etymology is Manetho's, frag. 42; Josephus, *Against Apion* 1.82–83.

25 The Hyksos retreated to Palestine ca. 1555 BCE, but remained a threat for another half century or more. The "New Kingdom" (eighteenth through twentieth dynasties) lasted from roughly 1569 BCE (shortly before the expulsion of the Hyksos) to around 1076 BCE. See "Chronology" and "New Kingdom" in Redford, ed., *Oxford Encyclopedia of Ancient Egypt*.

26 John J. Collins, "Reinventing Exodus: Exegesis and Legend in Hellenistic Egypt," in Randal A. Argall, Beverly A. Bow, and Rodney A. Werline, eds., *For a Later Generation: The Transformation of Tradition in Israel, Early Judaism, and Early Christianity* (Harrisburg, PA: Trinity, 2000), 52–62, explores this association of the Jews with the Hyksos, drawing out the political implications of the retelling of Exodus narratives by both Jews and Egyptians. On this, see also Philip Davies, "Judeans in Egypt: Hebrew and Greek Stories," in Grabbe, ed., *Did Moses Speak Attic?* 108–128.

27 *Oracle of the Lamb* is edited by K. Th. Zauzich, "Das Lamm des Bokchoris," in *Papyrus Erzherzog Rainer. Festschrift zum 100-jährigen Bestehen der Papyrussammlung der Österreichischen Nationalbibliothek* (Vienna: Brüder Hollinek, 1983), vol. 1:165–174. It is a composite text and difficult to date, but the extant version was put together some time after 168 BCE. For a survey of the scholar-

ship, see Roberto Gozzoli, *The Writing of History in Ancient Egypt during the First Millennium BCE: Trends and Perspectives* (London: Golden House, 2006), 293–297. On the genre of prophecy in Egyptian/Demotic literature, see Ludwig Koenen, "Die Prophezeiungen des Töpfers," *Zeitschrift für Papyrologie und Epigraphik* 2 (1968), 178–209.

28 See also frag. 1 of the first-century Egyptian priest Chaeremon, in P. W. Van der Horst, ed. and trans., *Chaeremon. Egyptian Priest and Stoic Philosopher* (Leiden: Brill, 1984), 8–9, 49–50. In this tradition the conflict was understood as an enduring confrontation between the followers of Isis and Osiris, and worshippers of Seth (= Baal). On this tradition's place in Egyptian anti-Judaism, see Jan-Willem van Henten and Ra'anan Abusch, "The Jews as Typhonians and Josephus' Strategy of Refutation in Contra Apionem," in Louis H. Feldman and John R. Levison, eds., *Josephus' Contra Apionem: Studies in Its Character and Context with a Latin Concordance to the Portion Missing in Greek* (Leiden: Brill, 1996).

29 One example is the Ipuwer papyrus. See Barry Kemp, *Ancient Egypt: Anatomy of a Civilization* (New York: Routledge, 2006), 66–69.

30 Redford, *Pharaonic King-lists*, 260–261, 264–265. Very early examples of such a lamentation are the fragments from the palace at Tod, celebrating the achievements of Senwosret I, of the Twelfth Dynasty (1971–1928 or 1958–1913 BCE).

31 Jan Assmann, *Moses the Egyptian: The Memory of Egypt in Western Monotheism* (Cambridge, MA: Harvard University Press, 1997), 28; Alan H. Gardiner, *Late Egyptian Stories* (Brussels: Édition de la Fondation égyptologique Reine Élisabeth, 1932), 85; and Hans Goedicke, *The Quarrel of Apophis and Seqenenre* (San Antonio, TX: Van Siclen, 1986), 10–11. See also Assmann's *Of God and Gods: Egypt, Israel, and the Rise of Monotheism* (Madison: University of Wisconsin Press, 2008).

32 On the parallels, see Assmann, *Moses the Egyptian*, 180–191. Other somewhat recent considerations of this relationship can be found in Carsten Knigge, "Überlegungen zum Verhältnis von altägyptischer Hymnik und alttestamentlicher Psalmendichtung: Zum Versuch einer diachronen und interkulturellen Motivgeschichte," *Protokolle zur Bibel* 9 (2000), 93–122; Paul Dion, "YHWH as Storm-god and Sun-god: The Double Legacy of Egypt and Canaan as Reflected in Psalm 104," *Zeitschrift für alttestamentliche Wissenschaft* 103 (1991), 43–71; and Donald Redford, "The Monotheism of the Heretic Pharaoh," *Biblical Archaeology Review* 13, no. 3 (1987), 16–32.

33 See Sigmund Freud, *Moses and Monotheism*, trans. Katherine Jones (New York: Knopf, 1939), e.g., 39–40 (on Moses's connections to the pharaonic house) and 93.

34 On Manetho's blurring of the Amenophis "trauma" with the figure of the foreign invader, see Assmann, *Moses the Egyptian*, 30. Assmann's "mnemohistory" emphasizes post-traumatic reworkings of the past. Cf. his "Freuds Moses und das kollektive Gedächtnis," in Eveline List, ed., *Der Mann Moses und die Stimme des Intellekts: Geschichte, Gesetz, und Denken in Sigmund Freuds historischem Roman* (Innsbruck: StudienVerlag, 2008), 81–96. Given the ideological

importance of "origins," and especially of the origins of monotheism and of the Jews, debates over the truth value of Manetho's Egyptian Moses will continue. Edward Said's *Freud and the Non-European* (New York: Verso, 2003), e.g., sees in Freud's theory the negation of any modern Jewish claim to ethnic or religious distinctiveness.

35 It is impossible to date all of the individual components of the text, but the composition as a whole is generally ascribed to the fifth century. See Jacob Neusner, *Lamentations Rabbah: An Analytical Translation* (Atlanta, GA: Scholars, 1989), 1–2.

36 Salomon Buber, ed., *Midrasch Echa Rabbati (Lamentations Rabbah)* (Vilna, 1899; Hildesheim: George Olms, 1967), 4:17, sect. 20, 152. Cf. Rashi on Lam. 4:17. See also Jer. 37:7: "Yahweh, God of Israel, says this, 'To the king of Judah who sent you to consult me make this reply: "Is Pharaoh's army marching to your aid? It will withdraw to its own country, Egypt. The Chaldeans will return to attack this city; they will capture it and burn it down." ' " According to the rabbis, Jeremiah had opposed this alliance with the Egyptians: Lamentations Rabbah 4:152; Louis Ginzberg, *The Legends of the Jews* (1913; Philadelphia, PA: Jewish Publication Society of America, 1939), 4:296–297, 6:389, n. 17.

37 Josephus, *Against Apion* 1.279.

38 Like Hecataeus and Manetho, we know of Artapanus only because fragments of his work are preserved in later histories, in Artapanus's case those of the Greek historian Alexander Polyhistor. For the fragments, see Felix Jacoby, *Fragmente der Griechischen Historiker* (Leiden: Brill, 1954), vol. 3, C no. 726, 680–686. On Artapanus, see Howard Jacobson, "Artapanus Judaeus," *Journal of Jewish Studies* 57 (2006), 210–221; Rob Kugler, "Hearing the Story of Moses in Ptolemaic Egypt: Artapanus Accommodates the Tradition," in Anthony Hilhorst and George H. van Kooten, eds., *The Wisdom of Egypt: Jewish, Early Christian, and Gnostic Essays in Honour of Gerard Luttikhuizen* (Leiden: Brill, 2005), 67–80; and Erkki Koskenniemi, "Greeks, Egyptians, and Jews in the Fragments of Artapanus," *Journal for the Study of the Pseudepigrapha* 13 (2002), 17–31.

39 Johannes Hermann and Friedrich Baumgärtel, *Beiträge zur Entstehungsgeschichte der Septuaginta* (Berlin: Kohlhammer, 1923), 48ff.; and Avigdor Tcherikover and Alexander Fuks, *Corpus Papyrorum Judaicarum* (Cambridge, MA: Harvard University Press, 1957) [henceforth *CPJ*], 1:32, 42. An Egyptian Jewish account of the tradition is provided by the second-century BCE *Letter of Aristeas* (Moses Hadas, trans., *Aristeas to Philocrates: The Letter of Aristeas* [New York: Ktav, 1973]; and André Pelletier, ed., *La Lettre d'Aristée à Philocrate* [Paris: Éditions du Cerf, 1962]), but scholarship is sharply divided about its reliability. Arie van der Kooij, e.g., preserves the hope that the letter can tell us something about the Septuagint and its Alexandrian context: "The Promulgation of the Pentateuch in Greek according to the Letter of Aristeas," in Anssi Voitila and Jutta Jokiranta, eds., *Scripture in Transition: Essays on Septuagint, Hebrew Bible, and Dead Sea Scrolls in Honour of Raija Sollamo* (Leiden: Brill, 2008), 179–191. Against that hope, see Paul Carbonaro, "Aristobule et Hécatée d'Abdère," *Ephemerides Theologicae Lovanienses* 84 (2008), 181–193. Tessa

Rajak attempts a mediation in "Translating the Septuagint for Ptolemy's Library: Myth or History?" in Martin Karrer and Wolfgang Kraus, eds., *Die Septuaginta: Texte, Kontexte, Lebenswelten* (Tübingen: Mohr Siebeck, 2008), 176–193. See also Erich S. Gruen, "The Letter of Aristeas and the Cultural Context of the Septuagint," in ibid., 134–156; and more generally Abraham Wasserstein and David J. Wasserstein, *The Legend of the Septuagint, from Classical Antiquity to Today* (Cambridge: Cambridge University Press, 2006).

40 Aryeh Kasher, in *The Jews in Hellenistic and Roman Egypt: The Struggle for Equal Rights* (Tübingen: Mohr, 1985), 328–332, argued, somewhat implausibly, that Manetho was himself motivated by the Septuagint to counter the humiliating picture of Egypt in the Hebrew Bible. Cf. Schäfer, *Judeophobia*,164. See also Erich S. Gruen, "The Use and Abuse of the Exodus Story," *Jewish History* 12, no. 1 (1998), 93–122. See esp. Philippe Borgeaud, "Moïse, son âne et les Typhoniens. Esquisse pour une remise en perspective," in Thomas Römer, ed., *La construction de la figure de Moise*, Transeuphratène Suppl. 13 (Paris: Gabalda, 2007).

41 Lysimachus, as quoted in Josephus, *Against Apion* 1.309.

42 Philo explicitly invokes the passage to counter Egyptian claims in *On the Special Laws* 1.9, 53, as does Josephus in *Against Apion* 2.237; and in *Antiquities* 4.207, from Josephus, *Jewish Antiquities*, bks. 4–6, trans. H. St. J. Thackeray and Ralph Marcus, Loeb Classical Library (1934; Cambridge, MA: Harvard University Press, 1998), 101.

43 Esther 3:8–9. The Greek version inserts into Esther 3:13 an entire letter from King Ahasuerus, detailing the bad character of the Jews and what must be done with them.

44 Josephus, the preserver and critic of Manetho's accusations, also provides a Greek version of Esther that parallels the Egyptian's charges. See *Antiquities* 2.6, 212–213: the Jews are "a wicked nation," "unfriendly and unsocial (*amikton asymphylon*), and "both by its custom and its practice it is the enemy (*echthron*) of your people and of all mankind (*hapasin anthrōpois*). If you wish to lay up a store of good deeds with your subjects, you will give orders to destroy this nation root and branch." Since Josephus is our sole source for Manetho's story, we should ask if his knowledge of the Greek Esther might have influenced his phrasing of Manetho's account, rather than vice versa. See Louis Feldman, "Hellenizations in Josephus' Version of Esther," *Transactions of the American Philological Association* 101 (1970), 143–170.

45 Diodorus, *Library of History* 34:1, 1–5, 53–55. The source here may have been Posidonius; see L. Edelstein and I. G. Kidd, eds., *Posidonius*, vol. 1: *The Fragments* (Cambridge: Cambridge University Press, 1972), frag. F278, gleaned from Josephus, *Against Apion* 2.79–80, 89, 91–96.

46 *CPJ* 3.520, quoted from David Frankfurter, *Elijah in Upper Egypt: The Apocalypse of Elijah and Early Christianity* (Minneapolis, MN: Fortress Press, 1993), 189–191.

47 3 Macc. 3:2–7. On the dating and authorship of 3 Maccabees (probably first century BCE), see Croy N. Clayton, *3 Maccabees* (Leiden: Brill, 2006), 11.

48 *Letter of Aristeas* 2.b.13.

49 On Onias and the temple at Leontopolis, see most recently Livia Capponi, *Il tempio di Leontopoli in Egitto. Identità politica e religiosa dei Giudei di Onia* (Pisa: Edizioni ETS, 2007).

50 Diodorus, *Library of History*, 17.52.5.

51 The reliability of this number (a million) is discussed in the commentary to Philo, *Against Flaccus*, 43, by Pieter Willem van der Horst, *Philo's Flaccus: The First Pogrom* (Leiden: Brill, 2003), 136–137.

52 For the artisans, see *CPJ* 1:46; John M. G. Barclay, *Jews in the Mediterranean Diaspora: From Alexander to Trajan* (Edinburgh: T & T Clark, 1996), 24. For Dositheos, see 3 Macc. 1:3; *CPJ* 1:127e; Barclay, *Jews in the Mediterranean Diaspora*, 33; and *CPJ* 1:127e. For Aristoboulos, see *P.Hib.* I 171, 243/2 BC; and Livia Capponi, "Aristoboulos and the Hieros Logos of the Egyptian Jews," *Proceedings of the 25th International Congress of Papyrology, Ann Arbor 2007* (Ann Arbor: American Studies in Papyrology, 2010), 109–120. According to Joseph Meleze Modrzejewski, Dositheos apostacized from Judaism, whereas other courtiers (such as the chronographer Demetrios) did not. See his *Jews of Egypt: From Rameses II to Emperor Hadrian* (Princeton, NJ: Princeton University Press, 1997), 56–65. For the mummy label, see W. Horbury and D. Noy, eds., *Jewish Inscriptions of Graeco-Roman Egypt* (Cambridge: Cambridge University Press, 1992), no. 133, 223. For Elephantine Jewish mummy labels (in Hebrew, Aramaic, and Demotic), see *TAD*, vol. 4: *Ostraka and Assorted Inscriptions* (Winnona Lake, IN: Eisenbrauns, 1999), 238 and 249–250; and for labels from Memphis (in Aramaic and Demotic), see Günter Vittmann, *Ägypter und die Fremden im ersten vorchristlichen Jahrtausend*, in *Kulturgeschichte der Antiken Welt* 97 (2003), 145.

53 Quote "undesirable and ineligible aliens" (interpreted as Jews) is from PSI 10 1160 = *CPJ* 2:150, the so-called Boulé papyrus (20–19 BC), published and commented by Tcherikover, "The Jewish Question in Alexandria," in *CPJ* 2:25–29. See also Herbert Musurillo, ed., *The Acts of the Pagan Martyrs: Acta Alexandrinorum* (Oxford: Clarendon Press, 1954), 1–3. BGU 4 1140 = *CPJ* 2:151 (5–4 BC) preserves an example of an Alexandrian Jew seeking such privileges, in this case an exemption from the poll tax. The document was published in *CPJ* 1:141 / SB 6:9564, and commented by Roger Rémondon, "Les Antisémites de Memphis (IFAO inv. 104 = CPJ 141)," *Chronique d'Egypte* 35 (1960), 244–261. For a translation see Roger S. Bagnall and Peter Derow, *The Hellenistic Period: Historical Sources in Translation* (Oxford: Blackwell, 2004), no. 175; and for a commentary Modrzejewski, *Jews of Egypt*, 154–157. The Greek phrase *bdelyssontai Ioudaious*, here translated as "loath the Jews," connotes a nauseous physical disgust. In *CPJ* 2:152 (41 AD), when tensions were at their height, a Greek merchant warns a business agent in Alexandria against borrowing money from the Jews there (lines 23–26): "Like everyone else, keep yourself away from the Jews."

54 There is a vast literature on anti-Jewish dynamics in Alexandria. In addition to works already cited, see John L. Collins, "Anti-Semitism in Antiquity? The Case

of Alexandria," in Carol Bakhos, ed., *Ancient Judaism in its Hellenistic Context* (Boston: Brill, 2005); and esp. Gideon Bohak, "The Ibis and the Jewish Question: Ancient 'Anti-Semitism' in Historical Perspective," in Menachem Mor et al., eds., *Jews and Gentiles in the Holy Land in the Days of the Second Temple, the Mishnah, and the Talmud* (Jerusalem: Yad Ben-Zvi Press, 2003), 27–43.

55 See Koen Goudriaan, "Ethnical Strategies in Graeco-Roman Egypt," in Per Bilde et al., eds., *Ethnicity in Hellenistic Egypt* (Aarhus: Aarhus University Press, 1992), 74–99, here 88–89. On the extraordinary complexity of corporate and ethnic privileges in Ptolemaic tax policy, see W. Clarysse and D. J. Thompson, *Counting the People in Hellenistic Egypt*, vol. 2: *Historical Studies* (Cambridge: Cambridge University Press, 2006).

56 On Cleopatra, Euergetes, and the drunken elephants, see Josephus, *Against Apion* 2.50–55. Compare 3 Macc. 3:1. On 3 Macc., see Tcherikover, "III Macc. as an Historical Source for the Age of Augustus" [Hebrew], *Zion* 10 (1945), 1ff.; and Arnaldo Momigliano, "Il decreto trilingue in onore de Tolemeo Filopatore e la quarta guerra di Celesiria," in *Quinto Contributo alla Storia degli Studi Classici e del Mondo Antico* (Rome: Ed. di Storia e Letteratura, 1975), 1:579–589 (originally published in *Aegyptus* 10 [1929],180–189). The quote about Euergetes's later treatment of the Greek citizens of Alexandria is from Valerius Maximus, *Factorum et Dictorum Memorabilium Libri Novem (Memorable Sayings and Doings)*, Loeb Classical Library 493 (Cambridge, MA: Harvard University Press, 2000), 9.2.5. On Cleopatra III and the sons of Onias, Josephus, *Antiquities* 13.285, 287, 349. On Ptolemy Lathyros's revenge, see Iordanis, *Romana et Getica*, chap. 81, ed. Theodore Mommsen, *Monumenta Germaniae Historica* [*MGH*] (Berlin: Weidmannnos, 1882), vol. 5.1, 9.

57 For a Jewish example of such triangulation, see Josephus, *Antiquities* 13.352–354, where Ananias, a descendant of Onias and a favored general of Cleopatra III, persuades the queen that she should not attack his kinsman, the Hasmonean king Alexander Jannaeus, because by killing Alexander she would risk making "all us Jews your enemies."

58 On Ptolemy XII, see M. Siani-Davies, "Ptolemy XII Auletes and the Romans," *Zeitschrift für Alte Geschichte* 46, no. 3 (1997), 306–340.

59 Less than a decade later (48/47 BCE) the Jewish garrison of Leontopolis made its final appearance, when Cleopatra VII (51–30 BCE), last of the Ptolemies, was besieged in Alexandria together with her friend and ally Julius Caesar. Onias's heirs marched once more to their relief. On the military relationship between the heirs of Onias and Cleopatra, see Josephus, *Antiquities* 13.284–287.

60 The date is debated, but it almost certainly falls between 41 and 53 CE. If after 43/44, the case was against Agrippa II. If earlier, it was against Agrippa I, whose visit to Alexandria had sparked the riots of 38 CE.

61 See Musurillo, *Acts of the Pagan Martyrs*, 18–26. For the nickname "pen-slayer," see Philo, *Against Flaccus*, 132.

62 On the Jewish privy council and sweating statue, see *Acta Hermaisci* 3.41–53, in Musurillo, *Acts of the Pagan Martyrs*, 45. Sweating statues were a standard type of marvel in antiquity. See, e.g., Plutarch, *Coriolanus* 38.1 and *Alexander*

14.8–9; and Arrian 1.11.2. Some centuries later, John Lydus stated that weeping or sweating statues portend internal disorder and civil strife; see his *De ostentis*, proem. 8, ed. C. Wachsmuth (Leipzig: Teubner, 1897), 16.

63 *Acta Appiani* (*P.Oxy.* I 33) 4.6–7, in Musurillo, *Acts of the Pagan Martyrs*, 67; see also 211–212: The *Acta Appiani* also seem to be modeled on the *Acta Hermaisci*—further evidence of a martyrological tradition.

64 Musurillo, *Acts of the Pagan Martyrs*, 168–172.

65 See, e.g., Aristotle, *Politics*, bk. 3.

66 Philo, *Against Flaccus*, 53–54, in F. H. Colson, trans., *Philo*, vol. 9: *Every Good Man Is Free; On the Contemplative Life; On the Eternity of the World; Against Flaccus; Apology for the Jews; On Providence*, Loeb Classical Library 363 (Cambridge, MA: Harvard University Press, 1941), 54.

67 Philo, *Against Flaccus*, 73–85.

68 On the liminal political status of Jews in Alexandria, see E. M. Smallwood, *The Jews under Roman Rule* (Leiden: Brill, 1976); Aryeh Kasher, "The Civic Status of the Jews in Ptolemaic Egypt," in Per Bilde, ed., *Ethnicity in Hellenistic Egypt*; and Sylvie Honigman, "Philon, Flavius Josèphe, et la citoyenneté alexandrine: vers une utopia politique," *Journal of Jewish Studies* 48 (1997), 62–90.

69 Josephus, *Against Apion* 2.60, 65, 125.

70 Josephus, *Against Apion* 2.68, 95, 121. On Josephus's reaction to Apion's concept of "Jewish misanthropy," see Monique Alexandre, "Le rapport aux étrangers dan le judaïsme selon Flavius Josèphe," in Jean Riaud, ed., *L'étranger dans le Bible et ses Lecteurs* (Paris: Cerf, 2007), 315–342.

71 Philo, *On the Embassy to Gaius*, in F. H. Colson, trans., *Philo*, vol. 10: *On the Embassy to Gaius*, Loeb Classical Library 379 (Cambridge, MA: Harvard University Press, 1962), sect. 353–367.

72 The precise terms of the ruling are unclear because its text has reached us in two different versions. One, given by Josephus, *Antiquities* 19.5.278–285, suggests that Claudius granted the Jews their entire petition, including citizenship. A contemporary papyrus copy of the edict (*CPJ* 2:153), however, urges Alexandrian tolerance of Jews, but also seems to bar Jews from claims of citizenship, and warns the Jews that if they aspire to more than their traditional privileges they will be treated as a "common plague for the whole world" (lines 99–100). For debates about the differences between these two versions see *CPJ* 2:36; Kasher, *Jews in Hellenistic and Roman Egypt*, 310–326; and Harold I. Bell, *Jews and Christians in Egypt: The Jewish Troubles in Alexandria and the Athanasian Controversy* (London: British Museum, 1924).

73 On the negative labeling of opponents as native Egyptians, see Goudriaan, "Ethnical Strategies in Graeco-Roman Egypt," here 86–94. On Aristeas's, Philo's, and Josephus's stock of negative Egyptian stereotypes, see Mary Ann Beavis, "Anti-Egyptian Polemic in the Letter of Aristeas 130–165 (The High Priest's Discourse)," *Journal for the Study of Judaism* 18, no. 2 (1987); Sarah Pearce, *The Land of the Body: Studies in Philo's Representation of Egypt* (Tübingen: Mohr Siebeck, 2007); Katell Berthelot, "The Use of Greek and Roman Stereotypes of the Egyptians by Hellenistic Jewish Apologists, with Special Reference to

Josephus' *Against Apion*," in *Internationales Josephus-Kolloquium Aarhus 1999* (Münster: LIT, 2000); and John M. G. Barclay, "The Politics of Contempt: Judeans and Egyptians in Josephus's *Against Apion*," in Barclay, ed., *Negotiating Diaspora: Jewish Strategies in the Roman Empire* (London: T & T Clark, 2004).

74 Philo says much the same about Helicon, the Egyptian who "poisoned" Caligula against the Jews: *On the Embassy to Gaius*, 166–177.

75 Josephus, *The Jewish War*, trans. H. St. J. Thackeray, Loeb Classical Library (Cambridge, MA: Harvard University Press, 1927), 2.490–497. See also Louis Feldman, *Jew and Gentile in the Ancient World* (Princeton, NJ: Princeton University Press, 1993), esp. 117–118.

76 *CPJ* 2:158a, col. 6; A. Fuks, "The Jewish Revolt in Egypt (A.D. 115–117) in the Light of the Papyri," *Aegyptus* 33 (1953) 131–158; M. Pucci Ben Zeev, *La rivolta ebraica al tempo di Traiano* (Pisa: Giardini, 1981); Pucci Ben Zeev, "La rivolta ebraica in Egitto (115–117 d.C.) nella storiografia antica," *Aegyptus* 62 (1982), 195–217; Pucci Ben Zeev, "CPJ II 158, 435 e la rivolta ebraica al tempo di Traiano," *Zeitschrift für Papyrologie und Epigraphik* 51 (1983), 95–103; Smallwood, *Jews under Roman Rule*, 389–427; and T. D. Barnes, "Trajan and the Jews," *Journal of Jewish Studies* 40 (1989), 145–162.

77 *CPJ* 2:158a, col. 1; Eusebius, *Historia Ecclesiae* 4.2–3.

78 Appian, *Civil Wars* 2.90; Historia Augusta, *Life of Hadrian* 5; Dio Cassius 68.32, 69.8; and Eusebius, *Historia Ecclesiae* 4.2–3. Cf. the papyri in *CPJ* 2:435ff., as well as Tcherikover's comments in *CPJ* 1:86–93, and Barclay, *Jews in the Mediterranean Diaspora*, n. 69, 79.

79 P.Giss. 24 = *CPJ* 2:437. The edition has "roasted" rather than "defeated," but see R. S. Bagnall and R. Cribiore, *Women's Letters from Ancient Egypt, 300 BC–AD 800* (Ann Arbor: University of Michigan Press, 2006), 157–158.

80 *CPJ* 2:450; see also Modrzejewski, *Jews of Egypt*, 224.

81 Tacitus, *Histories* 5.1–13.

CHAPTER 2: EARLY CHRISTIANITY

1 New Testament citations are from the *New Jerusalem Bible* translation.

2 Compare Paula Fredriksen on *vetus* vs. *verus* Israel in *Augustine and the Jews: A Christian Defense of Jews and Judaism* (New York: Doubleday, 2008), 77–78. On Luke's "historical" project, see Wayne Meeks's graceful "Assisting the Word by Making (Up) History: Luke's Project and Ours," *Interpretation* 57 (2003), 151–162.

3 As with all things related to the New Testament, the dating of its books is much debated, but there is something of a mainstream scholarly consensus at which all revisions aim. That consensus has long placed the seven genuine letters of Paul first, in the 50s and 60s CE. The Gospel of Mark is thought to be the earliest of the canonical gospels, written shortly after the destruction of the Jerusalem Temple in 70 CE, followed by Matthew later in the first century. Luke is generally dated to the 90s, and Acts, which proclaims itself to be by the same author, is increasingly dated as late as 115–120. John has almost universally been treated

as coming last and latest, closer to the middle of the second century. For a recent statement of the consensus, see Bart Ehrman, *The New Testament: A Historical Introduction to the Early Christian Writings*, 4th ed. (New York: Oxford University Press, 2007). Much debated, too, is the language in which Jesus preached. Most scholars favor an Aramaic-speaking Jesus, but there are some who point to the extensive Hellenization of the Galilee and champion Greek. For a small sampling of the debate, see M. F. Bird, "The Criterion of Greek Language and Context: A Response to Stanley E. Porter," *Journal for the Study of the Historical Jesus* 4, no. 1 (2006), 55–67; followed by Porter's counterargument in "The Criterion of Greek Language and Its Context: A Further Response," in the same issue, 69–74.

4 Compare Acts chapters 22 and 26.

5 Among the biographical details about Jesus that Paul reports is that "on the night he was handed over, the Lord Jesus took bread, and when he had given thanks he broke it and said, 'This is my body'" (1 Cor. 11:23–24). See also passages such as Rom. 1:3–4; and Gal. 4:14.

6 We will encounter a second-century example—that of Marcion—in the next chapter. For an excellent introduction to the Pauline corpus, including the question of pseudepigrapha, see Wayne Meeks and John T. Fitzgerald, *The Writings of St. Paul*, 2nd ed. (New York: W. W. Norton, 2007).

7 The gospel authors' knowledge of and relationship to Paul's writings are themselves complex questions. Richard Pervo argues powerfully that although he never refers to them specifically, the author of Luke/Acts utilized some version of Paul's letters: *Dating Acts: Between the Evangelists and the Apologists* (Santa Rosa, CA: Polebridge, 2006); and his *Acts: A Commentary*, in Hermeneia (Minneapolis, MN: Fortress Press, 2008). For Mark and Matthew, see n. 51 below.

8 Readers looking for an up-to-date commentary to Corinthians may turn to J. A. Fitzmyer, *First Corinthians*, Anchor Yale Bible Commentaries (New Haven, CT: Yale University Press, 2008).

9 Compare Matt. 11:25. Similar ideas can be found throughout Paul's writings, and in pseudepigraphical texts such as Eph. 2:7–10 (where the works of man are brought to naught by grace, "so that nobody can claim the credit"). On the general question of Paul's relationship to Greek philosophical traditions, see Sampley, ed., *Paul in the Greco-Roman World: A Handbook* (New York: Continuum, 2003); Bruce Winter, *Philo and Paul among the Sophists: Alexandrian and Corinthian Reponses to a Julio-Claudian Movement* (Grand Rapids, MI: Eerdmans, 2002); and Martin Hengel: *Judaism and Hellenism: Studies in Their Encounter in Palestine during the Early Hellenistic Period* (Eugene, OR: Wipf & Stock, 2003).

10 I put the words *Jew* and *Greek* in quotation marks because already in these very early texts we can see that these terms are being used to describe ethnic, cultural, and religious positions that do not map directly onto each other. In other words, insofar as *Jew* and *Greek* were used to describe cultural practices and qualities of thought, the labels could be and were applied across categories: ethnic Jews could be (and were) called Greeks for thinking, speaking, or acting a certain way; ethnic Greeks could be (and were) called Jews for the same reason. This holds true in every later period covered by this book as well.

11 J. Louis Martyn, *Galatians*, Anchor Yale Bible Commentaries (New Haven, CT: Yale University Press, 2007); and James D. G. Dunn, *The Epistle to the Galatians*, Black's New Testament Commentary (Peabody, MA: Hendrickson, 1993) have produced commentaries on Galatians that are alive to these questions, as has Daniel Boyarin, *A Radical Jew: Paul and the Politics of Identity* (Berkeley: University of California Press, 1994), although his work does not take commentary form. For Romans, see Robert Jewett, *Romans: A Commentary*, Hermeneia (Minneapolis, MN: Fortress Press, 2006); Joseph Fitzmyer, *Romans*, Anchor Yale Bible Commentaries (New Haven, CT: Yale University Press, 1993); and James D. G. Dunn, *World Biblical Commentary*, vol. 38A: *Romans: 1–8*, and vol. 38B: *Romans 9–16* (Nashville, TN: Thomas Nelson, 1988).

12 To designate non-Jews, Paul uses the words *Greek* (*Hellene*), and *gentiles* or *nations* (Greek *ethne*, analogous to Hebrew *goyim*) more or less interchangeably, regardless of the linguistic background of their object. In other words the term *Greek*, like the term *Jew*, has multiple referents that sometimes overlap but are not identical.

13 Compare Rom. 1:14–16 and 10:12, and Col. 3:11, which has "Barbarian nor Scythian."

14 There are a number of arguments against seeing in Paul's words anything like the revolutionary universalism attributed to them by some modern thinkers, perhaps the most obvious being that Paul did not intend this irrelevance to apply to all, but only to believers in Christ and his gospel. Denise Kimber Buell recently emphasized Paul's continuing dependence on the rhetoric of "race" and ethnicity (*genos, ethnos, laos, phylum*), in Buell, "Rethinking the Relevance of Race for Early Christian Self-Definition," *Harvard Theological Review* 94, no. 4 (October 2001), 449–476; Buell with Caroline Johnson Hodge, "The Politics of Interpretation: The Rhetoric of Race and Ethnicity in Paul," in *Journal of Biblical Literature* 123, no. 2 (Summer 2004), 235–251; and Buell, *Why This New Race: Ethnic Reasoning in Early Christianity* (New York: Columbia University Press, 2005). On barbarian/Scythian, see Douglas A. Campbell, "Unraveling Colossians 3.11b," *New Testament Studies* 42 (1996), 120–132.

15 Margaret Mitchell recently argued—focusing on the Corinthian correspondence—that Paul gave birth to Christian hermeneutics, in *Paul, the Corinthians, and the Birth of Christian Hermeneutics* (Cambridge: Cambridge University Press, 2010). My own argument focuses on the critical work done by "Judaism" in that birth. I am deeply grateful to Professor Mitchell for her generous help in improving that argument.

16 Antinomies were widespread in scripture and in popular oratory. They were also widespread in Greek philosophical thought, in rhetorical practice, and in Greek traditions about the cosmos being constructed out of "pairs of opposites." See G. E. R. Lloyd, *Polarity and Analogy: Two Types of Argumentation in Early Greek Thought* (London: Bristol Classical Press, 1992); and specifically on Paul, Norbert Schneider, *Die rhetorische Eigenart der paulinischen Antithese* (Tübingen: Mohr, 1970), 30ff. On the important ways in which, in Galatians, these traditions pressure Paul's presentation toward polarity, see J. Louis Mar-

tyn, "Apocalyptic Antinomies in Paul's Letter to the Galatians," *New Testament Studies* 31 (1985), 410–424. The cosmological use of polarity (e.g., in apocalyptic dualism) not only is Greek but also has important antecedents in the Hebrew Bible (e.g., Isa. 45:7), or in the (for Jews noncanonical) Wisdom of Ben Sirah, 33:15: "all the works of the most high / are in pairs, / one the opposite of the other."

17 Philo, *On Abraham* 147, in F. H. Colson, trans., *Philo*, vol. 6: *On Abraham; On Joseph; On Moses*, Loeb Classical Library 289 (Cambridge, MA: Harvard University Press, 1935), 75; the phrase "soul characteristics" is F. H. Colson's rendering of "*tropous psychēs*."

18 Philo, *On the Migration of Abraham* 92–93, in F. H. Colson, trans., *Philo*, vol. 4: *On the Confusion of Tongues; On the Migration of Abraham; Who is the Heir of Divine Things?; On Mating with the Preliminary Studies*, Loeb Classical Library 261 (Cambridge, MA: Harvard University Press, 1932), 185. On Philo's (and later Origen's) middle- and neo-Platonic use of the analogy of body and soul for text and meaning, see David Dawson, "Plato's Soul and the Body of the Text in Philo and Origen," in Jon Whitman, ed., *Interpretation and Allegory: Antiquity to the Modern Period* (Leiden: Brill, 2000), 89–107. See also A. J. M. Wedderburn, *Baptism and Resurrection: Studies in Pauline Theology against Its Graeco-Roman Background* (Tübingen: Mohr, 1987), 127.

19 Those interested in the New Perspective can begin with Krister Stendahl, "The Apostle Paul and the Introspective Conscience of the West," *Harvard Theological Review* 56 (1963), 199–215; E. P. Sanders, *Paul and Palestinian Judaism: A Comparison of Patterns of Religion* (Minneapolis, MN: Fortress Press, 1977), 474–511; Sanders, *Paul, the Law, and the Jewish People* (Minneapolis, MN: Fortress Press, 1983); Lloyd Gaston, *Paul and the Torah* (Vancouver: University of British Columbia Press, 1987); John Gager, *The Origins of Anti-Semitism: Attitudes toward Judaism in Pagan and Christian Antiquity* (Oxford: Oxford University Press, 1985), as well as Gager's highly accessible synthesis, *Reinventing Paul* (Oxford: Oxford University Press, 2000); W. D. Davies, *Paul and Rabbinic Judaism: Some Rabbinic Elements in Pauline Theology* (New York: Harper & Row, 1948); James D. G. Dunn, ed., *Paul and the Mosaic Law* (Tübingen: Mohr, 1996); and Dunn, *The New Perspective on Paul* (Tübingen: Mohr, 2005); and Steven Westerholm, *Perspectives Old and New: The Lutheran Paul and His Critics* (Grand Rapids, MI: Eerdmans, 2003). For a critical view, see Simon Gathercole, *Where Is Boasting? Early Jewish Soteriology and Paul's Response in Romans 1–5* (Grand Rapids, MI: Eerdmans, 2002); and Francis Watson, *Paul, Judaism, and the Gentiles: Beyond the New Perspective* (Grand Rapids, MI: Eerdmans, 2007).

20 Judaize: the Greek term (*ioudaizein*, translated into Latin as *judaizare*) appears already in the Septuagint (e.g., in Esther 8:17), where it is not, however, negative. Paul's use of it is in the long run transformative. On the verb's history, see Michele Murray, *Playing a Jewish Game: Gentile Christian Judaizing in the First and Second Centuries CE* (Ontario: Wilfred Laurier University Press, 2004), esp. 3–4; Róbert Dán, "Judaizare—The Career of a Term," in R. Dán and A. Pirnát,

eds., *Antitrinitarianism in the Second Half of the 16th Century* (Budapest and Leiden: Akadémiai Kiadó and Brill, 1982), 25–34; Gilbert Dagron, "Judäiser," *Travaux et Mémoires* 11 (1991), 359–380. The development of verbal forms from names of nations is far from unique. Aristophanes Grammaticus, *Fragmenta*, frag. 24, 4, described the practice: "[T]here are many slanderous expressions created as a verbal form from (the names of) nations, cities and peoples. From nations such is 'Kilikizein' and 'Aegyptiazein', meaning 'to act wickedly', or 'Kretizein', meaning 'to lie'. From cities, such is 'Lesbiazein', meaning 'to act filthily'" (*Aristophanis Byzantii grammatici Alexandrini fragmenta*, 2nd ed., ed. August Nauck [Halle: Lippert & Schmid, 1848], 178). Plutarch uses "Judaize" in such a derogatory sense in his *Life of Cicero* 7, 6, quoting a pun presumably made by Cicero (and entirely independent of Paul). On later readers of Gal. 2:13–14, see chap. 4.

21 For a general exposition (without particular attention to Judaism) of the generative potential of the Pauline system of antinomies, and of the parameters that tend to temper (or exacerbate) its polarity, see G. Caspary, *Politics and Exegesis: Origen and the Two Swords* (Berkeley: University of California Press, 1979), 108–116. Readers of Alain Badiou will recognize here my disagreement with his *Saint Paul: la Fondation de l'Universalisme* (Paris: PUF, 1998); and his *Circonstances, Tome 3: Portées du mot "Juif"* (Paris: Leo Schéer, 2005).

22 Part of Paul's obscurity stems from his complex vocabulary of flesh and body (*sarx, sōma*), soul and spirit (*psychē, pneuma*). The relationship between these key terms is not clear in Paul (at 1 Cor. 15:44 he can even speak of a "psychic body," *sōma psychikon*) and has produced much ancient and modern debate. For Origen's attempts to systematize the Pauline distinctions, see chap. 3. For modern scholarship on the relationship between matter and spirit in the historical Paul, see Troels Engberg-Pedersen, *Cosmology and Self in the Apostle Paul: The Material Spirit* (New York: Oxford University Press, 2010); and *Paul and the Stoics* (Louisville, KY: Westminster John Knox Press, 2000). See also Dale Martin, *The Corinthian Body* (New Haven, CT: Yale University Press, 1999). Marie E. Isaacs discusses the deployment of the term *pneuma* in service of a "new particularism," and specifically in supersessionism and "anti-Jewish polemic," in *The Concept of Spirit: A Study of Pneuma in Hellenistic Judaism and Its Bearing on the New Testament*, Heythrop Monographs 1 (London: Heythrop College, University of London, 1976), 144–145. On Philo's use of the trope of body as tomb, see D. Winston, ed. and trans., "Philo and the Contemplative Life," in A. Green, ed., *Jewish Spirituality from the Bible through the Middle Ages* (New York: Crossroad, 1988), 198–231, here 212.

23 On Paul's "moderate" dualism, see Boyarin, *Radical Jew*, 57–85.

24 The italicized portion is an allusion to Septuagint Gen. 15:16. The full import of the passage is that pagans persecute the Thessalonians just as Jews persecute the Judeans, but only the anti-Judaic conclusion seems to have had a historical future. Some scholars have argued that the passage is not genuinely Paul's but a later interpolation, since it 1) seems to look forward to the destruction of Jerusalem in 70 CE ("retribution") and 2) does not match what they see as Paul's more

conciliatory position in Rom. 9–11. See, e.g., Gager, *Origins of Anti-Semitism*, 255. It is nevertheless the version known to later Christianity, influencing such figures as Marcion (see my chap. 3), who retained the passage in his version of Thessalonians (Adolf von Harnack, *Marcion: Das Evangelium vom fremden Gott: eine Monographie zur Geschichte der Grundlegung der Katholischen Kirche* [Leipzig: Heinrich, 1924], 129ff., 294), and the rebels of Toledo, whom we will meet in chap. 5, who used it to justify their purity of blood statutes against descendants of converts from Judaism.

25 Vessels of wrath: adapting the New Jerusalem translation, which has "instruments" for the Greek *skeuē*, which also means "vessel." I prefer the latter because of its future in the Latin Vulgate: *vasa irae*. Augustine will develop the theme of "vessels of wrath" (see chap. 4) in his *Tractatus adversus Judeos* 7.9.

26 Blindness will quickly become a standard attribute applied to the Jews, e.g., in the second century by Irenaeus, *Adversus Haereses*, ed. Adeline Rousseau and Louis Doutreleau (Paris: Cerf, 1982), 4:30: "If therefore the Jews had not become the murderers of the Lord (which they also did to eternal life), and if they had not killed the apostles and persecuted the church and thus fallen into the bottomless pit of wrath, then we could not have been saved. For just as they received salvation through the blindness of the Egyptians, we have attained it through the blindness of the Jews." The New Perspective has produced suggestive rereadings of Romans in its rhetorical and historical context, some of which I have engaged in the treatment above. For a synthesis of these, see Gager, *Reinventing Paul*, 101–143. See also Lloyd Gaston, "Israel's Enemies in Pauline Theology," *New Testament Studies* 28 (1982), 400–423. Re "enmity": I intend no resonance with Jacob Taubes's treatment of Romans as "a political declaration of war" and Paul as an arch-theorist of enmity: *Die Politische Theologie des Paulus*, ed. A. Assmann and J. Assmann (Berlin: Fink, 1993), 27, 72. His reading of Paul is anachronistically inspired by Carl Schmitt's treatment of "enmity" as the fundamental political concept. It is curious that Schmitt himself, despite supporting National Socialism in Germany and despite maintaining that all modern political concepts derive from theological ones, did not explicitly treat Judaism as a "political enmity" in his theoretical writings. The oversight has been pointed out, first by Taubes in his *Ad Carl Schmitt: Gegenstrebige Fügung* (Berlin: Merve, 1987), and more recently by Jacques Derrida, *Politics of Friendship* (London: Verso, 1997), 84–85.

27 But compare Luke 18:32 on gentile complicity in the execution itself.

28 Compare John 4:44 and Matt. 13:57.

29 Compare Luke 3:7.

30 Compare Matt. 11:25–26. There is a long Hellenistic tradition of mockery aimed at scholars and the learned. For example, the Philogelos, an anthology of humor probably compiled in the fifth century, contains an entire section of jokes about the stupidity of the learned (*scholasticoi*). For an English translation, see Barry Baldwin, *The Philogelos or Laughter Lover* (Amsterdam: J. C. Gieben, 1983), 1–20.

31 On this topic, see above all Lloyd Gaston, *No Stone on Another: Studies in the Significance of the Fall of Jerusalem in the Synoptic Gospels* (Leiden: Brill, 1970).

32 Literature on the historical reconstruction of the communities associated with each gospel will be provided later. A good introduction to the question of gospel community and audience can be found in Richard Bauckham, ed., *The Gospels for All Christians: Rethinking the Gospel Audiences* (Grand Rapids, MI: W. B. Eerdmans, 1998). Readers interested in the literature on Mark, the only gospel not extensively discussed in this chapter, can see M. F. Bird, "The Markan Community, Myth or Maze? Bauckham's *The Gospel for All Christians* Revisited," *Journal of Theological Studies* 57, no. 2 (2006), 474–486; D. N. Peterson, *The Origins of Mark: The Markan Community in Current Debate* (Cologne: Brill, 2000); and Burton Mack, *A Myth of Innocence: Mark and Christian Origins* (Philadelphia, PA: Fortress Press, 1988).

33 This sectarian logic was common to a number of Second Temple Jewish communities. For examples from the Essene community at Qumran, see the essays collected in F. Garcia Martinez and M. Popovic, eds., *Defining Identities: We, You, and the Other in the Dead Sea Scrolls: Proceedings of the Fifth Meeting of the IOQS in Groningen* (Leiden: Brill, 2008), esp. George W. E. Nickelsburg, "Polarized Self-Identification in the Qumran Texts," 23–31; as well as Nickelsburg's earlier "Religious Exclusivism: A World View Governing Some Texts Found at Qumran," in M. Becker and W. Fenske, eds., *Das Ende der Tage und die Gegenwart des Heils: Begegnungen mit dem Neuen Testament und seiner Umwelt: Festschrift für Heinz-Wolfgang Kuhn zum 65. Geburtstag* (Leiden: Brill, 1999). For Paul's thinking in these terms see also Gaston, "Israel's Enemies."

34 The placement of the words from Luke 19:27 within the parable does not deprive them of significance, though it does complicate that significance.

35 In Matthew, e.g., the word *Iudaios* appears only in the formulation "King of the Jews," and in a line about Jesus's story "circulating amongst the Jews to this day" (Matt. 28:15). The synoptics prefer to give more specific names to the enemies of Jesus, pointing to subcategories of society such as scribes, lawyers, Pharisees, and Sadducees. On the terminology of "Jew" in early Christian writings, see Graham Harvey, *The True Israel: Uses of the Names Jew, Hebrew and Israel in Ancient Jewish and Early Christian Literature* (Leiden: Brill, 1996); Stephen Wilson, "'Jew' and Related Terms in the Ancient World," *Studies in Religion* 33, no. 2 (June 2004), 157–171; Luke Timothy Johnson, "The New Testament's Anti-Jewish Slander and the Conventions of Ancient Polemic," *Journal of Biblical Literature* 108, no. 3 (1989), 419–441; Urban von Wahlde, "The Johannine 'Jews': A Critical Survey," *New Testament Studies* 28 (1982), 33–60; and Steve Mason, "Jews, Judaeans, Judaizing, Judaism: Problems of Categorization in Ancient History," *Journal for the Study of Judaism* 38, no. 4–5 (2007), 457–512. See also Margaret H. Williams, "The Meaning and Function of *IOUDAIOS* in Graeco-Roman Inscriptions," *Zeitschrift für Papyrologie und Epigraphik* 116 (1997), 249–262.

36 On the widespread influence of the Gospel of Matthew in early Christianity, see the foundational work of Édouard Massaux, *L'Influence de l'Évangile de saint Matthieu sur la littérature chrétienne avant saint Irénée* (Louvain: Publications Universitaires, 1950).

37 The speech is one of Matthew's many additions to Mark's framework. Luke 3:7–9 has "crowds" instead of "Pharisees and Sadducees."

38 Cf. Pheme Perkins, "If Jerusalem Stood: The Destruction of Jerusalem and Christian Anti-Semitism," *Biblical Interpretation* 8, no. 1–2 (2000), 194–204.

39 The work of "The Jesus Seminar" represents one attempt to shift the blame for early Christian anti-Judaism from Jesus to the later evangelists. For a synthesis of that work, see Robert Funk and Roy Hoover, *The Five Gospels: A Search for the Authentic Words of Jesus* (New York: Macmillan, 1993), which treats as inauthentic the passages considered most antagonistic to Jews. More recent attempts to access or reclaim the Jewish Jesus, include Amy-Jill Levine, *The Misunderstood Jew: The Church and the Scandal of the Jewish Jesus* (San Francisco, CA: Harper, 2006); and Paula Fredriksen and A. Reinhartz, *Jesus, Judaism, and Christian Anti-Judaism: Reading the New Testament after the Holocaust* (Louisville, KY: Westminster John Knox Press, 2002). Particularly illuminating is Paula Fredriksen, *From Jesus to Christ: The Origins of the New Testament Images of Jesus*, 2nd ed. (New Haven, CT: Yale University Press, 2000).

40 Already in Matt. 2:1–12, the "Jew" Herod's murderous rejection of Jesus is contrasted with exaggerated gentile acceptance.

41 I am avoiding the important question of whether Matthew's Jesus here is or is not against law observance. He may well be arguing for more rigor rather than less. See, e.g., E. P. Sanders, *Jesus and Judaism* (Philadelphia, PA: Fortress Press, 1985), 260–264. My point is only that Matthew makes its case by deploying Pharisees as antithesis. The choice may have been motivated by the relative proximity of the Matthean community's positions to those of the Pharisees (on points like law observance, resurrection, etc.): intimacy is often a stimulus to invective. But whatever the historical intimacy, it was lost to later readers, whereas the antithetical invective remained in the gospel to generate meaning. On the social context of Matthew, see David C. Sim, *The Gospel of Matthew and Christian Judaism: The History and Social Setting of the Matthean Community* (Edinburgh: T & T Clark, 1998); Anthony J. Saldarini, "The Gospel of Matthew and Jewish-Christian Conflict," in D. L. Baich, ed., *Social History of the Matthean Community* (Minneapolis, MN: Fortress Press, 1991), 38–61; D. R. A. Hare, "How Jewish Is the Gospel of Matthew?" *Catholic Biblical Quarterly* 62 (2000), 264–277; and John F. O'Grady, "The Community of Matthew," *Chicago Studies* 40, no. 3 (2001), 239–250.

42 Neither the polarity nor the "hypocritical ontology" were original in themselves. Many Jewish groups (including the Pharisees and the Essenes) had already arrived at similar apocalyptically polarized solutions, and Hebrew scripture contained plenty of prophetic invective (in Jeremiah, Isaiah, Ezekiel, Psalms, and elsewhere) against hypocrites who honor God with their mouths but not with their hearts.

43 Absent from the Passion story unless we include the Pharisees among the "scribes" in 27:41.

44 I do not mean to minimize the potential dualism of the synoptics, nor their alignment of figures of Judaism with Satan. On the relationship between the

Notes to Pages 78–81

evolving notions of "Satan" and the position of Jews in early Christianity, see Elaine Pagels's sequence of articles: "The Social History of Satan, the 'Intimate Enemy': A Preliminary Sketch," *Harvard Theological Review* 84, no. 2 (1991), 105–128; "The Social History of Satan, Part II: Satan in the New Testament Gospels," *Journal of the American Academy of Religion* 62, no. 1 (1994), 17–58; and "The Social History of Satan, Part Three: John of Patmos and Ignatius of Antioch: Contrasting Visions of 'God's People,'" *Harvard Theological Review* 99, no. 4 (2006), 487–505.

45 On the terminology of "Jew" in early Christian writings, see n. 34 above. Concerning the fourth gospel and the roots of anti-Judaism, see Paula Fredriksen, "The Gospel of John and Christian Anti-Judaism," *SIDIC* 35, no. 1 (2002), 23–24; F. Vandecasteele-Vanneuville, "Johannine Theology of Revelation, Soteriology, and the Problem of Anti-Judaism," *Studien zum Neuen Testament und seiner Umwelt* 26 (2001), 165–188; and the essays collected in R. Bieringer, D. Pollefeyt, and F. Vandecasteele-Vanneuville, eds., *Anti-Judaism and the Fourth Gospel: Papers of the Leuven Colloquium, 2000* (Assen: Van Gorcum, 2001).

46 Conditional "if": John does not, however, use the unreal conditional, which would mark a much stronger skepticism. However, even the portrayal of the "believing" Pharisee Nicodemus leaves room for doubt about the nature of his belief. We meet him first in chap. 3, exasperating Jesus with his lack of understanding: "[Y]ou people reject our evidence. If you do not believe me when I speak of earthly things, how will you believe me when I speak to you about heavenly things?" (John 3:11–12). When we see Nicodemus again, he is embalming Jesus's body in a hundred pounds of myrrh and aloes—a pious act, but one that implies a still misplaced attention on the wealth and honors of this world, and a lack of faith in the resurrection (19:39).

47 The literature on this conflict is vast. See esp. J. Louis Martyn, *History and Theology in the Fourth Gospel*, 3rd ed. (Louisville, KY: Westminster John Knox Press, 2003); Wayne A. Meeks, "'Am I a Jew?'—Johannine Christianity and Judaism," in Jacob Neusner, ed., *Christianity, Judaism, and Other Greco-Roman Cults: Studies for Morton Smith at Sixty* (Leiden: Brill, 1975), 1:163–186; Meeks, "Breaking Away: Three New Testament Pictures of Christianity's Separation from the Jewish Communities," in Jacob Neusner and Ernest S. Frerichs, eds., *"To See Ourselves as Others See Us": Christians, Jews, "Others" in Late Antiquity* (Chico, CA: Scholars Press, 1985), 93–115; W.-H. Hwang and J. G. van der Watt, "The Identity of the Recipients of the Fourth Gospel in the Light of the Purpose of the Gospel," *HTS Teologiese Studies* 63, no. 2 (2007), 683–698; D. Reed, "Rethinking John's Social Setting: Hidden Transcript, Anti-Language, and the Negotiation of the Empire," *Biblical Theology Bulletin* 36, no. 3 (2006), 93–106; Y.-M. Blanchard, *Les écrits johanniques: Une communauté témoigne de sa foi* (Paris: Cerf, 2006); X. Levieils, "Juifs et Grecs dan la communauté johannique," *Biblica* 82, no. 1 (2001), 51–78; C. G. Lingad, *The Problems of Jewish Christians in the Johannine Community* (Rome: Editrice Pontificia Università Gregoriana, 2001); J. T. Townsend, "The Gospel of John and the Jews," in A. T. Davies, ed., *Anti-Semitism and the Foundations of Christianity* (New York:

Paulist, 1979), 72–97; and Bart Ehrman, "Heracleon, Origen, and the Text of the Fourth Gospel," *Vigiliae Christianae* 47 (1993), 105–118.

48 Compare Acts 18:6, 28:26–28.

49 Compare Acts 28:28.

50 On the topos of the Jewish killing of prophets, see Odil Hannes Steck, *Israel und das gewaltsame Geschick der Propheten* (Neukirchen: Neukirchener Verlag, 1967). The placement of agency for "unbelief" on the Jews so as to require the gentile mission seems a view distinctive to the author of Luke/Acts. On the communal context in which this view emerged, see Luke Timothy Johnson, "On Finding the Lukan Community: A Cautious Cautionary Essay," *Society for Biblical Literature, Seminar Papers* (1979), 87–100; and Dale C. Allison, "Was There a Lukan Community?" *Irish Biblical Studies* 10, no. 2 (1988), 62–70.

51 On Mark as interpreter of Paul (in this case, focusing on epiphanic vocabulary), see Joel Marcus, "Mark: Interpreter of Paul," *New Testament Studies* 46 (2000), 473–487; and Margaret M. Mitchell, "Epiphanic Evolutions in Earliest Christianity," *Illinois Classical Studies* 29 (2004), 183–204, here 191–194. Plentiful references to Matthew's critiques of Paul (such as the possible criticism of 1 Cor. 15:9 in Matt. 5:17–19) may be found in W. D. Davies and D. C. Allison's volumes on Matthew in the *International Critical Commentary* (London: T & T Clark, 2004).

52 On the messianic question, see also the classic statement by Rosemary Ruether, *Faith and Fratricide: The Theological Roots of Anti-Semitism* (New York: Seabury, 1974), 64–65, 116, 121.

CHAPTER 3: THE EARLY CHURCH

1 On the evolution of attitudes toward the disciples across the canonical gospels see Paula Fredriksen, *From Jesus to Christ* 190 [see chap. 2, n. 38]; on the disciples' unreliability in Mark, see 46.

2 Any count of discrete "works" found at Nag Hammadi must be only a provisional estimate, given the fragmentary condition of the texts. For an overview, see James M. Robinson, "Nag Hammadi: The First Fifty Years," in John Turner and Anne McGuire, eds., *The Nag Hammadi Library after Fifty Years: Proceedings of the 1995 Society of Biblical Literature Commemoration* (New York: Brill, 1997), 3–33. Condemned as heretical: see, e.g., Athanasius's Festal Letter of 367 CE, fragments of which can be found in L.-T. Lefort, ed., *Lettres festales et pastorales en copte* (Louvain: Durbecq, 1955), 15–22. On the Gospel of Thomas, fragments were known in the nineteenth century: D. D. Schmidt, "Early Gospel Fragments from Oxyrhynchus: POxy 1.654–655, 840, 1224," *Forum* 2, no. 2 (1999), 305–310. On the (seemingly) complete manuscript from Nag Hammadi, see H.-J. Klauck, "Geheime Worte Jesu? Das Evangelium nach Thomas aus Nag Hammadi," *Bibel und Kirche* 60, no. 2 (2005), 89–95. The identity of the synoptic Thomas with "Didymos Judas Thomas" (of the eponymous gospel) is not firmly established. Both "Didymos" and "Thomas" can mean "twin," and "Judas" might be the only "true" name invoked in the prologue of the Gospel of Thomas. The connection

between the two Thomases is nevertheless often made. See Robert J. Miller, *The Complete Gospels* (Salem, OR: Polebridge, 1995), 302, 305.

3 The Gospel of Thomas is sometimes dated to the late first century (70–100 CE). It therefore very possibly antedated John. Given these problems of chronology, considerations of the John-Thomas relationship often push their debate back into the decades before either gospel was formalized in the manner we now know; see Ismo Dunderberg, "John and Thomas in Conflict?" in Turner and McGuire, eds., *Nag Hammadi Library*, 361–380. The decision to capitalize the word *Word* in modern editions and translations of the gospel itself reflects the triumph of John's position. See Elaine Pagels, *Beyond Belief: The Secret Gospel of Thomas* (New York: Random House, 2003), 146–151. Care to cast Thomas: While this claim may lean on difficult-to-establish chronology, it is helped by the fact that John often refers to Thomas as "thomas ho legomenos didymos." See John 11:16, 20:24, 21:2. Close to the Jews: Recall John 5:1–18, 6:41–52, 7:45–52, etc.

4 "For if" quote is from Didache 6.2. On 1 Timothy, see Jouette M. Bassler, "1 Timothy," in James L. May, ed., *Harper Collins Bible Commentary* (San Francisco, CA: HarperOne, 2000), 1137. Didache: There is debate between scholars who believe that the primitiveness of the text is contrived, and the now-dominant argument that the Didache is genuine and may predate the synoptics, dating closer to Paul. While the earlier date is now more popular, the evidence remains scant: see Andrew Louth, *Early Christian Writings* (New York: Penguin, 1987), 187–189; Michael Holmes, *The Apostolic Fathers* (Grand Rapids, MI: Baker, 2007), 334–339; Clayton Jefford, ed., *The Didache in Context: Essays on Its Text, History, and Transmission* (Leiden: Brill, 1995); Jonathan Draper, ed., *The Didache in Modern Research* (Leiden: Brill, 1996); and H. W. M. Van de Sandt, H. van de Sandt, and D. Flusser, *The Didache: Its Jewish Sources and Its Place in Early Judaism and Christianity* (Assen: Royal van Gorcum, 2002). Translations of the Didache are taken from the Loeb Classical Library's *Apostolic Fathers*, ed. and trans. Bart D. Ehrman, 2 vols. (Cambridge, MA: Harvard University Press, 2003) [henceforth "Loeb translation"].

5 Didache 11:3–12:1. Compare the epistle of Ignatius to the Ephesians, 15:1, written ca. 108 CE: "It is good to teach, if the one who speaks also acts," i.e., if the teacher practices what he preaches (Loeb translation, 1:235).

6 "Christmonger" is from Didache 12:5. Quote with "final days" is from Didache 16:3–4. Phrase "World-deceiver" translated from *phanēsetai ho kosmoplanēs*.

7 Many other early Christians: for example, Ignatius to the Ephesians, 7:1, and to the Smyrnaeans, 4. The messianic overcoming of hypocrisy is a feature of writings like 2 Clement to the Corinthians 12:2–3: "For when the Lord himself was asked by someone when his kingdom would come, he said: 'When the two are one, and the outside like the inside, and the male with the female is neither male nor female.' Now 'the two are one' when we speak truth to one another, and when one soul exists in two bodies with no hypocrisy" (Loeb translation, 1:183). The same saying is attributed to Jesus by the Gospel of Thomas, and probably dates to the mid-first century. On Lord's yoke, see Didache 6:1.

8 For "spectators," see, e.g., the martyrdom of Pionius and his companions, chaps. 4.8 and 11, in Herbert Musurillo, *The Acts of the Christian Martyrs* (Oxford: Clarendon Press, 1972), 136–167. At chap. 13 the Jews' role as killers of prophets and crucifiers of Christ is explicitly invoked in an apologetic vein. For representations of Jews in the martyrdom of Polycarp, see also Musurillo, *Mart. Pol.* 13, 17; Freiherr von Hans Campenhausen, *Bearbeitungen und Interpolationen des Polykarpmartyriums* (Heidelberg: C. Winter, 1957), 24–26; and Judith M. Lieu, *Image and Reality: The Jews in the World of the Christians in the Second Century* (Edinburgh: T & T Clark, 1996), 57–102.

9 Thus the epistle of Barnabas, e.g., presents its author as attacked by Jews, but the danger is theoretical, not real. See Albrecht Oepke, *Das Neue Gottesvolk* (Gütersloh: Bertelsmann, 1950), 26; and Philipp Vielhauer, *Geschichte der urchristlichen Literatur*, 4th ed. (Berlin: De Gruyter, 1985), 605; against J. Schmid, "Barnabas," in the *Reallexikon für Antike und Christentum* (Stuttgart: Hiersemann, 1970), 1:1212–1275.

10 Justin Martyr, *Dialogue with Trypho, a Jew*, trans. M. Dods, in *The Ante-Nicene Fathers* (Grand Rapids, MI: Eerdmans, 1950), 1:16, 17. This volume's version of the *Letter to Diognetus* has also been consulted here. Hans Conzelmann, in *Gentiles, Jews, Christians: Polemics and Apologetics in the Greco-Roman Era* (Minneapolis, MN: Fortress Press, 1992), 250–251, nevertheless insists that "even if the Jews are not mentioned frequently in the stories of the martyrs," their participation in the persecutions of Christians "is not to be doubted" (290). His misplaced confidence is based on this same passage in Justin, as well as the anonymously authored *Letter to Diognetus* 5.17 ("they are assailed by the Jews as foreigners," etc.), and Adolf von Harnack's reading of Justin in *Ist die Rede des Paulus in Athen ein ursprünglicher Bestandteil der Apostelgeschichte? Judentum und Judenchristentum in Justins Dialog mit Trypho*, Texte und Untersuchungen zur Geschichte der altchristlichen Literatur 39.1 (Leipzig: J. C. Hinrichs, 1913), 47ff. The final quote is from Tertullian, *Ad nationes* 1.14: "*Quod enim aliud genus seminarium est infamiae nostrae?*" See also his *Adversus Judaeos* 13: "*Ab illis enim incepit infamia*"; *Scorpiace* 10; and Irenaeus, *Adversus Haereses* 4.28.3 [see chap. 2, n. 26]. For the Latin of Tertullian, consult Migne, *Patrologia Latina* [henceforth *PL*], vols. 1 and 2; for the Greek, Migne, *Patrologia Graeca* [henceforth *PG*], 7a–b. Eusebius, *Historia Ecclesiae* 5.16.12.

11 Ignatius's next sentence echoes Jesus on the Pharisees: "But if neither one speaks about Jesus Christ, they both appear to me as monuments and tombs of the dead, on which are written only human names" (6.1–2, Loeb translation, 1:289 [emphasis added]). Ignatius is the only one of the apostolic fathers to use the word *Judaize*. See Lieu, *Image and Reality*, 29–56, here 31. For a different view of the groups Ignatius opposed, see Einar Molland, "The Heretics Combated by Ignatius of Antioch," *Journal of Ecclesiastical History* 5 (1954), 1–6. On Christian Judaizing, see also Michelle Murray, *Playing a Jewish Game: Gentile Christian Judaizing in the First and Second Centuries CE* (Waterloo, Ontario: Wilfrid Laurier University Press, 2004). The counterpoint here is Thomas Robinson, *Ignatius of Antioch and the Parting of the Ways* (Peabody, MA: Hendrick-

son, 2009), which makes the strongest possible case for Ignatius's anti-Judaism (not just as figurative resource, but as concerning real Jews). See, e.g., 40 62, where Robinson attempts to estimate the number and typology of Antiochene Jews based on Ignatius's letters ("Nouveau Jews" or proselytes, "Near-Jews" or God-fearers). He also cites "post-Holocaust" and "postcolonial" sensibilities as contributing factors in readings of Ignatius that soften the "literalness" of his anti-Judaism (239–241). For another instance of the conflation of "Judaizers" with "Jews," see Louth on Magnesians and Philadelphians, in *Early Christian Writings*, 57, 92.

12 Or at least this is his position in the fragments Eusebius preserves of his work in his section on the origins of heresy, *Historia Ecclesiae* 4.22.4–5. See Conzelmann, *Gentiles, Jews, Christians*, 275–277. For the patristic sources on "Jewish Christians," see the useful collection by A. F. J. Klijn and G. J. Reinink, *Patristic Evidence for Jewish-Christian Sects*, Supplements to *Novum Testamentum* 360 (Leiden: Brill, 1973).

13 For a classic example, see Plato, *Timaeus* 68E, in *Plato: Timaeus, Critias, Cleitophon, Menexenus, Epistles*, trans. R. G. Bury, Loeb Classical Library (Cambridge, MA: Harvard University Press, 1929) on the "self-sufficing" and "most perfect" (*teleōtaton*) god.

14 Augustine, *City of God* 8.6.

15 See, e.g., Plato, *Timaeus* 41A–42D, for the supreme God's commissioning of the lesser gods, both visible and invisible, to create mortal things which could be matched up with his immortal creations.

16 On the human soul's characteristics, see Aristotle, *On the Soul*, ed. W. S. Hett, Loeb Classical Library 288 (Cambridge, MA: Harvard University Press, 1957), 430a, 17–23.

17 On "otherspeak," see Paula Fredriksen's felicitous itinerary (which I am following here) in *Augustine and the Jews*, 41–44 [see chap. 2, n. 2]. Peter T. Struck, *Birth of the Symbol: Ancient Readers at the Limits of Their Texts* (Princeton, NJ: Princeton University Press, 2004); and part one ("The Sources of Christian Allegory," 9–130) in R. P. C. Hanson, *Allegory and Event: A Study of the Sources and Significance of Origen's Interpretation of Scripture* (Louisville, KY: Westminster John Knox Press, 2002).

18 Some Docetists stressed the comedic effect of Jesus's playing to the audience, as in the Nag Hammadi text known as the "Gnostic" or Coptic Apocalypse of Peter: "I [Peter] saw him [Christ] apparently being seized by them. And I said, 'What am I seeing, O Lord?' Is it you yourself whom they take? And are you holding on to me? Who is this one above the cross, who is glad and laughing? And is it another person whose feet and hands they are hammering?' The Savior said to me, 'He whom you see above the cross, glad and laughing, is the living Jesus. But he into whose hands and feet they are driving the nails is the physical part [or fleshy thing], which is the substitute.'" See James Brashler, trans., "Apocalypse of Peter," in Birger Pearson, ed., *Nag Hammadi Codex VII* (Leiden: Brill, 1996), 241.

19 See also 1 John 2:18–22. The creed in Ignatius's letter to the Ephesians, 7:2,

reveled in such paradox: "For there is one physician, both fleshly and spiritual, born and unborn, God come in the flesh, true life in death, from both of Mary and God, first subject to suffering and then beyond suffering" (Loeb translation, 1:227).

20 Irenaeus, *Adversus Haereses* 3.3.4. In the Greek, Polycarp calls Marcion "*ton prōtotokon tou Satana*"; in the Latin, "*primogenitum Satanae.*" See Migne, *PG* 7.

21 The classic work is Harnack, *Marcion* [see chap. 2, n. 24]. See also Stephen G. Wilson, "Marcion and the Jews," in S. G. Wilson, ed., *Anti-Judaism in Early Christianity* (Waterloo, Ontario: Wilfrid Laurier University Press, 1986), 2:45–58; and the prudent revisions of Lieu, *Image and Reality*, 261–276.

22 Indeed in the second century the apostle to the gentiles seems to have been more popular among dualists than among those we consider proto-orthodox. See Elaine Pagels, *The Gnostic Paul: Gnostic Exegesis of Pauline Letters* (Philadelphia, PA: Fortress Press, 1975), 1–13.

23 Harnack, *Marcion,* 22.

24 Fredriksen, *Augustine and the Jews,* 55. Freiherr von Hans Campenhausen, *The Formation of the Christian Bible*, trans. J. A. Baker (Philadelphia, PA: Fortress Press, 1972), 148; cf. Bruce Manning Metzger, *The Canon of the New Testament: Its Origin, Development, and Significance* (Oxford: Clarendon Press, 1987), 90–99; and Bart Ehrman, *The Orthodox Corruption of Scripture: The Effect of Early Christological Controversies on the Text of the New Testament* (New York: Oxford University Press, 1993).

25 Tertullian, *Adversus Marcionem*, 1.19, ed. Ernest Evans (Oxford: Oxford University Press, 1972), 1.49. Justin, *Dialogue*, at, e.g., 43, 67. Quote with "poison" is from Tertullian, *Adversus Marcionem* 3.8 (1.191 in Evans's edition).

26 This does not mean that the thrusts of Justin's arguments could not also be felt by Jews. There may even be traces of a rebuttal of these arguments in the Talmud, e.g., in Babylonia Talmud [henceforth BT] Shabbat 116 a-b, on which see most recently Holger Zellentin, "Margin of Error: *Bavli Shabbat* 116a–b as Polemics, Apology, and Heresiology," in H. Zellentin and E. Iricinschi, eds., *Heresy and Identity in Late Antiquity* (Tübingen: Mohr Siebeck, 2006), 305–324.

27 Justin, *Dialogue*, 1, 2–3, 8.

28 Ibid., 8, 10.

29 Most pagan critiques of Christianity have reached us only in the works of their (eventually victorious) Christian opponents. The pagan argument presented here is a synthesis of positions attributed to pagans in works as diverse as the *Kerygma Petrou*, the *Epistle of Diognetus*, the *Apology of Aristedes*, Tertullian's *Apologeticum* against the pagans, and Minucius Felix's *Octavius*, among others.

30 Ignatius, epistle to the Magnesians, 8:2, 9:3. See also his epistle to the Philadelphians, 5:2. Both letters can be found in Dods, ed., *Ante-Nicene Fathers*, vol. 1.

31 Justin, *First Apology*, 46, also in Dods, ed., *Ante-Nicene Fathers*, vol. 1.

32 Justin, *Dialogue*, 16, 19, 26, 29. Cf. Tertullian, *Adversus Judaeos*, 3.

33 Justin, *First Apology*, 47, 50; translation modified and emphasis added.

34 In book 69 of his *Roman History* (Cambridge, MA: Harvard University Press, 1925), Dio Cassius gives the number of Jewish casualties as 580,000. Peter

Schäfer considers the number an exaggeration: *Der Bar Kokhba-Aufstand* (Tübingen: Mohr, 1981), 131–132. Others defend it: Hannah M. Cotton, "The Bar Kokhba Revolt and the Documents from the Judean Desert," in Schäfer, *The Bar Kokhba War Reconsidered: New Perspectives on the Second Jewish War* (Tübingen: Mohr Siebeck, 2003), 142–143; and Menahem Mor, "The Geographical Scope of the Bar Kokhba Revolt," in the same volume, 107–109. Justin, *Dialogue*, 1, 16. Compare Irenaeus, *Adversus Haereses*, 4.27.4. Like so many other references to the Jews in Irenaeus's work, this one is oriented by his struggle against the gnostics.

35 Tertullian, *Adversus Iudaeos*, ed. H. Tränkle (Weisbaden: Steiner, 1964). Tränkle posits a Christian and gentile audience on lxxi. Was Tertullian writing in a context of real competition with Jews and Judaism? W. H. C. Frend maintains that Christians in Tertullian's Carthage were adopting practices from Jewish neighbors. T. D. Barnes takes the opposite view, that there was little or no direct rivalry or contact, and that when Tertullian speaks of Jews he means those of the apostolic period as represented in scripture, not the real Jews of his own time. See Frend, "A Note on Jews and Christians in Third Century North Africa," *Journal of Theological Studies* n.s. 21 (1970), 92–96; Frend, "Jews and Christians in Third Century Carthage," in André Benoît, ed., *Paganisme, judaïsme, christianisme* (Paris: de Boccard, 1978), 185–194; Barnes, "Tertullian's Scorpiace," *Journal of Theological Studies* n.s. 20 (1969), 105–132, and Barnes, *Tertullian: A Historical and Literary Study* (Oxford: Clarendon Press, 1971), 90–93.

36 Origen, *Commentary on Romans,* trans. Thomas Scheck (Washington, DC: Catholic University of America Press, 2001), 9.25, 1226B. See Caspary, *Politics and Exegesis*, 142 [see chap. 2, n. 21] ; and Henri Crouzel, *Théologie de l'image de Dieu chez Origène* (Paris: Aubier, 1956), 193–196. For simplicity I use here the word *Jews*. Origen himself used multiple terms, sometimes intending distinct meanings. *Hebraioi*, e.g., he occasionally used to designate those who were the transmitters of his own philological knowledge of the Hebrew Bible, and *Ioudaioi* for those who rejected Jesus and were the general object of his polemics. See Nicholas de Lange, *Origen and the Jews: Studies in Jewish-Christian Relations in Third-Century Palestine* (Cambridge: Cambridge University Press, 1970), 32, 160, 193; the distinctions are not as systematic as de Lange takes them to be at, e.g., 30.

37 Origen, *On First Principles*, trans. G. W. Butterworth (Gloucester, MA: Smith, 1973), 4.1.7, 4.2.8, 4.3.11, and 4.2.4 (citing 1 Cor. 2:6–7; Rom. 7:14).

38 Ibid., 4.2.1, on the literalism of both the Jews and the "heretics"; 4.1.3, on the meaning of the destruction of Jerusalem. See also Origen, *Contra Celsum*, trans. Henry Chadwick (Cambridge: Cambridge University Press, 1953), 1.14–20, 5.43 on the virtues of Moses's teachings; 4.39, 7.30 on Plato's trip to Egypt. Justin had hinted at something similar in his *First Apology*, 59–60. Compare Numenius's roughly contemporary comment that Plato is Moses speaking in Attic Greek, discussed most recently by Myles Burnyeat, "Platonism in the Bible: Numenius of Apamea on Exodus and Eternity," in George H. van Kooten, ed., *The Revelation of the Name YHWH to Moses: Perspectives from Juda-*

ism, the Pagan Greco-Roman World, and Early Christianity (Leiden: Brill, 2006), 139–148. On Origen's hermeneutics, see Karen Jo Torjesen, *Hermeneutical Procedure and Theological Structure in Origen's Exegesis* (Berlin: De Gruyter, 1986).

39   Origen, *On First Principles*, 4.2.5.

40   Compare 1 Cor. 2:8.

41   See 1 Cor. 2:8; John 12:31, 14:30, 15:18; Rev. 18:1–20; 1 Peter 5.13; Tertullian, *De Idolatria* 19.1 (edited in the Corpus Christianorum Series Latina [henceforth CCSL] 2.1120). Others thought of earthly kings as *"exterae potestates,"* neither demonic nor salvific, but simply external and natural powers appointed for those who do not belong to the people of God. Irenaeus, for example, treats earthly kingdoms as godly institutions for the utility of the un-godly (*Adversus Haereses*, 5.24.2). *"Exterae potestates"* is from the council of Antioch (341), canon 5. On these issues Caspary, *Politics and Exegesis*, chap. 4, and Lester Field, *Liberty, Dominion, and the Two Swords: On the Origins of Western Political Theology (180–398)* (Notre Dame, IN: University of Notre Dame Press, 1998), are especially useful.

42   Indeed for many Christian thinkers, the Jews, by executing Jesus, provided the purest example of a people preferring Caesar's worldly sovereignty to Christ's, as Pseudo-Cyprian put it in his *Adversus Iudaeos* 42, 54 (CCSL 4.271, 273), and *De montibus* 7 (edited in the Corpus Scriptorum Ecclesiasticorum Latinorum [henceforth CSEL] 3.3.111). See also Justin, *Dialogue*, 41.1, and Melito of Sardis's *Homily on the Passion*. On debates over the dating (212?) and authorship of *Adversus Iudaeos*, see the works listed in Field, *Liberty, Dominion, and the Two Swords*, 280, n. 60.

43   Origen, *Commentary on Romans* 9.25, 1226B, on Peter and John. At times Origen seems to stress the Christian's goal of leaving the body behind, as in his commentary on the sacrifice of Isaac, "sicut in Domino corporeum nihil est, ita etiam tu in his omnibus corporeum nihil sentias; sed in spiritu generes . . ." (Migne, *PG* 12, 209b).

44   *Commentary on the Gospel of Matthew* (*Com. Mat.*) (Migne, *PG* 13) 17.27, 659–660: "imaginem enim Caesaris habet omnis res corporalis." On the fish, *Com. Mat.* 13.11, 208–209. Origen calls those Christians who err by refusing to acknowledge the debts of the flesh "Pharisaei" in *Com. Mat.* 17.27, 659–660. He characterizes Pneumatics who resist the earthly powers with material force as Judaizing Zealots in his commentary on Romans. On this, see Caspary, *Politics and Exegesis*, 149, 163.

45   The quote is from Caspary, *Politics and Exegesis*, 9. Origen comments on Pythagoras's beans in *Contra Haereses*, in Migne, *PG* 16.3, col. 3232. Origen probably followed his Alexandrian predecessor Clement in linking Pythagoras to Moses. See Clement, *Stromata*, in *Die griechischen christlichen Schriftsteller der ersten drei Jahrhunderte* [henceforth *GCS*], ed. O. Stählin (Leipzig: Hinrichs, 1906), 2:5.5, 342–346. Later church fathers such as Saint Ambrose considered Pythagoras a Jew (Letter 81, in Migne, *PL* 16, col. 1095–1098), a view credited by so distinguished an early modern scholar as John Selden.

46   Six thousand scrolls: Epiphanius, *Heresies* 64.63, found in Migne, *PG* 41, 1178–1179.

47 Eusebius, *Vita Constantini* 4.62.2 (*GCS* 7:146). The Greek word used for "type" is *typon*. See Averil Cameron, "Eusebius' *Vita Constantini* and the Construction of Constantine," in M. J. Edwards and Simon Swain, eds., *Portraits: Biographical Representation in the Greek and Roman Literature of the Roman Empire* (Oxford: Clarendon Press, 1997), 145–174. Translations of the *Vita* are here cited from Averil Cameron and Stuart G. Hall, *Eusebius, Life of Constantine, Translated with Introduction and Commentary* (Oxford: Clarendon Press, 1999). On Eusebius's use of Jews in his historical apologetics, particularly in the *Gospel Preparation* (*Praeparatio Evangelica*) and *Gospel Demonstration* (*Demonstratio Evangelica*), see Jörg Ulrich, *Euseb von Caesarea und die Juden: Studien zur Rolle der Juden in der Theologie des Eusebius von Caesarea* (Berlin: Walter de Gruyter, 1999). Also useful are the essays collected in sects. 5–8 of Harold W. Attridge and Gohei Hata, eds., *Eusebius, Christianity, and Judaism* (Leiden: Brill, 1992).

48 Eusebius, *Onomasticon: The Place Names of Divine Scripture*, ed. R. Steven Notley and Ze'ev Safrai (Boston: Brill, 2005). "New Jerusalem": Eusebius, *Vita Constantini* 3.33, cited from Cameron and Hall, *Eusebius*.

49 Quote "the facts about the Jews" is from Epiphanius of Salamis, *Panarion* 8.3.6 (*GCS* 25:189). Quote with "Anti-Christ" is from Cyril of Alexandria, *Catecheses* 15.15, found in W. K. Reischl and J. Rupp, *S. Cyrilli Hierosolymorum archiepiscopi opera quae supersunt omnia* (Hildesheim: Olms, 1967), 2:172. Cyril may have added these words in the 360s, after the reputed attempt of Emperor Julian "the Apostate" to rebuild the Temple. See Andrew S. Jacobs, *Remains of the Jews: The Holy Land and Christian Empire in Late Antiquity* (Stanford, CA: Stanford University Press, 2004), 37–44.

50 On jeering during sermons, see John's *On the Priesthood*, in *Nicene and Post-Nicene Fathers* 9 (Buffalo, NY: Christian Literature, 1889), 5.5, 48.675. By 380, when the emperor Theodosius forbade them from assembling in churches, the Arians were on the defensive. In 386 they scored a temporary victory, with the emperor restoring to them the right of assembly. See the *Theodosian Code* 16.1.2, 16.1.4.

51 John's sermons on the Arians are preserved in *Incomprehens.* 1 and 2, ed. and trans. in *Sources chrétiennes* 282 (Paris: Éditions du Cerf, 1970).

52 John Chrysostom, *Discourses against Judaizing Christians*, trans. Paul W. Harkins (Washington, DC: Catholic University of America Press, 1979), 1.1.4, 1.4.4.

53 James Parkes, *Prelude to Dialogue: Jewish-Christian Relationships* (London: Vallentine Mitchell, 1969), 153. "Judaizing" is here a loose translation of John's *Logoi kata Ioudaiōn*.

54 John Chrysostom, *Discourses,* 1.1.5, citing Hos. 4:16; and Jer. 31:18 (38:18 in the Septuagint).

55 John Chrysostom, *Discourses,* 1.2.6, citing Luke 19:27, the parable of the Ten Minas. John, like many ancient and modern readers, takes Christ to correspond to the character of "the King" in the parable. For a standard interpretation of this parable as pertaining to Christ see *Harper Collins Bible Commentary*, 951–952.

56 John Chrysostom, *Discourses,* 1.2.4.

57 The quotes are from the preface and introduction to the English translation by Harkins, in *Discourses*, ix, xxvi. For a leading example of the scholarship, see Robert L. Wilken, *John Chrysostom and the Jews: Rhetoric and Reality in the Late Fourth Century* (Berkeley: University of California Press, 1983), as well as his earlier collaboration with Wayne Meeks, *Jews and Christians in Antioch in the First Four Centuries of the Common Era* (Missoula, MT: Scholars Press, 1978).

58 John Chrysostom, *Discourses*, 1.6.

59 Ibid., 6.6.10–11.

60 Chrysostom was scarcely the only one to adopt such a strategy. See Christine Shepardson, *Anti-Judaism and Christian Orthodoxy: Ephrem's Hymns in Fourth-Century Syria* (Washington, DC: Catholic University of America Press, 2008), esp. chap. 4, "Ephrem, Athanasius and the Arian Threat." Specifically on Chrysostom, see her "Controlling Contested Places: John Chrysostom's *Adversus Iudaeos* Homilies and the Spatial Politics of Religious Controversy," *Journal of Early Christian Studies* 15 (2007), 483–516.

61 On the reconstruction plan, see among others Jeffrey Brodd, "Julian the Apostate and His Plan to Rebuild the Jerusalem Temple," *Bible Review* 11, no. 5 (October 1995), 32–38, 48; Yohanan H. Lewy, "Julian the Apostate and the Building of the Temple," in L. Levine, ed., *The Jerusalem Cathedra* (Detroit, MI: Wayne State University Press, 1983), 3:70–96; and David Levenson, "Julian's Attempt to Rebuild the Temple: An Inventory of Ancient and Medieval Sources," in Harold Attridge et al., eds., *Of Scribes and Scrolls* (Lanham, MD: University Press of America, 1990), 261–279.

62 John Chrysostom, *Discourses*, 5.11.4.

63 For an analysis of this event in a broader context, see Louis J. Swift, "St. Ambrose on Violence and War," *Transactions and Proceedings of the American Philological Association* 101 (1970), 533–543.

64 Ambrose, Letter 40.2, translated from Ambrose, *Select Works and Letters*, in *Nicene and Post-Nicene Fathers* 10, trans. H. de Romestin (New York: Christian Literature, 1896). See also J. H. W. G. Liebeschuetz, *Ambrose of Milan: Political Letters and Speeches* (Liverpool: Liverpool University Press, 2005), 95–123.

65 Ambrose, Letter 40.4; cf. Matt. 10:19–20.

66 Ibid., Letter 40.8.

67 Ibid., Letter 40.23.

68 Ibid., Letter 40.20.

69 Ibid., Letter 40.21.

70 Ibid., Letter 41.26.

71 Ibid., Letter 41.18.

72 Ibid., Letter 41.26.

73 Ibid., Letter 41.28.

74 Recall Luke 19:27. Medieval artists would later memorialize and monumentalize Ambrose's role as "expeller of Jews." See Walter Cahn, "The Expulsion of the Jews as History and Allegory in Painting and Sculpture of the Twelfth and Thirteenth Centuries," in Michael Signer and John Van Engen, eds., *Jews and Christians in Twelfth-Century Europe* (Notre Dame, IN: University of Notre Dame

Press, 2001), 94–108. I hasten to point out that unlike John, Ambrose never, so far as I know, applied Luke 19:27 to the Jews.

75 It is possible, though not necessary, that the church fathers themselves understood a clear difference between the threat posed to their community by "real" Jews and that posed by Christians or pagans with what they understood to be "Jewish" attitudes. For readers of their texts, whether in their own or later times, such clear distinctions became impossible.

76 Cf. Irenaeus, *Adversus Haereses*, 4.7.4, 3.6.2, 5.33, 4.26, 6.1.

77 Tertullian was among the theologians who argued against too sharp a differentiation between the figurative interpretation and the literal reality. His words in *Adversus Marcionem*, 4.40 are suggestive: "figura autem non fuisset, nisi veritatis esset corpus. Ceterum vacua res, quod est phantasma, figuram capere non posset." Or as he writes of the prophets in *De resurrectione carnis* 19, they expressed themselves in flesh as well as in allegorical shadows: "nec omnia umbrae, sed et corpora." How this caution affected his polemics against Judaism (e.g., in his *Adversus Iudaeos*) remains unexplored.

78 Concerning the influence of Origen on Jerome, see Megan Hale Williams, *The Monk and the Book: Jerome and the Making of Christian Scholarship* (Chicago: University of Chicago Press, 2006), esp. 83–89, 146–155.

79 Jerome credits Origen's inspiration in *De viris inlustribus* 54, in E. Richardson, ed., *Texte und Untersuchungen zur Geschichte der altchristlichen Literatur* (Leipzig: Akademie, 1896), 14.1.32–33. His Letter 52, to Bishop Nepotian, repeatedly represents Jews, Pharisees, and Sadducees in order to construct a negative foil for Christian clergy (e.g., chap. 13: "Do not broaden your fringes and wear phylacteries for show, or wrap yourself . . . in Pharisaic ostentation"). Quote with "but a figure" is from Letter 52, chap. 10, citing 1 Cor. 10:11; and Phil. 3:8 (F. A. Wright, trans., *Jerome: Select Letters*, Loeb Classical Library 262 (Cambridge, MA: Harvard University Press, 1933), 215–217. Jerome's friend Epiphanius of Salamis linked church wall-paintings to Pharisaism citing Acts 23:3: Epiphanius, *Testament*, in G. Ostrogorsky, ed., *Studien zur Geschichte des byzant. Bilderstreites* (Breslau: M & H Marcus, 1929), 67, frag. 2.

80 On this affair, see Jacobs, *Remains of the Jews*, 83–90.

81 Matt. 27; Mark 15; Luke 23; John 18–19.

82 Rufinus, *Apologia contra Hieronymum* 2.41 (CCSL 20:115).

83 On fourth-century worries about Origen's teachings, see the foundational work of Elizabeth A. Clark, *The Origenist Controversy: The Cultural Construction of an Early Christian Debate* (Princeton, NJ: Princeton University Press, 1992). On the increasing use of violence and physical coercion in the doctrinal debates of the imperial church, see Michael Gaddis, *There Is No Crime for Those Who Have Christ: Religious Violence in the Christian Roman Empire* (Berkeley: University of California Press, 2005).

84 For this and other relevant texts, see Norman Russell, *Theophilus of Alexandria* (New York: Routledge, 2007), esp. 89–174.

85 Serapion: Cassian, *Collatio* 10.3 (289:12–14); Clark, *Origenist Controversy*, 6.

86 Epiphanius of Salamis was among Jerome's allies in this affair. For a narration

of events, see Clark, *Origenist Controversy*, 44–47; F. Ledegang, "Anthropo-morphites and Origenists in Egypt at the End of the Fourth Century," in W. A. Bienert and U Kühneweg, eds., *Origeniana septima: Origenes in den Ausein-andersetzungen des 4. Jahrhunderts* (Leuven: Leuven University Press, 1999), 375–380; and Ágoston Schmelowszky, "The Origenist Controversy Revisited," in Péter Losonczi and Géza Xeravits, eds., *Reflecting Diversity: Historical and Thematical Perspectives in the Jewish and Christian Tradition* (Münster: LIT, 2007), 25–42.

87 Quote with "notable hatred" is from Jerome, Letter 84.3.3 (CSEL 55:123). Quote with "pure and hateful speech" is from the earlier *Praefatio in libro Iob* 41–48 (*Biblia Sacra*, 4th ed., ed. Robertus Weber et al. [Stuttgart: Deutsche Bibelgesellschaft, 1994], 732). On Jerome's strategy of appropriation, see Jacobs, *Remains of the Jews*, 83–87.

88 Augustine, *Confessions* 6.4, in Augustine, *Confessions*, trans. Henry Chadwick (Oxford: Oxford University Press, 1998), 94.

89 Augustine, *Confessions* 6.5, in ibid., 96.

90 Letter of Secundinus to Augustine, 3, found in John Rotelle and Boniface Ramsey, eds., *The Works of St. Augustine: A Translation for the Twenty-First Century* (Hyde Park, NY: New City Press, 2006), 1:357–362.

91 Augustine, *On Christian Doctrine*, trans. D. W. Robertson (Indianapolis, IN: Bobbs-Merrill, 1958), 3.v.9.

92 Some of Augustine's most virulently anti-Jewish language can be found in his sermons on the Gospel of John, the anti-Judaism of which we have already discussed. See, e.g., *Homilies on the Gospel of John* 3.19, 10.4, 114.40; Fredriksen treats these passages in *Augustine and the Jews*, 305–307, but ultimately explains them away as merely "rhetorical."

93 Augustine, *Confessions* 11.2.3.

94 Augustine, *The Spirit and the Letter* 21.13, in John Burnaby, trans., *Augustine: Later Works* (Philadelphia, PA: Westminster, 1955), 210.

95 On the epistolary exchange between Augustine and Jerome, see Ralph Hen-nings, *Der Briefwechsel zwischen Augustinus und Hieronymus und ihr Streit um den Kanon des Alten Testaments und die Auslegung von Gal. 2, 11–14*, Supplements to *Vigiliae Christianae* 21 (Leiden: Brill, 1994). See also *Aurelius Augus-tinus/Sophronius Eusebius Hieronymus, Epistulae mutuae/Briefwechsel*, ed. and trans. Alfons Fürst, *Fontes Christiani* 41, 1–2 (Turnhout: Brepols, 2002).

96 Augustine, Letter 28.4, in *Nicene and Post-Nicene Fathers* 1, ed. Philip Schlaff (Buffalo, NY: Christian Literature, 1896). I draw on this translation, except where otherwise indicated. For an example of Augustine's extensive attempts at preserving and sorting out the literal meanings of scripture, see his *De Genesi ad Litteram* (Migne, *PL* 34; CSEL 28), *Locutiones in Heptateuchem* (CCSL 33; ed. J. Fraipont and D. de Bruyne, 1958), and *Quaestiones in Heptateuchem* (also in CCSL 33).

97 Augustine, Letter 40.3.3.

98 Ibid., Letter 28.3.5.

99 Jerome, Letter 75.3.7, citing Acts 10:10–16.

100 Jerome, Letter 28.3.4, 40.3.3. For an example of the strength Augustine devoted to the task, and a restatement of his motives for doing so, see his work from the 410s, the *De Genesi ad litteram* (On the literal interpretation of Genesis), CSEL 28, 8.1, 231–232. He had undertaken but not completed a similar project in 393, *De Genesi ad litteram liber imperfectus* (CSEL 28.1).

101 Augustine, Letter 40.4.4.

102 Ibid.

103 Augustine, Letter 40.4.5. Jerome had interpreted Peter and Paul's quarrel as "simulatio," dissimulation or play-acting. See his *Commentarius in epistolam ad Galatas* 1.2.11–13 (Migne, *PL* 26:363C–367C). Hennings, Briefwechsel, 249–256, addresses the debate between Augustine and Jerome on this point; and Fürst, *Fontes Christiani*, 2–64, provides an excellent history of early Christian interpretations of the conflict between Peter and Paul, with special attention (29–36) to the view that it was an example of *simulatio/hypokrisis*.

104 Jerome, Letter 72.1.2.

105 Jerome, Letter 75.4.13.

106 Augustine, *Against Faustus* 19.17 (CSEL 25), found also in *Nicene and Post-Nicene Fathers* 4, trans. Richard Stothert (Buffalo, NY: Christian Literature, 1887).

107 On the Jewish plaintiff and the "Licinius" affair, see Fredriksen, *Augustine and the Jews*, 312–314.

108 Augustine, *Against Faustus* 18.1. On the encounter with Faustus, see also Fredriksen, *Augustine and the Jews*, esp. 213–234.

109 Augustine, *Against Faustus* 6.1.

110 Augustine, *On Christian Doctrine* 3.6.10; discussed in Fredriksen, *Augustine and the Jews*, 255.

111 Augustine, *Against Faustus* 12.9–13.

112 This exegesis was much cited in the Middle Ages, on which see Gilbert Dahan, "L'exégèse de l'histoire de Caïn et Abel du XIIe au XIVe siècle en occident," *Recherches de théologie ancienne et médiévale* 49 (1982), 21–89, and 50 (1983), 5–68, here (1982), 25–27. Augustine treats Cain quite differently in the *City of God* 15.7, where Cain is the founder of the earthly city. On this contrast, see the beautiful passage of Peter Brown, *Augustine of Hippo: A Biography* (London: Faber, 1967), 321. On the evolution of Augustine's views on religious coercion and his turn to other prooftexts (such as Ps. 59:12, "slay them not"), see Peter Brown, "St. Augustine's Attitude to Religious Coercion," *Journal of Roman Studies* 54 (1964), 107–116; and Jeremy Cohen, *Living Letters of the Law: Ideas of the Jew in Medieval Christianity* (Berkeley: University of California Press, 1999), 54–55. Curiously, Cain becomes a figure for penitential exile among pietist Jews in medieval Ashkenaz (see, e.g., Sefer Hasidim 38). Though the concept of penitential exile is found in the Talmud (e.g., BT Berachoth 56a; San. 37b), nowhere is Cain associated with it there: Could this be a Jewish response to the Christian figuration?

113 Cf. Paula Fredriksen, "Divine Justice and Human Freedom: Augustine on Jews and Judaism, 392–398," in Jeremy Cohen, ed., *From Witness to Witchcraft: Jews and Judaism in Medieval Christian Thought* (Wiesbaden: Harrassowitz, 1996),

29–54, here 48. Fredriksen, *Augustine and the Jews*, 235–259, also connects this revaluation of the fleshly and literal to Augustine's defense of the incarnation.

114 Quote with "milestones" is from *Sermo* 199.1.2, in Migne, *PL* 38:1027. For other examples, see Cohen, *Living Letters of the Law*. Compare Qur'an 62:5, with its image of donkeys carrying books.

115 Augustine, *Narrations on the Psalms* 59.17–19. A recent English translation is in Maria Boulding, trans., *Expositions of the Psalms* (Hyde Park, NY: New City, 2000).

116 On the plausibility of drawing connections between the Origenist and Pelagian controversies, see Clark, *Origenist Controversy*, chap. 5.

117 Ephraim of Bonn, *Book of Remembrance*, found in Shlomo Eidelberger, *The Jews and the Crusaders: The Hebrew Chronicles of the First and Second Crusades* (Hoboken, NJ: KTAV, 1996), 122.

118 Fredriksen, *Augustine and the Jews*, 352: "In the changed social context of medieval Christendom, Augustine's invocation of Psalm 59, interpreted literally, ultimately would safeguard Jewish lives." Peter the Venerable, Letter 130, in Giles Constable, ed., *Letters of Peter the Venerable* (Cambridge, MA: Harvard University Press, 1967), 1:327–330. See also the discussion in Jeremy Cohen, *Living Letters of the Law*, 245–270. Quote with "worse than death" is from Peter the Venerable, Letter 130.

119 Here, as elsewhere in this chapter, my appreciation for, but differences from, Paula Fredriksen's view should be clear. Augustine was not the forefather of Christian anti-Judaism, but neither are his criticisms of Judaism mere "lapses" (as Fredriksen puts it in *Augustine and the Jews*, 262). And as we will see, far from being a benign gift to future Jews that "ultimately would safeguard Jewish lives" (352), Augustine's writings played an important role in fashioning the exceptional status of Jews and Judaism in the medieval and modern Western political order.

120 On ancient theorizations of exile, see Giuliano Crifò, *L'esclusione dalla città: Altri studi sull'exilium romano* (Perugia: Edizioni Scientifiche Italiane, 1985). Augustine points toward these problems in *The City of God* 6.11, citing a quip about the Jews made by Seneca circa 70 CE in his lost *De Superstitione*: "The vanquished have given their laws to the victors" (*victi victoribus leges dederunt*). See Menachem Stern, *Greek and Latin Authors on Jews and Judaism* [henceforth *GLAJJ*], 3 vols. (Jerusalem: Israel Academy of Sciences and Humanities, 1974–1984), vol. 1, no. 186. Compare the complaint of Augustine's contemporary Rutilius Namatianus: "And would that Judea had never been subdued / by Pompey's wars and Titus' Military power! / The infection of this plague, though excised [*excisae pestis*] still creeps abroad to more: / and 'tis their own conquerors that a conquered nation keeps down." *De reditu suo* I, 391–398, in *GLAJJ*, vol. 2, no. 542. Both may find their inspiration in Horace's comment about captive Greece taming its Roman conquerors with her arts: *Epistularum liber* 2.1.156–157, found in H. Rushton Fairclough, trans., *Horace: Satires; Epistles; Art of Poetry*, Loeb Classical Library 194 (Cambridge, MA: Harvard University Press, 1929), 2:408.

121 Augustine, *City of God* 3.6, 15.4–5, 157. Cain's politics gives priority to flesh, "that part which the philosophers call vicious, and which ought not to lead the mind, but which the mind ought to rule and restrain by reason." The anthropology is Platonic, but more pessimistically than Plato (or Aristotle), Augustine explicitly assigns all earthly politics to the sphere of the appetites. His prooftexts here come significantly from Galatians (5:17) and Romans (7:17, 6:13). This link between Cain and the earthly city is mentioned briefly by Fredriksen (*Augustine and the Jews*, 346–347), but she does not refer it to the problem of Jewish political or legal status. Instead, she reads *The City of God* as beginning to dissociate Jews from Cain (so that Augustine can redeem the idea of "wandering" [*peregrinatio*]).

CHAPTER 4: "TO EVERY PROPHET AN ADVERSARY"

1 NOTE ON TRANSLITERATION: I have omitted all diacritical marks when converting words from Arabic, Aramaic, and other Near Eastern languages to Roman letters, with the exception of the signs for 'ayn (') and hamza ('). However, in citing the titles of other authors' works, I have retained any diacritics they used in those titles.

On Qur'an 6.112, see John Wansbrough, *Quranic Studies: Sources and Methods of Scriptural Interpretation* [henceforth *QS*] (Oxford: Oxford University Press, 1977), 61. Unless otherwise indicated, all translations from the Qur'an [henceforth Q] are my own, though I recommend to readers the translation of 'Abdullah Yusuf 'Ali, trans., *The Meaning of the Holy Qur'ān*, 11th ed. (Beltsville, MD: Amana, 2006).

2 On the Bahira legend, see Barbara Roggema, *The Legend of Sergius Baḥīrā: Eastern Christian Apologetics and Apocalyptic in Response to Islam* (Leiden: Brill, 2009).

3 Muhammad Ibn Ishaq, the author of the biography, died in AH 150/768 CE His work reaches us mainly through the recension of 'Abdu'l Malik Ibn Hisham (died ca. AH 218). The transliteration I cite here and throughout is that of A. Guillaume, *The Life of Muhammad: A Translation of Isḥāq's Sīrat Rasūl Allāh* (Karachi: Oxford University Press, 2000), 79–81. *Medina*: The name has additional resonances in Aramaic, "place of law (*din*)."

4 "Believers": Fred M. Donner, *Muhammad and the Believers at the Origins of Islam* (Cambridge, MA: Harvard University Press, 2010), 57. For reservations about Donner's thesis, see Patricia Crone, "Among the Believers: A New Look at the Origins of Islam Describes a Tolerant World That May Not Have Existed," *Tablet* (August 10, 2010) at http://www.tabletmag.com/news-and-politics/42023/among-the-believers/ (accessed January 3, 2012). Great systematizers: e.g., Ahmad ibn Hanbal, founder of one of the main schools of Islamic law, as reported by Abu Bakr al-Khallal, *Ahl al-milal wa-'l-ridda wa-'l-zanadiqa wa-tarik al-salah wa-'l-fara'id min kitab al-jamiʿ li-'l-Khallal*, ed. Ibrahim b. Muhammad al-Sultan (Riyadh, 1966), 55ff. Thomas Sizgorich argues that a hundred years earlier, by contrast, the traditionalist Dahhak ibn al-Muzahim could still treat the martyrs of Najran as simultaneously "Christian" and "people of

Islam"; see "'Become Infidels or We Will Throw You into the Fire': The Martyrs of Najran in Early Muslim Historiography, Hagiography, and Qurʾanic Exegesis," in Arietta Papaconstantinou, ed., *Writing "True Stories": Historians and Hagiographers in the Late Antique and Medieval Near East* (Turnhout: Brepols, 2010).

5   On the rarity of situating the message within Muhammad's life, see, e.g., sura 66. Muhammad is mentioned in 3:144, 33:40, 47:2, 48:29; and once as AHMaD, 61:6. Cf. Wansbrough, *QS*, 64.

6   Various prophets of the Arabs: Some of these names have a very uncertain history. James A. Bellamy argues, e.g., that Shuʿayb is not a prophet of the Arabs, but a misreading of Isaiah: see his "More Proposed Emendations to the Text of the Qurʾan," *Journal of the American Oriental Society* 116 (1996), 196–204 (197–198).

7   The Qurʾan uses two different terms, "Jews" (*Yahud*) and "Children of Israel," and the differences are significant.

8   Thus in the Targum (Aramaic translations of Hebrew scripture) Mount Sinai is referred to as *Tura de-sinai*. It is, however, impossible to be certain whether the influence here is Jewish or Christian.

9   BT Shabbat, 88a; BT Avodah Zarah 2b; D. Hoffman, ed., *Mekhilta de-Rabi Shim'on ben Yohai ʿal sefer hemot* (Frankfurt: Koyffmann, 1905), 100. Other Agadic traditions derive the same story from Cant. 8.5, "Under the Apple tree did I stir thee up"; see L. Grünhaut, ed., *Midrash shir-ha-shirim* (Jerusalem: Bidefus maʾarekhet ha-Tsevi, 1897), 47b and Cant. Rabba 45a col. B (top).

10   The Qurʾanic transformation of this phrase was itself deeply influenced by Rabbinic Jewish commentaries, as Julian Obermann brilliantly demonstrated in "Koran and Agada: The Events at Mount Sinai," *American Journal of Semitic Languages and Literatures* 58 (1941), 23–48. See also G. D. Newby, "Arabian Jewish History in the Sīrah," *Jerusalem Studies in Arabic and Islam* 7 (1986), 121–138, here 136–138; and I. de Mateo, "Il Tahrīf od alterazione della Bibbia secondo i musulmani," *Bessarione* 38 (1922), 64–111, 223–360. A recent argument for reading the Qurʾan in the light of these intertexts is Gabriel Said Reynolds, *The Qurʾan and Its Biblical Subtexts* (Oxford: Routledge, 2010).

11   The Muslim accusation against the Jews of *tahrif* (distortion, corruption) and *tabdil* (alteration, substitution) has a long bibliography. See esp. Camilla Adang, *Muslim Writers on Judaism and the Hebrew Bible* (Leiden: Brill, 1996), chap. 7, 223–248.

12   On the many prophetic traditions within the Qurʾan, see Brannon Wheeler, *Prophets in the Qurʾan: An Introduction to the Qurʾan and Muslim Exegesis* (London: Continuum, 2002). For some new methodological approaches to the study of intertexts, see Dirk Hartwig, Walter Homolka, Michael Marx, and Angelika Neuwirth, eds., *"In Vollen Licht der Geschichte": Die Wissenschaft des Judentums und die Anfänge der kritischen Koranforschung*, Ex Oriente Lux 8 (Würzburg: Ergon, 2008).

13   For Judeo-Christians, see S. Pines, "Notes on Islam and on Arabic Christianity and Judaeo-Christianity," *Jerusalem Studies in Arabic and Islam* 4 (1984), 135–152. On the Samaritans, see the (odd) article by John Bowman, "Banū Isrāʾīl in

the Qur'ān," *Islamic Studies* 2 (1963), 447–455, who argues that many Samaritans greeted Muhammad as the "prophet like unto Moses" promised in Deut. 18:18. See also Patricia Crone and Michael Cook, *Hagarism: The Making of the Islamic World* (Cambridge: Cambridge University Press, 1977), 14–15, 21–28. On the importance of Syriac Christian gospel commentaries and traditions in the Qur'anic community, see Joseph B. Witztum, "The Foundations of the House (Q 2:127)," *Bulletin of the School of Oriental and African Studies*, 72 (2009), 25–40, as well as the same author's PhD dissertation: "The Syriac Milieu of the Quran: The Recasting of Biblical Narratives" (Princeton University, 2011).

14 Q 2:61, 87, 91, and in many other suras.

15 Cf. Q 3:112: "Ignominy will be their portion wherever they are found."

16 Compare Q 16:123, 5:47, 42:13, and passim.

17 Yusuf ʿAli oddly leaves *musliman* untranslated, eliding the difficulty. *Hanif* is an obscure term meaning something like "natural monotheist." Cf. Donner, *Muhammad and the Believers*, 71.

18 The simile is also Talmudic: see Avodah Zarah 5b, which presents the image in a much less derogatory way.

19 See Muqatil ibn Sulayman, *Tafsir al-Qur'an*, commenting on Q 17:104, and discussed in Uri Rubin, *Between Bible and Qur'ān: The Children of Israel and the Islamic Self-Image* (Princeton, NJ: Darwin Press, 1999), 27–28. Such traditions seem to develop from debate over the ten tribes of Israel lost ca. 722 BCE, when the Assyrian conquerors of Israel deported them (see 2 Kings 7:6, 23; 2 Esd. 13:41–42, 46–47; Josephus, *Jewish Antiquities*, trans. Ralph Marcus [Cambridge, MA: Harvard University Press, 1937], 11.133). Might they also reflect knowledge of rabbinic stories like the Jerusalem Talmud's account (Kil'ayim 9.4) of Rabbi Meir's emigration to "Asia"? The idea that the ten lost tribes had settled in Central Asia was popular among medieval and early modern Europeans as well, including the famous historian Guillaume Postel in his *Des Histoires Orientales* (Paris, 1575), 34–37.

20 Qur'anic verses that allude to a believing fragment include 7:159, on a "group" (*umma*) of righteous people among the "people of Moses" (*qawm Musa*); 43:65; 61:14: "a faction [*ta'ifa*] of the Banu Isra'il believed, and a faction disbelieved." On the extensive writings of slightly later Muslim commentators about Jewish sects, see S. Wasserstrom, *Between Muslim and Jew: The Problem of Symbiosis under Early Islam* (Princeton, NJ: Princeton University Press, 1995), chap. 4.

21 Q 5:31–33. On early Islamic thinking about the inclusion of non-Muslims in Islamic society, see Yohanan Friedmann, *Tolerance and Coercion in Islam* (New York: Cambridge University Press, 2003).

22 The phrase is formulaically applied to hypocrites throughout the Qur'an. Note that these verses are aimed specifically at the Children of Israel.

23 The tradition will amplify the associative logic, as when Ibn Ishaq, 380, uses Jewish terms to describe the prophet's tribe of the Quraysh, because they are constantly questioning the prophet.

24 But see 2:142–145. On the change of direction of the *qiblah*, see recently (and helpfully) U. Rubin, "The Direction of Prayer in Islam: A Contribution to the

History of a Struggle between Rituals" [in Hebrew], *Historiya* 6 (5460/2000), 5–29.

25 "[S]triped cloaks" or alternatively, "propped up pieces of timber."

26 For traditions about Muhammad's ambivalent reaction to this first experience of revelation, see Ibn Ishaq, 106, and Uri Rubin, *The Eye of the Beholder: The Life of Muhammad as Viewed by the Early Muslims* (Princeton, NJ: Princeton University Press, 1995), 103–112.

27 I will suggest in subsequent text that the prophetic material eventually included in the Qur'an, on the one hand, and Islamic traditional accounts of the life of the Prophet, on the other, were structured and made intelligible through reciprocal and mutual reference to each other. The vast text-critical scholarship on the Qur'an is clearly of relevance to this question. It need not, however, be summarized here, since I intend what follows in the text to be coherent from the point of view of any of the three most influential text-critical approaches: those founded by Theodore Noldeke (*Geschichte des Qorans* [Göttingen, 1860; expanded by F. Schwally, Leipzig, 1909]); by John Wansbrough (*Quranic Studies; The Sectarian Milieu: Content and Composition of Islamic Salvation History* [Oxford: Oxford University Press, 1978]); and by Angelika Neuwirth (*Studien Zur Komposition der mekkanischen Suren* [Berlin: De Gruyter, 1981]); "Vom Rezitationstext über die Liturgie zum Kanon," in S. Wild, ed., *The Qur'an as Text* [Leiden: Brill, 1996], 69–105; and "Erzählen als Kanonischer Prozeß: Die Mose-Erzählung im Wandel der koranischen Geschichte," in R. Brunner et al., eds., *Islamstudien ohne Ende: Festschrift für Werner Ende* [Würzburg: Ergon in Kommission, 2002], 323–344).

28 The notes to this passage in Yusuf 'Ali's edition of the Qur'an are representative, identifying the "fools among the people" with the idolaters, Jews, and hypocrites, and comparing them to the Pharisees and Sadducees of Jesus's day ('Ali cites Matt. 22:15, 23). It is worth stressing the strong link in the Islamic tradition between this articulation of the crucial Islamic concept of "abrogation" (2:106) and the change of the *qiblah* as a way of confounding the Jews and their allies (2:142ff.). See, among countless examples of traditionists who emphasized this link, Ibn Ishaq, 258–259; and for a much later example, Abu 'Abd Allah Muhammad b. Ahmad Ansari al Qurtubi (d. 1272 CE), *Al-Jami' li-Ahkam al-Qur'an* (Cairo: al-Maktaba al-Tawfiqiya, n.d.), vol. 2, 55, 131ff. See also John Burton, *The Sources of Islamic Law* (Edinburgh: Edinburgh University Press, 1990), 174–183; Christopher Melchert, "Qur'anic Abrogation across the Ninth Century," in Bernard Weiss, ed., *Studies in Islamic Legal Theory* (Leiden: Brill, 2002), 84; and Rubin, "Direction of Prayer in Islam."

29 This may be one reason why the prophetic material collected in the Qur'an was not drawn on as a source of law in the early Islamic period, as it would be later on. On this point (made early by Joseph Schacht), see now Wael B. Hallaq, *A History of Islamic Legal Theories* (Cambridge: Cambridge University Press, 1997), 7–15, esp. 10.

30 I disagree with Fred Donner's conclusion, from the fact that the Believers' movement included some Jewish Believers, that critiques of Judaism in the

Qur'an and the tradition were a purely contingent reaction to "particular attitudes or political actions on their [the Jews'] part," so that in fact one should
not speak of a hostility to Judaism in the Believers' movement, any more than
the punishment or execution of some of Muhammad's opponents among his
own tribe of the Quraysh "should lead us to conclude that he was anti-Quraysh"
(*Muhammad and the Believers*, 74). On the contrary: like early Christianity, both
the Qur'an and the early Islamic tradition structure their engagement with previous scripture using ideas about Jews and Judaism adopted and adapted from
those earlier traditions. Their use of Judaism is in this sense structural, and it
affects how they perceived and represented the "particular attitudes" of living
Jews. As to the question of whether the Qur'an frequently takes the form of an
anti-Jewish polemic *because* it was redacted under the influence of the tradition, or whether the tradition frequently takes up Jewish enmity *because* Jewish
opposition to prophecy is such a prominent theme in the Qur'an, this cannot be
answered without taking a controversial position on the relative chronology of
both the Qur'an and the tradition. It is unnecessary to do so here.

31 His work, like that of many early traditionists, reaches us through redactions by
later authors, in this case 'Abdu'l Malik Ibn Hisham (died ca. AH 218) and others.
Ibn Ishaq is only one of several important early traditionists. I focus on his work
in part because his traditions (as redacted by Ibn Hisham) survive in a narrative
form, and in part because that narrative is the best known and the most easily
accessible in English translation (by A. Guillaume). But this narrative has a complex redaction history: even as redacted by Ibn Hisham, it circulated in multiple
forms. Moreover for each of the traditions Ibn Ishaq reported, there are traditions
from other traditionists that differ. I will mention some of these in the endnotes.
Marco Schöller, e.g., reconstructs traditions about the Prophet's conflict with the
Jews of Medina gathered by one of Ibn Ishaq's contemporaries: "Sīra and Tafsīr:
Muhammad al-Kalbī on the Jews of Medina," in Harald Motzki, ed., *The Biography of Muhammad: the Issue of the Sources* (Leiden: Brill, 2000), 18–48. These vari-
ances do not, however, affect my general arguments. Finally, this is not the place
to enter into the long debate about the reliability of the traditional material in
general as historical evidence for "what really happened" in early Islam, nor of Ibn
Ishaq's material in particular. For an accessible survey of this debate, see Rubin's
"Introduction: The Prophet Muhammad and the Islamic Sources," in Uri Rubin,
ed., *The Life of Muhammad* (Aldershot: Ashgate, 1998): xiii–xlvi.

32 Ibn Ishaq, 136–137. A similar story is related in the *Tafsir* (Qur'anic commentary) attributed to Muqatil b. Sulayman (d. 150/767), regarding Q 18:9. See the
analysis by Wansbrough, *QS*, 122–127.

33 Ibn Ishaq, 241–242.

34 Ibn Ishaq, 263–264.

35 The quotes are from Ibn Ishaq, 239–242.

36 Ibn Ishaq, 240. The episode was much debated, with some (like Mu'tazila) arguing that the prophet could not be bewitched, and others (Suhayli) opining that
he could be, since prophets were not immune to physical afflictions. For some
of the many traditions on the bewitching, see Michael Lecker, "The Bewitch-

ing of the Prophet Muḥammad by the Jews: A note à propos ʿAbd al-Malik b. Ḥabīb's Mukhtaṣar fī l-ṭibb," *Al-Qanṭara* 13 (1992), 561–569.

37 Ibn Ishaq, 364.

38 The warrior was Kaʿb b. al-Ashraf; his murder is described by Ibn Ishaq, 368. For a variant and interesting tradition about the killing of Kaʿb, see Michael Lecker, "Wāqidī's Account on the Status of the Jews of Medina: A Study of a Combined Report," *Journal of Near Eastern Studies* 54 (1995), 15–32.

39 Ibn Ishaq, 369.

40 Q 59:2; Ibn Ishaq, 438.

41 Ibn Ishaq, 464. On this episode, see M. J. Kister, "The Massacre of the Banū Qurayẓa: A Re-examination of a Tradition," *Jerusalem Studies in Arabic and Islam* 8 (1986), 61–96; and Michael Lecker, "On Arabs of the Banū Kilāb Executed Together with the Jewish Banū Qurayẓa," *Jerusalem Studies in Arabic and Islam* 19 (1995), 66–72.

42 The hypocrite was Muʿattib b. Qushayr. Some traditions specify that the case was brought to the Jew Kaʿb ibn al-Ashraf. Ibn Ishaq, 245, says only that "some Muslims" preferred to bring their cases to "Kahins" (pagan soothsayers). For a discussion of some of the many traditions, see Moshe Gil, "The Medinan Opposition to the Prophet," *Jerusalem Studies in Arabic and Islam* 10 (1987), 65–96 (here 81), an article important for many of the issues discussed here. On the constitution, see above all Michael Lecker, *The Constitution of Medina: Muḥammad's First Legal Document* (Princeton, NJ: Darwin Press, 2004). See also R. B. Serjeant, "The Sunnah Jāmiʿah, Pacts with the Yathrib Jews, and the Taḥrīm of Yathrib: Analysis and Translation of the Documents Comprised in the So-Called Constitution of Medina," *Bulletin of the School of Oriental and African Studies* 41 (1978), 1–42.

43 Ibn Ishaq, 466; cf. 521–523.

44 In making this comparative judgment I do not mean to minimize the violence of passages like Q 33:25–27, about how to deal with the "People of the Book" that opposed the Believers: "[S]ome you kill, and some you take captive. And He [God] made you inherit their lands and homes and property." Not surprisingly, this passage is linked by the traditionists to the treatment of the B. Qurayza after the Battle of the Ditch.

45 Ibn Ishaq, 517.

46 Ibid., 515–516. See 794 for Ibn Hisham's notes on Zaynab as a wife of the Prophet.

47 The first quotation in this paragraph can be found in Ibn Ishaq, 515; the second is from 523 and 689. The other tradition is from Malik b. Anas. The same words are attributed to ʿUmar when he expelled the Jews from Khaybar. On this tradition and its afterlife, see Maribel Fierro Bello, "A Muslim Land without Jews or Christians. Almohad Policies regarding the 'Protected People'," in Matthias M. Tischler and Alexander Fidora, eds., *Christlicher Norden-Muslimischer Süden. Ansprüche und Wirklichkeiten von Christen, Juden und Muslimen auf der Iberischen Halbinsel im Hoch- und Spätmittelalter* (Münster: Aschendorff Verlag, 2011), 231–247.

48 The influential modern Qur'anic commentator 'Afif 'Abd al-Fattah Tabbara cited Q 5:64 in support of Hitler's claim in *Mein Kampf* that the Jews were corrupting German youth. Cf. Suha Taji-Farouki, "A Contemporary Construction of the Jews in the Qur'an," in Taji-Farouki and Ronald Nettler, eds., *Muslim-Jewish Encounters: Intellectual Traditions and Modern Politics* (London: Routledge, 1998), 24–25. He also cited the related 7:167 ("your Lord proclaimed He would send forth against them, unto the Day of Resurrection, those who should visit them with evil punishment") as proof of the Qur'an's divine nature: "However, the certainty that this persecution, which became a historical fact and continued for a long time after the arrival of Islam, would shadow them until the Day of Resurrection, represents a statement concerning the unknown, which no human could possibly have made, furnishing undisputable evidence of the divine nature of the Qur'an." In Augustinian fashion, the Jews' degradation confirms the truth of a later scripture. For the eschatological *hadith* (in which I hear an echo of the Revelation of John 6:16), see Georges Vajda, "Juifs et Musulmans Selon le Hadit," *Journal Asiatique* 229 (1937), 57–127.

49 Phrase "farthest mosque," *Ar. al-masjid al-aqsā*: But where was that? The Qur'an makes no mention. It might well have been in heaven.

50 On Ka'b, who will figure more later, see Israel Wolfensohn, *Ka'b al-Ahbar und seine Stellung im Hadit und in der islamischen Legendenliteratur* (Gelnhausen: F. W. Kalbfleisch, 1933); Rubin, *Between Bible and Qur'ān*, 13–17, 56–57, 77; Rubin, *Eye of the Beholder*, 21–35. Thomas Sizgorich left incomplete a monograph tentatively titled "Ka'b and 'Umar Go to Jerusalem: Jewish Knowledge, Christian Stories, and Muslim Memory in the Early Islamic World" at his untimely death. I have benefited from reading his unpublished second chapter, which I cite with his permission. On the traditions about 'Umar as conqueror of Jerusalem, see Heribert Busse, "'Omar's Image as the Conqueror of Jerusalem," *Jerusalem Studies in Arabic and Islam* 8 (1986), 149–168; and Busse, "'Omar b. al-Ḥaṭṭāb in Jerusalem," *Jerusalem Studies in Arabic and Islam* 5 (1984), 73–119. The most famous traditional Islamic history of the conquests is that of Abu Ja'far Muhammad b. Jarir al-Tabari, *Ta'rīkh al-rusul wa-'l-muluk*, ed. M. J. de Goeje et al., 15 vols. (Leiden: Brill, 1887–1901). The sections concerning Palestine have been translated by Yohanan Friedmann, *The History of al-Ṭabarī*, vol. 12: *The Battle of al-Qādisiyyah and the Conquest of Syria and Palestine* (Albany: SUNY Press, 1992).

51 For Christian portrayals of the Muslims as rebuilding the Temple, see Crone and Cook, *Hagarism*, 161, n. 1–3. Following Sebeos's account, Crone and Cook also suggested that the Muslims installed a Jewish *Ishkhan* (governor) in Jerusalem (103). Sebeos was a seventh-century Armenian bishop. The (probably pseudonymous) account attributed to him was edited by Kerope Petrovich Patkanean, *Patmout'iun Sebēosi Episkoposi i Herakln* [History of Sebeos, Bishop of Heraclea] (St. Petersburg, 1879), here 111. See Robert Hoyland, "Sebeos, the Jews, and the Rise of Islam," in Ronald L. Nettler, ed., *Medieval and Modern Perspectives on Muslim-Jewish Relations* (Luxembourg: Harwood Academic, 1995), 89–102.

52 Tabari, *Ta'rikh*, 1:2408. For another version of this tradition, in which Ka'b is

portrayed as trying to reconcile the teachings of Muhammad and Moses, see Ibn 'Asakir, *Ta'rikh madinat Dimashq*, ed. Salah al-Din Munajjid (Damascus, 1951), 1:557. See Uri Rubin, "The Ka'ba: Aspects of Its Ritual Function," *Jerusalem Studies in Arabic and Islam* 12 (1989), 321–371.

53 The curse is attributed by al-Tabari to 'Abd Allah b. Abbas. See David T. Halperin and Gordon D. Newby, "Two Castrated Bulls: A Study in the Haggadah of Ka'b b. al-Aḥbār," *Journal of the American Oriental Society* 12 (1982), 631–638. The literature on *isra'iliyyat* is large, but see esp. Ismail Albayrak, "*Isrā'īliyyāt* and Classical Exegetes: Comments on the Calf with a Hollow Sound (Q.20.83–98/ 7.147–155) with Special Reference to Ibn 'Aṭiyya," *Journal of Semitic Studies* 47 (2002), 39–65; Albayrak, "Re-evaluating the Notion of *Isra'iliyyat*," *D.E.U. Ilahiyat Fakiltesi Dergisi* 13–14 (2001), 69–88; Jane Damen McAuliffe, "Assessing the *Isrā'īliyyāt*: An Exegetical Conundrum," in S. Leder, ed., *Storytelling in the Framework of Non-fictional Arabic Literature* (Wiesbaden: Harrassowitz, 1988); and Roberto Tottoli, "Origin and Use of the Term *Isra'iliyyat* in Muslim Literature," *Arabica* 46 (1999), 193–210. Tottoli and others have observed a resurgence of Islamic exegetical criticism of *isra'iliyyat* since the establishment of the State of Israel, criticism that I might interpret as a modern application of the tools of thought discussed in this section.

54 The quote with "faith of the Jews" is from Tabari's Qur'an commentary, as cited in Ze'ev Maghen, *After Hardship Cometh Ease: The Jews as a Backdrop for Muslim Moderation* (Berlin: De Gruyter, 2006), 56, n. 1. Compare Hava Lazarus-Yafeh, *Intertwined Worlds: Medieval Islam and Bible Criticism* (Princeton, NJ: Princeton University Press, 1992), 37.

55 The notion that Mosaic law was given as a punishment to the Jews will be well developed in Islamic thought: see Maghen, *After Hardship*, 52–71. Though this idea undoubtedly owes a good deal to Pauline Christianity, it also has roots in Hebrew scriptural and rabbinic traditions, as in Ezek. 20:25, "I gave them laws that were not good." On the exegetical history of this passage in the Second Temple and rabbinic periods, see P. W. Van der Horst, "'I Gave Them Laws That Were Not Good': Ezekiel 20:25 in Ancient Judaism and Christianity," in A. S. van der Woude et al., eds., *Sacred History and Sacred Texts in Early Judaism* (Kampen: Kok Pharos, 1992), 94–118. The notion will be amplified by Spinoza (see chap. 10) before being broadly diffused within European philosophical thought (see chap. 12).

56 The key Talmudic text, whose logic is closely followed by the Islamic debate, is Nedarim 20b. For the topic of anal sex, see also the medieval Tosafot commentary on the passage. The topic is explored with subtlety and acuity by Maghen, *After Hardship,* chap. 9: "Turning the Tables: The Muslim-Jewish Polemic over Sexual Positions," 161–209.

57 The confrontation with Byzantium does acquire apocalyptic overtones within the tradition over time, but I would nevertheless maintain the significance of my distinction.

58 For this quotation, see the entry for 'Uthmān b. 'Affān in the *Encyclopedia of Islam*, ed. M. T. Houtsma et al. (Leiden: Brill, 1987).

59 The charge was reportedly made by the Prophet's scribe Ubayy b. Kaʿab, who was angered that the caliph ʿUthman picked Zayd b. Thabit for the task of compilation. See Michael Lecker, "Zayd b. Thābit, ʿa Jew with Two Sidelocks': Judaism and Literacy in pre-Islamic Medina (Yathrib)," *Journal of Near Eastern Studies* 56 (1997), 259–273.

60 Ibn Ishaq, 308.

61 The executed leader was ʿUqba b. Abu Muʿayt, the mother of the first Umayyad caliph, Hind bt. ʿUtba. See also R. Sellheim, "Prophet, Caliph, und Geschichte: Die Muhammad-Biographie des Ibn Isḥaq," *Oriens* 18–19 (1965–66/7), 33–91.

62 The use of divining arrows was forbidden in the Qurʾan (2:219, 5:90). They had many uses, but the one intended here, the adjudication of genealogical claims, is discussed in Ibn al-Kalbi, *Kitab al-Asnām* (Cairo, 1965), 28. Ibn Ishaq, 67, describes a different method. For a full discussion of the tradition concerning ʿUqba, see Seth Ward, "Muḥammad Said: ʿYou Are Only a Jew from the Jews of Sepphoris': Allegations of the Jewish Ancestry of Some Umayyads," *Journal of Near Eastern Studies* 60 (2001), 31–41. The Umayyads are also assimilated to Jews in other ways, as in the tradition that reports a vision of the Prophet in which he sees the Umayyads climbing the *minbar* in the form of "apes and pigs"; see Rubin, "Apes, Pigs, and the Islamic Identity," *Israel Oriental Studies* 17 (1997), 89–105, here 101.

63 The traditionist was Shurahbil ibn Saʾd. An early analysis of Shurahbil can be found in Josef Horovitz, "The Earliest Biographies of the Prophet and Their Authors," trans. Marmaduke Pickthall, *Islamic Culture* 1 (1927), 552–553.

64 J. Fück, *Muḥammad ibn Isḥāq: literarhistorische Untersuchungen* (Frankfurt am Main: [n.p.], 1925), chap. 2; Guillaume, *Life of Muhammad*, xxxv–xl; Moshe Gil, "The Origins of the Jews of Yathrib," in F. E. Peters, ed., *The Arabs and Arabia on the Eve of Islam* (Brookfield, VT: Ashgate, 1998), 219. The story was often retold, as in Abu Hatim ibn Hibban's (d. AH 354) book on reliable narrators. Because of this anti-*israʾiliyat* sentiment Ibn Hisham, Ibn Ishaq's medieval editor, in fact suppressed the entire first book of Ibn Ishaq's work, called the *Kitab al-Mubtadaʾ*. That lost book has been recently reconstructed from citations in al-Tabari and other sources by Gordon Newby, *The Making of the Last Prophet: A Reconstruction of the Earliest Biography of Muhammad* (Columbia: University of South Carolina Press, 1989).

65 Among the early transmitters who came under suspicion were Kaʿb al-Ahbar (d. ca. 32/652–653) and Wahb b. Munabbih (d. ca. 110/728), as well as later ones like (to a much lesser extent) Ibn Ishaq. On the increasingly strident condemnations of *israʾiliyat*, i.e., stories, traditions, and memorabilia that the traditionists understood as Jewish, see among others Zeʾev Maghen, *After Hardship*, 73.

66 On these terms, see L. Kinberg, "*Muḥkamāt* and *mutashābihāt* (Koran 3/7): Implications of a Koranic Pair of Terms in Medieval Exegesis," *Arabica* 35 (1988), 143–172.

67 Or so the earliest commentaries understood it. See, e.g., Muqatil ibn Sulayman, *Tafsir al-Qurʾan*, ed. ʿAbdallah Mahmud Shihata, 5 vols. (Cairo: Al-Hayʾa al-Misriyya al-ʿAmma liʾl-Kitab, 1979), 1:264.

68 On the occasion of revelation of Qur'an 8:22, see Ibn Ishaq, 322. The Qur'an mentions the punishment of metamorphosis (*maskh*) into apes and pigs at 2:65, 5:60 (and the often associated 7:78), and 7:166. It does not identify the victims, but the tradition universally agrees that they were "Children of Israel," and specifically Jews (*Yahud*). The cause of the punishment varies according to the commentators. A Shi'i tradition says that the curse punished the Jews' killing of 120 prophets from the house of David (Ps.-Mas'udi, *Ithbat al-Wasiyah lil-Ilam 'Ali ibn Abi Talib 'alayhi al-Salam* [Qum: Manshūrāt al-Ridá, 1983], 80). On the Jews as apes and pigs, see I. Lichtenstaedter, "And Become Ye Accursed Apes," *Jerusalem Studies in Arabic and Islam* 14 (1991), 153–175; Michael Cook, "Early Muslim Dietary Law," *Jerusalem Studies in Arabic and Islam* 7 (1986), 222–223; and Rubin, *Between Bible and Qur'ān*, 213–220. Rubin shows how the punishment extended in the tradition to Muslim heretics (220–232). For the tradition that Q 8:22 refers to the hypocrites, see Ibn Ishaq, 322. On the Prophet's immunity to hypocrisy, see the traditions that attribute to Ka'b a prophecy drawn from the Torah, describing the coming prophet as the one who "says in private what he says in public, and his word and deed are equal," cited in Rubin, *Between Bible and Qur'ān*, 14.

69 For the many traditions linking the Khawarij to sura 3:7, see Rubin, *Between Bible and Qur'ān*, 147–167. Those cited here are from Ibn Abi Shayba, 15, no. 19748, and Ahmad, Musnad, 3, 224. Rubin provides numerous others. The quotation at the end of the paragraph can be found in Tabari, *Tafsir*, 16:27.

70 Tabari, *Ta'rikh* 6:82 (2:702), and further sources are found in Rubin, *Between Bible and Qur'ān*, 168ff. See also Steven M. Wasserstrom, "The Shi'is Are the Jews of Our Community': An Interreligious Comparison within Sunni Thought," *Israel Oriental Studies* 14 (1994), 297–324. On the "Jewish lineages" of all sects, see Wasserstrom, *Between Muslim and Jew*, 157–158. His use of the word "heresy" is a bit misleading here, since the denomination is relative. The Khawarij, e.g., probably considered their (eventually victorious) opponents a "Judaizing heresy."

71 Rubin, *Between Bible and Qur'ān,* 137. Cf. 117–146.

72 Ibn Ishaq, 103–104, quoting John 15:23, is here adopting John's claim that the divine plan requires the groundless enmity of the Jews toward the word, and redirects it forward in time, translating John's Greek "paraclete" through a Syriac variant (*menahhemana*, "comforter") into the Prophet Muhammad. For related traditions, see Rubin, *Eye of the Beholder*, 22–23.

73 *Revealing the Secrets and Disclosing the Concealed*, bk. 5, translated in "Disclosing the Fraudulence of the Jewish Doctors," by 'Abd al-Rahim al-Jawbari, trans. M. Perlman, "Notes on the Position of Jewish Physicians in Medieval Muslim Society," *Israel Oriental Studies* 2 (1972), 315–319, here 316.

74 'Abd Allah bin Buluggin, *Tibyan*, cited by Ross Brann, *Power in the Portrayal: Representations of Jews and Muslims in Eleventh and Twelfth Century Islamic Spain* (Princeton, NJ: Princeton University Press, 2002), 45–46.

75 Ibn Hazm, "The Refutation of Ibn Naghrila the Jew," trans. Moshe Perlmann, "Eleventh-Century Andalusian Authors on the Jews of Granada," *Proceedings*

of the American Academy for Jewish Research 18 (1948–49), 269–280, here 281–283. On this treatise, see Brann, *Power in the Portrayal*, 78–79.

76 The poem is by Muhammad ibn ʿAmmar, cited by Brann, *Power in the Portrayal*. Further examples given by Brann include the criticism of Khalaf b. Faraj al-Sumaysir (51–52); or the comment of the Tibyan that "most of the subjects in Granada . . . were only Jews" (44–45). Brann's book explores this Muslim "projection" of political anxiety onto Jews: "[T]he texts we will examine all prove to be concerned with issues of sovereignty, power, and control of knowledge and are reflective of concerns and paradigms internal to Islam for which the Jew serves as a speculum" (8).

77 ʿAli ibn Ahmad ibn Hazm, *Al-Fisal fi l-milal wal-ahwaʾ wal-nihal*, 6 vols. (Beirut, 1982), 1:325. See Camilla Adang, *Muslim Writers on Judaism and the Hebrew Bible: From Ibn Rabban to Ibn Ḥazm* (Leiden: Brill, 1996), 105. On Paul as a Jewish agent, see the citations in Moshe Perlmann, "Eleventh-Century Andalusian Authors," n. 37, 278.

78 On such complaints, Bernard Lewis's *Jews of Islam* (Princeton, NJ: Princeton University Press, 1987), 28–30, is a useful starting point. Lewis adduces an exemplary *fatwah* by the thirteenth-century scholar al-Nawawi (from his *Al-Manthurat*, ed. Ignaz Goldziher, *Revue des études Juives* 28 [1894], 94), which contains an explicit authorization of political critique: anyone who works to secure the monarch's dismissal of a nonbeliever will be rewarded by God, for "they will spare no pains to corrupt you" (Q 3.114). Ibn Khaldun, however, treats the use by Muslim monarchs of Christians and Jews in administrative posts as more or less a historical constant: 2:8–9, chap. 3, sect. 32 (Brann, *Power in the Portrayal*, 47)

79 For an attempt to compare the relative status of Jews under Islam and Christianity, see Mark Cohen, *Under Crescent and Cross: The Jews in the Middle Ages* (Princeton, NJ: Princeton University Press, 1995). Maribel Fierro Bello, in "A Muslim Land without Jews or Christians," shows well how arguments for expulsion (or extermination) of Jews drew on well-known traditions such as those of Muhammad's dying words, and suggests that the Almohads' expulsion and forced conversion of the Jews were attempts to implement those words. Other critiques akin to Ibn Hazm's include those of al-Turtushi, whose "mirror for princes" (Siraj al-muluk) criticized (in its chap. 51) various Islamic monarchs for empowering "dhimmis." I do not deal here with the most famous medieval "exception," Ibn Taymiyya (who died in Damascus in 1328 CE), whose influence on modern "Islamism" has been (perhaps too) widely noted. See Yossef Rapoport and Shahab Ahmed, eds., *Ibn Taymiyya and His Times* (Karachi: Oxford University Press, 2010), esp. the essay by Mona Hassan, "Modern Interpretations and Misinterpretations of a Medieval Scholar: Apprehending the Political Thought of Ibn Taymiyya," 338–366. An argument against the categorization of Ibn Taymiyya as an "extremist" can be found in Yahya Michot, *Muslims under Non-Muslim Rule: Ibn Taymiyya*, trans. Jamil Qureshi (Oxford: Interface, 2006).

CHAPTER 5: "THE REVENGE OF THE SAVIOR"

1 Ramon Martí, *Pugio fidei adversus mauros et judaeos* (1687; reprint Farnborough: Gregg Press, 1967), 2:24–27, translated by Cohen in *Living Letters of the Law*, 348–349 [see chap. 3, n. 112].
2 The choice to ignore the Greek Orthodox East is dictated by necessity, and with an eye to the future: it is the western Latin political theology of Judaism that had the greater impact on the modern world. But the parallel phenomenon in the Orthodox east is of tremendous interest and remains relatively unstudied.
3 *Crónica de 1344*, Biblioteca Nacional, Madrid, ms. 10,815, fol. 145 r-v.
4 *Castigos e documentos para bien vivir*, ed. Agapito Rey (Bloomington: Indiana University Press, 1952), 133.
5 Ibid., 31–32.
6 Ibid., 133.
7 Guibert of Nogent, *De Vita Sua* 3.16, in Edmond René Labande, ed., *Les Classiques de l'Histoire de France au Moyen Âge* (Paris: Belles Lettres, 1981), 34: 422–429; and John F. Benton, trans., *Self and Society in Medieval France. The Memoirs of Abbot Guibert of Nogent* (New York: Harper & Row, 1970), 209–211. Pucellina: Susan Einbinder, "Pucellina of Blois: Romantic Myths and Narrative Conventions," *Jewish History* 12 (1998), 29–46. The Estherke legend appears in Polish, Yiddish, and Hebrew sources. See Haya Bar-Itzhak, *Jewish Poland: Legends of Origin* (Detroit, MI: Wayne State University Press, 2001), 113–132. See also Salo W. Baron, *A Social and Religious History of the Jews* (New York: Columbia University Press, 1965), 10:321.
8 There were stories about other non-Christian groups. Muslim and Christian traditions had Alfonso VI of Castile married to the Muslim princess Zaida of Seville. László of Hungary was said by his enemies to have been led into paganism by his Cuman concubines. Nora Berend, *At the Gate of Christendom: Jews, Muslims, and "Pagans" in Medieval Hungary, c. 1000–c. 1300* (Cambridge: Cambridge University Press, 2000), 177.
9 On this genre, see Stephen K. Wright, *The Vengeance of Our Lord: Medieval Dramatizations of the Destruction of Jerusalem* (Toronto: University of Toronto Press, 1989); María Rosa Lida de Malkiel, *Jerusalén: el tema literario de su cerco y destrucción por los romanos* (Buenos Aires: Universidad de Buenos Aires, 1972). *Vindicta Salvatoris*, ed. Constantinus de Tischendorf, in *Evangelia apocrypha*, 2nd ed. (Leipzig: [n.p.], 1876), 471–486.
10 Juan Ruiz, *Libro de buen amor*, stanzas 1183–1184, trans. Raymond S. Willis (Princeton, NJ: Princeton University Press, 1972), 323.
11 On original commentaries, see Johannes Heil, *Kompilation Oder Konstruktion?: Die Juden in den Pauluskommentaren des 9. Jahrhunderts* (Hannover: Hahnsche Buchhandlung, 1998). The Bishop Agobard of Lyons was an exception, but his complaints about imperial favor shown to Jews were not influential, and probably owed something to his Visigothic background. On Agobard, see Heil, "Agobard, Amolo, das Kirchengut und die Juden von Lyon," *Francia* 25 (1998), 39–76.

12 Duke Bracizlao: *Chronica Boemorum* of Cosmas of Prague (d. 1125), in B. Bret-
holz, ed., *Monumenta Germaniae Historica* [*MGH*] SS rer. Germ., N.S. 2 (Ber
lin: MGH, 1923), sect. 3.5 (ad a. 1098), 166; and Hilsch, "Die Juden in Böhmen
und Mähran im Mittlelater und die ersten Privilegien (bus zum Ende des 13.
Jahrhunderts)," in F. Seibt, ed., *Die Juden in den bömischen Ländern* (Munich-
Vienna: Oldenbourg, 1983), 13–26. Normans: In 1086, Sichelgaita, Robert of
Apulia's widow, gave the Archbishopric of Bari all that city's Jews. See Raphael
Straus, *Die Juden im Königreich Sizilien unter Normannen und Staufern* (Heidelberg: C. Winter, 1910), 95. Four years later, Alfano II of Salerno received
a similar gift from Roger of Apulia: A. Marongiu, "Gli Ebrei di Salerno nel
Documenti dei Secoli X–XIII," *Archivio Storico per le Province Napoletane*, n.s.
23 (1937), 238–263, here 240–241.

13 The privileges granted by Henry IV in 1090 are similar in form to those granted
by their Carolingian predecessors. But these continuities in form obscure an
evolving relationship in which the sovereign's claim to absolute power over the
Jews grows continually stronger. See A. Patschovsky, "Das Rechtverhältnis der
Juden zum deutschen König (9.-14. Jahrhundert)," in *Zeitschrift der Savigny-
Stiftung für Rechtsgeschichte* 110 (1993), 331–371.

14 Laws of Edward: "quia ipsi Iudei et omnia sua regis sunt . . . tanquam suum
proprium," in Leges Edwardi Confessoris 25, in Felix Liebermann, ed., *Die
Gesetze der Angelsachsen* (1903; Halle: Max Niemeyer, 2007), 650. Alfonso II
and Frederick II: David Abulafia, "'Nam Iudei servi regis sunt, et semper fisco
regio deputati': The Jews in the Municipal Fuero of Teruel (1176–7)," in Harvey
Hames, ed., *Jews, Muslims, and Christians in and around the Crown of Aragon.
Essays in Honour of Professor Elena Lourie* (Leiden: Brill, 2004), 97–123. On
the Capetians, see Gavin Langmuir, "'Tanquam Servi': The Change in Jewish
Status in French Law about 1200," in his *Toward a Definition of Anti-Semitism*
(Berkeley: University of California Press, 1990).

15 Quoted in Cecil Roth, *A History of the Jews in England* (Oxford: Clarendon
Press, 1964), 33.

16 On Henry of Bracton, see F. I. Schechter, "The Rightlessness of Medieval English Jewry," *Jewish Quarterly Review* 4 (1914), 128; and F. W. Maitland and
F. Pollock, *History of English Law before the Time of Edward I*, 2 vols. (Cam-
bridge: Cambridge University Press, 1952), 1:472–473 [emphasis added]. For
the expulsion text, see David Abulafia, "The Servitude of Jews and Muslims
in the Medieval Mediterranean: Origins and Diffusion," *Mélanges de l'École
Française de Rome, Moyen Âge* 112 (2000), 687–714, here 691; and John A.
Watt, "The Jews, the Law, and the Church: The Concept of Jewish Serfdom in
Thirteenth-Century England," in Diana Wood, ed., *The Church and Sovereignty,
Studies in Church History*, Subsidia 9 (Oxford: Ecclesiastical History Society,
1991), 153–172.

17 See the reference to the *Chronica Boemorum* of Cosmas of Prague in n. 12.

18 Augustine of Hippo, *Sermones*, in Migne, *PL* 38:col. 56, "Behold, the Jew is slave
[servus] to the Christian," and col. 57, "Quomodo servi" [see chap. 3, n. 10].

19 For French exercises of *captio* by Capetian kings and magnates, see Robert

Chazan, *Medieval Jewry in Northern France: A Political and Social History* (Baltimore, MD: Johns Hopkins University Press, 1973), 38–40, 73, 78–80; and William C. Jordan, *The French Monarchy and the Jews: From Philip Augustus to the Last Capetians* (Philadelphia: University of Pennsylvania Press, 1989), 98–102.

20 Petrus Cantor, *Verbum Abbreviatum*, in Migne, *PL* 205: col. 158.

21 See Robert Stacey, "Parliamentary Negotiation and the Expulsion of the Jews from England," in Michael Prestwich, Richard H. Britnell, and Robin Frame, eds., *Thirteenth-Century England VI* (Woodbridge: Boydell & Brewer, 1997), 93–94. Among Stacey's many other valuable essays, see also "Anti-Semitism and the Medieval English State," in John Robert Maddicott and David Michael Palliser, eds., *The Medieval State: Essays Presented to James Campbell* (London: Hambledon Press, 2001), 163–177; as well as Robin R. Mundill, *England's Jewish Solution: Experiment and Expulsion, 1262–1290* (Cambridge: Cambridge University Press, 1998). For the cartoon, see Michael Adler, *Jews of Medieval England* (London: Jewish Historical Society, 1939), plate 1.

22 On lions, see among others Anna M. Adroer i Tasis, "La possessio de lleons, simbol de poder," in *XV Congreso de Historia de la Corona de Aragón (Jaca, 20–25 sept. 1993)* (Zaragoza, 1996), vol. 1, pt. 3, 257–268; and Asunción Blasco Martínez, "La casa de fieras de la Aljaferia de Zaragoza y los judios," in *XV Congreso de Historia de la Corona de Aragón, I: El poder real en la Corona de Aragón, siglos XIV–XVI*, 5 vols. (Zaragoza, 1996), 3:291–318.

23 On linens, see, e.g., Yom Tov Assis, *Jewish Economy in the Medieval Crown of Aragon (1213–1327): Money and Power* (Leiden: Brill, 1997), 173, 177. There were Jewish mint masters in Austria, the German empire, Bohemia, Poland, Moravia, and Hungary, as well as in the Iberian Peninsula: Daniel M. Friedenberg, *Jewish Minters and Medalists* (Philadelphia, PA: Jewish Publication Society, 1976); and Friedenberg, "Jewish Mint Masters of Medieval Hungary," *Shekel* 24, no. 4 (1991), 20–25. On Jews as treasurers and bailiffs (in Catalonia-Aragon) or *comites camere* (in Hungary and Austria), see J. Lee Shneidman, "Jews as Royal Bailiffs in Thirteenth Century Aragon," *Historia Judaica* 19 (1959), 55–66; and Shneidman, "Jews in the Royal Administration of Thirteenth Century Aragon," *Historia Judaica* 21 (1959), 37–52. On Hungary, see Berend, *At the Gate of Christendom*, 128–129. For the sake of this limited point, I am ignoring the prominence of Jews as royal physicians.

24 William Chester Jordan, "Jews, Regalian Rights, and the Constitution in Medieval France," *AJS Review* 23 (1998), 1–16, here 7. The ordinance is published in Alexandre Teulet et al., eds., *Layettes du Trésor des Chartes*, 5 vols. (Paris: Archives Nationales, 1863–1909), vol. 2, no. 2083, 192–193.

25 Quote with "we would rather die" is from David Nirenberg, "Une société face à l'altérité. Juifs et chrétiens dans la péninsule Ibérique, 1391–1449," *Annales. Histoire, Sciences Sociales* 62 (2007), 762.

26 William of Newburgh, *Historia rerum anglicarum*, ed. Hans Claude Hamilton (London: Sumptibus Societatis, 1856), bk. 3, chap. 26, 282–283, "De moribus regis Henrici." On the Magna Carta, see clauses 10 and 11 (both significantly omitted from the version reissued by John in 1216).

27 On Simon de Montfort's expulsion of the Jews from Leicester (1253), see J. R. Maddicott, *Simon de Montfort* (Cambridge: Cambridge University Press, 1994), 14–17; and H. G. Richardson, *The English Jewry under the Angevin Kings* (London: Greenwood Press, 1960), 187–192. On Grosseteste's involvement, see R. W. Southern, *Robert Grosseteste: The Growth of an English Mind in Medieval Europe* (Cambridge: Cambridge University Press, 1986), 246–249. For the letter (Epistle 5), see *Rerum Britannicarum Medii Aevi Scriptores* (London: Longmans, Green, 1862), 25:33–38. The strategic nature of these charges is suggested by the fact that the second issue pursued in the letter is a conflict between the Countess of Winchester's and Robert Grosseteste's churches over taxes.

28 On the sacking by Simon de Montfort's followers of the Jewries of Canterbury, London, and Northampton during Montfort's War of 1264, see Henry Richards Luard, ed., *Flores Historiarum*, 3 vols. (London: Rolls Series, 1890), 2:495. The quote is from Matthew Paris, *Chronica majora*, ed. Henry Richards Luard, 7 vols. (London: Rolls Series, 1872–1884), 5:487–488. For the argument that the clipped state of the coinage is imagined as the circumcision of the king, see Willis Johnson, "Textual Sources for the Study of Jewish Currency Crimes in Thirteenth-Century England," *British Numismatic Journal* 66 (1997), 23. For the Gulbenkian Apocalypse illumination, see Suzanne Lewis, "*Tractatus adversus Judaeos* in the Gulbenkian Apocalypse," *Art Bulletin* 68 (1986), 561.

29 For Philip V, see David Nirenberg, *Communities of Violence: Persecution of Minorities in the Middle Ages* (Princeton, NJ: Princeton University Press, 1996), 53. For a Castilian example, see the petition to Alfonso XI of the Cortes of Valladolid in 1322 (*Cortes de los antiguos reinos de León y de Castilla* [Madrid: Rivadeneyra, 1861], vol. 1, cap. 18, 342), and those of Madrid in 1329 (ibid., vol. 1, cap. 37, 415–416). My thanks to David Cantor-Echols for the reference to Alfonso XI.

30 On the accusations made by Castilian bishops against Alfonso X, see Peter Linehan, "The Spanish Church Revisited: The Episcopal *gravamina* of 1279," in Brian Tierney and Peter Linehan, eds., *Authority and Power: Studies on Medieval Law and Government Presented to Walter Ullmann on His Seventieth Birthday* (Cambridge: Cambridge University Press, 1980), 127–147; and Linehan, *The Spanish Church and the Papacy in the Thirteenth Century* (Cambridge: Cambridge University Press, 1971), 176, 219.

31 See the documents produced to justify the rebellion of Toledo against Juan II of Castile, cited in note 51. On Henry's IV's difficulties, see among others Ana Echevarria Arsuaga, "La conversion des chevaliers musulmans dans la Castille du XVe siècle," in Mercedes García Arenal, ed., *Conversions islamiques. Identités religieuses en Islam méditerranéen* (Paris: Maisonneuve et Larose, 2001), 119–140. On Isabel as "protector of the Jews and daughter of a Jewess," see the account of the Polish traveler Nicolas Popplau, in Javier Liske, *Viajes de extranjeros por España y Portugal en los siglos XV, XVI, y XVII: colección* (Madrid: Casa Editorial de Medina, 1878). On Ferdinand, see Maurice Kriegel, "Histoire sociale et ragots: sur l' 'ascendance juive' de Ferdinand le Catholique," in *Mov-*

imientos migratorios y expulsiones en la diáspora occidental (Pamplona: Universidad Pública de Navarra, 2000), 95–100.

32 The literature on the case, and on Frederick's privilege of protection, is vast. For a useful treatment of the legal issues, see Bernhard Diestelkamp, "Der Vorwurf des Ritualmordes gegen Juden vor dem Hofgericht Kaiser Friedrichs II. im Jahr 1236," in *Religiöse Devianz: Studien zur Europaischen Rechtsgeschichte*, special issue of *Ius Commune* no. 48 (1990), 19–39. On the people's surrender to the emperor of their sovereignty over Jews ("velut peculiarem commissum sibi populum"), see esp. 24–25.

33 František Graus, *Pest-Geissler-Judenmorde*, in *Veröffenlichungen des Max-Planck-Instituts für Geschichte* 86 (1987), esp. 208–214 on Nuremberg; Johannes Heil, "Vorgeschichte und Hintergründe des Frankfurter Pogroms von 1349," *Hessisches Jahrbuch für Landesgechichte* 41 (1991), 105–151, on Frankfurt.

34 Peter the Venerable, *Epistulae* 130, in Giles Constable, ed., *The Letters of Peter the Venerable*, 2 vols. (Cambridge, MA: Harvard University Press, 1967), 1:327–330 (emphasis added). On Peter, see Cohen, *Living Letters of the Law*, 245–270.

35 *Speculum adhortationis Judaice*, cited by Heiko Oberman, *The Roots of Anti-Semitism in the Age of Renaissance and Reformation* (Philadelphia, PA: Fortress Press, 1984), 33.

36 Gregory adapted the tale from a Greek version preserved by Evagrius Scholasticus of Antioch (ca. 536–600). Latin: "De quodam Iudeo," lib. 1, c. 10, in Migne, *PL* 71:col. 714; English: R. Van Dam, *The Glory of the Martyrs* (Liverpool: Liverpool University Press, 1988), no. 9, 29–32. See K. Winstead, "The Transformation of the Miracle Story in the Libri historiarum of Gregory of Tours," *Medium Aevum* 59 (1990), 1–15. William of Malmesbury's version is edited in *El libro de Laudibus et miraculis sanctae Mariae de Guillermo de Malmesbury OSB (d. 1143)*, ed. J. M. Canal (Rome: Alma Roma Libreria Editrice, 1968), no. 33, 137–138. He also invokes the story in his *Gesta Regum*, 2, ed. W. Stubbs (London, 1889) cc. 284–286, 338–342, as part of a refutation of theological errors about the nature of the Eucharist. For background on William, see P. N. Carter, "The Historical Context of William of Malmesbury's Miracles of the Virgin Mary," in R. H. C. Davis and J. M. Wallace-Hadrill, eds., *The Writing of History in the Middle Ages: Essays presented to Richard William Southern* (Oxford: Clarendon Press, 1981), 124–165. See more generally Miri Rubin, *Gentile Tales: The Narrative Assault on Late Medieval Jews* (New Haven, CT: Yale University Press, 1999), 8–28.

37 On William of Norwich's case, see *The Life and Miracles of St. William of Norwich by Thomas of Monmouth*, ed. Augustus Jessopp and Montague Rhodes James (Cambridge: Cambridge University Press, 1896); and Gavin I. Langmuir, "Thomas of Monmouth: Detector of Ritual Murder," *Speculum* 59 (1984), 822–846. "Ther was an Asye" quotation is from the "Prioress's Tale," cited from Geoffrey Chaucer, *The Riverside Chaucer*, 3rd ed., ed. Larry Dean Benson (Oxford: Oxford University Press, 2008), 209, lines 488–492.

38 I am here conflating the claims of a number of sources, notably the "Passio judaeorum secundum Johannes rusticus quadratus" and the "De caede judaeo-

rum pragensi." On these, see Rubin, *Gentile Tales*, 135–140; and Barbara New-
man, "The Passion of the Jews of Prague: The Pogrom of 1389 and the Lessons
of a Medieval Parody," *Church History* 81 (2012).

39 Joseph Naudet and Pierre Claude François Daunou, *Recueil des historiens
des Gaules et de la France*, 24 vols. (Paris, 1840), 20:34. The text dates to ca.
1276–1282, i.e., at much the same time that the story of Alfonso VIII entered
circulation.

40 Rigord presents Philip as an ideal Christian monarch for expelling the Jews
against the wishes of the bishops and the aristocracy. See *Œuvres de Rigord et
de Guillaume le Breton, historiens de Philippe-Auguste*, ed. Henri-François Dela-
borde, 2 vols. (Paris: Société de l'Histoire de France, 1882–1885), 1:27–31. For
the poem about Charles VIII as a second Vespasian, see Wright, *Vengeance of
Our Lord*, 126.

41 Jordan, "Jews, Regalian Rights, and the Constitution," 13. This strategy of
"compensation" was remarkably enduring. The Spanish expulsion of the Moriscos (Muslims converted to Christianity) in 1609, e.g., was proclaimed in the
same year as the Spanish defeat in the Low Countries: a "victory" of Spanish
Catholic arms meant to distract from their bitter defeat.

42 Jordan, *French Monarchy and the Jews*, 31.

43 Chazan, *Medieval Jewry in Northern France*, 186. See also David Abulafia,
"Monarchies and Minorities in the Christian Western Mediterranean around
1300: Lucera and Its Analogues," in Scott L. Waugh and Peter D. Diehl, eds.,
*Christendom and Its Discontents: Exclusion, Persecution, and Rebellion, 1000–
1500* (Cambridge: Cambridge University Press, 1996), 234–263.

44 Stacey, "Parliamentary Negotiation and the Expulsion," 77.

45 Clement IV to King James, December 31, 1266, in Santiago Domínguez Sán-
chez, *Documentos de Clemente IV (1265–1268) referentes a España* (León: Universidad de León 1996), no. 114, 224–227.

46 Berend, *At the Gate of Christendom*, 183–189.

47 The correspondence is transcribed in Joaquim Miret y Sans, "El proces de les
hosties contra.ls jueus d'Osca en 1377," *Anuari de l'Institut d'Estudis Catalans* 4
(1911–1912), 59–80.

48 See, e.g., the Cortes of Burgos of 1367, in *Córtes*, 2:150–151; and Julio Valdeón
Baruque, *Los Conflictos sociales en el reino de Castilla en los siglos XIV y XV*
(Madrid: Siglo Veintiuno, 1975), 132.

49 Recall that King Philip Augustus expelled the Jews from the French royal
domain (i.e., from the fiefs he governed directly) in 1181–1182. His example
was followed by a number of minor French lords in the 1190s and by more
major ones in the thirteenth century: of Brittany in 1240, of Gascony in 1287–
1288; of Anjou and Maine in 1289, of Niort in 1291, of Nevers in 1294. The
king of England expelled the Jews from his realms in 1290; the kings of France,
from theirs again in 1306 and 1322.

50 For the estimate of expulsions, see Phillip N. Bebb, "Jewish Policy in Sixteenth
Century Nürnberg," *Occasional Papers of the American Society for Reformation
Research* 1 (1977), 125–136, here 132–133. On the temporary privileges, Fried-

rich Battenberg, "Zur Rechtsstellung der Juden am Mittelrhein in Spätmittelalter und früher Neuzeit," *Zeitschrift für historische Forschung* 6 (1979), 129–183. See also František Graus, "Die Juden in ihrer mittelalterlichen Umwelt," in Alfred Ebenbauer and Klaus Zatloukel, eds., *Die Juden in ihrer mittelalterlichen Umwelt* (Vienna: Bohlan, 1991), 53–65.

51 Text in E. Benito Ruano, "El Memorial del bachiller Marcos García de Mora contra los conversos," *Sefarad* 17 (1957), 314–351, here 320–321. The representation of the synagogue as a "congregation of beasts" has a venerable tradition. Both Bede (in the eighth century) and Amalric of Metz (in the ninth) punned on the Latin "congregation" (a compound of the prefix *con* and the noun *grex*, meaning herd or flock) to describe the synagogue as a gathering of "sheep and inanimate objects." Both are cited in Kenneth Stow, *Jewish Dogs: An Image and Its Interpreters* (Palo Alto, CA: Stanford University Press, 2006), 6.

52 E.g., *Politics* 1279b. According to Aristotle, the natural life of subsistence we share with animals, but the human has a higher goal: "born with regard to life, but existing essentially with regard to the good life." *Politics* 1252b, 30. Cf. 1278b, 23–31; 1252a, 26–35. Citations from Aristotle are to *The Complete Works of Aristotle: The Revised Oxford Translation*, ed. Jonathan Barnes, 2 vols. (Princeton, NJ: Princeton University Press, 1984), citing, as is traditional, by the Bekker numbers. The influence of Aristotle's thought was expanding greatly in Spain, as in other parts of late medieval Europe. See, e.g., A. R. D. Pagden, "The Diffusion of Aristotle's Moral Philosophy in Spain, ca. 1400-ca.1600," *Traditio* 31 (1975), 287–313; and Christoph Flüeler, *Rezeption und Interpretation der aristotelischen Politica im späten Mittelalter*, 2 vols. (Amsterdam and Philadelphia: B. R. Grüner and J. Benjamins, 1992).

53 These lines have also been interpreted as an economic critique, an interpretation that is related to, though different from, the one proposed here. See Gabriel Egan, *Shakespeare and Marx* (Oxford: Oxford University Press, 2004), 36–38. See also J. H. Hexter, "Property, Monopoly, and Shakespeare's *Richard II*," in Perez Zagorin, ed., *Culture and Politics from Puritanism to the Enlightenment* (Berkeley: University of California Press, 1980), 1–24; Dennis R. Klinck, "Shakespeare's Richard II as Landlord and Tenant," *College Literature*, 25 (1998), 21–34; and William O. Scott, "'Like to a Tenement': Landholding, Leasing, and Inheritance in *Richard II*," in Constance Jordan and Karen Cunningham, eds., *The Law in Shakespeare* (Basingstoke: Palgrave Macmillan, 2006), 58–72.

CHAPTER 6: THE EXTINCTION OF SPAIN'S JEWS
AND THE BIRTH OF ITS INQUISITION

1 I do not mean to invoke through my metaphors the Freudian notion of the return of the repressed (on the relationship of Freud's notion to explanations of anti-Semitism, see chap. 1, n. 34). My metaphorical "dream" and "nightmare" were, for that matter, literal to some contemporaries like Ralph Josselin, whose diary for January 4, 1655, records a dream in which Oliver Cromwell's Secretary

of State "turned Jew." See *The Diary of Ralph Josselin, 1616–1683,* ed. Alain Macfarlane (Oxford: Oxford University Press, 1976), 337.

2 In 1391 Easter fell on March 26.

3 Words from Reuven are translated in Abraham Hershman, *Rabbi Isaac ben Sheshet Perfet and His Times* (New York: Jewish Theological Seminary of America, 1943), 194–196, emended here as per Jaume Riera in "Els avalots del 1391 a Girona," in *Jornades d'història dels jueus a Catalunya* (Gerona: Ajuntament de Girona, 1990), 156. Crescas's "Letter to the community of Avignon" is included in Shelomo Ibn Verga's much later *Das Buch Schevet Jehuda,* ed. M. Wiener (Hannover: H. Lafaire, 1924), 128. On the death toll in Gerona, see Riera, "Els avalots del 1391," 135. For Castile, see Lopez de Ayala, *Crónica de Enrique III de Castilla,* ed. Cayetano Rosell, Biblioteca de Autores Españoles 68 (Madrid: Rivadeneyra, 1877), 167, 177. Ayala lists as destroyed the Castilian aljamas of Seville, Córdona, Burgos, Toledo, Logroño, "y otras muchas," and in Aragon those of Barcelona, Valencia, Lérida, "y otras muchas." Those that escaped, he adds, "quedaron muy pobres."

4 See Archive of the Crown of Aragon, Chancery [henceforth ACA:C] 2042:23 v–24v (October 8, 1394), "in quo puteo quamplurima corpora judeorum tempore excidii seu destruccionis dicti calli etiam de mandato, ordinacionem seu licencia baiuli seu aliorum officialium Barchinone, ut dicitur tunch proiecta et modo etiam sepulta et subterrata existunt."

5 Some historians doubt this, explaining the 1391 attacks not in terms of Christian views of Judaism, but in terms of a contingent factor such as grain prices, the minority of the Castilian king, or (in the Crown of Aragon) the presence of foreigners inciting violence. See, e.g., Ph. Wolff, "The 1391 Pogrom in Spain: Social Crisis or Not?" *Past and Present* 50 (1971), 4–18; and A. Mackay, "Popular Movements and Pogroms in Fifteenth-Century Castile," *Past and Present* 55 (1972), 33–67.

6 See Arxiu Històric de la Ciutat de Barcelona [henceforth AHCB], Consell de Cent, Llibre del Consell, 19-A, n. 25, fols. 37r, 47r., August 23, August 27.

7 Valencia's 1397 ban: ACA:C 2209:149r–150r (February 22), with copy in ACA:C 2303:74v–75v. For royal attempts to resettle Jews in Barcelona, ACA:C 1882:188 v–189r, ACA:C 1884:132v–133r, ACA:C 2039:170 v–171r, and ACA:C 1910:12 r. For resistance by the city, AHCB, Consell de Cent, Llibre del Consell, 19-A, n. 25, fol. 93r. Ban of 1401: ACA:C 2196:102v–103v (May 18). Successors: AHCB, Consellers, Testaments de Consellers, XVII–2 (1399–1428), fol. 8v (1401). Cf. AHCB, Consellers, Testaments de Consellers, XVII–3 (1430–1448), fol. 9v (1431), shortly after the ban was made permanent.

8 Jaume De Puig i Oliver, "La *Incantatio studii ilerdensis* de Nicolau Eimeric, O.P.," *Arxiu de Textos Catalans Antics* 15 (1996), 7–108, here 47. Antoni was accused of this and other heretical opinions ca. 1393. "It has reached" is from ACA:C 2232:95v–96r (October 25, 1400).

9 See Robert E. Lerner, *The Feast of Saint Abraham: Medieval Millenarians and the Jews* (Philadelphia: University of Pennsylvania Press, 2001), esp. chap. 7.

10 For references to and analysis of these sources, see David Nirenberg, "Conver-

sion, Sex, and Segregation: Jews and Christians in Medieval Spain," *American Historical Review* 107 (2002), 1080–1081.

11 References can be found in ibid., 1081–1084, 1090.

12 Vincent Ferrer, *Sermons*, ed. Gret Schib et al., 5 vols. (Barcelona: Barcino, 1971–1985), 3:13–14. On Vincent's messianic inspiration, see José Guadalajara Medina, *Las profecías del anticristo en la edad media* (Madrid: Gredos, 1996), 232–247.

13 Hebrew accounts of the misery in Solomon Alami, *Igeret Musar*, ed. Adolph Jellinek (Vienna, 1872), 10b; and Abraham Zacuto, *Sefer Yuhasim ha-Shalem*, ed. Tsevi Filipowski (Edinburgh: Hevrat Mehorere Yeshenim, 1857), 225b, "the greatest persecution." Further references in Nirenberg, "Conversion," 1084–1085.

14 Alcañiz's privilege in ACA:C 2394:022 r–v (February 9, 1415). The bibliography on Tortosa is vast, but see most recently Jeremy Cohen, "Tortosa in Retrospect: The Disputation as Reported in Solomon ibn Verga's Shevet Yehudah [Hebrew]," *Zion* 76 (2011), 417–452; and Frank Talmage, "Trauma at Tortosa: The Testimony of Abraham Rimoch," *Mediaeval Studies* 47 (1985), 379–415.

15 Quoted in Eleazar Gutwirth, "Habitat and Ideology: The Organization of Private Space in Late Medieval *Juderías*," *Mediterranean Historical Review* 9 (1994), 205–234, here 208.

16 On the choice given converts in Mallorca, see the sources in Nirenberg, "Spanish 'Judaism' and 'Christianity' in an Age of Mass Conversion," in J. Cohen and M. Rosman, eds., *Rethinking European Jewish History* (Littman: Oxford, 2009), 158. For Barcelona, AHCB, Consell de Cent, Llibre del Consell, 19-A, n. 25, fol. 37 (August 27, 1391).

17 L. Batlle y Prats, "Un episodio de la persecucion judía de 1391," in *Per a una història de la Girona jueva* (1948; Girona: Ajuntament de Girona, 1988), 2:614–617. G. Secall i Güell, *La comunitat hebrea de Santa Coloma de Queralt* (Tarragona: Excma. Diputació Provincial de Tarragona, 1986), 118–119.

18 On the year's grace, see ACA:C 2374:77r–v (February 5, 1415). Gerona's complaint: ACA:C cr. Alfonso IV, box 4, no. 511 (May 12, 1417).

19 ACA:C 1950:107r (and cf: 1950:113r) (July 30, 1393). Conversely, see ACA:C 1862:71v–72r (October 10, 1394).

20 For extensive documentation on ceremonial and fiscal entanglements see Nirenberg, "Une société," 764–766 [see chap. 5, n. 25]. On Jewish relations with converted kin, see also Mark Meyerson's study of the community of Murviedro in the Kingdom of Valencia: *A Jewish Renaissance in Fifteenth-Century Spain* (Princeton, NJ: Princeton University Press, 2004), 184–224.

21 Though here I address only Christian (both "old" and "new") versions of this question, it was also of vital interest to Jews. For my understanding of Jewish responses, see "Mass Conversion and Genealogical Mentalities: Jews and Christians in Fifteenth-Century Spain," *Past and Present* 174 (2002), 3–41.

22 For the sources (including "quamplurimum frequentius judaytzant") on these concerns, and on royal inquiries into them, see Nirenberg, "Une société," 771.

23 Arxiu Municipal de Lleida [henceforth AML], Llibres de Crims, no. 803, ff.

115v–122r (November 17, 1407). For Franchesca's poisoning trial, see AML, Llibres de Crims, no. 802, fol. 69v–72r (Nov. 13, 1406). There were plenty of accusations of Judaizing made in conflictual situations. Bernat March of Barcelona, e.g., who was accused of unspecified crimes before the criminal justice, feared foul play in his trial because he had earlier denounced various converts for continuing to carry out Jewish ceremonies. See ACA:C 2360:96r (October 14, 1412).

24 All references are from Brian Dutton and Joaquín González Cuenca, eds., *Cancionero de Juan Alfonso de Baena* (Madrid: Visor Libros, 1993) [henceforth *Cancionero*]. Poems from cancioneros other than that of Baena will be cited from Brian Dutton's *El Cancionero del Siglo XV, c. 1360–1520*, 7 vols. (Salamanca: Universidad de Salamanca, 1990–1991). What follows in the text is a much-compressed summary of arguments found in my "Figures of Thought and Figures of Flesh: 'Jews' and 'Judaism' in Late Medieval Spanish Poetry and Politics," *Speculum* 81 (2006), 398–426, to which readers can refer for more sources and bibliography.

25 The eggplant quotes are from poems by Diego de Estuniga (no. 424) and Juan García (no. 384). See also no. 418. The reference to *adefyna* is by Juan de Guzmán (no. 404), the baptismal allusion by Ferrand Manuel (no. 370). For allusions to Juan Alfonso de Baena's sexual encounters with Jewesses, see among others the same poem by Juan Garçia. For the Mariscal's insult, see no. 418. It is entirely on the evidence of these poems that Baena's status as *converso* rests.

26 On these associations of eggplant in Spain, see Juan Gil, "Berenjeneros: The Aubergine Eaters," in Kevin Ingram, ed., *The Conversos and Moriscos in Late Medieval Spain and Beyond*, vol. 1: *Departures and Change* (Leiden: Brill, 2009), 121–142.

27 Examples of this underlying logic are legion: see the bibliography cited in Nirenberg, "Figures of Thought." Quote "half-converted Jews" is from Théodore de Puymaigre, *La cour littéraire de don Juan II, roi de Castille* (Paris: A. Franck, 1873), 131.

28 Suspicion of poetry has deep roots in Christian aesthetics. For the case of Augustine, see *De Civitate Dei* 11.18; *De Doctrina Christiana* 2.6 (7, 8) and 4.11 (26). For Thomas Aquinas's claim, see his *Quodlibetal Questions* 7.6.16. Elsewhere Thomas concedes that neither sacred scripture nor liturgical ritual can do without such "sensible figures." See *Summa Theologica* 1.1. 9, 1.2.101. For the theme in Spain, see the work of Karl Kohut, esp. "Der Beitrag der Theologie zum Literaturbegriff in der Zeit Juans II von Kastilien: Alonso de Cartagena (1384–1456) und Alonso de Madrigal, genannt el Tostado (1400?–1455)," *Romanische Forschungen* 89 (1977), 183–226; and *Las teorías literarias en España y Portugal durante los siglos XV y XVI* (Madrid: Consejo Superior de Investigaciones Científicas, 1973). On Saint Vincent Ferrer's opposition to the allegorization of poetry, see Pedro Catedra, "La predicación castellana de San Vicente Ferrer," *Boletín de la Real Academia de Buenas Letras de Barcelona* 39 (1983–1984), 235–309, esp. 278.

29 See the classic work of Ernst Robert Curtius, *Europäische Literatur und latein-isches Mittelalter* (Bern: A Francke, 1948), "Poesie und Theologie," 221–234; as well as the more modern bibliography cited in my "Figures of Thought." On the *Cancionero* de Baena in this context, see Karl Kohut, "La teoría de la poesia cortesana en el Prologo de Juan Alfonso de Baena," *Actas del coloquio hispano-aleman Ramón Menendez Pidal* (Tübingen: Niemeyer, 1982), 120–137, here 131, n. 27. On the theme of *gracia* in the *Cancionero*, see Julian Weiss, *Poet's Art: Literary Theory in Castile, c. 1400–60* (Oxford: Oxford University Press, 1990), 25–40.

30 Ferran's opening gambit is in no. 272, 472–474, lines 21–32. The allusion is to Matt. 11:25. Lope's response is no. 273, 473–474. Ferran counters in no. 274. Friar Lope attacks Villasandino on similar grounds in no. 117. That poem ends with a curse on those "hypocrites" who sow discord, and ends with the exhorta-tion that princes "abhor Jews" and "honor good men" (lines 89–96). Though here I am only concerned with "Judaization" in debates about the relative value of secular poetry and theology, it is worth noting that accusations of Judaism were also made in contests where both sides claimed theological authority. In a debate (nos. 323–328) between Franciscans and Dominicans over the immacu-late conception of the Virgin Mary, e.g., Fray Lope accuses Diego Martínez de Medina of reading like a Jew (no. 324, line 137: "La palavra mal entendida / mata e non da consuelo," a paraphrase of 2 Cor. 3:6), calls him a hypocritical Pharisee (lines 209–211), and suggests that he should join the people of Moses and the relatives of Cohen (no. 326, lines 61–63).

31 No. 96, 122–123, lines 28–45. See also no. 255, 453–455.

32 No. 359, 639, lines 1–4, 9–12. Baena says this explicitly in the challenge he issued to Villasandino and Lando in 1423 (no. 357, lines 28–30). The competi-tive exchange between Baena and Lando continues with Lando to Baena, no. 360, 639–640. Quote with "mule turds" is from Baena to Lando, no. 363, 641–642, lines 9–12. On the "truth claims" of insult, see Jean-Claude Milner, *De la syntaxe à l'interprétation: Quantités, insultes, exclamations* (Paris: Seuil, 1978), 174–223.

33 No. 365, 642–643.

34 *Cancionero*, no. 501, 343. For another example of a poem that combines the charge of Judaizing with that of being a bad lover, see no. 140, Alfonso Álva-rez de Villasandino against Alfonso Ferrández Semuel. To this charge, Alfonso Álvarez adds that his target is an apostate Jew with a big nose. On the place of love in the production of poetry and nobility in Castile during this period, see Julian Weiss, "Alvaro de Luna, Juan de Mena and the Power of Courtly Love," *Modern Language Notes* 106 (1991), 241–256.

35 Those critics: For examples, see Nirenberg, "Figures of Thought." Diego's poem about Symuel is in *Cancionero*, no. 511, 355–356. Of course the possibility of an ironic allusion to Jewish "literal" understanding should not be dismissed here. Cf., however, the Marqués de Santillana's comment on the writings of Rabbi Shem Tov de Carrion ("Being born in a vile nest / does not make the hawk worth less / nor are good examples diminished / because uttered by a Jew") in

his "Proemio," in *Obras Completas*, ed. Angel Gómez Moreno and Maximilian P. A. M. Kerkhof (Barcelona: Planeta, 1988), 451.

36 By way of contrast, note the distance claimed in the first line of Juan Ruiz's *Libro de Buen Amor*, written before the mass conversions.

37 For references, see Nirenberg, "Une société," 784.

38 References, together with a discussion of the events of 1434 and 1437, in Nirenberg, "Mass Conversion and Genealogical Mentalities," 23–25. The Council of Basel added an exhortation to converts that they marry "old" Christians. An extended narrative description and much of the bibliography on the Toledan revolt can conveniently be found in Benzion Netanyahu's *The Origins of the Inquisition in Fifteenth Century Spain* (New York: Random House, 1995).

39 The relevant texts are edited in Eloy Benito Ruano, "El Memorial" [see chap. 5, n. 51] and in his "La Sentencia-Estatuto de Pero Sarmiento contra los conversos toledanos," *Revista de la Universidad de Madrid* 6 (1957), 277–306. On the use of the word *raza* by contemporary participants in these debates, and on the question of whether these statutes can be understood as racial, see David Nirenberg, "Was There Race before Modernity? The Example of 'Jewish' Blood in Late Medieval Spain," in Miriam Eliav-Feldon, Benjamin Isaac, and Joseph Ziegler, eds., *The Origins of Racism in the West* (Cambridge: Cambridge University Press, 2009), 232–264.

40 For the relator's text, see Alonso de Cartagena, *Defensorium unitatis christianae*, ed. Manuel Alonso (Madrid: Escuela de Estudios Hebraicos, 1943), app. 2, 343–356, here 351–355. Note that though the relator condemns the anti-converso aspects of this genealogical approach, he nevertheless utilizes genealogical arguments as well, referring constantly to the converts as of the lineage of Christ. This seemingly contradictory strategy is common in pro-converso texts.

41 Max Horkheimer and Theodor W. Adorno, *Dialectic of Enlightenment*, trans. John Cummings (1944; London: Blackwell Verso, 1972), 186.

42 Hernando de Talavera, *Católica Impugnación,* ed. F. Márquez and F. Martín Hernández (Barcelona: Juan Floris, 1961), 186, cited and translated in Felipe Pereda, "Through a Glass Darkly: Paths to Salvation in Spanish Painting," *Judaism and Christian Art: Aesthetic Anxieties from the Catacombs to Colonialism*, ed. Herbert L. Kessler and David Nirenberg (Philadelphia: University of Pennsylvania Press, 2011), 264, 284. The charge against Donosa: "Nunca tuvo ni tiene ni costumbró tener en su casa oratorio de la Virgen María ni de Jhu. Xristo, ni de sus santos, segunt que xristianos costumbran tener e delant de los quales fazen oración." See B. Llorca, "La Inquisición española y los conversos judíos y marranos," *Sefarad* 8 (1942), 357–389.

43 The 1480 civic ordinances on painting are published in "Petición presentada en el Cabildo de Sevilla, el 18 de Septiembre de 1480" (*Actas Capitulares del Arch. Municipal de Sevilla*, 45–47), in J. Gestoso y Pérez, *Ensayo de un diccionario de artífices que florecen en Sevilla durante el siglo XIII al XVIII,* 3 vols. (Sevilla, 1899). On this episode see Pereda, "Through a Glass Darkly," 263–290.

44 The example of breast milk is drawn from Juan de Pineda, *Diálogos familiares de la agricultura Cristiana*, ed. Juan Meseguer Fernández (Madrid: BAE, 1963), vol.

3, 103b (Dialogue 15, sect. 21). This and other cases are discussed in Julio Caro Baroja, *Las formas complejas de la vida religiosa. Religión, sociedad y character en la España de los siglos XVI y XVII* (Madrid: Akal, 1978), 489–498. On *linajudos* in Seville, see Ruth Pike, *Linajudos and Conversos in Seville: Greed and Prejudice in Sixteenth and Seventeenth Century Spain* (New York: Peter Lang, 2000); and in Granada, see Enrique Soria Mesa, "Los Linajudos. Honor y conflict social en la Granada del siglo de oro," in Julián J. Lozano Navarro and Juan Luis Castellano, eds., *Violencia y conflictividad en el universo barroco* (Granada: Editorial Comares, 2010), 401–427. *Linajudo* more commonly means more or less the opposite of its use in these documents: someone of exceptionally pure lineage.

45 For Erasmus, see Marcel Bataillon, *Erasmo y España*, 2 vols. (Mexico City: Fondo de Cultura Económica, 1950), 1:90; 2:74–75; Erasmus, *Opus epistolarum*, 12 vols. (Oxford: Clarendon Press, 1906–1958), 3:6, 52. (Germany and Italy also had too many Jews for Erasmus's taste, and England too many riots.) On the development of the word *Marrano*, see esp. Arturo Farinelli, *Marrano (Storia di un vituperio)* (Geneva: L. S. Olschki, 1925), 53, 56, 66–67. The definition is from John Florio, *A Worlde of Wordes* (London, 1598; Hildesheim, NY: Georg Olms, 1972), 216. Farinelli also reports an amusing French dictionary of 1680 that defined *Marrane* as "an insult we apply to Spaniards, which means a Muslim." The Parisian graffiti is reported in G. Brunet et al., eds., *Jornal de Henri IV. Mémoires journaux de Pierre de l'Estoile* (Paris: Librairie des Bibliophiles, 1881), 5:39, 49, under August 1 and August 17, 1590. Further examples in J. N. Hillgarth, *The Mirror of Spain* (Ann Arbor: University of Michigan Press, 2000), 236–240; and Caro Baroja, *Las formas complejas*, 499–500. In the second half of the seventeenth century, *Portuguese* would similarly become a synonym for Jew throughout western Europe.

46 H. de Vocht, "Rodrigo Manrique's Letter to Vives," in *Monumenta Humanistica Lovaniensia* (Louvain: Librairie universitaire, Ch. Uystpruyst, 1934), 427–458, here 435. See also E. González González, "Vives, un humanista judeoconverso en el exilio de Flandes," in L. Dequeker and W. Verbeke, eds., *The Expulsion of the Jews and Their Emigration to the Southern Low Countries* (Leuven: Leuven University Press, 1998), 35–81, here 77.

CHAPTER 7: REFORMATION AND ITS CONSEQUENCES

1 All references from Luther's works are to the Weimar Edition [WA], *Dr. Martin Luthers Werke: Kritische Gesammtausgabe*, 121 vols. (Weimar: Hermann Böhlaus Nachfolger, 1883–2009). Unless otherwise indicated, all translations from the Latin and the German are my own.

   Insofar as secular and sacred were thoroughly interpenetrated in the existing political order, a call for spiritual freedom, even (or especially) one that argued for separation of the two spheres, could not be stripped of political implications. "I declare" is from *A Prelude on the Babylonian captivity of the Church*, which Luther published in Latin in 1520 (though German translations quickly followed). I cite from A. G. Dickens, *The German Nation and Martin*

Luther (London: Edward Arnold, 1974), 132–133. Eleutherius in WA, Br.1:83, 118, 122, etc. "Angel of the Apocalypse" is from Bugenhagen's valedictory oration, cited by Dickens, *German Nation*, 72.

2   Dickens, *German Nation*, 112–113.

3   For a brief synthesis of Luther's role in the formation of modern High German, see Heinrich Bach, "Die Rolle Luthers für die deutsche Sprachgeschichte," in *Sprachgeschichte. Ein Handbuch zur Geschichte der deutschen Sprache und ihrer Erforschung*, ed. W. Besch, O. Riechmann, and St. Sonderegger (Berlin: Walter de Gruyter, 1985), 2:1440–1447.

4   On prophet of the German nation, see Ernst Walter Zeeden, *The Legacy of Luther: Martin Luther and the Reformation in the Estimation of the German Lutherans from Luthers' Death to the Beginning of the Age of Goethe* (London: Hollis & Carter, 1954), 22, paraphrasing Johannes Mathesius. Luther also compared himself to the prophets, e.g., WA 51:598–599, 53:396.

5   WA 54:185–186.

6   "That Jesus Christ was Born a Jew," WA 11:314.

7   Philipp Melancthon, "History of the Life and Acts of Dr Martin Luther," in *Luther's Lives: Two Contemporary Accounts of Martin Luther*, trans. E. Vandiver, R. Keen, and T. D. Frazel (Manchester: Manchester University Press, 2002), 14–39, whence the quote about "just exercise of reason" in the previous paragraph is also drawn. The "Life" also highlights the young Luther's dependence on Saint Augustine's writings (esp. "On the Spirit and the Letter"). Melancthon is almost certainly correct in placing Luther's reading of "On the Spirit and the Letter" *before* Luther's epiphany rather than after. On Luther and Augustine, see Adolf Hamel, *Der junge Luther und Augustin*, part 1 (Gütersloh: Bertelsmann, 1934); and Bernhard Lohse, "Die Bedeutung Augustins für den jungen Luther," in his *Evangelium in der Geschichte. Studien zu Luther und der Reformation* (Göttingen:Vandenhoeck & Ruprecht, 1988), 11–30.

8   The sermon (on Jer. 23:5–8) was given on November 25, 1526 (WA 20:569.31–570b.12). He refers to the episode years later in "On the Jews and their Lies": WA 53:461–462. On the Thola episode with the rabbis (1525/6), see the fundamental work of von der Osten-Sacken, *Martin Luther und die Juden* (Stuttgart: Kohlhammer, 2002), 103–110. Both times he makes the same point.

9   Quote with "Hebrew rabbis" is from WA 55/1:8.8–10.15. For some examples of Luther's statements about the literal Christological sense (*sensus ad literam, sensus literalis*) of the Psalms, see WA 55/2, 65.18–19, 67.23–68.2. For the note, to Faber Stapulensis, see WA 4:468.25. Cf. Osten-Sacken, *Martin Luther*, 47–74, 147, n. 716. The best introduction to the *Dictata* is the (German) editorial apparatus to WA 55. For a treatment in English, see Scott H. Hendrix, *Ecclesia in via: Ecclesiological Developments in the Medieval Psalms Exegesis and the Dictata super Psalterium (1513–1515) of Martin Luther* (Leiden: Brill, 1974).

10 The Latin Vulgate's "chair of pestilence" follows the Greek Septuagint's mistranslation of the Hebrew: *cathedra loimōn* (hence the Latin version approved by Pope Pius XII in 1943 has "sits about with scoffers": *et in conventu protervorum non sedet*). Luther was aware of the correct reading (which he elsewhere

gave as "cathedra derisorum": WA 4:466–467), but he opted for the conventional error here to sharpen his point.

11 The influence of Augustine's Psalm commentary on Luther's is discussed by (among others) Gerhard Ebeling, "Die Anfänge von Luthers Hermeneutik" (1951), reprinted in his *Lutherstudien* (Tübingen: Mohr, 1971), 1:1–68, here 17; and Hamel, *Der junge Luther*. Both agree on Luther's heavy reliance on Augustine but disagree on the degree of Luther's innovation.

12 Osten-Sacken, *Martin Luther*, 58–60. Under the influence of Matt. 23:2, exegetes before Luther had identified those who sit in the seat of pestilence (*cathedra pestilentiae*) with the "Scribes and Pharisees" who sit in the seat of Moses (*cathedra Mosis*). An example well known to Luther, congenial because of its antipapal potential, was that of Faber Stapulensis: "'cathedra pestilentiae': pontificum, scribarum et pharisaeorum iudicaria potestas, qua corrupti abutebantur." See Reinhard Schwarz and Siegfried Raeder's introduction to WA 55/2, 3, 5. But the association of all three with Jesus's Jewish enemies was, so far as I know, an innovation.

13 Erasmus: "Si christianum est odisse Iudeos, hic abunde Christiani sumus omnes." *Epistolae*, ed. R. S. and H. M. Allen (Oxford: Oxford University Press, 1922), 4:46, no. 1006 (August 11, 1519). Cf. Luther's similar observation, but with the addition of "heretics and Turks": WA 5:429.9–11.

14 As Luther put it, "[T]he more Christological the interpretation, the more the Jews come into our field of vision" as enemies of Christ. WA 55/1: (Anmerkungen:) 46.9–10. For the shift, see Tarald Rasmussen, *Inimici Ecclesiae: Das Ekklesiologische Feindbild in Luthers Dictata Super Psalterium* (Leiden: Brill, 1989), 147ff.

15 Quote with "testimony to Christ's Cross" is from WA 55/1, 436–437; "scum in the streets" is from WA 55/2:32.11–17. The later expansion is in *Operationes in Psalmos* (1519–21), in WA 5:534.27–535.21. See Osten-Sacken, *Martin Luther*, 54, 57, 89. On "the shit of Rabbis," see WA 43:389.21–23.

16 A complete catalogue would include his letter of 1514 on the controversy between the Christian Hebraist Reuchlin and the convert from Judaism Pfefferkorn; his lectures on Romans from 1515/16; his letter of 1523 to the convert from Judaism Bernhard von Sommer; his interpretation of Psalm 109 for the queen of Hungary in 1526; his letter concerning the baptism of a Jewish girl in 1530; his letter to Josel von Rosheim, the head of the imperial Jewish communities, in 1537; his two other treatises of 1543, "On Schem Hamphoras and the lineage of Christ" and "On the last words of David"; as well as the sermons he gave on February 7, 1546, just before his death (on which more later).

17 On Jacob Perez, see Wilfred Werbeck, *Jacobus Perez von Valencia. Untersuchungen zu seinem Psalmenkommentar* (Tübingen: Mohr, 1959); Rasmussen, *Inimici*, 139–142; and J. Samuel Preus, *From Shadow to Promise: Old Testament Interpretation from Augustine to the Young Luther* (Cambridge, MA: Harvard University Press, 1969), 165.

18 WA 22:218.30–39.

19 WA 22:219.1–12.

20 WA 22:219.31–38.
21 Quote with "hands" is from Wilhelm Maurer, "Die Zeit der Reformation," in *Kirche und Synagoge. Handbuch zur Geschichte von Christen und Juden. Darstellung mit Quellen*, ed. K. H. Rengsfort and S. Von Kortzfleisch (Stuttgart: Klett, 1967), 1:363–452, here 394 (the sermon was from 1524). For quote from Pardoner, see Geoffrey Chaucer, *Riverside Chaucer* [see chap. 5, n. 37], 196, lines 474–475. Luther: WA 55/2:167.7–11. The frequent argument that such statements point to a solidarity of sin among all sinners, rather than to a "special" role for the Jews, seems to me unsustainable. At the very least we can say that the Jews' "special role" is that of "ur-example," and that their "special-ness" here derives from the important difference between being imagined as killers of Christ in the flesh (as the Jews were) and killers of Christ in the spirit (as Christian sinners and others might be).
22 Lectures on the epistle to the Hebrews: WA 57:168.5–11. "On the Jews and their Lies": WA 53: 427–439. Phrase "teufels Synagoga" is from "Wider das Bapstum zu Rom vom Teuffel gestifft," WA 54:206–299, here 245. The "Papensau" (so far as I know, the coinage is my own) is reproduced in Mark U. Edwards, *Luther's Last Battles: Politics and Polemics 1531–1546* (Ithaca, NY: Cornell University Press, 1983), 196, without comment about its relation to anti-Jewish imagery. The cartoons were executed by Lucas Cranach and are reproduced in WA 54. See Wolfgang Harms, *Deutsche illustrierte Flugblätter des 16. und 17. Jahrhunderts*, vols. 1–4 and 7 (Tübingen: Max Niemeyer, 1980–1997), here 2:146, with reference to the numerous editions of the print. See also Petra Schöner, *Judenbilder im deutschen Einblattdruck der Renaissance: ein Beitrag zur Imagologie*, Saecula Spiritalia 42 (Baden-Baden: Verlag Valentin Koerner, 2002). On Luther and the Wittenberg Judensau, see Isaiah Shachar, *The Judensau: A Medieval Anti-Jewish Motif and Its History* (London: Warburg Institute, 1974), 30ff., 43–51, and plates 26–27. The fact that Luther's anti-Jewish vocabulary was often aimed at the papacy is often used to excuse him from special animus: Luther thought himself to be in end-time, and was therefore concerned to fight any and all the forces of the Antichrist, without prejudice toward the Jews. See, e.g., Edwards, *Luther's Last Battle*, chap. 6; and Dietz Bering, "Gibt es bei Luther einen antisemitischen Wortschatz? Zur Widerlegung einer politischen Legende," *Zeitschrift für Germanistische Linguistik* 17 (1989), 137–161, esp. 143. It nevertheless seems relevant that in these contests Judaism provides the grounding enmity, the foundation of the anti-Christian. On Luther's apocalypticism in its medieval context, see Volker Leppin, "Luthers Antichristverständnis vor dem Hintergrund der mittelalterlichen Konzeptionen," *Kerygma und Dogma* 45 (1999), 48–64.
23 On Diet of Augsburg, see Selma Stern, *Josel of Rosheim in the Holy Roman Empire of the German Nation* (Philadelphia, PA: Jewish Publication Society, 1965), 95; Eric Zimmer, *Jewish Synods in Germany during the Late Middle Ages (1286–1603)* (New York: Yeshiva University Press, 1978), 62ff. See more generally J. Boendermaker, "Martin Luther—ein 'semi-iudaeus'? Der Einfluß des Alten Testaments und des jüdischen Glaubens auf Luther und seine Theologie,"

in H. Kremers et al., eds., *Die Juden und Martin Luther, Martin Luther und die Juden. Geschichte—Wirkungsgeschichte—Herausforderung* (Neukirchen-Vluyn: Neukirchener Verlag, 1987), 45–57. For letter to the convert Bernhard, see WA Br 3:101–103, here 101.34–36.

24 Osiander's treatise survived to the nineteenth century in only one copy, now lost. It was edited by Moritz Stern, *Andreas Osianders Schrift über die Blutbeschuldigung* (Kiel: Fiencke, 1893). Eck's refutation survives in multiple copies and editions. See *Ains Judenbuechlins verlegung: darin ain Christ, gantzer Christenhait zü schmach, will es geschehe den juden vnrecht in bezichtigung der Kristen kinder mordt* (Ingolstadt: Alexander Weissenhorn, 1542). "Judenvater" occurs at fol. A IIIv and elsewhere, Lutheran at A IIIr and elsewhere.

25 For the Jewish contemporary, see H. H. Ben-Sasson, "Jewish-Christian Disputation in the Setting of Humanism," *Harvard Theological Review* 59 (1966), 369–390, here 385–387. Luther's recommendations are excerpted from "On the Jews and their Lies," WA 53, 522–526. For expulsion, see WA 53:538.3–10; "sharp mercy," WA 53:522.34–35, 531.6–7; and "utter mercilessness," WA 53:541.30–33. See also Osten-Sacken, *Martin Luther*, 129.

26 For some of the expulsions by Protestant princes, see Stern, *Josel of Rosheim*, 195, 199–200. The quote is from Jonathan Israel, *European Jewry in the Age of Mercantilism, 1550–1750* (Oxford: Clarendon Press, 1985), 18; cf. 8, where the post-1530 campaign against the Jews is described as "a more systematic, total, and ideological assault than any which preceded it." For the Brunswick exile's condemnation of Luther, see H. H. Ben-Sasson, "The Reformation in Contemporary Jewish Eyes," *Proceedings of the Israel Academy of Sciences and Humanities* 4 (1971), 239–327, here 289.

27 Phrase "cruel as if written in blood" is the description of Luther's "On the Ineffable Name" given by Catholic deputies at the Diet of Worms (1545): see Stern, *Josel of Rosheim*, 307, n. 6.

28 Arguments about Jews and Judaism were central to many of the leading reformers of the day (as well as to Papists). John Calvin, e.g., depended on a distinction between law and gospel similar to Luther's, and deployed Judaism in similar ways. For examples of the vast literature on law and gospel in Calvin, see I. John Hesselink, *Calvin's Concept of the Law* (Allison Park: Pickwick, 1992); and M. S. Horton, "Calvin and the Law-Gospel Hermeneutic," *Pro Ecclesia* 6 (1997), 27–42. For examples of the almost equally vast scholarship on Calvin and the Jews, see Jack Hughes Robinson, *John Calvin and the Jews* (New York: Peter Lang, 1992). A useful (for German readers) survey of the sources and scholarship on all of these issues is Achim Detmers, *Reformation und Judentum. Israel-Lehren und Einstellungen zum Judentum von Luther bis zum frühen Calvin* (Stuttgart: Kohlhammer, 2001): see 80–85 on the struggle against Sabbatarians and other radical reform "Judaizers." On psalm exegesis, see G. Sujin Pak, "Luther, Bucer, and Calvin on Psalms 8 and 16: Confessional Formation and the Question of Jewish Exegesis," in Wim Janse and Barbara Pitkin, eds., *The Formation of Clerical and Confessional Identities in Early Modern Europe* (Leiden: Brill, 2006), 169–186.

29 Caspar Schwenckfeld, *Wider den Alten vnnd Newen Ebionitischen Irthumb/der Jhenigen/die Mosen mit dem Herren Christo/das gesetz mit dem Euangelio/sas Alt Testament mit dem Newen vermengen/und einen Zwang/des befreyten gewissens Im Christenthumb/daneben anrichtenn[.] Auff Oswald Glaids buchlenn Vom Sabbath* (dated January 1, 1532), ed. Chester David Hartranft, in *Corpus Schwenckfeldianorum*, vol. 4: *Letters and Treatises of Caspar Schwenckfeld von Ossig, December 1530–1533* (Leipzig: Breitkopf & Härtel, 1914), 444–518.

30 WA 50:330.5–6. Cf. H.-M. Kirn, "Israel als Gegenüber der Reformatoren: zur christlichen Sicht von Juden und Judentum im 16. Jahrhundert," V. Siegert, ed., in *Israel als Gegenüber. Vom Alten Orient bis in die Gegenwart. Studien zur Geschichte eines wechselvollen Zusammenlebens* (Göttingen: Vandenhoeck & Ruprecht, 2000), 290–321.

31 Thus Heiko Oberman, in *Wurzeln des Antisemitismus* (Berlin: Severin & Siedler, 1981), speaks of a "Jewish missionary offensive" and a "wave of Jewish conversions, a weakening of Christianity" (128, 139, 157). I imagine that he would have been shocked to discover that he was repeating what Shmuel Ettinger had called the "libel of the proselytes" (*'alilat ha-gerim*): "Ma'amadam ha-Mishpati ve-ha-Ḥevrati Shel Yehudei Ukraina Ba-Me'ot ha–15–17," *Zion* 20 (1955), 131. Contrast Osten-Sacken's lucid pages in *Martin Luther,* 124–127.

32 On Katarzyna's trial and execution, see Magda Teter, "The Legend of Ger Ẓedek of Wilno as Polemic and Reassurance," *AJS Review* 29, no. 2 (2005), 237–263, here 245–246. Katarzyna was in fact adopted as an early Protestant martyr, e.g., by Wojciech Węgierski, *Kronika Zboru Ewangelickiego Krakowskiego* (1651; Cracow, 1817), 3–4.

33 On the relationship between the rise of literalizing Protestant approaches to the Hebrew Bible and anti-Judaism, see the works of Jerome Friedman: "Sebastian Münster, the Jewish Mission, and Protestant Antisemitism," *Archiv für Reformationsgeschichte* 70 (1979), 238–259; *The Most Ancient Testimony: Sixteenth-Century Christian Hebraica in the Age of Renaissance Nostalgia* (Athens: Ohio University Press, 1983); and "Protestants, Jews, and Jewish Sources," in C. Lindberg, ed., *Piety, Politics, and Ethics: Reformation Studies in Honor of G. W. Forell* (Kirksville: Northeast Missouri State University, 1984), 139–156. The arguments marshaled against this view by Scott H. Hendrix in *Tradition and Authority in the Reformation* (Brookfield, VT: Variorum, 1996) do not challenge my conclusion that the reformers' turn toward the letter refigured the place of Jews and Judaism. On the Augsburg preacher, see the complaint of Sir Richard Morrison, England's ambassador to the court of Charles V, in *Calendar of State Papers, Spanish (1550–1552)*, ed. Royall Tyler (London: [n.p.], 1914), 236, 254.

34 For an early Protestant advocate of "tolerance" (the concept is anachronistic but useful) see Martin Brecht, "Ob ein weltlich Oberkait Recht habe, in des Glauben Sachen mit dem Schwert zu handeln. Ein unbekanntes Nürnberger Gutachten zur Frage der Toleranz aus dem Jahre 1530," *Archiv für Reformationsgeschichte* 60 (1969), 65–75. For Osiander's letter, see Reinhold Lewin, *Luthers Stellung zu den Juden. Ein Beitrag zur Geschichte der Juden in Deutschland während des Reformationszeitalters* (Berlin, Trowitzsch & Sohn Aalen,

1911), 99; and Gottfried Seebaß, *Das reformatorische Werk des Andreas Osiander* (Nürnberg: Verein für Bayerische Kirchengeschichte, 1967), 82. On Osiander and the Jews more generally, see G. Ph. Wolf, "Osiander und die Juden im Kontext seiner Theologie," *Zeitschrift für bayerische Kirchengeschichte* 53 (1984), 49–77.

35 WA 53:528.28–30; 538.25–27; cf. 520.33–36. Quote "worthy of hatred" is from WA 42:259.16. Compare, from a generation or two before, Nicholas of Cusa's dismissal of Jewish resistance to Christian theology as unthreatening because they were powerless (to him it was what the Muslims thought that mattered): *De pace fidei; cum epistola ad Ioannem de Segobia*, ed. R. Klibansky and H. Bascour (London: Warburg Institute, 1956), 39.

36 For Luther's millstones, see WA Tr.2:217.1–4 (no. 1795). The anecdote is reported by Claude Jordan, *Voyages historiques de l'Europe* (Paris: Nicholas le Gras, 1694), 4:82. The millstones are presumably inspired by Matt. 18:6 (a verse Luther elsewhere deploys against "Papists" in a sermon from 1544: WA 22:215.22–31) and Luke 17:2: "[I]t would be better for such a person to be thrown into the sea with a millstone around the neck than to be the downfall of a single of these little ones."

37 For Luther's letter of February 1 to his wife, see WA Br.11:275.4–276.19 (= Nr. 4195). "If they will not convert" is from his sermon of February 15: WA 51:196.14–17. His last four sermons were preached in Eisleben on January 31 (WA 51:148.17–163.6), February 2 (WA 51:163.7–173.22), February 7 (WA 51:173.23–187.15), and February 15 (WA 51:187.16–196.17). See A. Weyer, "Die Juden in den Predigten Martin Luthers," in Kremers et al., eds., *Die Juden und Martin Luther*, 163–70, here 167. On the entire episode, see Osten-Sacken, *Martin Luther*, 154–156.

38 *Handbuch der Judenfrage: Eine Zusammenstellung des wichtigsten Materials zur Beurteilung des jüdischen Volkes* (Hamburg: Hanseatische Druck-und Verlagsanstalt, 1907). On Fritsch, see Peter Pulzer and Massimo Ferrari Zumbini, *German Antisemitism Revisited / il caso Fritsch* (Rome: Archivio G. Izzi, 1999). On the "Institut zur Erforschung und Beseitigung des jüdischen Einflusses auf das deutsche kirchliche Leben" and other Nazi Christian institutions, see chap. 13. For Neo-Nazi websites, see, e.g., http://www.ety.com/berlin/deutsch2.htm (accessed September 5, 2006).

39 For the debate over Luther's "Antisemitism," see among others Lucie Kaennel, *Luther était-il antisémite?* (Geneva: Éditions Labor et Fides, 1997). On the reception of Luther's writings about Jews in the centuries after his death, see among many other works J. Wallmann, "The Reception of Luther's Writings on the Jews from the Reformation to the End of the Nineteenth Century," *Lutheran Quarterly* 1 (1987), 72–97; and Johannes Brosseder, *Luthers Stellung zu den Juden im Spiegel seiner Interpreten; Interpretation und Rezeption von Luthers Schriften und Äußerungen zum Judentum im 19. und 20. Jahrhundert vor allem im deutschsprachigen Raum* (Munich: M. Hüber, 1972). The quote is from Lewin, *Luthers Stellung*, 110.

40 On Luther and the Jews, see, in addition to the works cited in the previous

pages, the valuable study of Andreas Späth, *Luther und die Juden* (Bonn: Verlag für Kultur und Wissenschaft, 2001). Still useful as well are several older studies: Hayo Gerdes, *Luthers Streit mit den Schwärmern um das rechte Verständnis des Gesetzes Mose* (Göttingen: Göttinger Verlagsanstalt, 1955); Walther Bienert, *Martin Luther und die Juden: Ein Quellenbuch mit zeitgenössischen Illustrationen* (Frankfurt am Main: Evang. Verl.-Werk, 1982); and the essays edited by Kremers et al., *Die Juden und Martin Luther*.

41 WA Tr. 1:170.32–33. On Luther's economics, see Hermann Barge, *Luther und der Frühkapitalismus* (Gütersloh: C. Bertelsmann, 1951).

CHAPTER 8: "WHICH IS THE MERCHANT HERE, AND WHICH THE JEW?"

1 William Shakespeare, *The Merchant of Venice*, ed. Leah S. Marcus (New York: W. W. Norton, 2006). In-text citations are to act, scene, and line number in this edition. An earlier version of this chapter, with more extensive bibliography and footnoting, appeared as "Shakespeare's Jewish Question," *Renaissance Drama* 38 (2010), 77–113. On their explanations, see an elegant example combining both capitalism and homoeroticism: W. H. Auden, "Brothers and Others," in *The Dyer's Hand and Other Essays* (New York: Random House, 1962), 232–235.

2 Thomas Coryate, *Coryate's Crudities . . .* , 2 vols. (Glasgow: James MacLehose & Sons, 1905), 1:372–374. Henry Buttes, *Dyets Dry Dinner* (London, 1599), sig. k8r. For further examples and literature on the association of Jews with melancholy in medieval and renaissance humoral theories, see Nirenberg, "Shakespeare's Jewish Question," 105.

3 Citing here from the *Geneva Bible* (London, 1584). On Shakespeare's use of this translation (as well as others), see Richmond Noble, *Shakespeare's Biblical Knowledge* (London: Society for Promoting Christian Knowledge, 1935). On biblical (and particularly Pauline) allusions in *Merchant*, see Steven Marx, "The Merchant of Venice and Paul's Letter to the Romans," in *Shakespeare and the Bible* (Oxford: Oxford University Press, 2000), 103–124.

4 These exchanges are patterned on Matt. 6:16–21 and 23:1–36. Note that in act 2, scene 2, lines 175–183, Gratiano will promise to act precisely in this way, "like one well studied in a sad ostent."

5 For a description of this school, and a renewed insistence on the importance of acknowledging the presence of Jews and conversos in London, see Janet Adelman, *Blood Relations: Christian and Jew in the Merchant of Venice* (Chicago: University of Chicago Press, 2008), 4–12.

6 Augustine on love as diagnostic between literal and spiritual: *On Christian Doctrine* 3.v.9 [see chap. 3, n. 91]. George Herbert, *The Complete English Poems*, ed. John Tobin (London: Penguin, 1991), 160–161. On another school, see, e.g., Barbara Lewalski, "Biblical Allusion and Allegory in the *Merchant of Venice*," Shakespeare Quarterly 13 (1962); Frank Kermode, "The Mature Comedies," in J. R. Brown and R. Harris, eds., *Early Shakespeare* (New York: Capricorn Books, 1966), 224, and reprinted as a debate between Kermode and A. D. Moody in Sylvan Barnet, ed., *Twentieth Century Interpretations of the Merchant of Venice*,

97–108; and more subtle but still supersessionist, Steven Marx, "'Dangerous Conceits' and 'Proofs of Holy Writ': Allusion in *The Merchant of Venice* and Paul's *Letter to the Romans*," in *Shakespeare and the Bible*, 103–124.

7 Lewalski, "Biblical Allusion," 39, emphasizes Luke 18:9–13, and sees in Antonio "a perfect embodiment of Christian love." Joan Ozark Holmer stresses more the misanthropic publicans of texts like Matt. 5:39–47, and associates the word with usury: *The Merchant of Venice: Choice, Hazard, and Consequence* (Basingstoke: Macmillan, 1995), 151–153. The hypothesis of editing error is from H. B. Charlton, as cited in Edward Andrew, *Shylock's Rights: A Grammar of Lockian Claims* (Toronto: University of Toronto Press, 1988), 41. Lars Engle subtly stresses both the love and the economic interest in Antonio's "fawning": "'Thrift is a Blessing', Exchange and Explanation in *The Merchant of Venice*," *Shakespeare Quarterly* 37 (1986), 20–37, at 28.

8 Vincent Ferrer, *Sermons*, ed. Gret Schib (Barcelona: Barcino, 1984), 5:147. For a twelfth-century example, see Bernard of Clairvaux, Epistle 363, suggesting that Christian moneylenders should be called baptized Jews, not Christians. Sebastian Brant, *Das Narrenschiff. Faksimile der Erstausgabe Basel 1494*, ed. Dieter Wuttke (Baden-Baden: Verlag Valentin Koerner, 1994), chap. 93.

9 The lost play is mentioned in Stephen Gosson's *The School of Abuse* (1579), ed. Edward Arber (London: Murray & Son, 1868), 40. Some have argued that Shakespeare borrowed the device of the theme of the three caskets from this play. The anonymous treatise *The Death of Usury, or the Disgrace of Usurers* (Cambridge, 1594) is a good example of an attempt to distinguish between Christian and "Jewish" money-lending practices.

10 On John Shakespeare, see David Thomas, ed., *Shakespeare in the Public Record* (London: HMSO, 1985), 2–3. Francis Bacon's report is in his *De usura sive foenore*, in *The Works of Francis Bacon* (London: W. Baynes & Son, 1824), 10:107. For bibliography on the usury debates and the explosion of lawsuits for debt in this period, see Nirenberg, "Shakespeare's Jewish Questions," 106.

11 On canonical, see *Decretum Gratiani*, Prima Pars, Dist. 88, c.11. For examples of the association of merchants with covetousness and usury in medieval English literature, see e.g., William Langland, Piers Plowman, 100.9.22–42, and John Gower, Mirour de l'Omme, lines 7285–7320, 25192–25212. Henry Blount, *A Voyage into the Levant*, 2nd ed. (London, 1636), 113–122. On the expansion of English commerce in Shakespeare's day, see Keith Wrightson, *Earthly Necessities* (New Haven, CT: Yale University Press, 2000), arguing for a transformation of "earlier economic values" (204); and esp. Robert Brenner, *Merchants and Revolution: Commercial Change, Political Conflict, and London's Overseas Traders, 1550–1653* (Princeton, NJ: Princeton University Press, 1993), 3–91. For some of the vast literature on Shakespeare's interest in law and the language of law, see Nirenberg, "Shakespeare's Jewish Questions," 107. Quote with "profitable members" is from the anonymous treatise *A Breefe Discourse, Declaring and Approuing the Necessarie and Inuiolable Maintenance of the Laudable Customs of London* (London, 1584), cited in Markku Peltonen, "Citizenship and Republicanism in Elizabethan England," in M. van Gelderen and Q. Skinner, eds.,

Republicanism: A Shared European Heritage, 2 vols. (Cambridge: Cambridge University Press, 2002), 1:85–106, here 89–90. Quote "commodity of his Countrie" is from the English translation of the treatise by the Venetian Francesco Sansovino: *The Quintesence of Wit, Being a Corrant Comfort of Conceites, Maximes, and Poleticke Deuises*, trans. Robert Hitchcock (London, 1590), fol. 88v.

12 In his *Royal Exchange. Contayning Sundry Aphorismes of Phylosophie, and Golden Principles of Morall and Naturall Quadruplicities* (London, 1590), Robert Greene defended London's merchant oligarchy by aligning it with Venice's: sig. para. 2v. See also Markku Peltonnen, "Citizenship and Republicanism in Elizabethan England," in Martin van Gelderen, ed., *Republicanism: A Shared European Heritage* (Cambridge: Cambridge University Press, 2002), 85–106. For further examples, and on Venice's role as a model in English and European political thought more generally, see the bibliography in Nirenberg, "Shakespeare's Jewish Questions," 107. For Shakespeare's particular constructions of Italy, see the essays assembled in M. Marrapodi et al., eds., *Shakespeare's Italy: Functions of Italian Locations in Renaissance Drama* (Manchester: Manchester University Press, 1997).

13 For summaries of Shakespeare's investments, see E. K. Chambers, *William Shakespeare: A Study of Facts and Problems*, 2 vols. (Oxford: Clarendon Press, 1930), 2:170–174; Park Honan, *Shakespeare: A Life* (Oxford: Oxford University Press, 1998), 394–398. Two of the theatrical impresarios with whom Shakespeare was associated are known to have bonded players, including Francis Langley, owner of the Swan theater in which *The Merchant of Venice* may have first been staged. On the business of the stage (which included money lending), see the bibliography in Nirenberg, "Shakespeare's Jewish Questions," 108; and esp. William Ingram, *The Business of Playing: The Beginnings of the Adult Professional Theater in Elizabethan London* (Ithaca, NY: Cornell University Press, 1992). See more generally Luke Wilson, *Theater of Intention: Drama and Law in Early Modern England* (Stanford, CA: Stanford University, 2000).

14 For a survey of the many attacks on theater, see Jonas A. Barish, *The Antitheatrical Prejudice* (Berkeley: University of California Press, 1981), esp. "Puritans and Proteans," 80–131. For Jean-Christophe Agnew, theater and market raised similar questions of "representation and misrepresentation": *Worlds Apart: The Market and the Theatre in Anglo-American Thought, 1550–1750* (Cambridge: Cambridge University Press, 1986), 11. William Prynne, whose *Histriomastix* (1633) rabidly attacked theater, also produced tracts against Judaizing (e.g., *A short Demurrer to the Jewes* [1656]).

15 For another important context, that of debate about the obligations that bound citizen and sovereign, see bibliography in Nirenberg, "Shakespeare's Jewish Questions," n. 27. For an early and much-cited advocate of interpreting the play in economic and political context, see Walter Cohen, *Drama of a Nation: Public Theatre in Renaissance England and Spain* (Ithaca, NY: Cornell University Press, 1985), 195–211.

16 Shakespeare has just reminded us a few lines before, and will remind us again, that Jacob had indeed "stolen" his father Isaac's blessing from his older brother

Esau (the spiritual ancestor of the gentiles, according to biblical interpretation of the day). Shylock first marks Jacob's deception of Isaac in act 1, scene 3, lines 67–69, and Shakespeare restages it in act 2, scene 2, lines 31–108, Launcelot's "confusion" of his blind father Gobbo. The implications of this restaging are important but beyond my reach here. Shylock's economic argument is as significant as his exegesis, since the assimilation of the production of capital to agricultural reproduction plays a prominent role in economic theories of the seventeenth and eighteenth centuries, as Marx noted in his notes for book 4 of *Capital* ("Theorien über den Mehrwert," in Marx and Engels, *Werke* [see Introduction, n. 1], 26.1:319). Cf. Louis Dumont, *From Mandeville to Marx: The Genesis and Triumph of Economic Ideology* (Chicago: University of Chicago Press, 1977), 40–41.

17 Luther: *Von Kaufshandlung und Wucher* (1524), in WA 25:298–305 [see chap. 7, n. 1]. Sir Walter Raleigh, as cited in Auden, *Dyer's Hand*, 231.

18 In Aristotle's hierarchy, the management of household and agricultural estate is most honorable, retail trade and exchange is "justly censured," and the worst is lending at interest (*Politics* 1258b1–5). Luther: *Tischreden*, 6 vols. (Weimar: Böhlau, 1912–21), 5:no. 5429: "Pecunia est res sterilis." For the medieval background, see Nirenberg, "Shakespeare's Jewish Questions," n. 30.

19 The view that merchants and moneylenders treat their customers as enemies has both classical and biblical roots. For the classical, see my "Politics of Love and Its Enemies," *Critical Inquiry* 33 (2007). The Hebrew Bible's prescriptions are at Deut. 23:19–20, 28:12; and Lev. 25:35–37. Aquinas's summary: *Summa Theologica*, trans. Fathers of the English Dominican Province (New York: Benziger Brothers; Project Gutenberg ebook), 2.ii.Q.78.i. For a survey of this history, see Benjamin Nelson, *The Idea of Usury: From Tribal Brotherhood to Universal Otherhood*, 2nd ed. (Chicago: University of Chicago Press, 1969).

20 Defensibly "Christian": The desire for outer and inner conformity was an ideal in early Christian texts like 2 Clement to the Corinthians 12:2–3 and the Gospel according to Thomas, discussed in chap. 2. The casket's "scroll" may also be an allusion to "Jewish" hermeneutics, since scrolls were frequently opposed to Christian books as an iconographic device to identify Jews in medieval and renaissance art. Quote "vessell of golde" is from History 32 of the English *Gesta Romanorum*, trans. R. Robinson (1595 [Bodeleian, Douce R4]).

21 Modern critics have missed the humor, though the use of "hood," "cowl," and other items of clothing as puns for foreskin was noted by F. Rubinstein, *A Dictionary of Shakespeare's Sexual Puns and Their Significance*, 2nd ed. (London: Macmillan, 1989). Rubinstein cites Leclerq's translation of Rabelais as an analogue, e.g., "Priapus doffed his hood, discovering a red flaming face." In Spanish poetry such puns—as well as comments about the "cut" of clothing to imply circumcision—were so common as to necessitate word lists: see, e.g., Alicia Puigvert Ocal, "El léxico de la indumentaria en el *Cancionero de Baena*," *Boletín de la Real Academia Española* 67 (1987), 171–206.

22 Compare the Jew Barabas's reaction to his daughter's conversion in *The Jew of Malta:* "Oh my girl, / My gold, my fortune, my felicity . . . / O girl! O gold!

O beauty! O my bliss!" (2.1.47–54). Christopher Marlowe, *The Jew of Malta*, in David Bevington and Eric Rasmussen, eds., *Doctor Faustus and Other Plays* (Oxford: Clarendon Press, 1995); citation is to act, scene, and line number of this edition. Echoes of Marlowe in Shakespeare have been well studied. For references, see Nirenberg, "Shakespeare's Jewish Questions," n. 34.

23 I defer to my treatment of act 5 the question of whether the play's perils of communication apply only to Venice, or whether they extend to Belmont as well. For a treatment of the place of contract theory in English Protestant sectarian debates of the period, see David Zaret, *The Heavenly Contract* (Chicago: University of Chicago Press, 1985). Samuel Ajzenstat analyzes the play in terms of an opposition between conditional (justice-oriented) and unconditional (love/gift-oriented) notions of contract and exchange, mapped onto the opposition between Jew (conditional) and Christian (unconditional). See his "Contract in *The Merchant of Venice*," in *Philosophy and Literature* 21 (1997), 262–278.

24 On "chancering," see Edith G. Henderson, "Reliefs from Bonds in the English Chancery: Mid-Sixteenth Century," *American Journal of Legal History* 18, no. 4 (1974), 298–306. Shakespeare was not the only author of his day to use the example—which was in his source stories—for this purpose. Alexander Silvayn, in the 95th Declamation of his *Orator* (trans. Lazarus Piot [London, 1596]), also used a speech by a Jew "who would for his debt have a pound of flesh of a Christian" in order to explore the powers of contract "to binde" "not only the whole body but also the senses and spirits." Luke Wilson gives yet another legal context in "Drama and Marine Insurance in Shakespeare's London," in Jordan and Cunningham, eds., *Law in Shakespeare* [see chap. 5, n. 53].

25 Cicero, *De Officiis* 3.31.111, in *Remains of Old Latin,* vol. 3: *The Law of the Twelve Tables*, ed. and trans. E. H. Warmington, Loeb Classical Library 329 (Cambridge, MA: Harvard University Press, 1967), 512–513. Cicero himself claimed to have lived through a period of juridical revolution that transformed the Law of the Twelve Tables from a foundational text to a forgotten one: "[W]hen we were boys we used to learn the Twelve as a ditty, ordained by fate; no one learns them now" (Cicero, *De Legibus* 2.23.59).

26 Gellius, *Noctes Atticae,* 20.1.48–52. Cf. Gaius, *Inst.* 4.21, 3.78; Gaius, *Dig.* 42.1.4.5, 50.16.234.2; Gellius, *Noctes Atticae* 20.1.19, 15.13.11; Quintilian, *Institutio Oratoria* 3.6.84; Dio Cassius frag. 12., all in *Remains of Old Latin,* 438–441.

27 Tertullian, Apology 4, in *Ante-Nicene Fathers* [see chap. 3, n. 10] 3:31.

28 It is irrelevant to my argument whether Shakespeare knew of the critical attempts to reconstruct the Twelve Tables by A. du Rivail and others in the sixteenth century. Nor am I suggesting as some (H. J. Griston) have that Shakespeare set his play in Roman times and under Roman law. On the Twelve Tables as a myth of origin created by later Roman lawyers, see M. T. Fögen, *Römische Rechtsgeschichten: über Ursprung und Evolution eines sozialen Systems* (Göttingen: Vandenhoeck & Ruprecht, 2003), 63–79. William Blackstone gave this law a place in his genealogy of English legal thought first published in 1765–1769, *Commentaries on the Laws of England,* 4 vols. (New York: Oceana, 1966), 2:472–473, as did Max Weber in his more general historical sociology

of economic life, *Wirtschaft und Gesellschaft* (Tübingen: J. C. B. Mohr, 1922), 413–456.

29 Among the many who have commented on the mirroring implied in this line, see Richard Halperin, *Shakespeare among the Moderns* (Ithaca, NY: Cornell University Press, 1997), 184ff.

30 The attempted-murder charge follows that of a popular ballad of the day, the "Ballad of Gernutus," about a Jew who wanted to take a pound of flesh from his debtor. The ballad's ending makes clear the moral that many a Christian lender acts in the same way: "Good people that doe heare this Song, for truth I dare well say, / That many a wretch as ill as he doth live now at this day." Francis James Child, ed., *English and Scottish Ballads* (Boston: Little, Brown, 1860), 8:53, lines 65–68.

31 Shakespeare's contemporaries might not have noticed the cruelty of this mercy. The commutation of death sentences for Jews and Muslims who converted was a venerable and uncontroversial practice in Christian Europe.

32 For divergent opinions about whether a clear difference emerges between Shylock and Antonio over the course of the play, and hence between "Christian" and "Jew," compare Richard Halpern's sense (in *Shakespeare among the Moderns*) of a vanishing difference with Sylvan Barnet's conviction of a widening one in "Prodigality and Time in the Merchant of Venice," *PMLA* 87 (1972), 26–30. Portia's "Jewing" of Shylock has long been noticed by many critics. For an early example, see the anonymous essay "Shylock the Jew-ed," *Temple Bar* 45 (1875), 65–70.

33 These words have potentially "commercial" etymologies, e.g., the plausible derivation of *interpretation* from *inter* + *pretium*. On the Indo-European root **mei* and its Latin derivatives *munus, munera,* gifts that establish obligation (whence "communication"), see Emile Benveniste, "Gift and Exchange in the Indo-European Vocabulary," in *Problems in General Linguistics* (Coral Gables, FL: University of Miami Press, 1971), 271–280.

34 Francis Bacon, *The Advancement of Learning / De augmentis scientiarum* 6.1, in *Works of Francis Bacon,* 9:110. In his *New Organon,* Bacon used the phrase "Idols of the marketplace" to describe the dangerous attraction of words with unclear or nonexistent referents, which he claimed everywhere afflicted the philosophy of his day: *Novum Organum* (bk. 1, secs. 59–60), 2nd ed., ed. Thomas Fowler (Oxford: Clarendon Press, 1889), 233–237. The characterization of these semiotic errors in terms of money and market is important and closely related to the meaning of Judaism in Christian philosophies of language.

35 Cicero, *De Officiis* 1.4.12; Cicero *De re publica* 3.3.2 (cf. *De Officiis* 1.16.50). Hugo Grotius, *De jure belli ac pacis* (1625), bk. 2, chap. 16 ("De interpretatione"), here 2.16.1.1–2, in *The Rights of War and Peace,* trans. Richard Tuck (Indianapolis, IN: Liberty Fund, 2005), 2:848. Even atheists: "prolegomena," in Grotius's chap. 11. See also his chapter on the keeping of promises (3.19), e.g., 3.19.1.3. For a reading of Grotius within the context of English contract theory, see Victoria Kahn, *Wayward Contracts: The Crisis of Political Obligation in England, 1640–1674* (Princeton, NJ: Princeton University Press, 2004).

36 Thomas Hobbes, *Leviathan*, ed. Edwin Curley (Indianapolis: Hackett, 1994), chap. 5.36, 26. The idea of metaphor as a semi-fraudulent transaction is however much older, as in this example from Albert of Monte Casino in the eleventh century: "[I]t is the function of metaphor to twist, so to speak, its mode of speech from its property; by twisting, to make some innovation; by innovating, to clothe, as it were, in nuptial garb; and by clothing, to sell, apparently at a decent price." *Alberici Casinensis Flores rhetorici*, ed. M. Inguanez and H. M. Willard (Montecassino: Monaci di Montecassino, 1938), 45.

37 The "old proverb" is "The grace of God is gear enough," drawing on 2 Cor. 12:9: "My grace is sufficient for thee" (Authorized King James Version). On the "theological poetics" of grace invoked by some other late medieval and Renaissance defenders of secular poetry, see Nirenberg, "Figures of Thought" and the bibliography contained therein [see chap. 6, n. 24].

38 For a reading of act 5 as fulfillment of the Elizabethan audience's "contractual" expectations of comedy, see Lynda E. Boose, "The Comic Contract and Portia's Golden Ring," *Shakespeare Studies* 20 (1988), 241–254.

39 Or as Sir Philip Sidney put it more crudely, Christians "be flat contrary" to the Jews because the latter "take the sign for the thing signified." See Philippe de Mornay, *A Woorke Concerning the Trewnesse of the Christian Religion, Written in French, Against Atheists, Epicures, Paynims, Jewes, Mahumetists, and Other Infidels*, trans. Sir Philip Sidney and Arthur Golding (London, 1587), 581–582. Contemporaries might have heard echo here of Christian Eucharistic debates. As Bishop John Jewel would put it later, in differentiating the Church of England from the Papists, "[T]hree things herein we must consider; first, that we put a difference between the sign and the thing itself that is signified." *A Reply to Mr. Harding's Answer, in Works of John Jewel, Bishop of Salisbury*, ed. J. Ayre (Cambridge: Parker Society, 1845–1859), 1:449.

40 Augustine, *On Christian Doctrine*, trans. J. F. Shaw, in *Nicene and Post-Nicene Fathers*, first series, ed. Philip Schaff (1887; Grand Rapids, MI: Eerdmans, 1950), 2.560–561. Love's role in Shakespeare's economics is a topic in itself. See, e.g., John Russell Brown, "Love's Wealth and the Judgement of *The Merchant of Venice*," in *Shakespeare and His Comedies* (London: Methuen, 1957), 62–75.

41 James Shapiro, *Shakespeare and the Jews* (New York: Columbia University Press, 1996), 159, calls the allusion to Medea "the slightest hint of the possibility" of Jessica's relapse into Judaism and suggests an echo with John Studley's 1581 translation of Seneca's *Medea*.

42 "When a mouse" is from Thomas Calvert, "Diatriba of the Jews' Estate," preface to *The Blessed Jew of Marocco; or a Blackamoor Made White, by Rabbi Samuel [Samuel Marochitanus], a Jew Turned Christian* (York, 1648), 216, cited by Shapiro, *Shakespeare and the Jews*, 165. Lorenzo's musings on the music of the spheres echo commonplaces of Renaissance Neoplatonism and Neopythagoreanism from which Shakespeare elsewhere marks some distance (e.g., Cloten's speech in *Cymbeline*, act 2, scene 3, lines 11–31). For bibliography, see Nirenberg, "Shakespeare's Jewish Questions," n. 56. On the implications of this passage for Jessica's conversion, see

Mary Janell Metzger, "'Now by My Hood, a Gentle and No Jew': Jessica, *The Merchant of Venice,* and the Discourse of Early Modern English Identity," *PMLA* 113 (1998), 52–63; and Marc Berley, "Jessica's Belmont Blues: Music and Merriment in *The Merchant of Venice,*" in Peter C. Herman, ed., *Opening the Borders: Inclusivity in Early Modern Studies; Essays in Honor of James V. Mirollo* (Newark: University of Delaware Press, 1999), 185–205. For a more optimistic but less convincing view, see Camille Slights, "In Defense of Jessica: The Runaway Daughter in *The Merchant of Venice,*" *Shakespeare Quarterly* 31 (1980), 357–368.

43 Such is René Girard's argument in "'To Entrap the Wisest': A Reading of The Merchant of Venice," in Edward W. Said, ed., *Literature and Society* (Baltimore, MD: Johns Hopkins University Press, 1980); revised and expanded in René Girard, *A Theater of Envy: William Shakespeare* (New York: Oxford University Press, 1991), 243–255.

44 Jacques Derrida quoted in Elizabeth Weber et al., *Questioning Judaism: Interviews by Elisabeth Weber*, trans. Rachel Bowlby (Stanford, CA: Stanford University Press, 2004), 43, not, however, writing about Shakespeare.

45 The debate between Frank Kermode (one modern critic) and A. D. Moody (another) is reprinted in Barnet, *Twentieth Century Interpretations,* 97–108. It is curious that Shakespeare's irony is itself represented as "Jewish," even Shylockian (though with a positive valence), and this by even the most sophisticated critics (e.g., Halpern, *Shakespeare among the Moderns*, 219 [n. 114], 220, 226). The continuing "Jewishness" of irony in contemporary critical discourses demonstrates how entangled our reading practices remain within Christian hermeneutic structures.

46 Adam Smith, *The Wealth of Nations*, ed. Kathryn Sutherland (Oxford: Oxford University Press, 1998), bk. 1, chap. 4, 31. Compare this conclusion to the rather different argument of Stephen Greenblatt, who sees Shakespeare deploying a constant insistence on the difference between Christian and Jew in order to imagine the perfectibility of the Christian world, by contrast with Marlowe's *Jew of Malta,* in which all differentiation is dissolved in order to expose the relentless hypocrisy of the world. See Greenblatt's "Marlowe, Marx, and Anti-Semitism," *Critical Inquiry* 5 (1978), 291–307. Horkheimer and Adorno: *Dialectic of Enlightenment*, 187 [see chap. 6, n. 41].

CHAPTER 9: "ISRAEL" AT THE FOUNDATIONS OF CHRISTIAN POLITICS

1 The Augsburg treaty applied only to specific imperial German lands in which Luther's teaching had already taken deep root. It did not extend to other increasingly Protestant lands under the emperor's rule (most notably the Netherlands, soon to be flooded by the armies of the Hapsburg empire), much less to kingdoms like France, entirely outside it. Nevertheless, it is a representative example of the broader political and theological consensus I am trying to describe.

2 Justus Lipsius, *Six bookes of politickes or Civil Doctrine . . . done into English by William Jones* (London: R. Field, 1594); facsimile reprint, Amsterdam: The-

atrum Orbis Terrarum, 1970), 62. Cited in Richard Tuck, *Hobbes* (Oxford: Oxford University Press, 1989), 7.

3 For fourth- and fifth-century sources on these issues, see Gaddis, *There is No Crime for Those Who Have Christ* [see chap. 3, n. 83]. The quote from Calvin is from his *Defensio orthodoxae fidei* 46–47, cited in John Marshall, *John Locke, Toleration and Early Enlightenment Culture* (Cambridge: Cambridge University Press 2006), 325. Beza's *De Haereticis*, first published in 1554, exists in many editions. Melancthon is cited in J. Lecler, *Toleration and the Reformation*, 2 vols. (New York: Association Press, 1960), 1:161. On Servetus, see R. Bainton, *Hunted Heretic: The Life and Death of Michael Servetus* (Boston: Beacon Press, 1953). According to Marshall, *John Locke*, 255, Pierre Bayle treated that execution as a relic of Catholic cruelty in his *Philosophical Commentary* of 1686.

4 On Castellio and other "politique" writers, see Quentin Skinner, The *Foundations of Modern Political Thought* (Cambridge: Cambridge University Press, 1978), 2:250–251. On the *Exhortation*, see Lecler, *Toleration*, 2:50. The metaphor of heresy as cauterizable flesh is venerable: Saint Jerome, *Commentary on Galatians* III, on 5.9 (in Migne, *PL* 26, col. 403 [see chap. 3, n. 10]); Gratian, *Decretum* II, clause 24, q. 3, c. 37; Aquinas, *Summa Theologica* [see chap. 8, n. 19] II-II, qu. 11, art. 3.

5 Quote "we are born" is from Lipsius, *De constantia* 1.14; "Burn, cut" from Lipsius, *Politica* 4.2. See R. Bireley, *The Counter-Reformation Prince: Anti-Machiavellianism or Catholic Statecraft in Early Modern Europe* (Chapel Hill: University of North Carolina Press, 1990). On Lipsius, see G. Oestereich, *Antiker Geist und moderner Staat bei Justus Lipsius (1547–1606): Der Neustoizismus als politische Bewegung*, ed. N. Mout, Schriftenreihe der Historischen Kommission bei der Bayerischen Akademie der Wissenschaften, 38 (Göttingen: Vandenhoeck & Ruprecht, 1989); Richard Tuck, *Philosophy and Government 1572–1651* (Cambridge: Cambridge University Press, 1999), 58–59.

6 See Heinz Schilling, "Confessional Europe," in Thomas A. Brady Jr., Heiko Oberman, and James Tracy, eds., *Handbook of European History, 1400–1600*, vol. 2: *Visions, Programs and Outcomes* (Leiden: Brill, 1995). On the Geneva and King James Bibles, Christopher Hill, *The English Bible and the Seventeenth-Century Revolution* (London: Allen Lane, 1993), 58, 64.

7 Martin Luther, "How Christians should regard Moses," in *Luther's Works: American Edition*, ed. J. Pelikan and H. T. Lehman, 55 vols. (Philadelphia: Muehlenberg and Fortress, 1955–1986), 35:171, from the sermon of August 27, 1525. The title of the sermon makes clear the importance of Judaism to the political question it addresses.

8 On these debates in Reformation England, see, e.g., Michael C. Questier, *Conversion, Politics, and Religion in England, 1580–1625* (Cambridge: Cambridge University Press, 1996), esp. chaps. 5 and 6; and (with a helpful chapter on Henry VIII) Felicity Heal, *Reformation in Britain and Ireland* (Oxford: Oxford University Press, 2003).

9 The Thirty-nine Articles and Bishop Sandys are cited in David S. Katz, *Sabbath and Sectarianism in Seventeenth-Century England* (Leiden: Brill, 1988), 1.

10 There is much recent literature on Israel as a model for sixteenth- and seven-
    teenth-century political thought. See most recently Eric Nelson, *The Hebrew
    Republic: Jewish Sources and the Transformation of European Political Thought*
    (Cambridge, MA: Harvard University Press, 2010), which appeared after this
    chapter was written. Specifically on England, see Jason Rosenblatt, *Renaissance
    England's Chief Rabbi: John Selden* (Oxford: Oxford University Press, 2006);
    and Jeffrey Shoulson, *Milton and the Rabbis: Hebraism, Hellenism, and Chris-
    tianity* (New York: Columbia University Press, 2001). For a late-seventeenth-
    century shift away from Israel and toward Rome as a model, see Steven N.
    Zwicker, "England, Israel, and the Triumph of Roman Virtue," in Richard H.
    Popkin, ed., *Millenarianism and Messianism in English Literature and Thought,
    1650–1800* (Leiden: Brill, 1988), 37–64.

11 Thomas Hobbes, *Behemoth*, ed. F. Tönnies (London: Simpkin, Marshall, 1889),
    21–22. For a similar critique of clergy, see 53. Read together, the passages make
    clear that Hobbes's complaint is not about a lack of philological expertise, but
    about the normative nature of the claims.

12 Thomas Hobbes, *De Cive: Philosophical Rudiments Concerning Government
    and Society* (London: R. Royston, 1651; reprinted Whitefish, MT: Kessinger,
    2004), preface, 10.

13 Joseph Ben Gorion, *The Wonderful, and Most Deplorable History of the Later
    Times of the Jews* (London, 1652). The work saw at least six later editions. I
    cite from that of 1684, which also makes clear the causal relationship the author
    posits between the "Jewish Spirit" of revolutionary London, and the presence of
    real Jews in London in the 1680s: "Nay the Jews whereof there are Swarms now
    in this City will not stick to say [of Charles I's execution], that it was a murther
    beyond theirs" (A7v).

14 The database utilized was Early English Books Online is at eebo.chadwyck.com.
    See Meirav Jones, "The Image of Israel and the Development of Political Ideas
    in England, 1640–1660," PhD dissertation (Hebrew University of Jerusalem,
    2012). I am grateful to Dr. Jones for letting me read her dissertation before its
    completion.

15 Berkeley's remark cited in David S. Katz, *Philo-Semitism and the Readmission of
    the Jews to England, 1603–1655* (Oxford: Clarendon Press, 1982), 16–17, with
    further examples. On the Fifth Monarchy Men, see David S. Katz and Richard
    H. Popkin, *Messianic Revolution: Radical Religious Politics to the End of the Sec-
    ond Millennium* (New York: Hill & Wang, 1998), 73–76; and Bernard S. Capp,
    *The Fifth Monarchy Men: A Study in Seventeenth-Century English Millenarian-
    ism* (London: Rowman & Littlefield, 1972).

16 On Selden, see Rosenblatt, *Renaissance England's Chief Rabbi* (48–49 on the
    correspondence with Modena). On Selden's theories of natural and civil law,
    see J. Somerville, "John Selden, the Law of Nature, and the Origins of Govern-
    ment," *Historical Journal* 27 (1984), 437–447.

17 J. G. A. Pocock, *The Machiavellian Moment: Florentine Political Thought and
    the Atlantic Republican Tradition* (Princeton, NJ: Princeton University Press,
    1975), 383–422; and Pocock, *Politics, Language, and Time: Essays on Political*

Thought and History (New York: Atheneum, 1971), 104–147. For arguments against this view, see David Wooton, "Introduction: The Republican Tradition: From Commonwealth to Common Sense," in David Wooton, ed., *Republicanism, Liberty, and Commercial Society* (Palo Alto, CA: Stanford University Press, 1994), 10–19.

18 Compare *Leviathan*, 42.37–41. All quotes from *Leviathan* are to Curley's edition [see chap. 8, n. 36], by chapter and section number.

19 Hobbes's biblical philology was motivated by the same logic that drove him to insist on the careful definition of words: "Seeing the foundation of all true ratiocination is the constant signification of words . . . [I]t is necessary . . . to determine out of the bible the meaning of such words as by their ambiguity may render what I am to infer upon them obscure or disputable" (34.1). He pointed out that the books of Moses were not written in that prophet's own lifetime, and noted that the New Testament could have been falsified by ecclesiastics who "thought such frauds as tended to make the people the more obedient to Christian doctrine to be pious" (33.20). But he did not explicitly doubt the scriptures as "true registers of those things which were done and said by the prophets and apostles" (33.20). On the debate over Hobbes's sincerity on this point, see A. P. Martinich's summary: "The Bible and Protestantism in *Leviathan*," in Patricia Springborg, ed., *The Cambridge Companion to Hobbes's* Leviathan (Cambridge: Cambridge University Press, 2007), 375–389.

20 Quote with "sharp distinction" is from A. P. Martinich, *The Two Gods of* Leviathan*: Thomas Hobbes on Religion and Politics* (Cambridge: Cambridge University Press, 1992), 132.

21 One part of the debate between Strauss and Schmitt over Hobbes is available in Carl Schmitt, *The Concept of the Political*, trans. George Schwab (Chicago: University of Chicago Press, 1996), with Leo Strauss's comments as an appendix. But see esp. Franz Neumann, *Behemoth: The Structure and Practice of National Socialism*, written in 1942 against Carl Schmitt's *Der Leviathan in der Staatslehre des Thomas Hobbes: Sinn und Fehlschlag eines politischen Symbols* (Hamburg: Hanseatische Verlagsanstalt, 1938). Schmitt's children's book (as he called it) was entitled *Land und Meer: Eine weltgeschichtliche Betrachtung* (Leipzig: Philipp Reclam jun., 1942); pages 9–10 suffice to justify the tag anti-Semitic.

22 J. G. A. Pocock, "Time, History and Eschatology in the Thought of Thomas Hobbes," in his *Politics, Language, and Time*, 200; and Joel Schwartz, "Hobbes and the Two Kingdoms of God," *Polity* 18 (1985), 10.

23 Small communities can be found in Alsace, in Avignon, in parts of Italy (esp. Livorno/Leghorn), and from ca. 1600 on, in a few cities of the Netherlands' United Provinces, particularly Amsterdam.

24 On Arias Montano, and more generally on the Hebraism involved in his monumental Polyglot Bible, see Theodore Dunkelgrun, "Radical Philology: The Confluence of Textual Traditions in the Making of the Antwerp Polyglot Bible (1568–1573)," PhD dissertation (University of Chicago, 2012). Buxtorf produced (again, among other works) a Hebrew and Aramaic grammar in 1602, a history of the Jews in 1603, and an edition of the Hebrew Bible with rabbinic

commentaries in 1618–1619: Stephen G. Burnett, *From Christian Hebraism to Jewish Studies: Johannes Buxtorf (1564–1629) and Hebrew Learning in the Seventeenth Century* (Leiden: Brill, 1996). The phenomenon was not confined to western Europe; see, e.g., David Frick, *Polish Sacred Philology in the Reformation and Counter Reformation: Chapters in the History of the Controversies (1551–1632)* (Berkeley: University of California Press, 1989).

25 By the seventeenth century some scholars advocated the abandonment of the Hebrew Bible as hopelessly corrupt, urging a turn to the Greek Septuagint (Vossius) or the Samaritan Bible (Morin) instead. For Vossius, J. C. H. Lebram, "Ein Streit um die hebräische Bibel und die Septuaginta," in Th. H. Scheurleer and G. H. M. Meyjes, eds., *Leiden University in the Seventeenth Century: An Exchange of Learning* (Leiden: Brill, 1975). For Morin on the Samaritan Bible, see his *Exercitationes biblicae, de Hebrai Graecique textus sinceritate* (Paris, 1669).

26 Serjeant Sir Henry Finch's *Worlds Restauration. Or the Calling of the Iewes* (1621) got him thrown in prison as blasphemer by King James I, but a decade or two later his views would seem moderate within the increasingly millenarian English landscape. The Talmud translation project was advocated by Oliver Cromwell's agent John Drury. On these and others, see Katz, *Philo-Semitism*, 218–219.

27 The *Cratylus* explores a number of approaches but endorses none of them (see, e.g., Socrates's reservations at 435c). On Laputa, see Jonathan Swift, *Gulliver's Travels*, ed. H. Davis (Oxford: Oxford University Press, 1965), pt. 3, chap. 5, 185–186. Others, such as Pierre-Charles Fabiot Aunillon in a travel fantasy from 1750 (*Azor, ou le Prince enchanté, histoire nouvelle, pour servir de chronique à celle de la terre des Perroquets*), were more optimistic than Swift. See Paul Cornelius, *Languages in Seventeenth and Early Eighteenth-Century Imaginary Voyages* (Geneva: Droz, 1965). On the correspondence between Mersenne and Descartes, see Marin Mersenne, *Correspondance*, ed. Tannery et al. (Paris: Éditions du CNRS, 1945), 2:323–329. Hobbes's description of Mersenne is in Tuck, *Hobbes*, 13–14. G. W. Leibniz's comments are in his *Opuscules et fragments inédits*, ed Louis Couturat (Paris: Félix Alcan, 1903), 27–28. See also James Knowlson, *Universal Language Schemes in England and France, 1600–1800* (Toronto: University of Toronto Press, 1975), 44–70.

28 On Hebrew as the original common speech of mankind, see Augustine, *City of God* 16.11. Samuel Purchas, *Pvrchas his Pilgrimage*, 4th ed. (London: W. Stansby, 1626), 45. Aspects of the universal-language debates most relevant to our topic can be followed in Katz, *Philo-Semitism*, 43–88.

29 These fields were much wider than we might today imagine, since the reach of the Bible was much longer. See, e.g., Peter Harrison, *The Bible, Protestantism, and the Rise of Natural Science* (Cambridge: Cambridge University Press, 1998).

30 See, in addition to Katz, *Philo-Semitism*, the important works of Hans Joachim Schoeps: *Philo-Semitismus im Barock* (Tübingen: Mohr Siebeck, 1952); and *Barocke Juden, Christen und Judenchristen* (Bern: Francke, 1975).

31 Opposition from the merchants played a significant role in the defeat of read-

mission. Drury's postscript is from a letter of 1656, published in *The Harleian Miscellany*, ed. William Oldys and John Malham (London: Robert Dutton, 1810), 6:444. William Prynne, *A Short Demurer To the Jewes*, 2nd ed. (London, 1656), i. sig. A3v. The preacher Ralph Josselin prayed that if the Jews were readmitted, God would "keep us from turning aside from Christ to Moses, of which I am very heartily afraid." *Diary of Ralph Josselin*, 358, entry for December 16, 1655 [see chap. 6, n. 1]. For Harrington's settlement proposal, see his *Commonwealth of Oceana and a System of Politics*, ed. J. G. A. Pocock (Cambridge: Cambridge University Press, 1992), 6.

32 On the role of Jews in French Catholic-Protestant polemics, see Myriam Yardeni, *Anti-Jewish Mentalities in Early Modern Europe* (Lanham, MD: University Press of America, 1990). On French views of Spain as Jewish, see Hillgarth, *Mirror of Spain* [see chap. 6, n. 45]. On La Peyrère, see above all Richard H. Popkin, *Isaac La Peyrère (1596–1676): His Life, Work, and Influence* (Leiden: Brill, 1987). Even more controversial than La Peyrère's French brand of political messianism was his attempt in the Pre-Adamites (*Prae-Adamitae*, 1655) to rescue the validity of biblical chronology by arguing that although the Jews were indeed descendants of Adam, more ancient peoples like the Egyptians were not.

33 Quote "whiteness of their complexion" is from Dean Phillip Bell, *Jews in the Early Modern World* (Lanham, MD: Rowman & Littlefield, 2007), 204. Balthazar Grangier de Liverdis, describing Avignon's ghetto in his *Journal d'un voyage de France et d'Italie* (Paris, 1667), 72–73, borrowed also by Jouvin de Rochefort, *Le voyageur d'Europe* (Paris, 1672). Compare, on Italy, Nicolas Audeber's *Le voyage et observations de plusieurs choses qui se peuvent remarquer en Italie* (Paris, 1656), 127: "No matter what, no matter where, they are almost recognizable by their sheer facial features," since "for reason of race they all have a face that is different from that of Christians." Moreover they "smell rather bad, with a dull and pungent odor." For a Turkish example, see Antoine Morison, *Relation historique d'un voyage nouvellement fait au Mont Sinaï et à Jerusalem* (Toul: A. Laurent, 1704), 296, who remarks that "the Jews are regarded by the other nations as the refuse and filth of the world." For these and other examples, see Yardeni, *Anti-Jewish Mentalities*, 139–154.

CHAPTER 10: ENLIGHTENMENT REVOLTS AGAINST JUDAISM

1 In their efforts to caricature the badness of bad King John, medieval English chroniclers suggested that the excommunicated king had toyed with the idea of converting the kingdom to Islam, but they hardly meant the possibility to be taken seriously. The situation was very different with the religious legislation of Henry VIII, or with the shifting confessional allegiances of his successors over the next century. On the rumors about King John, see John Tolan, *Saracens: Islam in the Medieval European Imagination* (New York: Columbia University Press, 2002), 183.

2 The passage continues: "Jews were of two kinds: one kind had pagan sensitivities, the other Christian ones." See Blaise Pascal, *Pensées* (1670; Oxford: Oxford

University Press, 1995), 85, cited in Adam Sutcliffe, *Judaism and Enlightenment* (Cambridge: Cambridge University Press, 2003), 189.

3   All three quotations are from the same page in the translation of Samuel Shirley, *Theological-Political Treatise*, 2nd ed. (Indianapolis, IN: Hackett, 2001). The standard edition of the *Treatise* [henceforth *TTP*] is that of Carl Gebhardt in Spinoza, *Opera*, 4 vols. (Heidelberg: Carl Winter Universitätsverlag, 1925; reprint 1972 [henceforth Geb.]). Citations in the text and notes are in parentheses, with the Shirley pagination followed by the Gebhardt volume and page numbers. For publication history, see Fritz Bamberger, "The Early Editions of Spinoza's Tractatus Theologico-Politicus, a Bibliohistorical Re-examination," *Studies in Bibliography and Booklore* 5 (1961), 9–33; and J. Kingma and A. K. Offenberg, "Bibliography of Spinoza's Works up to 1800," *Studia Rosenthaliana* 2 (1977), 1–32. Steven Nadler's *Book Forged in Hell: Spinoza's Scandalous Treatise and the Birth of the Secular Age* (Princeton, NJ: Princeton University Press, 2011) appeared after this chapter was written, but readers interested in the *Tractatus* may profit from it.

4   Graeme Hunter interprets the *TTP* as a radical Protestant document: *Radical Protestantism in Spinoza's Thought* (Hampshire: Ashgate, 2005), 182–184. The Jewish philosopher Hermann Cohen also presented Spinoza as a pro-Christian and anti-Jewish author: *Jüdische Schriften* (Berlin: Schwetschke 1924), 3:290–372. On Spinoza's view of Jesus and Christianity, see esp. Yitzhak Y. Melamed "'*Christus secundum spiritum*': Spinoza, Jesus and the Infinite Intellect," in Neta Stahl, ed., *The Jewish Jesus* (London: Routledge, 2012).

5   According to Charles Levier's *La Vie et l'Esprit de Mr. Benoît de Spinosa*, ed. Silvia Berti (1719; Turin, 1994), 36, the false titles were used to evade the Inquisition's ban on Spinoza's work. The choice is nevertheless significant. Spinoza's motives are from Letter 30, addressed to Henry Oldenburg: *Spinoza: Complete Works*, trans. Samuel Shirley (Indianapolis, IN: Hackett, 2002), 844. See also Spinoza's preface to the *TTP*, where he provides similar reasons; and Spinoza's correspondence with Blyenberg (Letters 18–24, 27), which may itself have stimulated Spinoza to undertake the project.

6   Spinoza mocks such beliefs in his letter correspondence with Hugo Boxel, Letters 51–56 (*Spinoza*, 893–906). His dismissal was precocious but not unprecedented: Hasdai Crescas criticized belief in demons in his *Refutation of Christian Principles*, trans. Daniel Lasker (Albany: SUNY Press, 1992), chap. 10, a text probably known to Spinoza. (On precedents to some of Spinoza's positions in Jewish anti-Christian polemics, see Daniel J. Lasker, "Reflections of the Medieval Jewish-Christian Debate in the *Theological Political Treatise* and the *Epistles*," in Yitzhak Y. Melamed and Michael Rosenthal, eds., *Spinoza's Theological Political Treatise: A Critical Guide* [Cambridge: Cambridge University Press, 2010]). Antonius van Dale (1638–1708) expanded and provided historical evidence for some of Spinoza's claims in his *De oraculis ethnicorum* (Amsterdam, 1683) and his *Dissertationes de origine ac progressu idololatriae et superstitionum: de vera ac falsa prophetia; uti et de diviniationibus idololatricis judaeorum* (Amsterdam: Henricum & viduam Theodori Boom, 1696).

7 In Spinoza's _Ethics_ it becomes clear that this freedom of choice is itself an illusion. On the tension between biblical and secular history in Spinoza's treatise, see Martin D. Yaffe, "'The Histories and Successes of the Hebrews': The Demise of the Biblical Polity in Spinoza's _Theologico-Political Treatise_," _Jewish Political Studies Review_ 7 (1995), 57–75. On Spinoza's relationship to the Bible more generally, see J. Samuel Preuss, _Spinoza and the Irrelevance of Biblical Authority_ (Cambridge: Cambridge University Press, 2001).

8 On complete subjection, see, e.g., _TTP_, chaps. 19 and 20, where Spinoza suggests that preaching on religion should be permitted only to those licensed by the sovereign; or chap. 16 (183/3.199), "it belongs completely to the sovereign power . . . to make what decisions it thinks fit concerning religion." See also his _Political Treatise_, chap. 8 (Geb. 3.345) on the treatment of religions that are not the official ones of the state.

9 John Aubrey, _Brief Lives_, ed. Andrew Clark (Oxford: Clarendon Press, 1898) 1:357, following Edwin Curley, "'I durst not write so boldly,' or, how to read Hobbes' _Theological-Political Treatise_," in _Hobbes e Spinoza, scienza e politica_, ed. D. Bostrenghi (Naples: Bibliopolius, 1992), lxviii.

10 On La Peyrère and his milieu, see among others Popkin, _Isaac La Peyrère_ [see chap. 9, n. 32]; Anthony Grafton, _Defenders of the Text: The Traditions of Scholarship in an Age of Science, 1450–1800_ (Cambridge, MA: Harvard University Press, 1991), esp. 204–213; and Leo Strauss, _Spinoza's Critique of Religion_ (Chicago: University of Chicago Press, 1997), chap. 3.

11 On Fisher, see Nicholas McDowell, _The English Radical Imagination: Culture, Religion, and Revolution, 1630–1660_ (Oxford: Oxford University Press, 2003), chap. 5.

12 Spinoza's circle produced treatises that anticipated parts of the _TTP_'s arguments. For an extended discussion of that circle, see Jonathan Israel, _Radical Enlightenment: Philosophy and the Makings of Modernity, 1650–1650_ (Oxford: Oxford University Press, 2001), 159–257.

13 "Nothing more than the order of nature" is from Johann Heinrich Heidegger's attack on Spinoza, cited in Israel, _Radical Enlightenment_, 449.

14 On Spinoza's knowledge of Maimonides and of the Jewish tradition, see Shlomo Pines, "Spinoza's _Tractatus Theologico-Politicus_ and the Jewish Philosophical Tradition," in I. Twersky and B. Septimus, eds., _Jewish Thought in the Seventeenth Century_ (Cambridge, MA: Harvard University Press, 1987), 499–521; Zev Warren Harvey, "A Portrait of Spinoza as a Maimonidean," _Journal of the History of Philosophy_ 19 (1981), 151–172; Harvey, "Maimonides and Spinoza on the Knowledge of Good and Evil," _Binah: Studies in Jewish Thought_ 11 (1989), 131–146; and Richard A. Cohen, "Levinas on Spinoza's Misunderstanding of Judaism," in Melvyn New et al., eds., _In Proximity: Emmanuel Levinas and the Eighteenth Century_ (Lubbock: Texas Tech University Press, 2001), 23–51.

15 Sutcliffe, _Judaism and Enlightenment_, 122. For Spinoza on elitism, see _TTP_, chap. 7 (Geb. 3.116).

16 Justin Martyr, _Dialogue with Trypho_, chaps. 18 and 19 [see chap. 3, n. 10].

17 Quote "in Hebrew" is from _TTP_, chap. 1 (Geb. 3.22); stiff-necked from _TTP_,

chap. 13 (157/3.172). His presentation of Christian superstition in Letter 73 (*Spinoza*, 942–943) makes such a reading plausible. Spinoza knew: Instead of choosing Matt. 5:43, he might have cited Hebrew sources such as Ps. 139:21 to make a case.

18 I. S. Revah's work on Spinoza's break with the rabbis is foundational: "Aux origines de la rupture spinozienne: Nouveaux documents sur l'incroyance dans la communauté Judéo—Portugaise d'Amsterdam à l'époque de l'excommunication de Spinoza," *Revue des études juives*, 4th series, 3/113 (1964); and his *Spinoza et le Dr. Juan de Prado* (Paris: Mouton, 1959). Israel, *Radical Enlightenment*, 164–173, provides a recent synthesis. Spinoza was admiringly portrayed in two biographies that appeared shortly after his death: John Lucas, *The Life of the Late Mr. de Spinosa* (in *The Oldest Biography of Spinosa*, ed. A. Wolf [New York: Dial, 1927]); and John Colerus, "The Life of Benedict de Spinosa" (edited in Frederick Pollock, *Spinoza. His Life and Philosophy*, 2nd ed. [London: Duckworth, 1899]).

19 Spinoza makes the accusation of Judaizing explicit in a number of places, e.g, chap. 12 (145/3.158) and chap. 15 (165/3.180). "Song of the Pharisees" is from his Letter 76 (*Spinoza*, 949). Though I see Spinoza's focus on the Old Testament as crucial, there are some who understand it as merely a convenient example of his general thesis, e.g., Sylvain Zac, *Spinoza et l'interprétation de l'écriture* (Paris: Presses Universitaires de France, 1965), 12. Scholars have also noted the rhetorical (i.e., oriented toward persuasion) nature of the *TTP*. Fokke Akkerman studied the treatise's classical rhetorical techniques in his "Le caractère rhétorique du *Traité théologico-politique*," in *Spinoza entre lumière et romantisme*, ed. J. Bonnamour (Fontenay-aux-Roses: E. N. S. Fontenay, 1985), 381–390. Leo Strauss's much-criticized reading of the *TTP* as having both an exoteric and an esoteric meaning is also a "rhetorical" approach ("How to Study Spinoza's *Tractatus Theologico-Politicus*," in *Persecution and the Art of Writing* [Westport, CT: Greenwood, 1973]). My suggestion that strategic reasons encouraged Spinoza's focus on the Hebrew Bible and on Jewish superstition might be considered another. Spinoza himself gave a simpler reason that I take to be disingenuous—namely, that he could not criticize the New Testament because he did not know Greek (but note that in the *Hebrew Grammar*, he does bring Greek examples).

20 Again Spinoza was not univocal, and at times suggests some forms of *Hebraica veritas*, as in the *Ethics*, pt. 2, prop. 7, scholium: "[S]ome of the Hebrews seem to have seen this [Spinoza's parallelism] as if through a cloud" (a metaphor borrowed from but also targeting Maimonides! [Geb. 2.90]); and Letter 73 (*Spinoza*, 942), where Spinoza suggests that his own pantheism was anticipated by "the ancient Hebrews, as far as may be conjectured from certain traditions, though these have suffered much corruption." In both examples, Spinoza's Hebrew predecessors were close to the truth. For an example from the *TTP*, see chap. 13 (Geb. 3.69), approving of the Hebrews' claim that the Tetragrammaton is the only name of God that indicates God's absolute nature (though Spinoza makes the point in order to show that the patriarchs did *not* know

God's true nature). The Hebrew Grammar contains further claims to "Hebrew truth," such as the claim that the grammatical structure (binyan) of Hitpael is the best to express God's action as an immanent cause. For other examples, see Zev Warren Harvey, "Spinoza's Metaphysical Hebraism," in Heidi M. Ravven and Lenn Evan Goodman, eds., *Jewish Themes in Spinoza's Philosophy* (Albany: SUNY Press, 2002), 107–114.

21 For some examples, see Israel, *Radical Enlightenment*, 447–464. For a study of Old Testament philology with excellent coverage of the Dutch milieu, see Cees Houtman, *Der Pentateuch: die Geschichte seiner Erforschung neben einer Auswertung* (Kampen: Kok Pharos, 1994). See more generally Jonathan Sheehan, *The Enlightenment Bible: Translation, Scholarship, Culture* (Princeton, NJ: Princeton University Press, 2005), which focuses on England and Germany in the eighteenth century. On Bayle's King David, see Walter Rex, "Pierre Bayle: The Theology and Politics of the Article on David," *Bibliothèque d'Humanisme et Renaissance* 24 (1962) 168–189, and 25 (1963), 366–403.

22 "But what I esteem most" is from Lucas, *Life*, 69; "Once again" is from Sutcliffe, *Judaism and Enlightenment*, 140. I would only add that Spinoza, like every prophet in this book, contributed to his "subliminally" messianic impression by deliberately casting his emancipation of reason as an overcoming of Judaism.

23 Quote with "godlessness" is from Israel, *Radical Enlightenment*, 291. For the survey of the *TTP*'s German reception, see Manfred Walther, "*Machina civilis* oder *Von Deutscher Freiheit*: Formen, Inhalte und Trägergeschichten der Reaktion auf den Politiktheoretischen Gehalt von Spinozas *Tractatus Theologico-Politicus* in Deutschland, bis 1700," in Paolo Cristofolini, ed., *The Spinozistic Heresy: The debate on the* Tractatus Theologico-Politicus, *1670–1677, and the Immediate Reception of Spinozism* (Amsterdam: APA-Holland University Press, 1995), 184–221. The *Presentation of Four Recent Worldly Philosophers* (Fürstellung Vier Neuer Welt-Weisen) was published anonymously in Cothen in 1702, and is cited in David Bell, *Spinoza in Germany from 1670 to the Age of Goethe* (London: Humanities Press, 1984), 6. On Spinoza as a new Muhammad, see Israel, *Radical Enlightenment*, 572–573.

24 Henry More's comment to Robert Boyle cited in Israel, *Radical Enlightenment*, 604. It is not easy to decide what Bayle thought about Spinoza. His tendency to ventriloquize dangerous ideas through the mouths of others is everywhere evident in his *Historical and Critical Dictionary* (trans. Richard Popkin and Craig Brush [Indianapolis, IN: Bobbs-Merrill, 1965]), for example at 313, and it may be that he was using his critique of Spinoza as a mask to say some things that could not otherwise be safely said. At times he even suggests that Spinoza's thought could support orthodoxy. Yet Bayle's critique was certainly extensive, and it influenced other early Enlightenment thinkers.

25 On Wagenseil, see Peter Blastenbrei, *Johann Christoph Wagenseil und seine Stellung zum Judentum* (Erlangen: Fischer, 2004). Eisenmenger's work, first published in Frankfurt in 1700, was republished throughout the eighteenth and nineteenth centuries, at least up to the 1893 edition put out by Brandner in Dresden. Müller discussed in Israel, *Radical Enlightenment*, 629–630. See also

Richard H. Popkin, "Jewish Anti-Christian Arguments as a Source of Irreligion from the Seventeenth to the Early Nineteenth Century," in Michael Hunter and David Wooton, eds., *Atheism from the Reformation to the Enlightenment* (Oxford: Clarendon Press, 1992), 159–181.

26 Johann Georg Wachter, *Der Spinozismus im Jüdenthumb* (Amsterdam: Johann Wolters, 1699), 57, 65, 69. On Wachter, see Popkin, "Spinoza, Neoplatonic Kabbalist?" in Lenn E. Goodman, ed., *Neoplatonism and Jewish Thought* (Albany: SUNY Press, 1992); and Gershom Scholem, "Die Wachtersche Kontroverse über den Spinozismus und ihre Folgen," in K. Gruender and W. Schmidt-Biggemann, eds., *Spinoza in der Frühzeit Seiner Religiösen Wirkung* (Heidelberg: Lambert Schneider, 1984), 15–25. Wachter may have been using the cover of an anti-Spinozan treatise to defend some Spinozan positions about natural reason. He also deployed Judaism against more traditional rivals: of Bishop Huet's *Demonstratio Evangelica*, a defense of the Hebrew Bible against Spinoza, he wrote that only the Jews should be thankful for it (*Spinozismus*, 63–64).

27 Cf. Sutcliffe, *Judaism and Enlightenment*, 185–189, here 189. I quote Basnage's subject headings from the English translation of his *History of the Jews, from Jesus Christ to the Present* by Thomas Taylor (London: Beaver, Lintot, et al., 1708), 228–230.

28 Leo Strauss, "Introduction," in his *Spinoza's Critique of Religion*, reprinted in K. Green, ed., *Leo Strauss, Jewish Philosophy and the Crisis of Modernity* (Albany: SUNY Press, 1997), 143.

29 Ronald Schechter, *Obstinate Hebrews: Representations of Jews in France, 1715–1815* (Berkeley: University of California Press, 2003), 19, and in general, chap. 1. Schechter demonstrates as well the poverty of most of these Jews. In the eastern provinces, up to 80 percent of Jews were classified as beggars and secondhand peddlers, many depending on charity. In the western Sephardic populations, traditionally thought of as much wealthier, the proportion of Jews listed as dependent on charity still approached 50 percent.

30 Ibid., 36. I have adapted and expanded the searches to correct for his overlooking of variant forms, and applied them to a much-expanded database. I did not repeat Schechter's searches for Basques, nor within the Voltaire corpus.

31 See Michael Sonenscher, *Before the Deluge: Public Debt, Inequality, and the Intellectual Origins of the French Revolution* (Princeton, NJ: Princeton University Press, 2009); and the articles collected in the special issue titled "Money and the Enlightenment" of *Historical Reflections/Réflexions historiques* 31 (2005).

32 The comment about the London Stock Exchange is from Voltaire's *Lettres philosophiques* (Paris: Flammarion, 1964), Letter 6, "On the Presbyterians," 47. On the medieval constraints that pushed Jews into commerce, see his *Dictionnaire Philosophique*, in *Oeuvres* (Paris: Garnier, 1879), 19:524–525. For Jewish exemplars of commercial cruelty, see his *Candide, ou l'optimisme* from 1759 (Paris: Hachette, 1913), 208, 216. His lover's judgment (Mme. Denis, writing in 1754) is quoted in Theodore Besterman, *Voltaire*, 3rd ed. (Chicago: University of Chicago Press, 1976), 350. The banker's opinion is cited in Jerry Z. Muller, *Capitalism and the Jews* (Princeton, NJ: Princeton University Press, 2001), 31.

33 Montesquieu, *De l'esprit des lois* (1755; reprint Paris: Belles Lettres, 1958), bk. 21, chap. 20, 121–122; Montesquieu, *Lettres persanes* (Amsterdam, 1721; Paris: Roches, 1929), Letter 60, 127–128 (and cf. Letter 67, 151ff.). "Juif," in *Encyclopédie, ou Dictionnaire raisonné des sciences, des arts et des métiers*, ed. D. Diderot and J. le Rond d'Alembert (Paris: Mouton, 1751–1772), 9:25. Kant summarizes the logic well in his note on Jewish ("Palestinian") merchants/ cheaters in *Anthropology from a Pragmatic Point of View*, ed. Robert Louden (Cambridge: Cambridge University Press, 2006), sect. 46, 100.

34 See Paul Cheney, *Revolutionary Commerce: Globalization and the French Monarchy* (Cambridge, MA: Harvard University Press, 2010).

35 The first edition appeared as *Traité sur la circulation et le credite* in 1771. I cite from *An essay on circulation and credit, in four parts; and a letter on the jealousy of commerce. From the French of Monsieur de Pinto*, trans. S. Baggs (London: J. Ridley, 1774), 13, 39–40, 52, 171, 174–175. Other works by de Pinto include treatises on luxury, stock markets, and the East India Company.

36 Montesquieu, *De l'esprit des lois*, bk. 25, chap. 13, 279–282. The theme of the persecuted Jew is a frequent one in Montesquieu's work. See also in *De l'esprit*, bk. 12, chap. 4, 113; bk. 21, chap. 20, 122; bk. 28, chaps. 1 (34) and 7 (44); and in his *Lettres persanes*, Letter 78 (19). On Montesquieu's Jews, see Schechter, *Obstinate Hebrews*, 40–43. The quote from Voltaire is from his *Oeuvres* [see n. 32], 8:136 (translated in Schechter, *Obstinate Hebrews*, 49). Spinoza had made similar points about the Inquisition.

37 D'Argens, "Lettre dédicatoire," as cited in Jonathan Israel, *Enlightenment Contested: Philosophy, Modernity, and the Emancipation of Man, 1670–1752* (Oxford: Oxford University Press, 2006), 32.

38 See, e.g., De Lisle de Sales's *De la Philosophie de la nature* (Amsterdam, 1770), or his lost letter to Voltaire of 1773, discussed in Arthur Hertzberg, *The French Enlightenment and the Jews: The Origins of Modern Anti-Semitism* (New York: Columbia University Press, 1990), 307. Pierre-Louis Lacretelle's brief is "LVIIIe cause. Question d'état sur les Juifs de Metz," in *Causes célèbres, curieuses et intéressantes, de toutes les cours souveraines du royaume, avec les jugemens qui les ont décidées* (Paris, 1776), 23:64–98, cited by Schechter, *Obstinate Hebrews*, 104. The statement became standard in treatises arguing for the improvement of the Jews, ranging from (among the more famous) Christian Wilhelm von Dohm's *On the Improvement of the Jews for Citizenship* (Berlin, 1781) to Abbé Henri Grégoire's *Essay on the Physical, Moral, and Political Regeneration of the Jews* of 1789.

39 The word *regénération* was made famous in this context by Mirabeau in his *L'ami des hommes* of 1756. Jean Starobinski, "Eloquence et liberté," *Revue suisse de l'histoire* 26 (1976), 549–563, here 562.

40 Montesquieu, *Lettres persanes*, Letter 60, 127–128 (and cf. Letter 67, 151ff.); *De l'esprit des lois*, bk. 25, chap. 13, 282. On Montesquieu's toleration more generally, see Diana Schaub, "Of Believers and Barbarians: Montesquieu's Enlightened Toleration," in Alan Levine, ed., *Early Modern Skepticism and the Origins of Toleration* (Lanham, MD: Lexington Books, 1999), 225–247.

41 The most recent critical edition of this work can be found in *Œuvres Complètes de Voltaire*, vol. 56C, ed. John Renwick (Oxford: Voltaire Foundation, 2000). The English translation followed here is that of Simon Harvey, *Voltaire, Treatise on Tolerance and Other Writings* (Cambridge: Cambridge University Press, 2000).

42 On the Calas affair, see David Bien, *The Calas Affair* (Princeton, NJ: Princeton University Press, 1960); José Cubero, *L'Affaire Calas: Voltaire contre Toulouse* (Paris: Perrin, 1993); and Janine Garrisson, *L'Affaire Calas: Miroir des Passions Françaises* (Paris: Fayard, 2004).

43 Elsewhere Voltaire characterized some of these places quite differently. In his *Essai sur les moeurs*, e.g., he cast China as a battlefield between tolerant Confucians and intolerant Buddhists.

44 Among the more influential responses were those by relatively liberal Catholic theologians like Antoine Guénée, who adopted a Jewish persona to respond to the *Treatise on Tolerance* in his *Lettres de quelques Juifs portugais et allemands à M. de Voltaire*, 2nd ed. (Paris, 1769). The best-known responses by Jews are those of Jacob Rodrigues Péreire (better known as the inventor of a sign language for deaf-mutes), whose defense of Judaism appeared in 1767, and Isaac de Pinto, whose *Apology for the Jewish Nation* of 1762 criticizing the representation of Jews in Voltaire's *Philosophical Dictionary* elicited a response from Voltaire himself. On Péreire's contribution on behalf of the deaf, see Marjoke Reitveld-van Wingerden and Wim Westerman, "'Hear, O Israel': The Involvement of Jews in Education of the Deaf, 1850–1880," *Jewish History* 23, no. 1 (2009), 41–56. On the correspondence between de Pinto and Voltaire, see Sutcliffe, *Judaism and Enlightenment*, 244–245. Voltaire responded to some of these in his late *Christian against Six Jews* and *The Bible Finally Explained*, both published in 1776. See the Paris *Oeuvres* of 1879, 29:499–582 (for "Un Chrétien") and 30:1–316 (for "*La Bible*"). It is worth asking why Jewish authors (including Moses Mendelssohn in his 1783 *Jerusalem, oder Über religiöse Macht und Judentum*, translated by Alfred Jospe as *Jerusalem, and Other Jewish Writings* [New York: Schocken, 1969]) assigned to Judaism many of the same exceptional characteristics as Christian authors did, but that question lies outside the boundaries of this study.

45 D'Holbach, *L'esprit du judaïsme ou Examen raisonné de la loi de Moyse et de son influence sur la religion chrétienne* (London: Rutilius Itixerar, 1770), 200–201, translated by Hertzberg, *French Enlightenment*, 310. The work is in large part a translation of a treatise by the English deist Anthony Collins. In his *Philosophical Dictionary* Voltaire also portrayed Judaism as a religion plagiarized from the Egyptians, but he added that "their stubbornness, their new superstitions, and their hallowed usury" were proper to the Jews (cited in Hertzberg, *French Enlightenment*, 303).

46 Some of the participants in these debates understood themselves to be part of a very long tradition. We have already seen Voltaire and his allies take up Egyptian and Hellenistic traditions of argument against the Jews. On the other side, there were also those who took up patristic arguments to defend the Jews (and

more important, Christianity) from philosophical attack. (One even wrote a debate between Voltaire and Trypho, the protagonist of Justin Martyr's second-century attack on Judaism discussed in chap. 3; see Charles Louis Richard's *Voltaire Parmi les Ombres*, as mentioned in Hertzberg, *French Enlightenment*, 257.) An important result of all this activity was the creation of a dossier of ancient anecdotes and arguments about the Jews that would henceforth serve as an archive for anti-Semites.

47 Locke, *A Letter Concerning Toleration*, in David Wootton, ed., *Political Writings of John Locke* (Penguin: New York, 1993), 390 (on what was forbidden by the Savior, citing Luke 22:25), 395–396 and 420 (on coercion and hypocrisy), 399 (on the lack of coercion in the New Testament), 407 (on zealots), 414 (on the Jews being commanded while the Christians are free), and 419 (on the law of Moses as absolute theocracy applicable only to Jews, and only during their kingdom of God in the land of Canaan). On the context of Locke's writings, see esp. Marshall, *John Locke* [see chap. 9, n. 3].

48 Immanuel Kant, *Religion within the Bounds of Reason Alone*, ed. Allen Wood and George de Giovanni (Cambridge: Cambridge University Press, 1998), 130–135 (italics in original). "So many evils . . ." is my loose translation of Kant's quote from Lucretius, "tantum religio potuit suadere malorum," *De rerum natura* 1.101. Kant's appropriation of Spinoza on Judaism was influenced by the writings of the Jewish philosopher Moses Mendelssohn, particularly his *Jerusalem, or on Religious Power and Judaism* (1783). On Kant's view of Jesus as Greek, see *Reflexionen Kants zur Anthropologie, Aus Kants handschriftlichen Aufzeichnungen*, ed. Benno Erdmann (Leipzig: Fues's Verlag, 1882), 213–214. Kant's arguments are aimed both at the clerical establishment (whose authority depended on claims about the historicity of scripture) and against new schools of biblical scholarship—beginning with Lessing's publication of the Reimarus fragments in 1774–1778—whose search for the "historical Jesus" led them to a recognition of his (and hence early Christianity's) "Jewishness." This historical recognition played an important role in Mendelssohn's defense of Judaism (in *Jerusalem*) as well. Kant's attack against it was therefore also very much an attack against contemporary Judaism, and was immediately recognized as such by contemporary Jewish writers (see chap. 12).

49 Italics in original. For this last quotation, and for "win over to the new faith," see Kant, *Religion Within the Boundaries*, 135; for "statutory law" and "mere fetishism." Kant repeats these arguments in the last book he published, *The Conflict of the Faculties* (*Der Streit der Fakultäten*) of 1798. *Euthanasie des Judenthums*: German in *Immanuel Kant: Gesammelte Schriften* (Berlin: Koniglich Preussische Akademie der Wissenschaften,1902–38), 6:52–53; English in *The Conflict of the Faculties*, trans. Mary J. Gregor (Lincoln: University of Nebraska Press, 1979), 93–95. Quasi-Pauline because Kant's Jews must first convert to rationality and humanity before they can then convert to the universal religion. (Similar views would be expressed by the second generation of enlightened Jews in Berlin, but that is beyond my subject here.)

50 Kant, "Beantwortung zur Frage: Was ist Aufklärung?" *Gesammelte Schriften*,

8:34–36. See Jonathan M. Hess, *Germans, Jews, and the Claims of Modernity* (New Haven, CT: Yale University Press, 2002), 178.

CHAPTER 11: THE REVOLUTIONARY PERFECTION OF THE WORLD

1 The Declaration of the Rights of Man and of the Citizen in French can be found on the website of the Assemblée Nationale, http://www.assemblee-nationale.fr/histoire/dudh/1789.asp.

2 See Edmund Burke's *Letter to a Noble Lord*, in *Works*, vol. 5 (New York: Georg Olms, 1975), 175. On the role of philosophy, see Israel, *Enlightenment Contested* [see chap. 10, n. 37]; and Israel, *Democratic Enlightenment: Philosophy, Revolution, and Human Rights, 1750–1790* (Oxford: Oxford University Press, 2011), which appeared too late for these pages. Leibniz meant "revolution" more in the sense of "upheaval." On the history of "revolution" as a concept, see Reinhart Koselleck, "Revolution, Rebellion, Aufruhr: Bürgerkrieg von der frühen Neuzeit bis zur französischen Revolution," in Otto Brunner, Werner Conze, and Reinhart Koselleck, eds., *Geschichtliche Grundbegriffe* (Stuttgart: Klett-Cotta, 1972–1997), 5:689–788. Leibniz's worry was expressed in his *Nouveaux Essais sur l'Entendement* (Paris: Charpentier, 1847), 4.xvi.4, 480. See Israel, *Enlightenment Contested*, 9.

3 Rousseau, *Considérations sur le gouvernement de Pologne et sur sa réformation projetée*, in *Oeuvres complètes*, 4 vols. (Paris: Gallimard, 1964), 3:960–961 on "national physiognomy" and 956 on Moses. Moses as legislator was a useful subject for the political sciences of the day. See, e.g., the tome published in Paris in 1788 by the Marquis de Pastoret (Claude Emmanuel Joseph Pierre): *Moyse, consideré comme législateur et comme moraliste* (Paris: Buisson, 1788). The phrase "mosaic moment" is from Philip S. Gorski, "The Mosaic Moment: An Early Modernist Critique of Modernist Theories of Nationalism," *American Journal of Sociology* 105 (2000), 1428–1468.

4 Although some revolutionaries advocated granting political (in addition to civil) rights to women, the proposition was never seriously considered. See Lynn Hunt, *The French Revolution and Human Rights: A Brief Documentary History* (Boston: St. Martin's, 1996), 26–29, 119–139.

5 Abbé Grégoire, the Marquis de Condorcet, and the Comte de Mirabeau, among other revolutionaries, were members of the abolitionist Société des Amis des Noirs. The National Assembly granted full rights to free blacks in May of 1791 but soon revoked the status. French policy on slavery would fluctuate throughout subsequent decades. For an introduction to this history, see David Brion Davis, *The Problem of Slavery in the Age of Revolution, 1770–1823* (New York: Oxford University Press, 1993).

6 From the outset of the revolution, distinctions were made between levels of citizenship: the poor might be "passive" (unpropertied, nonvoting) but not "active" (propertied, voting) citizens. This passive-active distinction was abolished in August of 1792, but the extension of suffrage still had its limits, some of which were addressed in the (never-implemented) Constitution of 1793. For

a survey of these debates, see Malcolm Crook, "The Rights of Man and the Right to Vote: The Franchise Question during the French Revolution," in Gail Schwab and John Jeanneney, eds., *The French Revolution of 1789 and Its Impact* (Westport, CT: Greenwood, 1995), 191–198.

7 Schechter, *Obstinate Hebrews*, is fundamental here [see chap. 10, n. 29]. On the number of discussions in the National Assembly, see 154; on the calculation of new citizens, 152; on the "right to pronounce," 151.

8 *Prix proposés en 1788, par la Société royale des sciences et des arts de Metz, pour les concours de 1789 et 1790* (Metz, 1788). On the Hell affair, see Schechter, *Obstinate Hebrews*, 67–73. Grégoire's quotes are from *Archives Parlementaires de 1787 à 1860, Premier Série (1789 à 1799)* (Paris: Librairie Administratif de Paul Dupont, 1878) [henceforth *AP*], 10:764. Robespierre's is in *AP* 10:757, while Clermont-Tonnere's is in *AP* 10:754–756. The count's more famous formulation was that "[t]he Jews should be denied everything as a nation, but granted everything as individuals": Paul Mendes-Flohr and Jehuda Reinharz, *The Jew in the Modern World: A Documentary History*, 2nd ed. (New York: Oxford University Press, 1995), 114–115. For more on the count, see Hertzberg, *French Enlightenment*, 355–368 [see chap. 10, n. 38].

9 On the vote of 408 to 403, see *AP* 10:758; Hertzberg, *French Enlightnement*, 339–340. On the debates of 1791, *AP* 31:441, translated in Mendes-Flohr and Reinharz, *Jew*, 118. Somewhat exaggerated: For decades the French state continued to treat Jews as exceptional in both its legislation and its tax policy. See Schechter, *Obstinate Hebrews*, 153, and his later discussion of Napoleonic policy. For bibliography on revolutionary debate about Jewish emancipation, see (in addition to the works of Hertzberg and Schechter) Richard Ayoun, ed., *Les Juifs de France: de l'émancipation à l'intégration (1787–1812)* (Paris: L'Harmattan, 1997); and Frederic Cople Jaher, *The Jews and the Nation: Revolution, Emancipation, State Formation and the Liberal Paradigm in America and France* (Princeton, NJ: Princeton University Press, 2002), 59–102.

10 On "regeneration," see Mona Ozouf, *L'homme régénéré : essais sur la Révolution française* (Paris: Gallimard, 1989), as well as her "Regeneration," in *A Critical Dictionary of the French Revolution*, ed. F. Furet and M. Ozouf, trans. Arthur Goldhammer (Cambridge, MA: Belknap Press, 1989). See also Antoine de Baecque, *The Body Politic: Corporeal Metaphor in Revolutionary France* (Stanford, CA: Stanford University Press, 1997), 131–156. On Talleyrand and language, see Sophia Rosenfeld, *A Revolution in Language: The Problem of Signs in Late Eighteenth-Century France* (Stanford, CA: Stanford University Press, 2001), 123–124. For a much earlier French example, see Montaigne, *Essais*, 2.12.508–509 (in *Oeuvres complètes*, ed. Albert Thibaudet and Maurice Rat [Paris: Gallimard, 1962]): "La plus part des occasions des troubles du monde sont Grammairiennes."

11 The sermon is discussed in detail in David A. Bell, *The Cult of the Nation in France: Inventing Nationalism, 1680–1800* (Cambridge, MA: Harvard Univer-

sity Press, 2001), 169–174. The text is available as an online appendix: https://jshare.johnshopkins.edu/myweb/davidbell/cnsermet.htm (accessed September 15, 2011).

12 Rabaut and his treatise are discussed in Bell, *Cult of the Nation*, 1–6, 161. On education in revolutionary France, see among many others Mona Ozouf, *L'Ecole de la France: essais sur la Révolution, l'utopie et l'enseignement* (Paris: Gallimard, 1984).

13 Dan Edelstein, *The Terror of Natural Right: Republicanism, the Cult of Nature, and the French Revolution* (Chicago: University of Chicago Press, 2009). Chénier cited at 191; Quinette, at 150.

14 See ibid., 197–199; and Keith Baker, *Condorcet: From Natural Philosophy to Social Mathematics* (Chicago: University of Chicago Press, 1975), 320–326.

15 See Edelstein, *Terror*, chap. 3.

16 "Considering the depths" and "All must be new" are quoted in Bell, *Cult of the Nation*, 156. "We have revolutionized" is cited in Rosenfeld, *Revolution in Language*, 164. My suggestion here is related to Mona Ozouf's description of two ways in which the revolutionaries thought about the creation of the "new man," which she calls the "miraculous" and the "laborious," in *L'homme régénéré*, 116–157.

17 See Jean-Clément Martin, *La Vendée et la France* (Paris: Seuil, 1987).

18 "Let us not be fooled" is from Claude Royer on August 10, 1793, citing Danton. See Edelstein, *Terror*, 175.

19 Eugen Weber discusses some relationships between millennialist and Enlightenment thought in *Apocalypses: Prophecies, Cults, and Millennial Beliefs through the Ages* (Cambridge, MA: Harvard University Press, 1999), 99–117.

20 For "The republic does not know," see Patrice Higonnet, *Goodness beyond Virtue: Jacobins during the French Revolution* (Cambridge, MA: Harvard University Press, 1998), 237.

21 On "relicks," see William Wordsworth, *The Prelude* (New York: W. W. Norton, 1979), bk. 9.65–70. Quote "pamphlets swarmed" is from Nicholas Roe, *Wordsworth and Coleridge: The Radical Years* (New York: Oxford University Press, 1990), 18. Giambattista Vico in 1725, *New Science*, trans. David Marsh (New York: Penguin, 1999), 482–491.

22 All citations will be to Burke, *Reflections on the Revolution in France*, ed. J. C. D. Clark (Stanford, CA: Stanford University Press, 2001). Original pagination will be cited first, followed by the page numbers for Clark's edition. In places, the edition by J. G. A. Pocock (Indianapolis, IN: Hackett, 1987) has also been consulted. On the original work's "best-seller" status, see Clark's introduction, 68.

23 Early readers recognized Burke's intended audience. As Philip Francis wrote him after reading an early draft, "[Y]our appeal in effect is to all Europe." See Francis to Burke, February 19, 1790, in Burke, *Correspondence* (Cambridge: Cambridge University Press, 1958–1978), 6:85–87. For Burke on regicide, see his *Reflections*, 123/245. On Burke's contacts (encouraging or otherwise) in France, and on the genesis of the *Reflections*, see Clark's introduction, 43–68.

24 On "low lawyers" and "litigious minds," see Burke, *Reflections*, 123/197–198; for "Jew brokers," 70/203–204; and dying Moses, 96/224: "Then viewing, from the *Pisgah* of his pulpit, the free, moral, happy, flourishing and glorious state of France as in a bird's-eye landscape of a promised land, he breaks out in the following rapture." For "Change Alley," see Burke, *Reflections*, 156/269; "Hebrew brethren," 125/247; "money-jobbers," 72/205; "sophisters," 113/238; "hypocritical professors," 94/223. The above-mentioned sermon, by the dissenting minister Richard Price, was given on November 4, 1789, and published as "A Discourse on the Love of our Country." Some twenty-seven published responses to it survive, not including Burke's. See Gayle Trusdel Pendleton, "Towards a Bibliography of the *Reflections* and *Rights of Man* Controversy," *Bulletin of Research in the Humanities* 85 (Spring 1982), 65–103. On the meetinghouse, see Clark's edition, 155, n. 32. However, neither Clark nor (so far as I know) any other commentator treats the phrase "Old Jewry" as meaningful. On "Pisgah," see Burke, *Reflections*, 96/224. The reference is to Deut. 3:27, 34:1–4, where Pisgah is the name of the mountain in Moab from which Moses sees the distant land of Israel before his death.

25 On this, see Pocock's introduction in his edition, xxxi, and n. 68. Clark's note is from his edition, 204, n. 195.

26 Burke, *Reflections*, 143–144/260–261.

27 On "stock-jobbing," see Burke, *Reflections*, 77/209; for "metaphysics" and "loose counters," 272–274/357–358.

28 "Beiträge zur Berichtigung der Urtheile des Publicums über die französische Revolution," in Reinhard Lauth and Hans Jacob, eds., *Gesamtausgabe der Bayerischen Akademie* (Stuttgart: Friedrich Fromann, 1962–), I.i., 193–404. For "Does a people have any right . . . ?" see 210; *Handelsleute*, 239–240; "dead book" and "inflexible letters," 250–252. I have tried to approximate the meaning of the word *Staatsverfassung* that Fichte uses with the clunky phrase "constitution or basic political contract." On the role of the revolution in the development of Fichte's philosophy, see Manfred Buhr, *Revolution und Philosophie. Die ursprüngliche Philosophie Johann Gottlieb Fichtes und die Französische Revolution* (Berlin: Deutscher Verlag der Wissenschaften, 1965); and Anthony J. La Vopa, *Fichte: The Self and the Calling of Philosophy, 1762–1799* (Cambridge: Cambridge University Press, 2001), 100–130. On Fichte's views of Judaism, see Paul Lawrence Rose, *Revolutionary Anti-Semitism in Germany from Kant to Wagner* (Princeton, NJ: Princeton University Press, 1990), 117–132; Walter Grab, "Fichtes Judenfeindschaft," *Zeitschrift für Religions- und Geistesgeschichte* 44 (1992), 70–75; and Paul R. Sweet, "Fichte and the Jews: A Case of Tension between Civil Rights and Human Rights," *German Studies Review* 16 (1993), 37–48.

29 Fichte on *Judenthum*: "Beiträge," 291–292; on Moses, 235; on decapitation of Jews, 293.

30 Friedrich Nietzsche, *Sämtliche Werke: Kritische Studienausgabe*, ed. Giorgio Colli and Mazzino Montinari (New York: De Gruyter, 1988), 2:446.

31 See Robespierre's speech of May 7, 1794, translated in George Rudé, *Robespierre* (Englewood Cliffs, NJ: Prentice Hall, 1967), 71.

32 For musket production, see Ken Alder, *Engineering the Revolution: Arms and Enlightenment in France, 1763–1815* (Chicago: University of Chicago Press, 1997), 274, 333. At the national manufacturer at Saint-Étienne, firearms output reached almost 10,000 per year in 1794–1795, a number that would not be reached again until 1810. Napoleon spoke often of bringing about an era of "general peace." See, e.g., R. M. Johnston, *The Corsican: A Diary of Napoleon's Life in His Own Words* (Boston: Houghton Mifflin, 1910), e.g., 297; or on 490 (from St. Helena), Napoleon's comparison of himself with "the Savior of the world."

33 On the development of an ideology of "total war" in this period, see David Bell's *The First Total War: Napoleon's Europe and the Birth of Warfare as We Know It* (Boston: Houghton Mifflin Harcourt, 2007).

34 The debate over the nature and periodization of the "modern" is important but not central to the concerns of this book. See, among many other titles on the subject, Hans Blumenberg, *The Legitimacy of the Modern Age*, trans. Robert M. Wallace (Cambridge, MA: MIT Press, 1983); Jürgen Habermas, *The Philosophical Discourse of Modernity*, trans. Frederick Lawrence (Cambridge, MA: MIT Press, 1987); and Hans Ulrich Gumbrecht, "Modern," in *Geschichtliche Grundbegriffe*, 4:93–131.

35 On Wordsworth's and Coleridge's early radicalism, see Roe, *Wordsworth and Coleridge*. The story of meeting at Racedown Farm is often told, most recently by Adam Sisman, *The Friendship: Wordsworth and Coleridge* (New York: Viking, 2007). "The Wanderings of Cain" was never completed. After its failure Coleridge began the "Rhyme of the Ancient Mariner." On the Ancient Mariner as the Wandering Jew, see *The Notebooks of Samuel Taylor Coleridge*, ed. Kathleen Coburn (New York: Pantheon, 1957), 1:Note 45. On the wandering Jew more generally, see Alan Dundes and Galit Hasan-Rokem, eds., *The Wandering Jew: Essays in the Interpretation of a Christian Legend* (Bloomington: Indiana University Press, 1986). For some influences on Coleridge's adaptation of the legend, see John Livingston Lowes, *The Road to Xanadu* (London: Constable, 1927), 244–246. Coleridge uses Fichte especially heavily in his *Biographia Literaria*, vol. 7 of *The Collected Works of Samuel Taylor Coleridge*, ed. James Engell and W. Jackson Bate (Princeton, NJ: Princeton University Press, 1983), passim, usually translating whole passages without attribution (see appendix 2:253–254).

CHAPTER 12: PHILOSOPHICAL STRUGGLES WITH JUDAISM,
FROM KANT TO HEINE

1 Numbers in parentheses in the text refer to pages from the translation of R. F. Jones and G. H. Turnbull (1922), as reprinted in Johann Gottlieb Fichte, *Addresses to the German Nation*, ed. George A. Kelly (New York: Harper, 1968). Elsewhere Fichte writes: "If a German does not establish the government of the world through knowledge . . . it will be the North American tribes that will do it and put an end to the current state of affairs." Cited in ibid., xxviii.

2 Ernst Moritz Arndt, "a Jew People," cited in Karen Hagemann, *Mannlicher Muth und Teutsche Ehre: Nation, Militär und Geschlecht zur Zeit der Antinapoleonischen Kriege Preußens* (Paderborn: Ferdinand Schöningh, 2002), 249.

3 On Holy Synod, see Bell, *First Total War*, 256 [see chap. 11, n. 34]. Others also characterized Napoleon as the Jews' Messiah, e.g., Johann Gottfried Herder, "Bekehrung der Juden" (The Conversion of the Jews) of 1802, in *Herders Sämmtliche Werke*, ed. B. Suphan (Hildesheim: Georg Olms, 1967), 24:61–75, here 67. Saul Ascher (1767–1822), *Eisenmenger der Zweite. Nebst einem vorangesetzen Sendschreiben an den Herrn Professor Fichte in Jena* (Berlin, 1794), 32–35. Fichte is the "Second Eisenmenger" of Ascher's treatise. On Ascher, see chap. 4 of Jonathan M. Hess, *Germans, Jews, and the Claims of Modernity* (New Haven, CT: Yale University Press, 2002); and Walter Grab, "Saul Ascher: ein jüdisch-deutscher Spätaufklärer zwischen Revolution und Restauration," *Jahrbuch des Instituts für deutsche Geschichte* 6 (1977), 131–179.

4 For Kant, see *Critique of Pure Reason*, trans. Werner S. Pluhar (Indianapolis, IN: Hackett, 1996), 61–65 and passim. On the increasing rapidity of philosophical change, see Hegel as cited in Karl Rosenkranz, *Georg Wilhelm Friedrich Hegels Leben* (Berlin, 1844; Darmstadt: Wissenschaftliche Buchgesellschaft, 1977), 544. Hegel was born in 1770 (the same year as Wordsworth), five years before Friedrich Wilhelm Joseph von Schelling (1775–1854), but Schelling was only two years behind him at the Tübingen seminary, where both were much influenced by the poet Friedrich Hölderlin. The letter is quoted from Herbert Marcuse, *Reason and Revolution* (New York: Humanity Books, 1999), 11. Compare from the same year Hegel's claim, worthy of Robespierre, in "The Life of Jesus" (1795): "Pure reason . . . is divinity itself," translated in *Three Essays, 1793–1795*, ed. Peter Fuss and John Dobbins (Notre Dame, IN: University of Notre Dame Press, 1984), 104.

5 René Descartes, *Discourse on the Method*, pt. 6, in *The Philosophical Writings of Descartes*, ed. and trans. J. Cottingham, R. Stoothoff, and D. Murdoch (Cambridge: Cambridge University Press, 1985), 1:142–143; John Locke, *An Essay concerning Human Understanding*, ed. Peter H. Nidditch (Oxford: Clarendon Press, 1975), bk. 3, chap. 3, sect. 11; and David Hume, *An Abstract of a Treatise on Human Nature* (Cambridge: Cambridge University Press, 1938), 16.

6 I will skip over the "transcendental apperception" by which this universal subjectivity becomes a unified subject and a thinking ego's active role in the production of its own experiences: a point on which Fichte's own philosophy would focus.

7 On "unbekannten Etwas" and "Dinge an sicht selbst" as noumena, see Kant, *Critique of Pure Reason*, 320. On "Verstand" as "der Quell der Gesetze der Natur," see ibid., 173.

8 On Kant's attempt to establish the independence of practical reason from empirical conditions, see Dieter Henrich and Richard Velkley, *The Unity of Reason: Essays on Kant's Philosophy* (Cambridge, MA: Harvard University Press, 1994), 93. Quote "carefully cleansed of everything empirical" is from Kant's 1785 *Groundwork of the Metaphysics of Morals*, ed. Mary Gregor (Cambridge:

Cambridge University Press, 1998), 2. Steven Miller suggests a comparison between Paul and Kant in "The 'Fulfillment of the Law' in Paul and Kant," *A Journal of Culture and the Unconscious* 2, no.1 (2002), 33–45.

9   The dichotomies are from Hegel's *The Difference between Fichte's and Schelling's Systems of Philosophy*, trans. H. S. Harris and Walter Cerf (Albany: SUNY Press, 1976), 90. Hegel then adds the "critical" version of these dichotomies: "[r]eason and sensibility, intelligence and nature, . . . absolute subjectivity and absolute objectivity."

10 Cf. Robert B. Pippin, *Idealism as Modernism: Hegelian Variations* (Cambridge: Cambridge University Press, 1997), 12: "[S]ince Kant, . . . a kind of Holy Grail for modern philosophy has been finding a way to argue that 'our natures' are not properly accounted for by 'subsumability to causal law' without basing such an argument on any metaphysical dualism."

11 Jesus: Kant, *Religion within the Bounds*, 97 [see chap. 10, n. 48]. Kant's separation of the "thing-in-itself" from cognition was itself grounded in his "cognitive dualism," separating the faculty of sensibility from that of understanding. See, for example, *Critique of Pure Reason* A52/B56. [A refers to the section number of the 1781 edition; B, to that of the 1787 edition]. The difficulties this dualism created were first pointed out by Solomon Maimon in his *Versuch über die Transcendentalphilosophie* (An Essay on Transcendental Philosophy) of 1790 (Hamburg: Felix Meiner, 2004). (Kant praised Maimon's critique but complained that Maimon, like all Jews, promoted himself at the expense of his betters.)

12 Pure submission: One important example is Kant's claim that while other ancient societies had the concept of *Eigentum* (private property), Jews had only *Besitz* (natural possession) because God was the owner of all. Since only *Eigentum* could produce autonomous rationality and ethics, the Jews never developed these. On this distinction (whose influence on Hegel and Marx I discuss in chap. 13), see Michael Mack, *German Idealism and the Jew: The Inner Anti-Semitism of Philosophy and German Jewish Responses* (Chicago: University of Chicago Press, 2003), 30. For Kant on Mendelssohn's refusal to convert, see *Conflict of the Faculties*, 275 [see chap. 10, n. 49].

13 For Fichte's introductions, see Fichte, *The Science of Knowledge: With the First and Second Introductions*, ed. P. Heath and J. Lachs (Cambridge: Cambridge University Press, 1970). The Idealists were well versed in the dualists. Schelling's dissertation was on Marcion's edition of Paul (*De Marcione Paullinarum epistolarum emendatore*). Hegel mentions reading the work in a letter of August 30, 1795. On Hegel and Schlegel's reading preferences, see Günther Nicolin, ed., *Hegel in Berichten seiner Zeitgenossen* (Hamburg: Felix Meiner, 1970), 13.

14 F. H. Jacobi, *Über die Lehre des Spinoza, in Briefen an den Herrn Moses Mendelssohn* (Breslau: Gottlieb Löwe, 1785; revised edition, 1789, reprinted Hamburg: Felix Meiner, 2000). Johann Wolfang von Goethe's comment is from *Dichtung und Wahrheit*, 3, 681, in K. Richter et al., eds., *Sämmtliche Werke* (München: Hanser, 1985–), 16:681. For more of Jacobi's critique of Kant's thing-in-itself, see the appendix to his *David Hume on Faith, or Idealism and Realism, a Dialogue* (1787), trans. by B. Sassen as "'On Transcendental Idealism," appendix to

David Hume über den Glauben oder Idealismus und Realismus, in *Kant's Early Critics: The Empiricist Critique of the Theoretical Philosophy* (Cambridge: Cambridge University Press, 2000), 169–175, here 173.

15 For a synthesis of these debates, see Frederick Beiser, *The Fate of Reason: German Philosophy from Kant to Fichte* (Cambridge, MA: Harvard University Press, 1987). On Jacobi and the influence of the Spinoza debate in German Idealism, see George Di Giovanni, *Freedom and Religion in Kant and His Immediate Successors: The Vocation of Humankind, 1774–1800* (Cambridge: Cambridge University Press, 2005); and Giovanni, "Hen kai pan. Spinozafigurationen im Frühidealismus, in Walter Jaeschke and Birgit Sandkaulen, eds., *Friedrich Heinrich Jacobi: Ein Wendepunkt der geistigen Bildung der Zeit* (Hamburg: Felix Meiner, 2004), 88–106.

16 For "Messias of speculative Reason," see Jacobi, "Open Letter to Fichte, 1799," trans. Diana I. Behler, in Ernst Behler, ed., *Philosophy of German Idealism* (New York: Continuum, 1987), 119–141, here 122. For "Moses unserer Nation," see Friedrich Hölderlin, *Sämtliche Werke. Große Stuttgarter Ausgabe,* ed. Friedrich Beissner and Adolf Beck (Stuttgart: W. Kohlhammer Verlag, 1943–1985), vol. 6, pt. 1, 304. Against Kant's portrayal of the noumenal realm as transcendent and unknowable, Hölderlin posited (in "Über Religion") "a higher, more than mechanical inter-relationship (Zusammenhang)" which he called "das All," "das Ganze" (ibid., vol. 4, pt. 1, 275).

17 For "[strip] off," see G. F. W. Hegel, *Lectures on the Philosophy of Religion*, trans. E. B. Speirs and J. B. Sanderson, 3 vols. (New York: Humanities Press, 1962), 1:23. He makes a similar point in his first published essay, *The Difference between Fichte's and Schelling's System*, 90–91, as well as in his draft "Fragments of a Philosophical System" from the same year. Quote "ideal does not come " is from *Über die wissenschaftlichen Behandlungsarten des Naturrechts* of 1802, in *Gesammelte Werke,* ed. Hartmut Buchner and Otto Pöggeler (Hamburg: Felix Meiner, 1968), 4:432. See also *Faith and Knowledge*, trans. Walter Cerf and H. S. Harris (Albany: SUNY Press, 1977), 72. Quote "the Jewish principle" is from *The Spirit of Christianity and Its Fate*, translated by T. J. Knox, *Early Theological Writings* (Chicago: University of Chicago Press, 1948; reprint Philadelphia: University of Pennsylvania Press, 1971), 259ff. On the philosophically exemplary nature of the death of Christ, see the references to the *Philosophy of Religion* in n. 24.

18 "Judeo-Prussian" Kant is from Walter Cerf's introduction to Hegel's *Difference between Fichte's and Schelling's System*, xiv. "Jewish—and Kantian—ethics" is from Werner Hamacher, *Pleroma: Reading in Hegel* (London: Athlone Press, 1998), 55, and more generally 46–88. *The Spirit of Christianity and Its Fate* was first published in 1907. The text has since inspired many readings, including Jacques Derrida, *Glas* (Paris: Galilée, 1974).

19 "The Spirit of Judaism," in Knox, *Early Theological Writings*, 194, 196, 199, 202, and passim. Given the important place of it in Hegel's philosophy, his frequent stress on the "lovelessness" of the Jews is significant. See Joseph Cohen, *Le spectre juif de Hegel* (Paris: Galilée, 2005).

20 Quote "the ridiculous anti-Semitism" is from Walter Kaufmann, "The Young

Hegel and Religion," in his *From Shakespeare to Existentialism: An Original Study* (Princeton, NJ: Princeton University Press, 1980), 154. Other writers have confronted the difficulties of the younger Hegel's writings about Jews. See, e.g., Bernard Bourgeois, *Hegel à Frankfort au Judaïsme, Christianisme, Hegelianisme* (Paris: J. Vrin, 1970). Emmanuelle Levinas responds to Bourgeois in his "Hegel and the Jews," published in his *Difficult Freedom: Essays on Judaism* (Baltimore, MD: Johns Hopkins University Press, 1990), 235–239.

21 Marcuse describes Hegel's view of Kant's "alienation" (*Entfremdung*) of mind as one in which "the world of objects, originally the product of man's labor and knowledge, becomes independent of man and comes to be governed by uncontrolled forces and laws in which man no longer recognizes himself." Marcuse, *Reason and Revolution*, 23. Cf. Marx's views in the next chapter.

22 "Fulfillment" = Greek *plērōma*: Knox, *Early Theological Writings*, 214, 253.

23 In the *Philosophy of History*, Hegel asserts that every "Ecclesiastical principle" contains within itself the negative principles of "slavish deference to Authority," the "adamantine bondage" of the spirit to what is "alien to itself," "hypocrisy," etc. (New York: Dover, 1956), 413. He thinks this alienation stronger among the "Romanic nations": "Italy, Spain, Portugal, and in part France" (420). The French Revolution was a key moment in the spirit's achievement of freedom. But (like Fichte) Hegel declares that this French philosophy was "only abstract thought, not the concrete comprehension of absolute Truth [that the Germans would achieve]—intellectual positions between which there is an immeasurable chasm" (446). This "abstract Thought" is not here called "Jewish," though the association may be implied.

24 Goethe and Schiller in Kaufmann, *From Shakespeare to Existentialism*, 164. The quotes from *Logic* are in Marcuse, *Reason and Revolution*, 67–69. I set aside the task of exploring the Christological roots of Hegel's distinction in the *Logic* between the "good" and the "bad" infinity of objects. Phrase "*imitatio christi*": Compare Hamacher, *Pleroma*, 199–200, who concludes that for Hegel "all of world history is an *imitatio Christi*." "It is in connection" is from Hegel, *Lectures on the Philosophy of Religion*, 3:96–97, 98; cf. 2:220–224, and Hegel's *Phenomenology of Spirit,* trans. A. V. Miller (Oxford: Oxford University Press, 1977), 470–478. On the *Philosophy of Religion* as a Trinitarian demonstration of the rational structure of reality, see Peter C. Hodgson's "Editorial Introduction," in Hegel, *Lectures on the Philosophy of Religion*, ed. Peter C. Hodgson, 3 vols. (Berkeley: University of California Press, 1984–1987), 1:63–64. See Laurence Dickey, *Hegel: Religion, Economics, and Politics of Spirit, 1770–1807* (Cambridge: Cambridge University Press, 1987).

25 See Hegel, *Vorlesungen über die Geschichte der Philosophie 3*, ed. Eva Moldenhauer and Karl Markus Michel (Frankfurt a.M.: Suhrkamp, 1986), 162–163; Cf. Hegel, *Encyclopedia Logic*, ed. and trans. T. F. Geraets, W. A. Suchtig, and H. A. Harris (Indianapolis, IN: Hackett, 1991), 97, 226. According to Yitzhak Melamed, Hegel's reading here derives from Salomon Maimon: "Salomon Maimon and the Rise of Spinozism in German Idealism," *Journal of the History of Philosophy* 42 (2004): 67–96, here 95.

26 On Kant and Fichte as Manichaeans, see Hegel, *Lectures on the Philosophy of Religion*, ed. Hodgson, 2:612–613. On un-digestible remnant, see Hamacher's tracing (in *Pleroma*) of digestive metaphors as marking limits of dialectical incorporation in Hegel's philosophical system. Quote "Most despicable" (Verworfenste): The term occurs both in the *Phenomenology of Spirit* (206, 228) and in the *Lectures on the Philosophy of Religion* (2:108). For debate over its meaning, compare Yirmiyahu Yovel, *Dark Riddle: Hegel, Nietzsche, and the Jews* (University Park: Pennsylvania State University Press, 1998), 55, and M. Mack, *German Idealism and the Jew*, 53–54. I do not agree with Yovel that because Hegel's Berlin lectures on religion "recognize Judaism's essential contributions" they "thereby, do dialectical justice to it," and "overcome the principle bias of his youth" (80). Rather he has brought the place of Judaism in his dialectic into closer conformity with its place in Lutheran Christology, and thereby done "justice" to Christianity, not to Judaism.

27 Hegel tried to claim that love had its own "law" independent of any positive or external law. But his recourse to the mysterious appeal of "forgiveness" in chap. 6 of *Phenomenology of Spirit* suggests that he himself found the argument wanting.

28 Quote "a totally new kind of adversary" is from Ascher, *Eisenmenger der Zweite*, 77, also cited by Katz, *From Prejudice to Destruction*, 68 [see Introduction, n. 6].

29 *Hegel's Philosophy of Right*, trans. T. M. Knox (Oxford: Clarendon Press, 1942), notes to 168–169. On the episode in Heidelberg, see Shlomo Avineri, "A Note on Hegel's Views on Jewish Emancipation," *Jewish Social Studies* 25 (1963), 145–151. On "German-ness," the pun is between Deutsch*tum* and Deutsch-*dumm*. Letters about the episode can be found in J. Hoffmeister, ed., *Briefe von und an Hegel* (Hamburg, 1953), 2:455ff. For more general background on Hegel's relations with the Burschenschaften, see Jacques d'Hondt, *Hegel en son temps* (Paris: Editions Sociales, 1968), 147–170. Yovel, *Dark Riddle*, discusses the episode at 89–92 from whence the quote in the next paragraph.

30 Quote the "connecting bonds" is cited by Bell, *First Total War*, 237. Walt Whitman, "Passage to India," in *Walt Whitman: Complete Poetry and Collected Prose* (New York: Library of America, 1982), 534–535.

31 On "suffering," see Arthur Schopenhauer, *The World as Will and Representation*, ed. J. Norman, A. Welchman, and C. Janaway (Cambridge: Cambridge University Press, 2010), vol. 1, sect. 56. On "Jewish realism," see Schopenhauer, "Über die vierfache Wurzel des Satzes vom zureichenden Grunde," in A. Eigner, ed., *Urwille und Welterlösung: Ausgewählte Schriften* (Gütersloh: Bertelsmann, 1958; Wiesbaden: Fourier, 1982), 131. On Schopenhauer's relationship to the Idealists, see Bryan Magee, *The Philosophy of Schopenhauer* (Oxford: Oxford University Press, 1997), 271–285. Schopenhauer believed that Judaism and Islam "consider appearance [Erscheinung] to be the highest reality," and aligned them not with the Vedic but with what he called the Zend religions. On these points, see M. Mack, *German Idealism and the Jew*, 8–9. For a pithier formulation, see Schopenhauer's *Briefwechsel*, in *Arthur Schopenhauers Sämtliche Werke*, vol. 15, ed. Paul Deussen (Munich: Piper, 1933), no. 659, 581–582: "[E]verything Jewish and Islamic is repellent to me."

32 *Foetor judaicus* was for Schopenhauer a frequent and general term of oppro-
    brium, although he sometimes applied it to real Jews such as Spinoza and
    Moses Mendelssohn. For Spinoza's *foetor*, see Schopenhauer, *Parerga and Para-
    lipomena: Short Philosophical Essays* (Oxford: Oxford University Press, 1974),
    73. *Ecce judaeus* and Spinoza, see Henry Walter Brann, *Schopenhauer und das
    Judentum* (Bonn: Bourier Verlag, 1975), 39, 57. Quotes "plaster daubers," etc.
    (*Pflasterschmierer, Pillendrechsler, Klystiersetzer*) are from Schopenhauer, *Brief-
    wechsel*, no. 620, 508–509. "men are born": Brann, *Schopenhauer*, 7.

33 On Schopenhauer's fondness for insults, see the letter sent to him by his disciple
    and literary executor, Julius Frauenstädt, in November of 1850, in Brann, *Scho-
    penhauer*, 80. Quotes "entire Old Testament" and "philosophy must be" are
    from Brann, *Schopenhauer*, 19–20 and 7, respectively.

34 Schopenhauer to Frauenstädt, August 21, 1852 in *Briefwechsel*, no. 437, 154–
    158 (emphasis in original). Frauenstädt was a convert (he converted as a twenty-
    year-old in 1833, before meeting Schopenhauer), not a Jew, as Brann would have
    it (*Schopenhauer*, 76). Like too many historians (and not only historians), Brann
    seems not to see any distinction between Jews and converts from Judaism.

35 Some of Schopenhauer's comments on the status of Jews and converts appear in
    his *Parerga und Paralipomena*, vol. 2 (Berlin: A. W. Hahn, 1851), for example,
    279–281, against emancipation of the unconverted and in favor of strategic con-
    version and mixed marriages.

36 Schopenhauer on Heine's *foetor Judaicus*: Brann, *Schopenhauer*, 39.

37 Quote with "European civilization" is from Heinrich Heine, "Ludwig Börne.
    Eine Denkschrift," in Hans Magnus Enzensberger, ed., *Ludwig Börne und Hein-
    rich Heine, ein deutsches Zerwürfnis* (Nördlingen: Franz Greno, 1986), 127.

38 Quote with "prophet of Orient" is from *Heine's Werke* (Berlin: Aufbau Verlag,
    1968), 5:197–198.

39 Penis: ibid., 279.

40 "Elementargeister," in *Heinrich Heine, Sämtliche Schriften*, 2nd ed., ed. Klaus
    Briegleb (Munich: Hanser, 1978), 3:651 (dwarves), 685 (Judaism vs. Hellenism).

41 Translation adapted from *The Works of Heinrich Heine*, trans. Charles Godfre
    Leland (Hans Breitmann) (London: William Heinemann, 1906), 1:249.

42 Heine, "Ludwig Börne," bks. 1 and 2. Thomas Mann would later (1908)
    praise *Ludwig Börne* as Heine's greatest book, precisely for its "psychology
    of the Nazarene type," and call it the greatest work of German letters before
    Nietzsche: *Rede und Antwort* (Berlin: S. Fischer, 1922), 382. For the attributes
    Heine assigns to Nazarenes/Jews and to Hellenes, see "Ludwig Börne," 128; for
    the "Zweykampf" between Hellenism and Judaism, 127; for "Der Jude Pust-
    kuschen . . . pharisäisches Zeter," 158; for Shakespeare, 157. On Hegel's Greece
    as a union of real and ideal, see his *Philosophy of History*, 215, 238.

43 Quote with "blank mirror" is from F. Nietzsche, "Menschliches, Allzumenschli-
    ches," 2, sect. 218, in Friedrich Wilhelm Nietzsche, *Werke*, ed. K. Schlechta, 3
    vols. (Munich: C. Hanser, 1954), 1, 818–819. Nietzsche on Heine as German's
    greatest writer: *Ecce Homo* 2.4.

44 "Whither now the Talmud?": "Wozu jetzt noch der Talmud? . . . Denn was

überflüssig ist, ist schädlich," is from Heine, [*Zur Geschichte der Religion und Philosophie in Deutschland* (Stuttgart: Reclam, 1997), 83. We should pause to admire both the polemic (Heine can simultaneously mock Catholicism as Jewish, and Talmudic Judaism as Catholic) and the suggestion that the Talmud is a response to and defense against Christianity, a position adopted (without reference to Heine) by many modern scholars of Rabbinic Judaism. "Do not laugh": ibid., 143.

45 Quote with "creeping calamity" is from Nietzsche's *Ecce Homo* 1.7, trans. Walter Kaufman, *"On the Genealogy of Morals" and "Ecce Homo"* (New York: Vintage, 1989), 232. Quote with "mushrooms" is from Marx and Engel's *Werke* [see Introduction, n. 1], 1:97.

46 On Matthew Arnold, see Lionel Gossman, "Philhellenism and Antisemitism: Matthew Arnold and His German Models," in *Comparative Literature* 46 (1994), 1–39. Richard Wagner (1813–1883) published his *Das Judenthum in der Musik* in 1850, under the pseudonym of K. Freigedank ("Free-thought"), in the *Neue Zeitschrift fuer Musik* 33, no. 19 (September 3), and no. 20 (September 6). He revised the text—but in no way moderated it—for a new edition that appeared in 1869. For an English translation, see W. A. Ellis, ed. and trans., *Richard Wagner's Prose Works* (London, 1897).

47 James Joyce, *Ulysses* (New York: Random House, 1934), 492. The sentiment survived Joyce's spleen, e.g., in the term "Judeo-Christian" to describe European civilization. There is some irony in the fact that this term came into broad circulation only in the 1950s, after the extermination of the vast majority of Europe's Jews had made clear the brutal limits to the "harmony" of any synthesis. The irony is instructive, in that it points to a potentially lethal asymmetry in these dialectical models of European culture: One side of the fundamental oppositions they claim to "sublate" and synthesize is more stigmatized than the other. Only one is meant to be fully overcome, and only one has living representatives whose refusal to disappear seems to challenge the triumphant claims of synthesis itself. Joyce, too, was attracted to *The Merchant of Venice* as a foil for his own critiques of (in his case) Irish Catholic fantasies of political perfection. In this same "Circe" chapter of *Ulysses*, e.g., Stephen Bloom is temporarily cast as the messianic savior and most Catholic monarch of Ireland: "A Daniel did I say? Nay! A Peter O'Brien!" (477).

48 Schopenhauer's complaint: "One should not equate Judaism and Reason," is from *World as Will and Representation*, 575.

49 What is implied here is a process in which both the "habit" and "world," "figures of Judaism" and "real Jews," are constantly changing. The figures of Judaism deployed in ideas are re-formed by the work to which they are put in understanding the changing world, but both the world and the real Jews in it are also re-formed by being thought through figures of Judaism.

50 Quote "[I]f Satan" is from "Shakespeare's Maidens," 400, on which see also Anton Schütz, "Structural Terror: A Shakespearian Investigation," in Peter Goodrich, Lior Barshack, Anton Schütz, ed., *Law, Text, Terror: Essays for Pierre*

Legendre (Glass House Press, 2006), 71–91; and Heine, *Sämtliche Schriften*, 4:265.

CHAPTER 13: MODERNITY THINKS WITH JUDAISM

1 Goebbels's speech is printed in *Die Bücherverbrennung: Zum 10. Mai 1933*, ed. Gerhard Sauder (Munich: Carl Hanser Verlag, 1983), 254–257. I cite the first line: "Meine Kommilitonen! Deutsche Männer und Frauen! Das Zeitalter eines überspitzten jüdischen Intellektualismus ist nun zu Ende." "Un-Spirit": *Ungeist der Vergangenheit*.

2 The bibliography on the Nazis' university politics begins with E. Y. Harteshorne's *The German Universities and National Socialism* (London: Allen & Unwin, 1937). Max Weinreich's *Hitler's Professors: The Part of Scholarship in Germany's Crimes against the Jewish People*, published in 1946 (2nd ed. New Haven, CT: Yale University Press, 1999) is a classic statement. On fears of "Judaization" in Nazi thought, see S. Aschheim, "'The Jew within': The Myth of 'Judaization' in Germany," in J. Reinharz and W. Schatberg, ed., *The Jewish Response to German Culture* (Hanover, NH: University Press of New England, 1985), 212–241.

3 The Vatican's official translation of "Rerum Novarum" is available at http://www.vatican.va/holy_father/leo_xiii/encyclicals/documents/hf_l-xiii_enc_15051891_rerum-novarum_en.html (accessed September 28, 2011). The subject of the wage contract is at the heart of the encyclical: "43. We now approach a subject of great importance, and one in respect of which, if extremes are to be avoided, right notions are absolutely necessary. Wages, as we are told, are regulated by free consent." Benedict XVI's 2009 encyclical "Caritas in veritate" (Love in Truth) represents a further effort within this tradition of articulating the limitations of contract by Christian love, this time in the context of twenty-first-century debates about neoliberal globalization.

4 According to Börne, *The Merchant of Venice* was a parable for the transcendence of Jewish materialism. See Ludwig Börne, *Sämtliche Schriften*, ed. I. and Rippman, 5 vols. (Düsseldorf: Joseph Melzer, 1964–1968), 1:103. Börne also reviewed other plays relevant to our theme, such as an 1819 performance of Richard Cumberland's *The Jew* (written in 1794): 288. Quote with "mirrors" is from Shelley's "A Defence of Poetry," in *The Major Works*, ed. Z. Leader and M. O'Neill (Oxford: Oxford University Press, 2003), 701.

5 Jerry Z. Muller provides an accessible survey in *The Mind and the Market: Capitalism in Modern European Thought* (New York: Knopf, 2003).

6 Emphasis in original. My thanks to Eran Shalev for bringing this editorial to my attention.

7 "Real humanism" is from Marx and Engels, *Werke* [see Introduction, n. 1], 2.7. "*Mediating activity*," "in my production," and "true nature" quotes are from *Karl Marx and Frederich Engels, Collected Works*, vol. 3: *Marx and Engels (1843–44)* (New York: Progress, 1975), 212, 228 (emphasis in original).

8 Karl Marx, *Economic and Philosophical Manuscripts of 1844*, trans. Martin Mil-

ligan (1961; Mineola, NY: Dover, 2007), 137–138 on Shakespeare (quoting *Timon of Athens* 4.3, "Thou common whore of mankind," rather than *Merchant* 3.2, "pale and common drudge / 'Tween man and man"); quote "philosophy is nothing else" is from 145. He exempted only Feuerbach from this critique. For the history of these debates, see among many others Warren Breckman, *Marx, the Young Hegelians and the Origins of Radical Social Theory* (Cambridge: Cambridge University Press, 1999).

9 *Hegel's Philosophy of Right*, trans. T. M. Knox (Oxford: Clarendon Press, 1942), par. 40, 38. For an explicit example of Hegel's mapping of interpersonal relations onto Trinitarian theology, see his *Lectures on the Philosophy of Religion, The Lectures of 1827*, ed. Peter C. Hodgson (Oxford: Clarendon Press, 2006), 427–429.

10 "[T]he origin of property" is from Lectures 1824, 2:448 (cited Yovel, *Dark Riddle*, n. 23, 77–81 [see chap. 12, n. 26]). Quotes with "no freedom" and following are from *Lectures on the Philosophy of Religion, together with a work on the Proofs of the Existence of God*, trans. from the 2nd German ed. by E. B. Speirs and J. Burdon Sanderson, 3 vols. (London: Kegan Paul, 1895), 2:209–219. On Kant's earlier distinction between property and possession see chap. 11, n. 12. These distinctions appear already in Hegel's *Spirit of Christianity*, where he interprets the Jews' lack of permanent individual ownership of land (according to the land laws of the Hebrew Bible, land must revert to its originally equitable distribution every fifty years) as a symptom of their slavery to God, whereas he considers the Greeks' poor law as a sign of charity.

11 On these grounds Bauer denies them even the "rights of man": "Can the Jew really take possession of them? As long as he is a Jew, the restricted nature that makes him a Jew is bound to triumph over the human nature that should link him as a man with other men, and will separate him from non-Jews." (Hegel manifested sympathy for this line of thought in a footnote to the *Philosophy of Right*, trans. Knox, 168–169). Marx does provide an argument against this particular charge.

12 The translations are my own, from the text in *Karl Marx-Friedrich Engels Werke* (Berlin: Dietz, 1957), 1:360.

13 The extended quote is from *Werke*, 1:372–373. This Judaization of the United States is potentially present already in the Introduction to Hegel's *Philosophy of History*, ed. Sibree [see Introduction, n. 6] (84–86), where without using the word *Jewish*, he describes the Americans' relation to property, law, and community in terms of a similarly failed dialectic. Börne and other radical Hegelians would pursue the analogy. I will return to its uses in German thought and propaganda in the early twentieth century. Its uses in the later twentieth and the twenty-first centuries would repay further study.

14 The quotes from Marx can be found in *Werke*, 1:372–374.

15 Hans Liebeschütz emphasizes patristic influences: "German Radicalism and the Formation of Jewish Political Attitudes during the Earlier Part of the Nineteenth Century," in Alexander Altmann, ed., *Studies in Nineteenth Century Jewish Intellectual History* (Cambridge, MA: Harvard University Press, 1964),

141–170. For Spinoza, see David McLellan, *Marx before Marxism* (London: Macmillan, 1970), 52. Orlando Figes argues for Börne's influence: "Ludwig Börne and the Formation of a Radical Critique of Judaism," *Leo Baeck Institute Year Book* (1984), 351–382. Julius Carlebach's *Karl Marx and the Radical Critique of Judaism* (London: Routledge & Kegan Paul, 1978) remains an excellent introduction. Quote with "patricide" is from Yuri Slezkine, *The Jewish Century* (Princeton, NJ: Princeton University Press, 2004), 63, 98–99.

16 Börne on his father: "das Geld an die Stelle der Liebe gesetzt findet," cited in Martin Schneider, *Die kranke schöne Seele der Revolution. Heine, Börne, das "Junge Deutschland," Marx u. Engels* (Franfurt am Main: Syndikat, 1980), 99. On Shylock, see n. 4. Throughout his "Briefe aus Paris," Börne treats France after the July revolution of 1830 as a Jewish state.

17 Marx's anti-Semitism is much debated. Hannah Arendt dismissed the charge on the grounds that Marx was himself Jewish, and even argued that "the Jew Marx's" anti-Judaism in fact exonerates non-Jewish radical critics of Judaism from the charge of anti-Semitism as well. But compare Francis Kaplan, *Marx Anti-Semite?* (Paris: Berg International, 1990), 52 (citing Arendt); and Edward Silberner, "Was Marx an Anti-Semite?" *Historia Judaica* 11 (1949), 3–52. Although I have focused on Marx's early essays, similar views are reflected in his mature published and unpublished work. In *Capital*, e.g., he characterizes capitalists as Jews ("innerlich beschnitten Juden," interiorly circumcised Jews, a phrase Marx suppressed in the French translation), and frequently characterized Jews as capitalists. Marx also invoked a broad range of thinkers from the traditions we have been studying, from Manetho to the Enlightenment. For these and other examples, see Kaplan, *Marx*, 97–138.

18 On 1873 and the rise of political anti-Semitism, see Katz, *From Prejudice to Destruction*, 247–272 ("Ninety percent" from 250) [see Introduction, n. 6]; and Peter G. J. Pulzer, *The Rise of Political Anti-Semitism in Germany and Austria* (New York: John Wiley & Sons, 1964). An abridged version of Roscher's 1875 article was published by Solomon Grayzael in *Historia Judaica* 6 (1944), 13–26, with an introduction by Guido Kisch (3–12). The date of their engagement is enough to suggest how pernicious these two scholars thought the influence of Roscher's work had been. Both are cited, along with additional references, in Paul R. Mendes-Flohr, "Werner Sombart's the Jews and Modern Capitalism— An Analysis of Its Ideological Premises," *Leo Baeck Institute Year Book* (1976), 87–108, here 95–96.

19 On Weber's role in German politics, see Wolfgang J. Mommsen, *Max Weber und die deutsche Politik, 1890–1920* (Tübingen: Mohr, 1959).

20 All citations from *The Protestant Ethic* are given from the English translation by T. Parsons (1930; London: George Allen & Unwin, 1985). For the complex publication history of Weber's work, I have relied on Wolfgang Schluchter, *Rationalism, Religion, and Domination. A Weberian Perspective* (Berkeley: University of California Press, 1989); and the essays collected in H. Lehmann and G. Roth, ed., *Weber's Protestant Ethic: Origins, Evidence, Contexts* (Cambridge: Cambridge University Press, 1993).

21 "Israel" quote is from Werner Sombart, *The Jews and Modern Capitalism*, trans.
    M. Epstein (Glencoe, IL: Free Press, 1951), 13. Gordon Marshall, *Presbyter
    and Profit: Calvinism and the Development of Capitalism in Scotland, 1560–1907*
    (Oxford: Oxford University Press, 1980), 23–24, discusses Weber's citations of
    Sombart's early work in the first version of *Protestant Ethic*.

22 The quotes are from Sombart, *Jews*, 30, 38, 44, 121, 192, 249 (emphasis in
    original). Sombart's Judaizing of the Puritans is an explicit restatement of early
    modern theological polemics that accused the Calvinists of Judaism (e.g., "Der
    Calvinische Judenspiegel").

23 Among many contemporary reactions, see those of the Münster historian Her-
    mann Wätjen: "Das Judentum und die Anfänge der modernen Kolonisation,"
    Vierteljahrschrift für Sozial- und Wirtschaftsgeschichte 11 (1913), 338–368; and
    *Das Judentum und die Anfänge der modernen Kolonisation: kritische Bemerkun-
    gen zu Werner Sombarts: Die Juden und das Wirtschaftsleben* (Berlin: Kohlham-
    mer, 1914).

24 The quotes with "free of magic" and "world-historical" are from Max Weber,
    Ancient Judaism, trans. H. Gerth and D. Martindale (Glencoe, IL: Free Press,
    1952), 4.

25 Quotes are from *Protestant Ethic*, 165–166, 270–271, and *Ancient Judaism*, 3.
    Innovation vs. diffusion: The distinction is Schluchter's, in *Rationalism, Reli-
    gion*, 199.

26 Weber expands his treatment of the Jew as pariah in *The Sociology of Religion*
    trans. E. Fischoff (Boston: Beacon Press, 1964), e.g., 108. Weber himself was
    presumably aware of the resonances between his historical argument and Chris-
    tian theologies of supersession. In his lectures of 1919–1920, entitled "Universal
    Social and Economic History," he stressed as key moments in the economic
    history of the West "the miracle of Pentecost, the fraternization in the Chris-
    tian Spirit," and "the day of Antioch (Galatians 2:11) where Paul (in contrast
    to Peter) fostered a cultic community with the uncircumcised." For references
    and fuller treatment, see my "Birth of the Pariah: Jews, Christian Dualism, and
    Social Science," *Social Research* 70 (2003), 201–236.

27 Quote "equipped with extraordinary vitality" is from Mendes-Flohr, "Werner
    Sombart's," 93. For more recent and detailed studies of Sombart's thought, see
    Jürgen G. Backhaus, *Werner Sombart (1863–1941): Klassiker der Sozialwissen-
    schaft. Eine kritische Bestandsaufnahme* (Marburg: Metropolis, 2000). Weber
    and Sombart were not the only sociologists to ponder the role of Jews in the
    formation of modern economies. For others, see Arthur Mitzman, *Sociology and
    Estrangement, Three Sociologists of Imperial Germany*, 2nd ed. (New Brunswick:
    Transaction, 1986); and more broadly Jeffrey Herf, *Reactionary Modernism:
    Technology, Culture, and Politics in Weimar and the Third Reich* (New York:
    Cambridge University Press, 1984), 130–151.

28 The original title page of the thesis is lost, but the Heidelberg library replace-
    ment page gives the title as "Wilhelm von Schütz als Dramatiker: ein Beitrag
    zur Geschichte des Dramas der romantischen Schule." Romantics a "mirror"
    from 8, 11; Schlegel, "dancing before the Golden Calf," etc., from 14–15; false

synthesis ("Aufhebung"), "irony" etc., from 17ff. Quote with "overthrow" is from 21, and with "new type of Philistinism" from 23–26. All citations are to the copy of the dissertation at Heidelberg University Library (my thanks to Astrid Lembke for facilitating my access to the copy). It should be noted that despite Goebbels's critique of the Romantics' corruption by philosophy, many of his own key concepts (such as the national literary folk spirit) were in fact developed by the Romantics in their own attempts to criticize "reason." See among others Erich Auerbach's essay of 1949, "Vico and Aesthetic Historism," in his *Scenes from the Drama of European Literature* (Gloucester, MA: Peter Smith, 1973), 186–187.

29 Similar ideas inspired Goebbels's associate Walter Frank, future director of the Nazis' "Reich Institute for the History of the New Germany," whose *Kämpfende Wissenschaft* (Hamburg: Hanseatische Verlagsanstalt, 1934) stressed that the "greatest enemy of creativity (Schöpfung)" is the intellectual (30).

30 Jeffrey Herf, *The Jewish Enemy: Nazi Propaganda during World War II and the Holocaust* (Cambridge, MA: Harvard University Press, 2006), 64, 71–75.

31 Thousands of anti-Semitic postcards were collected by Wolfgang Haney and are now available from Zeno.org as "Spott und Hetze: Antisemitische Postkarten 1893–1945." On the Seifert Collection, see Wolfgang Wangerin, ed., *Der rote Wunderschirm: Kinderbücher von der Frühaufklärung bis zum Nationalsozialismus* (Göttingen: Wallstein, 2011). For Friedrich Köper's diary, see "Köper, Lottmann & Cia., Guatemala, Plaudereien über Handelsmarken, Etiquetten, Wappen, etc.," typescript, February 1, 1945, 16, StAHB 7,13, *Köper, Friedrich* [papers], cited and discussed in Lars Maischak, "A Cosmopolitan Community: Hanseatic Merchants in the German-American Atlantic of the Nineteenth Century," PhD dissertation (Johns Hopkins University, 2006), 434.

32 On Judaism of neo-Kantians, see Ulrich Sieg, "Deutsche Kulturgeschichte und Jüdischer Geist: Ernst Cassirer's Auseinandersetzung mit der Völkischer Philosophie Bruno Bauchs. Ein unbekanntes Manuskript," in *Bulletin des Leo Baecks Institut* 88 (1991), 59–71, 73–91. The latter pages are Cassirer's unpublished response, "Zum Begriff der Nation: Eine Erwiderung auf den Aufsatz von Bruno Bauch." Cassirer did publish a book of essays defending his school's approach to philosophy, revealingly entitled *Freedom and Form: Studies in German Intellectual History (Freiheit und Form: Studien zur deutschen Geistesgeschichte)*, 2nd ed. (Berlin: Bruno Cassirer, 1922). On Troeltsch, see Thomas Meyer, *Ernst Cassirer* (Hamburg: Ellert & Richter, 2006), 78.

33 On Davos, see esp. Peter Gordon, *Continental Divide: Heidegger, Cassirer, Davos* (Cambridge, MA: Harvard University Press, 2010). The quote from Lévinas is on p. 2. Cf. my review of that work: "When Philosophy Mattered," *New Republic*, February 3, 2011, 39–43.

34 Scheler and Einstein quoted in Gordon, *Continental Divide*, 71 and 17, respectively.

35 Philipp Lenard, *Deutsche Physik*, 4 vols, 1st ed. (Munich: J. F. Lehmann, 1936), 1:6.

36 The axiom of well-ordering states that any set x can be provided with a linear

order in such a way that any nonempty subset of x will have a first element. More formally, for any set x there exists a relation $<$ between its members such that for any z and y and w in x we have either $y<z$, or $z<y$, or $z = y$, and so that $<$ is transitive (i.e., $y<z$ and $z<w \to y<w$), and in such a way that any nonempty subset of x will have a first element (y is the first element of x means that $y \in x$ and $z \in x$ and $z \neq y \to y<z$).

37 The preceding quotes are from Gordon, *Continental Divide*, 8, 17, 31–32, 134, 212.

38 "Mere brokerage": "bloße Vermitteln." The word may also be translated as "mediation." Cited in Gordon, *Continental Divide*, 212. Toni Cassirer is cited at p. 264. The extensive controversy and bibliography about Heidegger's anti-Semitism are not directly relevant to my point.

39 There is a vast bibliography on the relationship between theology, critical religious studies, and Nazi anti-Semitism, beginning with Cardinal Michael von Faulhaber, *Judaism, Christianity and Germany* (New York: Macmillan, 1934). Among recent studies, see Suzanne Heschel, *The Aryan Jesus: Christian Theologians and the Bible in Nazi Germany* (Princeton, NJ: Princeton University Press, 2008); and Uriel Tal, *Religion and Ideology in the Third Reich: Selected Essays* (London: Routledge, 2004). Schechter quoted in Adina Hoffman and Peter Cole, *Sacred Trash: The Lost and Found World of the Cairo Geniza* (New York: Shocken, 2011), 49.

40 For an outline of this history, see my "Judaism of Christian Art," 387–428 [see chap. 5, n. 42]. On the topic of Nazi policy toward art Hildegard Brenner's *Die Kunstpolitik des Nationalsozialismus* (Reinbeck bei Hamburg: Rowohlt, 1963) remains foundational. On the 1937 exhibition, see among others Stephanie Barron, ed., *"Degenerate Art": The Fate of the Avant Garde in Nazi Germany* (Los Angeles: Los Angeles County Museum of Art, 1991).

41 All the disciplines: Each has a separate and ample bibliography. On music, see Ruth HaCohen, *The Music Libel against the Jews* (New Haven, CT: Yale University Press, 2012). W. Bialas and A. Rabinbach bring together essays on various humanistic disciplines in *Nazi Germany and the Humanities* (Oxford: Oneworld, 2007). Numerous studies trace the work of Aryan and anti-Semitic theories in specific disciplines, among them Suzanne L. Marchand, *German Orientalism in the Age of Empire: Religion, Race, and Scholarship* (New York: Cambridge University Press, 2009); and Maurice Olender, *The Language of Paradise: Race, Religion, and Philology in the Nineteenth Century*, trans. A. Goldhammer (Cambridge, MA: Harvard University Press, 2008).

42 Kant did not inoculate: Hans Jonas occasionally suggests that he did in his *Memoirs*, ed. Christian Wiese (Hanover, NH: University Press of New England, 2008), 32, 147–148 (citing Julius Ebbinghaus: "[W]ithout Kant I wouldn't have been able to survive this period.") The "Eighteenth Brumaire" is cited from Karl Marx, *Selected Writings*, ed. L. Simon (Indianapolis, IN: Hackett, 1994), 188.

43 For a comparative study of English and German antifinancial discourses, see Mark Loeffler, "Producers and Parasites: The Critique of Finance in Germany and Britain, 1873–1944," PhD dissertation (University of Chicago, 2011). On asked to

predict, see Johannes Heil, "Antisemitismus, Kulturkampf und Konfession—Die antisemitischen 'Kulturen' Frankreichs und Deutschlands im Vergleich," in Olaf Blaschke and Aram Mattioli, eds., *Katholischer Antisemitismus im 19. Jahrhundert Ursachen und Traditionen im internationalen Vergleich* (Zurich: Orell Füssli Verlag, 2000). For a study that makes clear just how politically powerful anti-Semitism was in France, see Pierre Birnbaum's *Anti-Semitic Moment: A Tour of France in 1898* (New York: Hill & Wang, 2002). On American citizens, see Charles Herbert Stember et al., *Jews in the Mind of America* (New York: Basic Books, 1966), 127–129. On fears of a Jewish "fifth column" among U.S. policy and military leaders, see Joseph W. Bendersky, *"The Jewish Threat": Anti-Semitic Politics of the U.S. Army* (New York: Basic Books, 2000), 287–348.

44 Herf, *Jewish Enemy*, 63, translates a Reich Press Office Directive from October 23, 1939, that sets out the strategy. See also 67 and for Goebbels's diary entry of 1942, 314.

45 "Peculiarities": I borrow the phrase from one of the leading contributions to the debate, David Blackbourn and Geoff Eley, *The Peculiarities of German History: Bourgeois Society and Politics in Nineteenth-Century Germany* (Oxford: Oxford University Press, 1984).

46 The sociologist Wolfgang Seibel is studying differential deportation rates in occupied countries. His results for France were recently published as *Macht und Moral: Die "Endlösung der Judenfrage" in Frankreich, 1940–1944* (Constance: Constance University Press, 2010).

EPILOGUE: DROWNING INTELLECTUALS

1 Hannah Arendt, "Antisemitism" in *The Jewish Writings*, ed. Jerome Kohn and Ron H. Feldman (New York: Schocken Books, 2007), 46–124; and Arendt, *The Origins of Totalitarianism* (New York: Harcourt, 1968).

2 "Why the Jews?": Arendt, "Antisemitism," 47; Arendt, *Origins*, 5. The admonition remains necessary, since recent definitions (such as Gavin Langmuir's) treat the *irrationality* of a belief about the Jews as the precondition for its being classified as anti-Semitic.

3 The quotes with "perfect innocence," "Arbitrarily," and "specifically Jewish functions" are from Arendt, *Origins* 5, 7, 9; cf. "deny all specific Jewish responsibility," from ibid., 8; "[a]ll economic statistics" is from Arendt, "Antisemitism," 53–54.

4 Arendt, "Antisemitism," 95–99. Note that at the time Arendt wrote these words, she was employed by a philanthropic organization headed by a Rothschild. On these subjects see Bernard Wasserstein, "Blame the Victim—Hannah Arendt among the Nazis: The Historian and Her Sources," *Times Literary Supplement*, October 30, 2009. For more on Frank, see Helmut Heiber, *Walter Frank und sein Reichsinstitut für Geschichte des neuen Deutschlands* (Stuttgart: Deutsche Verlags-Anstalt, 1966) and Alan E. Steinweis, *Studying the Jew: Scholarly Antisemitism in Nazi Germany* (Cambridge, MA: Harvard University Press, 2006). *Kämpfende Wissenschaft* was the name of one of Frank's own books (Hamburg: Hanseatische Verlagsanstalt, 1934).

5 Quote with "defined as a Jew by others" is from Arendt, *Origins*, xv; "specific Jewish responsibility" is from ibid., 8. She would doubtless have rejected my approach as well, not least because I set aside all questions of "responsibility" for complex historical phenomena. On methodological grounds alone, the degree of Jewish "co-responsibility" for anti-Semitism seems to me as impossible to determine as that of African co-responsibility for the Atlantic slave trade, the co-responsibility of the colonized for colonialism, or of labor for capital.

6 So much anti-Semitic literature: Walter Laqueur, "The Arendt Cult: Hannah Arendt as Political Commentator," *Journal of Contemporary History* 33, no. 4 (1998), 483–496.

7 Quote with "repulsive" is from a letter to Gertrud and Karl Jaspers, April 18, 1966, in Lotte Köhler and Hans Sahler, ed., *Hannah Arendt Karl Jaspers: Correspondence, 1926–1969* (New York: Houghton Mifflin, 1993), 634.

8 Horkheimer and Adorno, *Dialectic of Enlightenment*, 187 [see chap. 6, n. 41]. For Horkheimer's description of how "the perceived fact is co-determined by human ideas and concepts," see his *Critical Theory: Selected Essays*, trans. Matthew J. O'Connell (New York: Continuum, 1995), 199–201. On the Horkheimer and the Frankfurt School's repudiation of their earlier association of Jews with the sphere of circulation, see Dan Diner, "Reason and the 'Other': Horkheimer's Reflections on Anti-Semitism and Mass Annihilation," in *On Max Horkheimer: New Perspectives*, ed. Seyla Benhabib, Wolfgang Bonß, and John McCole (Cambridge, MA: MIT Press, 1993), 335–363.

9 "Letter to Traugott Fuchs," 22.10.38, in "Scholarship in Times of Extremes: Letters of Erich Auerbach (1933–46) on the Fiftieth Anniversary of his Death," ed. M. Elsky, M. Vialon, and R. Stein, *PMLA* 102 (2007), 742–762, here 752–755. Though a Protestant, Traugott Fuchs was also in exile in Istanbul, barred by the Nazis from the German university for having protested the expulsion of his Jewish teacher, the philologist Leo Spitzer, from his professorship.

10 "Figura" was first published in *Archivum Romanicum* 22 (1938), 436–489. An English version was included in Auerbach's *Scenes from the Drama of European Literature* (New York: Meridian, 1959), 11–76; "Figural interpretation" is from 53. On the dates of composition, see Jesse M. Gellrich, "*Figura*, Allegory, and the Question of History," in Seth Lerer, ed., *Literary History and the Challenge of Philology: The Legacy of Erich Auerbach* (Palo Alto, CA: Stanford University Press, 1996), 107–123, here 111. "Divine Providence" is from Auerbach, *Mimesis: The Representation of Reality in Western Literature*, trans. W. Trask (Garden City, NY: Doubleday, 1957), 64. On allegory versus figura, see A. D. Nuttall, "Auerbach's *Mimesis*," *Essays in Criticism* 54 (2004), 68.

11 See Carl Landauer. "*Mimesis* and Erich Auerbach's Self-Mythologizing," *German Studies Review* 11 (1988), 83–96.

12 Curiously absent: The reasons for that absence are beyond my reach here. I am grateful to Avihu Zakai for letting me read his unpublished "Erich Auerbach and the Crisis of German Philology: An Apology for Western Judeo-Christian Tradition in an Age of Peril, Tyranny and Barbarism," which orients much of my argument. The "Old Testament" quote is from Rosenberg, as quoted in Peter

M. Head, "The Nazi Quest for an Aryan Jesus," *Journal for the Study of the Historical Jesus* 2 (2004), 69.

13 As I have tried to show throughout this book, the Christian tradition (like the Islamic) had the potential to authorize and generate many different attitudes toward Israel and Judaism. We may find the arguments in "Figura" about the place of the Hebrew Bible in early Christian interpretive practices a more congenial potential within early Christianity than say, Marcion's, but we should not treat it as normative, or as the "correct interpretation of Christian orthodoxy."

14 "Our purpose" quote is from Auerbach, *Scene*, 76. "Is the beginning" is from Edward Said, *Beginnings: Intention and Method* (New York: Basic Books, 1975), 43. Among Said's last writings was his introduction to a new edition of *Mimesis* (Princeton, NJ: Princeton University Press, 2003).

15 Nirenberg, *Communities of Violence*, 249 [see chap. 5, n. 29].

INDEX

Badr, Battle of, 171, 172–73
Baena, Juan Alfonso de, 230, 231, 236–37,
    529
    in contest with Villasandino, 234–35,
    529
    "poetic grace" theory of, 232
    poetic manifesto of, 233–34
Bahira, 135–36, 154
"Ballad of Gernutus," 543
Banu Nadir, 159, 161
Banu Qaynuqa`, 158
Banu Qurayza, 159–60, 161, 513
baptism, 60, 70, 110, 225, 226–27, 230,
    237–38, 263, 265–66, 351, 367
    see also Jews, mass conversions of
barbarism of reflection, 377
barbarism of sense, 376–77
Barcelona:
    converts in, 226, 237
    Holy Week massacre in, 219, 220
    Jews forbidden from, 210, 220, 221
    royal lions in, 195
Barère, Bertrand, 373–74
Bar Kochba revolt, 103
Barnabas, 497
Barnes, T. D., 500
Baruch, Aldonça, 226
Baruch, Samuel, 226
Basnage, Jacques, 342
Bastille, 361, 376, 385
Battle of Britain, 447
Bauch, Bruno, 449
Bauer, Bruno, 433–34, 435–36, 437, 572
Bayle, Pierre, 342, 347
    David criticized by, 337
    Spinoza criticized by, 340, 554
Becanus, Johannes Goropius, 321
Bede, Venerable, 525
Beginnings: Intention and Method (Auer-
    bach), 469
Being and Time (Heidegger), 449
Béla IV of Hungary, 209
Believers, 137, 511–12, 513
Bell, David, 368
Bello, Maribel Fierro, 518
Benedict XIII, 225, 226
Benedict XVI, Pope, 571
Benjamin, Walter, 11, 470
Berbers, 180

Berkeley, Robert, 310
Berlin, 422, 425
Berlin Academy, 388
Bernard of Clairvaux:
    Jews protected by, 132, 202
    moneylending criticized by, 539
    use of images criticized by, 240
Besitz, 565
"Beyond Good and Evil" (Nietzsche), 476
Beza, Theodore, 304
Bible, 27, 54, 105, 291, 355
    canon of, 99
    doctrinal disputes and, 93
    Hobbes's philology of, 548
    literal vs. spiritual exegesis of, 58–59,
        60–61, 64, 100, 104–6, 120, 121,
        124–26, 130, 212, 213–14, 233,
        248–50, 291, 333, 382, 420, 430, 439,
        470, 504
    translations of, 247–48, 306–7; *see also*
        specific translations
    see also Hebrew Bible; New Testament
Bible Finally Explained, The (Voltaire),
    557
Bielefeld, 425
Bin Laden, Osama, 10
Birmingham, 425
Blackstone, William, 542
blasphemy, 26, 31, 141, 203, 209, 229, 259,
    260, 262, 303–5, 354, 549
blindness, 76, 100, 103, 104, 145, 232,
    339, 349, 491
"Blood Clot, The," 150
bloodline, *see* genealogy (bloodline)
Blount, Henry, 276
Boccaccio, 231
Bocchoris, Pharaoh, 30
body, *see* flesh
Bonafos, Shaltiel, 225
book-burnings, 10
Book of Good Love (Ruiz), 188
Bordeaux, 344, 367
Börne, Ludwig, 572–73
    Heine's critique of, 416
    Jewish background of, 417, 418, 438
    Merchant of Venice seen by, 427
    United States and, 441
Boston Patriot, 428–29
Boxel, Hugo, 551

mathematics, 450–53
Matthew, Gospel of, 50, 491
    dating of, 486–87
    exhortation to love in, 273, 335
    hesitant apostles in, 88
    hypocrisy in, 74, 76, 90, 149
    Jesus as fulfillment of prophecy in,
        69–70, 83
    Jesus on spiritual meaning of scriptures
        in, 105
    Jews rarely mentioned in, 69, 492
    John the Baptist's prophecy in, 70, 71
    and law of observance, 493
    Merchant of Venice's allusion to, 270
    Pharisees in, 69, 70, 73, 74–77
    Qur'an's similarity to, 149
    "render unto Caesar" passage in, 106,
        107, 108
    Sabbath laws in, 73
    "Whosoever will save his life" passage
        in, 270
Maximus, Emperor of Rome, 118
Measure for Measure (Shakespeare), 427
Mecca, 136, 151, 153, 157, 165
Medea, 544
Medina, 136, 153, 155, 156, 157–58,
    159–60, 161
Mein Kampf (Hitler), 514
Melancthon, Philipp, 251, 265, 532
Memphis, 35
Men Before Adam (La Peyrère), 33
Mendelssohn, Moses, 396–97, 418, 558,
    569
Menzel, Wolfgang, 417
mercantilism, 218, 276, 422
Merchant of Venice (Shakespeare), 269–99,
    538–45
    Antonio's melancholy in, 269–71, 277
    Börne's interpretation of, 438, 571
    contract in, 276, 280, 284–87, 288, 289,
        290, 292, 294, 295, 298, 299
    conversions in, 273, 280, 283, 287,
        289–90, 296
    and critical school emphasizing real
        London Jews, 272
    Jessica's escape in, 282–84, 296
    Joyce's fondness for, 570
    literal vs. figurative in, 292–94, 544
    marriage in, 281, 294, 296
    money lending in, 275

nineteenth- and twentieth-century per-
    formances of, 427
"publican" analogy in, 273
Shylock and Antonio's dispute in,
    279–80
Shylock's linguistics in, 278, 291–93
sympathy for characters in, 273–74
three chests in, 280–82, 288
merchants, stigmatization of, 275–76
Mersenne, Marin, 321, 549
metaphor, 544
    Augustine and, 124–25, 129–30
    in definitions of history, 470
    Hegel's use of, 400
    Hobbes on, 292
    Luther and, 255
    in scripture, 76, 77, 124
    see also spirit, letter vs.
Metz, 344, 366, 367
Mibtahiah, 16
Michelangelo Buonarroti, 51
Michelet, Jules, 7–8, 475
Middle Kingdom, 25
middle-Platonism, 55
Mill, James Stuart, 430
millennialists, 319–20
millennium, 375
*Mimesis: The Representation of Reality in
    Western Literature* (Auerbach), 467
Mirabaud, Jean Baptiste de, 356
Mirabeau, comte de, 366
misanthropy, Jews accused of, 21, 22–24,
    30–31, 42–43, 46, 273, 335, 355, 366,
    382
Mitchell, Margaret, 488
Moderates, 338
Modern Capitalism (Sombart), 441
modernity, 239–40, 384–85, 456
Modrzejewski, Joseph Meleze, 483
monarchy, absolute, 377
money, as Jewish, 3, 4, 345–47, 352, 437,
    439, 463
money economy, Judaizing of, 344–47,
    427–29, 430–31, 434–37
money lending:
    Aristotle on, 279
    by Christians, 275
    by Jews, 194, 197, 206–7, 274–76,
        279–80, 351–52, 539
    see also usury

Index   603

Ostend, 319
Othello (Shakespeare), 284
otherspeak, 96, 124, 498
Ottomans, 218, 323
Oxyrhynchus, 45
Ozouf, Mona, 561

pagans, 101–6, 115
Paintings of the Old Masters (Schlegel),
    455
Palatinate, 262
Palencia, Alonso de, 230–31
Palestine, 5, 34, 355
Pamphilus, 109
pantheism, 397, 404, 418, 419, 422, 553
papacy, 378
paper currency, 345, 380
Paris, 422, 425
Paris, Matthew, 198–99
Pascal, Blaise, 326, 327, 550–51
Passion story, 75
Passover, 18–19
Passover letter, 16–17, 18
Paul, 51–66, 77, 81–85, 86, 87, 94, 96, 98,
    106, 107, 137, 198, 232, 233, 417,
    436, 469–70, 487, 490, 515
  on Christian synthesis of love, 389
  circumcision opposed by, 55–56,
    58–59, 96, 353, 393
  cognitive revelation started by, 53–56,
    62
  conversion of, 51–53
  on conversion of Jews, 84, 221, 319–20,
    359, 373
  dualism of, 55–56, 58, 61, 63, 98, 107–
    8, 488–89
  French Revolutionaries influenced by,
    367–70, 373
  images criticized by, 240, 241
  influence of, 52
  Jews considered enemies of God by,
    64–65, 92, 189
  Judaizing and, 59, 60, 126–27, 189,
    229, 272, 353, 489
  on justice of God, 249–50
  Luther's reading of, 263
  Mark as interpreter of, 495
  Muslim critique of, 181
  paintings of, 51

  Peter's quarrel with, 60, 353, 506
  racial rhetoric used by, 488
  reading theory of, 57–58, 61, 212, 248,
    256, 258–59
  relation to Greek philosophical tradi-
    tion of, 487
  on two vessels, 65, 131
  universalism of, 56, 488
Peace of Westphalia, 303
Peasants' War, 307, 373
Pelagius, 132
penis, 415
Pensées (Pascal), 326, 327, 550–51
Péreire, Jacob Rodrigues, 557
Perez, Jacob, 256
Persia, 17, 19, 25, 33, 34, 37, 353
Persian Letters (Montesquieu), 346,
    351–52
Pervo, Richard, 487
Peter, Coptic Apocalypse of, 498
Peter, Saint, 60, 127, 353, 501
  circumcision insisted on by, 353
  Paul's quarrel with, 60, 353, 506
2 Peter, 54–55
Peter the Ceremonious, King of Aragon,
    197, 200, 209–10
Peter the Chanter, 194
Peter the Venerable, 132–33, 202
Petrarch, 231
Pfefferkorn, Johannes, 202–3, 533
Pharisees, 85, 142, 147, 149, 232, 261, 270,
    271, 273, 277, 328, 393, 401, 492,
    493, 497, 504, 511
  as advocates of exclusive Jewishness,
    71
  as desiring empty wisdom, 10
  as enemies of Jesus, 66–67, 70, 71, 72,
    73, 74–75, 76, 77, 80, 83, 84, 174,
    281, 282, 331, 337, 401
  French Revolutionaries compared to,
    378
  heretics and, 115
  John the Baptist's criticism of, 70, 71
  as personification of hypocrisy, 86
  pride in descent from Abraham, 62
  and salvation through merits, 251, 258
  Shylock compared to, 278, 280
Phenomenology of Spirit (Hegel), 568
Philip II, King of France, 207, 211, 524